Legal Theory Today

Law after Modernity

Legal Theory Today

Founding Editor
John Gardner, Professor of Jurisprudence, University College, Oxford

TITLES IN THIS SERIES

Law after Modernity

Sionaidh Douglas-Scott

·HART·
PUBLISHING

OXFORD AND PORTLAND, OREGON
2013

Published in the United Kingdom by Hart Publishing Ltd
16C Worcester Place, Oxford, OX1 2JW
Telephone: +44 (0)1865 517530
Fax: +44 (0)1865 510710
E-mail: mail@hartpub.co.uk
Website: http://www.hartpub.co.uk

Published in North America (US and Canada) by
Hart Publishing
c/o International Specialized Book Services
920 NE 58th Avenue, Suite 300
Portland, OR 97213-3786
USA
Tel: +1 503-287-3093 or toll-free: (1) 800-944-6190
Fax: +1 503-280-8832
E-mail: orders@isbs.com
Website: http://www.isbs.com

British Library Cataloguing in Publication Data
Data Available

ISBN: 978-1-84113-029-3

Typeset by Compuscript Ltd, Shannon
Printed and bound in Great Britain by
TJ International Ltd, Padstow, Cornwall

Preface

This book must speak for itself but its inspirations are manifold. It did not spring from thin air, fully formed, but is the product of the influences and conversations that have helped shape my thinking about law, and my desire to write about jurisprudence in a way that clearly links it to other forms of life.

The most immediate of these influences have been my colleagues at Oxford and at King's College, London, and the many students to whom I have taught jurisprudence at both of these universities. The original debt of gratitude should go to John Gardner, who, longer ago than I care to remember, asked me to write a book about postmodern jurisprudence for the *Legal Theory Today* series. For the fact that this book is not, or at least not only, a work of postmodern jurisprudence, I owe the pleasure of several years of co-teaching a course in Law and Social theory at the University of London. This stimulated many conversations with students and colleagues, and in particular with co-teachers Alan Norrie and Roger Cotterrell, and enriched my understanding of law in countless ways. My interest in legal pluralism, and its pitfalls, owes much to my parallel career as an EU and human rights lawyer.

This book places law in its cultural context. It is somewhat unusual in employing images and works of art to illustrate and reinforce its messages. My debts in this field are long-standing, and originally derive from my good fortune in being taught aesthetics by the late Richard Wollheim, and learning about Renaissance art from John White. I was also extremely lucky to be taught political philosophy by Ted Honderich and the late Jerry Cohen—and it was through them that I first encountered theories of justice. Not all of them would agree with the message and methodology of this book but all of these tutors at University College, London captured my imagination and inspired me in their different ways.

I also owe another large debt of gratitude to Richard Hart, for continuing to encourage me in this project, and to all those at Hart Publishing who have worked hard to prepare the book for publication. Special thanks are due to Scott Veitch, who read a much earlier draft and provided some invaluable commentary. His comments, and those of many other readers, enabled me to avoid numerous pitfalls, but those errors that do remain are very much my own.

I also would not have been able to complete this book, without two periods of sabbatical leave from my fellowship at Lady Margaret Hall, University of Oxford—which has in any case provided a very congenial environment in which to work.

Last of all, I thank my family, and of course, Peter.

Sionaidh Douglas-Scott,
Oxford, February 2013.

Table of Contents

Table of Figures

1

Introduction: Beyond the 'Degree Zero' of Law after Modernity

Jurisprudentia

The aim of this book is to investigate the shape and character of law in the contemporary world. It argues for a pluralistic conception of law and focuses on the richness of law, its historical embeddedness and its cultural contingencies, rather than on a vision of law as singular, autonomous and systematic—a view that was more prevalent in some nineteenth- and twentieth-century jurisprudence and was characteristic of a certain type of modernity. However, this book aims for more than analysis. Several recent accounts of law have embraced legal pluralism as an appropriate paradigm for the twenty-first century. However, very few have gone further by enquiring whether pluralism is normatively attractive, and productive of justice. This is an important question, and I will argue that the answer to it must be, at best, equivocal. Law after modernity is liable to be no more just than its predecessors.

These opening remarks are in need of a caveat. The title of this book makes use of two key concepts—'law' and 'modernity'—and moreover implies that we are now 'after modernity'. All of these concepts are challenging. Undeniably, law has taken more than one form in modernity. Modernity itself has many meanings. Even the assertion that we are now in a 'postmodern' era is controversial. Therefore, although I believe that it is possible to identify particular understandings of law which became dominant during the modern period and are now being superseded, it should be acknowledged that any attempt to write about law in modernity and postmodernity as if these concepts possessed singular, straightforward meanings is doomed to fail.

Indeed, in order to capture the troubled, perplexing nature of this enterprise, I have found it best to start with a pictorial image of law, to proceed by way of metaphor, in the belief that this metaphorical expression of law crystallises some of my major concerns—for sometimes art can capture in a more immediate way that which becomes garbled and unclear in words. The work I shall use to do this is Gustav Klimt's *Jurisprudentia* (Figure 1-1).

Figure 1-1: Gustav Klimt, *Jurisprudentia* (1903) (since destroyed)

The *Jurisprudentia* was painted by Klimt in 1903 as part of a series commissioned by the University of Vienna to represent the faculties of law, medicine and philosophy. These works were to be prominently displayed in the central hall of the University, and their overarching theme was to be 'the triumph of light over darkness'.[1] The *Jurisprudentia* was a large work that depicted Truth, Justice and Law in its upper section, looking down on an old, naked man who was enveloped in the tentacles of an octopus-like figure and was surrounded by three (also naked) women. The women have been interpreted as the three goddesses of Fate—Clotho, Lachesis and Atopos.

The painting's fate was closely entwined with twentieth-century history. In fact, the work was never displayed, as it (and the other two from the series) proved too controversial, and Klimt, while protesting his artistic freedom of expression, ended up buying it back from the University.[2]

---

[1] F Whitford, *Klimt* (London, Thames and Hudson, 1990); and E Pirchan, *Gustav Klimt, Ein Künstler aus Wien* (Vienna, Wallishauser, 1956).

[2] The paintings were requested for an international exhibition in St Louis, United States, in 1904, but the Austrian government declined, anxious of the reaction of a foreign public. The Austrian authorities initially refused to sell the series back to Klimt, asserting that the paintings were state property, but apparently handed them over when Klimt threatened the

Klimt died in the great flu pandemic of 1918, and the *Jurisprudentia* later became part of the collection of the Austrian Lederer family. However, the Lederers were of Jewish origin, and in another historical twist emblematic of the twentieth century, their entire collection was seized in 1938. Shortly after, the three faculty paintings were displayed in the Österreichische Galerie in Vienna. In 1943, because of the war they were moved for protection to the Schloss Immendorf in lower Austria, where all three were destroyed by fire two years later, when the retreating German forces attempted to prevent Allied occupation of the castle. There are no remaining good quality reproductions of the *Jurisprudentia*, only some old, rather obscure black and white ones, which, it is said, fail to bring out the rich gold and black of the original.

Apparently, Klimt had originally intended the work to represent Justice, as a symbol of the (perceived) liberal Austria of the time.[3] In the late nineteenth century, the Austrian state had been receptive to cultural modernism, seeing in it a possible cosmopolitan, counter-phenomenon to the particular, ethnic divisions of the Austro-Hungarian empire.[4] However, public antagonism to modern art had rendered state support for it politically unwise, and as a result, Klimt, reacting against this criticism, refused to affirm the rational, Enlightenment theme of a triumph of light over dark. Therefore, after earlier censure of the *Philosophy* and *Medicine* paintings, Klimt revised his conception.

Instead of a confident Justice enveloped in the security of law and order, Klimt presented a bleak representation of a very different character. At the top of the picture, Justice, in the centre, was not freestanding but rather flanked by Law on the right and Truth on the left. The emaciated old man before them appeared like a condemned prisoner, head lowered, hands (perhaps tied) behind his back. This painting therefore represented not the benefits of a legal system but rather the isolation of the human being, insecure in the modern world—a portrayal of law in which justice is uncertain and opaque, seemingly dependent on the fates. Moreover, the old man was trapped within the tentacles of the octopus-like figure, perhaps representing capricious societal forces. In such an environment, what hope could there be for Law, Justice and Humanity? This vision is dystopian,

---

removal staff with a shotgun! See G Fliedl, *Gustav Klimt* (Cologne, Benedikt Taschen Verlag, 1998); H Bahr, *Gegen Klimt* (Vienna, 1903), reprinted in CE Schorske, *Fin-de-siècle Vienna: Culture and Politics* (New York, Vintage, 1981); and P Vergo, 'Gustav Klimts Philosophie und das Programm der Universitätgemälde' (1978–79) 22–23 *Mitteilungen der Österreichischen Galerie* 69–100.

[3] 'Perceived', because many did not see Austria as liberal in the early twentieth century—some have interpreted Kafka's *The Trial* as a commentary on Austrian law and procedure of the time. See T Zjolkowski, *The Mirror of Justice* (New York, Princeton University Press, 1997) 224.

[4] See further on this, Schorske (above n 2).

hellish, in sharp contrast to the usual, bland, confident, artistic expressions of Justice to be found in courthouses everywhere of that period.

I have chosen the *Jurisprudentia* because this work, painted just over 100 years ago, expresses the anxieties and insecurities of the late modern era, and it places law firmly at the centre of these anxieties, while at the same time universalising these themes through classical allusion. It might be seen as an attack on the very rule of law itself. Indeed, one interpretation of the *Jurisprudentia* reads it as explicitly demonstrating the gap between two different conceptions of law: namely a formal, rationalist, systematic conception of law, more prevalent in the modern era, offering certainty and clarity (these elements to be found in the upper part of the painting, with the three allegorical figures of Justice, Truth and Law); and a contrasting vision of law as it really is—irrational, chaotic and uncertain (these elements to be found in the lower part of the work).[5] In this way, the work distinguishes its representation of law from associations of order and stability, foreshadowing the postmodern concerns of the later twentieth century in its attempt to demythologise and displace law's orderly role, as well as prefiguring some of the more sinister events to come in the twentieth century. These themes will be explored in the course of this book.

Law and the Image

This book is somewhat unusual for a work of legal scholarship in that it makes frequent use of images—very often of works of art—to aid and clarify the points it seeks to make. Their use is grounded in the view that the study of law is enlightened by reflection on other socio-cultural norms that create and enable laws and legal meaning. Cultural influences play a vital role in the forging and fashioning of law. The use of cultural images in particular, far from conflicting with or having nothing to say about legal meanings and arguments, actually helps us to refine and amplify them. Law is a creature of culture, with as much claim to be an art as a science, and it is grounded in and composed of images as much as of rules. Yet this relationship is sometimes missed or denied. A strong connection is usually asserted between law and reason, science and deduction, rather than with art and the imaginary, the latter being perceived as imprecise, overly creative and imbued in subjective emotions, in the face of law's perceived need for certainty. Indeed, certain types of jurisprudence such as legal positivism (or legal realism) have made specific connections between law and science, often invoking a correlative separation of law from art, as well as from morality.

---

[5] For this interpretation, see A Likhovski, 'Czernowitz, Lincoln, Jerusalem, and the Comparative History of American Jurisprudence' (2003) 4 *Theoretical Inquiries in Law* 621.

Yet art may function in a role of rescue and deliverance of law.[6] The reference to art reveals other criteria by which law may be improved and can expose covert assumptions that underpin the law and shape and structure law's work—values and concepts that, though taken for granted, favour some modes of being and work to the detriment of others. A turn to art provides another language with which to address and assess the experience of law and to resist law's sometimes coercive fabrications. It provides an imaginative empathy, by which the self, with its very human attributes, may be recovered from the more formal, rational language of the law.

In this cultural context, the image is particularly powerful: 'In its ability of disclosing things, the image is promiscuous and forceful.'[7] In its organisation of our mental representations, the firing and underpinning of our imagination, and in its reinforcement and support of all types of experience—poetic and prosaic—the image is potent and all-encompassing.[8] We may be disturbed, perplexed, overwhelmed or provoked to violence by images.[9] Plato wished to banish painters and poets from his ideal republic, believing the influence of art to be both far-reaching and potentially subversive.[10] Images can evoke powerful reactions—ranging from a formal ban on tobacco advertising to the toppling of a statue of a former dictator—and for that reason, society will over time seek to use, misuse and censor them. The image creates both an emotional experience and a force in society. It not only addresses the viewer but also imposes a relation on the viewer.[11]

The notion of image is given a very broad remit in this book, and a wide variety of examples will be used, encompassing not only the 'high' art of Klimt, Giotto and art galleries but also images as they are found in everyday life—advertisements, photographs and other images that are all around us. The question of what art is, is every bit as difficult to resolve as the question of what law is (the latter to be addressed in chapter two), and I shall not attempt to answer it. Instead, I will note the omnipresent, pervasive, presence of images as a particularly powerful, cultural reference for and influence on law, as on all other forms and aspects of life. Although

[6] See, eg, J Boyd White, *The Legal Imagination* (Chicago, University of Chicago Press, 1973).

[7] C Douzinas, 'A Legal Phenomenology of Images' in O Ben-Dor (ed), *Law and Art* (London, Routledge, 2011) 248.

[8] Cf D Freedberg, *The Power of Images* (Chicago, University of Chicago Press, 1989); and A Young, *Judging the Image: Art, Value, Law* (London, Routledge, 2005).

[9] For example, on the opening day of a notable exhibition of 'Young British Art', named 'Sensation,' at the Royal Academy in London, a portrait of the notorious child murderer Myra Hindley, entirely compiled in paint using the handprints of small children, was attacked, and a can of paint thrown at it. As a result, it had to be removed from the display.

[10] Plato, *Republic*, Desmond Lee (trans) (Harmondsworth, Penguin Books, 1983) 10.424b–c.

[11] See, eg, J Berger, *Ways of Seeing* (London, Penguin Books, 1972) 7: 'It is seeing which establishes our place in the surrounding world; we explain that world with words, but words can never undo the fact that we are surrounded by it.'

Western law has tended to oppose reason to emotion, it is the case that images, often strongly grounded in our emotions, may provide the most compelling motivation for action—regardless of whether the images are in fact trustworthy or whether they form the basis of sound argument, as the power of advertising illustrates.

Further, law is itself a 'deeply aesthetic practice'.[12] Law institutionalises images, as well as other notions, as official ways of seeing,[13] creating and approving particular domains of visibility—ways of living that we constantly experience. Indeed, it has been suggested that 'Law's force depends partly on the inscription on the soul of a regime of images. . .'[14] The practice of law is enclosed and manifested in images, its history marked and traced in images as custom, usage, practice, tradition or precedent, and publicised through visual depictions, or notions, that persist due to the power of the images. To give more specific examples, law's ardour for images is expressed by means of an iconography of justice, illustrated in the architecture of the law, of courts and their organisation and design, which reproduce and uphold an appearance of official authority, equity, symmetry, drawing on an aesthetic of harmony and order. Law depends and builds on a panoply of images to create and enforce its authority, as well as to implement its reasoning and judgement: wigs, robes, the sword and scales of justice, gavels, black caps, prison bars—these are all constitutive of a particular sensory perception of the world which law itself has brought into being and worked upon. Familiar concepts of the law—the 'reasonable man', 'the officious bystander'—form and present themselves as images impressed by and within the legal consciousness. Therefore, should law deny any explicit connection with images or with art, such a denial is undermined by the pervasiveness of law's own aesthetic.

But notably, any relationship that law *openly* acknowledges with the image is one of assertion, of control, of image as object and subject to manipulation, in the same way that religion has manipulated images— banning them or strictly controlling them, as Judaism, Islam and the Catholic Counter-Reformation have all done in the past. Medieval Christian art, with its unique iconography, is a clear case in point: every element has a specific permitted meaning, every saint an allotted 'attribute'. Likewise, law polices its own image by filtering it through its own iconography: the forms of authority, sovereignty, rationalism, legality and order. Law manipulates its images rather than permitting a dialogue with them or establishing any other more equal relationship. Yet why should we allow law to dominate the relationship in this way?

---

[12] C Douzinas and L Nead (eds), *Law and the Image: The Authority of Art and the Aesthetics of Law* (Chicago, University of Chicago Press, 1999).

[13] See again Berger (above n 11).

[14] C Douzinas and L Nead, 'Introduction' in Douzinas and Nead (eds) (above n 12) 9.

Law's relationship to the image is therefore complicated. Law may be interpreted as an art form, one of the liberal arts, but that is not all that it is. It makes use of images but is not reducible to images. Nor can art be straightforwardly compared to law. There exists no unambiguous analogy between art and law, and there are of course many points of distinction between them. Alison Young identifies the relationship between art and law as one of *co-implication*, 'in which law and image are enfolded within each other, their contours and substance passing through and around each other', a relationship that 'interrupts any straightforward story of legal governance'.[15] This relationship is one of entanglement and implication, 'a responsive dance'.[16] Such a relationship of co-implication is adopted in this book as the basis on which law and art interact, the argument being that, while law's own management of images must be scrutinised with care, law itself may be illuminated, enhanced or attenuated by the work that images do and our own understanding of law thus enriched, or even undermined.

'Modernity'

To get beyond modernity and to understand the contemporary legal age, we must first have some sort of conception of modernity itself—to make sense of the present, we must first understand the past. Yet 'modernity' is an ambiguous, over-broad term, spanning too extensive a period of time for any unified description. Indeed, the question arises as to whether modernity should be understood as a period of time, a state of mind or a concept or series of concepts. Indeed, perhaps it is capable of being all of these things.

If we see modernity in its simplest, temporal sense, then it is absolute contemporaneity—for example, Rimbaud's *'il faut être absolument moderne'*.[17] But in this sense, modernity is not an historical era; it is *now*, this minute, no time past, and its content is always changing. What was absolutely contemporary in 1900 will obviously be very different from the contemporary of 2000 or 2100. This sense is captured by Walter Benjamin's notion of the *Jetztzeit*, namely 'the present as a moment of revelation'.[18] Understood in this way, it could also be seen as a state of mind—one does not *have* to be modern in this sense; one can choose to be old-fashioned. In this book, modernity will not be understood in this sense but rather in the sense of the two understandings of modernity outlined below.

The second usage of modernity occurs when we make reference to the 'modern' era, by which we do not necessarily mean now, this very minute,

---

[15] Young (above n 8) 14.
[16] Ibid.
[17] A Rimbaud, *Une Saison en Enfer*, 1999 reprint (Paris, Gallimard, 1873).
[18] See J Habermas, 'Modernity v Postmodernity' (1981) 22 *New German Critique* 6.

but rather a period in time spanning many years. Yet *which* period in time modernity comprises is not so clear. In this sense, modernity is not a state of mind but a professional periodisation, and professional opinions differ. Inevitably, the choice of any historical period as 'the modern era' will be controversial. With an awareness of this controversy, in this work, I take the modern era to span the period from the Peace of Westphalia Treaties (1648)— itself a contentious starting point—up to the later twentieth century. There are of course many other candidates for the modern period. One could arguably start earlier, with the Renaissance and growth of humanism. Michel Foucault, on the other hand, dates modernity from a later point, distinguishing it from the 'classical' age (which he saw as stretching from the late sixteenth century to the second half of the eighteenth century). For Foucault, the main characteristic of this earlier classical age was the monarchical state, constructed round the integrity of law and the sovereign.[19]

I justify the identification of the onset of modernity with the Peace of Westphalia by the fact that these treaties are often characterised as the birth of the era of the nation state, and as will be seen, this book identifies 'modern' law with state law to a large extent.[20] The Peace of Westphalia, which ended the Thirty Years War,[21] one of the most brutal wars in history, marked the end of the Holy Roman Empire as an effective institution and initiated huge power shifts in Europe, with worldwide ramifications, inaugurating the modern state system, which is founded on the notion of sovereignty, as well as the beginning of some religious toleration in the West.[22] The Peace of Westphalia has been described as marking 'the end of an epoch and the opening of another', as well as representing 'a majestic portal which leads from the old world into the new,'[23] a turning point in European history and 'the genesis of the inter-state order'.[24] Indeed, it has been argued that references to the crucial nature of Westphalia for the international order of states dates back at least to mid-nineteenth-century law treatises.[25] The notion of a Christian

---

[19] See M Foucault, *The Order of Things: An Archaeology of the Human Sciences* (London, Routledge, 1974).

[20] For example, Neil MacCormick has written, 'The world of modernity owes much to the epoch of reformation and religious wars in the 16th and 17th century Europe. . . . Not until the Peace of Westphalia in 1648 was it settled that the new order would prove durable.' See N MacCormick, *Questioning Sovereignty* (Oxford, Oxford University Press, 1999) 123.

[21] CV Wedgwood, *The Thirty Years War*, 1990 edn (London, Jonathan Cape, 1936).

[22] V Gerhardt, 'On the Historical Significance of the Peace of Westphalia: 12 Theses' in *1648: War and Peace in Europe I*, Council of Europe Exposition (Münster, Osnabrück, 1998/99); and W Spellman, *European Political Thought* (Basingstoke, Macmillan, 1998).

[23] L Gross, 'The Peace of Westphalia, 1648–1948' (1948) 42 *American Journal of International Law* 28.

[24] A Eyffinger, 'Europe in the Balance: An Appraisal of the Westphalian System' (1998) 45 *Netherlands International Law Review* 164.

[25] See, eg, S Beaulac, 'The Westphalian Legal Orthodoxy: Myth or Reality?' (2000) 2 *Journal of the History of International Law* 148.

commonwealth, governed by the spiritual and temporal leaders of Pope and Emperor,[26] was to become a thing of the past, gradually to replaced by principles of religious equality as part of the peace under an international guarantee. For the first time, Europe received 'what may fairly be described as an international constitution, which gave to all its adherents the right to interfere to enforce its engagements'.[27] It thus became the starting point for modern, international law and also for the growing secularisation of law, separate from any religious source, and 'the unravelling of concepts and institutions' that had given guidance for centuries.[28] The 'balance of power' (namely, the principle that enemies were not to be obliterated, as this would lead to an unbalanced vacuum and a threat to peace) rather than Christendom therefore became the key organising concept.

Around this time, one of the first notably 'modern' accounts of law was published by Thomas Hobbes, who wrote, 'It is not wisdom but authority that makes a law',[29] arguing that reason dictated that men seek the protection of law in a well-organised community. The Peace of Westphalia was notably the first European peace to be concluded not militarily but by diplomatic means.[30] Article II of the 1648 Treaty of Münster (one of the key Westphalia treaties) declared, 'That there shall be on the one side and the other a perpetual Oblivion, Amnesty or Pardon of all that has been committed since the beginning of these Troubles.'

The Peace of Westphalia was also significant in being pictorially represented on an unprecedented scale. Works of art were exchanged as gifts and used as diplomatic instruments to proclaim power, and copies and prints were widely circulated as a means of propaganda to a wider public, spreading images of the diplomatic negotiations, their personnel and the peace process itself. One such well known pictorial representation is 'The Swearing of the Oath of the Treaty of Münster' by Geraert ter Borch,[31] one of the greatest artists of the Dutch Golden Age. Ter Borch's famous 1648 canvas (a popular choice for the cover of international law textbooks) represents the actual swearing of the oath—the culmination of the whole Westphalia peace process. Law itself becomes critical and central

---

[26] On which see further Gross (above n 23).

[27] DJ Hill, *A History of Diplomacy in the International Development of Europe, Vol II* (London, Longmans, Green and Co, 1925) 602. But for a contrary view, see Beaulac (above n 25); and A Osiander, 'Sovereignty, International Relations and the Westphalian Myth' (2001) 2 *International Organization* 261.

[28] Eyffinger (above n 24) 165.

[29] T Hobbes, *Leviathan* (Oxford, Oxford University Press, 1998 reprint).

[30] It involved the participation of thousands of diplomats, 145 delegations, 55 different jurisdictions and three years of hearings and bargaining. See further Eyffinger (above n 24).

[31] The painting is part of the collection of the National Gallery London but was recently on loan to the Peace Palace in The Hague. See also SJ Gudlaugsson, *Geraert ter Borch* (The Hague, Martinus Nijhoff, 1959–60); and SJ Gudlaugsson, *Geraert Ter Borch* (Münster, Landesmuseum für Kunst und Kulturgeschichte, 1974).

Figure 1-2: Geraert ter Borch, *Swearing of the Oath of Affirmation of the Treaty of Münster* (1648), collection of the National Gallery, London

in this performative act. It is a complex group portrait in which we see the exchange of copies of the treaty, richly encased in velvet covers with silver clasps, between the Dutch (who are behind the table in the centre) and Spanish delegations (who are to the right) in the Town Hall of Münster, known ever since as the 'Friedensaal'.[32]

Ter Borch's image conveyed the importance of the Peace of Westphalia to a much wider European public than that of the royal courts when it was very exactly reproduced as a print by Jonas Suijderhoef. The only change was that Suijderhoef substituted for ter Borch's signature high up on the left hand side the adage 'Pax Optima Rerum'.[33] One could therefore say that the onset of modernity in Europe (in its particular legal manifestation) literally became a vision that entered the popular psyche.

[32] Ie, 'Hall of Peace'.

[33] Ie, literally 'peace, the best of things'. See further J Israel, 'Art and Diplomacy: Gerard ter Borch and the Munster Peace Negotiations 1646–1648' in J Israel, *Conflicts of Empires: Spain, the Low Countries and the Struggle for World Supremacy* 1585–1713 (London, Hambledon Press, 1997).

Yet modernity connotes more than a period of history; it may also be conceived in a different, third sense, which has been subject to very different interpretations. For even within even a 350-year timespan, it is impossible to settle upon a single agreed concept or definition of modernity. For Kant in *What is Enlightenment?*[34] Enlightenment was a process of maturity, of thinking for oneself. Modernity is often connected with this notion—with modernity came Enlightenment and a reluctance to rely on traditional authority, ritual and magic. Instead, Kant proposed his now famous injunction to dare to think for oneself: 'Sapere Aude!' With this process came the recognition of an ability to reason in clear and distinct perceptions, a breaking down of beliefs into components and scrutiny of Lockean 'atomic bits',[35] a thinking that claims to be objective, to grasp the world as it is, from a disengaged perspective. 'Modernity' also spans and overlaps with other concepts related to the Enlightenment, such as scientific method, positivism,[36] secularism, foundationalism, individualism and capitalism, as well as the process of industrialisation, although is not necessarily coterminous with them.

However, for many prominent theorists, modernity is identified with capitalism.[37] This involves a perception of capitalism as a particular social form and the product of specific historical circumstances, such as the onset of Western liberalism, the classical school of economics, the industrial revolution and the growth of colonialism. In this process, the concepts of the rational individual and the protection of private property, along with equal and free bargaining power, are necessarily linked with the growth of a market-based organisation of society. Contract law is seen as enabling new varieties of relationship between individuals, extricating the free, rational individual from the fixed, status-bound forms of pre-modern relational organisation.[38]

Max Weber interpreted modern history as the advance of rationalisation, both of the state in the form of bureaucratic organisation and of the economy

---

[34] I Kant, 'An Answer to the Question "What is Enlightenment?"' in I Kant, *Political Writings*, HS Reiss (ed) (Cambridge, Cambridge University Press, 1991).

[35] J Locke, *An Essay Concerning Human Understanding* (Oxford, Clarendon Press, 1975).

[36] John Gray has written, 'For Positivism, modernity is the transformation of the world by the use of scientific knowledge'. J Gray, *Al Qaeda and What It Means to Be Modern* (London, Faber, 2003) 38.

[37] It should be noted, however, that for many recent authors, modernity is to be associated with only a particular type of capitalism. For Fredric Jameson, the postmodern era is distinguished from the modern era and identified with 'late capitalism' (F Jameson, *Postmodernism, or, The Cultural Logic of Late Capitalism* (Durham, Duke University Press, 1991), while David Harvey identifies a transition from Fordism to 'flexible accumulation' in capitalism (D Harvey, *The Condition of Postmodernity* (Oxford, Blackwell, 1990). For a theory of 'disorganised capitalism', see also S Lash and J Urry, *The End of Organised Capitalism* (Cambridge, Polity Press, 1987). See also EM Wood, 'Modernity, Postmodernity or Capitalism?' (1997) 4 *Review of International Political Economy* 539.

[38] On which see further, H Sumner Maine, *Ancient Law*, 1976 edn (London, John Murray, 1861).

in the form of industrial capitalism. Weber also perceived European law as contributing to this rationalisation process by virtue of its particular features (which Weber identified as law's differentiation from other areas of society, as well as its more general nature), which he believed rendered it more 'rational' than law in other civilisations and thus particularly conducive to capitalism.[39] Weber, however, believed this process to have both positive and negative effects: while the progress of reason and freedom associated with Enlightenment enabled the freeing of humanity from traditional constraints, on the other hand rationalisation promoted a new form of oppression—the 'iron cage' of modern bureaucratic organisational forms and structures.

Capitalism and modernity of course also came together in Karl Marx's historical materialism, which characterised the historical process as a series of modes of production, proceeding through the dialectic of class struggle, eventually to culminate in the classless society of communism. Karl Polanyi also viewed the process of modernisation as one of capital development, of the subjection of society to economy, of Maine's progress from status to contract, a distinctly modern form; but along with Marx, he was highly critical of its negative aspects, identifying it with a destructive violence of accumulation. Polanyi argued that 'however natural it may appear to us . . . a [market] system is an institutional structure which, as we all too easily forget, has been present at no time except our own.'[40] Polanyi saw in market capitalism a singular moment in history, in which was to be found:

> ...a motive only rarely acknowledged as valid in the history of human societies, and certainly never before raised to the level of justification and behavior in everyday life, namely, gain. The self-regulating market was uniquely derived from this principle. The mechanism that the motive of gain set in motion was comparable in effectiveness only to the most violent outbursts of religious fervor in history...[41]

Therefore, modernity, or at least the later modern era, has been less positively identified with the downsides and flaws of capitalism. Modernity has also been associated with disenchantment and with suppression of the sense of wonder of life. Weber's perception of the negative effects of rationalisation has already been mentioned, and Weber also stated, 'The fate of our times is characterised by rationalisation and intellectualisation and above all, disenchantment of the world.'[42] One response to rationalisation

---

[39] M Weber, *On Law in Economy and Society*, M Rheinstein (ed) (Cambridge, MA, Harvard University Press, 1954).

[40] K Polanyi, *The Great Transformation: The Political and Economic Origins of Our Time* (Boston, Beacon Press, 1957) 40.

[41] Ibid, 31.

[42] M Weber, 'Science as a Vocation' in HH Gerth and C Wright Mills (trans and eds), *From Max Weber: Essays in Sociology* (New York, Oxford University Press, 1946) 156. Weber conceived rationalisation, namely the instrumentalisation of reason, using practical knowledge to achieve a given end, as part of a larger theory of bureaucracy.

and disenchantment was the late eighteenth- and early nineteenth-century Romantic movement, which prized aesthetic experience and irrationalism even, as well as looking to custom and ethnicity as sources of authenticity—as exemplified by the works of Johann Gottfried Herder and Johann Gottlieb Fichte. Such romanticism censured modernity for being dominated by instrumental reason, preferring instead to look to a romantic-expressive notion of authenticity as the way to recover one's true nature.[43] Romanticism also engaged in a melancholy belief that, with modernity, something important had been lost, involving the alienation of important values—a sort of nostalgia of the soul. Indeed, for Isaiah Berlin, Romanticism was part of a larger tendency of counter-Enlightenment.[44]

Kantian optimism about Enlightenment has also been derided as a desire for mastery and control of the environment rather than a more innocent autonomy and freedom from medieval superstition. Even as early as 1818, Mary Shelley's *Frankenstein* presented a negative image of modernity and Enlightenment as an overwhelming desire for knowledge and a dangerous attempt to master nature, devoid of ethical context. Shelley portrayed Dr Frankenstein as an enlightened scientist who views magic and alchemy with contempt, and yet his creation, the awful, nameless monster, causes terrible harm and finally destroys him. Theodor Adorno and Max Horkheimer, presenting their *Dialectic of Enlightenment*, wrote, 'Enlightenment behaves towards things as a dictator toward men. He knows them in as far as he can manipulate them.'[45]

These approaches ultimately link Enlightenment and modernity with destruction and self-destruction. They perceive modernity as at risk of degeneration into the pathological, or even as a suicidal impulse.[46] According to Jacques Derrida, the post-war conflicts of the twentieth and twenty-first centuries—the Cold War and the more recent 'war on terror'—are 'auto-immune' responses generated by modernity itself.[47] Derrida has noted that an auto-immune condition is one in which 'a living being, in a *quasi-suicidal* fashion, "itself" works to destroy its own protection, to immunise

---

[43] See further, C Taylor, *The Ethics of Authenticity* (Cambridge, MA, Harvard University Press, 1991).

[44] I Berlin, 'The Counter-Enlightenment' in H Hardy (ed), *Against the Current: Essays in the History of Ideas* (London, Hogarth Press, 1979).

[45] T Adorno and M Horkheimer, *The Dialectic of Enlightenment*, (London, Verso, 1979).

[46] This perception was already prefigured in Romanticism with Goethe's depiction of the suicide of the melancholic Werther. Goethe's own synopsis, sent to a friend, of *The Sorrows of Young Werther* reads as follows: 'I present a young person gifted with deep, pure feeling and true penetration, who loses himself in rapturous dreams, buries himself in speculation, until at last, ruined by unhappy passions that supervene, in particular an unfulfilled love, puts a bullet in his head.' *Werther* has been interpreted as representative of certain young Germans of his time, jaded and sickened by a futile, stagnant and spiritless social order. See, eg, JM Coetzee, 'Storm over Young Goethe', *New York Review of Books* (26 April 2012).

[47] See the interview with Derrida in G Borradori (ed), *Philosophy in a Time of Terror* (Chicago, Chicago University Press, 2003).

itself *against* its own immunity.'[48] John Gray, for example, sees Al Qaeda as uniquely modern: 'Like Marxists and neo-liberals, radical Islamists see history as a prelude to a new world. All are convinced they can remake the human condition. If there is a uniquely modern myth, this is it.'[49]

Given these substantial definitional problems,[50] it might be safest to understand modernity by what it is not—not medieval, not the Dark Ages—thereby reaching a sort of 'degree zero' of modernity.[51] Admittedly, this does not take one very far, although in its element of negation this notion of modernity carries a late modern or postmodern twist that is itself redolent of Derrida or Martin Heidegger: instead of ~~Being~~, we have ~~Medieval~~.[52] I suggest, however, that there is some accuracy in both the 'Enlightenment' and the 'pathological' visions of modernity. Indeed, it is the complex, contested nature of modernity that provides tensions within and problematises much of modern law.

'After' Modernity

The title 'Law *after* Modernity' implies some sort of transformation or rupture—if not of law, then of time, perhaps of both. If law has moved beyond modernity, what does that mean? Where are we now, and how has law altered? Where does modernity end? Has it ended yet?

According to Jürgen Habermas, modernity is still an 'unfinished project'.[53] For Fredric Jameson, it is over and buried.[54] Millennial times have indeed produced some momentous features and events, which signal or threaten huge changes in culture and society: the Internet, global warming, global terrorism, failed states and the threat of deadly pandemics. For some, modernity might seem to have waned or metamorphosed around the time of the first Gulf War (1991) (described by Jean Baudrillard as a 'virtual'

[48] Derrida continues, 'For let us not forget that the US had in effect paved the way for and consolidated the forces of the "adversary" by training people like Bin Laden, who would here be the most striking example, and by first of all creating the politico-military circumstances that would favour their emergence and shifts in allegiance.' Ibid, 94 and 95.

[49] Gray (above n 36) 3.

[50] Fredric Jameson has written, 'The words "modernisation" and "modernity" have been degraded to fashionable concepts under which you can think anything at all.' F Jameson, *A Singular Modernity* (London, Verso, 2002) 9.

[51] The term 'degree zero' derives from R Barthes, *Le degré zero de l'écriture* (Paris, Seuil, 1953), a work that starts with a series of definitions to show what writing is not.

[52] The strikethrough was a device often used by Heidegger to signify 'inadequate but necessary' (see M Heidegger, *Being and Time* (New York, Harper & Row, 1962)) and was also used by Derrida as *sous rature*—'under erasure' (see, eg, J Derrida, *Writing and Difference* (London, Routledge, 1978).

[53] J Habermas, 'Modernity: An Unfinished Project' in MP D'Entrèves and S Benhabib (eds), *Habermas and the Unfinished Project of Modernity* (Cambridge, Polity Press, 1996).

[54] Jameson, *The Cultural Logic of Late Capitalism* (above n 37).

and thus possibly the first 'postmodern' war).[55] For others, the change came ten years later with September 11 and the new world order.[56] David Harvey sets an actual date for the change: 'There has been a sea-change in cultural as well as in political-economic practices since around 1972.'[57] Yet we can go further back in search of transformation—highly significant change predates the millennium by a considerable period of time. The English historian Alfred Toynbee described the First World War as the first postmodern war.[58] Since earlier in the twentieth century and certainly by the end of the Second World War, the post-Westphalian order had started to break down. In a now famous speech at Humboldt University Berlin in 2000, then German foreign minister Joschka Fischer suggested:

> The core of the concept of Europe after 1945 was and still is a rejection of the European balance-of-power principle and the hegemonic ambitions of individual states that had emerged following the Peace of Westphalia in 1648, a rejection which took the form of closer meshing of vital interests and the transfer of nation-state sovereign rights to supranational European institutions.[59]

Robert Cooper also sees 1945 (but additionally 1989) as a key date. He writes:

> What happened then was more far reaching than the events of 1789, 1815 or 1919 because it wrought a fundamental change in the European state system itself ... [H]istorically the best point of comparison is 1648 ... In both cases, 1648 and 1945, the result was a recognition that there had been a radical failure and the system was changed.[60]

Some writers assert that there has been a shift seismic enough to be called paradigmatic or, in Foucaultian terms, an 'epistemic' break. In his novel *Atomised*, the French writer Michel Houellebecq discusses the 'metaphysical mutations' that have transformed the way people think, writing:

> Once a metaphysical mutation has arisen, it moves inexorably towards its logical conclusion. Heedlessly, it sweeps away economic and political systems, ethical considerations and social structures. No human agency can halt its progress—nothing but another metaphysical mutation.[61]

---

[55] J Baudrillard, *The Gulf War Did Not Take Place* (Bloomington, Indiana, 1995).

[56] For example, at a speech to the Labour Party conference in October 2001, then UK Prime Minister Tony Blair announced, 'In retrospect, the Millennium marked only a moment in time. It was the events of September 11 that marked a turning point in history.'

[57] Harvey (above n 37) vii.

[58] A Toynbee, *A Study of History*, vol 8 (Oxford, Oxford University Press, 1954).

[59] J Fischer, 'From Confederacy to Federation: Thoughts on the Finality of European Integration', speech given at Humboldt University, Berlin (12 May 2000).

[60] R Cooper, *The Breaking of Nations* (London, Atlantic Books, 2003) 2–3.

[61] M Houellebecq, *Atomised* (London, Vintage, 2001) 4. Houellebecq's fictional 'metaphysical mutation' concerns the elimination of human desire and the creation of a new

As Houellebecq highlights, such transformations are rare in the course of history. The emergence and spread of the Christian and Islamic religions was one such seismic shift, the Enlightenment and growth of scientific method another. The environmentalist George Monbiot cites Houllebecq's theory of 'metaphysical mutation' in his own book, *The Age of Consent*, suggesting that we are on the verge of another such mutation, this time caused by globalisation, which tears down old barriers and bonds, forcing states to relinquish nationhood.

Similarly, Michael Hardt and Antonio Negri, in their grandly titled *Empire*, refer to a new 'logic and structure of rule—a new form of sovereignty'—proclaiming that 'the sovereignty of nation states has declined' and that 'sovereignty has taken a new form . . . what we call Empire', which they envisage as a sort of planetary 'Gestalt' of flows and hierarchies of networks of power on a global scale with its own constitutional system.[62] Hardt and Negri make further ambitious claims for 'Empire', suggesting its creative forces may be directed toward emancipatory ends.

Hardt and Negri are not alone in boldly claiming a new legal order (in their case, constitutional and economic) for a new era. Boaventura de Sousa Santos provides another manifesto, with the perhaps less grandiose title *Towards a New Legal Common Sense*.[63] For de Sousa Santos, modernity (by which he means the dominant mode of thought from the sixteenth century to the mid-twentieth century) has broken down and is in the process of being replaced by a postmodern paradigm in which a constellation of different legalities operate in local, national and transnational time spaces. De Sousa Santos' vision is, however, also utopian, calling for a 're-enchanted' common sense.

Of course, writers have been claiming paradigm shifts long before Hardt, Negri and de Sousa Santos came up with their millenarian theories. Postmodern writers have been announcing the onset of a new legal era for quite some time. But what does such postmodernism amount to? The term 'postmodern' has been as contested as 'modernity'.[64] A key theme in the literature on postmodernism is taken from Jean-François Lyotard's *The Postmodern Condition*, which identified postmodernity with an absence of grand narratives. For Lyotard, 'grand narratives' were linked to modernity and Enlightenment and portrayed humanity as an heroic agent of its own

---

world in which 'a new, rational species' relies on cloning rather than sexuality as a means of reproduction, as part of an attempt to achieve immortality.

[62] M Hardt and A Negri, *Empire* (Cambridge, MA, Harvard University Press, 2000) xii.

[63] B de Sousa Santos, *Towards a New Legal Common Sense: Law, Globalisation, and Emancipation*, 2nd edn (London, Butterworths, 2002).

[64] See, eg, S Connor, *Postmodernist Culture: An Introduction to Theories of the Contemporary* (Oxford, Blackwell, 1989); and Harvey (above n 37) for a discussion of the problems of identifying and defining postmodernity and postmodernism.

liberation through the advancement of knowledge.[65] In contrast, Lyotard's postmodern condition is defined by the loss of credence in these meta-narratives, which have been replaced by a plurality of different types of story and argument, a proliferation of paradoxes, a fragmentation and dispersal of knowledge and of 'language games' and the recognition that science is just one more language game among others. Indeed, according to Lyotard, even science, through new concepts such as microphysics, fractals and chaos, is 'theorising its own evolution as discontinuous, catastrophic and paradoxical'.[66]

The 'postmodern' as a concept also has important roots in the arts. In the 1972 work *Learning from Las Vegas*,[67] the architect Robert Venturi and his associates criticised the purist orthodoxy of modernist architect Mies van der Rohe. In 1977, the first edition of Charles Jencks' *Language of Postmodern Architecture*[68] appeared. According to Jencks, this 'language' employs a radical eclecticism and hybrid forms of modern and historical syntax, providing a tribute to the past, yet in a new form. Since the publication of these architectural works, a primary association of the term 'postmodern' has been with new forms of built and designed space. Indeed, the spatial has been a key element of the postmodern in other disciplines as well—a theme that will be picked up in later chapters of this book.

However, translated into legal theory, postmodern work seems to be not so much exemplary of a new paradigm as constituting a body of critique of existing legal theories, which takes the following form: it is suspicious of 'reason', hierarchies and unity, and is therefore often identifiable as much for its *methods* as for any substantive new way of visualising law. Postmodernism can be whimsical, poetic, averse to 'hard' legal language, disrespectful or metaphorical. However, very often much of its message is nihilistic or negative.

The term 'postmodern' is in any case inextricably linked to the concept of modernity—dependent on it and shadowing it. Therefore, it may be difficult to ascertain how postmodern thinking can lead to a postmodern way of life, although it is likely that those urging such a lifestyle might invoke the recognition of incommensurable differences, inclusion of the

---

[65] Examples of such thought might be found in Kant's *Idea of a Universal History with a Cosmopolitan Purpose*, as well as in the work of the nineteenth-century English Whig historians, such as WEH Lecky, Lord Acton and JR Seeley, which illustrate the tendency to present history as an ineluctable progress toward advancement and Enlightenment; or additionally, in those theories of nineteenth-century social evolutionists such as Auguste Comte and Herbert Spencer.

[66] J-F Lyotard, *The Postmodern Condition* (Manchester, Manchester University Press, 1984).

[67] R Venturi, D Scott Brown and S Izenour, *Learning from Las Vegas: The Forgotten Symbolism of Architectural Form*, revised edn (Cambridge, MA, Massachusetts Institute of Technology Press, 1977).

[68] C Jencks, *The Language of Postmodern Architecture* (New York, Rizzoli, 1977).

marginal, or empowerment of the excluded[69]—which sounds somewhat Christ-like, imposing demands that only a messiah might fulfil. However, I prefer to take 'postmodernism' not as a paradigmatic or accurate description of twenty-first-century law but rather as a methodology that presents useful insights, but whose methods should not be followed slavishly. Therefore, the project of this book is not, strictly speaking, 'postmodern'.[70]

Nevertheless, there exists evidence to indicate some sort of shift with a past, 'modern' era, even if it does not take the form of a clean break or rupture. The present age might be described as a transitional, rather ambiguous era, which continues with some of the trappings of the past. The changes in legal form will be closely detailed in later chapters of this book, and they involve the growth of informal, flexible, private or non-state 'governance' organisations and networks, as well as a growing awareness of the pluralism and plurality of legal orders. One further characteristic of the present age is its loss of confidence and of certainty. During modernity, however we characterise it, there existed greater confidence in the ability to deliver a persuasive, comprehensive account of law, or of society in general.

'Law'

The starting point is therefore the assumption that there is an era identifiable as 'modernity' (albeit 'modernity' understood in a complex way), and during this era, law was conceived and theorised according to the various ideational structures of modernity; but that era is coming to an end, and both law itself and theories about law are changing in this new post-millennial age. Benjamin sought to capture the nineteenth-century arcades at the moment of their decay and thereby developed a theory about history—that you can best understand the present from the standpoint of the immediate past, whose fashions are just a little out of date.[71] Similarly, the nature of twenty-first-century law may become clearer if we consider what might be meant by law in 'modernity' and how law—or our perceptions of law—appear to be changing. In other words, what is law changing from? Is it possible to identify a recognisably 'modern' conception of law? What

---

[69] As advocated, for example, in the works of Lyotard (see, eg, above n 66) or those of Emmanuel Levinas (for example, *Time and the Other* (Pittsburgh, Dusquesne University Press, 1990).

[70] For a similar approach, see W Twining, *Globalisation and Legal Theory* (London, Butterworths, 2000) ch 8, which includes an interesting discussion of Susan Haack's views on postmodernism in her book *Manifesto of a Passionate Moderate* (Chicago, University of Chicago Press, 2000).

[71] W Benjamin, *The Arcades Project* (Cambridge, MA, Belknap Press, 1999), cited by F Jameson, 'Future City' (2003) 21 *New Left Review* 66.

is unworkable or outdated about this conception, and how then should we shift our perceptions of law?

At first this seems an impossibly over-ambitious task. 'Modern' law is not a unified body of doctrine. As Nigel Simmonds has suggested, 'Legal thought of any period is likely to resemble an ancient palimpsest. Modern law contains layers of meaning, one superimposed on and partially obscuring the other.'[72] Within the long period of time that could be said to constitute 'modernity', there have existed a wide variety of candidates for the concept of law, seemingly with little in common. No complex legal order ever forms a fully coherent legal system in any case. We are again faced with the problem of getting beyond the definitional degree zero. These definitional problems of providing a unified concept of law in modernity are well illustrated by the following sample of theories, all of which are candidates for a 'modern' concept of law.

One (perhaps somewhat obvious, in Western Jurisprudence at least) starting point is the relentlessly schematic *Province of Jurisprudence* by John Austin,[73] formulated in the nineteenth century and further formalised as an object of doctrinal study by his successors, including TH Holland.[74] Seen from this perspective, law is not only a domain, or province, with somewhat imperialist connotations, but also an expression of a nineteenth-century desire for a scientifically organised study of living things and concepts. Austin believed he could establish a 'science of jurisprudence'. Austin's theory was positivist in that it identified law on the basis of its sources only (in this case a sovereign) with the aim of keeping law as it is separate from law as it ought to be. 'Positivism' is of course a term of multiple meanings. John Gray has described the nineteenth-century French positivists Henri de Saint-Simon and Auguste Comte as 'the original prophets of modernity', as they believed in the power of science to organise society.[75] Scientific positivism focuses on empirical observations and the making of regular connections. Austin exhibited some of these techniques but was generally more conceptual. Weber and HLA Hart, on the other hand, while also being positivist, were more interpretative in method.

A later nineteenth-century investigation of law is to be found in Max Weber's 'The Sociology of Law', which forms part of his larger work

---

[72] N Simmonds, *The Decline of Juridical Reason* (Manchester, Manchester University Press, 1984) 23.

[73] J Austin, *The Province of Jurisprudence Determined* (Cambridge, Cambridge University Press, 1995).

[74] Of course, Austin was himself a disciple of Jeremy Bentham, who was a more original legal thinker. Yet, as much of Bentham's work on law remained unavailable for so long, it was Austinian positivism that was disseminated in the Anglo-Saxon legal world and its colonies. See, for example, TH Holland, *Elements of Jurisprudence* (Oxford, Clarendon Press, 1880).

[75] Gray (above n 36) 27.

Economy and Society.[76] Weber's study is also an explicit reflection on the relationship between law and modernity. Weber saw modern law as made up of a formal legal system that presents itself as universal and a class of professional technocrats whose task is to apply the system. Law thereby epitomises the modern by its techniques of rendering things calculable, its strategies of control, its measure, systematisation, and bureaucracy—to the exclusion of non-rational elements such as religion, aesthetics and ethics. So, like Austin, Weber separated law from morality, but he did so as part of a broader investigation of modernity. Weber's methodology and theorising about law also influenced twentieth-century positivists such as Hart and Hans Kelsen, whose theories have also played a very important part in modern theorising about law.

A third item in our sample of 'modern' theories of law takes us to the United States in the 1930s. The American legal realists were also positivists in that they sought to locate law in social fact, but their social science-driven legal theory focused not on abstract notions such as Austin's trilogy of command-sovereign-sanction or Weber's formally rational law but on empirical research—what courts actually do in practice. Therefore, the realists' work was scientific and positivist in an empirical or statistical way rather than in the more conceptual sense in which Austin's theory was positivist, but it very clearly aspired to be 'modern' and scientific. William Twining has located the roots of legal realism within a broader attempt to come to grips with modernity and to address the problems of rapid societal and legal change in late nineteenth- early twentieth-century America—and the related problems of trying to achieve a unified system of modern doctrine.[77]

Jumping forward in time almost 70 years but staying with a writer who consciously places himself within the paradigm of modernity (although he anticipates many of the anxieties and problematics of postmodernity), we find a self-conscious attempt to provide a theory of law that, as its title states, locates it *Between Facts and Norms.*[78] The German theorist Jurgen Habermas presents law as neither an object of doctrinal study nor empirical research but instead focuses on the problem of the legitimacy of law in an era Weber characterised as 'disenchanted'. The search for legitimacy has become one of the most pressing problems of modern law. In modern times, when neither religion nor morality are part of the fabric of everyday life for every citizen, how may law be legitimised and become something other than brute force of the powerful or a soulless bureaucratic rationality, which seems to embody nothing other than good order? Habermas'

---

[76] Weber, *On Law in Economy and Society* (above n 39).

[77] W Twining, *Karl Llewellyn and the Realist Movement* (London, Butterworths, 1973).

[78] J Habermas, *Between Facts and Norms* (Cambridge, MA, Massachusetts Institute of Technology Press, 1996).

solution derives law's legitimacy from the democratic process itself, a democracy that is understood as a powerful consensual process in which citizens accord each other a range of both public political rights and rights of private autonomy. Habermas, however, stresses not only the democratic process but also the productive power of reason or rationality (so, in this way, he remains self-consciously modern, although Habermas invokes a communicative, intersubjective rationality), itself a concept derided by some postmodern writers.

Habermas' account is optimistic—he sees a possible emancipatory role for law. He also introduces something not to be found in the three earlier accounts—the issue of law's legitimacy and its problematic relationship with morality. All is not optimism, however. Our final choice of a 'modern' theory of law presents law in a less positive light. Marxist writings aim to expose law, or at least Western law, as ideological. The Marxist critique is premised on the claim that supposedly liberating doctrines such as the rule of law and human rights in fact justify or mask a legal regime that is based on the self-interest of a few. In other words, Marxists claim, law is not transparent, not to be taken at face value, but a key bearer of ideological messages, which, because of law's (wrongly) generally assumed legitimacy, serve to reinforce its ideology. Such visions of law are still to be found in contemporary writings (eg, the critical legal studies movement and critical race theory) and by no means died with the demise of Soviet communism. Indeed, they are enjoying a resurgence in an era in which there exists censure of the power and dominance of global capital.

I have deliberately chosen the above five 'modern' visions of law (which I shall continue to deploy throughout this book) to illustrate the varieties of legal thought over the period of time characterised as 'modernity'. They provide diversity—historically, geographically and theoretically—although all are the product of white Western males, most of them dead, not all of whom were, strictly speaking, lawyers. All could with accuracy be called modern, and yet they exhibit very different visions of what law is, what its role must be. This diversity is to be expected, especially since no universally acceptable conception of the term 'modernity' itself can be identified. However, part of the explanation of their diversity lies in their historical and cultural contexts—a theme that I shall explore throughout this book.

Beyond the 'Degree Zero' of Law in Modernity

My attempt to summon up law in modernity (and thus provide a starting point for the differentiation of law after modernity) aims at least to take us a little further from what I have termed the 'degree zero'—the 'not-medieval'—definition of law in modernity. This book does not seek to provide a concept of law, nor to define law. Nor does it propose only one way of theorising law, one path for jurisprudence. It proceeds instead by setting out a short list of features that seem salient, or paradigmatic, of law in modernity. Most attempts to characterise law, including the five accounts of Austin, Weber, the legal realists, Habermas and Marxism, feature at least some of the items on the list, but not necessarily all, which is why the accounts of law discussed above seem different, although if one follows the logic of this list, one begins to see some sort of Wittgensteinian 'family resemblance'. The items of the list are clearly not comprehensive, but they are enough to take us beyond the 'degree zero' of law in modernity.

The argument is that theorising about law within the modern era— loosely understood as the period from the mid-seventeenth century to the late twentieth century—exhibited the following traits:

1. a belief in the relative autonomy or 'closure' of law;
2. a characterisation of law as systematic, fairly orderly and capable of existing in the context of separate 'legal systems'; and
3. a tendency to identify law with the nation state, or at least to stress the importance of state law, and a reluctance to delve too deeply into the multidimensionality or pluralisms of law, whether on a global, regional or sub-national level.

Chapters two through four of this book examine these three features and aim to demonstrate their problematic nature.[79] Although few legal theorists would these days unreservedly promote a jurisprudence based on law's autonomy and systematic quality, this orthodox view continues to have a relatively strong normative pull. The aim of this project is therefore to move beyond a prevailing orthodoxy in the modern period and to investigate the nature of a legal theory with which to replace it—which will be a theory of a more complicated, nebulous nature. The remaining chapters of the book continue with this task.

It will be argued that the contemporary legal space is becoming a space of overlapping jurisdictions, segmented authority and multiple loyalties, characterised by the growth of informal, flexible, private or non-state 'governance' organisations and networks, as well as by an increasing number of transnational and supranational legal orders. In a landscape in which national legal sovereignty is weakened and jurisdictions compete (and overlap) globally, there is a risk of conflict and of officials being compelled

---

[79] See, by contrast, de Sousa Santos' selection of what he takes to be the '3 structural features of modern law': rhetoric, bureaucracy, violence. See de Sousa Santos (above n 63). Alternatively, Nonet and Selznick suggest three classic paradigms—or, in their preferred terminology, 'postures'—of law, in modern legal theory: repressive law, autonomous law and responsive law. See P Nonet and P Selznick, *Law and Society in Transition: Toward a Responsive Law* (New York, Harper Colophon, 1978).

to choose between their loyalties to different institutions. This raises the prospect of untidy collisions, legal tangles and apparently irresolvable dilemmas. These developments will be discussed in subsequent chapters. This legal landscape also has a tendency to display some attributes that have been commonly identified as postmodern: namely, a fragmentation, indeterminacy and discontinuity of form; the growth of multiple and different discourses; an acceleration of time and compression of space and chaotic flurry of change; a tendency to heterarchical rather than hierarchical relationships; and the strengthening of globalism at the expense of national sovereignty. Undeniably, this contemporary legal landscape is challenging.

In the face of this prospect, how to conceptualise law? It appears impossible to categorise such complex legal landscapes by a neat, self-contained conception of law, such as those associated with various legal theories of the modern era. Is law now better conceptualised as 'postmodern? Rather than taking this path, this book affirms a theory of legal pluralism. Many contemporary theorists believe legal pluralism to be the most convincing and workable theory of law, and this book is sympathetic to many of these claims. Legal pluralism describes a state of affairs in which two or more legal orders occupy the same legal space, sometimes peacefully coexisting but sometimes in direct competition with each other.[80] Chapter four argues that the notion of legal pluralism better captures the nature of law in the contemporary era.

This book therefore presents contemporary law as a complex, pluralist phenomenon not readily capable of systematisation, in contrast to an earlier paradigm of a more formal, autonomous, systematic law. Yet is this a transformation to be welcomed? While I believe legal pluralism empirically workable, I have reservations about its normative attractions. Later in the book I argue that in the contemporary landscape, where 'formal' law may sometimes be thin on the ground, the most crucial and often unanswered questions are of justice and accountability. In particular, there are many situations in which there is either a weak or, indeed, no functioning rule of law. Such environments undermine accountability and the possibility of justice. Justice is further compromised in the global arena, where there exists either little or no trace of formerly familiar mechanisms of state accountability.

Justice therefore becomes a key issue for law in the era of legal pluralism. Rather than, or at least in addition to, exploring questions of ordering[81] and attempting to interpret pluralism, we should ask how justice

---

[80] For further on legal pluralism, see, eg, J Griffiths, 'What Is Legal Pluralism?' (1986) 24 *Journal of Legal Pluralism* 2–55, 2. The origins of legal pluralism lie in anthropology, sociology and colonial experience. See, eg, E Ehrlich, *Fundamental Principles of the Sociology of Law*, WL Moll (trans) (New York, Russell and Russell, 1936).

[81] See, eg, M Delmas Marty, *Ordering Pluralism* (Oxford, Hart Publishing, 2009).

is achievable, given this complexity and the wide variety of legal forms and experiences. Ultimately, how is justice possible? The later chapters of this book focus on this issue.

In the present age, the notion of justice has often been overshadowed by other concepts. For example, human rights, democracy and accountability tend to be used as frequently as the concept of justice as conceptual tools for diagnosing, treating and solving the normative problems that arise in the legal domain. Yet perhaps we should remember the plea for the priority of justice as articulated by John Rawls:

> Justice is the first virtue of social institutions, as truth is to thought. A theory however elegant and economical must be rejected or revised if it is untrue; likewise laws and institutions no matter how efficient and well-arranged must be reformed or abolished if they are unjust.[82]

While I will not argue for the application of Rawls' actual theory of justice to law after modernity, I do argue that justice—or perhaps rather *injustice*—raises especially salient issues for the contemporary legal world. Analysing contemporary law's actions in terms of justice highlights their impact on its peoples and accentuates law's imbalances of power. However, the solutions to these instances of injustice are not readily apparent; nor may answers easily be found in the other concepts such as human rights, democracy or accountability.

My argument is that some solution to the problem of justice may be found in the particular relation of justice to law, in a concept I name 'critical legal justice', which is explored later in this book, particularly in chapter eight. However, justice is not confined to legal justice. While justice in a broader sense may be so elusive as to be an ideal or utopian, it is the diagnosis of *injustice* that is crucial, as justice is more likely to move people in its absence than it is as an academic or rhetorical exercise that fails to convince. It is *injustice* that motivates and propels action, and the highlighting of injustice does its own work.

Methodology

This book is, to a certain extent, interdisciplinary and historical. This is also characteristic of much postmodern writing,[83] which turns away from the more abstract scholarship of the modern era, although as already stated, this book is not intended as another contribution to the postmodern genre

---

[82] J Rawls, *A Theory of Justice* (Cambridge, MA, Harvard University Press, 171) 3.

[83] For example, de Sousa Santos in the first edition of *Towards a New Common Sense: Law, Science and Politics in the Paradigmatic Transition* (New York, Routledge, 1995) spends much of the earlier part of the book discussing modern scientific developments.

as such. Rather, it proceeds on the basis that it is impossible to achieve an adequate understanding of law unless some attempt is made to situate it within its historical, societal, cultural and political context. I conclude this introductory chapter, therefore, by reflecting in a more general form on the argument already made for the relevance of art and the image to law, to stress once again the role that cultural influences play in fashioning law and the ways in which we understand it. Law is as much a matter of culture as it is a system of rules.

Law has been interpreted as a symbolic form that attempts to construct its own ostensible domain of meaning.[84] It asserts its intrinsic ways of seeing and, in so doing, structures our consciousness and creates ways of being in the world—a myriad of complex, intricate forms and traditions. Yet it is not the autonomous discipline it sometimes asserts itself as, bound and influenced only by its own forms and creations. The permeability of law to other areas of knowledge has long been recognised in the course of a deep, historical relationship between law and the humanities, and many of the most famous philosophers—Plato, Aristotle, Hobbes, Kant and Hegel, for example—have either been students of law or possessed a rich knowledge of it and understood law as irrevocably tied to society and morality, as both productive of culture and shaped by it.[85] The study of law also played its part in the curricula of medieval universities, in the *trivium* of the liberal arts, and more generally, law has been approached as part of a broader exploration of human civilisation, culture and tradition, both in the context of accepted orthodox beliefs but also within critical, dissident and irreverent traditions. Law cannot be understood only in terms of doctrinal science. The increasing recognition of interdisciplinary approaches and the growth of interdisciplinary journals acknowledge this.[86] Law itself has its own aesthetic and may be envisioned as a creative art form as much as a science. Most importantly perhaps, 'the study of law as a human discipline is concerned with the capacity of humans to engage with the environment and to reform it through the use of the imagination'[87]—to ensure that law is not investigated only in terms of its own, self-chosen forms of understanding.

But we may ask again, what does this relationship amount to? Many things. Surely not just the simplistic understanding of law itself as literature

---

[84] P Kahn, *The Cultural Study of Law: Reconstructing Legal Scholarship* (Chicago, University of Chicago Press, 1999); cf E Cassirer, *The Philosophy of Symbolic Forms* (New Haven, Yale University Press, 1965).

[85] See further Douzinas (above n 7).

[86] For example, the following journals: *Yale Journal of Law and the Humanities*, founded in 1988; *Law, Culture and the Humanities* (Sage), founded in 2005; and *Law and Humanities* (Hart), founded in 2007. There also exists a Law and Humanities blog at http://lawlit.blog-spot.co.uk/.

[87] *Law and Humanities*, 'Editorial' (2007) v.

or art, nor merely a study of the way law has been portrayed in literature or art. For theorists such as James Boyd White, the study of literature and its relationship to law enriches the legal imagination.[88] This is no anodyne, trivial function. Understanding law in this broader way and relating it to literature or art expands our sympathetic identification with those in very different contexts and experiences. Some scholars have used a narrative jurisprudence or storytelling, or even offered personal accounts of their own experiences,[89] often with great immediacy and abundance of detail. The voices expressed in such narratives are not those of the judges, lawyers or lawmakers who more usually occupy scholarly attention; they are often from those who are dispossessed, for example, on account of gender, race or poverty. Thus an interdisciplinary approach has beneficial counter-hegemonic effects, bringing to our awareness the impact of power and the effects of exploitation and oppression. It retrieves and rescues the law, becoming a means through which we learn to improve the law and become better lawyers. We could take this further. In the view of Matthew Arnold, culture could be seen as a bulwark against anarchy.[90] For Sir Philip Sidney, poetry is the best means of inspiring readers to virtuous action—it possesses a unique power to demonstrate social and political desires, to evoke disaffection with government: 'The poet with that same hand of delight doth draw the mind more effectually than any other art doth'. [91]

To be sure, one should not make inordinate claims for an approach that seeks to understand law in terms of a relationship between law and the humanities, culture and art. We cannot equate the creative process for judges, who write judgments, with that of literary authors, who write fiction. Rhetoric and cultural issues bestride these two domains, but artists are not practising law, nor are great judgments literary novels. *Bleak House* may enhance our knowledge of the Victorian legal system, but Charles Dickens was not a legal scholar. Lord Denning's legal opinions often tended to be narrative in style, but he was not a novelist. As suggested earlier, the relationship between law and culture is a complex one, of co-implication, not simplistically causal but rather one that illuminates and enriches our understanding of law.

Law is continuous with and a reflection of other aspects of social and cultural practices. This is of course a two-way process, for laws also organise the way in which we see the world. As Roberto Unger has written, 'A society's law constitutes the chief bond between its culture and its

---

[88] Boyd White (above n 6).

[89] See, eg, P Williams, *The Alchemy of Race and Rights* (Cambridge, MA, Harvard University Press, 1992).

[90] M Arnold, *'Culture and Anarchy' and Other Writings*, S Collini (ed) (Cambridge, Cambridge University Press, 1993).

[91] Sir Philip Sidney, *The Defence of Poesy*, 1595 (London, Penguin Classics, 2004). See also *Law and Humanities*, 'Editorial' (2007) vi.

organisation: it is the external manifestation of the embeddedness of the former in the latter.'[92] An appraisal of the broader cultural context reveals all sorts of interesting connections and correspondences that can enrich our understanding of law and bring fresh perspectives to bear on old puzzles and problems. It may also illuminate, as Philip Selznick suggests, 'how legal rules and concepts . . . are animated and transformed by intellectual history; how much the authority and self-confidence of legal institutions depends on underlying realities of class and power.'[93] William Twining has pointed out how the term 'discipline' usually connotes visions of solid physical structures that enjoy relative autonomy. These disciplines occupy and defend separate territories in which 'each seems to have its own quite distinctive culture', forming 'an aggregation of sovereignties connected by a common heating plant'.[94] But so much is lost if we take the 'separate physical structures' approach. EP Thompson wrote of history that it was 'a discipline of context and process' in which 'every meaning is a meaning-in-context'.[95] I believe this to be just as true of law.

It is often said that the postmodern condition entails a crisis of values and a loss of faith,[96] which are created by the dissipation of traditional forms of value. In this situation, an economic, instrumentalist logic, a creature of capitalism, has tended to dominate and function as a place marker for legitimacy. Law has frequently adopted this logic, as well as its technical reason, its reliance on contract and property (the attributes of commerce) and its belief in the 'rational actor' of the law and economics doctrine, while often presenting them in the guise of law as doctrinal science. While a well functioning economy may help create the prosperity necessary for human freedom and well-being, there are many types of human flourishing and other understandings of law that do not rely on market relations, and this reductionist (albeit far from neutral) model, which limits complex human behaviour to the maximisation of preferences, must be rejected. This book will examine this often unhappy alliance between law and capitalism. An interdisciplinary approach, looking to law's undeniable relationship with a broader culture, is a way of resisting both this reductionist approach to law and the acontextual and unhistorical view of law as doctrinal science.

---

[92] R Unger, *Law in Modern Society* (London, Macmillan, 1976) 250.

[93] P Selznick, '"Law in Context" Revisited' (2003) 30 *Journal of Law & Society* 177. See also Robert Cover, who uses the concept of 'Jurisgenesis' to explain how the creation of legal meaning always 'takes place through essentially cultural meaning.' R Cover, 'Nomos and Narrative' (1983) 97 *Harvard Law Review* 4.

[94] W Twining, *Blackstone's Tower: The English Law School* (London, Hamlyn Press, 1994) 64, quoting RM Hutchins from M Mayor, *RM Hutchins: A Memoir* (Berkeley, University of California Press, 1993) 97.

[95] EP Thompson, *The Poverty of Theory* (London, Merlin, 1978).

[96] Eg, Lyotard (above n 66).

Therefore, while this book is not an excursus into law, art and the humanities, it does employ much of the methodology of such approaches, believing that an interdisciplinary, contextual approach that shapes our understanding of law in its cultural context not only provides an important form of resistance against a contemporary drift but also provides a richer understanding of law—indeed, as argued later in this book, it aids us in our search for justice.

And I keep Klimt's *Jurisprudentia* in mind—its provocative images are a reminder of the uncertainties, complexities and contradictions of law, as well as of the elusiveness of justice.

2

Autonomous Law or Redundant Law? The Elusive Nature of Legal Theory

Autonomous Law

Why start with legal autonomy? What does it mean? Why does it seem important? Legal autonomy can mean a number of things: that law forms a distinct sphere of practical reasoning; that law has its own epistemology (ie, there is such a distinct thing as purely 'legal' knowledge, as Hans Kelsen believed);[1] or the even stronger claim that law as a concept should be understood only on the basis of internal 'legal' sources rather than on external elements such as culture or politics. It can also be the claim that law's foundations are self-grounding, that its validity is not dependent on some external source, such as religion or morality—in this sense we could perhaps more specifically refer to it as legal 'closure'. Very closely linked with this is Niklas Luhmann's point that law insists on its authority to determine whether something is legally relevant or significant.[2]

These are not identical claims, but they are related and emblematic of much theorising about law in the modern era, which is why they are discussed at this early stage of the book. Many of the theorists holding these views have been positivists,[3] engaged in analytical jurisprudence concerned with the clarification and explication of legal concepts, most particularly with legal theory—ie, theorising about the nature of law itself.

---

[1] H Kelsen, *Pure Theory of Law*, M Knight (trans) (Berkeley, University of California Press, 1967).

[2] N Luhmann, *Das Recht der Gesellschaft*, (Frankfurt, Suhrkamp, 1995) 93.

[3] Which I consider to include: J Austin, *The Province of Jurisprudence Determined* (Cambridge, Cambridge University Press, 1995); Kelsen, *Pure Theory of Law* (above n 1); HLA Hart, *The Concept of Law* (Oxford, Clarendon Press, 1961); J Raz, *Practical Reason and Norms*, 2nd edn (Oxford, Oxford University Press, 1999); W Waluchow, *Inclusive Legal Positivism* (Oxford, Clarendon Press, 1994); M Kramer, *In Defence of Legal Positivism: Law without Trimmings* (Oxford, Clarendon Press, 1999); J Coleman, *The Practice of Principle* (Oxford, Clarendon Press, 2001); T Campbell, *The Legal Theory of Ethical Positivism* (Dartmouth, Aldershot, 1996); and J Gardner, 'Legal Positivism: 5½ Myths' (2001) 46 *American Journal of Jurisprudence* 199.

In this chapter I shall consider these views, although I acknowledge that legal positivism is not a unified field, and clearly not all positivists have the same objectives. More recent Anglo-American legal positivism has acknowledged law as a social phenomenon—most famously, in the case of HLA Hart's description of *The Concept of Law* as 'an essay in descriptive sociology'.[4] But even more recent positivism has tended to emphasise the institutional distinctiveness of law from other areas of society—most particularly, morality—hence casting law as an autonomous, discrete discipline with an existence in its own right, which, crucially, may be identified without recourse to moral, value-laden principles.[5] This is a claim that will be examined seriously in this chapter.

Although a stress on law's autonomy has been a key feature of 'modern' legal theory, such views continue to be asserted beyond the modern era. In particular, such theories proceed analytically, focusing on the analysis of particular concepts rather than situating law within a broader societal context, even if they acknowledge, as most contemporary legal positivists do, the connectedness of law to other social facts. They stress the value of a conceptual approach to law.[6] The nature of this approach is neatly summarised by the American theorist Stanley Fish, who does not believe in the formal existence or autonomy of the law but has written:

> The law wishes to have a formal existence. That means, first of all, that law does not wish to be absorbed by, or declared subordinate to, some other non-legal structure of concerns; the law wishes, in a word, to be distinct, not something else. And, second, the law wishes in its distinctness to be perspicuous; that is, it desires that the components of its autonomous existence be self-declaring and not be in need of piecing out by some supplementary discourse; for were it [so] … that discourse would be in the business of specifying what the law is, and consequently its autonomy would have been compromised indirectly.[7]

In contrast, many contemporary theorists, particularly those of a critical or postmodern persuasion, contend that claims of legal autonomy are ultimately unsustainable.[8] Nonetheless, it is worthwhile exploring both the claim for legal autonomy and its critique, because the assertion of legal

---

[4] See Hart's own Preface to *The Concept of Law*. Other examples are to be found: for example, Austin located the source of law in the command of the sovereign, backed up by a habit of obedience, ie, a social fact.

[5] This last claim is often described as the 'sources' thesis, a feature of theories of law, such as those of Raz, for example, who believes that law must be identified only in terms of its social sources.

[6] For further on this, see W Twining, *General Jurisprudence: Understanding Law from a Global Perspective* (Cambridge, Cambridge University Press, 2009) ch 2.

[7] S Fish, 'The Law Wishes to have a Formal Existence' in S Fish, *There's No Such Thing as Free Speech, and It's a Good Thing Too* (Oxford, Oxford University Press, 1994) 141.

[8] See, eg, M Davies, *Delimiting the Law: 'Postmodernism' and the Politics of Law* (London, Pluto, 1996); and C Douzinas and R Warrington, *Postmodern Jurisprudence: The Law of Text in the Texts of Law* (London, Routledge, 1991).

autonomy is highly representative of legal theory in modernity—a sort of orthodoxy or 'gold standard' that is adhered to, sometimes subconsciously, by many lawyers and theorists.[9]

Purity

Why is legal autonomy considered important? For earlier positivists, attributing autonomy to law had an important clarificatory aim. In the seventeenth century, Thomas Hobbes rejected custom, 'natural' reason and tradition as sources of law. A century and a half later, Jeremy Bentham was scornful of the way in which law, custom and morality were intermingled in Blackstone's *Commentaries* and insisted that they should be kept separate.[10] Both natural law and common law theory had envisioned law as part of something larger, whether of the natural order of things or of the timeless, accumulated wisdom of the ages. Prior to the modern era, law had not been so sharply differentiated from other aspects of life. Religious, human and natural 'laws' were liable to be conflated. As Walter Ullmann wrote, 'For the larger part of the Middle Ages there was no splitting up of human activities into different compartments. The Christian idea itself militated against any kind of departmentalisation.'[11] So with the onset of modernity, autonomy became an important perceived attribute of law, signifying a key change in the way that law was viewed.

For John Austin, the point of providing (in his own words) a 'map of the law' was to draw up a science of jurisprudence, enabling an objective test to separate law from non-law. For this, by way of definitional fiat, Austin, in somewhat paedogogical and determinative language, insisted on identifying the law 'properly so-called'[12]—which for Austin, was the law of the realm, the aggregate of the general commands of the sovereign. Austin dismissed constitutional and international law as not law 'properly so-called' but rather 'positive morality', because they do not, according to Austin, emanate from a sovereign.

Related thoughts can also be found in the work of Max Weber, whose *Sociology of Law* analyses modernity as the history of emptying law of cultural references (although, as I shall later discuss, Weber's account of law is in fact a deeply historical one). Conceiving of law in this way precludes any

---

[9] As well as featuring in those theories that explain law in terms of various paradigms (eg, those of Nonet and Selznick, Weber, Unger and Habermas).

[10] See W Blackstone, *Commentaries on the Laws of England*, 3rd revised edn (Clark, NJ, Lawbook Exchange, 2004); and J Bentham, *A Fragment on Government: Being an Examination of What Is Delivered on the Subject of Government in General in the Introduction of Sir William Blackstone's Commentaries* (Cambridge, Cambridge University Press, 1988).

[11] Ullmann, *Mediaeval Political Thought* (Harmondsworth, Penguin, 1979) 16.

[12] Austin (above n 3) Lecture I.

identification of law by its content and instead acknowledges some notion of law as having an essence and existence in its own right. Weber described modern law as 'legal rational authority' and wrote that while it was not the only variety of legal authority, it was the 'purest'.[13] Similarly, Kelsen's twentieth-century theory is a 'pure' one, requiring the banishment of ethics, politics, sociology and religion from its domain of identification. Indeed, Kelsen's list of exclusions has been described as 'more comprehensive than that found in most insurance contracts'.[14] In addition to treating law as self-contained and constructing its own objects of discourse, Kelsen went so far as to claim that norms of law and morality cannot conflict because they exist in autonomous, separate spheres.[15] Kelsen's language is revealing: he wanted to avoid 'adulteration' and 'methodological syncretism', which would 'obscure the science of law'. His concern was to identify what is 'peculiarly legal' in social life. Indeed, the French social theorist Bruno Latour argues that to be modern is to define oneself as a purifier who, in contradistinction to premodern thinkers, is skilled in separating the natural from the cultural.[16]

Perhaps the most abstract, sophisticated and technical assertion of law's closure or autonomy is provided by autopoiesis,[17] which insists on the gapless nature of law and its capacity to regulate its own creation; going well beyond traditional legal positivism, it insists on law's ability to 'think' independently of individuals.[18] Autopoiesis gives another explanation of legal autonomy in terms of the fact that, as social complexity has increased, elements of society have become more and more separate and specialist: politics, law, economics and art have developed separately in subsystems to the point that they may appear unintelligible to non-specialists and require expert knowledge.[19] Autopoiesis views law as a distinct social system in itself, which should be understood in this way rather than in relation to other aspects of society. Luhmann suggested that 'autonomy is not a desired goal but a fateful necessity. Given the functional differentiation

---

[13] M Weber, *Essays in Sociology* (Oxford, Oxford University Press, 1958) 299.

[14] C Sampford, *The Disorder of Law* (Oxford, Blackwell, 1989) 24.

[15] H Kelsen, *A General Theory of Law and State*, A Wedberg (trans) (Cambridge, MA, Harvard University Press, 1945) 374–75.

[16] B Latour, *We Have Never Been Modern* (Cambridge, MA, Harvard University Press, 1993) 1.

[17] See N Luhmann, *Law as a Social System*, K Ziegert (trans) (Oxford, Oxford University Press, 2004).

[18] By which autopoiesis theories seem to mean that when persons communicate within institutions, such as corporations or universities, such communications, in addition to being individual communications, are also institutional expressions. In this way, social systems are able to create their own reality. For further on this, see G Teubner, 'How the Law Thinks: Towards a Constructivist Epistemology of Law' (1989) 23 *Law & Society Review* 727.

[19] A point also made by Habermas in *Knowledge and Human Interests* (Boston, Beacon Press, 1971).

of society no subsystem can avoid autonomy'.[20] Law is to be identified and theorised in terms of its distinctness and separation from other social systems, and according to this theory, a legal system will only recognise something as 'law' if it emanates from recognised, law-making institutions. Social systems such as law are seen to interpret actions according to their own logic and binary codes, and autopoiesis insists that law itself determines what is to count as law by the application of the legal/illegal code, achieving structural stability through recursivity. This is extreme—a theory from which humans have been effaced, and almost a clinical example of Kelsen's 'purity'.[21] It is far removed from law in its huge, complex unwieldiness, as actually experienced by human beings.

A Culture of Autonomy?

A concern with autonomy cuts across disciplines, and perversely, as a result, autonomy has its own interdisciplinarity and can be seen as a feature of a broader culture of modernity. We find it in the history of art, for example, in late nineteenth-century theorists such as Heinrich Wölfflin, who sought to free art history from the history of civilisation. The language used by Wölfflin is the same as that of legal theorists—to confine oneself to a 'pure' vision and to the 'pure' consideration of a work of art, to develop a theory of the autonomous development of art that is focused on form, ignoring techniques, historical circumstances and patronage,[22] to prefer formal and conceptual analysis. Interestingly, and by contrast, the art historian Aby Warburg—who was the founder of the Warburg institute[23] and part of the generation following Wölfflin in the 1930s, but who worked co-terminously with Kelsen—was relentlessly interdisciplinary in his approach. Warburg created his unfinished *Bilderatlas*, or photographic library, entitled *Mnemosyne* (Figure 2-1), in order to help users elude the boundary claims of academic disciplines and what he called the 'border police' of disciplinary specialism.

---

[20] N Luhmann, 'The Self-Production of Law and its Limits' in G Teubner (ed), *Dilemmas of Law in the Welfare State* (Berlin, de Gruyter, 1986) 112.

[21] Indeed, the origins of autopoiesis lie in biology, which classifies cells as separate entities that develop self-reproductively even if in complex relations with others. Autopoiesis as a term was first used by the Chilean biologist Maturana. See HR Maturana and FJ Varela, *Autopoiesis and Cognition: The Realization of the Living* (Dordrecht, D Reidel Publishing, 1980).

[22] H Wölfflin, *Classic Art* (London, Phaedon, 1994).

[23] According to its website, the Warburg Institute of the University of London, which stems from the personal library of the Hamburg scholar Aby Warburg, exists principally to further the study of the classical tradition, that is of those elements of European thought, literature, art and institutions that derive from the ancient world. See its website at http://warburg.sas.ac.uk/home/about-the-institute/.

Figure 2-1: Aby Warburg, *Mnemosyne Display* (1924), courtesy of the Warburg Institute

This historically non-linear compilation of images of diverse types, which he continually changed, was an explication of Warburg's method and of his vision of the complicated inter-relatedness of things.[24] He mixed pictures of classical sculpture with medieval manuscripts and cheap popular prints to produce a mosaic, or montage, of almost Dadaistic effect. As the choice of name, *Mnemosyne*, suggests,[25] Warburg was concerned to preserve the memory and aid the survival of a disparate range of references, opening the borders of human knowledge and collective memory.[26] The world of social exchange was especially important to Warburg's methodology, and the exchange and migration of forms essential to his work. Indeed, along with Klimt's *Jurisprudentia*, I see Warburg's *Bilderatlas* as a metaphor for much that I seek to achieve in this book, my project being to reveal the *Mnemosyne*-like nature of the contemporary legal world.

[24] See, eg, M Iversen, 'Retrieving Aby Warburg's Tradition' (1993) 16 *Art History* 541.

[25] Mnemosyne is the Greek word for memory. Indeed, Warburg had originally intended to call the project *Nachleben*, meaning afterlife.

[26] A concern with memory and history also pervades the work of certain legal scholars. For example, Peter Goodrich has argued that a 'defining feature of formalism is the rejection of history': P Goodrich, *Legal Discourse: Studies in Linguistics, Rhetoric, and Legal Analysis* (New York, St Martin's Press, 1987) 5–6.

This concern for autonomy is also to be found elsewhere in the arts, for example, in the purist and puritanical modern architecture of Mies van der Rohe and in the school of formalism within literary theory. Literary formalism holds that a literary text is not a cultural artefact but an autotelic, or unified, self-contained and self-defining work; a reader does not need specialised or detailed contextual knowledge to understand its meaning.[27] This high level of formalism mirrors the legal formalism of much late nineteenth-century jurisprudence.[28] Twentieth-century literary formalism was derided by postmodernists—the American critic William Spanos set up the postmodern literary journal *Boundary 2* at the height of the Vietnam War with the aim 'to get literature back into the world, to demonstrate that postmodernism is a kind of rejection, an undermining of the ethic of formalism and the conservative politics of the new criticism'.[29]

References to art and literature are not misplaced. Hart, at the outset of *The Concept of Law*, puzzled over the prevalence of the question 'What is Law?', suggesting a certain uniqueness to it in the fact that scholars of other disciplines did not agonise over questions such as 'What is Chemistry?' And yet the question 'What is Art?' (or indeed, 'What is Philosophy?') has generated as much, if not more, scholarship as the question 'What is Law?' Indeed, many similar responses to the nature of art conundrum have been given to that of the question 'What is Law?', such as those that rely on the autonomy of art as a discipline or on 'institutional' theories of art,[30] suggesting a particular mindset and way of looking at the world in the modern era. So comparisons are by no means spurious.

The growth in formalism also parallels the growth of law as an autonomous university discipline in England: for example, a separate school of jurisprudence was not founded at Oxford until 1870.[31] Indeed, John Austin was one of the first professors of law at the newly established University College London in the 1820s. German formalist 'legal science' was intimately linked to university legal education during the nineteenth century, and a central theme in Weber's work is the connection between university

---

[27] Eg, IA Richards, *The Principles of Literary Criticism* (New York, Harcourt, 1924); and W Empson, *Seven Types of Ambiguity* (London, Chatto and Windus, 1930).

[28] For example, Thomas Holland, Austin's disciple, describes jurisprudence as 'the formal science of law', T Holland, *Elements of Jurisprudence* (Oxford, Clarendon Press, 1880) ch 1. See also the highly formalist work of Christopher Columbus Langdell, nineteenth-century Dean of Harvard Law School, eg: CC Langdell, *A Selection of Cases of the Law of Contracts with a Summary of the Topics covered by the Cases*, 2nd edn (Boston, Little, Brown and Co, 1879). For an example of contemporary legal formalism, see also E Weinrib, ' "Legal Formalism": On the Immanent Rationality of Law' (1988) 97 *Yale Law Journal* 949.

[29] See P Anderson, *The Origins of Postmodernity* (London, Verso, 1998) 16.

[30] For general discussion on theories of the nature of art, see, eg, G Dickie, *Art and the Aesthetic: An Institutional Approach* (Ithaca, Cornell University Press, 1974); and R Wollheim, *Art and its Objects* (Harmondsworth, Penguin, 1975).

[31] See F Lawson, *The Oxford Law School* (Oxford, Clarendon, 1968) 69–85.

law teaching and conceptual, systematised legal theory.[32] Professional autonomy also became important, with the growth in self-governance of the legal professions (in England, the Bar and the Law Society) encouraging the development of a separate group of professional legal practitioners who could assert a monopoly of legal expertise.[33] These provide examples perhaps of Michel Foucault's claim that the assertion of disciplinary autonomy furnishes the validity of certain claims to knowledge—and with knowledge comes power[34] (if we can possibly say that jurisprudence, as a new discipline, wielded any power[35]).

Moral Functions of Legal Autonomy

The attempted separation of law from non-law, as well as the staking out of an independent territory for law, also had an important moral purpose, which should not be ignored. For only if a separation of law from morality was made, Austin and Bentham insisted, could law be recognised for what it was—an act of will, of human conduct, and no brooding omnipresence in the sky or any such metaphysical entity. As a human act rather than an intractable moral or religious entity—an act of 'artificial'[36] rather than natural reason—law was capable of being legislated, changed and disobeyed. And thus the moral imperative of legal closure.

The desire for legal autonomy and closure also has a further moral, or at least practical, function. It aims to provide security—not just the security of order but also of (aspired for) legitimacy. It recognises the need for a 'stable and predictable stock of common norms in response to the regulation and co-ordination problems facing any significantly complex societal group'.[37] In this way, it is believed, social cohesion may be attained, even in a multicultural, morally pluralist society. Relatedly, as Gerald Postema has noted, there is a moral propulsion to the desire to transcend the con-

---

[32] M Weber, 'The Sociology of Law' in M Rheinstein (trans), *Max Weber on Economy and Society* (Cambridge, MA, Harvard University Press, 1954) 274–78.

[33] See on this T Halliday and L Karpik (eds), *Lawyers and the Rise of Western Political Liberalism* (Oxford, Clarendon Press, 1997) 22.

[34] M Foucault, *The Archaeology of Knowledge* (London, Routledge, 1969).

[35] Although the proliferation of John Austin's theories throughout the common law world in the later nineteenth century suggests that at least at one stage it did. See WL Morison, *John Austin* (Stanford, Stanford University Press, 1982).

[36] In the famous opinion in *Prohibitions del Roy* (1607) 12 Co Rep 63, Sir Edward Coke held that cases were not to be decided by natural reason 'but by the artificial reason and judgment of Law'.

[37] HP Olsen and S Toddington, *Law in its Own Right* (Oxford, Hart Publishing, 1999) 6. See also T Campbell, 'The Point of Legal Positivism' (1999) 9 *King's College Law Journal* 66, which elaborates a theory of 'ethical positivism', which is also a theory of how law *ought* to be.

troversy of what constitutes right action by establishing legal institutions that act with authority.[38] It is suggested that this can only be achieved if we remove law from the sphere of intractable moral, political and cultural disagreement. This argument lays claim to a distinctiveness for law—its particular ability to resolve conflict, a function that, it is asserted, law is particularly and singularly well-placed to perform. (We shall return to this argument later in the chapter.) As has been noted,[39] this might be seen as a 'progressive' argument, for it perceives value in law's role in handling moral pluralism by resolving society's co-ordination problems by account-able and predictable legal procedures.

Another important argument in favour of legal autonomy is the claim that if law is not perceived as autonomous, it may become redundant—a criticism levelled at natural law theories.[40] For if law's authority depends on morality, what room is left for law?[41] Or, as Joseph Raz has asserted, law must be identified on its own terms, without relying on the same consider-ations it is there to settle; otherwise it will lose its ability to serve the medi-ating role of authority as law.[42] This view is sometimes expressed in the following way by modern legal positivism: if the identification of an auton-omous body of law is to be possible, then positivism must be 'hard'—in other words, law's validity and identity must be determinable exclusive of morality or politics.[43] Autonomy is therefore perceived as serving a (pos-sibly moral, and certainly practical) purpose of preserving institutional integrity. The choice of language of positivism is interesting. Whereas earlier positivists sought 'proper' law (Austin) or 'pure' law (Kelsen), later ones seek to be 'hard' or 'exclusive'; but in each case the implied contrast is to some less worthy approach—improper, impure or soft.

'Hard' positivism states that a basic function of law is to provide pub-licly ascertainable statements and directives and clear reasons for action. Moreover, if this is to happen, then determining what the law actually *is* must not, and indeed does not, involve value judgments.[44] Adherents of

---

[38] See Postema's 'autonomy thesis' in G Postema, 'Law's Autonomy and Public Practical Reasoning' in RP George (ed), *The Autonomy of Law: Essays on Legal Positivism* (Oxford, Oxford University Press, 1996) 79; and Olsen and Toddington (ibid) 31.

[39] Olsen and Toddington (above n 37) 35.

[40] For examples of natural law theories, see J Finnis, *Natural Law and Natural Rights* (Oxford, Clarendon Press, 1980); AP D'Entrèves, *Natural Law: An Introduction to Legal Philosophy*, 2nd revised edn (London, Hutchinson University Library, 1970).

[41] This is not an argument accepted by the prominent contemporary natural law theorist John Finnis, who asserts a unique and essential role for law in the co-ordination of human affairs, while stressing law's moral nature. See Finnis (ibid).

[42] J Raz, *The Authority of Law* (Oxford, Clarendon Press, 1979).

[43] See on this point, eg, Raz, *The Authority of Law* (ibid); Gardner, '5½ Myths' (above n 3); and MH Kramer, *In Defence of Legal Positivism* (Oxford, Oxford University Press, 1999).

[44] See Raz, *The Authority of Law* (above n 42); and Gardner, '5½ Myths' (above n 3).

hard positivism claim that law's universal claim to function as an authority is hampered if in order to identify law we have to make all sorts of morally-based evaluations. Thus, hard, or exclusive, positivists embrace a 'sources' thesis, by which the existence, content and validity of the law are always to be determined according to its social sources (ie, legislation and judicial acts) without recourse to moral argument.[45] In any case, from whence could these evaluations derive, it might also be added, in a pluralist 'disenchanted' modernity in which there is no general consensus as to value.

The preceding sections summarise the claims for legal autonomy made by modern schools of analytical jurisprudence. This summary is clearly no comprehensive introduction to analytical jurisprudence and the notion of legal autonomy, but rather, it is an attempt to highlight the prevalence of a certain type of thinking about law in modernity. However, claims for legal autonomy have been increasingly challenged, by critical and postmodern theories in particular, as well as by the contemporary developments in transnational law wrought by globalisation. This critique will now be addressed.

Failures of Legal Autonomy

Much contemporary and postmodern writing about law asserts that attempts to achieve legal closure and autonomy inevitably fail, normatively and descriptively. On closer analysis, it becomes challenging to find anything singular or unique about legal thinking. Law's techniques of practical reasoning, its methods of interpretation and problem-solving procedures, are not categorically different from non-legal approaches. However, a lack of uniqueness in method and practice need not necessarily rule out law's existence in its own right, so a more detailed investigation of legal autonomy is required.

What Is So Special about Law?

The assertion of autonomy for law relies on the belief that there is something distinctive about law, even if law does share many of its methods with other areas of social life. But just what makes law so (supposedly) distinctive?

---

[45] See, eg, Raz, *The Authority of Law* (above n 42) 47. However, 'inclusive' or 'soft' positivists hold that the existence and identification of a valid law may be determined by moral considerations if the rule of recognition so requires. This view was taken by Hart in his later work. For example, see HLA Hart, *The Concept of Law*, 2nd edn (Oxford, Clarendon Press, 1994) 204; WJ Waluchow, *Inclusive Legal Positivism* (Oxford, Clarendon Press, 1994); and J Coleman, *The Practice of Principle: In Defence of a Pragmatist Approach to Legal Theory* (Oxford, Oxford University Press, 2003).

Hart believed that with the concept of rules, rather than Austin's trilogy of command–sanction–sovereign, he had found the 'key to the science of jurisprudence' and had identified the distinguishing feature of law.[46] However, it is very hard to distinguish legal rules from other types of social rules. What makes legal rules distinctively legal? To state that legal rules are obligatory rules of an institutionally significant sort[47] that exert a serious social pressure (as indeed do many moral rules) is to beg the question of why they are significant, and why they are obligatory.[48] Do they fulfil some specific function singular to law?[49]

Hart's jurisprudence does not provide a very satisfactory answer. His 'internal point of view,'[50] which he asserted that officials take toward legal rules, seems to suggest some degree of institutional autonomy, but it is problematic. Hart rejected the Austinian command model of law, which identifies coercion as characteristic of the distinctively legal. According to Hart, a legal system is a complex of primary rules (those that regulate behaviour by, ie, imposing obligations on individuals) and secondary rules (those that regulate primary rules by, for example, making provision for appointment of judges or the adoption of legislation). For a legal system to be in force in a given society, not only must the rules be generally obeyed, but these secondary rules must also be practised and accepted by officials.[51] This latter feature is crucial for Hart's theory. In this way, Hart sought to explain how laws may be seen as authoritative even though they might not be backed by penalties for noncompliance. To accept the rules is to take the 'internal point of view' (a standard required by Hart of officials but not necessarily of the whole community). As Hart explained:

> [This requires] that there should be a critical reflective attitude to certain patterns of behaviour as a common standard, and that this should display itself in criticism (including self-criticism), demands for conformity, and in acknowledgments that such criticism and demands are justified, all of which find their characteristic expression in the normative terminology of 'ought' 'must' and 'should', 'right' and 'wrong'.[52]

---

[46] See Hart (ibid) chs 4 and 5.

[47] Hart and Weber distinguish law as 'institutional law enforcement'.

[48] Hart, however, does of course spend much time on the distinction between 'being obliged' and 'being under an obligation', ie, distinguishing obligation from coercion. See Hart, *The Concept of Law* (above n 3). This leads to his stipulation of an 'internal point of view', which is, however, problematic. See further the discussion on the next few pages.

[49] The legal realist Karl Llewellyn suggested a specific 'law jobs' thesis, namely, a series of functions for law—ie, to prevent conflicts and resolve disputes—but many of these may be accomplished by other aspects of social life. See Llewellyn, 'The Normative, the Legal and the Law-Jobs: The Problem of Juristic Method' (1940) 49 *Yale Law Journal* 1355.

[50] See Hart, *The Concept of Law* (above n 3) 79 et seq.

[51] Ibid, 113; cf 88.

[52] Ibid, 56.

Hart's introduction of the 'internal point of view' is generally seen as an advance on older theories of positivism, and important for that reason.[53] Yet what exactly is the internal point of view? Hart further elucidated it in this way:

> Those who accept the authority of a legal system look upon it from the internal point of view, and express their sense of its requirements in internal statements couched in normative language which is common to both law and morals ... Yet they are not thereby committed to a moral judgment that it is morally right to do what the law requires.[54]

So the internal point of view involves 'normative language' but does not commit one to 'moral judgement', nor to a moral obligation to obey the law. What, however, might be the meaning of 'normative' here?

One way of approaching the internal point of view might be to argue that legal rules function rather like the rules of a game (and Hart drew many analogies between laws and games in *The Concept of Law*) whose requirements and procedures are accepted as legitimate by participants. However, this analogy breaks down, as those who participate in games have decided to do so voluntarily. In the case of law, unlike the rules of chess or bridge, for example, authority is demanded regardless of whether all have chosen to take part, and the 'critical reflective attitude' is not a position connected to any activity that is anything other than mandatory. So the comparison with a game is inapposite.

But is it possible to make sense of a normative approach that is not moral? Raz suggests that it is possible to make 'statements from a legal point of view', ie, to presuppose the existence of a normative system without accepting it as binding or as possessing full normative commitment or force.[55] But surely these do not adequately explain law's normativity for its *participants*? One is drawn toward the following conclusion. If the internal

---

[53] Indeed, for many, *The Concept of Law* is the most important work of twentieth-century analytical jurisprudence. For example, Brian Simpson writes of it in the following way: 'However success is properly to be judged, it has to be conceded that this book is the most successful work of analytical jurisprudence ever to appear in the common law world.' B Simpson, *Reflections on* The Concept of Law (Oxford, Oxford University Press, 2011) 1.

[54] Hart, *The Concept of Law* (above n 3) 198–99.

[55] J Raz, *Practical Reason and Norms* (Oxford, Oxford University Press, 1990) 171–72. Links have also been drawn between Hart's internal point of view and Max Weber's concept of 'Verstehen', by which Weber meant that to understand the actions of a person or a group is to understand what they are trying to achieve—ie, to understand them in the light of their purpose for insiders. See M Weber, *The Methodology of the Social Sciences* (New York, Free Press, 1949). Hart himself does not appear to make any such explicit links, referring instead to the work of Peter Winch, who believed it was possible to understand a social practice only if one understood the perceptions of its participants. See P Winch, *The Idea of a Social Science and Its Relation to Philosophy* (London, Routledge, 1958). For a discussion of the influence of Weber and Winch on Hart, see N Lacey, *The Life of HLA Hart: The Nightmare and the Noble Dream* (Oxford, Oxford University Press, 2004) 230.

point of view indicates some sort of moral attitude toward law, a perception that it is 'right' or just, then it is uncomfortably redolent of natural law thought and imbues law's autonomy with an uncomfortable dose of morality. Yet if law's significance is alternatively just a product of power, then law's legitimacy is at stake and legal autonomy lost, for law is reduced to power, and legal officials' internal point of view is little different from that of mafia supremoes.[56] The middle position, a non-moral point of view, is either mysterious, lacking further explanation, or indicative of a banal, bureaucratic approach that, again, lacks substance.

Raz offers an alternative explanation for the nature of laws in terms of exclusionary reasons:[57] legal rules offer us reasons for excluding from deliberation a range of otherwise sound reasons bearing upon present options. As such, legal rules are executive rather than deliberative—ie, they exclude any further deliberation. To explain the executive/deliberative distinction further: before the law in a particular area comes into being, when there exist no legal authorities and precedents, all sorts of arguments (political, moral, as well as legal) are used to promote and devise what will become the relevant law. This constitutes the 'deliberative' stage, which constitutes a process designed to create and give content to the law. In contrast, the 'executive' stage, which occurs after the adoption of a legal standard, consists in the application and enforcement of the laws devised in the deliberative stage. According to Raz, only executive considerations are authoritative and binding: they are the law, and the courts are bound to apply them. In theory, morality and politics play a part only in the deliberative and not in the executive stage, thus preserving the positivist distinction between law and morality, and the autonomy of law. In this way, Raz proffers another argument for the traditional positivist thesis of the separation of law from morality: laws are matters of institutional fact.

Raz acknowledges that statutes may contain provisions that require judicial deliberation, in which case the deliberation stage persists at the adjudicative level, requiring the courts to use non-legal considerations and create law. However, Raz gives the impression that such deliberation is relatively rare.[58] Yet in many cases, it is extremely hard to draw a line between the deliberative and the executive elements of a law. For example, the application of a particular area of human rights law may require both

---

[56] Also, further: why focus only on officials' point of view? In contrast, Oliver Wendell Holmes preferred to focus on the perceptions of the 'Bad Man', and John Finnis prefers to work with an ideal or 'focal' point of view. For further discussion on this point, see the section below on 'The Subjective Nature of Legal Autonomy'.

[57] See Raz, *The Authority of Law* (above n 42) ch 1. Raz's view is in contrast to the legal realists, who denied that rules could provide reasons of any sort and paid little attention to law's normativity.

[58] Raz, 'The Problem about the Nature of Law' in J Raz, *Ethics in the Public Domain* (Oxford, Clarendon Press, 1994) 208.

the application of legal precedents and broad, abstract, apparently value-laden provisions in Bills of Rights. In such cases, the distinction between the authoritative and the evaluative, or the legal and the non-legal, is by no means as clear as Raz would have us believe.[59]

Yet even if Raz is correct in asserting this executive/deliberative distinction (which shifts the key role in maintaining legal autonomy onto the courts, which ensure that law is identified in terms of its social sources and not by any act of evaluation), surely legal rules are not the only rules to function by means of this distinction? Other types of rules (religious, bureaucratic) might also be said to exhibit these features and reasoning processes. However, one of Raz's central claims is that law's claim to distinctiveness lies in its assertion of exclusionary authority for itself. According to Raz, all legal systems make this claim. However, this claim to authority is, as Raz stresses, very extensive and very hard to justify (indeed Raz believes that much of the time it will not be justified), as the authority claimed by law is, first, *comprehensive* (namely, the authority to regulate any type of behaviour) and, secondly, *supreme* (namely, the authority to regulate any other institutionalised normative system within their jurisdiction).[60] Raz, however, as discussed, makes clear that it is law's *claim* to authority, not the existence of any actual legitimate authority, that is the hallmark of law's claim to distinctiveness.

Yet moral and religious rules often function very effectively as exclusionary rules for many people.[61] They may also claim the same sort of comprehensiveness and supremacy that law asserts. In other words, laws seem a lot less distinctive and more porous than modern schools of analytical jurisprudence allow.

Problems of Closure

As already stated, positivists believe that it is morally and practically important that laws are *identifiable* as valid laws without reliance on moral, or non-legal, deliberations, even if contemporary positivism tends to deny a broad version of the 'separation thesis,'[62] and acknowledge complex

---

[59] Further, we should note, however, that where there exists *no law* at all on any particular subject, then Raz, in common with other legal positivists, acknowledges that judges act in a deliberative way, just like a legislature (Raz, *The Authority of Law* (above n 42) 113); or to put it otherwise, they exercise a 'strong' discretion—a feature of legal positivism that Dworkin assailed in his earlier work as being counter-democratic (judges are not elected, unlike legislatures) and an example of retrospective lawmaking (Dworkin, 'The Model of Rules I' in R Dworkin, *Taking Rights Seriously* (Cambridge, MA, Harvard University Press, 1978).

[60] Raz, *The Authority of Law*, 2nd edn (Oxford, Oxford University Press, 2009) ch 1.

[61] This is most obviously the case with religious fundamentalism.

[62] The separation thesis traditionally held that there is no necessary connection between law and morality—expressed by Hart as 'the simple contention that it is in no sense a necessary truth that laws reproduce or satisfy certain demands of morality, though in fact they

interactions and links between law, politics and other social factors. In the absence of a strict sources thesis, hard positivists fear, law will not be able to function as an authority by providing publicly ascertainable statements, directives and clear reasons for action. Initially, this seems a matter of common sense. How can a citizen know and follow the law if he or she must engage in a sort of moral philosophy to work out what it is?[63] Laws would quickly become defunct if this were the case. Surely we all know that the law of England prohibits theft, and if I walk into a supermarket, pick up a loaf of bread and leave without paying, I have committed theft. No value judgement is involved in working out the applicable law—apparently only identification and application of the relevant provisions of law.

Hard Cases

However, judicial discretion—the capacity of judges to make policy decisions when deciding cases—creates particular problems. A formalist approach to law considers the function of a judge to be purely analytical, the logical application of existing law to the case at hand. Few now subscribe to such a view.[64] Hart's discussion of adjudication in *The Concept of Law* refers to the 'open texture of rules', and Hart also drew a distinction between a 'core of settled meaning' to legal provisions and 'a penumbra of uncertainty'.[65] In easy cases, pre-existing rules may simply be applied, maintaining a clear distinction between law as it is and law as it ought to be. In penumbral cases, however, the law is not clearly covered by a rule and is more indeterminate. In such cases, Hart allowed that judges have discretion whether to bring the case within an existing rule and, in exercising this discretion, will rely on extra-legal considerations, such as morality or politics. In such cases, therefore, the judges will be making rather than applying the law. However, according to Hart, such lawmaking is not widespread, just occurring within the 'interstices' of existing rules.

To be sure, not every legal case is a hard case or a matter of complex interpretation. Sometimes law's content and application is unproblematic.

---

often have done so'. See Hart, *The Concept of Law*, 2nd edn (above n 45) 185–86; and HLA Hart, 'Positivism and the Separation of Law and Morals' (1958) *Harvard Law Review*. It has been rejected in this form by many contemporary positivists (eg, Gardner, '5½ Myths' (above n 3); and L Green, 'Positivism and the Inseparability of Law and Morals' (2008) 83 *New York University Law Review* 1035).

[63] A criticism that has been made, for example, of Dworkin's work, especially *Law's Empire* (Oxford, Hart Publishing, 1998). See Raz, *Ethics in the Public Domain* (above n 58) 224.

[64] But cf the view of Lord Hailsham, UK Lord Chancellor (who sat as a judge in the House of Lords), that adjudication is not dependent on the subjective opinion of the individual judge but on the strict application of the clearly formulated rule of law. Lord Hailsham, *The Dilemma of Democracy* (London, Collins, 1978) 106.

[65] Hart, *The Concept of Law* (above n 3) 120 et seq; and Hart, 'Positivism and the Separation of Law and Morals' (above n 62).

However, there are many cases in which the identification of a valid law is not so straightforward, and in this way, the autonomy and closure of law become much harder to assert, even in the cases of apparently clearly drafted provisions.[66] Lon Fuller illustrated this point with his very simple example of a statute that prohibits sleeping on railway station benches.[67] This, he said, is directed not at an exhausted commuter who dozes off for five minutes at the end of a busy day while waiting for the train but rather at the tramp who is sprawled all over a bench, occupying it to the exclusion of others, barely conscious but not actually asleep. But in order to determine this and exclude the commuter, who on a literal interpretation might be caught, we need to consider the purpose of the statute, its spirit, its aim. And when we do this, Fuller suggested that we arrive at a conclusion that the law is actually what it ought to be: law and morals (in a certain sense) are blended in our identification of the law. The law is not simply a matter of plain or institutional fact but requires personal, and indeed perhaps even moral, engagement.

Much law is open-ended or controversial, intimately connected with and animated by a broader realm of morality, fairness and other non-legal values. The complications of Raz's executive/deliberative distinction have already been mentioned. The interpretation of legal texts more generally can appear to pose a grave threat to legal autonomy. A formalist theory of interpretation asserts that provisions may be drafted with sufficient clarity and precision to deny manifold interpretations and provide one fixed meaning, that law may have a sense deducible from the very words of the text. Formalists deny the possibility of an anarchy of countless, subjective interpretations. As already argued, however, to claim such a formalism is to assert the impossible. Meaning is not always self-evident in this way. Ideally, the application and interpretation of legal provisions should take place according to public and stable methods of interpretation. But this is impossible to realise completely in practice. It would be reassuring, however, to believe that on the one hand, meaning is not completely arbitrary, subjective and at the whim of judges and, on the other hand, that interpretation need not be automatic and formalistic. Furthermore, it is surely not the case that in order to be coherent, interpretation must be accompanied by a complete background moral theory of interpretation. Such a moral theory would have to be of such comprehensive proportions,

---

[66] For legal indeterminacy, see, eg, S Fish, *The Trouble with Principle* (Cambridge, MA, Harvard University Press, 1999) 295; and the works of the Critical Legal Studies movement more generally.

[67] LL Fuller, 'Positivism and Fidelity to Law: A Reply to Professor Hart' (1958) *Harvard Law Review* 630–72. Similar points are made by Dworkin in *Law's Empire* (above n 63) in his dismissal of what he terms 'plain fact' theories of law.

demonstrating the self-evidence of certain values, that it would require a universalism that few believe in.

None of these extremes—formalism, indeterminacy or a belief in the possibility of an objective moral theory of interpretation—really captures how judging works. Rather, judges are thrown into legal disputes, which they have to rationalise and make sense of. But making sense does not require a morally realist theory of interpretation, nor a belief such as Ronald Dworkin's that there can be 'one right answer' out there[68] (even if this requires Dworkin's superhuman judge Hercules to find it) within a range of legal materials that can be interpreted according to legal principles of coherence and integrity. Indeed, reality seems to be rather more banal and pragmatic. Judges do look for coherence within the law, and their decisions are taken in the context of a public culture of openness and criticism, where open debate and need for justification of argument, the giving of reasons and reference to earlier precedents ideally help to create a culture of shared interpretive understandings and to prevent caselaw being too obviously a tool for subjective judicial preference. Yet these techniques may not always be satisfactory, nor as determinate as many would desire. Where precedents do not apply, moral principles, ideas of justice, fairness, expediency, practicality and all sorts of arguments may figure; argument itself becomes 'open textured', whereby there is no one right approach, no single test for determining the law, and standards are applied because they are seen to be appropriate rather than necessarily applicable. The law is never completely certain but often underdetermined. The rule of law is an ideal as much as a reality.

Foundations?

Problems of closure, however, become even more pressing at the level of law's ultimate foundations. The 'redundancy' argument mentioned earlier, which requires autonomy for law to secure its continued relevancy, has usually been applied against natural law thought, to deny that law's ultimate authority may rest on morality; but logically, this argument may also apply if politics[69] or God are substituted for morality—which would also deprive law of its autonomy. (However, not all writers about law have addressed the problem of law's ultimate closure directly. Weber, for example, described modern law as formally rational and self-contained but did

---

[68] R Dworkin, 'No Right Answer?' (1978) 53 *New York University Law Review* 1.

[69] Much recent critical thought stresses the political sources of law, namely critical schools of thought, such as CLS, as well as schools of public law that stress the 'political' constitution (eg, J Griffiths, *The Politics of the Judiciary*, 5th edn (London, Fontana Press, 1997) as opposed to legally autonomous constitutional law.

not posit a fundamental concept by which law actually all hangs together, as did Hart and Kelsen.)

When theorists attempt to identify such fundamental concepts, problems of closure appear. An obvious problem of closure arises with Hart's 'rule of recognition', with which he supplanted Austinian 'sovereignty', in a more democratic, liberal age. Hart defined the rule of recognition as a mechanism whereby citizens and officials 'are provided with authoritative criteria for identifying primary rules of obligation'.[70] Hart told us that it may be viewed from two perspectives: externally, as a statement of fact; and internally, as a statement of validity. But Hart also referred to the rule of recognition's 'essentially factual' characteristics.[71] This mix of descriptions results in contradiction and confusion if, as Hart appeared to do, one seeks a unified, authoritative source for law. What is the nature of the rule of recognition—internally valid or an observable fact? Furthermore, the consequence of asserting essentially factual characteristics for the rule of recognition would be to derive normative laws from an essentially factual precept—a contradiction of Hume's naturalistic fallacy.[72] Ultimately, either way, Hart's account is problematic. Either the rule of recognition is an externally valid, reductionist statement of what people do (what JR Harris described as 'a refined version of behaviourism'[73])—and why then should others do alike? Or the rule relies on some internal justificatory sense—and from whence is this justificatory sense derived?

Kelsen's 'Basic Norm' (ie, the concept Kelsen asserted as providing an underlying basis for the legal system) provides no greater clarity. According to Kelsen, the Basic Norm is not a social fact but a concept or presupposition, so it cannot be identified empirically.[74] But as a source for law, it is equally unsatisfactory. Indeed, Kelsen acknowledged the Basic Norm as a hypothetical postulate and in later years came to call it a 'fiction', which renders it metaphysical or obscure (or both). Carl Schmitt famously attacked Kelsen, insisting that 'like every other order, the legal order rests on a decision and not on a norm' and that no norm, or legal rule, could be sovereign. Schmitt also made the well-known statement, 'Sovereign is he who decides on the state of exception', meaning by this that all law and order is ultimately based on human actions, decisions and authority, not on

---

[70] Hart, *The Concept of Law*, 2nd edn (above n 45) 101.

[71] Ibid, 108.

[72] See D Hume, *A Treatise of Human Nature*, Book III (Oxford, Clarendon Press, 1978). Hume's argument is that moral values cannot be derived from observable facts.

[73] JR Harris, *Law and Legal Science* (Oxford, Clarendon, 1979) 52.

[74] See Kelsen, *Pure Theory of Law* (above n 1); and Kelsen, *A General Theory of Law and State* (above n 15).

norms. Schmitt wrote, 'The exception, the power of real life breaks through the crust of a mechanism that has become torpid by repetition.'[75]

Neither the rule of recognition nor the Basic Norm can be derived from law itself. But then law must be derived from something extra-legal, and closure fails.[76] Blaise Pascal wrote, 'Anybody can see that those principles that are supposed to be ultimate do not stand by themselves but depend on others, which depend on others again, and thus never allow of any finality.'[77]

Nor do modern so-called 'anti-positivists' escape problems of closure. Dworkin has moved away from positivism by denying that law can be a matter of plain, historical fact, instead asserting that law is entirely interpretative and discursive.[78] Yet Dworkin still relies on the autonomy and coherence of law due to what he posits as law's underlying discursive unity—the constructive legal interpretation that he argues for in his monograph *Law's Empire*. For Dworkin, law's meaning may only be extracted from within shared understandings of life and community. But such a discursive unity and sense of principled, community morality surely exist now only in the weakest of forms.[79] 'Community' plays a very important role in Dworkin's theory, and yet in the contemporary world, where communities may be transient, nebulous or overlapping[80] (bound but also split by national, regional, ethnic, cultural or occupational ties), the concept of community appears inappropriate, in both a normative and descriptive sense, as a vehicle for legal closure (even if it has surfaced in other areas, for example, as a vehicle for politics and morality in a resurgence of communitarian thought in the 1990s[81]). It may be impossible to distil a single, coherent set of interpretive practices (ie, a sort of unified moral and political philosophy) from the political history and culture of a particular community, as Dworkin's theory

---

[75] C Schmitt, *Political Theology: Four Chapters on the Theory of Sovereignty* (1922), G Schwab (trans) (Cambridge, MA, Massachusetts Institute of Technology Press, 1986). See also the discussion in ch 7 of this book.

[76] Davies (above n 8).

[77] B Pascal, *Pensées* (London, Penguin, 1995) 62.

[78] Dworkin, *Law's Empire* (above n 63).

[79] Brian Simpson argued that legal coherence was achieved through institutional arrangements rather than by a system of rules, writing that the English common law system 'consists of a body of shared practices observed by a caste of lawyers'. AWB Simpson, 'The Common Law and Legal Theory' in AWB Simpson (ed), *Oxford Essays in Jurisprudence, Second Series* (Oxford, Oxford University Press, 1973) 94. Similar problems of a perceived lack of shared understandings are faced by Émile Durkheim's master concept of 'solidarity', which is now accepted by few as an appropriate concept with which to characterise society. See É Durkheim, *The Division of Labor in Society*, G Simpson (trans) (New York, Free Press, 1933).

[80] R Cotterrell, *The Politics of Jurisprudence*, 2nd edn (London, Lexis-Nexis Butterworths, 2003) 258.

[81] For example, see C Taylor, *Sources of the Self: The Making of the Modern Identity* (Cambridge, Cambridge University Press, 1989); and M Sandel, *Liberalism and the Limits of Justice*, 2nd edn (Cambridge, Cambridge University Press, 1998).

requires.[82] Furthermore, should transnational, international and foreign law principles form part of the corpus of legal materials[83] for Dworkinian interpretation in legal disputes? Yet given the changes and developments of globalisation and the burgeoning of international and transnational law regimes, would this not be an impossibly ambitious task? If a communal morality, productive of legal integrity, is hard to locate at a national level, how much harder in an era of cosmopolitan or global legal concerns.

On the other end of the analytical jurisprudence spectrum, autopoiesis insists that legal closure presents no problem and even acknowledges the paradox and 'epistemic trap' of modern law, attempting to make productive use of the paradoxes of law's self-referentiality.[84] One such paradox cited by autopoiesis is that law is forced to produce an autonomous legal reality and yet cannot at the same time immunise itself from the conflictual realities produced by other social systems. So autopoiesis acknowledges that law is not completely closed after all. While being normatively closed, there is 'cognitive openness'.[85] Autopoiesis identifies what it names 'structural couplings'—eg, contract law makes possible translation between specific autonomous worlds of law and commerce. Yet as autopoietic theory acknowledges, this is problematic: the supposed closure of the legal system can result in law's inability to make sense of other systems in their own terms; it tends to 'juridify' them. For example, in the case of insanity, law continued to operate its own doctrine—the M'Naghten rules—in spite of criticism of this test from the psychiatric community.[86] As will be discussed in chapter nine, the 'juridification' of human rights has been particularly problematic. This is hardly 'productive'.[87]

These approaches are unsatisfactory. The almost incomprehensible 'productive paradoxes' of autopoiesis take us little or no further than

[82] Dworkin states, 'Interpretive theories are by their nature addressed to a particular legal culture, generally the legal culture to which their authors belong.' See *Law's Empire* (above n 63) 102.

[83] See, eg, on this, M Poiares Maduro, 'Interpreting European Law: Judicial Adjudication in a Context of Constitutional Pluralism' (2007) 1 *European Journal of Legal Studies*.

[84] See, for example, N Luhmann, *Essays on Self-Reference* (New York, Columbia University Press, 1990).

[85] See Luhmann, *Law as a Social System* (above n 17). As Habermas has stated, it is very hard to reconcile these two statements: J Habermas, *Between Facts and Norms* (Cambridge, Massachusetts Institute of Technology Press, 1994) 53.

[86] See, eg, Department of Health and Social Security, *Report of the Committee on Mentally Abnormal Offenders* (CMND 6244, 1975).

[87] See G Teubner, 'Legal Irritants: Good Faith in British Law or How Unifying Law Ends Up in New Divisions' (1998) 61 *Modern Law Review* 12. Indeed, Teubner's development of reflexive law was apparently partly inspired by the need to explain the failure to shape society through law. See further, R Cotterrell, *Law's Community* (Oxford, Clarendon Press, 1995) 106.

the 'fiction' (or Kierkegaardian glorification of the absurd[88]) of Kelsen's Basic Norm. It appears that closure is not a feature of law but rather a subjective or ideological approach generated by specific historical circumstances. Law's ultimate foundations are inevitably non-legal, and law rests on something else. That 'something else' can be drawn from a large range of possibilities: for example, a metaphysical foundation[89] or God (a 'self-causing cause', according to Benedictus de Spinoza[90]); social contract theories, such as those of Hobbes, Locke, Rousseau or Kant, grounded in the consent (usually theoretical) of the governed; or Schmitt's 'decision on the exception'.[91]

The most extreme reaction to the assertion of legal closure or autonomy comes from certain postmodern theories. These theories subvert this problematic lack of foundation by ultimately deriving law from the 'unrepresentable', the 'sublime', force or violence.[92] Jacques Derrida, for example, located the essence (ie, a necessary rather than a contingent feature) of law in its foundation outside of law—in a violence 'without ground'.[93] For Derrida, the foundation of law is of necessity violent because it cannot be justified by any pre-existing law. Such a foundation is therefore a performative, self-legitimising act—what Derrida, following Montaigne and Pascal, termed the 'mystical foundation of authority'. Derrida argued that, however distant, 'the foundation of all states occurs in a situation that we can call revolutionary', and for any revolution to succeed in establishing a new authority beyond law, it is necessary for that authority to create, after the coup, belatedly, a 'discourse of self-legitimation'.[94]

Ultimately, the source identified as law's foundation tends to be the expression of a particular point of view or period of time. The 'sovereign' was designated at a time when parliamentary sovereignty tended to be absolute and participatory democracy almost non-existent, but later conceptions of law's foundations have relied on Kantian metaphysics (in Kelsen's case), mid-twentieth-century social science statistics (legal

---

[88] For a comparison of law's foundation with Kierkegaardian mysticism, see J Gardner, 'Law as a Leap of Faith' in P Oliver, S Douglas Scott and V Tadros (eds), *Faith in Law: Essays in Legal Theory* (Oxford, Hart Publishing, 2000).

[89] In some ways Kelsen comes close to this. For example, Raz writes, 'Though Kelsen rejects natural law theories, he consistently uses the natural law concept of justified normativity.' Raz, *The Authority of Law* (above n 42) 144.

[90] B Spinoza, *Ethics*, GHR Parkinson (trans) (London, Everyman Classics, 1989).

[91] C Schmitt. *The Crisis of Parliamentary Democracy*, E Kennedy (trans) (Cambridge, MA, Massachusetts Institute of Technology Press, 1988); and C Schmitt, *Die Diktatur* (Munich, Duncker & Humblot, 1928). See below ch 7 for further discussion of Schmitt.

[92] For this approach see, eg, J Derrida, 'Force of Law: The Mystical Foundation of Authority' in D Cornell, M Rosenfeld and DG Carlson (eds), *Deconstruction and the Possibility of Justice* (London, Routledge, 1992); and W Benjamin, 'Critique of Violence' in M Bullock and M Jenkins (eds), *Walter Benjamin: Selected Writings* (Belknap, 1996).

[93] Derrida (ibid).

[94] Ibid, 36.

realism), or more bureaucratic notions of officialdom and rules in the case of Hart and Weber. The contemporary era is more existentially uncertain, so accounts vary, for example, between the cynical or pessimistic postmodern identification of force, the hermetically sealed recursivity of autopoiesis or the negation of law and its subsumption in politics in the critical legal studies movement.

The Subjective Nature of Legal Autonomy

It is important to recognise that identifying law as autonomous by means of characterising law according to a single origin or central case (ie, state institutionalised law) in fact depends on a certain way of perceiving the law, of recognising what is significant or 'central' about it, however much such claims for legal autonomy may assert themselves as value-neutral legal philosophy. Kelsen explicitly stated that 'the function of the science of law is not the evaluation of its subject but its value-free description,'[95] and Hart's description of *The Concept of Law* as 'an essay in *descriptive sociology*' (italics added) is well-known.[96] However, even a belief in the possibility of purely descriptive natural sciences may these days raise a sceptical eyebrow,[97] and within the social sciences, which include law, the possibility of value-free description is usually regarded as futile. Theorising about any subject requires some value judgements that are selective and a focus on those aspects of a practice considered by theorists to be the most important. In this respect, every apparent 'description' of law is value-laden. Each account reflects what that theorist considers to be most important.[98] Very often in the case of law, theorists have highlighted those aspects considered by legal insiders, such as lawyers and judges, to be most important—hence Hart, with the 'internal point of view'.[99] Given that all types of theorising appear to involve evaluation to some extent—and indeed, contemporary legal positivists tend not to deny the role of evaluation in legal theory—legal philosophy is what Julie Dickson describes as 'indirectly evaluative'.[100] What present-day positivists deny is that evaluations need be moral ones, such as are to be found in the works of, eg, John Finnis or Dworkin.

---

[95] Kelsen, *Pure Theory of Law* (above n 1) 68.
[96] Hart, *The Concept of Law*, 2nd edn (above n 45) v.
[97] Ie, in the light of the work of theorists such as Kuhn who assert that various 'paradigms' govern the expression of scientific thought. See T Kuhn, *The Structure of Scientific Revolutions*, 3rd edn (Chicago, University of Chicago Press, 1996); and WVO Quine, 'Two Dogmas of Empiricism' (1951) 60 *Philosophical Review* 20–43.
[98] On evaluation and law, see J Dickson, *Evaluation and Legal Theory* (Oxford, Hart Publishing, 2001).
[99] On this, see Dickson (ibid) 39–44.
[100] Ibid, chs 2 and 3.

Finnis argues that the attitude toward law that is most significant and therefore most important for evaluation is that of the person who appreciates the moral value of law. Therefore, Finnis acknowledges the evaluative element involved in theorising about law but claims his own evaluation (which in fact resuscitates natural law as a 'focal case' of law[101]) is objective because it is based on 'sound judgement' and 'authentic practical reason'.[102] Yet Finnis cannot make his evaluation objective so easily. It still reflects his 'world view'.

In this context, as Margaret Davies pointedly asks, why should we accept one view over another? In modern times, there has been a focus on what lawyers and policymakers designate as law, to see a practical point of view (ie, one with a view to decision and action) as important, and this results in a concomitant overemphasis on disputes and adjudication—on what is in fact the pathology of social life.[103] However, why should we acknowledge Hart's 'internal point of view' or Kelsen's viewpoint of the 'man of legal science' as the key to understanding the mystery of law and legal systems? In contrast, over 100 years ago, Oliver Wendell Homes focused on the point of view of the 'Bad Man', who cares only about the material consequences of the law on him personally.[104] If the 'Bad Man' viewpoint is considered relevant, why not also that of a feminist or anarchist? Why, as Davies suggests, do we consider some views 'balanced' and others 'political', and as she also comments, 'Is it an overreaction to be so angry about this?'[105]

Law's ultimate foundation derives from cultural contexts and characteristics—a feature that many of modernity's dominant conceptions of law have failed to acknowledge, either by asserting an independent, closed, autonomous source and existence for law (such as in the case of Kelsen's Basic Norm) or by stipulating a foundation for law that, though it may be derived from non-legal sources (such as Austin's Sovereign), still attempts to derive a general, autonomous theory of law from a particular subjective, monist perspective of the author, thus distinguishing 'proper' from 'improper' law. These theories all assume that if a concept such as 'law' is to be used at all meaningfully, there must be some sort of common essence to all uses of the word, a common quality shared by all laws. Such approaches tie the theory to one particular vision and, inevitably, are challenged by examples of law that do not fit within their accounts. If law is, by definitional fiat, the command of the sovereign, then law that cannot be sourced in the sovereign is not 'proper' law. If law is seen as part of

---

[101] See Finnis (above n 40).
[102] Ibid.
[103] This was, for example, Eugen Ehrlich's complaint, writing over 100 years ago: E Ehrlich, *Gesetz und Lebendes Recht* (Berlin, Duncker and Humblot, 1986 reprint).
[104] O Wendell Holmes, 'The Path of the Law' (1897) *Harvard Law Review* 457.
[105] Davies (above n 8) 23–24.

an official system of primary and secondary rules, unified by a rule of recognition, then norms that are hard to place within this 'system' (such as principles that are not rule-like in nature[106]) cannot be law. Such approaches to law are troubling because they appear to draw firm lines, distinguishing the 'legal' from the 'non-legal', which inevitably gives rise to hard cases, grey areas and all sorts of problems that are hard to resolve.

The worry underlying an assertion of legal autonomy appears to be the following one: if law is not autonomous from other areas of social life such as politics or morality, is it not indeed redundant? Why not apply Ockham's Razor and ensure the economy of entities by erasing law and proceeding directly to the sources that underlie it—religion, politics or morality? And yet there is a strong intuition that law is not redundant: to make a legal claim is to do something more than to make a moral argument, assert a political preference or exert coercive force. What might this something else be? Is it possible to allow that law may be *distinctive* in nature from other areas of society without insisting on its autonomy from them?

There is another way to envision law, and I seek to do this in the ensuing sections of this chapter and elsewhere in this book. This project involves not so much a denial of professional lawmakers' views of law but rather an attempt 'to supplement, expand, interpret and explain law in its broader context'.[107] Nor do I believe that the acknowledgement of law's ultimate porosity, its dependence on extra-legal sources, makes law redundant. As will become clear, I believe law has never been so pervasive nor, in so many senses, important to us.

Replacements and New Understandings

As a first step, it is suggested that those extreme sceptic theories of law, such as Derrida's, which deny legal autonomy by identifying law's very essence as violence, are unsatisfactory and incomplete. Undoubtedly, law relies on coercion for efficacy, and it is hard to conceive of a legal system surviving without coercion, but it is too extreme to render violence as law's main distinctive feature. For this reason, Kelsen's theory of law, which understands the essence of law as organised by force, also seems unsatisfactory. Further, as Roger Cotterrell highlights, within those theories in which violence is identified as the foundation of law, the concept

---

[106] The example Dworkin gives is the principle that 'no man may profit from their own wrongdoing'—a maxim that he says does not apply in an all-or-nothing fashion in the way that legal rules are supposed to apply; nor can it automatically be sourced in a rule of recognition. Dworkin, 'The Model of Rules I' (above n 59).

[107] R Cotterrell, 'Subverting Orthodoxy, Making Law Central: A View of Social Legal Studies' (2002) 29 *Journal of Legal Studies* 632.

of violence itself 'remains opaque, generalised, indeterminate and usually unconnected with any detailed historical or social enquiries'.[108]

Such an identification of law with violence ignores the distinction between legal and non-legal violence, as well as the fact, highlighted by Hart, that law relies on legitimation and acceptance rather than, or at least in addition to, coercion for its continued authority. If all legal regimes are perceived to be in essence derived from violence, then how to distinguish those systems in which justice prevails from those regimes that are fundamentally unjust? If violence is at the essence of all, then we are denied the conceptual tools to make these distinctions. It is necessary to develop a more discriminating jurisprudence, one that can take account of such distinctions between legal systems.

Law may have a close relationship with coercion and power, but power at least is a complex notion (for example, capable of being productive or empowering, as Foucault pointed out), not just reducible to violence. Further, those postmodern accounts, which excoriate traditional jurisprudence for its insistence on a separation of law from other societal norms, risk committing the very same error of essentialising law, of limiting it to one elemental feature, one master narrative (in this case a negative one) of force or violence. This leaves no room for critical and discerning assessments of law, for substance in the belief that, eg, the Nazi legal system really was more unjust than those legal regimes that adhere to human rights norms and are based on the rule of law, however imperfect they may seem. The certainties of modern, analytical legal thought have been deconstructed, but a troubling nihilism takes their place.

A preferable view is to concede (as indeed some contemporary analytical jurisprudence has done) that law may not be analysed successfully in isolation from its social sources—any attempt so to do so will inevitably be circular[109]—but this need not lead to the conclusions that law has its origins only in violence or the unrepresentable. Instead, as Cotterrell urges:

> Rather than close off law analytically, legal theory should interpret it in ever widening perspectives. As the attempt to understand law as a social phenomenon, legal theory should *require* that the limited views of law held by different kinds of participants in legal processes ... be confronted with wider theoretical perspectives that can incorporate and transcend these partial views and thereby broaden understanding of the nature of law.[110]

As Cotterrell continues, however, this is not what legal theory has done; rather, it has 'typically asked how it is possible to organise in intellectually satisfying ways diverse doctrinal materials and modes of juristic

---

[108] Cotterrell, *The Politics of Jurisprudence* (above n 80) 247.
[109] Ibid, 246.
[110] Ibid, 15.

thought'[111]—an enterprise that will always be fraught with circularities as well as personal prejudices. In the remainder of this chapter, I will consider other ways of theorising about law that do not assert law as autonomous but instead seek to situate law within a broader social context and allow for a variety of perspectives.

Marx and Weber: More Limited Autonomy

With those writers whose treatment of law is more historical, we find either a rejection of autonomy or a more ambiguous attitude towards it. Not all 'modern' legal theory asserts autonomy for law. Marxist theory allowed law only a 'relative autonomy'. According to Marxism, 'in the last instance' or 'long run', economic conditions take causal priority and determine the characteristics and content of law; law is an element of the superstructure and dependent on an economic base. Therefore, Marxism resists the modernist orthodoxy of treating law as autonomous and capable of study in its own right. A clear expression of this Marxist view is also found in the work of EP Thompson, who denied the possibility of separating law from economy and society, writing of England in the eighteenth century:

> The last instance ... actually grabbed hold of the law, and throttled it and forced it to change its language, and to will into existence new forms appropriate to the mode of production, such as enclosure acts and new case law excluding customary common law rights.[112]

Marx's *Capital* is a study of a society dominated by the dull compulsion of economic forces.[113] It is significant that around the time that legal autonomy asserted itself as a concept, law was developing in a certain way that drew heavily on its relationship with capitalism. A self-contained, systematic legal order was perceived as a clear aid to the growing commercial community, which needed predictable and calculable rules to govern its transactions. However, in Marxist visions, not only does law lack autonomy but it also becomes an ideological tool for the furtherance of economic interests. In this way, law and capitalism were perceived to be essentially linked, but with oppressive effects. Evgeny Pashukanis understood the form of law as essentially capitalist in nature, as having achieved its highest flowering in capitalist society.[114] Even the supposedly neutral rule of law, along with individual rights and the separation of powers, could appear to

---

[111] Ibid, 16.
[112] EP Thompson, *The Poverty of Theory* (London, Merlin, 1978) 288; but see also Thompson's views on the rule of law, which are discussed below in ch 8.
[113] R Fine, *Political Investigations: Hegel, Marx, Arendt* (London, Routledge, 2001).
[114] E Pashukanis, *Law and Marxism* (London, Pluto Press, 1983).

further this purpose where disproportionate economic power lurked behind the apparently neutral mask of law.[115] Therefore, Marx was deeply suspicious of 'neutral', semi-autonomous, liberal law.

In contrast to Marxism, Weber's positivist theory of legal rational authority links law's perceived authority to its *legality* rather than asserting any moral foundations for law; Weber seemed less willing to cede law's autonomy. For Weber, valid law was a bureaucratic, formally rational structure, with an emphasis on posited legal rules.[116] Weber, unlike Marx, did not see the relationship between law and capitalism as one in which law was causally determined by the economy, but nonetheless the relationship between the two was a continually pressing issue for Weber. In seeking to determine why capitalism had arisen only in certain societies, Weber pondered whether law had an essential impact, questioning whether a particular type of law was necessary for capitalism to arise—a thought that comes close to reversing the causal relationship suggested by Marx. However, rather than positing a causal relationship between law and capitalism, Weber believed them to be rooted in the same beliefs and attitudes and thus to share an exegesis. Yet Weber did believe that formal legal rationality, with its systematic rule-governed procedures, had been significant,[117] especially modern contract law:[118] 'The most essential feature of modern substantive law ... is the greatly increased significance of legal transactions, particularly contracts, as a source of claims guaranteed by legal coercion.'[119] Indeed, Weber designated modern society as 'contractual', devoting a huge part of the *Rechtssoziologie* to contracts.

Therefore, Weber seems to have perceived modern contract law at least as contributing to the growth of capitalism, increasing societal wealth and personal freedom, in comparison with former societies which had consisted of feudal practices. Such a view is compatible with legal autonomy. However, Weber's approach to law and its relationship with capitalism was ambivalent. Weber was not, unlike Marx, fiercely critical of the effects of capitalism, nor was he, however, ingenuous about it, realising that freedom of contract could aggravate inequalities, with economic power producing

---

[115] See K Marx, 'On the Jewish Question' in K Marx, *Early Writings*, R Livingstone and G Benton (trans) (London, Penguin, 1992).

[116] Weber, 'The Sociology of Law' (above n 32) 274–78.

[117] But that this was not a direct causal connection was recognised by Weber in his discussion of the 'England problem', in which the legal security required as a background for capitalism was more of a product of legal training and precedent than formally coherent law. Indeed, Weber distinguished the common law as 'essentially different from and of a type inferior than that of continental Europe'. See S Ewing, 'Formal Justice and the Spirit of Capitalism: Max Weber's Sociology of Law' (1987) 21 *Law & Society Review* 487.

[118] In which he was followed by Karl Renner's pioneering account of contract as the principal exponent of exchange relations: K Renner, *The Institutions of Private Law and their Social Functions* (London, Routledge and Kegan Paul, 1949).

[119] Weber, 'The Sociology of Law' (above n 32) 274–78.

a special kind of coercive situation, which might in its turn rebound on law. For all his emphasis on 'formal rationality', Weber's account of law was deeply historical: law is embedded in certain historical contexts and, if not fully dependent on them, in a symbiotic relationship with society. This militates against law's closure and hardly posits a watertight autonomy, suggesting that once we move away from conceptual approaches and situate law historically, it becomes difficult to make successful claims for its autonomy. In other words, legal autonomy tends to be the property of a particular type of conceptual or doctrinal jurisprudence.

Habermas: Law and Democracy

However, Marx and Weber are both somewhat unsatisfactory as guides to understanding twenty-first-century law. Weber, although furnishing an historical account of law, nonetheless, by conceiving law as formal, rational authority, identified it clearly with modern analytical accounts that stress its rational, official nature. Marxist theories tend to be too one-dimensional in their positing of a causal relationship between law and capitalism, largely ignoring other non-economic relationships between law and culture, and types of oppression other than those provoked by class. Marx also posits a strong relationship between state and law, which is something that does not apply so strongly in the twenty-first century.[120]

A more recent theory of law, one that tries to give an account of how law may be perceived to be legitimate and to possess an authority derived neither from violence on the one hand nor from a value-free rationality on the other, is provided by Jürgen Habermas. Habermas has explicitly stated that it is his aim to articulate 'a convincing understanding of law that is connected with a constitutional project tailored for complex societies'.[121] In many ways, Habermas provides the most satisfactory current theory of law's foundations and legitimation, and notably, he makes no claims for complete legal closure or autonomy.

In *Between Facts and Norms*, his *magnum opus* published in the 1990s, Habermas considered the question of how valid law is possible. In an age in which there exists a 'legitimation gap', in which, as Weber[122] asserted, law has lost its metaphysical dignity and indisponibility (because unlike in ancient institutions where there existed a fusion of fact and value, this is not the case in 'disenchanted' modernity), modern positivism separates law from morality, deriving legitimacy from law's formal properties only, as does

---

[120] See below chs 3 and 4 for further discussion of these points.

[121] Habermas, *Between Facts and Norms* (above n 85) 361.

[122] M Weber, *The Protestant Ethic and the Spirit of Capitalism* (London, George Allen & Unwin, 1948) 183.

Weber's account of legal rational authority. For Habermas, as for many of us, this is inadequate. But Habermas does not turn to natural law instead. For Habermas, *democracy* is the only late modern or post-metaphysical source of legitimacy. Law cannot be valid merely because it is 'legal' but rather because it is the concurring and united will of free and equal citizens who are the authors of the law to which they are subjects as addressees. Habermas stipulates that 'just those norms are valid to which all possibly affected persons could agree as participants in rational discourse'.[123] This is termed the principle of universalisability by Habermas, and though it is offered as an alternative to the Kantian tradition, it clearly has ties with Kant's categorical imperative.[124] But whereas Kant's categorical imperative is monological, with *individual* reasoning at its centre, for Habermas, these universal norms are dialogical and discursive in nature, taking all relevant interests into account; and in this way, a consensus is reached. The emphasis is on human rights and justice over any substantive conception of the good and on procedure over substance.

The principle of universalisability is very closely linked to and derives from Habermas' belief in communicative rationality and presentation of 'the ideal speech situation'.[125] It also serves to continue the Enlightenment project, to assert a belief in the possibility of truth and justice, without some of the undesirable metaphysical baggage of Enlightenment thought. This needs a little further explanation in order to understand how the Habermasian concept of the 'ideal speech situation' may contribute to an understanding of the concept of law and of law's legitimacy.

Habermas argues that in the act of speaking, we make an implicit commitment to truth, reason and some sort of justice, because we proffer ourselves as sincere, believable and reliable. Habermas' theory of communicative action is therefore a universalising principle that claims to counter relativism by asserting that there exist basic standards which underlie our behaviour, such as reason and justice.[126] And so the validity of rules underlying communication exceeds the particular instances of concrete cases. In this way, contrary to most postmodern thought, Habermas' theory presents a world that is not just a murky mess of language games or power. However, Habermas' theory

---

[123] Habermas, *Between Facts and Norms* (above n 85) 132.

[124] Kant asserted that the fundamental principle of morality is a *categorical imperative*. One formulation of it requires us to 'act only in accordance with that maxim through which you can at the same time will that it become a universal law'. I Kant, *Groundwork of the Metaphysics of Morals*, A Wood (trans and ed) (New Haven, Yale University Press, 2002) 4:421.

[125] J Habermas, *Theory of Communicative Action* (Boston, Beacon Press, 1985).

[126] For this and the ensuing discussion, see Habermas, *Theory of Communicative Action* (ibid); and J Habermas, 'Reflections on the Linguistic Foundations of Sociology', lecture (1997), reproduced in J Habermas, *On the Pragmatics of Social Interaction* (Cambridge, MA, Massachusetts Institute of Technology Press, 2001).

also involves a counterfactual and idealistic conception of reason—founded on this notion of the 'ideal speech situation' as a paradigm for communication and discourse. The construct of the ideal speech situation stipulates that discourse should be free from coercion and power differences, offering equal chances for participation, with no topic to be excluded and the only accepted force to be that of the better argument. This is obviously not how much communication in the world actually operates—language is frequently used to deceive or manipulate—but Habermas argues that these are 'strategic' uses of language that go counter to the spirit of language; they are parasitical on open, honest ethical use. For example, Habermas characterises terrorism as distorted communication.[127] Therefore, even if communication is not always just, honest and domination-free, it has the possibility of being so. Therefore, Habermas attempts to counter relativism on the basis of communicative rationality.

How does this relate to law? In *Between Facts and Norms* Habermas adds to the principle of universalisability the condition that the legitimacy of law depends on a system of fundamental rights. This includes both private rights to equal subjective liberties and freedom of action (without which individuals would be unwilling to submit themselves to the demands a coercive legal order), along with rights of public autonomy (such as the right to equal participation in the democratic will formation), which require popular sovereignty and are not premised on the atomistic, individualist, autonomy-based foundations of much of human rights theory.[128] Habermas therefore presents politics as a matter of collectively realising public autonomy—that it is the freedom of 'we the people' that is crucial rather than of each private individual. However, unlike other republican theorists, Habermas, by uniting private and public autonomy, insists that human rights and popular sovereignty are equally primordial and reciprocal, and each depends on the other. Law and morality are inextricably connected: it is not a question of moral priority for natural law, nor of legitimating law through its formal properties. Indeed, for Habermas, formal properties of law have an implicitly moral dimension, since, although law is a system formally administered by professional jurists, it will contribute to legitimacy only if we take moral justifications into account; and the judiciary do not apply law blindly, but moral views are involved in interpretation. Therefore, we have an amalgam of fact and norm, acknowledging the Janus-faced duality of law—constituted by its facticity, its actual existence as positive law and its normative ability to bind us, arising out of its origins in the democratic will of people legitimised by public and private rights.

---

[127] G Borradori, *Philosophy in a Time of Terror: Dialogues with Jürgen Habermas and Jacques Derrida* (Chicago, University of Chicago Press, 2003) 19 and 35.
[128] For further on human rights, see below ch 9.

Habermas' account is attractive, persuasive in sourcing rights and the democratic process as the joint foundations for law's legitimacy, thus avoiding both the focus on officials that permeates theories such as Hart's and the reliance on judicial practice in theories such as Dworkin's. This also fits with current practices in many legal systems that link democracy and human rights to the rule of law as legitimating principles of public law and of the state more generally.[129] It also provides a more satisfactory general theory of law than both those analytical jurisprudential theories that find it difficult to explain why law should claim authority (ie, Hart's circularity of officials who recognise a rule of recognition which authorises them) and natural law theories that, with their metaphysical or religious foundations, appear inappropriate for understanding the nature of twenty-first-century law. As such, Habermas' theory is one of the most persuasive and successful contemporary theories of law.

Despite its attractiveness, Habermas' theory is more problematic when it comes to transnational, global and more informal types of law, which will be discussed in many chapters of this book. However much we might wish it to be the case, the democratic process figures little in the creation of many of these types of law. International institutions, including the European Union, are not known as paragons of democracy, and the types of business regulation that Gunther Teubner and others have written about in the context of a growing global *lex mercatoria*[130] seem to have almost no democratic input. This means that Habermas' theory is unsuited to types of law that appear not to have originated in any democratic process, a point which will be further developed in later chapters. Indeed, Habermas' procedural paradigm appears to take a normative form rather than being presented as an accurate empirical description of existing legal systems.[131] As such, it may function as a persuasive attempt to account for the legitimacy of law in more developed legal systems, but for other types of law, it will be aspirational as a guide but not reflective of their current nature.

A Broader Definition of Law?

The critique of legal autonomy has asserted that it is difficult to distinguish laws from other normative elements in society—whether one looks

---

[129] For example, see the decision of the German Constitutional Court in the *Lisbon Treaty Judgment*, which found the Act Approving the Treaty of Lisbon compatible with the Basic Law, BVerfG, 2 BvE 2/08 vom 30.6.2009, Absatz-Nr (1–421), available at http://www.bverfg.de/entscheidungen/es20090630_2bve000208en.html

[130] See further below chs 3, 4, 5 and 11.

[131] Although it may be driven by the development of the postwar German Constitution, see, eg, M Specter, *Habermas: An Intellectual Biography* (Cambridge, Cambridge University Press, 2010).

to their function, essence or origin in order to do so. Given this fact, it is suggested that 'law' is a much broader phenomenon than is often acknowledged. This has been acknowledged by early pluralists such as Ehrlich or Malinowski,[132] who saw law everywhere, merging law with religion, custom, morality, decorum, fashion and etiquette. It has also been acknowledged by legal anthropologists such as Sally Falk Moore, who perceive law as 'semi-autonomous' and dynamically interrelated with other fields,[133] as well as by Fuller, who objected to the positivist tendency to equate law with the authority of the state, insisting rather that law results from human interaction and could be a matter of degree (and he therefore found it in universities, clubs and societies).[134] Similar points have been made more recently by Boaventura de Sousa Santos, for whom much of our social world takes the form of law, including instances that are very informal or unwritten.[135] A further, crucial dimension of law after modernity is its existence at regional or global level, above and beyond the nation state, as I shall discuss in the next chapters. In these contexts, legal pluralism has become a popular legal theory. Indeed, legal pluralism is no longer a controversial theory, and its current proponents are exuberant and expansive, and claims such as the following have become typical: 'Law is everywhere ... There has been and still is law without jurisprudence, even law without laws, without legal doctrine, without lawyers.'[136] While such claims may be overblown, they are evidence of a perception of law's prevalence and ubiquity, an indication that this is something that should be taken into account.

The writings of Foucault are of relevance to a perceived pervasiveness of law. Foucault himself adopted a rather anachronistic definition of law to which few would now subscribe, separating law from 'governmentality' and defining law as a sovereignty that manifests the coercive power of the state.[137] Foucault thus perceived law as a negative representation of power—a prohibition. This was a rather old-fashioned definition of law for a theorist with such radical views. He saw the rise of administration, technologies and governance generally as signalling the decline of law, which for Foucault had become increasingly ineffectual and epiphenomenal.

---

[132] See, eg, Ehrlich (above n 103); and B Malinowski, *Crime and Custom in Savage Society* (London, Routledge and Kegan Paul, 1926).

[133] S Falk Moore, 'Law and Social Change: The Semi-Autonomous Social Field as an Appropriate Subject for Study' (1972/73) *Law and Society Review* 719.

[134] LL Fuller, *The Morality of Law* (New Haven, Yale University Press, 1965).

[135] B de Sousa Santos, *Towards a New Legal Common Sense*, 2nd edn (London, Butterworths, 2002).

[136] MT Fogen, 'Rechtsgeschichte—Geschichte der Evolution eines sozialen Systems. Ein Vorschlag' (2002) 1 *Rechtsgeschichte* 15, quoted in S Roberts, 'After Government? On Representing Law without the State' (2005) 68 *Modern Law Review* 3.

[137] M Foucault, *Power/Knowledge* (Harvester, Wheatsheaf, 1980) 201.

Foucault identified the huge increase in new forms of power as characteristic of modernity. For Foucault, this increase took the form of the 'management' of things—ie, strategies of control, or practices. In his earlier work, Foucault tended to characterise such practices as disciplinary or 'normalising' in nature; in his later work, he understood them as elements of 'governmentality' or 'governance'[138]—a 'productive' rather than prohibitive force.

Foucault was wrong to be so dismissive of law and define it so narrowly. On the contrary, much of what he designated 'governance' might in fact be characterised as law. There has been a massive and persistent increase in the range, scope and detail of legal intervention, as well as great expansion in the legalisation and juridification of social life. To use Foucauldian terminology, one might say that the instruments of law have become integrated into technologies for the government of life. This was earlier recognised by Karl Llewellyn, who made a plea for an integrated vision of 'law-government', noting the attenuation of distinctively legal institutions and an absorption of law into the larger realm of administration.[139]

Traditional theories of analytical jurisprudence often appear unwilling to capture the vast diversity of regulatory practices of contemporary law and governance, focusing instead on institutional law (Hart and Kelsen) or the courts (Dworkin). Law creates organisations that supervise as well as prohibit, and they do so in diverse and apparently 'non-legal' ways. Teubner suggested in the late twentieth century that a 'reflexive' law[140] should be developed, relieved of the burden of direct regulation, the key being self-regulation. This was a move away from his earlier interest in autopoiesis, which he had come to believe was inadequate for the roles required of law. An example of such reflexivity might be found in the fulfilment of the claims of those who wish the internet to become self-regulating rather than subject to state regulation, with the distribution of domain names by the Internet Corporation for Assigned Names and Numbers (ICANN).[141] For Teubner, restricting law to an external, constitutional role of procedural regulation drastically reduces the cognitive requirements of the legal system.

Given the challenges of contemporary law and regulation, it is tempting to dispense with the notion of legal autonomy altogether and simply see law as part of a broader field of social regulation—indeed, of what Foucault

---

[138] M Foucault, 'Governmentality' (1979) 6 *Ideology and Consciousness* 5–21.

[139] KN Llewellyn, *Jurisprudence: Realism in Theory and Practice* (Chicago, University of Chicago Press, 1962).

[140] G Teubner, 'Substantive and Reflexive Elements in Modern Law' (1983) 17 *Law & Society Review* 239.

[141] ICANN is an internationally organised nonprofit corporation that has responsibility for Internet Protocol (IP) address space allocation, protocol identifier assignment, generic (gTLD) and country code (ccTLD) Top-Level Domain name system management.

called 'governmentality'—as a response that functions in many social sites. Predating Teubner's 'reflexive' law, Philippe Nonet and Philip Selznick identified a movement from autonomous to 'responsive' law, which involved an evolving concept of law that is less formal and more purposive and interdisciplinary.[142] They recalled the argument of Jerome Frank that a key purpose of the legal realists was to make law 'more responsive to social needs'.[143] This approach regards law not as a separate tool external to social life with which to shape society but rather an aspect of social experience, or of the 'social imagination', as Clifford Geertz expressed it.[144]

We may also note a corresponding dwindling of the distinction between public and private law, along with what de Sousa Santos has described as 'a dislocation of power from formal institutions to informal networks'[145] (a feature of law after modernity that will be discussed from a critical viewpoint in subsequent chapters). Such an approach, as Cotterrell suggests, 'highlights regulation's fluidity, ubiquity and varied consequences, making it possible to describe law as a continuum network or web of regulatory practices or techniques'.[146] It involves the creation of special-purpose institutions endowed with broad discretionary powers, less concerned with prescribing conduct than enlisting co-operation. Additionally, this awareness of a broader spectrum of law highlights the complex interrelations between state agencies, 'quasi-government' and 'private' disciplinary strategies and normative practices that pervade social life—thus avoiding the increasingly implausible public–private dichotomy.[147] For example, EU law makes use of a wide range of alternative regulatory instruments, such as the Open Method of Co-ordination (OMC), benchmarking, peer pressure, networks and standardisation, in order to circumnavigate the problem of trying to attain a (often impossible) consensus under traditional international intergovernmental law-making.[148] Many of these methods, such as OMC, are characterised by inclusiveness, learning from others, deliberation, confidence-building and exchange of experience, and they can often be more effective than sanctions in making people comply. Such governance lacks the 'command and control' measures of traditional law

---

[142] P Nonet and P Selznick, *Law and Society in Transition: Towards Responsive Law* (New York, Harper Colophon, 1978).

[143] J Frank, 'Mr Justice Holmes and Non-Euclidian Legal Thinking' (1932) 17 *Cornell Law Quarterly* 568, 586.

[144] C Geertz, *The Interpretation of Cultures* (New York, Basic Books, 1973).

[145] B de Sousa Santos, 'Law and Community: The Changing Nature of State Power in Late Capitalism' (1980) *International Journal of the Sociology of Law* 379, 391.

[146] Cotterrell, 'Subverting Orthodoxy' (above n 107) 632 et seq. See also N Rose and M Valverde, 'Governed by Law?' (1998) 7 *Social and Legal Studies* 541–51.

[147] Cotterrell, 'Subverting Orthodoxy' (above n 107). See also below chs 4 and 5.

[148] See European Commission, *White Paper on European Governance* (COM(2001) 428 final); and subsequently, European Commission, 'Inter-institutional Agreement on Better Lawmaking' (2003/C 321/01).

and government.[149] It derives instead from multiple sources of authority; rather than legal hierarchy and the monopoly of force, it often takes the form of flexible, voluntary measures and fluid, soft law.[150] On account of its multiple and diverse origins, which derive from a plurality of social and cultural sources, it requires a broader investigation from legal, social, cultural and political perspectives if we are to fully evaluate and understand it. This in turn leads us to revisit our conceptions of justice, authority, power, legitimacy and authority, as well as the concept of democracy and the nature of 'legal' institutions.

For example, François Ewald has illustrated this growth or relocation of law by an example from the insurance industry.[151] Given the inability of law enforcement agencies to protect against theft and housebreaking, insurance companies have developed the practice of insisting on the installation of alarms in private houses as a condition of insurance. Monetary compensation through insurance claims has tended to replace the pursuit of offenders through the criminal justice system—a shift of the limits of the law that involves a significant expansion of contract law. In such a case, legal regulation provides an example of the complex interconnection with other regulatory techniques.

Further examples of such an expansion in the regulatory field is to be found in the provision of detailed standards across many areas—welfare, education, health and safety, credit transfers—an interpenetration and interplay of law and regulation. There have also been important shifts of focus from 'state' action to a broader field involving policies, programmes, strategies, projects and tactics such as censuses, medical returns and storage of information—a 'decentring' of law in new forms of regulation. Indeed, legal systems have become increasingly pervaded by forms of knowledge and expertise that are usually perceived as non-legal. Law has been supplemented by the knowledge claims of medicine, psychology, education and so on, and the authorities who produce, define and delimit areas for government by law may not be legal at all.

This broader approach to law has several advantages. It allows an escape from legal philosophy's 'What is law?' conundrum because it denies essentialism, allowing law to be many things.[152] It picks up a Wittgensteinian

---

[149] Such characterisation has of course provoked opposition, eg, that of Simon Roberts, who contests those who reject the orienting link between law and domination. See S Roberts, 'After Government? On Representing Law without the State' (2005) 68 *Modern Law Review*. Such views will be further considered below in chs 4 and 5.

[150] See generally U Mörth (ed), *Soft Law in Governance and Regulation* (Cheltenham, Edward Elgar, 2004).

[151] F Ewald, 'Insurance and Risk' in G Burchell, C Gordon and P Miller (eds), *The Foucault Effect: Studies in Governmentality* (Chicago, University of Chicago Press, 1991).

[152] This evolution of law also brings with it risks and a lack of accountability. These issues are discussed below in ch 5.

intuition[153] that there may be no such thing as a 'correct' definition of certain concepts, no single, common essence or denominator but merely complex patterns of overlapping resemblances. The philosopher Morris Weitz described art as an 'open' concept,[154] namely one in which the necessary and sufficient conditions for the operation of a concept cannot be given because new and unforeseen cases may arise that do not share any asserted common denominator. It is also worth pointing out that while historically and culturally certain groups or institutions have made decisions identifying various practices as law, these are not finally determinative of law's nature, and indeed, we should be aware of the fact that the designation 'law' is often a product of those who have an investment in identifying law in a certain way—for example, those colonialists who recognised only imperial state 'law' and not the laws of conquered and indigenous peoples. The identification of law as an 'open' concept asserts that law is not to be understood as homogeneous, insular and closed but instead to encompass very plural entities and diverse opportunities.

However, one could feel some concern at this conclusion. To acknowledge law as so diverse and miscellaneous in nature might suggest that there is nothing special about it at all and deny it any distinctiveness. It might indeed be tempting to label law merely as 'some form of normative predictability'.[155] This is enticing, perhaps, for those who have had enough of the abstract, doctrinal approaches of analytical jurisprudence, and of attempts to 'straitjacket' law within one all-embracing definition. Nonetheless, such a wide account may seem to efface and collapse law out of independent existence—the very fear of those modern theorists who insisted on legal autonomy in the first place. Dennis Galligan has described this predicament as:

> ... the dilemma of either not taking law seriously enough or taking it too seriously. If the view prevails that there is nothing distinctive about it and that its place and importance are marginal to society, law is not taken seriously enough. If, on the other hand, it is thought that law is simply a system of rules that exerts authority over society while being insulated from it, then its character is mis-described and its importance exaggerated.[156]

However, denying complete autonomy to law and recognising the need to understand it in a broader social context do not necessarily debar law from any distinctiveness. It is possible to capture this sense of distinctiveness without overblown claims for legal autonomy based on theorists' own

---

[153] L Wittgenstein, *Philosophical Investigations*, 3rd edn (Oxford, Blackwell, 1967).

[154] M Weitz, 'The Role of Theory in Aesthetics' in A Neill and A Ridley (eds), *The Philosophy of Art: Readings Ancient and Modern* (New York, McGraw-Hill, 1995) 183–91.

[155] An expression mentioned but not necessarily recommended by Olsen and Toddington (above n 37).

[156] D Galligan, *Law in Modern Society* (Oxford, Clarendon Press, 2007) 4.

subjective preferences. Part of the problem has been caused by past attempts to distinguish law from other social practices by finding some common element to all law. But law is an immensely diverse, fluid, complex phenomenon—one that supports a continuous variation and reinvention of itself. To try to find elements common to all trivialises its richness and reduces it to banal definitions such as normative predictability, which is why theorists such as Llewellyn believed that it was best to avoid becoming involved in general efforts at definition altogether.[157] There is no one 'right' way of understanding law. In order to understand the nature of law it is necessary to consider it from different perspectives and different social environments.

'Banal' Positivism

However, even those who insist on a contextual understanding of law also concede that it may often be necessary provisionally to identify some sort of 'organising concept' of law,[158] although this need not depend on some conceptual theory of law's autonomy. Admittedly, at such a general level, such a concept would most probably be so broad as to be banal and uninformative, if unobjectionable. At this modest level, such an organising concept might be found in Roberto Unger's characterisation of law:

> In the broadest sense, law is simply any recurring mode of interaction among individuals and groups, together with more or less explicit acknowledgement by these individuals and groups that such patterns of interaction produce reciprocal expectations of conduct that ought to be satisfied.[159]

Or we might consider William Twining's formulation, which as he expresses it, 'can serve as a prism and as an organising concept for viewing the phenomenon of law from a global perspective'.[160] Twining's formulation is as follows:

> From a global perspective it is illuminating to conceive of law as a species of institutionalised social practice that is oriented to ordering relations between subjects at one or more levels of relations and ordering.[161]

Twining has stressed that this is not 'his' definition of law and that he uses different conceptions of law for different purposes in other contexts. He

---

[157] See WL Twining, *Karl Llewellyn and the Realist Movement* (London, Weidenfeld and Nicholson, 1973) 178.

[158] Twining, *General Jurisprudence* (above n 6) 119. See also Cotterrell, *The Politics of Jurisprudence* (above n 80) 18.

[159] R Unger, *Law in Modern Society* (London, Macmillan, 1976) 59.

[160] Twining, *General Jurisprudence* (above n 6) 116.

[161] Ibid, 117.

also has discussed further ideas that could be built into the formulation as 'optional extras', such as rules, system and normative order.

The use of such a broad 'organising concept' of law represents the acknowledgment of what I would term 'banal positivism', namely the identification of phenomena of law by reference to social facts and not by reference to their merits. The existence of law is determined by the presence of the very extensive range of criteria, regardless of whether the norms concerned are perceived to be just, efficient or desirable. Banal positivism acknowledges law as a social construction, determined by a broad and varied range of social standards. To the extent that I accept the organising concept of 'banal positivism', then my general approach to law is positivist. But banal positivism tells us very little that is interesting about law. It amounts to little more than nominalism—that whatever interactive and reciprocal practices a particular society or social grouping considers to be law are to be treated as law. It does not require laws to take any particular form as rules, nor that laws should form part of a unified system. It need not accord any special role to officials, nor to states. It is capable of being embraced by social theorists such as Marx and Weber, as well as by legal realists. It does little, if anything, to separate the notion of law from other social activities and practices with interactive, normative elements, such as customs, rites, traditions, conventions, manners, mores, usages and so on. It tells us little about why law might be considered valuable or distinctive and also seems to give us little authoritative basis to obey it if we do not feel inclined to do so—a feature of positivist thinking that has often been raised as unsatisfactory. For example, Fuller questioned how 'an amoral datum called law could have the peculiar quality of creating an obligation to obey it'.[162] Legal positivism has generally always insisted that law's moral authority must be separated from the question of its existence and identity as a matter of social fact, an approach uncongenial to natural lawyers such as Finnis.[163] Recent legal positivism has stressed that it is law's *claim* to authority rather than any actual authority that it might possess that makes it distinctive.[164]

The problem then is that banal positivism presents us with a concept of legal validity, which tells us nothing about why law may be thought capable of having authority or creating obligations to obey it. It severs law from justice, leaving an apparently intractable (from the positivist point of view

---

[162] Fuller, 'Positivism and Fidelity to Law' (above n 67) 656.

[163] Nigel Simmonds reminds us that an 'older tradition of thought preceding analytical jurisprudence assumes inquiry into law as a distinct form of human institution would reveal the basis of its justificatory power'. N Simmonds, *Law as a Moral Idea* (Oxford, Oxford University Press, 2008) 1–2.

[164] Raz, *The Authority of Law* (above n 42). See also Raz, 'Law, Authority and Morality' in Raz, *Ethics in the Public Domain* (above n 58) ch 9, where Raz asserts that there is no general obligation to obey the law.

at least) issue of why there should be an obligation to obey the law. These are perceived as distinct issues. Yet law not only is a normative practice but also enforces its norms with coercion. It requires certain behaviour and uses force when necessary. It is usually perceived as important that law be able to justify the use of force and give us reasons to believe that the obligations it imposes are justified. Banal positivism tells us nothing about this, merely that laws may be identified as social practices. Anti-positivist theories such as Dworkin's insist that a legal system is to be identified by those standards that courts would be morally justified in applying consistently with their interpretation of that society's legal practices, regardless of social sources. By separating the identification of valid law from justice, law becomes somewhat of an empty vessel, capable of being filled with all sorts of different ideological content. As this book argues in later chapters, it is these issues of justice that have been all too often ignored.

With banal positivism as our baseline, it is hard to substantiate a case for the distinctiveness of law, given its overlap with other aspects of the regulation of our lives. The best candidate for distinctness appears to be that laid out by Raz—namely, law's *claim* to a supreme, comprehensive authority. Law may satisfy its assertion of distinctiveness by its claim to end moral and political disagreement through its open, public system of norms (although whether law actually succeeds in resolving such conflict is a different matter). Humans need to agree to a common code of conduct and authority; otherwise, communal life becomes impossible. Some theorists take this claim further. For Finnis, this achievement of co-ordination by law should be acknowledged as a form of human flourishing.[165] In this way, the form and substance of law coalesce.[166] This is, at base, a moral claim. The claim is that law, by providing some sort of order in the face of value pluralism and co-ordination conflicts, offers something morally valuable. But this may not always be substantiated. To be sure, order need not necessarily be valuable of and in itself—anarchy may indeed sometimes be preferable to order[167] if law is unable to support its claims with actual justified reasons for obedience,[168] and claims as to the moral value of law would be denied by certain schools of, eg, Marxist thought that understand law as the tool of the capitalist class.[169] So banal positivism allows for law's distinctness in a weak way—in terms of a claim to authority that may not

---

[165] Finnis (above n 40). Although Finnis does not claim that every existent legal system exemplifies the common good, he believes law to be valuable for its capacity to improve society.

[166] See further S Veitch, E Christodoulidis and L Farmer, *Jurisprudence: Themes and Concepts* (London, Routledge-Cavendish, 2007) 25.

[167] See further Green (above n 62).

[168] See further Raz, *Ethics in the Public Domain* (above n 58) ch 10, for elucidation of the 'normal justification thesis'.

[169] For further on this, see below ch 8.

always be justified, a function of co-ordination that, although it may take the form of human flourishing for some, for others amounts to an amoral capacity for organisation.

However, law may also seek to distinguish itself by what Leslie Green has described as its 'aptness for justice'.[170] Law may not be alone in this regard, but legal systems are undoubtedly apt for appraisal as just or unjust in the way that other practices, such as carpentry, cookery or rock climbing, are not. Law may not always be just, but it is always possible—and indeed, often necessary—to ask if it is actually just. This is an important issue and will be further addressed later in this book.

Therefore, law—even understood within the very general organisational concept of 'banal' positivism—may claim distinctiveness, by virtue of its role in addressing conflict in society and its 'aptness' for justice; and though this distinctiveness may fail to render law unique or completely autonomous from other elements in society, it helps to explain law's claim to do so.

Against the 'One Big Thing'

Ultimately, attempts to answer the question 'What is Law?' are liable to produce subjective, monist accounts, to assume the existence of the 'standard case' of law or the generality of banal positivism. Brian Simpson pithily characterised this monistic approach as the 'One Big Thing', attributing such an approach to Hart, Austin and Kelsen: 'to foxes the problem is to see how it can possibly contribute to an enhanced understanding of the multifarious legal system of the complex legal word we inhabit.'[171]

In order to gain greater insight into the nature of law, it is necessary to study law from many different perspectives, including but not limited to those of legal participants, such as lawyers and judges. It is necessary to take account of law's origins in society (and in different types of society, which produce different types of law) and different concepts of law. In addition to conceptual and doctrinal issues of analytical jurisprudence, it is also necessary to study the history, the evolution, indeed the very architecture of legal institutions. And this must be done not only at national but at transnational level, to take account of the manifold, complex legal developments across

---

[170] Green (above n 62).

[171] Simpson, *Reflections on* The Concept of Law (above n 53) 128. Simpson, in writing of the fox, is using Isaiah Berlin's reference to the ancient Greek poet Archilocus, who is said to have written, 'The fox knows many things. The hedgehog knows one big thing.' See I Berlin, 'The Hedgehog and the Fox: An Essay on Tolstoy's View of History' (London, Weidenfeld and Nicolson, 1953). Berlin was distinguishing two different types of thinkers: those who relate everything to a universal organising principle and those who pursue many ends, often unrelated. Simpson classified himself as a fox.

borders.[172] As Twining has argued, legal phenomena invoke 'continuous variation along several axes, eg, institutional, normative and social'.[173] Therefore it is necessary to work with different conceptions of law in different contexts, as well as the different functions of law: dispute processing, allocation of authority, the provision of infrastructure for commerce are not necessarily linked. This entails what has been described in the context of Simpson's work as an 'anti-grand theory' theory of legal scholarship.[174]

It is a question of taking law sufficiently seriously without denying its necessary connections with other aspects of society. Galligan concludes his own work, *Law in Modern Society*, with a quotation from David Garland, adopting Garland's characterisation of punishment for the case of law:

> We need to think in terms of complexity, of multiple objectives, and of overdetermination. We need to think of it … as a distinctive form of life which is also dependent on other forms and other social relations … Such a way of thinking may involve a degree of difficulty, and it certainly lacks the spare elegance of some of the more reductionist approaches.[175]

An investigation into law after modernity therefore must proceed without the 'spare elegance' of Simpson's castigated 'One Big Thing'.

---

[172] See further Cotterrell, *The Politics of Jurisprudence* (above n 80) 15.

[173] Twining, *General Jurisprudence* (above n 6) 103.

[174] See C McCrudden, 'Introduction' in Simpson, *Reflections on* The Concept of Law (above n 53) vi.

[175] Galligan (above n 156) 353, quoting D Garland, *Punishment and Modern Society* (Oxford, Clarendon Press, 1990).

3

Law as System: The Missing Multidimensionality of Law

Methodical Law

Modern law has sought to present itself as an orderly landscape.[1] Since the times of Hobbes and Grotius in the seventeenth century, 'Law has presented itself as the antithesis to fragmentation, leading from the chaos of civil war to unified nation, from inter-state anarchy to an international legal community.'[2] John Austin wished the *Province of Jurisprudence* to be 'a region of order and light' by analogy to his impressions of the Roman *Corpus Iuris Civilis*, and he believed that once law was presented as a well-organised subject, it would gain respect within the university environment. For HLA Hart, modern law could be distinguished from 'primitive' law by its systematic quality, which for Hart took the form of law as the union of primary and secondary rules, with the rule of recognition as the overarching, unifying feature of the system. Hart described this union as the key to the science of jurisprudence—believing that only when rules form a *system* can we overcome the defects of 'primitive' law, namely its uncertainty, its static nature and its inefficiency. Of course, concern with system is not singular to legal positivism. We also find it in Durkheim and Parsons, Hegel and Marx—concern with 'system' is one of the key features of modernity.

It is not very clear what Hart had in mind by 'primitive' law—whether he was influenced by Sir Henry Maine's concept of ancient law or Max Weber's concept of 'traditional' authority. In any case, the common law, although it could certainly not be termed 'primitive', provides a good contrast to modern law's desire for order, as well as illustrating some of the motivations behind positivist theory, given that early positivists defined their views against the common law mindset. SFC Milsom evoked the

---

[1] As Mireille Delmas-Marty has written, 'An orderly landscape. That is what we want. We ask law for a little order, to protect us from disorder.' M Delmas-Marty, *Towards a Truly Common Law* (Cambridge, Cambridge University Press, 2002) 7.

[2] M Koskenniemi, 'Global Legal Pluralism: Multiple Regimes and Multiple Modes of Thought', paper given at Harvard Law School (5 March 2005).

chaotic quality of the early common law, writing, 'In the fourteenth century there was no law of England, no body of rules complete in itself with known limits and visible defects.'[3] Brian Simpson described the common law as 'inherently incomplete, vague and fluid'.[4] This was not necessarily perceived as a problem by earlier generations of common lawyers, for the authority of the common law was seen to derive not from systematic clarity and a single identifiable source but from its application since time immemorial. According to Blackstone, the common law judges were 'living oracles' who distilled legal principle from this collective fabric of wisdom, and thus, even when faced with an original problem, their decision was presented as the accumulation of this great legacy of collective wisdom rather than the judge's own original thought.

However, common law thought struggles to support an adequate legal theory. For one thing, common law theory presents law as rooted in society and yet itself lacks any explicit concept of society.[5] Common law theory also has further problems in explaining the relationship between judge and legislation, and struggles to explain the nature of law's authority, relying as it does on myths of time immemorial rather than justice or reason. For Jeremy Bentham, the common law was 'sham law' and derided as 'power everywhere arbitrary'.[6] It was Bentham's ambition to 'demystify' the common law, which he described as showing itself 'in a mask' and full of 'fictions'. Austin described the state of English law in his time as 'an Empire of darkness'.[7] With the passage of time, while Anglo-American lawyers continued to respect certain aspects of common law methodology, such as judicial precedent and its pragmatic, empirical approach, they shed its more romantic claims, such as the myth of an ancient constitution. More recent theorists, such as Lon Fuller and Ronald Dworkin, have sought to present common law as unified by principles and maxims which have their own immanent logic, as a holistic body of wisdom. Fuller suggested, 'By acting as if there existed a body of legal principle that could simply be called "The Law" they (the common law judges of many states) have brought into existence something not wholly undeserving of that name . . .'[8] Yet both Dworkin and Fuller's theories seem to suffer from the same deficit as common law theory—namely, where may we find such a discursive

---

[3] Cited in N Simmonds, *The Decline of Juridical Reason* (Manchester, Manchester University Press, 1984).

[4] B Simpson, 'The Common Law and Legal Theory' in W Twining (ed), *Legal Theory and the Common Law* (Oxford, Blackwell, 1986).

[5] See on this point R Cotterrell, *Law's Community* (Oxford, Clarendon Press, 1995); and R Cotterrell, *The Politics of Jurisprudence*, 2nd edn (London, Butterworths, 2003) 32.

[6] CK Ogden, *Bentham's Theory of Fictions, 1932* (London, Taylor and Francis, 2000).

[7] See J Austin, *Lectures on Jurisprudence, or The Philosophy of Positive Law*, 5th edn, R Campbell (ed) (London, John Murray, 1885) 467, describing English law as an 'empire of chaos and darkness'.

[8] LL Fuller, *Anatomy of the Law* (Harmondsworth, Penguin, 1968) 140.

community, such a holistic society, a web of law, in the legal world today? Such a unified body of wisdom simply does not exist.

Yet if common law theory is inadequate, modern legal positivism, with its preference for an orderly legal world, has its own problems, which will now be considered. To start with, we may note the historical particularity of modern legal positivism's orderly impulse. Weber described the modern law era as one of 'disenchantment', and the positivist project to 'demystify' the law may well be seen as a parallel enterprise. Legal positivism, a theory that has tended to pay little attention to history (usually preferring the 'ahistorical' techniques of abstract thought), is itself historically significant in seeking to distinguish itself from the perceived 'disorder' of the earlier common law vision. Yet as was noted in the last chapter, law's historical situatedness was acknowledged by Weber, who characterised modern law as 'formal legal rationality' in contrast to the 'charismatic' or 'traditional' authorities of former times. Weber believed that modern law, or at least modern Western law of his time, was *rational* in that it was governed by rules and principles, systematic, intentionally created, logical, clear and self-contained.[9] For Weber, formally rational law found its best examples in the nineteenth-century 'legal science'[10] codes of the German Pandectists (for example, those of Bernhard Windscheid, a now rather forgotten figure, who infamously suggested that political, moral and economic arguments were irrelevant to the 'lawyer as such', being out of step with argumentative legal reality.[11] Weber distinguished legal rational authority from law emanating from 'traditional' types of authority, which he identified as lacking the impersonal, formal characteristics of modern law. For Weber, modern law had two key features: comprehensiveness (in that no social actions lay beyond its reach) and organisational clarity (such that the principles according to which it was constructed were organisationally clear and self-contained).[12]

Such a wish for organisational clarity was also manifested by Hans Kelsen, as well as by the English positivists—and Weber's influence is surely to be found in Hart's work.[13] Austin presented a formal, scientific

---

[9] M Weber, 'The Sociology of Law' in M Rheinstein (trans), *Max Weber on Economy and Society* (Cambridge, MA, Harvard University Press, 1954).

[10] The work of the Pandectists is matched by similar developments in the US (eg, formalists such as Christopher Columbus Langdell). The purpose of the Restatement projects in the US was to establish a grand consensus, enlightened by legal science, on fundamental principles of common law; to give precision to legal terms; and to make law uniform throughout the US. The scientific impulses of John Austin's work have already been noted.

[11] Bernhard Windsheid's major work was *Lehrbuch des Pandektenrechts* (1862) (Aalen, Scientia, 1963). See also R Ihering, *Briefe an Windscheid* (Göttingen, Vandenhoeck & Ruprecht, 1988).

[12] See A Kronman, *Max Weber* (Stanford, Stanford University Press, 1983).

[13] Although Hart himself makes no explicit link to Weber. See further N Lacey, *A Life of HLA Hart: The Nightmare and the Noble Dream* (Oxford, Oxford University Press, 2004) 384.

classificatory scheme in *The Province of Jurisprudence Determined* and urged his followers to 'imitate the methods so successfully pursued by geometers'[14]—an aspiration to a pure, abstract form of reasoning. Austin's 'map of the law' supposedly makes sense of the chaotic jumble of legal materials.[15] The geometry ideal survives today in moral and political theory—and so, for example, John Rawls suggested that 'We should strive for a kind of moral geometry with all the rigor that this name connotes.'[16] As far back as the seventeenth century, Thomas Hobbes used entertaining architectural and spatial metaphors in order to expound his theory. He suggested that if a constitution is to be anything other than 'a crasie building, such as hardly lasting out of their own time', then it must be constructed with 'the help of a very able Architect', continuing, 'The skill of making and maintaining Common-wealths consisteth in certain Rules, as doth Arithmetique and Geometry; not (as Tennis-Play) on Practise onely.'[17]

Hobbes' theory was of course propelled by the need for social order and peace in the face of a perceived brutal state of nature. However, 300 years on from Hobbes, similar architectural metaphors were employed in the context of the European Union. The European Union, which came into being with the Maastricht treaty of 1992,[18] was composed as a structure with 'three pillars',[19] across which it was seen to be necessary for there to be consistency and unity rather than an undesirable, unsystematic Europe of 'bits and pieces'.[20] The modern legal world has witnessed an impulse toward 'constitutionalisation', revealing a desire for a systematic, unified and comprehensive law. Such impulses have their roots in the earlier constitutional codifications of the eighteenth century, particularly those following the French and American revolutions, but they continue today in the move toward constitutionalisation of EU law and international law.[21]

---

[14] J Austin, *The Province of Jurisprudence Determined*, W Rumble (ed) (Cambridge, Cambridge University Press, 1995) 77–78. The philosopher Gottfried Leibniz stated that a perfect legal system would be derivative of his calculus. In the eighteenth and nineteenth centuries it was quite common to compare the scholars of Roman law to Euclid. See M Hoeflich, 'Law and Geometry: Legal Science from Leibniz to Langdell' (1986) 30 *American Journal of Legal History* 95.

[15] Austin's follower, TH Holland, complained that 'the old fashioned English lawyer's idea of a satisfactory body of law was a chaos with a full index'. Quoted in (1870) 5 *American Law Review* 114.

[16] J Rawls, *A Theory of Justice* (Cambridge, MA, Harvard University Press, 1971) 121.

[17] T Hobbes, *Leviathan*, R Tuck (ed) (Cambridge, Cambridge University Press, 1991) 145.

[18] As opposed to the EEC, which had been in existence since the treaty of Rome (1957).

[19] The three pillars that made up the EU being the EEC itself (which retained its separate EC treaty), the EU's common foreign and security policies and, thirdly, policies in the area of justice and home affairs. The tripartite pillar structure was abolished by the treaty of Lisbon in 2009, which consolidated all three pillars into a single, unitary structure.

[20] D Curtin, 'The Constitution of the Union: A Europe of Bits and Pieces?" (1994) *Common Market Law Review*.

[21] For further discussion of constitutionalisation, see below ch 10.

Indeed, in much legal theory, the terms 'law' and 'legal system' have been used interchangeably. For Joseph Raz, to understand the nature of law is to understand it as a legal *system*.[22] The use of the term 'system' implies a wholeness, a unity of constituent parts or elements that are related in ways that aggregates or collections are not. 'System' connotes some sort of a pattern or an order of interlocking parts—sense, not randomness.[23] In conceiving law as system, the aim of such an organisational project was, at least for the earlier legal positivists, to provide some sort of certainty and unity of the law. In this way, the law could appear predictable, and people would know where they stood—which was seen as particularly important to a growing business community.[24] A complete and unified system of norms would appear to offer the possibility of determinate answers in an increasingly uncertain world—a world in which, for many, religion has lost its capacity to supply some sort of underlying order to life. Law might appear huge and complex, but if presented in a systematic way then it could be transformed into something manageable, something that individuals could comprehend. It could also be perceived as something mechanically amoral but free from arbitrariness. This unity was presented both as unity of law as a mode of organisation and also as a unified understanding of legal experience, and by so doing it provided law with self-validation. It also serves an aesthetic function: an organised system presents an orderly if somewhat austere beauty.[25] It is, however, important to stress once again that law-as-system is a mode of construction, an organisational project, rather than a mere representation of laws that actually are organised and clear.[26]

Undermining the System

Law is not so easily pigeonholed. Austin's systematic account was at the expense of constitutional and international law, which, lacking (at least in Austin's day) the 'sanctions' that Austin considered an essential component of law 'properly so-called', Austin instead considered to be examples of

---

[22] J Raz, *The Concept of a Legal System* (Oxford, Clarendon Press, 1980) 2.

[23] For further on this, see, eg, C Sampford, *The Disorder of Law* (Oxford, Blackwell, 1989) 15 et seq.

[24] The connection between law and capitalism is explored more particularly below in chs 8 and 10.

[25] See K Llewellyn, 'On the Good, the True and the Beautiful in Law' in K Llewellyn, *Jurisprudence: Realism in Theory and Practice* (Chicago, Chicago University Press, 1962) 167.

[26] Although Austin and Hart did sometimes write as if their work in fact described existing practice, eg, Hart's characterisation of *The Concept of Law* as 'an essay in descriptive sociology' (already discussed above ch 2).

custom or positive morality but not law. Also, as Hart so famously pointed out, Austin ignored the variety of laws by restricting laws to the concept of a command, ignoring the ways in which laws function as powers or permissions, ie, the way in which law facilitates, as do areas of contract or testamentary law. Yet Hart's own system was not watertight. His categories overlap and intermesh in a way that undermines his system. For Hart, as for Weber, law was institutionalised norm enforcement. However, Hart's neat division of laws into primary (duty-imposing) and secondary (power-conferring) rules distorts a less tidy reality. Are primary rules necessarily duty-imposing when much of contract law (which Hart seems to term 'primary') confers *power* on parties to organise, regulate and change their affairs (something that Hart himself termed 'private acts of legislation'[27])? Such problems also beset the all-important rule of recognition, supposedly the linchpin of Hart's system, distinguishing 'law' from all other social means of control. Is it, to use Hart's terminology, duty-imposing or power-conferring? It seems to be duty–imposing—requiring officials to recognise things as laws—but if so, it takes on an unfortunate circularity, because officials end up recognising the rule that recognises them as officials. Which is to come first?

A focus on law as unified and systematic has been understood as requiring a unity of law within the state. Yet is it the case that there should be only one linchpin, just one rule of recognition or 'Basic Norm', as stipulated by Hart and Kelsen, for whom the unity of a legal system is essential? Surely laws may derive their essential validity from different sources? English domestic law may derive its validity from one source (namely an Act of Parliament or judicial decision), but EU law as applied in England may derive its validity from another source (through a decision of the European Court of Justice (ECJ) in Luxemburg, from the EU treaties or from secondary legislation).[28] Judge-made common law and legislation may also have different sources, as suggested by Raz.[29] Hart's solution was to dismiss such examples as 'substandard', 'abnormal' or 'deviant' cases.[30] Yet one could hardly call EU law deviant, given its prevalence and huge importance.

For the earlier positivists (but also later legal thinkers such as Carl Schmitt), divided sovereignty was simply a contradiction in terms, and the

---

[27] HLA Hart, *The Concept of Law*, 2nd edn (Oxford, Clarendon Press, 1994) 96.

[28] Some interpretations of the nature of EU law would dispute this, deriving the ultimate authority of EU law in its member states from national constitutions, ie from those domestic state acts that gave effect to EU law in those territories. In the UK this being the European Communities Act 1972.

[29] J Raz, *Practical Reason and Norms*, revised edn (Oxford, Oxford University Press, 1999) 147. Yet Raz, while providing a more flexible account that could accommodate some element of pluralism, still refers to law as a 'system.'

[30] See Hart, *The Concept of Law*, 2nd edn (above n 27) 123.

doctrine of sovereignty was the doctrine of the *unity* of states (*pace* Bentham and the framers of the US federal Constitution[31]). A unified legal system was perceived as a key advancement of modernity, rectifying the fragmented forms of feudalism and the common law.[32] AV Dicey, for example, criticised federalism as leading to weak government. He attacked Irish home rule, accusing it of undermining the British constitution, of which he wrote, '[The] secret source of strength is the omnicompetence, the sovereignty of Parliament.'[33] Modern law was statist, and the state was perceived as able to guarantee the triumph of order over chaos. Where foreign or international law was included at all by twentieth-century positivists, it was appropriated by their schematic approach (usually at the price of distortion), which squeezed it into a well-worn hierarchy. Modern law was also monist: even though Kelsen took international law seriously, he stipulated a monist unity of laws, with international law at its apex, tantamount to an account of national law with global dimensions.[34] Where writers were more pluralistic in approach, they tended to be perceived as marginal (sometimes literally—as in the case of Eugen Ehrlich, who wrote at the University of Czernitz at the fringes of the old Austro-Hungarian empire, in present day Romania. Ehrlich lamented 'the tragic fate of juristic science', which he stated to be devoted 'exclusively to state law'.[35] But legal pluralism may no longer be dismissed as 'marginal', and there is now a growing recognition of its highly significant advances, dating back at least as far as those of the framers of the US Constitution, who 'split the atom of sovereignty'.[36]

If the notion of 'legal system' is taken as the baseline, then there will be some requirement of orderliness and structure, which will make it hard to accommodate flailing loose ends, or overlapping or conflicting sources of authority. Even more problematic are the developments in law beyond the state, which will now be addressed.

---

[31] See HLA Hart, 'Bentham on Sovereignty' in HLA Hart, *Essays on Bentham: Jurisprudence and Political Theory* (Oxford, Oxford University Press, 1982) for consideration of Bentham's views on the possibility of divided sovereignty. The US federal Constitution of course provides possibly the first example of federalism—a division of sovereignty par excellence.

[32] In contrast, Harold Berman has described the radical legal pluralism of feudalism as 'perhaps the most distinctive feature of the Western legal tradition.' H Berman, *Law and Revolution: The Formation of the Western Legal Tradition* (Cambridge, MA, Harvard University Press, 1983).

[33] AV Dicey, *England's Case against Home Rule* (London, John Murray, 1886).

[34] H Kelsen, *Pure Theory of Law*, M Knight (trans) (Berkeley, University of California Press, 1967) 328–44.

[35] E Ehrlich, *Fundamental Principles of the Sociology of Law* (New York, Russell & Russell, 1962) ch 1. Ehrlich's work was 'rediscovered' by the legal anthropologist Leopold Pospisil. See L Pospisil, *The Anthropology of Law: A Comparative Theory*, 2nd edn (New Haven, Yale University Press, 1972).

[36] On this, see *US Term Limits v Thornton* (1995) 514 US 779, 838 (per Kennedy J).

Beyond State Law

One immediate way in which the multidimensionality, complexity and lack of unity of law can be identified is to look at law beyond state boundaries. If we do so, law becomes very hard to systematise. Yet much modern legal theory has tended to focus on municipal law, ignoring the broader picture. Austin placed the (national) sovereign at the apex of the legal system, denying international law the status of law at all. For Kelsen, state and law were the same thing, expressed in different ways. Hart tended to see international law as a deviant form of law, if indeed as law at all.[37] For Jeremy Waldron, however, 'The neglect of international law in modern analytical jurisprudence is nothing short of scandalous.'[38] With some notable exceptions, such as Neil MacCormick, William Twining, Julie Dickson, Keith Culver and Michael Giudice,[39] analytical jurisprudence has not expressed great interest in developing a theory of law beyond the state. Yet as Culver and Giudice have asserted, there is a need 'to capture legal phenomena outside the model of the law-state'.[40] In these non-state contexts, legal norms and institutions are forming new and interesting relationships, and the concept of a legal 'system' at least may be, as Culver and Giudice suggest, 'outdated and outmoded' and of little conceptual value in explaining what is going on.[41] For example, the European Union, which will be discussed further below, describes itself as 'a new legal order'[42] and seeks to differentiate itself from state forms of law, to distinguish itself as a legal order of a different kind. However, not all theorists accept that the concept of legal 'system' is inadequate to conceptualise the contemporary legal world, including that of the European Union. For example, Dickson prefers to retain the concept of 'legal system' but to investigate new

---

[37] For example, Hart wrote, 'It is indeed arguable, as we shall show, that international law not only lacks secondary rules of change and adjudication . . . but also a unifying Rule of Recognition . . . These differences are striking and the question "Is international law really law?" can hardly be put aside.' Hart, *The Concept of Law*, 2nd edn (above n 27) 214. He went on to conclude that international law was primitive because it lacked the secondary rules that qualify for a mature, fully developed legal system.

[38] J Waldron, 'Hart and the Principles of Legality' in M Kramer et al (eds), *The Legacy of HLA Hart: Legal Moral and Political Philosophy* (Oxford, Oxford University Press, 2008) 69.

[39] See, eg, N MacCormick, *Questioning Sovereignty* (Oxford, Oxford University Press, 1999); W Twining, *Globalisation and Legal Theory* (London, Butterworths, 2000); W Twining, *General Jurisprudence* (Cambridge, Cambridge University Press, 2009); J Dickson, 'Towards a Theory of European Union Legal Systems' in J Dickson & P Eleftheriadis (eds), *Philosophical Foundations of European Union Law* (Oxford, Oxford University Press, 2012); and K Culver and M Giudice, *Legality's Borders* (Oxford, Oxford University Press, 2010).

[40] Culver and Giudice (ibid) xvi.

[41] Ibid, 74.

[42] This is the famous description of the ECJ in Case 26/62 *Van Gend & Loos* (1963) ECR 1.

conceptions of its deployment beyond the state.[43] Dickson cites the example of Scotland in support of her argument that the concept of a legal system may still meaningfully be used in the context of a non-state entity. For Dickson, it is the claim to normative self-determination that is crucial in distinguishing a legal system from other entities.

In contrast, Culver and Giudice, in denying the usefulness of the term 'system', have themselves propounded an 'inter-institutional theory of legality', arguing that laws should be understood not as separate and differentiated legal systems but rather as 'variegated combinations of legal institutions and function oriented, content led peremptory norms and associated normative powers' in which varying relations characterise legality rather than a particular relation to the state.[44] They see legality as 'shorn from officials, states and geography', to be understood in terms of intra-state, trans-state, supra-state and super-state institutions and norms, which interact and engage in 'mutual relations of varying intensity' and appear in individuals' lives as 'upwellings of normative force'.[45] Admittedly, Culver and Giudice substitute for the concept of a legal system the rather imprecise notion of a legal 'order'. Yet imprecise is very much what the great variety of new forms of legal norms and relationships appear to be.

The difficulties in systematising and regularising law so far described have been revelled in as productive paradoxes by autopoiesis.[46] Yet it might be queried what is 'productive' about an account that is deceptive, suggesting an orderly landscape when the legal world in fact may be much more chaotic? Contradictions, aporia and a lack of closure are also enjoyed by deconstruction theory. Jacques Derrida, who described law as 'essentially deconstructible',[47] therefore looked not for unity but difference in concepts generally. Derrida argued that it is force or violence, not some sort of Basic Norm, that holds the 'system' together, in which case, law is indistinguishable from institutionalised power. This characterisation of law was rejected above in chapter two as overly essentialist and unsatisfactory in its focus on only one dimension of the legal field.

More generally, attempts to systematise law have been characterised as examples of 'grand narratives'[48] in postmodern terminology. Jean-François

---

[43] See, eg, Dickson (above n 39).

[44] Culver and Giudice (above n 39) xxviii.

[45] Ibid, 165, 112 and 105.

[46] See, eg, N Luhmann, 'The Autopoiesis of Social Systems' in, F Geyer and J van der Zouwen (eds), *Sociocybernetic Paradoxes* (London, Sage, 1986) 172–92. For further discussion of autopoiesis, see above ch 2.

[47] J Derrida, 'Force of Law' in D Cornell, M Rosenfeld, DG Carlson (eds), *Deconstruction and the Possibility of Justice* (London, Routledge, 1992).

[48] For such an example, see C Douzinas and R Warrington, *Postmodern Jurisprudence: The Law of the Text in the Text of the Law* (London, Routledge, 1991).

Lyotard referred to the ideology of the 'system', with its pretensions to totality. He characterised systematic totality as a silencing of other knowledges, identifying it as a form of 'terror'.[49] Drucilla Cornell alludes to Franz Kafka's metaphor of the penal colony, likening the legal subject to the prisoner of modern law and jurisprudence, with its legal propositions etched on its backs, just as the sentence of Kafka's prisoner in the penal colony.[50] This is in contrast to the conception of Hobbes, who saw social order (and with it, organised law) as essential to peace and well-being. The point to note is that a propulsion toward order, legal 'system' and the organisational impulse is capable of becoming oppressive and is not always benign in nature.

Complexity and Interesting Relationships

In spite of the difficulties involved in constructing a coherent system, modern lawyers and legal theorists have continued to have a preference for order. The German Pandektist school believed that the formal structures of rules could be conceived with technical perfection and logical coherence, 'converting the science of law into the science of maths'.[51] Such extreme attempts have not always been taken particularly seriously. Hart strongly denied that legal positivism could be equated with 'mechanical jurisprudence',[52] ie, 'a series of calculating machines where definitions and answers come tumbling out when the right levers are pushed'.[53] Yet when law is the subject of academic study, usually it is presented in some sort of orderly way—ie, 'duty-breach-damage', as if one concept followed logically from another. Dworkin's legal theory seeks to find coherence and integrity in law, and a contemporary legal formalist, Ernest Weinrib, seeks in legal rules 'an internal coherent whole . . .'[54] Ockham's Razor suggests that we do not multiply entities or hypotheses unnecessarily. Modern lawyers have tended to prefer the orderly and structured to the disorderly and complex—and to compartmentalise arguments.

Yet the legal landscape is not that clear. Legal ensembles are tangled and fluid, untidy and unsettled, and law's image blurred, because law's

---

[49] J-F Lyotard, *The Postmodern Condition: A Report on Knowledge*, G Bennington and B Massumi (trans) (Minneapolis, University of Minnesota Press, 1984).

[50] See D Cornell, *The Philosophy of the Limit* (London, Routledge, 1992) 94.

[51] See R Ihering, *The Struggle for Law* (Chicago, Callaghan, 1915). Similar impulses were to be found in the nineteenth-century US formalists.

[52] HLA Hart, 'Positivism and the Separation of Law and Morals' in HLA Hart, *Essays in Jurisprudence and Philosophy* (Oxford, Oxford University Press, 1984).

[53] W Douglas, 'The Dissent as a Safeguard of Democracy' (1948) 32 *American Judicature Society* 104, 105.

[54] E Weinrib, 'The Jurisprudence of Legal Formalism' (1993) 16 *Harvard Journal of Law and Public Policy* 583.

landmarks and boundaries are not so easily identifiable. Writers such as Dworkin and Fuller have identified the importance of principles, or law's 'internal morality', complicating a positivist focus on rules or 'norms', but the landscape is far more complex than such writers have allowed for. Indeed, Simpson referred to the 'mindboggling complexity' of UK law, including commonwealth and colonial laws, in 1961, the date of publication of the first edition of Hart's *The Concept of Law*.[55] There exists a profusion of different types of norm—rules, principles, maxims, provisos, ratio decidendi, obiter dicta—and their relationship to each other is not always clear, nor hierarchical. Different jurisdictions and areas of law interlock in contemporary law in imprecise and weak or non-hierarchical ways—contrary to Hart's account, whereby rules relate to each other in a clearly hierarchical fashion. The legal world, while it may contain some examples of straightforward, hierarchical 'system', is also a world of crossings, hybrids, inverse hierarchies, fluctuations and fluidity of space. The law is complex in complex and sometimes strange ways. Indeed, as one of Thomas Pynchon's characters relates (in a work to which I shall return), once we look carefully, 'Things do not delay in turning curious.'[56]

The Missing Multidimensionality of Law

If we look to law on a broader plane, the attempts at neat diagrammatic configuration tend to fall apart, as we have already seen in the last section. Law becomes ambiguous and difficult to place, rather than systematic. One simple way of illustrating this ambiguity and complexity is by attempting to draw a list of the many types of law that exist in the world today.[57] It is not clear how they interact together, if indeed they do. Trying to map them, let alone to schematise them, is a formidable task. My list set out below is not comprehensive; rather, it is a device to tease out the implications of law's complex, multidimensional nature. The great varieties of law make neat configurations impossible. So, for example, we can include on the list:

1. *International Law*, including the law of international organisations, mainly identified through the United Nations (UN), World Trade Organization (WTO), International Monetary Fund (IMF), International Criminal Court (ICC), etc, and related international principles, such as human

---

[55] B Simpson, *Reflections on the Concept of Law* (Oxford, Oxford University Press, 2011) 139.

[56] T Pynchon, *The Crying of Lot 49* (Jonathan Cape, Vintage, 1996) 28.

[57] In compiling this list I have drawn on the work of Twining, *Globalisation and Legal Theory* (above n 39); and JH Wigmore, *A Panorama of the World's Legal Systems*, 2nd edn (Washington, Washington Law Books, 1936) for examples of lists and of mapping the world's law.

rights, *jus cogens*, democracy and international humanitarian law. (Even this brief synopsis raises the further and common question: how much of international law takes the form of what has been traditionally recognised as law rather than morality or international relations, and is there indeed a clear distinction to be made?)

2. *Transnational (rather than international) Law*, eg, transnational commercial law, law of capital markets or the *lex mercatoria* revival, which is taking place on the fringes of or alongside international law. These types of law are more 'lawyerly' (ie, practitioner-based) than public international law and may have very little state input, tending to be private rather than public in nature (although there is a growing transnational criminal law in the aftermath of the attacks of September 2001).

3. *Regional Integration Law*, most notably in the context of the European Union, but also including the North American Free Trade Agreement (NAFTA), Association of Southeast Asian Nations (ASEAN), European Economic Area (EEA), etc. Should these associations be categorised as merely regional examples of 1, or something of a more singular nature? To what extent do they differ from international law? Some assert a different status for themselves—the European Union deliberately distinguishes itself by the term 'supranational' rather than 'international', partly on the basis of the direct effect and supremacy of its laws, and it calls itself a 'new' legal order, implying something of a different nature than international, transnational or state law.

4. *State Law*, which includes different families of state law, eg, common law, civil law and socialist law, as well as jurisdictions that are not themselves states (eg, Scotland). It also includes the subdivisions of state law into federal and non-federal law; public and private law; regulatory, self-regulatory and 'meta-regulatory' law.

5. *Religious Law*, for example, Islamic Sharia law, Jewish law and so on, which often run in parallel with municipal law, covering the same ground, sometimes interacting.

6. *Local Indigenous or Customary Law*, for example, that of the Adat (Indonesia) or Pasagarda (Brazil). Again, as with religious law, these often co-exist with official state law and interact with it in different ways.

7. *Alternative Dispute Resolution and Arbitration*, which are often not recognised as 'law' but may possess similar normative effect.

8. *'Laws' of Sub-National Organisations*, such as of universities, corporations, clubs or churches. Their status as law may be disputed, but for some people they may exercise a greater normative pull than municipal law and function in similar if not identical ways to what is traditionally recognised as law. Ehrlich, writing in Bukowina at the turn of the twentieth century, preferred to focus on what he saw as the 'living law' applicable to his community, rather than on the official law imposed

by the Austro-Hungarian administration, which seemed to him to be largely irrelevant.[58] As Felix Cohen wrote of Ehrlich, 'under Ehrlich's terminology, law itself merges with religion, ethics, custom, morality, decorum, tact, fashion and etiquette.'[59]

9. *Natural Law*, a centuries-old tradition of thinking about law as necessarily incorporating certain moral standards, usually associated with pre- or early modern thinkers such as Thomas Aquinas but enjoying a renaissance following the publication of John Finnis' *Natural Law and Natural Rights*. There is also the question of the relationship of natural law to international human rights standards, or *jus cogens*, which also embody what are seen as essential and universal moral standards.

10. *Roman Law*, which is dead yet undead, in being as it is a formative influence or foundation of many modern legal systems, especially 'Restatements' and Common Codes.

11. *Legal Principles, Rules and Maxims*, such as principles of equity. For example, the principle that 'no man may profit from his own wrongdoing' is used by Dworkin to argue his case against legal positivism, making the point that law is more than a system of rules.[60]

12. *'Soft' Law*, an expression used to describe any system of regulation other than traditional legislation and caselaw. 'Soft' law is not legally binding but is capable of exercising a strong normative pull in some quarters.[61]

Many of the types of law listed above have found little place in treatises of modern legal theory. This is understandable in some cases. It is hard enough to analyse one's own system and harder still to penetrate a foreign culture, let alone a foreign legal system. Yet not all of these categories relate to 'foreign' law, and even the unofficial types of law play a crucial part in the contemporary world of law, often being more important than municipal law. Some of the categories in the list fit together in unexpected but interlocking ways. Some coexist peacefully. Some conflict, threatening each others' stability. Some initially seem not to interact at all. For example, religious law and transnational commercial law seem unrelated, and yet there can be unexpected connections (eg, adaptation of commercial law to provide 'sharia-friendly' loans to Moslems). Some elements of this plurality of laws well illustrate that society is no longer bounded by the state. Social

---

[58] E Ehrlich, *Gesetz und Lebendes Recht* (Berlin, Duncker and Humblot, 1986).

[59] F Cohen, 'Fundamental Principles of the Sociology of Law' in F Cohen, *The Legal Conscience: Selected Papers*, LK Cohen (ed) (New Haven, Yale University Press, 1960) 187.

[60] R Dworkin, 'The Model of Rules I' in R Dworkin, *Taking Rights Seriously* (London, Duckworth, 1996 reprint).

[61] See, eg, H Hillgenburg, 'A Fresh Look at Soft law' (1999) 10 *European Journal of International Law* 499.

relations of many kinds exist (eg, commercial and financial links and inter-dependencies; ethnic, religious, ideological and cultural bonds), many of which operate on a transnational basis. New regulatory forms are emerging that encapsulate these kinds of relationship, and legal scholarship must find ways to capture these changes. Yet much analytical jurisprudence continues to focus on state law forms. New and distinct conceptions and ways of envisioning law are needed.[62]

Multiple Relationships: 'Strange Loops and Tangled Hierarchies'[63]

In addition to the proliferation of new legal forms, major landmarks of modern law seem to have lost their prominence in a way that produces many crossings and fluidities of law. State sovereignty has become weaker in a post-Westphalian age, and government and governance no longer necessarily follow the structures of state sovereignty, even if states are still important in the world order. Philippe Nonet and Philip Selznick have described a situation in which 'the symbolism of sovereignty is weakened and gives way to an image of a loose aggregate of public corporations, each with its own mission and own public'.[64]

Michael Hardt and Antonio Negri[65] argue that state-centred systems of power are swiftly unwinding in the face of the forces of world capitalism, and they characterise 'empire' as a system of governing principles without boundaries—an expansive, fluctuating territory that presents a challenge to conventional national sovereignty. In many circumstances, such as the Single Market of the European Union, borders are less relevant, and legal judgments are now frequently enforced across borders. There exist many situations in which jurisdiction is asserted beyond the bounds of national

---

[62] Some do already exist: the work of MacCormick, Twining, Dickson and Culver and Giudice has already been mentioned (above n 39). Also worthy of mention in this context are: M Delmas-Marty, *Ordering Pluralism* (Oxford, Hart Publishing, 2009); S Besson and J Tasioulas (eds), *The Philosophy of International Law* (Oxford, Oxford University Press, 2010); N Krisch, *Beyond Constitutionalism* (Oxford, Oxford University Press, 2010); D von Daniels, *The Concept of Law from a Transnational Perspective* (Farnham, Ashgate, 2010); GP Callies and PC Zumbansen, *Rough Consensus and Running Code* (Oxford, Hart Publishing, 2010); also much of the work of Neil Walker, eg, N Walker, 'Beyond Boundary Disputes and Basic Grids: Mapping the Global Disorder of Normative Orders' (2008) 6 *International Journal of Constitutional Law* 373.

[63] This expression was originally used by Douglas Hofstader in *Gödel, Escher, Bach: An Eternal Golden Braid* (New York, Basic Books, 1979) and more recently adopted by Delmas-Marty as a way of capturing contemporary developments fostering the complexity of law. See Delmas-Marty, *Towards a Truly Common Law* (above n 1) 58 et seq.

[64] P Nonet and P Selznick, *Law and Society in Transition: Toward Responsive Law* (New York, Harper Colophon, 1978) 103.

[65] M Hardt and A Negri, *Empire* (Cambridge, MA, Harvard University Press, 2000).

sovereignty, for example, the extraterritorial application of US or EU antitrust and competition laws. The UN Convention on Torture permits inspection of prisons by those authorised to do so, without any warning, within the territory of any party to the Convention. The Internet also challenges the geographical model of sovereignty, exceeding territorial jurisdiction in cyberspace, if not real space, making it very hard for states that wish to prohibit certain websites (such as Nazi propaganda in Germany) to do so. The state has therefore become decentred as a source of law and regulation, with other non-state institutions playing a variety of roles generating regulation.[66] For example, the sixteenth-century French jurist and political philosopher Jean Bodin described the coining of money as one of the 'traditional marks of sovereignty', and yet this is now done by the EU Central Bank for those countries that are members of the Euro rather than by their national banks.

In other areas, institutions relate to each other in complex, not straightforwardly hierarchical ways. Consider the Good Friday agreement, which created a power-sharing assembly in Northern Ireland itself but also a North–South council (ie, Eire–Northern Ireland) and East–West (Northern Ireland–Westminster) institutions. In another context, Judge Gilbert Guillaume, President of the International Court of Justice, worried that the proliferation of international tribunals (ie, specialist tribunals on human rights, law of the sea, environmental law, the ECJ, the Court of Justice of the European Free Trade Association States (EFTA Court), the ICC, the International Criminal Tribunal for the former Yugoslavia (ICTY) and the International Criminal Tribunal for Rwanda (ICTR))—which has taken place without any overall plan—might give rise to serious conflicts between judgments. He identified this as a 'danger of the fragmentation of the law'.[67]

In some parts of the world (ie, parts of Africa, parts of Russia, Afghanistan, Iraq in the early twenty-first century, Kosovo, Chechnya), there exist failed or collapsed states in which there is nothing resembling the effective modern state. Rather, there are networks of crime and irregular militias not controlled by any state, which become part of a global criminal economy. Within some of these (Bosnia, Kosovo, Afghanistan), international enterprises have worked within the framework of the North Atlantic Treaty Organization (NATO), the United Nations and the

---

[66] For examples of such regulation, see C Scott, 'Analysing Regulatory Space: Fragmented Resources and Institutional Design' (2001) *Public Law* 329–53. See also P Legendre, *Remarques sur la refeodalisation de la France* (Paris, LGDJ, 1997).

[67] Judge Guillaume, speech to UN General Assembly, 20/10/2000. See also 'Report of the Study Group on Fragmentation and International Law' UN GA OR 55th Session Supp No 10, UN Doc A/CN. 4/L.628; and M Koskenniemi and P Leino, 'Fragmentation of International law' in (2002) *Leiden Journal of International Law* 553.

European Union; and it has been suggested that 'imperial government is being quietly reinvented as the only remedy for the dangers that flow from failed states'.[68]

The familiar distinctions of core/penumbra[69] and centre/margin are hard to apply, as apparently 'marginal' events may transform into central ones. The dissolving boundaries of public and private law have already been mentioned. The distinctions between foreign and domestic policy have also become much less clear within the European Union. For example, Single Market matters relating to trade fall within both domestic and foreign policy. The ICC has been described as 'a striking example of the postmodern breakdown of the distinction between domestic and foreign attitudes, whereby moral consciousness applies to international relations as well as domestic affairs'.[70] 'Soft' law has also become more important and increasingly used. It is a term less used by national lawyers but beloved of international and EU lawyers for some time.[71] 'Soft' law statements emanating from the European Commission, for example, may have a serious effect on the competition practices of companies, and although not officially legally binding, they may be capable of overriding some 'firm' legal rules.[72] Transnational lawyers negotiate directly with each other, creating binding rules for clients (eg, netting clauses for insolvency in the context of derivatives trading on global insolvency markets). These informal binding norms acquire such force that national governments are then under pressure to transform them into nationally binding legal norms.[73]

Human rights law is another example that illustrates problems of complexity, classification and fluidity of boundaries.[74] Within any field of law, national or international, human rights rarely if ever function as rules—whether primary or secondary in Hartian terms. Sometimes they function as 'exclusionary reasons'[75]—the US First Amendment protecting freedom of speech sometimes seems to function in this way[76]—operating with an almost peremptory force, excluding the possibility of actions contrary to

---

[68] J Gray, *Al Qaeda and What It Means to be Modern* (London, Faber, 2003) 97.

[69] See, eg, Hart, 'Positivism and the Separation of Law and Morals' (above n 52) for use of the 'core–penumbra' distinction.

[70] R Cooper, *The Breaking of Nations* (London, Atlantic Books, 2003) 31.

[71] See, eg, 'Soft Law in the European Union', a discussion paper by the National Consumer Council (NCC, 2001). See also K Wellens and G Borchardt, 'Soft Law in European Community Law (1989) 14 *European Law Review* 267.

[72] See M Cini, 'The Soft Law Approach: Commission Rule-Making in the EU's State Aid Regime' (2001) 8 *Journal of European Public Policy* 192.

[73] See the discussion below in the context of the 'lex mercatoria'.

[74] Human rights are discussed further below ch 9.

[75] See J Raz, *The Authority of Law* (Oxford, Clarendon Press, 1979) ch 1, for an examination of laws as exclusionary reasons.

[76] For example, Hugo Black, Justice of the US Supreme Court, was famous for having said of the First Amendment, which reads 'Congress shall pass no law abridging the freedom of speech' that 'no law' means 'no law'. See *Smith v California*, 361 US 147, 157 (1959).

their provisions. However, more often, like Dworkin's definition of legal principles,[77] they have a 'dimension of weight'—ie, freedom of expression may sometimes be outweighed by pressing societal interests such as national security. Rights may be phrased very simply in terms of brevity and concision (eg, 'Congress shall pass no law abridging the freedom of speech') yet be epistemologically complex[78] in relying on general, transcendent ideas—as to, for example, what it is that constitutes 'speech'.[79] So it is with human rights in the European Convention on Human Rights (ECHR), the UK Human Rights Act and the US Bill of Rights. Their complexity depends on their culture, which determines how these provisions are understood, but they also therefore introduce contestation into the concept of human rights, rendering them less than straightforward to apply.

In addition to substantive complexity, human rights law adds a level of structural complexity. Judge Guillaume's reservations concerning the proliferation of international tribunals have already been cited. This proliferation increases the risk of conflicting judgments.[80] Furthermore, the interpretation of a right may depend on a reverse hierarchy. For example, within the ECHR reference is frequently made to a 'margin of appreciation', namely state cultural standards, which are sometimes allowed to determine the ruling of the higher court, the European Court of Human Rights.[81] This 'margin of appreciation' may result in a differentiated impact, as illustrated by the coexisting decisions of *B v France* and *Rees v UK*,[82] which resulted in the different treatment of transsexuals in the UK and France for about 10 years under ECHR law. Another example of structural complexity in the human rights field is provided by the European Union, which for the first 40 years of its existence, did not have its own Bill of Rights,[83] so it imported rights from national and international legal systems and then applied them to those same national systems in a two-way process of

[77] Dworkin, 'The Model of Rules I' (above n 60).

[78] See N Rescher, *Complexity: A Philosophical Overview* (New Brunswick, NJ, Transaction, 1998) 19.

[79] Eg, the question of whether 'symbolic' speech (acts such as flag burning or cross burning) constitute speech. See, eg, the US Supreme Court case *Texas v Johnson*, 91 US 397 (1989).

[80] This fear has been frequently expressed in the context of a possible conflict between the European Court of Human Rights and the European Court of Justice exercising their human rights jurisdictions. So far there has been no real conflict. However, the European Court of Human Rights in *Loizidou* (1995) Series A No 310 gave an interpretation of 'territorial reservations' that was different than that of the ICTY in *The Prosecutor v Tadic* IT-94-1-A 15/7/99.

[81] See, eg, *Handyside v UK* (1976) (Series A No 24) for the European Court's explication of the 'margin of appreciation' doctrine.

[82] *Rees v UK* (1987) 9 EHRR 56; and *B v France* (1993) 16 EHRR 1.

[83] The EU Charter of Fundamental Rights, proclaimed in December 2000, finally became legally binding with the coming into force of the Treaty of Lisbon in 2009.

first upward and then downward incorporation.[84] In this way, the state monopoly of broadcasting in Greece was challenged[85] by virtue of a right of freedom of expression derived initially from national law but applied through EU law in a circular looping route, illustrating a relationship of inversely commutative hierarchies.

Since 2000, human rights protection in the European Union has taken on a further dimension. In 2000 the European Union was given its own dedicated Bill of Rights, the EU Charter of Fundamental Rights, which was in 2009 accorded legally binding force by the treaty of Lisbon. In the *Kadi* case, which concerned the freezing of the applicant's assets on grounds of alleged terrorism, the ECJ referenced the Charter and stressed the primacy and importance of fundamental rights as constitutional principles of the EU Treaty, even in the face of obligations under international law. This judgment raised the possibility of a fragmentation of international law and even ultimately the insulation of the ECJ from any international human rights standards, because of its choice to look instead to autonomous EU standards.[86] Therefore, within Europe there now exists a plurality of human rights jurisdictions—national, EU and ECHR[87]—as illustrated by the *Bosphorus* case, in which a Turkish airline, whose aircraft had been seized under sanctions against former Yugoslavia, sued in all three of these jurisdictions over a total of 13 years—and lost in all three, illustrating that more choice does not always necessarily equate with success for litigants.[88] On a related point, the first European court to refer to the EU Charter of Fundamental Rights was not the EU Court of Justice but the Council of Europe Court of Human Rights[89]—an example of a 'crossing' of legal jurisdictions. However, since the EU Charter became binding in 2009, the ECJ has frequently used it as a basis for its caselaw, so ECJ caselaw on fundamental rights is also likely to become a reference point for the ECHR, thereby providing an example of further crossings. Indeed, the relationship between the European Union and the Convention will be further complicated by the planned accession of the European Union to the ECHR.[90]

---

[84] See S Douglas-Scott, *Constitutional Law of the European Union* (Harlow, Longman, 2002) ch 13.

[85] As in Case C-260/89 *ERT* [1991] ECR I-2925.

[86] Joined Cases C-402/05P and C-415/05P *Kadi and Al Barakaat v Council* [2008] ECR I-6351; K Ziegler, 'Strengthening the Rule of Law, but Fragmenting International Law: The *Kadi* Decision of the ECJ from the Perspective of Human Rights' (2009) 9 *Human Rights Law Review* 288; and S Douglas-Scott, 'The EU and Human Rights after the Treaty of Lisbon' (2011) 11 *Human Rights Law Review* 645.

[87] And indeed, sometimes even a fourth, international dimension may also be at issue.

[88] For a comment on *Bosphorus*, see S Douglas-Scott, 'Case Note on *Bosphorus*' (2006) 1 *Common Market Law Review* 83.

[89] In *Goodwin v UK* [2002] 35 EHRR 18.

[90] At the time of writing, this accession process was struggling with somewhat tortuously drafted provisions to ensure that autonomy of EU law might be preserved within a system that

Mireille Delmas-Marty, writing about European law generally, has described it as a situation in which 'incomplete pyramids surrounded by strange loops are mocking the old hierarchies'.[91] European law reveals further interesting interactions and relationships between pluralities of laws and legal systems. Indeed, it is probably one of the best contemporary examples of legal pluralism. EU law is one of the most striking examples of rapid legal development and different (sometimes incompatible) legal sources—indeed, it may provide an example that will be taken up elsewhere in the world in future.[92] On the one hand, EU law sees itself as a distinct legal order—it has acquired what MacCormick[93] has named 'self-referentiality'. It has developed its own doctrines and constitutional principles and, as in the *Kadi* case, stresses the autonomy of EU law. Yet EU law also interlocks and interacts with municipal laws in a post-sovereign Europe, where there are no longer any absolutely sovereign states. In introducing the concepts of direct effect and supremacy of EU law, the ECJ has, in the words of one commentator, 'pierced the protective veil around national law'.[94] But the European Union relies on its Member States to enforce and apply EU law, and most EU law is litigated in national courts rather than the ECJ—a feature that is problematic for those legal theories which designate 'norm-applying' institutions (ie, courts) as indicative of distinct legal systems.[95] For if Member State courts function as both national and EU courts, then which legal 'system' is at issue when a national court is determining a point of EU law?[96] EU law therefore illustrates that legal systems may not be solid and palpable entities. Furthermore, in spite of the detailing of some areas as being within the 'exclusive' competence of the European Union,[97] it is generally the case that competence is not neatly divided between the European Union and its Member States but rather overlapping, symbiotic, incremental and unpredictable in nature. Whether the European Union or its Member States have competence depends on contingent past events

---

nonetheless appeared to give the last word to the ECtHR. For further on this, see Douglas-Scott, 'The EU and Human Rights after the Treaty of Lisbon' (above n 86).

[91] Delmas-Marty, *Towards a Truly Common Law* (above n 1).

[92] Should the EU survive the crisis of the Euro, which is current at time of writing.

[93] N McCormick, *Questioning Sovereignty* (Oxford, Oxford University Press, 1999). See also an early attempt to theorise the EU's legal system, FE Dowrick, 'A Model of the European Community's Legal System' (1983) 3 *Yearbook of European Law* 161.

[94] Krisch (above n 62) 7.

[95] See, eg, Raz, *Practical Reason and Norms* (above n 29) 134–37.

[96] For further on this, see Dickson (above n 39).

[97] These specifications of EU competence were set out for the first time in the 2009 Treaty of Lisbon amendments. There are few areas of exclusive EU competence. According to Article 3 of the Treaty on the Functioning of the EU, the Union has exclusive competence in the areas of the customs union; the establishment of the competition rules necessary for the functioning of the internal market; monetary policy for Member States whose currency is the Euro; the conservation of marine biological resources under the common fisheries policy; common commercial policy; and the conclusion of certain international agreements.

(ie, on whether the European Union has taken some previous action, however small, to 'occupy the field'—another spatial metaphor) or on the interpretation or application of vague principles, such as the doctrines of proportionality and subsidiarity.

The European legal space is hence one of overlapping jurisdictions, segmented authority and multiple loyalties, carrying with it the risk of con-stitutional crisis and of officials being compelled to choose between their loyalties to different public institutions. It has been characterised as a legal space of interlocking normative spheres in which there are border points (eg, supremacy of EU law, pre-emption of Member State competence to act by the European Union) and bridging mechanisms (direct effect) rather than clear boundaries.[98] Within the myriad of legal relationships that characterise the European legal space, we might say more generally that some exemplify a *plurality* of legal norms—ie, one type of law sits along-side another type, without vying for supremacy—while others illustrate a legal *pluralism*—ie, different legal orders vie for authority within the same legal space.[99]

Further examples of the sort of complex relationships occurring in law, many of them taken from the fertile history of EU law, can be given.[100] Various types of transfer, or transplant, have taken place. An obvious example is that of replication, which occurs all over the place. This is where a rule or concept is adopted because it seems appropriate on the basis of its use elsewhere—sometimes surprisingly so. For example, China has systematically adopted capitalist laws in recent years. The European Union has copied previous creations of the Council of Europe, such as those on money laundering or mutual assistance in criminal matters, and in this way a European norm or heritage is created. Replication involves a crossing of the tracks, as it were, principles jumping legally from one order to another like a stepping stone. Indeed, Alan Watson has controversially suggested that 'imitation' was the main agent of legal change.[101]

---

[98] For this type of analysis, see Z Bankowski and A Scott (eds), *The European Union and its Order: The Legal Theory of European Integration* (Oxford, Blackwell, 2000).

[99] The issue of legal pluralism will be further discussed below ch 4.

[100] In using these terms I loosely follow the terminology of C Harding, 'The Identity of European Law: Mapping out the European Legal Space' (2000) 6 *European Law Journal* 128. Other comparative lawyers use their own, different terminology. Lawrence Friedman suggests that we should distinguish between the processes of 'borrowing', 'diffusion' and 'imposition'. L Friedman, 'Borders: On the Emerging Sociology of Transnational Law' (1996) 32 *Stanford Journal of International Law* 65. Some writers simply use the term 'transplants' to cover all these situations. For another analysis, see also Walker (above n 62).

[101] A Watson, *Legal Transplants: An Approach to Comparative Law*, 2nd edn (Athens, GA, University of Georgia Press, 1993). But of course this leaves open the question of what exactly is 'received' when something is transplanted, and by whom is it received?

Related to replication is cross-referring conditionality.[102] This is where a norm from one legal order is specifically adopted from another as a precondition for future legal action. This is more complex and less clear-cut than replication, but an example might be provided by the principle of proportionality, originally a creation of German law but applied by the ECJ to both state and EU action and thereafter gradually recognised by other EU states.[103] Often there seem to exist legal oscillations rather than straightforward itineraries.

Another process that has been identified is that of 'cross-sanctioning',[104] whereby sanctions are cross-applied from one regime to another. For example, regulators of EU structural funds expenditure often check for compliance with other regimes of EU law such as its public procurement or environmental regulation, and they can impose sanctions for breaches of those regimes. Professional bodies, interest groups and trade associations are thus empowered to formulate or enforce each other's legal rules—resulting in a hybridisation of the law.[105]

A last example is the practice of exportation, which has its origins in Roman law, mediaeval canon law and the growth of the common law world. One interesting contemporary illustration concerns the European Economic Area (EEA), which is not part of the European Union. In this case, the European Union has managed to export its laws in the context of co-operation rather than integration, creating novel legal problems.[106] For example, the same legal principles may apply in the context of EU law and EEA law but with different enforcement and adjudication mechanisms. A special EEA court (the EFTA Court[107]) rather than the ECJ adjudicates. Thus, although the EEA states have imported and assimilated EU laws, a parallel development has taken place at the level of norm application (unlike the 'Europe agreements', made with central and eastern European states in which accession to the European Union and full integration were always intended). As a result, new terminology has evolved: EEA institutions engage in 'decision-shaping' rather than the 'decision-making' of the EU bodies, and there are 'shadow' enforcement bodies, such as the EFTA Court.[108] These practices cannot be compared to traditional conflicts mechanisms nor to the European Union's standard harmonisation process.

---

[102] Harding (above n 100).

[103] A proportionality analysis has also been advocated by some members of the US Supreme Court. See, eg, S Breyer, *Making Our Democracy Work: A Judge's View* (New York, Knopf, 2010).

[104] Scott (above n 66).

[105] Ibid.

[106] For further on the EEA, see, eg, T-I Harbo, 'The European Economic Area Agreement: A Case of Legal Pluralism' (2009) 78 *Nordic Journal of International Law* 201.

[107] The EFTA being the forerunner of the EEA.

[108] For these terms, see Harding (above n 100) 138.

Their aim is not to identify the applicable law nor to harmonise rules but rather to shadow and track different orders.

One specific and interesting example of the widely varied form that law can take is Gunther Teubner's 'global Bukowina' or 'global living law',[109] so-called because Teubner has retrieved Ehrlich's 'living law'[110] from the early history of the sociology of law. 'Global living law' is a particularly good example because it sheds light on how modern legal theory approaches may prove inadequate to the complexities and varieties of contemporary law. Teubner's 'global living law' is private law and sometimes called a new 'lex mercatoria' (the original 'lex mercatoria' being a body of mercantile custom in the Middle Ages, associated with Lombard merchants who traded all over Europe). This 'global living law' is said to arise in aspects of commercial law relating to banking and negotiable instruments, without need for state legislation. It is nourished from self-reproducing global networks, or discourses, as Teubner would prefer to call them—or we could just call them business communities. It therefore grows from the peripheries, and Teubner's claim is that it can produce valid law without the authority or control of the state.[111] The best such example is the 'self-validating contract', which is formed outside the operation of ordinary contract law and enforced by means of 'closed-circuit arbitration'—ie, states are supposedly not involved. Therefore, according to Teubner's argument, it lacks what for many theorists are essential characteristics of law, given that:

(i) It is not formed by 'core territories' but by less clearly visible professional communities or social networks;
(ii) Its sources lie not in state or international bodies but the self-organising process of 'structural coupling' of law and technical global processes;
(iii) It is closely dependent on its social context and has very limited autonomy; and
(iv) It is not unified.

According to Teubner, our tendency to think in terms of legal positivism makes us think this 'global living law' is not law at all. For Teubner, traditional legal theory cannot explain it, and to understand it we should reject the focus on state and power and municipal law.

---

[109] G Teubner, 'Global Bukowina: Legal Pluralism in the World Society' in G Teubner (ed), *Global Law without a State* (Dartmouth, Aldershot, 1997) 3–30. This global living law or *lex mercatoria* is also discussed by other writers. Teubner draws on work such as T Carbonneau (ed), *Lex Mercatoria and Arbitration* (New York, Yonkers, 1998); and Y Dezelay and B Garth, *Dealing in Virtue: International Commercial Arbitration and the Construction of a Transnational Legal Order* (Chicago, University of Chicago Press, 1996).

[110] Ehrlich, *Gesetz und Lebendes Recht* (above n 58).

[111] But for a different and contrary view, see P Muchlinski, '"Global Bukowina" Examined: Viewing the Multinational Enterprise as a Transnational Law-Making Community' in Teubner (ed) (above n 109).

A further example of non-state law creation is offered by Culver and Giudice, in the form of the Greenland Conservation Agreement, which imposed a seven-year moratorium on commercial salmon fisheries in Greenland's territorial waters. The agreement was signed by various non-government organisations (NGOs) such as the Atlantic Salmon Federation of North America, and thus Culver and Giudice argue it as an example of the ability of non-state bodies to create legally enforceable norms at international level.[112] They use this in support of their argument that the concept of a legal system is inadequate to explain the manifold forms of contemporary law.

Yet it is worth stressing that the crossing of boundaries is hardly new. Legal systems have never been truly solid and palpable entities. As already argued, modern systematised law is as much a matter of vision as of fact. Common law judges have for some time looked to various precedents with disregard for political and jurisdictional boundaries.[113] For example, California courts may look to Massachusetts, to New South Wales or to Ontario. Interlegality is not new, just previously understated and probably under-theorised.

The contemporary obsession with globalisation, whether of an economic or cosmopolitan humanist sort, explains a recent sharpened awareness of the richer varieties of law. Yet globalisation has long been around as a force to be reckoned with—the colonial clashes of laws of the European powers in their Empire-building days illustrated that extra-municipal law could not be ignored,[114] although it was often perceived as marginal. Furthermore, globalisation often stresses how the world is becoming more homogeneous rather than the richness in variation of the legal world. In any case, some of the varieties of laws listed above, such as rules of corporations or churches, are not products of globalisation but rather of a focus on the sub-national level (although admittedly, corporations are at their most normatively powerful when they are multinational).

And of course not all crossings or transplants are desirable. There is an awareness of the dangers of animal to human transplants, which raise questions of identity[115] and allow viruses to cross the species barrier. In *A Thousand Plateaux*, Gilles Deleuze and Félix Guattari referred to life's productions as 'lines of flight', whereby mutations and differences produce

---

[112] Culver and Giudice (above n 39) 'Introduction'.

[113] As was remarked by Fuller, who wrote of these common law judges, 'They borrow legal wisdom back and forth across political boundaries.' LL Fuller, *Anatomy of the Law* (Harmondsworth, Penguin, 1968) 138.

[114] For a full discussion of legal pluralism and its origins, see S Engle Merry, 'Legal Pluralism' (1988) *Law & Society Review* 869. See also below ch 4.

[115] See, eg, M. Rosengarten, 'A Pig's Tale: Porcine Viruses and Species Boundaries' in A Bashford and C Hooker (eds), *Contagion: Historical and Cultural Studies* (London, Routledge, 2001).

not just the progression of history but disruptions, breaks, new beginnings and 'monstrous births'.[116] Legal transplants can be dangerous in their own way, and Teubner has written of 'transplants as irritants'[117] in the context of the Europeanisation of domestic contract law.

Cubist Law? The Lack of a Singular Perspective

Michel Foucault famously likened France's legal system to one of the diverting and frenzied constructions by the modern Swiss artist Jean Tinguely (see Figure 3-1) in the following words: 'one of those immense pieces of machinery, full of impossible cog-wheels, belts which turn nothing and wry gear systems: all these things which "don't work" and ultimately serve to make the thing work'.[118] Delmas-Marty has described a legal world that has gone from the 'complicated' (multiple and hetero-geneous) to 'complex' (interactive and unstable).[119] The great fluidity, crossings and spatial morphologies of the legal world recall the innova-tions of recent science—of quantum mechanics, non-Euclidean geometry, chaos theory, string theory, twister space, Borromean knots, Moebious bands, 'rubber maths' (whereby figures are pulled and twisted and reshaped in different ways)—all of which offer alternative conceptions of space and time. This is in contrast with the modernist paradigm, which tends towards a more mechanical order, with a precise, clockwork-like nature.[120]

Chaos theory concerns complex systems and has produced the idea of fractal dimensions. The disorder and order of legal life could be mapped or replicated even in these chaotic ways.[121] Deleuze and Guattari intro-duced the concepts of the 'striated' space of modernity and 'smooth space of postmodernity'.[122] Hardt and Negri adopt this distinction, writing:

> The striated space of modernity constructed places that were continuously engaged in—founded on a dialectical play with their outsides. The space of imperial sovereignty in contrast is smooth. It might appear to be free

---

[116] G Deleuze and F Guattari, *A Thousand Plateaux* (London and New York, Continuum, 2000). The reference is made throughout the work.

[117] G Teubner, 'Legal Irritants: Good Faith in British Law, or How Unifying Law Ends Up in New Directions' (1998) 61 *Modern Law Review* 11–32.

[118] M Foucault, 'Governmentality' (Lecture at the Collège de France, 1 February 1978) in G Burchell, C Gordon and P Miller (eds), *The Foucault Effect: Studies in Governmentality* (London, Harvester Wheatsheaf, 1991) 87–104.

[119] Delmas-Marty, *Ordering Pluralism* (above n 62) 12.

[120] See, eg, R Dawkins, *The Blind Watchmaker* (Harmondsworth, Penguin, 1988).

[121] See below ch 4 for some examples of how this might be done.

[122] Deleuze and Guattari (above n 116) 353.

Figure 3-1: Jean Tinguely, *Méta-Harmonie IV: Fatamorgana* (1985), Tinguely Museum, Basel © ADAGP, Paris; and DACS, London 2012

of the binary divisions—or striations—of modern boundaries, but really it is criss-crossed by so many faultlines it appears as a continuous, uniform space.[123]

It is impossible to categorise complex legal landscapes by a neat map of the law, as earlier positivists attempted. Indeed, as I have already suggested, it is challenging, perhaps impossible, to theorise a single, unified concept of law or to find a single metaphor for law. Rather, law is made up of cross-references, strange loops, alternative hierarchies (eg, coexisting supreme courts, as in the European Union, or international tribunals), inverted hierarchies (wherein norms are determined by lower levels, eg, by a margin of appreciation) and swiftly shifting landmarks. To be comprehended, law must be studied from a variety of perspectives—yet even so, relationships of authority can be difficult to trace because what might appear to be strictly hierarchical relationships in fact involve mutual incorporation or mutual influence. This is troubling and can lead to injustice and uncertainty—issues that will be explored in detail later in this book.

A further artistic analogy is of value here, perhaps somewhat of a provocation, in order to take the notions of spatial representation, mapping and landscape further. In the early Renaissance, artists attempted

---

[123] Hardt and Negri (above n 65) 190.

a more realistic depiction of pictorial space than had previously been achieved. They discovered (or rediscovered) perspective,[124] whereby figures could be placed within an orderly spatial grid and thereby gain greater realism and depth. This perspective was very often based on complex mathematical propositions and orders. Sometimes artists overdid or belaboured their attempts to order space. For example, some of the works of the fifteenth-century Florentine artist Paolo Uccello have an over-schematised, almost wooden appearance, due to too great a focus on a mathematical scheme of perspective (see Figure 3-2), as is illustrated in his mathematically-based studies for a headdress (Figures 3-3 and 3-4) depicted in his painting of the Battle of San Romano.

In these works, space becomes a mental construction that 'abstracts fundamentally from psycho-physiological space'.[125] In other words, perspective does not represent the world as we experience it but rather orders, corrects and unifies space. Indeed, the history of perspective has been described as 'the triumph of the distancing and objectifying feeling for reality and as a triumph of a distance-denying struggle for power . . . a fixing and a systematising of the external world as an extension of the ego's sphere'.[126]

I am of course not suggesting a direct relationship between modern legal theory and Italian Renaissance art. Indeed, such a connection might seem to involve a regrettable cranking of gears. And yet the comparison with pictorial perspective, schematisation and the mental construction and categorisation of space is instructive and helps us detect by analogy the processes of modern legal thought. The German art historian Erwin Panofsky wrote about visual perspective as a 'symbolic form',[127] drawing on the work of Emmanuel Kant and the twentieth-century German philosopher Ernst Cassirer. And indeed, the philosophical implications of perspective have been acknowledged for some time.[128] Panofsky saw

---

[124] See J White, *The Birth and Rebirth of Pictorial Space* (Cambridge, MA, Harvard University Press, 1987).

[125] E Panofsky, *Perspective as Symbolic Form*, CS Wood (trans) (New York, Zone Books, 1997).

[126] E Panofsky, 'Die Perspektive als "symbolische Forme"' in F Saxl (ed), *Vorträge der Bibliothek Warburg, 1924–25* (Leipzig, BG Teubner, 1927) 268.

[127] Panofsky, *Perspective as Symbolic Form* (above n 125) 477. It should be noted that Panofsky's interpretation of perspective is not accepted by all art historians. See, eg, E Gombrich, *Art and Illusion* (Princeton, Princeton University Press, 1956).

[128] As far back as the late fifteenth century, Cristoforo Landino considered perspective to be 'part philosophy and part geometry'. See J Elkins, *The Poetics of Perspective* (Ithaca, Cornell University Press, 1994) 263. Also relevant here is W Pollack, *Perspektive und Rechtswissenschaft* (Berlin, Rothschild, 1912); and O Spengler, *The Decline of the West* (New York, Oxford University Press, 1991) esp 'Volume II: World History Perspectives'.

Figure 3-2: Paolo Uccello, *Battle of San Romano (c 1435–40), Louvre Museum, Paris*

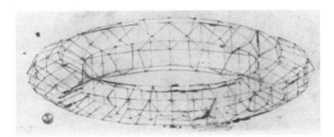

Figure 3-3: Paolo Uccello, *Study of Headdress* (c 1430–40), Uffizi Gallery, Florence, Gabinetto dei disegno e delle stampe

Figure 3-4: Paolo Uccello, detail of headdress in *Battle of San Romano* (c 1435–40)

perspective as an artifice appropriate to a particular way of apprehending the world and believed that a direct correlation could be drawn between forms of spatial organisation and the modes of perception of particular periods.

Kant departed from the view that knowledge of the empirical world consists in a straightforward mirroring of a pre-existing, independent reality, arguing that consciousness brings to experience certain forms that both structure and constitute our experience in a way that makes knowledge possible.[129] Cassirer built on the Kantian critique in an attempt to extend it to other aspects of human cultivation, arguing that cultural forms such as language, art, myth, science and technology are 'symbolic forms', structuring—not mirroring—reality.[130] For Cassirer, these symbolic forms are representations of the world that aid our efforts to make the world intelligible and to occupy the ground between the individual and the external world. As Jürgen Habermas has written:

> Cassirer derives philosophical thoughts from allegories—changes in the philosophical concept of freedom, for example, from the transformation of the symbol of Fortuna: 'Fortuna with the wheel which seizes hold of man and spins him around, sometimes raising him high, sometimes plunging him into the depths, becomes Fortuna with the sail—and it is no longer she alone who steers the ship, but rather man himself who (now) sits at the rudder.'[131]

If language, art and myth may be interpreted as symbolic forms, then why not law?[132] There is a strong case to be made that law, as a form, is used to structure reality, to render the world intelligible and to permit certain understandings of our experience and relations with others. As argued in the last chapter, different theories of law highlight different features of law as they see them to be important. These are constructions. In particular, there is a clear spatial dimension to the work of those theorists who conceive law in terms of 'system'—a rationalised conception of a

---

[129] I Kant, *Critique of Pure Reason*, N Kemp Smith (trans) (New York, St. Martin's Press, 1963).

[130] E Cassirer, *The Philosophy of Symbolic Forms*, Vols 1–3, R Mannheim (trans) (New Haven, Yale University Press, 1953–57).

[131] J Habermas, 'The Liberating Power of Symbols: Ernst Cassirer's Humanistic Legacy and the Warburg Library' in J Habermas, *The Liberating Power of Symbols: Philosophical Essays* (Cambridge, MA, Massachusetts Institute of Technology Press, 2001) 6, quoting E Cassirer, *Individuum und Kosmos in der Philosophie der Renaissance* (Leipzig, Studien der Bibliotek Warburg, 1927) vol 10, 81.

[132] Indeed, Cassirer spent much time on Kant's theory of law as well as working on a study of the Swedish legal philosopher Axel Hägerström. See E Cassirer, *Axel Hägerström: Eine Studie zur Schwedischen Philosophie der Gegenwart* (Göteborg, Göteborgs Högskolas Årsskrift, 1939) 45.

form of human experience and an intelligible organisation of often rather disorganised social practices. Legal 'systems' as devised, are architectural in form, structured in hierarchies, creatures of human agency. As with visual perspective, they imply, indeed often rely on, a particular point of view. Panofsky himself was particularly interested in a single-point perspective construction and revived the term *costruzione legittima*—ie, the perspective that offers the 'legitimate position'.[133] Is it a flight of fancy to compare this viewpoint device to 'the internal point of view', to the 'man of legal science' or at least to the strong focus on officials and their role in the legitimation of law?

Perhaps. Yet even a flight of fancy may serve as a useful heuristic device, and some modern legal theory seems to illustrate a similar schematising process to the overly rigid perspectives of artists such as Uccello. The argument of this chapter has been that these schematisations are inappropriate to an understanding of law after modernity. There are few orderly perspectives to be found in the contemporary legal world. Theories and conceptualisations of law must therefore now adapt.

A further artistic analogy may be employed here. Twentieth-century art witnessed a movement away from a conception relying on a single viewpoint perspective—a rejection of the *costruzione legittima*. This was particularly obvious in works by the Cubists (but also in the late nineteenth-century art of Paul Cézanne), in which forms are represented as composite images from multiple viewpoints which may conflict with each other. Rather than seeking fidelity to a particular visual perception, these works have their basis in mental conceptions and series of perceptions but nevertheless are still attempts to communicate the nature of an object. In works such as these, space and volume are disrupted and restructured within the art form, in order to create a new way of conceiving space. Perspectival objectivity, or the belief in a privileged or objective point of view, is rejected. Perspectives are instead dependent on the viewpoint of observers. Therefore, a better artistic analogy for law than the early Renaissance *costruzione legittima* might be a work executed in the Cubist style, in which order and design are very definitely present, but overall composition is difficult to read, partly because the work's spatio-temporal presentation is multi-dimensional, shifting, partial, tentative, not from a fixed universalisable point of view. Juan Gris' portrait of Pablo Picasso

---

[133] Thought to have been devised by the fifteenth-century Florentine artist Leon Battista Alberti, who described the drawing of a chequer-board floor stretching away behind the picture plane towards a 'centre point', now known as a 'vanishing point', where all the orthogonals (lines perpendicular to the picture plane) met. This classic demonstration became known as the 'costruzione legittima', and its use may be seen in the study of a headdress by Uccello (above Fig 3-3).

Figure 3-5: Juan Gris, *Portrait of Pablo Picasso* (1912), Art Institute of Chicago

(Figure 3-5) is particularly apposite here. And so it is with law. There is no one right viewing point, no aerial perspective. This implies a pluralism that is more complex than the world of the old common law.

4

Reconfiguring the Legal Landscape: The Sojourn of Legal Pluralism

Disorder, Entropy, Chaos: Is Law Like Literature?

The account of law given so far may seem discouraging. It paints a dystopian image of a legal world descending into chaos, prompting anxiety, despair and nihilism. Such a vision of law finds parallels with other perceptions of the world—in literature, architecture, science and the pictorial arts. Examples from these other disciplines can help us comprehend and decipher law, given that law does not exist in a vacuum but is rather a cultural artefact made up of many symbols, rituals, traditions, texts and objects which produce an inevitable richness of meanings and identities. Law is an assemblage of thought, not merely sets of rules, and as already suggested, it is not amenable to a single, one-size-fits-all definition. In this chapter, I start by looking more deeply into comparisons from literature and art, which provide insights into life 'after modernity', and while the messages from these media are mixed, they tend to be pessimistic and negative.

My first example is taken from the American author Thomas Pynchon, most particularly his novel *The Crying of Lot 49*.[1] Pynchon, whose work is sometimes described as 'postmodern', has a well-known interest in chaos theory.[2] Indeed, Pynchon's fiction has been referred to as 'the *Triste Tropiques* of Western civilisation'.[3] In *The Crying of Lot 49*,

---

[1] T Pynchon, *The Crying of Lot 49* (New York, Bantam, 1966). Pynchon's work is of increasing interest to lawyers: whole symposiums have been devoted to Pynchon and law, eg, (1999) 24(3) *Oklahoma City University Law Review*.

[2] Pynchon even wrote a short story entitled 'Entropy' in 1960. See, eg, D Witzling, *Everybody's America: Thomas Pynchon, Race and the Cultures of Postmodernism*, Studies in Major Literary Authors (London, Routledge, 2008).

[3] Claude Lévi-Strauss's autobiography *Tristes Tropiques* has been interpreted as a study of the destructive impact of modern Western civilisation. Louis Menaud made the comparison between Pynchon and Lévi-Strauss in 'Entropology', *New York Review of Books* (12 June 1997). Richard Rorty in *Achieving Our Country: Leftist Thought in Twentieth-Century America* (Cambridge, MA, Harvard University Press, 1998) interpreted Pynchon's work in a similar way.

Pynchon uses entropy, ie, the second law of thermodynamics, as a metaphor for a society in which there exists a multiplicity of signs, meanings and sources of authority. Pynchon's use of entropy suggests a society of increasing disorder, randomness and chaos. This work is a mystery story (or rather a parody of a 'Californian' detective novel of the sort written by Raymond Chandler) in which the central character, Oedipa Maas, is unexpectedly appointed executor of a former lover's will and undertakes an investigation. This investigation leads her to discover the mysterious, elusive 'Tristero' organisation, in which nothing is as it seems—confusing entropic forces lie all around, and language cannot fulfil its function of communicating and representing the world because there are no stable signifiers.[4] This is partly due to information overload: the inundation of messages renders communication unclear and leads to entropy. Sometimes, in our late (or post-) modern world, law seems to behave in this way. As in Pynchon's compelling and frenzied world, so too, our legal world appears unstable in its many norms and sources of authority. Some may be blind alleys.

Another writer whose work highlights the chaos and multiplicity of the world is Paul Auster, whose novel *City of Glass* forms part of his 'New York Trilogy'.[5] While Auster's work is comparable to that of Pynchon, it is generally less frenzied, less overloaded with metaphors and references, less frenetically comic, and thus less exhausting to read, if ultimately even more depressing. On the face of it, *City of Glass*, like *The Crying of Lot 49*, is a detective or mystery story. Both novels are thus part of a genre that has as its focus the sifting through of signs and, ultimately, the possibility of deriving order from a chaos of conflicting clues and meanings. In many ways, this is what lawyers, too, try to do.

City of Glass is a detective story about a writer of detective stories—Daniel Quinn, the protagonist, who (like Oedipa Maas, an antihero) writes under the name of William Wilson and whose own protagonist is called 'Max Work'. Quinn writes of his own interest in detective fiction: 'The detective is one who . . . moves through this morass of objects and events in search of the idea that will pull all these things together and make sense of them.'[6] In this way, the task of a detective is like that of a lawyer or judge—or an academic writing about law. 'Work' allows Quinn's (fictional) text to accomplish an end, to create order.[7] However, *Auster's* work is a

---

[4] For example, Oedipa takes the word 'WASTE' not to be the sign on a litter bin but an acronym for communication between the Tristero—'We await silent Tristero's Empire'—but she cannot be sure, and for others, these are just ordinary litterbins, receptacles for the unwanted products of a consumer society.

[5] P Auster, *City of Glass* (London, Faber and Faber, 1987).

[6] Ibid, 9.

[7] However, Auster's novel is also about the frustration of work, how it often fails to provide us with satisfactory completion of tasks.

postmodern anti-detective novel, so order and closure are elusive. Indeed, the critic William Spanos suggested that 'the most immediate task' of the postmodern writer is that of 'undermining the detective-like expectations of the positivistic mind.'[8] Quinn becomes caught up in a 'real' detective story—he takes on a case when he is mistaken for the 'detective' Paul Auster. Involved in a situation with no ends or limits, where the circumference becomes the centre, no principle can draw an end to Quinn's travails. He cannot solve the puzzle. Auster is noted for his unresolved endings, and one might interpret this lack of resolution as an option that frees one to see infinite possibilities, to choose any or none of the potential solutions available—rather in the way that Boaventura de Sousa Santos has suggested that the pluralism of law can offer individuals multiple possibilities.[9] But is the existence of multiple possibilities a positive element? On the whole, Pynchon and Auster seem to suggest not. On the contrary, presenting individuals with endlessly insoluble dilemmas in their lives is liable to lead to anxiety and despair.

Further images of entropy, disorder and chaos exist elsewhere in the contemporary arts and are worth considering for the light they shed on law as a form of life in our age. The contemporary architect Rem Koolhaas has coined the term 'junkspace' as part of an effort to create a new language to critique what he has designated a new moment in history: 'Junkspace is what remains after modernism has run its course.'[10] Koolhaas describes 'junkspace' as 'a fuzzy Empire of blur [that] fuses high and low, public and private, straight and bent . . . a kingdom of morphing'.[11] Commenting on Koolhaas, Fredric Jameson has described 'junkspace' as 'a massive and terrifying vision' of 'angular geometric remnants invading stormy infinities . . . crucial space in an infernal feedback loop' in which 'trajectories are launched as ramp, turn horizontal without any warning, intersect, fold down, suddenly emerge . . .'[12] Figure 4-1 presents a photographic image of what 'junkspace' may look like.

It would be a profligate strain on an analogy between law and art to suggest a new conjecture—'junk law'—to rival Koolhaas' dystopic confection, and to be sure, not every contemporary urban environment provides an example of 'junkspace'. It may also be argued that not every postmodern novel deals with chaos or uncertainty. Authors exist who proclaim a more positive message and determinate conclusion. Yet it is rare to find

[8] W Spanos, 'The Detective and the Boundary: Some Notes on the Postmodern Literary Imagination' (1972) 21 *Boundary 2* 147–68.

[9] B de Sousa Santos, *Towards a New Legal Common Sense*, 2nd edn (London, Butterworths, 2002).

[10] R Koolhaas, 'Junkspace' in *The Project on the City 2: The Harvard Design School Guide to Shopping* (Cologne, Taschen, 2002).

[11] Ibid, 176.

[12] F Jameson, 'Future City' (2003) 21 *New Left Review* 65–79.

Figure 4-1: Urban sprawl (Los Angeles): 'junkspace'?

contemporary literature with the unambiguous moral purpose of Victorian novels, or architecture with either the orderly discipline of the classical period or the 'pure', bare stripped back modernism of Le Corbusier and Mies van der Rohe. Law follows a present drift. Law has its own 'Empire of blur and morphing', its own feedback loops.

I have compared law to a blur of forces in motion, finding parallels with the lack of resolution and with the chaos and entropy that figure in contemporary art and literature. Yet undeniably, law is more usually presented as a form of social ordering. Faced with instability and uncertainty, an established reaction is to seek to organise and reorder in a more rational way—an impulse that gave rise to the social contract theory of the state, which originated with Thomas Hobbes' attempt to define a structure of government that would overcome what he perceived as the chaos of England in the aftermath of the Civil War.[13] Indeed, the modern paradigm of law might be characterised as one of 'reverse entropy' whereby the chaotic, disordered, random collision of elements, or litigants, crystallises into a clear structure of orderly systematic governance. Law is often complex but not necessarily entropic. To be sure, law is still used (more or less successfully) to guide and structure societal relations, promote understandings, define lines of authority, facilitate projects, limit risk and encourage trust. Abstruse relationships, multidimensionality, even morphings, are complex, but complexity need not lead to chaos and entropy. Therefore, is there space for optimism, a hope that law may prove more rewarding than the gloom and unsettled nature of some postmodern literature?

[13] T Hobbes, *Leviathan* (Cambridge, Cambridge University Press, 1991).

A Plurality of Laws and Legal Pluralism

Undeniably, the contemporary legal landscape is challenging. One recent theorist has characterised it as 'a rugged mountainous terrain,'[14] and another has described its primary characteristics as 'imprecision, uncertainty, and instability or . . . the fuzzy and the soft'.[15] Rather than interpreting the legal landscape as a rugged mountainous terrain, I believe it may be more usefully captured by the image of the *Carina Nebula* (Figure 4-2).

The *Carina Nebula* is a vast complex of dust, stars, gas, forces and energy situated 7,500 light-years from Earth. Interestingly, this particular image is a mosaic, compiled from 50 frames taken by the advanced camera for surveys on board the Hubble Space Telescope—interesting, because a mosaic is itself a pattern of complexity and intricacy, composed of many interlocking pieces and patterns,[16] and so appears particularly apposite as a technique for portraying contemporary complexity. The image of the *Carina Nebula* portrays a region many hundreds of light-years across, with huge quantities of solar material: stars of all sizes, masses, temperatures and brightnesses, forming as well as dying, and gas and dust blowing and whirling into all sorts of shapes. There are black holes, dark matter and all manner of imponderable, perplexing shapes. This is a beautiful but

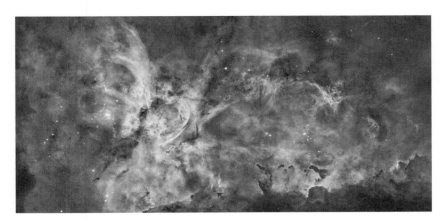

Figure 4-2: The *Carina Nebula* (image from the Hubble Space Telescope), source: NASA

[14] N Krisch, *Beyond Constitutionalism: The Pluralist Structure of Postnational Law* (Oxford, Oxford University Press, 2010) 225.

[15] M Delmas-Marty, *Ordering Pluralism* (Oxford, Hart Publishing, 2009) 10.

[16] For further discussion of the mosaic metaphor, see, eg, S Douglas-Scott, 'Europe's Constitutional Mosaic: Human Rights in the European Legal Space—Utopia, Dystopia, Monotopia or Polytopia?' in N Walker, J Shaw and S Tierney (eds), *Europe's Constitutional Mosaic* (Oxford, Hart Publishing, 2011).

disturbing image. With its hugeness, its mysteries and multiplications, its black holes (to which contemporary law has not been immune[17]), it might be compared to the contemporary legal landscape.

Legal Pluralism

In the face of this nebulous, indeterminate prospect, how to conceptualise law? Many contemporary theorists believe legal pluralism to be the most convincing and workable theory of law, and I am sympathetic to many of their claims. Legal pluralism has been defined as 'that state of affairs, for any social field, in which behaviour pursuant to more than one legal order occurs'.[18] As one writer has commented, 'legal centralism is like monotheism in that it posits one all-powerful god. Pluralism replaces one god with a pantheon.'[19] Building on the analysis in the previous chapter of the many and varied forms of contemporary law and their complex interactions, I now proceed on the basis that legal pluralism provides a more accurate depiction of the legal landscape than monist or unified accounts of law, and in this chapter I explore further the implications of this approach.

Legal pluralism is not, however, itself uncomplicated. Indeed, its very definition is contested, and a voluminous academic literature now explores its complexities and many versions. An immediate distinction to be aware of is that between the empirical and normative dimensions of pluralism. For example, Margaret Davies has suggested that an 'ethos of pluralism'[20] should be adopted, implying a normative domain to this concept. For many theorists, pluralism is an ethically superior theory because it appears more open to acknowledging as legal a variety of norms and activities, thus avoiding the privileging of certain types of law—for example, state law—for which more centralising, unified theories have been castigated.[21] Indeed, legal pluralism seems attractive not only because it apparently provides a more accurate description of the legal world, in that it fits the contemporary legal experience (so it is epistemologically superior) but also because it is perceived by some as providing an additional normative basis for its claims, given its more inclusive nature than those of unitary, systematic

---

[17] See, eg, J Steyn, 'Guantanomo Bay: The Legal Black Hole' (2004) *International and Comparative Law Quarterly* 1.

[18] J Griffiths, 'What is Legal Pluralism?' (1986) 24 *Journal of Legal Pluralism* 2–55, 2. The origins of legal pluralism lie in anthropology, sociology and colonial experience. See, eg, E Ehrlich, *Fundamental Principles of the Sociology of Law*, W Moll (trans) (New York, Russell and Russell, 1936). See also further discussion below.

[19] See D Manderson, 'Beyond the Provincial: Space, Aesthetics, and Modernist Legal Theory' (1996) 20 *Melbourne University Law Review* 1048, 1060.

[20] M Davies, 'The Ethos of Pluralism' (2005) *Sydney Law Review* 4.

[21] Eg, by Griffiths, 'What is Legal Pluralism?' (above n 18).

theories. As Ralf Michaels has noted, 'It is quite hard to be against pluralism' given its respect for other ways of life and 'a willingness to let a thousand flowers bloom'.[22]

I want for the present to set the ethical superiority or not of pluralism aside (though it will be considered later in detail). My immediate concern is to focus on legal pluralism's empirical dimension—its claim to provide a more accurate depiction of the legal world. Legal pluralism is usually taken to imply more than just a plurality of laws; rather, it is a situation in which two or more legal systems coexist—sometimes in a contradictory way—in the same societal field, in which each may have equally plausible claims to authority.[23] In this way, pluralism introduces incommensurability as a feature of legal life to be reckoned with, and rather than a centralised unity of the legal field, legal relationships are seen to be characterised by the heterarchical interactions of different levels and sources of law. Many pluralists also include the further and distinct claim that not all law-like phenomena have their source in institutionalised law—in contrast to views of positivists such as Max Weber and HLA Hart, for whom law took the form of institutionalised enforcement of norms.[24]

It is also important not to conflate legal pluralism with another type of pluralism, with which I am not really concerned in this section of the book but which, for the sake of clarity, I will briefly mention—that is *moral* pluralism rather than legal pluralism.[25] For some theorists, moral pluralism—a broad and incommensurable variety of beliefs and values[26]—might seem to require legal pluralism, so that different legal norms could enforce and support different values. (For example, Sharia law courts alongside state courts might be required to protect and enforce certain religious beliefs.[27]) But the two types of pluralism do not necessarily go together. For example, for liberal theory, moral pluralism tends to require legal *monism*. This is due to liberal theory's assertion that different moral values may co-exist only within a system that asserts a single, unified but neutral, anti-perfectionist concept of law. (Accounts of this sort of moral pluralism are to be found

[22] R Michaels, 'Against Pluralism', paper delivered at University of Helsinki conference 'Rethinking Law and Legal Thinking' (August 2010).

[23] Eg, S Falk Moore, 'Law and Social Change: The Semi Autonomous Social Field as an Appropriate Object of Study' (1973) 7 *Law and Society Review* 719; and SE Merry, 'Legal Pluralism' (1988) 22 *Law and Society Review* 869.

[24] Although it should be noted that for Weber law was not necessarily connected to the institutions of the state. Weber wrote, 'It does not constitute a problem for sociology to recognise the co-existence of different, mutually contradictory valid legal orders.' M Weber, *Economy and Society* (Berkeley, University of California Press, 1977) 25.

[25] Also to be distinguished is political pluralism, as is found for example in Robert Dahl's theory of Democracy. See R Dahl, *Dilemmas of Pluralist Democracy: Autonomy and Control* (New Haven, Yale University Press, 1986).

[26] Eg, I Berlin, 'Two Concepts of Liberty' in I Berlin, *Four Essays on Liberty* (Oxford, Oxford University Press, 1969).

[27] See, eg, *Refah Partisi v Turkey*, Grand Chamber (2003) 37 EHRR 1, 70.

in the work of John Stuart Mill, Will Kymlicka and John Rawls.) Such theories assume that it is possible for a singular, autonomous, culturally neutral legal system to exist, in order to allow diverse moral viewpoints to flourish. Yet the claim for the existence of such monist systems of law is undermined by the richness, variety and competitive pluralism of contemporary laws, in turn problematising liberal theories of moral pluralism.

Pluralism (of whatever sort) is, to be sure, not a new concept. It has been valued and theorised for millennia in, for example, the works of ancient Greek philosophers such as Empedocles and in the Tao of Lao Tzu.[28] More recently, a strong recommendation of it is to be found in William James' pragmatist works.[29] Nor is *legal* pluralism a new phenomenon. Earlier chapters of this book have given examples of legal pluralism in pre-modern law.[30] However, the more recent roots of legal pluralism lie in anthropology, sociology and colonial experience.[31] Eugen Ehrlich's work in early twentieth-century Bukowina has already been cited in the last chapter. Ehrlich's concern was that law should respond to social needs, and his conception of law was in sharp contrast to the legal formalism prevalent in the late nineteenth century. Ehrlich believed accounts of law as a unified hierarchy to be inadequate and also suggested that what passed as state law in the turn-of-the-century Austro-Hungarian Empire was in fact incoherent—a melée of different norms. Indeed, Ehrlich conceived the terrain of law as enormous. He maintained that jurists should study banks, factories, railways and many other industries and professions as sources of law.[32]

While Ehrlich's ambitions for the scope of law were gargantuan, the context of his work in the multicultural, fragmented, Austrian Empire raises interesting comparisons with the pluralism of the contemporary

---

[28] For these and further references, see Delmas-Marty (above n 15).

[29] See W James, *A Pluralistic Universe* (Cambridge, MA, Harvard University Press, 1977) 177.

[30] Roman law was pluralist in employing the concepts of *ius gentium* and *ius civile*. See B Nicholas, *Introduction to Roman Law* (Oxford, Oxford University Press, 1962). In medieval England there existed the customary law of the realm and divergent manorial, ecclesiastical and mercantile legal regimes. See JH Baker, *Introduction to English Legal History* (London, Butterworths, 1979).

[31] See, eg, Ehrlich (above n 18); L Pospisil, *The Anthropology of Law: A Comparative Theory* (New York, Harper and Row, 1971). For classic recent accounts of legal pluralism, see Merry (above n 23); Falk Moore (above n 23); F von Benda-Beckmann, 'Who's Afraid of Legal Pluralism?' (2002) 47 *Journal of Legal Pluralism* 38; and Griffiths, 'What is Legal Pluralism?' (above n 18). The *Journal of Legal Pluralism* was started in 1962 and still contains much empirical and anthropological scholarship. Other important sources for legal pluralism lie in the work of Harold Laski and other pluralists at the London School of Economics early in the twentieth century. The international jurist Hans Morgenthau also criticised international law in the interwar years for its lack of pluralism and sociological grounding. See H Morgenthau, 'Positivism, Functionalism, and International Law' (1940) 34 *American Journal of International Law* 260.

[32] As did Fuller. See L Fuller, 'Human Interaction and the Law' in K Winston (ed), *The Principles of Social Order* (Durham, NC, Duke University Press, 1981).

European Union. However, Ehrlich's work suffered from Hans Kelsen's[33] critique of it, and Kelsen's assertion that the term 'legal' should be used only for norms that could be derived from one unifying Basic Norm as their source of their validity appeared to leave no room for Ehrlich's legal pluralism. Ehrlich was, however, later rediscovered and re-elevated, eg, by the legal anthropologist Leopold Pospisil (and then more latterly by Gunther Teubner[34]). Pospisil has written that 'every functioning subgroup in a society has its own legal system which is necessarily different from those of other subgroups'[35]—and by 'subgroup', Pospisil had in mind the family, community, politics or lineage.[36] For self-acknowledged pluralists such as Ehrlich and Pospisil, and more latterly, de Sousa Santos,[37] law is everywhere—omnipresent, even overlapping and doubling back on itself.

Legal pluralism has long since moved beyond its earlier locus in the anthropology of law. As Sally Engle Merry has expressed it, 'The intellectual odyssey of the concept of legal pluralism moves from the discovery of indigenous forms of law among remote African villages and New Guinea tribesmen to debates concerning the pluralistic qualities of law under advanced capitalism.'[38] Many present-day advocates of legal pluralism, instead of focusing on anthropology and the unequal power of colonial and indigenous law, draw attention to the fact that not all law takes place in the courts but rather is a product of extra-judicial groups such as disciplinary bodies or trade groups. They assert that 'law is to be found in the courtroom no more than health is to be found in hospital.'[39]

Notably, one crucial strand in contemporary pluralism is situated at the transnational or global level, where a rich and often competing proliferation of rules and norms are to be found.[40] As already discussed, whereas the state once defined the geographical boundaries of law, there now exists a multitude of laws and legal orders at supranational and international levels.[41] Indeed, William Twining has suggested that the Westphalian state legal order should be viewed as the exception—existing for a mere two

---

[33] See, eg, B van Klink, 'Facts and Norms: The Unfinished Debate between Eugen Ehrlich and Hans Kelsen' in M Hertogh (ed), *Living Law: Reconsidering Eugen Ehrlich*, Oñati International Series in Law and Society (Oxford, Hart Publishing, 2009) 127.

[34] G Teubner, 'Global Bukowina: Legal Pluralism in the World-Society' in G Teubner (ed), *Global Law without a State* (Aldershot, Dartmouth, 1996) 3.

[35] Pospisil (above n 31) 107.

[36] Merry (above n 23) 72.

[37] See further below.

[38] Merry (above n 23) 869.

[39] M Galanter, 'Justice in Many Rooms: Courts, Private Ordering and Indigenous Law' (1981) 19 *Journal of Legal Pluralism and Unofficial Law* 1, 8.

[40] Although there exist other forms of pluralism that articulate a resistance to globalisation or EU integration. See Krisch, *Beyond Constitutionalism* (above n 14) 227.

[41] See, eg, N Walker, 'Beyond Boundary Disputes and Basic Grids: Mapping the Global Disorder of Normative Orders' (2008) *International Journal of Constitutional Law* 373, who writes that legal frontiers have shifted beyond the 'Keynesian-Westphalian frame'.

centuries or so in the North, an anomaly in a broader historical mass of legal experience of co-existing multiple legal orders.[42] Anomaly or not, traditional Western legal thought over the past two centuries tended to reflect either a monism that recognised the municipal law of sovereign states as the locus of legal order, or a dualism of national and international laws, which if not hermetically sealed, existed independently of each other with relatively clear boundaries and mechanisms for organising their interrelationships (if any) governed by conflict of laws, itself a creature of domestic law. To be sure, *plurality* and contestation are not alien to state law—witness the undecided ultimate claims to authority left open in the US Federalist Papers or Carl Schmitt's accentuation of the undecided 'suspended' character of ultimate authority in nineteenth-century European federalism.[43] The United Kingdom comprises a 'Union'[44] of different legal systems—a plurality regulated by instruments such as the Scotland Act 1998 and the Government of Wales Acts under the British constitution. However, transnational organisations such as the European Union present a particular challenge to the unified state law framework by introducing new means of interactions and also new types of conflict. For example, the concept of direct effect,[45] whereby EU law—whether it be the law of the EU treaties or secondary legislation such as directives or regulations—has the capacity to become a directly applicable and justiciable part of the national legal orders of the EU Member States, raises pertinent questions as to how and whether EU law actually becomes an organic part of national law, and if it does, whether there still exist 27 separate and autonomous state orders in addition to the legal order of the European Union itself, or whether such a piercing of the veil of Member State laws involves a greater loss of autonomy and welding into one large, monist order of EU law.[46]

A prominent and widespread view among theorists is that there exists, at least within the European Union, a constitutional pluralism of orders,[47] consisting of state legal orders but also of the Union itself, in which no

---

[42] W Twining, 'Normative and Legal Pluralism: A Global Perspective' (2010) 20 *Duke Journal of Comparative and International Law* 47.

[43] C Schmitt, *Die Verfassungslehre* (Munich, Duncker and Humblot, 1928).

[44] Perhaps not for much longer, given the declared intention of the First Minister of Scotland, Alex Salmond, to hold a referendum on Scotland's continued membership of the UK.

[45] Introduced by the European Court of Justice as a foundation of the 'new legal order' of the (then) EEC in the case of *Van Gend en Loos* (1963) ECR 1.

[46] See further on this, J Dickson, 'How Many Legal Systems? Some Puzzles Regarding the Identity Conditions of and Relations between Legal Systems in the European Union' (2008) 2 *Problema* 9–50.

[47] Eg, N MacCormick, *Questioning Sovereignty: Law, State and Nation in the European Commonwealth* (Oxford, Oxford University Press, 1999); N Walker, 'The Idea of Constitutional Pluralism' (2002) 65 *Modern Law Review* 317; and M Kumm, *The Jurisprudence of Constitutional Conflict: Constitutional Supremacy in Europe before and after the Constitutional Treaty* (2005) 11 *European Law Journal* 262.

order may be identified as ultimately controlling the legal space overall—whatever that legal order's insiders such as judges and lawyers may claim from an internal point of view. In this context, the courts have become particularly important in that they are often seized with boundary conflicts,[48] as evidenced by the fundamental rights disputes that were played out in the European Court of Justice (ECJ) in *Internationale Handelsgesellschaft*[49] and in the German Constitutional Court's *Solange* line of jurisprudence.[50] On those and other occasions, both courts have claimed for themselves the role of the ultimate guardian of fundamental rights. The *Kadi* case,[51] in which the applicant sought to challenge the freezing of his assets by an EU legal measure deriving from a United Nations (UN) Security Council order, adds a more global dimension to these conflicts, pitting the EU and UN legal orders against each other. In *Kadi*, the ECJ, by asserting the autonomy of the EU constitutional order and the fundamental status of human rights within that order, maintained an ultimacy of the EU legal order in the face of the UN order, a creature of international law. Intriguingly, by deriving the foundational nature of fundamental rights from the stipulated autonomy of the EU legal order, the ECJ in *Kadi* assisted a fragmentation of relations under international law[52] by denying the status traditionally claimed for it[53]—that of unifying, monist supremacy.

The sizeable literature on (constitutional) pluralism, whether in the context of the European Union or in the broader global field,[54] tends to be concerned with relationships *between* legal fields that are conventionally and uncontroversially 'legal'.[55] Indeed the appellation 'constitutional' pluralism highlights the orthodox nature of their legal existence. So these debates do not raise the sorts of issues as to legal status that are to be found in writings of de Sousa Santos or Ehrlich, whose legal pluralism is a different and more catholic sort, welcoming other social normative

---

[48] See on this Walker, 'Beyond Boundary Disputes and Basic Grids' (above n 41).

[49] Case 11/70 *Internationale Handelsgesellschaft* [1970] ECR 1125.

[50] BVerfGE 37, 271 2 BvL 52/71 *Solange I-Beschluß*. For the most recent pronouncements of the German Constitutional Court on this issue, see *Re Ratification of the Treaty of Lisbon*, Bundesverfassungsgericht BVerfG2 BvE 2/08 [2010] 3 CMLR 13; and *Re Honeywell*, Bundesverfassungsgericht BVerfG 2 BvR 2661/06 [2011] 1 CMLR 33. See further M Payandeh, 'Constitutional Review of EU Law after *Honeywell*: Contextualising the Relationship between the German Constitutional Court and the EU Court of Justice' (2011) 48 *Common Market Law Review* 9.

[51] Joined Cases C-402 & 415/05P *Kadi & Al Barakaat International Foundation v Council & Commission* [2008] ECR I-6351.

[52] See, eg, K Ziegler, 'Strengthening the Rule of Law, but Fragmenting International Law: The Decision of the ECJ from the Perspective of Human Rights' (2009) 9 *Human Rights Law Review* 288.

[53] See, eg, H Kelsen, *The Legal Process and International Order* (London, Constable, 1935).

[54] See, eg, N Krisch, 'The Pluralism of Global Administrative Law' (2006) 17 *European Journal of International Law* 247.

[55] See, eg, the literature cited above n 47.

orders into the field 'legal'. Note, however, that the *lex mercatoria* identified by theorists such as Teubner as an example of legal pluralism (and discussed in previous chapters) raises the question of the *status* of a measure as law, being located in lawyers' and other professionals' discourses, as well as the nature of its relationship and possible conflict with other legal orders.

Interactions

It is important to be clear that there exist many and varied ways in which laws and legal orders may combine, conflict and overlap. 'Legal pluralism' has often been used as a loose umbrella term to convey a myriad of complex legal relationships, by no means all of which are examples of legal orders in conflict. These interactions were discussed in the last chapter, so they will be only briefly noted here in order to stress the dynamic way in which contemporary laws may overlap and inform each other, as well as compete for territory.

Much has been written about the relationship between the ECJ and the German Constitutional Court, the *Solange* cases being a high-profile site of contestation between them.[56] While their relationship is sometimes taken as a paradigm example of 'constitutional pluralism', it would be misleading to focus on such agonistically competitive relations as typical of plurality and inter-legality. There are many forms of interrelation: convergence, repression, borrowing, recognition and incorporation are examples of the varied means by which legal orders make provision for the reception of legal elements from other legal systems. These examples range from consideration or acknowledgement of salient norms of other orders to full incorporation, such as when states implement and incorporate EU law or the European Convention on Human Rights (ECHR) into their domestic legal orders. Accordingly, there exist many and varied types of interconnectivities, overlaps, hybridities and 'interlegalities',[57] indicating a porosity of legal orders, as well as the competition of norms recognised by classical legal pluralism.[58] It is very common to find all of these types of interaction heaped together within discussions of 'pluralism', and yet they raise very

---

[56] Joseph Weiler has likened the scenarios of this caselaw to a form of MAD, or 'mutually assured destruction', the Cold War term for the nuclear standoff (namely the threat of the German Constitutional Court to rule EU law inapplicable in Germany for breach of fundamental rights). J Weiler, *The Constitution of Europe: 'Do the New Clothes Have an Emperor?' and Other Essays on European Integration* (Cambridge, Cambridge University Press, 1999).

[57] A term used by de Sousa Santos, *Towards a New Legal Common Sense*, 2nd edn (above n 9).

[58] See, eg, Twining, 'Normative and Legal Pluralism' (above n 42); Walker, 'Beyond Boundary Disputes and Basic Grids' (above n 41); and Delmas-Marty (above n 15).

different issues. For example, at one extreme, there are issues of threats to national legal sovereignty in the case of the European Union; at another, there may be questions about the particular status of a 'persuasive' legal precedent in a foreign legal system which is not binding on the domestic law; and a further example is provided by the claim of certain practices to be law.[59]

Problematic Pluralism

Pluralism has become very popular in some quarters—so much so as to be described as 'the new orthodoxy', or possibly 'uninteresting' when so prevalent.[60] Some writers assert that legal pluralism *is* the new paradigm for law. For example, John Griffiths insisted (several decades ago now) that 'anyone who does not accept this [ie, pluralism] is simply out of date and can safely be ignored'[61]—thus displaying a breath-taking arrogance (redolent of critical legal studies (CLS) 'trashing' techniques or avant-gardism of twentieth-century art movements). While I find pluralism to be persuasive as an empirical description of the current legal state of affairs (ie, if we accept it as what Twining has termed 'social fact' pluralism[62]), I believe some authors may claim too much for pluralism's popularity—or even desirability. Indeed, references have even been made to 'the folly of legal pluralism'.[63] Its allure is not apparent to all.

Pluralism is as difficult and contested as any other legal theory. As has been suggested,[64] it is not always an easy place to be, accentuating as it does a lack of stability, certainty and orderliness—which of course may not be perceived by all as qualities in the first place. As Neil MacCormick wrote, 'The diffusionist (pluralist) picture is a happy one from many points of view, but its proponents must show that the Hobbesian problems (about societal insecurity) can be handled even without strong central authorities, last-resort sovereigns for all purposes.'[65] Hart warned of this instability

---

[59] Eg, the 'common law movement' of militias in the US, which challenges the legitimacy of most US federal and state law. See, eg, SP Koniak, *When Law Risks Madness* (1996) 8 *Cardozo Studies in Law and Literature* 65.

[60] See N Barber, 'Legal Pluralism and the European Union' (2006) 12 *European Law Journal* 306, who states, 'If everyone is pluralist, pluralism ceases to be an interesting theory.' See also S Roberts, 'After Government? On Representing Law without the State' (2005) 68 *Modern Law Review* 3, referring to the 'heady expansive mood' of legal pluralism.

[61] Griffiths, 'What is Legal Pluralism?' (above n 18).

[62] See further Twining, 'Normative and Legal Pluralism' (above n 42).

[63] Eg, B Tamanaha, 'The Folly of Legal Pluralism' (1993) 20 *Journal of Law and Society* 192. See also S Roberts, 'Against Legal Pluralism: Some Reflections of the Contemporary Enlargement of the Legal Domain' (1998) *Journal of Legal Pluralism* 95.

[64] MacCormick, *Questioning Sovereignty* (above n 47) 78.

[65] Ibid.

when he characterised the possibility of a multiplicity of rules of recognition as a 'substandard, abnormal case, containing with it the threat that the legal system will dissolve'.[66]

In the following pages, I focus on three particular problems raised by legal pluralism. The first relates to an incoherence produced by a pluralism of definitions of law, which I shall call 'expansive' legal pluralism; the second to the difficulties of finding some sort of overarching meta-principles suitable to organise competing, fragmented or interlocking legal orders; and the third to the charge that legal pluralism brings increased risks of lack of accountability and legitimacy of law. Very little space will be devoted to this last issue in this chapter, as it will be the theme of much of the later sections of the book.

Expansive Legal Pluralism

A popular definition of legal pluralism interprets it as an empirically verifiable situation in which two or more legal orders exist in the same juridical space. Presented thus, legal pluralism appears deceptively straightforward. This still leaves the question of what is to count as a 'legal' order, however. What first appears to be a question of social fact or description becomes therefore normatively charged by evaluations[67] as to what features are to be included in the category 'law'—an issue already encountered earlier in this book. Expansive legal pluralism insists that we be aware of a rich variety of conceptions of law, some of which are incommensurable, suggesting that the dominant Western unitary concept of law is not universal, as some of its proponents present it to be, but instead limited and culturally specific—although it has sometimes succeeded rather well in marginalising other types of law as 'primitive' or defective.

Expansive legal pluralism urges that we acknowledge the continuation or overlap between law and other forms of life. Yet there are tricky questions here. Crucially, by which conceptual scheme will certain features be identified as 'legal'? For example, there is no necessary conflict between legal positivism and legal pluralism if one adopts a social-fact positivism, or what I named a 'banal' positivism in chapter two, which does not tie law to municipal legal orders (as for example Hart's positivism seemed to do). Even if most forms of positivism do not leave the category of law open enough to include all of the social practices that might fight to be included as legal, there is no logical reason why positivism should reject

---

[66] HLA Hart, *The Concept of Law*, 2nd edn (Oxford, Oxford University Press, 1994) 123.

[67] See J Dickson, *Evaluation and Legal Theory* (Oxford, Hart Publishing, 2001).

them, if it does not commit itself to a definition of law linked to official recognition or state monopoly of force. But there is of course a rather large 'if' here.

The strong pull of legal autonomy asserts itself as a challenge to expansive legal pluralism, partly because too great a broadening of the concept of law appears to lead to trivialisation. If law can span many features of society, when do we dispense with the term 'law' and find ourselves on the larger plane of social interaction? Twining refers to these problems as that of 'definitional stop'—of where to draw the line between the legal and the non-legal?[68] Definitional stop is less worrisome to some theorists than others. As already mentioned, Ehrlich's claims for law were prodigious—so much so that he believed jurisprudence to be merely a branch of sociology. Nor did Lon Fuller believe law to be a unitary phenomenon. In 'Human Interaction and the Law', he wrote that we should be interested in 'not only the legal systems of states and nations, but also the smaller systems—at least "law-like" in structure and function—to be found in labour unions, professional associations, clubs, churches, and universities',[69] which he proclaimed to be 'miniature legal systems'.[70] De Sousa Santos has referred to a cluster of 'interpenetrating legalities' whereby law moves from the old and familiar to the new and innovative, becoming in the process tangled, fluid and difficult to pin down.[71] Indeed, Griffiths has suggested that law should be identified only by its place at one end of a normative spectrum.

Ultimately, such an elastic application of the designation 'legal' might stifle one's ability to talk about 'law' at all. Some writers go so far as to eschew the term 'law', using instead 'regulation'[72] or some other yet more general term to encompass the myriad of practices involved. For example, Nikolas Rose and Mariana Valverde employ the concept of a 'governable space', which consists of a patchwork of local laws, bylaws and regulation which does not partake of the abstract, universal nature of statute law. 'Governable spaces' are made up of different types of authority—merchants' associations, landlords, shopping complexes and local authorities—which produce codes that embody specific types of desirable or undesirable conduct.[73]

It seems an extreme solution to dispense with the term 'law' altogether. Yet if everything is complex and variable, how can it be possible to pin down law or to use the term in anything other than a bland and imprecise

---

[68] See W Twining, *General Jurisprudence: Understanding Law from a Global Perspective* (Cambridge, Cambridge University Press, 2009) 131.

[69] Fuller, 'Human Interaction and the Law' (above n 32) 59.

[70] Ibid.

[71] de Sousa Santos, *Towards a New Legal Common Sense*, 2nd edn (above n 9).

[72] 'Regulation' is itself as flexible and problematic a concept as 'law'.

[73] N Rose and M Valverde, 'Governed by Law?' (1998) 7 *Social and Legal Studies* 541–51.

manner, rendering it useless as a conceptual tool? Brian Tamanaha[74] has suggested that there exist so many competing visions of what is meant by 'law' that the assertion that law exists in a plurality itself leads to a plurality of legal pluralisms. Does legal pluralism commit one to a wide nominalism or radical indeterminacy about law? Perhaps all that can be said is that there is this type of law, and those types of law—or should we go even further and cease searching for a precise usage of the term 'law' and instead focus on what is practically treated as law?[75]

If 'law' simply is whatever people identify and treat through their social practices as law, there is a danger of a resigned nominalism taking over, rendering law ephemeral and contingent in nature. This is a disturbing conclusion for some theorists, who assert that there is an 'ideological quality' in legal pluralism's insistence in attaching the label 'law' to different normative orders that may be fundamentally different.[76] Will they all concur with their rescue as 'legal'? Does such nominalism as to the meaning of the law benefit subaltern or non-official types of law, or does it further empower those who are already powerful enough, such as an elite international business community, enabling it to fashion client-friendly practices into a more official sounding *lex mercatoria* to suit its own needs? Further, if one legal order takes precedence over others, perhaps this is not because it represents some 'focal' or 'core' instance of law but rather a matter of political power—of its ability to impose itself on the rest? This of course says nothing about the desirability of the more peripheral types of law either. Indeed, for this reason, there is nothing necessarily ethically superior about pluralism—each of the plurality may be good, bad or indifferent.

Notwithstanding these vexing questions, I believe it is necessary to engage with legal pluralism, because it provides a plausible—though ultimately both complicated and demanding—account of the current legal space. Legal pluralism is not itself perfect as a theory. Benda-Beckmann, for example, has referred to legal pluralism as a 'useful analytical tool' but not a theory or explanation.[77] While apparently at first offering a better empirical 'fit' of contemporary practices, on closer inspection, it fails to dissolve some of the old problems of legal theory (such as that of the nature of law), which, perhaps unsurprisingly, rear their heads as soon as the simple cover of social-fact legal pluralism, or 'banal' legal positivism, is lifted.

---

[74] B Tamanaha, 'A Non-essentialist Version of Legal Pluralism' (2000) 27 *Journal of Legal Studies* 296.

[75] J Griffiths, 'The Idea of Sociology of Law and Its Relation to Law and to Sociology' (2005) 8 *Current Legal Issues* 49.

[76] Eg, Roberts, 'After Government?' (above n 60).

[77] von Benda-Beckmann (above n 31) 40.

Definitional Stop or False Conundrum?

These are issues that concern how we theorise or identify law and raise again the question of law's autonomy, which was discussed above in chapter two. For many, the distinction between law and non-law remains crucial, and the idea of law as a continuum will not appeal. For example, international law is often denied the status of 'law', and yet this very issue can be of critical importance in, eg, a dispute as to whether a particular source has gained the status of *jus cogens*.[78] These problems are not resolved by the admission that the term 'legal' is imprecise and unhelpful, that 'law' is simply a matter of positioning on a wide spectrum. Such disquiet is also to be found among pluralists. For example, Merry believes that some uses of the term 'law' are more central than others.[79] Are there then solutions to Twining's problem of 'definitional stop', namely a workable solution to the issue of where to draw the line between law and non-law?[80]

It may be that at least some of these problems present false conundrums. This is because of a tendency to present definitions of the concept 'law' in the misleading guise of a straightforward 'either/or' choice between a single, unified concept of law with clear boundaries or a messy over-inclusive pluralism. A better claim is that these different definitions are dependent on context. From one perspective—that of empirical, descriptive investigation—the contemporary legal space already exists as a messy pluralist world. It could not be transformed into an orderly, united, uncomplicated one if only it were possible to find the right analytical tools to do so—there exists no such Holy Grail or 'key to the science of jurisprudence'. Seen differently, however, from the internal perspective of a practising legal profession, 'law' may look very different, as a working assumption of coherence, containment and integrity even.

Therefore, a more constructive approach begins with an awareness that different concepts of 'law' may be used for different legal purposes: context is important. This is something that all legal theorists surely know but frequently seem to forget. Law may be theorised and worked with from different perspectives. A legal anthropologist studying a distant legal culture will not use 'law' in the same way as judges or advocates who work within (what they perceive as) a single, unified state system and have to apply 'the law' as defined in the normative logic of their professional organisations. A lawyer advising a client or communicating with a judge in court will tend to take an 'internal point of view' about 'the law' (ie, assume their legal

---

[78] The House of Lords famously recognised the *jus cogens* nature of the torture prohibition in the *Pinochet* case: *R v Bow Street Metropolitan Stipendiary Magistrate and Others, ex parte Pinochet Ugarte* [2000] AC 147.

[79] Merry (above n 23). See also the discussion on the next few pages.

[80] Twining, *General Jurisprudence* (above n 68) 88–121 and 362–75.

system's holism and integrity)—otherwise communication with the bench and 'learned friends' is difficult. A more independent observer might, however, reflect that effective advocacy or economic might[81] are as likely to determine what the law is, rather than any systematic coherence.

Another basic observation in response to a standard critique of legal pluralism is to acknowledge that phenomena may belong to more than one category. For example, property rights qualify as legal but are often also social, economic or political in nature—ie, the categories are not watertight or mutually exclusive, and by assessing something as 'legal' we are not necessarily permanently removing it from some other category, engaging in some latter-day pluralistic imperialism. To acknowledge this much is compatible with legal pluralism but is unlikely to be objectionable to many modern theorists who prefer to see state law as a central case.

Second, it must be acknowledged that many theorists, even some of those who are self-styled pluralists, continue to preserve a special place for state or centralised law, while acknowledging a role for other practices as 'law'. A longstanding pluralist, Merry nonetheless differentiates state law from other types of law, suggesting that it is 'fundamentally different in that it exercises the coercive power of the state and monopolises symbolic power associated with the state authority' and arguing that 'calling all forms of ordering that are not state law "law"' confounds analysis'.[82]

Simon Roberts, a legal anthropologist, has written an article entitled 'Against Pluralism',[83] which suggests that whatever is included in the category 'law', at its core will still be the category of 'state' law, 'because its provenance and confidence is hard to get away from'.[84] Roberts has drawn on historical evidence for an essential link between law and government going back as far as Hammurabi in ancient Mesopotamia, and also for his assertions that it is very difficult to conceptualise law without government, and that there is something particularly distinctive about institutionalised, municipal law.

Yet contemporary developments of globalisation, and international and supranational law such as the European Union, as already discussed in the last chapter, surely illustrate how state power has shifted and waned and how 'governance' has become separated from the state. Also, social science research has revealed how state law often does not have the coercive might and impact claimed for it and may sometimes prove powerless to shape and change society, even if it does have the power of state coercion. For example, the drastic law reforms of Ataturk, which introduced a Turkish

---

[81] Ie, the ability to pay for expensive legal representation or to choose to litigate in a jurisdiction likely to favour a particular claim.

[82] Merry (above n 23) 72.

[83] Roberts, 'Against Legal Pluralism' (above n 63).

[84] Ibid.

civil code based on Swiss law, sweeping away the old Ottoman law, were not able to fundamentally change the position of women in local villages.[85] Many state laws, coercive or not, lack the ability to resist the practices of powerful multinational corporations or global financial markets.[86] So accounts that seek to establish law's centre of gravity in state law remain problematic.

Klaus Günther has suggested that rather than looking to state law as a paradigmatic or focal example of law, we should acknowledge a 'universal code of legality'—a universal but basic language of law and legal concepts that virtually all cultures share, a bare minimum of features that are recognisably legal. Günther's aim is to address the fear that 'if law is the ephemeric and contingent result of multi-level negotiations between many different actors it does not make any sense to attribute any truth value to propositions of law'.[87] Günther's 'universal code of legality' therefore seeks to explain how communication between various networks is possible—by means of what might be described as a legal 'meta-language'. Günther's 'universal code' consists of certain concepts such as rights, sanctions and competence, which he asserts have been widely used throughout history.[88] Günther has also suggested that this code is 'more than a fiction or at best the kind of law talk of Western lawyers which immediately disappears in the face of the fact of legal pluralism'.[89] For Günther, the universal code provides a means of escape from the vicious circle of the radical indeterminacy and unfoundability of law (discussed in chapter two), which Jacques Derrida attributed to a 'mystic foundation' in violence, devoid of rational explanation or legitimacy. However, Günther asserts that the universal legal code is not the same as the monist universal concept of law so often asserted by modern theories. Beyond the rather minimal universal code, there will be wide differences, which legal social science, legal anthropology and legal theory will explore—from what might be termed an 'an external point of view' (ie, that of someone who is not an official or committed member of the system). The universal code does not render law determinate or self-contained in nature but simply accentuates particular features cardinal to law. In this way, 'law' may provide a starting point or criterion by which phenomena are to be adjudged legal or by which similarities and differences in several dimensions may be looked at in a consistent way. So

---

[85] Merry (above n 23) cites J Straw and J Pool, 'The Impact of Legal Revolution in Rural Turkey' (1974) 8 *Law and Society Review*.
[86] This point is discussed below in later chapters.
[87] K Gunther, 'Legal Pluralism or Uniform Concept of Law? Globalisation as a Problem of Legal Theory' (2008) *NoFo: An Interdisciplinary Journal of Law and Justice* 5.
[88] Ibid.
[89] Ibid.

in the sense outlined, communication is possible—we can talk about law meaningfully, and chaos is not come again.

Günther's attempt to provide a basic functional definition of law may, however, overreach itself as an account of law in a 'pre-interpretive' sense. 'Overreach', because some of the features he includes within the code, such as rights, simply may not have the universality he claims for them but instead derive from a particular Western strain of law emerging in the seventeenth and eighteenth centuries.[90] Claims for universality are therefore tendentious. Yet Günther's account is attractive because he seeks to include those features within law (eg, rights) that distance it from a bare exercise of power and propel it instead to a notion of authority founded in a co-original exercise of right and power.[91] But even such a minimalist account as Günther's universal code illustrates the problems of any general, overarching theory of law. Perhaps it is safer to limit the definition of law for these purposes still further—to law as an institutional normative order[92] directed at ordering relations between subjects.

One further approach might be to seek to dissolve the problem as a particular problem of legal pluralism by asserting that complexity or 'definitional stop' are not unique problems of pluralism. The phenomenon of plurality also applies to what is conventionally assumed to be singular or unified. A single legal 'system' displays different threads, features and multiple layers, as well as contradictions of the sort well noted by CLS—strands of authorities that reflect different cultural contexts or concepts. For example, within Anglo-American contract law there exists a strong bias towards autonomy of bargaining and freedom to contract but also a more paternalistic impulse to protect weaker parties such as minors from undue influence.[93] On a larger scale, David Sugarman noted the fact that within eighteenth-century England, struggles existed between local courts, special courts and the formal state courts.[94] Similarly, twentieth-century anthropological studies noted how what was normally taken to be a singular, indigenous or 'native' law had itself been shaped by conquests and events in previous centuries. For example, Clifford Geertz described how law in Java derived from Chinese settlers and trading companies, North Vietnam, India, Islamic missionaries, Dutch and British colonisers, the

---

[90] See below ch 9 for a further discussion of these matters.

[91] Linking his work to that of Jürgen Habermas. See, eg, J Habermas, *Between Facts and Norms: Contributions to a Discourse Theory of Law and Democracy* (Cambridge, MA, Massachusetts Institute of Technology Press, 1996).

[92] See, eg, N MacCormick, *Institutions of Law: An Essay in Legal Theory*, 2nd edn (Oxford, Oxford University Press, 2008).

[93] See, eg, C Dalton, 'An Essay in the Deconstruction of Contract Doctrine' (1985) 94 *Yale Law Journal* 97.

[94] D Sugarman, 'Law, Economy and State in England, 1750–1914' in D Sugarman (ed), *Legality, Ideology and the State* (London, Academic Press, 1983) 213.

Japanese occupation force and, in contemporary times, the Indonesian state.[95] Federalism as a doctrine, while requiring systemic unity, allows for plurality and uses meta-principles of organisation with a concern for distinctiveness and autonomy of concomitant parts.[96] So even what we might commonly think of as singular and unified is usually in fact a plural, diversified phenomenon. We should not compare pluralism to some idealised, alternative monist vision.

The Search for Meta-principles

Moving on from the issue of what is rightfully defined as law, the further problem of how to interpret the interactions of those entities acknowledged as 'law' arises. Many theorists understandably wish to go beyond the simple comment that there exist this and that type of law, and the different types sometimes interconnect; they wish to engage more deeply with the multiplicity of laws. How, if at all, to make sense of this complex jumble of legal materials, this legal world of energy being released, of collisions and crossings? Are we doomed to the sort of pessimism adopted by Pynchon or Auster in which there is no room for an 'internal morality of law'? Are we living in a legal 'city of glass'? Teubner's assertion is that 'any aspiration to the organised and doctrinal study of law is surely a chimera . . . [T]he only realistic option is to develop heterarchical forms of law that limit themselves to creating loose relationships between the fragments of law.'[97] Yet if order and structure are so difficult to achieve, how are we to avoid the chaos and pessimism of, for example, postmodern literature?

Contemporary theory does attempt to impose or identify structures or orderings so that the plurality of laws need not be interpreted as infinite, chaotic and entropic in nature. Mireille Delmas-Marty advocates a 'pluralism ordonée', and indeed, most pluralists tend to seek some sort of overarching principles that can hold things together. System and order continue to beguile, and a lack of order prompts uneasiness. Further, although law is not akin to an extremely crumpled tablecloth, to be ironed out and straightened at all accounts, 'system' in this context need not be highly

---

[95] See C Geertz, *Local Knowledge: Further Essays in Interpretive Anthropology* (New York, Basic Books, 1983); and B Malinowski, *Crime and Custom in a Savage Society*, (Totowa, NJ, Littlefield Adams, 1926).

[96] For a looser definition of federalism in the context of the early EEC, see P Pescatore, 'The Doctrine of "Direct Effect": An Infant Disease of Community Law' (1983) 8 *European Law Review* 155, 167.

[97] A Fischer-Lescano and G Teubner, 'Regime Collisions: The Vain Search for Legal Unity in the Fragmentation of Global Law' (2004) 25 *Michigan Journal of International Law* 1017.

structured and well ordered, nor imply logical coherence and systematic or 'taxonomic collectivity'.[98]

The *Carina Nebula* was earlier proposed as a model for contemporary legal chaos. However, a different model may be found in another mosaic—that of a dodecahedral tessellation, which possesses a clearer structure of its own, as illustrated below in Figure 4-3. This mathematical mosaic obviously provides a greater vision of order than the *Carina Nebula*. It is highly complex, polytopic, hugely multiple, overlapping and yet still clear in structure—indeed all of its components share the same structure. There are no black holes. We might posit this shared structure as a meta-principle for legal ordering—an overall priority, as seen by the clarity of this form, reproduced again and again, and salient as the central, dominant image. As a pictorial metaphor, this dodecahedral tessellation has its attractions. As will be discussed, some of the suggested solutions for bringing overall structure and resolution to pluralism by positing overarching meta-principles might seem closer to this model. Yet of course, it is merely a projection, one way of looking at things, as also is the mosaic of the *Carina Nebula*. As such, it is an aspiration, not a representation of reality.

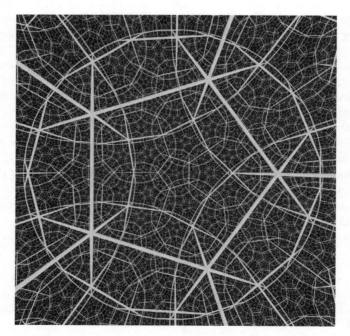

Figure 4-3: A perspective projection of a dodecahedral tessellation in H3, http://en.wikipedia.org/wiki/Order-4_dodecahedral_honeycomb (accessed 4 January 2013)

[98] von Benda-Beckmann (above n 31) 63.

Generally, approaches to legal pluralism fall into one of two camps: 'radical' or strong pluralists, who posit an insurmountable pluralism—an irreducible set of legal orders with no clear, overarching way of resolving conflicts; and 'weak' pluralists, who acknowledge that different 'laws' exist but believe that conflicts between them are resolved by a dominant law or meta-principle—as was the case in colonialism.[99] Weak pluralists tend to be much more common; indeed, radical pluralism may ultimately be indefensible.

Radical Pluralism

Griffiths, writing within the anthropology and sociology of law, has advocated radical pluralism, rejecting claims for any dominant structure or framework of ordering. However, much contemporary literature on radical pluralism emanates from work on EU law. Does the European Union provide such an example of radical pluralism, with its different legal orders in different Member States flourishing alongside the EU law? MacCormick's work has been very influential in this area and has inspired much of the constitutional pluralism literature in EU law. Given the co-existence and sometimes competition of legal orders within the European Union, MacCormick asserted that there existed 'no hierarchical relationship in the rank-order international law-community law-Member State law'.[100] He concluded:

> [R]elations between states inter se and between states and Community are interactive rather than hierarchical . . . It follows also that the interpretive power of the highest decision-making authorities of the different systems must be, as to each system, ultimate. It is for the ECJ to interpret in the last resort and in a finally authoritative way the norms of Community law. But equally, it must be for the highest constitutional tribunal of each member state to interpret its constitutional and other norms, and hence to interpret the interaction of the validity of EC law with higher level norms of validity in the given state system.[101]

MacCormick described this view as 'radical pluralism', suggesting:

> [I]t is possible that the European Court interprets Community law so as to assert some right or obligation as binding in favour of a person within the jurisdiction of the highest court of a member state, while that court in turn denies that such a right or obligation is valid in terms of the national constitution.[102]

He believed, however, that such conflicts were 'not logically embarrassing' because 'strictly, the answers are from the point of view of different

---

[99] Griffiths, 'What is Legal Pluralism?' (above n 18) 5.
[100] MacCormick, *Questioning Sovereignty* (above n 47) 117.
[101] Ibid, 118.
[102] Ibid.

systems'.[103] Yet such conflicts are problematic in other respects, especially from that of the rule of law critique discussed below,[104] as they may dictate different legal rights and obligations under different legal systems yet within the same legal space. A further dilemma is also to be noted in the face of divided loyalties and contradictory laws—that of conflicted loyalties of 'national' lawyers who will not necessarily see their allegiance as lying with 'national' law but might apply EU law in case of conflict.[105]

Interestingly, radical pluralism is not so far from a monism in which national legal orders do not interact at all and in which different legal systems exist as separate entities, failing to recognise other legal systems as having any claim within their territory. Although MacCormick stressed the interaction of legal systems within the European Union, the consequence of this radical pluralism appears to be more a *failure* of interaction, in which systems are not communicating with each other, given that each legal system affords no recognition to the other's demand for compliance.[106] This is a surprising consequence for a theory that started as apparently open to mutual recognition of legal systems.

MacCormick later moderated his views on pluralism in the European Union in any case, looking to international law as a source of resolution of conflicts, writing, 'The obligations of international law set conditions upon the validity of state and of Community constitutions and interpretations thereof and hence impose a framework on the interactive but not hierarchical relations between systems.'[107] MacCormick thereby suggested that both national law and EU law are hierarchically subordinate to international law, a view which must at the very least be suspect as far as EU law in the human rights field is concerned, following *Kadi*.[108] This change of view by MacCormick suggests a fear of the consequence of instability emanating from radical pluralism, of chaos and of noncompliance with obligations.

Outside of the European Union, other examples of potentially radical pluralism may be found. We have seen that in the context of the increasing proliferation of special tribunals and conventions in international law, there has been a fear of 'loss of overall control'.[109] European human rights law presents a plurality of human rights orders, with national, ECJ and ECHR judges very often all having jurisdiction over one single rights

---

[103] Ibid, 119.
[104] See also below chs 7 and 8.
[105] For an interesting discussion of these issues, see Barber (above n 60).
[106] See P Eleftheriadis, 'Pluralism and Integrity' (2010) *Ratio Juris* 365–89.
[107] MacCormick, *Questioning Sovereignty* (above n 47) 118.
[108] Above n 51.
[109] Speech by HE Judge Gilbert Guillaume, President of the International Court of Justice to the General Assembly of the United Nations (30 October 2002).

violation—a fact that Judge Luzius Wildhaber, former President of the European Court of Human Rights (ECtHR), referred to as a 'détriplement' of functions.[110] This situation may often result in a literal tripling of actions, as in the *Bosphorus* case,[111] which was determined by the Irish Supreme Court, the ECJ and the ECtHR (with a negative result for the applicant in each case, after 13 years of litigation). A potential for conflict also exists—ie, the Strasbourg and Luxembourg courts might decide cases in different ways, or national courts might refuse to apply a Strasbourg ruling.[112]

A radical pluralist interpretation has been also advocated for the field of private law. Jan Smits has argued against identifying the state and its democratic procedures as the sole ground for private law and its legitimacy.[113] Indeed, given the profusion of sources for private law in national, European and other areas of law and their 'equal claim' to validity and lack of hierarchy, Smits doubts whether private law should be termed a 'system'. Smits' claim approaches radical pluralism in that he advocates that this pluralism should not be harmonised or eliminated by uniformisation, nor structured through private international law rules, nor managed through overarching policy or principle, such as, eg, the EU Open Method of Coordination.[114] Smits prefers to leave the plurality as it is and to encourage it. Along with other legal pluralists, Smits stresses the capacity of people to belong to several different groups and suggests that they should be free to choose which laws apply to them. Smits prefers to conceive of private law as a market in which the most attractive systems would survive. In some ways, his approach has something in common with de Sousa Santos, although de Sousa Santos' work is prompted by very different concerns.[115]

However, radical pluralism is unsatisfactory.[116] It implies no communication exists between legal orders, but this is not always so. Strategies of peaceful compliance are sometimes employed, and in the context of the

---

[110] 'The Coordination of the Protection of Fundamental Rights in Europe', address by Luzius Wildhaber, President of the European Court of Human Rights, Geneva (8 September 2005).

[111] *Bosphorus v Ireland* [2006] 1 EHRR, also mentioned above ch 3.

[112] See also S Douglas-Scott, 'A Tale of Two Courts: Luxembourg, Strasbourg and the Growing European Human Rights *Acquis*' (2006) 43 *Common Market Law Review 629*.

[113] J Smits, 'Plurality of Sources in European Private Law, or: How to Live With Legal Diversity?' in R Brownsword, H Micklitz, L Niglia and S Weatherill (eds), *The Foundations of European Private Law* (Oxford, Hart Publishing, 2011).

[114] The Open Method of Coordination was introduced by the European Council of Lisbon in March 2000. It was designed to help Member States progress jointly in the reforms needed to reach the Lisbon goals.

[115] See de Sousa Santos, *Towards a New Legal Common Sense*, 2nd edn (above n 9); and the discussion above at n 71.

[116] For a different view, see N Krisch, 'Who's Afraid of Radical Pluralism? Legal Order and Political Stability in the Postnational Space' (2011) 24 *Ratio Juris* 386–412.

European Union at least, concepts such as direct effect suggest a very real intermingling of laws, which undermines the claims of radical pluralism. It also raises particularly strong dilemmas for the rule of law and accountability, to be discussed later in the chapter.

Weaker Pluralism

A more common response to pluralism, whether at national, regional, or international level, is to seek to structure and stabilise the proliferating institutions and rationalities by way of meta-principles, or by some sort of 'order of orders'.[117] A wide variety of suggestions has been made by theorists as to how this unruly pluralism might be ordered. Delmas-Marty has looked to devices such as those already familiar in European law— the margin of appreciation, subsidiarity and proportionality—as 'fuzzy' guiding principles (rather than as precise codes). Her image of ordered pluralism is that of a land of 'organised clouds', more structured by a post-modern, non-Euclidean geometry than a rigid logic. So the dodecahedral mathematical mosaic, constructed from principles of Euclidean geometry would not be an appropriate image for her. She emphasises a need for sustainability and equilibrium, rather than hegemonic processes or ultra-liberal, self-regulating autonomous systems. Indeed, Delmas-Marty's cloud metaphor is in many ways particularly apposite for the European Union, with its constantly shifting forms and ambitions. Delmas-Marty's land of 'ordered clouds' is hence intriguing, but it is ultimately perhaps vague and unsatisfying due to its extremely nebulous and ephemeral nature. Other theorists have looked to more settled, co-ordinated or systematic means of ordering complexity.

More familiarly, legal units have been organised by choice of law rules, jurisdictional rules or even 'constitutionalism'—both at EU level and also, more latterly, at international level.[118] If governed by a constitution, law may satisfy a perceived yearning for a complete system and not therefore subsist as an aggregate of incommensurable regimes. Constitutionalism is not in itself a form of legal pluralism. But in common with its half-sibling, constitutional pluralism, it seeks some sort of overarching arrangement whereby plural legal elements may be ordered. Those who argue for the growth of constitutionalism at international level maintain that it posits a web of laws, conventions and *jus cogens*, which supposedly provide a whole with no legal gaps.

---

[117] Walker, 'Beyond Boundary Disputes and Basic Grids' (above n 41).

[118] Eg, N Krisch, 'Global Administrative Law and the Constitutional Ambition', LSE Legal Studies Working Paper No 10/2009.

At EU level, constitutionalism appears able to straighten out the messy complexity of EU versus Member States by means of allocated competences and the express primacy of EU law.[119] Yet constitutionalism may still appear inadequate—at supra- or inter-national level, at least—to providing overarching ways of dealing with conflicts between special systems (such as the International Criminal Court or the International Criminal Tribunal for former Yugoslavia) and general international law, or between EU law and national law. There exists no *Grundnorm* of *Kompetenz-Kompetenz* at international level. An EU rule may derogate from the Law of the Sea, but it is not clear which rule or tribunal[120] is to govern. Nor has the EU developed in its relationships with its Member States in a way that provides possibilities for a clear division of competence. The tensions between the universal and particular are hard to resolve, and there is little indication as to who should have a final say. Sometimes there is comity—as between the Hamburg tribunal and the ECJ in the Irish *Mox Plant* case, or between the ECJ and the ECtHR in *Bosphorus*—but this is not always the case. Nor is there any international people, no *pouvoir constituent*, to have the final say. Further, at European level, organised constitutionalism has so far largely failed, resulting in the strong 'No' of the French and Dutch people in their national referenda on the draft European Constitution in 2005. Indeed, it might even be the *lack* of a clear hierarchy that appears to keep the system in motion (pre-empting the sort of constitutional crisis that occurs when attempted solutions such as the EU draft Constitution are imposed on an unwilling populace). Without firm hierarchy, it is left suspended but balanced, in a workable situation (rather like the Tinguely machine[121]), unsatisfactory though this might seem.

This is perhaps where the large residuum of the majority of those interested in pluralism are grouped—not allied to constitutionalism as such, nor to radical pluralism, seeking no firm hierarchy but rather some sort of balance. There exists a considerable variety of suggestions as to the form that this less than rigid ordering may take. We may start by looking at those that have been offered in the more limited geographical context of the European Union, rather than more generally applicable. In the EU context, Matthias Kumm, for example, has written of a 'cosmopolitan constitutionalism'—an adaptation of constitutionalism to pluralism, and

---

[119] See the EU draft Constitutional Treaty, Chapter I-6 and Chapter I-Title III. The Lisbon Treaty moves Article I-6 of the Constitution referring to the primacy of Community law to Declaration No 17 attached to Lisbon.

[120] Namely whether it should be the ECJ or UN Law of the Sea tribunal in Hamburg. See *Ireland v UK (Mox Plant)* provisional measures, reports of Judgments, Advisory Opinions and Orders 5 (2001), Part II, 51–54, in which the Hamburg tribunal eventually yielded jurisdiction in favour of the ECJ in an action brought by Ireland concerning operation of the Sellafield nuclear enrichment plant in England.

[121] See above ch 3, Figure 3-1, and below, Figure 4-4.

he looks to 'principles of common European constitutionalism' derived from the heritage of the European constitutional tradition, in turn drawn from the practises of the highest European courts, especially the German Constitutional Court. Miguel Poiares Maduro, former Advocate General at the ECJ, has highlighted the need for 'meta-teleological reasoning' as a way of managing conflict, which he terms 'contrapunctual law'.[122] Contrapunctual law could be interpreted as a sort of 'internal pluralism' of the European Union, acknowledging that courts have loyalties to both the EU and national levels but urging or (perhaps even requiring) them to strive for coherence and integrity in the overall legal order. Competing claims to sovereignty are moderated by contrapunctual legal principles.

The problem with both of these approaches, however, is that they strive for (or even assume) a coherence that may simply not be present. Within the geographical area of the 27 Member States of the European Union there exists a great diversity of legal principles. Even within the constitutional order of the European Union itself, there exists contradiction and incoherence. The 'constitutional' law of the European Union has not been created in a structured and determined way, under the auspices of a written constitution, as was, eg, the US federal Constitution or the German Basic Law. The European Union started out as an economic community, a free trade area, and principles more clearly constitutional in nature, such as primacy of EU law, human rights, subsidiarity, proportionality, democracy and so on, were later accrued in an *ad hoc* way, either through the case law of the ECJ or by treaty amendments at intergovernmental conferences, the impact or even justiciability of which was not always immediately evident. The economic imperative very often outweighed or directed other values. Therefore, EU law itself lacks the coherence[123] and principle that some scholarship attributes to it.[124]

If we add to primary EU law (ie, treaties and legislation) principles derived from Member State constitutional laws, the picture becomes even more complicated. Although there exists to a certain extent a common fund—with principles such as proportionality enjoying almost universal recognition, and human rights and general principles of law also playing an important part—constitutional traditions in the European Union are extremely varied, ranging from the historically evolved convention-driven British constitution to the more rational, structured German Basic Law. The different

---

[122] MP Maduro, 'Contrapunctual Law: Europe's Constitutional Pluralism in Action' in N Walker (ed), *Sovereignty in Transition* (Oxford, Hart Publishing, 2003).

[123] See, eg, A Williams, *The Ethos of Europe* (Cambridge, Cambridge University Press, 2010).

[124] Much of such scholarship is German in origin, eg, M Kumm, 'Constitutional Rights as Principles: On the Structure and Domain of Constitutional Justice' (2004) 2 *International Journal of Constitutional Law* 595; and A von Bogdandy and J Bast (eds), *Principles of European Constitutional Law*, 2nd edn (Oxford, Hart Publishing, 2009).

ideologies of these constitutions may often be very hard to reconcile. If we add to these varied resources Maduro's plea for European judges when working within the field of EU law to 'universalise' their decisions beyond their immediate jurisdiction, then it truly seems to require Ronald Dworkin's ideal judge Hercules to manage this.[125] Even disputes involving similar facts and areas of law can take on a very different character, depending on the Member State of litigation, and a particular remedy such as injunctive relief or declaration may not exist in every jurisdiction, making legal suits almost impossible to universalise in the way suggested by Maduro. While it is undoubtedly the case that it is the judiciary who are most often placed to determine boundary disputes between different legal orders (and a growing focus on transnational judicial reasoning and dialogue illustrates this fast growing trend)[126] and a search for common ground and co-operation in disputes is preferable to conflict, the notion of meta-principles as a means of defining relations is far more aspirational and prescriptive than immanent and descriptive. There is no 'dominant overall grid'.[127]

Weiler's suggested solution for the European Union is that of a *Sonderweg*, highlighting the distinctiveness and singular nature of the European Union and implying almost the absence of a meta-principle and offering instead a constitutional tolerance in which unity and distinctiveness are balanced against each other.[128] The least ambitious of suggestions for some sort of organising grid or structure is that of a conflict-of-laws approach, a 'bottom-up' conception with mechanisms for conflict emanating from subordinate orders rather than from above.[129] As such an approach already exists and has done for centuries, it at least has the merit of being tried and tested, but it is hardly revolutionary.

After this short survey of European law scholarship, one returns to the metaphor of the Tinguely machine (Figure 4-4). Suspended balance, rather than the *Carina Nebula* or a mathematical mosaic, may be the best we can achieve. Rather like Jean Tinguely's own creations, the current state of law within the European Union has an impermanent, provisional feel to it, with a certain balance and harmony but also bringing the fear that this is a fragile, not a robust state of affairs that is somewhat tentative in nature.

[125] In R Dworkin, *Law's Empire* (Cambridge, MA, Harvard University Press, 1986), Dworkin introduced the ideal judge, 'Hercules', as a judge of superhuman intellectual power and patience who accepts and applies law as integrity.

[126] Eg, A-M Slaughter, 'A Typology of Transjudicial Communication' (1994) 29 *University of Richmond Law Review* 99; and Douglas-Scott, 'A Tale of Two Courts' (above n 112) on the relations between the ECJ and the ECtHR.

[127] Walker, 'Beyond Boundary Disputes and Basic Grids' (above n 41).

[128] J Weiler, 'In Defence of the Status Quo: Europe's Constitutional Sonderweg' in J Weiler and M Wind (ed), *Constitutionalism beyond the State* (Cambridge, Cambridge University Press, 2003).

[129] Eg, R Michaels, 'Global Legal Pluralism' (2009) 5 *Annual Review of Law and the Social Sciences* 243–62.

Figure 4-4: Jean Tinguely, *Méta Harmonie IV: Fatamorgana* (1985), Tinguely Museum, Basel © ADAGP, Paris; and DACS, London 2012

Flexible, Imaginative Reworkings

Although EU law currently drives much of the contemporary scholarship on legal pluralism, it cannot be allowed to occupy the field, and we will complete this section by comparing two different arrangements of legal pluralism, both from outside the tradition of European law. One such example of ordering may be found in the work of Masaji Chiba, who is critical of the alleged monism and ethnocentrism of Western jurisprudence, which he takes to be based on Hellenistic and Christian values and believes to have a history of colonisation or influence on other systems, particularly those of African and Asian countries.[130] Chiba has identified various levels of law, which he believes cannot be unified. He instead prefers to evoke legal pluralism as '6 concepts in 3 dichotomies', namely:

1. state/official versus unofficial but valid law;
2. indigenous versus transplanted law (ie, received from other cultures); and
3. clearly formulated legal rules versus legal postulates or ideologies that base or revise rules.

---

[130] M Chiba, 'Legal Pluralism in the Contemporary World' (1998) 11 *Ratio Juris* 228, 241.

Chiba has suggested that these three 'dichotomies' may be arranged in various combinations. In this way, he believes it possible to give a more meaningful account of the richness of law (or as he calls it, '*the 3 dichotomies of law under the identity postulate of a legal culture*').[131] Indeed, Chiba has maintained that his conceptualisations have been verified and shown their utility by his successful applications of them in Japan and Sri Lanka.[132] Chiba has acknowledged of his account that, 'as the first attempt of its kind, it may leave much room for improvement'.[133] However, his methodology provides some structure and order to an analysis of law without being too rigidly schematic.

Another writer who attempts to express the richness of law but in a less than formulaic way is de Sousa Santos, who uses the metaphor of mapping[134] (as of course did John Austin,[135] with his 'province of Jurisprudence' and his desire to provide a 'map' of the law). However, unlike Austin, de Sousa Santos' map is not one-dimensional but designed to take account of the fact that law is not a single entity but operates in different forms and on different levels and scales that interrelate in complex ways. Law is not, according to de Sousa Santos, a clearly articulated system—an approach that may be contrasted to other perceptions of 'modern' legal theory, for example Fuller's revealingly chosen title, *An Anatomy of the Law*,[136] which at the very least implies an organic wholeness. De Sousa Santos has distanced himself from what he terms the 'theoretical gulag' by looking to the ways in which law, like any map, misreads or distorts reality: our images of law create only 'credible illusions of correspondence'. De Sousa Santos' subtitle, 'A Map

---

[131] M Chiba, 'Three Dichotomies of Law in Pluralism: An Analytical Scheme of Legal Culture' (1987) *Tokai Law Review* 1.

[132] See, eg, M Chiba, 'Legal Pluralism in Sri Lankan Society: Toward a General Theory of Non-Western Law' (1993) 33 *Journal of Legal Pluralism* 197–212.

[133] In fact, it is doubtful whether Chiba's is the first such attempt: see the references at n 31 above.

[134] De Sousa Santos sees 'spatial metaphors' as emblematic of postmodernism. B de Sousa Santos, *Towards a New Legal Common Sense*, 1st edn (London, Butterworths, 1996) 400. See also B Janz, 'Philosophy as if Place Mattered: The Situation of African Philosophy' in H Carel and D Gamez (eds), *What Philosophy Is* (London, Continuum, 2004).

[135] B de Sousa Santos, 'Law: A Map of Misreading—Toward a Postmodern Conception of Law' (1987) 14 *Journal of Law and Society* 279 (reprinted in *Towards a New Legal Common Sense* (above nn 9 and 134)). De Sousa Santos and Austin have not been the only theorists to use the metaphor of mapping. Twining (who ultimately prefers 'mental maps' of the law to actual cartography) and John Henry Wigmore have also done so. See W Twining, 'Mapping Law' in W Twining, *Globalisation and Legal Theory* (London, Butterworths, 2000); and JH Wigmore, *Panorama of the World's Legal System* (St Paul, West Publishing Company, 1928). Gottfried Leibniz also talked of a '*theatrum legale mundi*', and Italo Calvino drew abstract maps of idealised geographical itineraries. See G Leibniz, *Nova Methodus Discendae Docendaeque Jurisprudentiae (New Method for the Learning and Teaching of Jurisprudence)*, original edition 1667, reprint in L Dutens (ed), *Leibniz Opera Omnia* (Geneva, Fratres de Tournes, Tomus Quartus, III, Jurisprudentiam, 1768) A.6.1, 293–345; and I Calvino, *Invisible Cities*, W Weaver (trans) (New York, Harcourt, 1978). Mapping is becoming more and more popular.

[136] L Fuller, *Anatomy of the Law* (Harmondsworth, Penguin, 1968).

of Misreading', is taken from the literary critic Harold Bloom's theory that a misreading occurs whenever a text is read, because the reader is involved in attributing meaning and thus attributes his/her interpretation according to context.[137] So de Sousa Santos' focus is not on cartography as clarity but rather on the deceptive functions of mapping. According to de Sousa Santos, law's misreadings, like those of cartography, take various forms.

The first form it takes is that of *scale*. In other words, a large-scale legal map would involve a particular local legal practice (eg, a bylaw), whereas a small-scale legal map would be focused on international or global law. In either case, only part of the picture of a particular legal terrain is given. Information is necessarily omitted, just as with any small-scale geographical map, which omits all local detail.

Secondly, like maps, laws tend to use distorting *projections*. Some projections, such as that of 'legal modernity', place Western law at the centre (just as Mercator's map placed Europe at the centre of the world, exaggerating its size). Not only modern maps distort. The medieval 'Mappa Mundi' (Figure 4-5) placed Jerusalem at its centre, east at the top, and countries were misshapen and forced into the map's circular form. The map represented what was important to its creators (ie, Christianity) and ignored what was not.

Thirdly, according to de Sousa Santos, the *symbolic* plays its part in representations of law and maps. He illustrates this by comparing the symbols on an ordnance survey map to those of the Mappa Mundi. Those of the Mappa Mundi are pictorial rather than schematic; but an ordnance survey map is far more abstract in character—a geometric grid with lines of latitude and longitude whereby (in principle at least) all places are knowable

Figure 4-5: Medieval *mappa mundi*

[137] H Bloom, *A Map of Misreading* (New York, Oxford University Press, 1975).

a priori, if we follow the formula and symbols of those who constructed the grid. Similarly, law may be formalistic (which de Sousa Santos has designated 'Homeric', a term borrowed from Erich Auerbach in his classical account of the different forms of representation of reality in Western literature[138]) and schematic (as in the case of pleadings, in which an error in drafting may result in serious harm to the litigant); or law may be more flexible or emotive in nature (what de Sousa Santos terms 'biblical'—ie, inscribed 'through iconic, emotive and expressive signs'[139]), seeking to deliver justice, as in Lord Denning's 'deserted wives' equity'[140]. The 'Homeric' and the 'biblical' are perpetually in tension.

The point of this 'map of misreading' for de Sousa Santos is that we cannot think of law from just one standpoint or internal point of view. Rather there *is* no right way of presenting it overall: law is porous and overflowing, and different aspects or inter-legalities may be seen from different angles. Unity and fragmentation are matters of narrative perspective. What from one angle appears a terribly distorted and chaotic image of something may from another appear just as 'a finely nuanced and sophisticated reflection of deeper unity'.[141] This may be a positive feature, empowering individuals who are no longer compelled to see law as solely repressive or bureaucratic. Under legal polystemy, not only are multiple points of view valuable and worthy of study, but subjective or internal perspectives may be actively adopted, with individuals as active agents for the choice of alternative rules, thus engaging in a productive, creative vision of the law. This could mean that ultimately what law means is a question for each of us to resolve.[142] In this way, pluralism could be able to accommodate the different and competing choices, affiliations and loyalties that for many people are a feature of contemporary life. De Sousa Santos uses the expression 'living on the frontier' to capture the sense in which we never belong fully to one space or another.

However, such a conclusion also provokes the question of how power may be critical in determining who decides which laws are to apply. The

---

[138] E Auerbach, *Mimesis: The Representation of Reality in Western Literature* (Princeton, Princeton University Press, 1968) 23. According to de Sousa Santos, law tends to the Homeric, 'where the legal symbolisation of reality has the following characteristics: the conversion of the everyday continuous flux of reality into a succession of disparate solemn moments (contracts, legal disputes, etc) described in abstract and formal terms through conventional cognitive and referential signs.' De Sousa Santos, 'Law: A Map of Misreading' (above n 135) 295.

[139] De Sousa Santos, 'Law: A Map of Misreading' (above n 135).

[140] See, eg, Lord Denning's holding in *H v H* (1947) 63 TLR 645, one of his rulings to establish a common law right in a deserted wife to remain in the matrimonial home.

[141] M Koskenniemi, 'Global Legal Pluralism: Multiple Regimes and Multiple Modes of Thought', paper delivered at Harvard University (5 March 2005).

[142] See P Fitzpatrick, 'The Desperate Vacuum' in P Fitzpatrick (ed), *Dangerous Supplements: Resistance and Renewal in Jurisprudence* (London, Routledge, 1991).

choice may not always lie with the individual. For example, in *Refah Partisi*[143] the Turkish Welfare Party challenged their ban in Turkey (for advocating the introduction of sharia (ie, Islamic law) and for challenging the non-amendable provisions of the Turkish Constitution, which were designed to keep Turkey forever as a secular, liberal democracy). Refah Partisi claimed that 'the citizen must be able to choose for themselves which legal system is most appropriate'.[144] This plea was firmly rejected by the European Court of Human Rights as an infringement of both the neutral role of the state as a guarantor of rights and freedoms and of the principle of non-discrimination, and indeed to the very values of the European Convention itself.

The European Court has itself clearly stressed that pluralism may contribute to the proper functioning of society,[145] most particularly when individuals participate in many different kinds of groups and associations. However, in *Refah Partisi*, the Court showed itself to be less confident of a pluralism that results in a compartmentalising of society, where members of different groups have little contact with each other and there are separate communities, and it therefore rejected a notion of legal pluralism of different legal orders for different groups—or put otherwise, they rejected a radical pluralism.

Lack of Legitimacy and Potential for Abuse

Unlike some contemporary theorists, I do not believe that pluralism, plurality, interlegality and the like are necessarily normatively superior (as opposed to more descriptively accurate) to those monist or dualist accounts that cleave to notions of a more unified legal space, although clearly some legal pluralists do believe this. For example, Davies' reference to an 'ethos' of legal pluralism implies that 'pluralism is more about practical ethical positioning in the world than scholarly theory'.[146] On the contrary, it is important to be aware that legal pluralism brings with it increased risks of a lack of accountability, of self-regulating institutions or localised laws being

---

[143] *Refah Partisi v Turkey*, Grand Chamber (2003) 37 EHRR 70.

[144] 'There must be several legal systems. The citizens must be able to choose for himself which legal system is most appropriate for him, within a framework of general principles ... Why then, should I be obliged to live according to another's rules? ... The right to choose one's own legal system is an integral part of the freedom of religion.' *Refah* (ibid) paras 28–29.

[145] Eg, in *Handyside v UK*, ECtHR, 7 Dec 1976, the Court held that freedom of expression was also applicable to ideas that 'offend, shock or disturb the State or any sector of the population. Such are the demands of that pluralism, tolerance and broadmindedness without which there is no "democratic society".'

[146] Davies (above n 20) 6.

captured by special interests and of 'a fragmented and impotent polity in which the public interest is emptied of meaning'.[147] Indeed, fragmentation and instability can benefit the powerful, who can, for example, engage in the practice of 'forum shopping' to find those laws that best suit their needs. Accountability may be very weak in a pluralistic landscape, and institutional design and effective tutelage become ever more important. Further, in the face of a pluralism of competing laws, how are conflicts to be settled, and by which standards? How to identify those 'like' cases which are to be treated alike? How to treat persons with equal concern and respect if there is no uniform system? Ultimately, how is legal legitimacy possible?

Traditional legal pluralism has not paid a great deal of attention to these questions. One way to approach these issues would be to insist on a separation of the empirical description from the justification and evaluation of law—a distinction that would satisfy traditional positivism.[148] The social fact of multiple legal orders says nothing as to their moral worthiness or capacity for justice, which for a positivist would fall to be determined by extra-legal standards. This approach might, however, be unavailable to those who assert that law necessarily has some sort of normative dimension. Some members of this latter category might even fall within the legal pluralist camp. Fuller, whose inclusion of wider social practices within the concept of 'law' we noted earlier, insisted that the enterprise of law embodies certain moral principles—what he termed the 'internal morality of law', which has more broadly been explained as the 'rule of law', or a set of formal principles, such as treating like cases alike, and ensuring that laws are sufficiently prospective, clear and predictable—a way of keeping law 'in good shape'.[149] This 'internal morality' of the rule of law impacts on human dignity, enabling individuals to plan their conduct and enabling a reciprocity between government and citizen in the working out of the law. Legal pluralism does not seem to encourage such an internal morality of law. By its very definition, pluralism acknowledges the possibility of contradictory laws, of different legal orders imposing competing demands

---

[147] P Nonet and P Selznick, *Law in Society: Toward Responsive Law* (New York, Harper Colophon, 1979) 103; TJ Lowi, *The End of Liberalism: The Second Republic of the United States*, 2nd revised edn (New York, Norton, 1979); and C Scott, 'Analysing Regulatory Space: Fragmented Resources and Institutional Design' (2001) *Public Law* 329–53, for the view that institutional design is increasingly important. Note, however, that Miguel Maduro makes the strong argument that transnational organisations benefit democracy, by taking account of interests (ie, those of migrants) that are often ignored by the domestic political process. M Maduro, 'Europe and the Constitution: What if This Is as Good as It Gets?' in J Weiler and M Wind (eds) (above n 128) 74–102.

[148] Twining, 'Normative and Legal Pluralism' (above n 42).

[149] J Waldron, 'Legal Pluralism and the Contrast between Hart's Jurisprudence and Fuller's' in P Cane (ed), *The Hart–Fuller Debate in the Twenty-First Century* (Oxford, Hart Publishing, 2010).

on citizens—a legal space that is not 'in good shape'.[150] This conclusion works against pluralism as a normative theory or as an 'ethical positioning', in the sense that pluralism appears to run the risk of opening up too many opportunities for abuse of power and law, of undermining the rule of law, of glorying in the beauty and wonder of a *Carina Nebula* without sufficiently acknowledging its black holes.

Positive Crossings, Engagements and Perspectives: Turbulent Beauty?

The law of the excluded middle, a key element of modern logic, dictates that an entity is either *A* or *not-A*. It cannot be both. However, postmodernism asserts the inadequacy of the binary 'either/or' of the modern world. In Auster's work there is usually no rosy conclusion. *City of Glass* shows the unsatisfactory nature of the traditional positivist 'either/or' expectations but offers no alternative liberating possibilities, nor individual empowerment. One can only, as Auster concludes, 'grope ahead, faltering in darkness'.[151] Auster's readers are often left perplexed or depressed at the end of his work. Likewise, for many interpreters, the jurisprudence that we can extract from Franz Kafka's novels is one of despair and offers no prospect of a coherent future.[152] The innocent are endlessly punished. Bureaucracy destroys us in arbitrary meaningless ways. Yet for all Kafka's negative undercurrents, his legal and social criticism was not only nihilistic in output. Kafka worked in a legal capacity assisting in workers' compensation schemes, and we have evidence that he went to work every day with the hope of improving life for injured workers.[153] So he believed positive outcomes to be possible.

Pynchon's work often seems a little more hopeful. Towards the close of *The Crying of Lot 49*, Oedipa believes herself near to the truth of the elusive Tristero organisation, proclaiming, 'Either you have stumbled indeed ... onto a network ... maybe even onto a real alternative to the exitlessness, to the absence of surprise in life ... or you are hallucinating it ...'[154] There might be hope for Oedipa amid the chaos. She may be able to resolve the mystery of the Tristero, thus showing her usefulness as a defence against

[150] Ibid. Also, Eleftheriadis for this reason rejects pluralism, as he believes that it cannot provide for integrity, which requires that 'government speak with one voice ... act in a principled manner to all ... same substantive standards of justice and fairness'. P Eleftheriadis, 'Pluralism and Integrity' (2010) *Ratio Juris* 365. He therefore advocates a return to dualism.

[151] P Auster, *The Locked Room* (the final episode of *The New York Trilogy*) (London, Faber and Faber, 1987) 370.

[152] F de Coste, 'Kafka: Legal Theorising and Redemption' (1994) 27 *Mosaic* 161.

[153] D Litowitz, 'Franz Kafka's Outsider Jurisprudence' (2002) 27 *Law and Social Inquiry* 103.

[154] Pynchon (above n 1) 170–71.

the chaotic, thermodynamic pull toward heat and death. On the other hand, the 'clues' she finds may be random events or even the product of her own imagination. Either she is paranoid, or a real sinister Tristero exists. Neither is an attractive option. Along with her ancient Greek namesake, Pynchon's Oedipa is striving to answer a riddle that stands between peace and the plague of disorder affecting her society. Pynchon makes clear in his work that the struggle for unity, order and holism is impossible from the beginning. However, excluded middles may lie behind the limiting 'either/ ors' that Oedipa intones.[155] This leaves room for possibilities behind the binary poles of certainty and chaos, and anticipates the conceptualisation of fuzzy logic—not the constricting 'either/or' but 'both/and'. The novel ends with the repetition of its title, with an auctioneer crying the enigmatic Lot 49 and perhaps about to reveal the 'truth'—but we are never to know, as the book stops at this point.

Legal monism or centralism no longer appears a plausible thesis, nor yet has it been replaced by a radical legal pluralism. Rather, the current experience of law appears as a rapid proliferation of layers and types of law, with all manner of structured attempts to tame and manage it. My preferred interpretation makes room for context, allowing that law may be uniform and contained if experienced from a particular internal point of view, but pluralist if looked at from another perspective. In this way, the most undesirable consequences of pluralism—of law that is not in 'good shape' and pulls the individual in numerous conflicting directions—may be avoided.

As Adolf Merkel long ago pointed out, 'Many legal terms have a blurry quality. Their areas of application are not delineated by insurmountable fences, but rather they spill over into neighbouring areas.'[156] An illustration is provided by Hart's famous hypothetical ordinance proclaiming 'No vehicles in the Park', which Hart used to illustrate that legal concepts have a 'penumbra' as well as a 'core'.[157] But what is to count as a vehicle? We can identify a skateboard as a vehicle to a certain degree, but it is also an 'aid to pedestrians'. Fuller provides the example of a war monument taking the form of a statue of a tank and soldiers put up by patriots in the park: whether this is a vehicle depends completely on context. Hart's example illustrates that the law of contradiction does not apply completely in the legal field. Not only do legal terms have a 'penumbra of uncertainty', acknowledged by Hart, but their meaning may also be determined by context, as asserted by Fuller. Another example is offered by the status of

---

[155] Ibid. See also G Rose, *The Broken Middle* (Oxford, Blackwell, 1992).

[156] Cited in M Grunhut, *Begriffsbildung und Rechtsanwendung in Strafrecht* (Tubingen, Mohr, 1926).

[157] See HLA Hart, *Positivism and the Separation of Law and Morals* (1958) 71 *Harvard Law Review* 593.

foreign law in municipal legal systems. Foreign law may have 'persuasive' authority and thereby move beyond the binary binding/nonbinding. In other words, rather than black and white, cut and dried, there are shades of grey in the legal landscape. There is little by way of straightforward either/or.[158]

Indeed, why should logical principles apply so rigidly to legal reasoning? One reason is that the rule of law appears to depend on logic, and as Fuller stressed, the rule of law seems essential if law is to have any aspiration to guide conduct. Yet sometimes it is possible to have inconsistent rules without forcing citizens to act unlawfully, and this may in fact reflect realities of political compromise. While the rule of law remains important and failure to respect it will often render law meaningless, the rule of law does not lose its meaning if language is sometimes indeterminate, nor if law is sometimes illogical, nor if there is no 'right answer'.[159]

There are also other reasons to accept a legal world in which there exist no clear, certain outcomes. For example, there may be tacit political agreement not to disagree so as not to promote a constitutional crisis (as in case of the German Constitutional Court and the Maastricht Treaty),[160] so long as citizens are not placed in an impossible situation requiring inconsistent action. The proliferation of human rights remedies in contemporary Europe may be a force for good rather than a neurotic, needlessly overlapping and complex state of affairs, provided that individuals can get their remedy. For example, in the case of *Poirrez*, the litigant, after failing in the French courts and at the ECJ, finally succeeded on their third human rights action, in the European Court of Human Rights.[161] Yet it must be acknowledged that for every *Poirrez* there may be a *Bosphorus*, which was a prolonged and unsuccessful 'détriplement' of litigation, with the lawyers waiting with bated breath to see how much judicial concord actually exists.

As already mentioned, Weber's claim was that the modern era suffers from disenchantment—the loss of the magic, the mystical and the substantive, which were replaced by rational calculation and formal procedure. This suggests that we have lost the ability to think beyond the present system and to create another more enlivening or engaging one. This was a bleak vision, and of course Weber wrote elsewhere of the 'iron cage' imprisoning humans in modernity.[162] Yet there can be

---

[158] L Fuller, 'Positivism and Fidelity to Law: A Reply to Professor Hart' (1958) 71 *Harvard Law Review* 630.

[159] These issues are pursued below in subsequent chapters.

[160] A situation likened by Joseph Weiler to containment during the Cold War by MAD (mutual assured destruction). See Weiler, *The Constitution of Europe* (above n 56).

[161] *Koua Poirrez v France* (Judgment of 30 September 2003), No 40892/98, ECtHR.

[162] M Weber, *The Protestant Ethic and the Spirit of Capitalism*, T Parsons (trans) (New York, Scribner, 1930).

little hope if we have replaced Weber's bleak, mechanical legal world with one of entropy, confusion and chaos. William James wrote that 'As compared with all these rationalist pictures the pluralistic empiricism which I profess offers but a sorry appearance. It is a turbid muddled gothic sort of affair, without a sweeping outline and with little pictorial nobility.'[163] Turbulence and chaos are not always beautiful; they can be the product of oppression. Not all instability is desirable. Hobbes wrote of the insecurity and 'Babel of incomprehension' in the state of nature, which prompted his notion of Leviathan, a situation unfortunately realised today in collapsed states.

However, the complex world of legal crossings and multiplicity that I have tried to describe might—in addition to producing complexity, confusion or even entropy—be capable of fostering enchantment or the beauty of turbulence. One commentator has described the aesthetic power of chaos, writing, 'Modernism seems to have missed the beauty of pluralism … [C]haos it turns out is beautiful and colourful; in architecture, art, and human life, we value the non-linear and the fractal, and on the contrary we find linearity deeply alienating.'[164] These elements of unpredictability 'require us to abandon the relentless and arrogant system building of modernity … and direct our attention instead to the poetry and power of the local and particular. In this sense, the new science is ultimately empowering.'[165] Fredric Jameson is also open to the enchanting elements of even so derogatory a concept as 'junkspace', writing of 'matter ceaselessly mutating all round us, with moments of breath-taking beauty', 'railway stations unfold like iron butterflies'.[166] If we take another look at the image of urban sprawl junkspace in Figure 4-1, we may be able to see its beauty—its huge swerving expanse and strange symmetries. Indeed, science may even view chaos as a source of order. Ilya Prigogine and Isabelle Stengers, the originators of chaos theory, authored a work entitled *Order out of Chaos*.[167] Chaos is even treated as normal science by scientists who employ all the usual scientific procedures to study and record it.

Jane Bennett has written in a more general context, 'The dynamism of crossings could revive wonder at life, their morphings inform our reflections on freedom … [T]heir flexibility stretches your moral sense of the

---

[163] W James, *A Pluralistic Universe* (New York, Longmans, Green and Company, 1909).

[164] D Manderson, 'Beyond the Provincial: Space, Aesthetics and Modernist Legal Theory' (1996) 20 *Melbourne University Law Review* 1048.

[165] Ibid.

[166] Jameson (above n 12).

[167] I Prigogine and I Stengers, *Order out of Chaos: Man's New Dialogue with Nature* (London, Fontana, 1984). See also NK Hayles, *Chaos Bound: Orderly Disorder in Contemporary Literature and Science* (Ithaca, Cornell University Press, 1990).

possible.'[168] Crossings can show the world to be capable of inspiring order and 'might just help to induce the kind of magnanimous mood that seems to be crucial to the ethical demands of a sociality that is increasingly multicultural, multispecied and multitechnical'.[169] Bennett's examples are exotic and not taken from the legal world; she writes of Kafka's Rotpeter the 'ape-man' and of Gilles Deleuze's and Pierre-Félix Guattari's 'body without organs'. This body without organs (BwO) consists of an assemblage or body with no underlying organisational principles and therefore no organs within it, a 'post-Enlightenment entity'. As Deleuze and Guattari wrote:

> People ask, So what is this BwO? But you're already on it, scurrying like a vermin, groping like a blind person, or running like a lunatic; desert traveller and nomad of the steppes. On it we sleep, live our waking lives, fight—fight and are fought—seek our place, experience untold happiness and fabulous defeats.[170]

Bennett has also discussed the marvels of nature, such as the satyrion root, which was, according to Paracelsus, formed 'like the male privy parts'.[171] Yet the legal world too has its exotic hybrids. There exist special panels such as those established by the UN: a special court in East Timor that was empowered to apply both the law of East Timor and international treaties; the special court of Sierra Leone, which was also hybrid; and the Iraqi special tribunals for crimes against humanity. In these courts we find the intersection of national and international—which can also counterbalance fragmentation and accommodate difference at national level by including the local and international.

De Sousa Santos is perhaps the legal theorist who has argued most vigorously for an emancipatory potential in the complex world of pluralism. De Sousa Santos' project is utopian:[172] he aspires to realise the imaginative potential in this legal and social complexity and thereby to advance in particular the perspective of oppressed groups and to invoke a 're-enchanted common sense'. 'Common sense' for de Sousa Santos is a form of knowledge that individuals and communities create and use to give meanings to their practices. It is not monolithic, so there are different forms of common sense for different *loci*. For de Sousa Santos, the 'narrow and reductionist' modernist legal canon 'arrogantly discredits, silences or negates the legal

---

[168] J Bennett, *The Enchantment of Modern Life* (Princeton, Princeton University Press, 2001) 32.

[169] Ibid.

[170] G Deleuze and F Guattari, *Anti-Oedipus: Capitalism and Schizophrenia*, R Hurly, M Seem and HR Lane (trans) (Minneapolis, University of Minnesota Press, 1983) 150.

[171] Bennett (above n 168) 35; and Paracelsus, *Selected Writings*, J Jacobi (ed) (Princeton, Princeton University Press, 1979) 133.

[172] Similarly utopian is Roberto Unger's earlier work, eg, R Unger, 'False Necessity: Anti-necessity Social Theory in the Service of Radical Democracy' in R Unger, *II POLITICS: A Work of Constructive Social Theory* (London, Verso, 1987) 531.

experiences of large bodies of the population'.[173] For him, the wealth of the legal landscape makes possible a sociology of emergences. De Sousa Santos' vision is a positive place with which to conclude this section—legal pluralism at its most optimistic.

Visualising Law Today

Law students are sometimes presented with pyramidical drawings to aid to their understanding of Kelsonian jurisprudence. The Grundnorm is placed at the apex, with the rest of Kelsen's 'dynamic system of norms' extending throughout the base. However, if we use diagrams to represent our contemporary legal world of complexity and multidimensionality, then I suggest we should replace Kelsonian pyramids with scientific 'visualisations'. A visualisation is an image used to structure and communicate information—a type of 'cognitive art'.[174] 'Visualisation' sounds a dull term, yet visualisations can be anything but dull—they are certainly capable of fostering enchantment. They can turn into images train timetables, maps, musical scores, structures of social relations, rhythms of the heart, landscapes of numbers—so why not law? Visualisations were first used in the sciences with the 'Lorenz Attractor' (Figure 4-6).

Figure 4-6: Example of a graph of a Lorenz Attractor plotted from the mathematical model for atmospheric convection first developed by Edward Lorenz in 1963

[173] De Sousa Santos, *Towards a New Legal Common Sense*, 2nd edn (above n 9) 494.
[174] See, eg, E Tufte, *Visual Explanations* (Cheshire, CT, Graphics Press, 1997).

In the 1960s, Edward Lorenz worked with long-term meteorological data, seeking patterns in it. He used a 3-D co-ordinate system, reduced meteorological data to three variables and plotted them. He discovered striking and previously unnoticed patterns in the data, which he named an 'attractor'—ie, points that coalesce around a particular area in a butterfly-like shape.

Visualisations offer methods for seeing the unseen and thus provoke unexpected insights. They can be used to organise complex systems that may seem random and chaotic but, when plotted, produce coherent if unpredictable patterns. They may be applied to art and literature, revealing deep structures, symmetries, asymmetries, order and complexities. Social scientists have also used visualisations. For example, Lothar Krempel's visualisations for social science networks (Figure 4-7) would not be inappropriate for plotting highly complex organisations such as the European Union.

In the same way that looking at Cubist art leads one to reassess our conceptions about pictorial space, so too visualisations confront us with richly varied abstract spaces. They are dense with information and allow us to see elements we would not have notice if they were not so spatially organised. They make it possible to track movements, to make new connections and to spot new relationships in phenomena. Visualisations of our multidimensional legal world could provide illustrations of the breathtaking beauty and literally new visions of the legal space, as well as shedding new light on law's polymorphy. (They would, however, be rather difficult to produce freehand on a classroom whiteboard.)

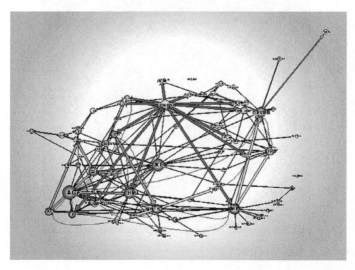

Figure 4-7: Lothar Krempel, network visualisation, http://www.mpi-fg-koeln.mpg. de/~lk/netvis/access.html (accessed 4 January 2013)

Conclusion

However, my conclusion, unlike that of de Sousa Santos, is not completely positive and emancipatory. Friedrich Nietzsche[175] re-described Greek culture as existing within a creative tension between Dionysian and Apollonian forces—the former nihilistic and dangerous, full of emotional abandon and forces in motion, the other an illusion that enabled the ancient Greeks to live on a daily basis. The legal world likewise seems to be caught in a taut balancing act between these two forces—between potentially chaotic, overly exuberant multiplicity and the fiction of autonomy, of an orderly landscape. If law is as I have described it, then much of the time it will simply appear (to many people at least) so confusing as to be alienating and Kafkaesque, bringing with it risks of constitutional crises and competing loyalties. It may be impossible to draw sufficient connections to make sense. The breath-taking beauty of legal crossings and hybrids may be inadequate compensation, except for a few privileged legal aesthetes. But a focus on and awareness of plurality, of local or singular acts, will empower some and provide opportunities where none existed before.

However, if it is to have this positive, empowering effect, then there must be supportive institutional conditions. Greater legal energies need to be spent in designing and considering institutional arrangements. There will have to be 'new modes of supervision, new organisational units, new structures of authority, new incentives'.[176] Above all, what will be important is a focus on good institutional design, ways of providing accountability, legitimacy and, most importantly, justice—where there are no straightforward channels. I turn to this in subsequent chapters.

---

[175] F Nietzsche, *The Birth of Tragedy* (Cambridge, Cambridge University Press, 1999).
[176] Nonet and Selznick (above n 147).

5

The Injustice of Law
after Modernity

Injustice, Insecurity and Flexible, Private Justice

It is now time to enquire more closely into the ways in which complexity, fragmentation, pluralism of laws and globalisation can perpetuate injustice. The last chapters have presented law as a complex, pluralist phenomenon not readily capable of systematisation, in contrast to an earlier paradigm of a more formal, autonomous, systematic law. Yet is this a transformation that should be welcomed? In chapter four it was argued that legal pluralism provides a realistic and persuasive analysis of law but may be less satisfactory from a normative perspective. In this chapter, I proceed to argue that in the contemporary landscape, where 'formal' law may sometimes be thin on the ground, the most crucial and often unanswered questions are of justice and accountability. In particular, many situations exist in which there is either a weak or, indeed, no functioning rule of law. This is visible in the growth of informal, flexible, private or non-state 'governance' organisations and networks. This undermines accountability and the possibility of justice. Justice is further compromised in the global arena where there exists either little or no trace of formerly familiar mechanisms of state accountability. Too little attention has been paid to this.

It is worth highlighting that what is also particularly interesting—or perhaps we should say dismaying—about these 'little or no rule of law' situations is that they are in part implicated by a politics of fear and security, which gives rise to a growing spiral of further injustices and destruction of human rights—a point that will be elucidated later in this chapter.

The concept of justice will be discussed later in this book, along with, in particular, the role that human rights and a critical application of the rule of law, fuelled by a politics of resistance, may play in its realisation. The task of this chapter will be to highlight in greater detail the ways in which contemporary law is highly problematic and may cause injustice—in other words, to look at law's shadowy underside.

As Costas Douzinas and Ronnie Warrington have written, '[L]aw is expanding, but at the price of assuming characteristics of contemporary society, thus becoming open, decentred, fragmented, nebulous and multiform.'[1] Significant but somewhat intangible challenges are posed to justice and the rule of law by the character and development of contemporary law and regulation. These developments include: the increasing privatisation, fragmentation and technicisation of state functions; the expansion of law-creation beyond the state; a growing flexibility of law; a growing informality and shift from hard to soft law, which blurs categories of norms; and a shift towards heterarchical global governance.[2]

> So, are Gunther Teubner and the idea of reflexive law to blame for the current financial crisis that many associate with the exorbitant degree of liberalisation and deregulation? Are post Welfare State approaches to a more responsive, adaptive and learning form of law responsible for the triumph of the market and the situation we find ourselves in now?[3]

This question, recently posed, in the aftermath of the 2008 financial crisis, likely in jest, raises the issue of the particular perceived injustice of a certain type of contemporary lawmaking and its possible disastrous consequences. All too often, the rather nebulous, plural character of much contemporary law has been assessed with a certain breathless enthusiasm, as if only benefits could spring from its complex nature. Yet on the contrary, privatisation, technicisation and greater flexibility may threaten human well-being, by removing state benefits or failing sufficiently to regulate certain measures. In the aftermath of the banking crisis, light-touch or reflexive regulation seems less attractive.

In a situation of global legal pluralism in which 'laws' emanate from a variety of sources and are created in a multiformity of ways, there are no clear answers to troublesome questions of legal validity and authority. When law is no longer created only by recognised state institutions and fragmentation of legal sources exists, many laws operate independently from familiar structures of political accountability. Legal pluralism leaves rights and duties less clearly articulated and can lead to conflicts of loyalty, especially in the case of the radical pluralism discussed in the last chapter. Law becomes amenable to manipulation by the powerful. This promotes the privatisation of justice and dereliction of rule-of-law values.

It is time to look at these phenomena in greater detail, which involves an excursion into existing legal practices. Much of this discussion will concern transnational law, which should, however, be distinguished from the 'cosmopolitan' norms that characterise some international law in the field

---

[1] C Douzinas and R Warrington, *Justice Miscarried: Ethics, Aesthetics and the Law* (London, Harvester Wheatsheaf, 1994) 3.

[2] These phenomena have been discussed in previous chapters.

[3] P Zumbansen, 'Post Regulatory Law: Chronicle of a Career Foretold', Faculty Seminar, McGill University Faculty of Law (18 February 2009).

of human rights, environmental or humanitarian law.[4] The latter tend to have a public interest element, with humanitarian concerns or public good at their centre.

Globalisation and International Commerce

These tendencies toward fragmentation, technicisation, and flexibility and informality in law, as well as the expansion of law-creation beyond the state, have been particularly notable in the international commercial sector. Since the end of the Cold War, there has been an ascendancy of transnational market forces, along with a globalisation of the liberal ethos. The largest multinational enterprises (MNEs) have budgets, outputs and turnovers exceeding those of many of the world's sovereign states, and they exercise economic power superior to small or even medium-size states. In this environment, corporations become, as Ulrich Beck has described them, 'private sector quasi states'.[5] Within states themselves, sovereignty has been divided and transformed, leading to the growth of new centres of power (eg, independent central banks, media conglomerations, financial markets) that rival state power. For example, in the field of banking regulation, private law-making and enforcement has been carried out[6] by national and international organisations, such as those that prescribe technical standards for credit cards. In other areas, functions have been delegated to national bodies such as the Bar or Stock Exchange. Many individuals serve on influential boards and are active in private acts of standard-setting. This saves money and time for governments as well as providing requisite expertise. Yet such arrangements have rarely included adequate representation from consumers or small businesses and tend to be industry-dominated, with the largest firms disproportionately influenced—illustrating a 'regulatory capture' by these concerns.[7]

The growth of deregulation in the banking sector led to the repeal (after heavy lobbying by the banking and insurance industries) in 1999 in the United States of the Glass-Steagall Act 1933, which had mandated the strict separation of speculative investment banking from ordinary deposit banking. After the repeal, banks were no longer troubled by rules restricting how and where they could invest their funds. Along with this came

---

[4] Cosmopolitan law is discussed below ch 10.
[5] U Beck, *Power in the Global Age* (Cambridge, Polity Press, 2005) 75.
[6] Or not carried out, as the global financial crisis revealed!
[7] See, eg, TA Canova, 'Financial Market Failure as a Crisis in the Rule of Law: From Market Fundamentalism to a New Keynesian Regulatory Model' (2009) *Harvard Law & Policy Review* 369.

an increasing complexity in the nature of financial instruments and the laws concerning them. How to explain complex financial products such as credit default swaps or the use of 'securitisation' by banks to increase their borrowing?

In the examples given, these private actors are unelected and are not expected to serve in the public interest. Their roles have also been relatively well insulated from judicial, executive and legislative oversight and thus not very amenable to rule-of-law type procedures. Rather than resting on a democratic basis, the legitimacy of important and extensive international and national regulation often depends on technical, specialist expertise— sometimes described as 'epistemic communities'.[8] This has involved the splitting of law into functionally different areas of co-operation (such as environment, trade and human rights), each managed by a different group of experts—causing fragmentation and transforming law into regulation steered by technocrats.[9] 'Networks' is a further term used in the context of law beyond the state, referring to groupings that are dispersed, fluid, unhierarchical and flexible—indeed, rhizomatic and 'Deleuzian' in nature.[10] Yet it should not be overlooked that something as nebulous and free-flowing as a 'network' is just as capable of being a radical counter-cultural or terrorist network, as a transglobal linkage of experts. Boaventura de Sousa Santos, for example, describes a category of counter-hegemonic networks that are 'animated by a redistributive telos' and 'based on equality and recognition of difference'.[11] This suggests a growing resemblance of law-making, law-resisting and law-breaking forms, alike in their lack of recognised institutional grounding and febrile nature.

These new forms of association for norm creation present themselves as solutions to the problems of governing ever more complex societies. Many rely on the idea of self-regulation, a notion that has much in common with Gunther Teubner's 'reflexive law' and Philippe Nonet and Philip Selznick's

---

[8] This concept was originally developed by neofunctionalist theories of integration, suggesting that international cooperation could be enhanced by delegating certain issues to experts, who could employ managerial, technical methods to decide in a non-political way. See, eg, PC Schmitter, 'Ernst B Haas and the Legacy of Neofunctionalism' (2005) 12 *Journal of European Public Policy* 255.

[9] See, eg, G Majone, 'The Rise of the Regulatory State in Europe' (1994) 22 *Western European Politics* 1.

[10] In *A Thousand Plateaux* (Minneapolis, University of Minnesota Press, 1987) 23, Deleuze and Guattari describe the rhizome thus: 'The rhizome connects any point to any other point, and its traits are not necessarily linked to traits of the same nature; it brings into play very different regimes of signs, and even nonsign states. The rhizome is reducible to neither the One or the multiple.'

[11] B de Sousa Santos and C Rodríguez-Garavito, 'Law, Politics and the Subaltern in Counter-Hegemonic Globalisation' in B de Sousa Santos and C Rodríguez-Garavito (eds), *Law and Globalisation from Below: Towards a Cosmopolitan Legality* (Cambridge, Cambridge University Press, 2005) 1–26.

'responsive law'.[12] For example, the 'Libor' rate (namely, the London inter-bank lending rate) scandal arose in 2012 when it was revealed that banks were falsely manipulating these rates to increase their profits and inflate their creditworthiness.[13] However, a lack of accountability in the financial system was also revealed. The Libor rate is set neither by governments nor the UK Financial Services Authority but by the banks themselves—ie, it is an exercise in self-regulation. Yet the increase in self-regulation and the growing complexity of regulation of modern society threatens freedom and democracy, because what were previously governmental functions are now developed by or completely transferred to many different actors, resulting in more responsibility for unelected officials and private parties and the often incomplete supervision of activities in which the public has an interest. For example, the 'regulatory state' and 'epistemic communities' are supposedly associated with highly specialised, technical matters, in which experts are needed for their expertise, and laws are 'legitimated' as a product of direct deliberation of experts with an enhanced specialist knowledge, rather than of volatile electorates. Yet if matters of public interest[14] or individual liberty are at stake—eg, criminal law penalties or access to essential resources—then this type of norm creation, with its supposed legitimation by experts, is less attractive. Informal, flexible networks may also be amenable to capture by powerful voices.

This problem may be further illustrated by contemporary trends in commercial law. As William Scheuerman has suggested, a traditional belief in an 'elective affinity' between the rule of law and economic liberalism has obscured the way in which the growing power of global capitalism in fact threatens the main features of the rule of law.[15] It has been argued that in the eighteenth and nineteenth centuries, the rule of law aided the growth of capitalism, as it provided fixed, stable rules that could be relied upon by traders, as well as shielding freedom of contract and property laws from government interference.[16] The recognition of such a traditional 'affinity' between capitalism and the rule of law suggests that the rule of law is not ethically neutral but has facilitated the growth of business.

---

[12] On this, see above ch 2.

[13] See, eg, 'The Libor Scandal: The Rotten Heart of Finance', *The Economist* (7 July 2012).

[14] Such 'technical' issues can prove surprisingly controversial, such as the BSE crisis, which converted animal feed into a political issue and created much publicity for the EU veterinary standards committee.

[15] W Scheuerman, 'Globalisation and the Fate of Law' in D Dyzenhaus (ed), *Recrafting the Rule of Law: The Limits of Legal Order* (Oxford, Hart Publishing, 1999) 243. This relationship is discussed in greater detail below ch 8.

[16] Max Weber famously argued this. Niall Ferguson also makes this point in a 2012 BBC Reith lecture entitled 'The Rule of Law and its Enemies'.

Whether we see this 'affinity' between capitalism and the rule of law as something positive or not, the argument of this book is that this affinity has in any case waned, and the correlation may no longer be clearly made.[17] Global capitalism has evolved in the twentieth and twenty-first centuries, taking on a significantly different shape from that of past times.[18] As already discussed, MNEs and large corporations have created their own powers of law-making[19] and function at high velocity, continually finding new ways to increase productivity, which do not always involve the constraints of the rule of law, because they involve a singular privileged treatment for certain entities rather than the equal application of the law, and they also make use of highly complex, quasi-private regulation rather than a clarity and generality of law-making as prescribed by the rule of law. For example, MNEs have profited from regulatory regimes governing specific activities, such as certain legal enclaves or even a kind of 'privatisation of sovereignty'.[20] This can involve the use of 'flags of convenience' (the convenience being the avoidance of laws that would otherwise govern, eg, employment conditions of workers[21]) for international shipping and havens for tax avoidance. Some jurisdictions, such as the Cayman Islands and Lichtenstein, even offer 'comprehensive packages of arrangements' for avoidance purposes, or 'designer jurisdictions'—which are by no means marginal phenomena. This has been described as a 'commercialisation of sovereignty'[22] and is certainly to the benefit of those who have sufficient revenue to forum-shop.

Another example of self-serving, corporate tailored law and justice, conventionally presented as beneficial to poorer nations, is provided by the growing phenomenon of bilateral investment treaties. These are treaties in which MNEs draft or broker agreements for large-scale projects such as oil or mineral exploitation. These agreements often include provisions that exclude domestic law, as well as international law or human rights obligations, and typically replace local, state law enforcement with arbitration

---

[17] For a more detailed discussion of this point, see below ch 8.

[18] See also D Harvey, *The Condition of Postmodernity: An Enquiry into the Origins of Cultural Change* (Oxford, Blackwell, 1989) 240; and S Strange, *Casino Capitalism* (Oxford, Blackwell, 1986).

[19] See, eg, P Muchlinski, *Multinational Enterprises and the Law* (Oxford, Oxford University Press, 2007); and N Chomsky, 'Power in the Global Arena', *New Left Review* (Jul–Aug 1998).

[20] S Picciotto, 'Offshore: The State as Legal Fiction' in M Hampton and J Abbott (eds), *Offshore Finance Centres and Tax Havens: The Rise of Global Capital* (London, Macmillan, 1999) 43.

[21] For example, the EU *Viking Line* case (Case C-438/05, *Viking* [2007] ECR I-10779) concerned the issue of how far trade unions could take social action against a reflagging of a shipping company from a 'high-wage' country (Finland) to a 'low-wage country' (Estonia). The ECJ found that the free movement of services and goods under the EU Treaty outweighed the right to collective action.

[22] See S Picciotto, 'Constitutionalising Multilevel Governance?' (2008) 6 *International Journal of Constitutional Law* 457.

under the International Chamber of Commerce or World Bank. Such arrangements thereby create systems of privately arranged justice, with choice of applicable laws and arbiters to suit corporate needs, ensuring that the economically powerful are 'fortified with their own custom made justice'.[23] Bilateral investment treaties of this sort create their own hierarchy, placing commercial needs above the public interest and ensuring that the public cannot always rely on a supposedly neutral judiciary to lessen their impact. Although some see such developments in a positive light, as an important step on the way to a transnational legal order or an 'economic constitution', such contracts clearly prejudice the interests of very poor states,[24] which may even be coerced into accepting certain contractual provisions.[25] Given the enormous disparities in assets and power between the parties to these contracts, as well as the important disadvantages that developing countries face in the case of disputes, international investment contracts can represent bargaining 'as much in the shadow of power as in the shadow of the law'.[26] This results not in the neutral procedure praised by supporters of commercial arbitration but rather in a privatisation of justice, for the benefit of the few who can afford to pay for it.

Notably, state court litigation and international commercial arbitration differ radically in the way that state parties to a contract are characterised. Commercial arbitration treats a state as a private party to a contract. In the court system, however, the state is expected (at least in theory) to take the public interest into account in developing and implementing policy and in the prosecution of claims. Such different approaches mean that international commercial arbitration and adjudication maintain very differing roles for state parties to a dispute. This eclipse, or evaporation, of the public interest threatens accountability and justice. For example, it seems that if investment contract cases go to state adjudication under, eg, the US

---

[23] Y Dezalay and B Garth, *Dealing in Virtue: International Commercial Arbitration and the Construction of a Transnational Legal Order* (Chicago, University of Chicago Press, 1996) 210.

[24] See, eg, J Stopford and S Strange, *Rival States, Rival Firms: Competition for World Market Shares* (Cambridge, Cambridge University Press, 1991).

[25] For example, in drafting the contract for the Baku pipeline project (between the government of Turkey and the state oil company of the Azerbaijan Republic, BP Exploration (Caspian Sea Ltd), Statoil BTC Caspian AS, Ramco Hazar Energy Ltd, Turkiye Petrolleri AO, Unocal BTC Pipeline Ltd, ITOCHU Oil Exploration (Azerbaijan) Inc and Delta Hess (BTC) Ltd), a major US law firm representing the oil consortium partners is described as having 'proposed, cajoled [and] coerced' partners Turkey, Georgia and Azerbaijan into accepting certain contract provisions. D Eviatar, 'Wildcat Lawyering', *American Lawyer* (Nov 2002). Such procedures are hard to reconcile with Article 1 of the UN Charter of Economic Rights and Duties of States, which provides, 'Every State has the sovereign and inalienable right to choose its economic system as well as its political, social and cultural systems in accordance with the will of its people, without outside interference, coercion or threat in any form whatsoever.' See Charter of Economic Rights and Duties of States, Article 1, GA Resolution 3281(XXIX), United Nations General Assembly, 1974.

[26] Y Dezalay and B Garth, *Dealing in Virtue: International Commercial Arbitration and the Construction of a Transnational Legal Order* (Chicago, University of Chicago Press, 1996) 204.

Alien Tort Claims Act 1792 rather than arbitration, courts are more likely to find liability for human rights abuses.[27]

The compression of time and space is also a notable feature of the contemporary commercial world.[28] We no longer live in a world in which it can take months to reach another continent. Financial transactions across different trading blocks take place at high speed using very advanced technology. Capitalism no longer has a need for steady, enduring laws.[29] Much regulation of international finance and banking consists of flexible guidelines or sets of informal 'best practices' rather than clear and stable norms. A premium is set on actions that are smart and original.[30] This situation has been described as a 'space of flows' rather than a 'space of places',[31] evoking fluidity but also evasiveness and something unsettled in nature. The predictability and calculability associated with more traditional legal forms and the rule of law have been supplanted by actions and measures that may be very obscure or even irrational. Indeed, one cause of the international banking crisis of 2008 seems to have been the very lack of clear, stable, banking law and regulation. One finds similar phenomena within international trade and tax law. Overall, the body of national and international tax law is extremely complex, and corporations have been able to exploit and increase this complexity. MNEs have been able to profit from incoherent international taxation regimes—resulting in an under-taxing of their profits and a complete lack of reciprocity between the benefits they receive and the burdens that fall on them as a result—the opposite of the reciprocity lauded by Lon Fuller as a benefit of the rule of law.[32] The World Trade Organization (WTO) is supposedly based on the rule of law, on rules considered to be binding and precise and on the interpretation of rules undertaken by a third-party adjudicator. Yet WTO adjudication requires great skill to navigate the extremely complex labyrinth of legal rules and WTO-related regimes.[33] The WTO obligations are also expressed in abstract general principles involving a high degree of indeter-

---

[27] For example, a California court held that oil multinational Unocal might be liable for human rights violations by the government of Myanmar in relation to a pipeline project, under the doctrine of vicarious liability. P Waldman, 'Unocal to Stand Trial', *Wall Street Journal* (11 Jun 2002).

[28] Harvey, *The Condition of Postmodernity* (above n 18); and D Harvey, *Justice, Nature and the Geography of Difference* (Oxford, Blackwell, 1996).

[29] But for a different view—that 'economic globalisation is about securing certainty'—see D Scheiderman, 'Investment Rules and Regulations' (2001) *Constellations* 521.

[30] Harvey, *The Condition of Postmodernity* (above n 18).

[31] M Castells, *The Rise of the Network Society* (Oxford, Blackwell, 1996).

[32] See L Fuller, *The Morality of Law* (New Haven, Yale University Press, 1965), which is discussed below chs 7 and 8.

[33] As Scheuerman comments, anyone who studies the massive body of WTO materials 'is minded of the Egyptian hieroglyphics' that concerned Bentham. W Scheuerman, *Liberal Democracy and the Social Acceleration of Time* (Baltimore, Johns Hopkins University Press, 2004) 168.

minacy and uncertainty. Both the WTO and the International Monetary Fund (IMF) have institutional arrangements that are undemocratic in that they do not operate on the basis of one vote for each of their members. The United States has a large vote share, and thus a more dominant role in both of these organisations and is able to veto measures. Indeed, the United Nations High Commissioner for Human Rights has suggested that WTO rules are based on unfair assumptions, reflecting an agenda that serves only to promote rich countries and dominant corporate interests—eg, by the use of quotas and tariffs to protect the rich.[34] Thomas Pogge, a political philosopher, has argued that it is just these specific designs of global institutions and structures of world trade that have had a crucial, causal impact on world poverty—these rules and practices shaped and developed by the better-off are imposed on the worse-off in ways that produce radical inequality and exclusion from natural resources. The nature of this injustice will be further explored in chapter six, but for the moment the main point to be argued is that the nature of global institutions and the laws underpinning them contribute to injustice in a significant way.

The same criticism may be made of European Union law—that it fails to respect the rule of law. For example, the question of what will constitute a 'restriction' on trade under the EU Internal Market law, what restrictions on the free movement of goods or services will be proportionate, has become ever more uncertain,[35] dependent on a string of European Court decisions based on the very broad and abstract wording of the EU Treaty.[36] The recent Eurozone economic governance rules have been derided as failing 'the test of transparency, because of their near-total complexity and unreadability, scattered across a dozen primary, secondary and soft-law sources, with more to come'.[37]

One final example of injustice and a lack of the rule of law may be cited here: the unequal enforcement of the law against different groups of lawbreakers or perceived lawbreakers. There has been a lack of prosecution regarding the financial crisis, giving the impression that some actors are above the law and immune from prosecution. The general message seems

[34] 'The Realisation of Economic, Social and Cultural Rights: Globalisation Admits Impact on the Full Enjoyment of Human Rights', UN Economic and Social Council Commission Human Rights Preliminary Report, UN DocE/CN.4/Sub.2/2000.

[35] See, eg, the *Viking* case (above n 21), in which trade union collective action was considered to be a restriction on the free movement of services. Also, in Case C-60/00 *Carpenter* [2002] ECR I-6279, the European Court of Justice held that the deportation of the Philippine spouse of an EU national could be construed as a restriction of his freedom to provide services.

[36] For example, Article 34 of the Treaty on the Functioning of the EU, which is the key provision stating the principle of the free movement of goods, holds: 'Quantitative restrictions on imports and all measures having equivalent effect shall be prohibited between Member States.'

[37] S Peers, 'Analysis: Draft Agreement on Reinforced Economic Union (REU Treaty)', *Statewatch* (21 Dec 2011).

to be that whereas conduct leading to the financial crisis was unethical and irresponsible, it was not always necessarily illegal.[38] This failure to use the criminal law in the context of the financial crisis is in sharp contrast with the severity of the punishment imposed on those found to be guilty of more visible crimes, such as those committed in the course of the London riots of 2011[39] or indeed those not guilty of any criminal acts at all, such as those innocent bystanders who have been 'kettled' or confined in small spaces for many hours at a time.[40] The law has been vigorously enforced to manage public protest and deny protesters the right to take to the streets. Such a dissonance between the lack of prosecution of bankers and the law's response to public protests such as the Occupy movement suggests that rules are written for and by elites—an exploitative capture of regulators and politicians.

All of this undermines the rule of law. Law has become increasingly unpredictable and prone to regulatory capture and manipulation. Zygmunt Bauman, drawing on radical and revolutionary writings, has described a 'liquid modernity'.[41] The Communist Manifesto's revolutionary description of 'all that is solid melts into air' and Gramsci's description of late modern existence as flexible and fluid have in common the recognition of a drive, a spirit of change, and revolutionary destruction of tradition and anything likely to stand in their way. Bauman's liquid modernity is composed of endless processes with no solid end in sight. Indeed, global capital even shares one of the features that Hannah Arendt identified as characteristic of totalitarian regimes, namely, rather than a framework of stability, instead the experience of motion and flexible decision-making, resulting in an ever changing 'law' as a mystery to the public, undermining any faith in the capacity of law to do good.[42]

Many of the measures described here rely not on the formal rule of law but on openly antiformalist practices designed with very specific interests of business in mind, such as highly complex financial trading rules (eg, the concept of a 'derivative', which has much in common with gambling). Contemporary law possesses anti-formal trends—often flexible and discretionary, with vague clauses and general principles. These are evidence

---

[38] E Holder, 'Preventing and Combating Financial Fraud', speech at Columbia University Law School (23 February 2012), available at http://www.justice.gov/iso/opa/ag/speeches/2012/ag-speech-120223.html (accessed 21 November 2012).

[39] For example, immediately following the London riots, an electrical engineering student with no previous convictions was jailed for the maximum permitted six months after pleading guilty to stealing bottles of water worth £3.50 from Lidl in Brixton. 'UK Riots: In Courtrooms across Country, There Was Little Room for Leniency', *The Guardian* (11 August 2011).

[40] For further on this, see *Austin v Metropolitan Police Commissioner* [2009] UKHL 5, upheld by the European Court of Human Rights in *Austin v UK* [2012] ECHR 459.

[41] Z Bauman, *Liquid Modernity* (Cambridge, Polity Press, 2000).

[42] H Arendt, *The Origins of Totalitarianism* (New York, Harcourt Brace, 1973).

of ad hoc, discretionary trends rather than traditional virtues associated with the rule of law.

There exists a variety of analyses as to the nature of global capital and corporate power, but less of a consensus as to how they might be tamed. Claire Cutler[43] has described ascendancy of corporate power as a 'global mercatocracy', suggesting that law has been progressively captured by these factions, becoming an unalloyed vehicle of disciplinary neoliberalism, a view shared by postmodern, Marxist and neo-Marxist critiques. However, other commentators are more welcoming of these developments, characterising them as examples of a postmodern proliferation of multiple justices, each with its own language game, in some cases formulated by corporate power. The great diversity of law-creating regimes, networks and epistemic communities has even been described as bringing 'power to the people', empowering people as lawmakers for themselves, to 'realise some of the benefits of democratic theory and in this way achieve greater legitimacy'.[44] Similarly, Anne-Marie Slaughter welcomes a 'new world order' of cooperative networks and transnational actors, which she suggests might amount to 'a kind of disaggregated global democracy based on individual and group self-governance'—a type of 'horizontal democracy'.[45]

Michael Hardt and Antonio Negri[46] have offered a more messianic *Zeitdiagnose* of this globalisation of power—as an evolving system of totalising domination, a planetary gestalt of flows and hierarchies, of anonymous networks of global powers replacing the former Westphalian state-dominated world. Hardt and Negri's use of language is dramatic, and they quote Virgil to illustrate what they perceive to be the magnitude of the change: 'The final age that the oracle foretold has arrived; the great order of the centuries is born again.'[47] (This image possesses dramatic intensity that is similar to Michel Houellebecq's 'metaphysical mutation', which was discussed in chapter one.) Hardt and Negri also draw on the work of the Roman writer Polybius (an unlikely entrant in twenty-first-century globalisation), who attempted to explain to his puzzled contemporaries how the Roman Empire came to possess such great power. Hardt and Negri identify a 'constitution' for this Empire, but the 'mixed' world constitution they delineate is not the traditional ancient one of monarch, aristocracy and democracy, but instead comprises the United States as supreme monarch,

---

[43] AC Cutler, *Private Power and Global Authority* (Cambridge, Cambridge University Press, 2003).

[44] D Snyder, 'Molecular Federalism and the Structures of Private Lawmaking' (2007) *Journal of Global Legal Studies* 434.

[45] AM Slaughter, 'Global Government Networks, Global Information Agencies and Disaggregated Democracies' in KH Ladeur (ed), *Public Governance in an Age of Globalisation* (Aldershot, Ashgate 2004) 148.

[46] M Hardt and A Negri, *Empire* (Cambridge, MA, Harvard University Press, 2001).

[47] Ibid.

an 'aristocracy' of G8 and corporate economic wealth, and the 'democracy' of the internet. Non-profit organisations (NGOs) are given an apparently attractive role—compared to the Dominicans and Franciscans of the late medieval world, their charitable campaigns forming the 'mendicant orders' of Empire. However, Hardt and Negri's attitude to this Empire is somewhat ambiguous. For all its energy, it is not portrayed as entirely benign (but nor yet entirely to be condemned), and it is notable that Hardt and Negri characterise Empire as existing in a permanent state of emergency—a waft of exceptional measures being necessary to sustain it.

Hardt and Negri have included within their regime of Empire international institutions such as the WTO and also cosmopolitan institutions of the 'postnational constellation', such as international human rights regimes. Hardt and Negri (who are far more critical of these international institutions than, for example, Jürgen Habermas) believe all of them to lack democratic accountability and to serve a global elite. In taking this approach, Hardt and Negri share a view similar to that of Antonio Gramsci, who explored and deplored 'imperial cosmopolitanism' in his *Prison Notebooks*.[48] What is clear is that Hardt and Negri believe this Empire to be controlled not centrally but though diverse networks and sites of power, and therefore it is very difficult to control and render accountable—a feature, however, not particularly highlighted by Hardt and Negri, who appear keener to pronounce on the novelty of its flows, multitudes and rhizomatic networks.

Yet any concentration of power—whether public, private or mixed—risks abuse, arbitrariness and corruption. So it has been necessary for societies to develop systems of checks and balances to control the abuse of power and to protect citizens. Yet if power is abused or exercised in an arbitrary way by non-state actors, then surely this conduct is every bit as in need of constraining as arbitrary, abusive conduct by the state? What is revealed is a serious problem of governance. Global institutions are too weak to deal with the huge problems and risks thrown up by occurrences such as the financial crisis. They also lack accountability and responsibility. As the Governor of the Bank of England, Mervyn King, stated, 'Banks may be global in life, but they are national in death.'[49] This gives rise to a 'mortality mismatch'[50] in which a dissonance exists between, on the one hand, the increasing move toward a harmonisation and globalisation of financial regulation and, on the other, the need for governments to strengthen

---

[48] A Gramsci, *Prison Notebooks* (New York, Columbia University Press, 1982). Contrast this to the more optimistic view of cosmopolitanism presented below ch 10.

[49] Quoted in J Black, 'The Credit Crisis and the Constitution' in D Oliver, T Prosser and R Rawlings (eds), *The Regulatory State: Constitutional Implications* (Oxford, Oxford University Press, 2010) 122.

[50] J Black, 'Managing the Financial Crisis: The Constitutional Dimension', London School of Economics Law, Society and Economy Working Papers 12/2010, 35.

national supervision and regulation to protect their citizens and to guard against increasing budget deficits. The result is that problems are dealt with in unilateral and ad hoc ways.

Such situations raise salient questions of justice. Surely the conclusion to be drawn from this brief excursion into contemporary global lawmaking and lawyering is not to reject the rule of law and its capacity to place formal constraints on power, but rather to require large corporate interests, as well as other powerful non-state sources of 'law', to conform to standards that the rule of law can enforce and thereby to ensure that they do not produce regimes of injustice. Vague, flexible measures are all too easy for MNEs and nebulous networks to exploit. So accountability is crucial.

Privatisation, Flexible Law, Governance and Insecurity

The matters discussed above do not exhaust the concerns over the growth and abuse of power. Outside of the commercial context, there exists considerable input of the non-state sector into law creation and enforcement. There has also been a huge growth in administrative agencies, or what in the United Kingdom is known as the 'contracting out'[51] of once public functions to the private sector.

One of the most worrying developments concerns the growth of private or mixed control over areas such as nursing, biomedical data, residential care and even prisons. In the modern era, incarceration became a matter intrinsically governmental in nature,[52] and yet many privately employed prison officers now exercise control over human rights and liberties of prisoners such as access to visitors, showers, meals and so on. These developments raise possible conflicts between a private interest in maximisation of profits and a public interest in sound correctional policies. Equally troubling is the growth of involvement of private enterprise in areas such as biomedical science and genetics, and the rise in data banks of personal information—where, again, practices are driven by commercial imperatives rather than by public welfare.

Given these developments, dispute resolution has also adopted a different form from the traditional mechanisms of public law. In the case of contracting out nursing care or residential care for the elderly, in the event of complaints, a contract-based system relies on enforcement of private law on behalf of agency rather than on public law rights enforced by citizens.

---

[51] See, eg, M Freedland, 'Government by Contract and Public Law' (1994) *Public Law* 86.
[52] In contrast to the pre-modern era, when there existed many non-state prisons and police. See, for example, M Foucault, *Discipline and Punish* (New York, Vintage, 1979).

A patient facing eviction from a privately provided but government-funded nursing home, in breach of an agency-provided contract, may face a legal lacuna, as they may have no contractual right due to privity of contract and no administrative law rights, such as legitimate expectations, because the service is privately provided.[53] Similar issues arise in the context of prison services. These situations involve the intervention of private law concepts, especially contract and property law, but also others such as business confidentiality, into areas formerly governed by public law, and exclusion of the former supervision of public law, with its greater concern for the public interest. AV Dicey[54] feared that the growth of the welfare state, with its centralisation of power and discretion, would threaten the rule of law, yet surely it is the intrusion of private power into welfare matters that should cause greater concern? In the latter case there exists no presumption, as in the case of the state, that the exercise of power should be subject to certain controls of public law, such as a duty to give reasons or proportionality. The field of private law has no such concept of the public interest but rather is based on individual concepts, such as consent, or the autonomous bargaining power of the parties in contract law. However, the basis of judicial review is that, unlike in the case of individual contracts, the parties have no choice as to the imposition of government power, and therefore certain protections and safeguards should apply, whereas contractual situations are seen as consensual, to be determined by the parties to the contract. Yet in many contracting-out situations, the public also have no choice as to who provides a service—relations are not consensual.[55]

Security

Private law creation and enforcement also pervade the field of security—a troubling development. One common phenomenon of the contemporary era is the huge growth in surveillance, especially notable in the form of the ubiquitous closed-circuit television (CCTV) cameras that overlook high streets, railway stations and shopping malls. Huge data banks of

[53] For relevant UK caselaw, see *YL v Birmingham City Council* [2007] UKHL 27; and s 145, UK Health and Social Care Act (2008), introduced in order to ameliorate the situation of care home residents.
[54] AV Dicey, *Introduction to the Study of the Law of the Constitution*, 10th edn (London, Macmillan, 1959) 195.
[55] For further on this see, eg, M Freedland, 'Law, Public Services and Citizenship: New Domains, New Regimes?' in M Freedland and S Sciarra (eds), *Public Services and Citizenship in European Law* (Oxford, Oxford University Press, 1998); and L Turano, 'Charitable Trusts and the Public Service: The Public Accountability of Private Care Providers' (2007) 18(3) *King's Law Journal* 427.

information are held about us, some of it biometric, taken from personal, intimate areas of the human body. The taking and storing of this data is often justified on the basis that security will thereby be enhanced, because dangerous individuals can be located by this information, although there is little evidence that this is indeed the case. Much of this data is gathered by private institutions, for example passenger name records (which are now required to be retained by airlines) and telecommunications data (which must now be retained up to three years by telecommunications companies).[56] Such extensive surveillance and data storage raises considerable questions of privacy rights. The European Court of Human Rights, in the *Marper* case,[57] found the UK to have breached the right to privacy in its practice of retaining DNA samples of those (even children) who were acquitted of crimes, or arrested but not subsequently charged.

Cases like *Marper*, because they involve a finding against a state, in this case the United Kingdom, encourage us to think in Orwellian terms, of a Big Brother security state, watching our every movement and hoarding all sorts of our very private data. Notably, in the early twenty-first century, the state is reinventing itself as the 'security state'. However, in reality, the surveillance is just as likely to be carried out by non-state bodies, either as agents on behalf of the state or for purely commercial private concerns. The many CCTV cameras that adorn Britain's high streets and communal areas are likely to be there to protect property owners' interests. All sorts of issues arise as to how and by whom these huge flows of information are to be controlled, indeed as to who owns the data, who is to be held accountable and responsible for exchange of data, whether it can be sold and how it can be tracked. There exists no body with overall control (which in any case would not be an encouraging prospect but rather one with Orwellian overtones), just a fragmented collection and processing of information. A surely crucial question is whether there is any quantifiable benefit from this immense collection and retention of data and biometrics—at great financial cost? More information is not necessarily preferable. Is it necessary? Is it proportionate to any threats we face? Can it help anticipate or prevent dangerous activities? Does it make us more secure? Or does it invade our privacy and increase surveillance of individuals without promoting

---

[56] For an account of airline passenger record retention, see, eg, E Brouwer, 'The EU Passenger Name Record System and Human Rights: Transferring Passenger Data or Passenger Freedom?' CEPS Working Document No 320, Centre for European Policy Studies, Brussels (2009). On data retention in the EU, see EC Directive 2006/24 of 15 March 2006 on the retention of data generated or processed in connection with the provision of publicly available electronic communications services or of public communications networks, [2006] OJ L105/54.

[57] *S and Marper v United Kingdom* [2008] ECHR 1581.

individual and collective safety? Does it increase suspicion and undermine social cohesion?

Indeed, Mark Poster has used the expression 'database anxiety' to describe the concern of people over the data collected about them by governments, but by also private bodies such as credit agencies and insurance companies, because this data storing affects behaviour.[58] Poster relates this anxiety to the power of the Panopticon device described by Michel Foucault in *Discipline and Punish* (and of course by Jeremy Bentham)—a means conceived in the early nineteenth century to survey all prisoners from 'one central viewpoint—and designates all existing databases 'Superpanopticon'.

Figure 5-1 illustrates the Orwellian-sounding 'Total Information Awareness Program', whose mystical logo (depicting an eye positioned at the apex of a pyramid peering over the Earth) conjures up the image of a giant Panopticon.

This was the initiative of the US Defense Department's 'Defense Advanced Research Project Agency' (DARPA). It was designed to unite a number of databases so as to be able to search for terrorist activities but was blocked in the US Senate in 2003, due to civil liberties concerns.[59] The image, curiously redolent of secret societies and freemasonry—given the giant, all-seeing eye on the pyramid—suggests a not entirely benevolent power; and the slogan beneath it, 'scientia est potentia' ('knowledge is power'), is open to sinister as well as benign interpretations. This giant

Figure 5-1: Defense Advanced Research Project Agency (DARPA), US Department of Defense, 'Total Information Awareness'

[58] M Poster, *The Second Media Age* (Cambridge, Polity Press, 1995) 85.
[59] See the Defense Advanced Research Project Agency (DARPA) 'Information Awareness Office and Total Information Awareness Project' (2002).

Panopticon may be no more, but others are on the way. For example, the European Union has mooted the possibility of joining its databases together in one central location.[60]

The issue of private data is part of a broader phenomenon that has been described as 'the governance of security'.[61] This has involved an increasing 'polycentring' of security. For example, there are now many more non-state policing agents than there are regular police forces.[62] In the modern era, provision of security became seen as a crucial state function, with the creation of centralised police forces and state militaries instead of private police and militia. In a reversal of this process, there now exists a proliferation of contracts with private security firms, and not only in war zones such as Iraq or Afghanistan. There has also been a growth of transnational private military and security companies involved in training military forces. In addition, citizens have been encouraged to take responsibility for their own security, for example through neighbourhood watch groups—practices that sociologists have described as part of a trend of 'responsibilisation'.[63]

Governance

In parallel with areas such as health, prison service and public procurement, where states have contracted-out government services that were once seen as at the core of their public role, the field of security has similarly seen government rely increasingly on contract law.[64] As much as in the commercial law field, this has led to new forms of governance outside the state, involving much more than a devolution of state functions. This

[60] There are already diverse EU-wide databases in existence over the field of justice and home affairs. For example, states exchange immigration and crime-related information through the Schengen Information System. Crime related information is also exchanged through the Europol Information System, to which the Europol Convention applies. The Eurojust Information System applies to national prosecutors and courts exchanging information, and the Customs Information system applies to data of, eg, smuggling that is collected by customs officers.

[61] Eg, by former UK Metropolitan Police Commissioner Ian Blair. See C Shearing, 'Nodal Security' (2005) 8 *Police Quarterly* 57.

[62] See, eg, R van Stedena and R Sarre, 'The Growth of Private Security: Trends in the European Union' (2007) 20 *Security Journal* 222.

[63] See, eg, D Garland, 'Governmentality and the Problem of Crime: Foucault, Criminology, Sociology' (1997) 1 *Theoretical Criminology* 173; and J Wood and C Shearing, *Imagining Security* (Devon, Willan Publishing, 2006).

[64] C Shearing and J Wood, 'Nodal Governance, Democracy and New Denizens' (2003) 30 *Journal of Legal Studies* 300.

has been described as 'government at a distance',[65] and a distinction has been drawn between the 'rowing' and 'steering' of functions[66]—'steering' remaining with more traditional or core organisations of government and 'rowing' being taken on by a diverse group of bodies. Moreover, there are now references made to 'hybrid' policing and security structures and even 'bubbles' of private governance, which indicates a rather motley patchwork of governance. In any case, the role of the state has been reduced to one of regulation of the activities of non-state actors.

The notion of citizenship is traditionally associated with the sovereign state, but in many of these diverse contexts it is more appropriate to refer to 'denizens', who enjoy social or civil rights but not political inclusion. Denizenships (which need not even involve non-nationals) of all sorts of spaces can exist, but these spaces have in common the fact that the term 'communal' would seem to describe them better than either the term public or private. Examples of these may be found in that favourite of contemporary life, the shopping mall, where individuals (nationals and non-nationals) each have different expectations, duties and rights, thick or thin, some with greater social capital. Property owners rather than public authorities play a very large role in the governance of these spaces, and for some theorists, the resonance is akin to that of medieval common spaces controlled by feudal authorities. The Occupy movement was unable to protest in its preferred space in front of the London Stock Exchange, which was privately owned by the Stock Exchange, so ended up in the space adjoining St Paul's Cathedral, from where it was eventually evicted. Indeed, the lack of public spaces in the City of London has meant that political protest is impossible in the vast majority of the City's open spaces—which, although nominally public, are owned and controlled by private estates. Access to these is conditional and enforced by private security and continued surveillance. Activities such as filming, taking photos, cycling, eating and public protest are very often forbidden.

In such environments, there exists a commodification of services, whereby consumers have some control, and those with little or no purchasing power are less able to participate. Poorer people are seen as flawed consumers, excluded by coercion or banishment, to live in 'communities of fate' such as sink estates or squatter camp settlements—what Alan Minc has described as 'zones grises'[67]—localised ghettos, geographical areas or social contexts in which the rule of law does not function. This bears some

---

[65] N Rose and P Miller, 'Political Power beyond the State: Problematics of Government' (1992) 43 *British Journal of Sociology* 174, drawing on Bruno Latour's concept of 'action at a distance'.

[66] See D Osborne and R Gaebler, *Reinventing Government* (New York, Addison Wesley, 1992).

[67] A Minc, *Le nouveau Moyen Âge* (Paris, Gallimard, 1993).

resemblance to the durable disorder of feudalism, a situation of relative and increasing entropy that is reminiscent of the Middle Ages.[68] A free market in security is much more likely to deliver only to the rich rather than to the poor, as well as to engender very deep inequalities. This in turn leads to more inequalities, fragmentation of effective government and multiplication of quasi fiefdoms.[69]

Foucault, in his later work, seemed to describe a similar phenomenon—what he regarded as a move away from the direct authority and control by the state to the management of affairs through a singular and more complex scheme of power, 'which has as its target population, political economy, and as its specific technique means apparatus the management of security'.[70] This trend involves near universal surveillance through, eg, auditing, monitoring, self-reporting and evaluation. In his depiction of how power no longer derives only from the state but has become dispersed, Foucault described new types of regulatory discipline and the production of new apparatuses of security and surveillance, which he referred to as 'governmentality'.[71] Foucault contrasted this situation with earlier, traditional—what he termed—'juridical' forms of sovereignty that had centred on the state. However, Foucault maintained that 'governmentality' creates a form of power that organises and constructs society by operating through diverse networks and 'a proliferation of a whole range of apparatuses pertaining to government and a complex body of knowledges and "know-how" about government',[72] This therefore involves 'government at a distance', as well as 'networks of interests allied with each other through the adoption of shared vocabularies, theories and explanations'.[73] In this way, law is converted, and perhaps downgraded, into a series of regulatory mechanisms—mechanisms of power.

Foucault used the term 'governmentality', but it has become more usual to replace 'government' with 'governance' as a term. Unlike government, which is institutional and constitutional in character, 'governance' extends beyond the traditional domain of governments; it denotes the existence of multiple actors (often private authority), is usually non-hierarchical in nature and does not necessarily encompass a normative agenda. Along

---

[68] P Cerny, 'Globalisation and the Erosion of Democracy' (1999) 36 *European Journal of Political Research* 1.

[69] See J Braithwaite, 'The New Regulatory State and the Transformation of Criminology' (2000) 40 *British Journal of Criminology* 222.

[70] M Foucault, 'Governmentality' in G Burchell, C Gordon and P Miller (eds), *The Foucault Effect: Studies in Governmentality (with Two Lectures by and an Interview with Michel Foucault)* (London, Harvester Wheatsheaf, 1991) 102. But note that Foucault relates this disciplinary society to the condition of modernity. See M Foucault, *The Order of Things: An Archaeology of the Human Sciences* (London, Routledge, 2002).

[71] Foucault, 'Governmentality' (ibid).

[72] Rose and Miller, 'Political Power beyond the State' (above n 65) 174.

[73] N Rose and P Miller, 'Governing Economic Life' (1990) 19 *Economy and Society* 10.

with the rise in 'governance' come other new beliefs—the perceived need for responsive or reflexive regulation described in earlier chapters, along with the belief that we have become a 'risk society' in which preventive governance has become more important,[74] justifying vast databanks of information, linked with the practice of risk assessment in the belief that this will make the future safer.

Once again these practices raise formidable questions of justice and accountability. Certainly, too little attention has been given to the issue of abuse by non-state or inchoate lawmaking. We should remember that Thomas Hobbes, for example, grounded the necessity for law in protection of citizens' rights against private intrusion in the state of nature. The issue of imposing constraints on power is surely not limited to that frequently asked in public law of whether the body concerned is exercising a 'public function' in order to justify imposing public law constraints, which tends to lead to tortuous analysis of core and functional public authorities and also tends to focus on activities that were in the past within the remit of the state, rather than in perceiving private abuse of power as a problem per se.[75] Nor is the solution necessarily to return many of these functions to the state. Is it the case that the only legitimate possessor of coercive power should be the state, and all other bodies should be essentially voluntary in nature? Or is it permissible for non-state organisations to wield coercive power legitimately? If so, what should this legitimacy rest on—a capacity for those bodies to produce some sort of public benefit such as charitable organisations or trade unions, or even commercial bodies in their wealth creating capacities? Yet if this is the case, there is then the question of whether private actors should be obliged to have regard for the public interest in setting standards in the first place—this is sometimes expressed in terms of a need to 'responsibilise' the private sector. If the state is subject to a public law system of judicial review on the basis that the matters which it regulates are of common interest, then surely when private parties dominate, control or affect matters of public interest, similar accountability measures should exist? What should the rule of law mean in such contexts? At the very least, enforceable and more formalised national, transnational and international standards are required to constrain and control the tyranny of powerful economic interests. The sort of 'horizontal democracy' embraced by Slaughter, for example, is inadequate, given that the only parties in this horizontal democracy tend to be experts, bureaucrats and commercial interests rather than those ultimately affected by their actions. As Scheuerman has suggested, the only solution to the

---

[74] Eg, U Beck, *Risk Society: Towards a New Modernity* (London, Sage, 1992); C Shearing, 'Justice in the Risk Society' (2005) 38 *Australian & New Zealand Journal of Criminology* 25.

[75] See, eg, D Oliver, 'Functions of a Public Nature under the Human Rights Act' (2004) *Public Law* 329.

crisis of the rule of law is thus more of the rule of law, operating also on a transnational level.[76]

Insecurity

It is apparent that society has become obsessed with security, very often at the expense of freedom and justice, and law has partaken of this obsession. Two apparently diverse phenomena—the exercise of executive power in the face of the 'war on terror'[77] and the growth of non-hierarchical governance—both display an obsession with security and are linked. The adoption of indefinite detention measures, the collection of huge data banks about us, the growth in numbers of CCTV cameras in public spaces, along with pre-emptive arrests of those who have committed no criminal acts and other deprivations of liberty, such as 'kettling' of ordinary members of the public, intrusive stop and search measures without the need for reasonable suspicion[78]—all involving considerable intrusions into personal freedom—are justified on the basis that they will somehow make us more secure and free from terror, although there is little to no evidence to support this claim.

The very mechanisms that are involved in creating and processing security in fact may operate to its detriment and make us more insecure. Jacques Derrida captured this situation generally as one of an 'autoimmune crisis', in which a mechanism 'works to destroy its own protection, to immunise itself against its own immunity'.[79] One manifestation of this autoimmunity is the vicious cycle of repression, whereby by declaring a war on terrorism, the West has declared a war on itself on account of reductions in civil liberties, human rights, tolerance and credibility associated with the fight against terror.

For Bauman, this focus on security is a key attribute of late modernity, something that has come about as a result of certain shifts and passages in the way governance is conducted, such as a separation of power from politics to a more uncontrolled private or global sphere and capricious market forces.[80] Therefore, globalisation and the transnational pluralism of laws play their part in a perceived growing need for security. The consequence has been that traditional political institutions appear less relevant.

---

[76] Scheuerman, 'Globalisation and the Fate of Law' (above n 15) 265.

[77] Discussed below ch 7.

[78] A measure that was at least found to be incompatible with the right to respect for private life under Art 8 ECHR in *Gillan v UK* [2010] 50 EHRR 45.

[79] 'A Dialogue with Jacques Derrida' in G Borradori (ed), *Philosophy in a Time of Terror* (Chicago, University of Chicago Press, 2003) 90.

[80] Z Baumann, *Liquid Fear* (Cambridge, Polity Press, 2006); and Z Baumann, *Liquid Times* (Cambridge, Polity Press, 2007).

This has also been accompanied by the gradual, consistent withdrawal of welfare state mechanisms—of communal state insurance against individual failure. Increasing deregulation, flexibility and the multiplicity of forms of governance have in fact made us more insecure. The withdrawal of much state social subsistence has sapped social solidarity and community, resulting in alienation and anomie, as well as distrust and fear of aliens, of the Other.

An immediate and graphic example of an enforced move from social welfare to austerity (and consequent sapping of social solidarity) is provided by the handling of the recent financial crisis within the Eurozone. New measures on economic governance have been adopted, and austerity measures have been institutionalised through mandatory limits on public spending and adjustment of labour market policies in favour of more flexibility and lower wages. These dramatic changes have been advanced speedily and without great transparency, under the pretext of restoring stability in the Eurozone. Notably, what is often missed in the widespread commentary on the Euro's troubles is that this crisis is as much of governance as of economics and finance. Neither the EU Member States nor its institutions have been able to find adequate solutions to the crisis in the face of action by the financial markets. Once we examine the details of what the European Union has actually done in its attempts to solve the Eurozone crisis, we can see that the scope and impact of these measures has been formidable, as for example, those imposed by the 'conditionality' clauses in bailout agreements, involving drastic intervention in Eurozone states' economic and social policy.[81] Yet all of these measures were adopted with little debate and a minimum of public awareness. Most Europeans have little idea that such changes, involving such inroads into their governments' economic sovereignty, have taken place. The European Union and its Member States' response to the crisis of its currency has been characterised by a continuous flurry of untransparent and undemocratic measures, which impose conditions of severe austerity on Member States, distancing economic governance from the control of elected governments and national parliaments, in an extremely complex and confusing melée of arrangements of EU law and international agreements between the states, without, however, any apparent beneficial effects.

Further, it would seem that many of these measures have brought the EU into conflict with both human rights and social and welfare values proclaimed in its own treaties. For example, the Lisbon Treaty sets the

---

[81] These have required, inter alia, reductions in pensions; large-scale privatisation programmes; reduction of public investment; and reform of wage legislation in the public sector. See, eg, Greek Bailout: Council Decision 2010/320, [2010] OJ L145/6 (as amended by Council Decision 2010/486 [2010] OJ L241/12) respectively Articles 2(1)(e), 2 (1) (n), 2(2) (d).

objective of 'a highly competitive social market economy' (Article 3(3)). It would be hard to argue that the measures and reforms detailed above are compatible with a social market economy, nor with the provisions of Article 9 of the Treaty on the Functioning of the European Union (TFEU), which states:

In defining and implementing its policies and activities, the Union shall take into account requirements linked to the promotion of a high level of employment, the guarantee of adequate social protection, the fight against social exclusion, and a high level of education, training and protection of human health.

Nor do measures that impose unilateral cuts on wages, pensions and public spending, as well as restrict collective bargaining, enhance the objective of social justice set out in Article 3 of the Treaty on European Union (TEU) or with the freedom of association recognised in both the European Convention on Human Rights (ECHR) and the EU Charter of Fundamental Rights.[82] Solidarity between the EU Member States has not been greatly in evidence; insecurity and resentment of outsiders has increased.

The Eurozone crisis provides a particularly compelling example, but more generally, the result of these passages and shifts is that, as Bauman has suggested, although many of us are more free than we have ever been (in the sense of having more money and time and less drudgery), this freedom comes at a price—insecurity, anxiety or a more complex *Unsicherheit*—that is just as likely to be experienced by the wealthy as by the poorest in society. Indeed, in a transformation of roles and values, security has itself become seen as the primary freedom.

At the same time, this transformation has been accompanied by rising expectations that insecurity is something that can be solved by technology— that a life free from fear can be assured by expensive technical expertise. People want to feel secure, and apparently a climate of suspicion requires special management techniques. Therefore, political dilemmas have been reduced to technical solutions. Indeed, much commercial capital is to be gained from prompting insecurity and fear, along with the belief that technology can help protect us from it. The media contributes to this insecurity—choices of newsworthiness or advertising strategies can subject people to largely irrational forces.[83] Advertisers deliberately exploit fears

---

[82] Further, all 27 EU Member States have ratified the International Labour Organization (ILO) Convention No 154 on Promotion of Collective Bargaining and ILO Convention No 87 on Freedom of Association. Greek trade unions complained to the ILO regarding the imposition of bailout conditions and, in particular, restrictions on collective bargaining. In this context, the CEACR Report of the ILO held that 'restrictions on collective bargaining should only be imposed as exceptional measures and only to the extent necessary, without exceeding a reasonable period.' See the Report of the Committee of Experts on the Application of Conventions and Recommendations (CEACR) (2011) 83.

[83] A Curtis, *The Power of Nightmares: The Rise of the Politics of Fear*, BBC documentary (2004).

of catastrophic terrorism—Baumann has given as an example an advertising shot of a sport utility vehicle (SUV) escaping from a burning city, with the implicit suggestion that only this car can help us escape from the Armageddon to come.[84] So fear can be turned to commercial as well as political profit. Increasingly, security has become understood as the management of risk, which engages the discourses of economics, insurance and technology rather than politics and policing. Yet this is inadequate—computer technology cannot stand in for humans, nor can biometrics and database profiles predict future behaviour, and security is not increased.

The connection between globalisation, flexibility, deregulation and security becomes more apparent if we consider the role of the state. States cannot compete with a powerful global elite of MNEs or financial markets, so they seek to compensate for their lack of power and to legitimise themselves by attending to national security, declaring states of emergency, issuing continual warnings of terrorism or other threats and enacting repressive measures. State actions take the form of 'speech acts' that, being productive rather than descriptive in nature, have just as much a capacity to *create* threats as to identify existing objective threats. This in turn justifies the taking of exceptional measures going beyond ordinary state policies. Yet this merely increases the climate of fear, and the state cannot compensate for its citizens' insecurities. For due to the very fact that we live in an era of globalisation and increased mobility of persons, provision of security is no longer something that the state can provide by its own efforts alone. Commercial enterprises and security firms are involved. International or regional cooperation is necessary. So the legal orders of the West are now in transition from constitutional criminal law to a transnational security order.[85] There exists much intergovernmental co-ordination and co-operation in the security field, and networks of police and law enforcement authorities exchanging information, again involving an intermeshing of public and private, resulting in a transnational security law. International securitisation has been given further justification by the lifting of internal border controls in the context of the EU Internal Market programme, which has also increased the free movement of criminals, which in turn is giving rise to a further perceived need for EU cooperation in criminal justice matters. Such internationalisation was already in existence by the turn of the twenty-first century but became accelerated by the response to the attacks of September 11.

Yet such a move to transnational or privatised security brings with it considerable adverse consequences. It removes many of the constraints of the

---

[84] Baumann, *Liquid Fear* (above n 80) 45.
[85] See K Günther, 'World Citizens between Freedom and Security' (2005) 12 *Constellations* 379.

democratic state. It creates a democratic deficit of worrying proportions in the context of great intrusions into individual liberty by biometric regulation, exchanges of data and automatic surrender of suspects without complementary protection of suspects' rights—all of which are measures, for example, taken by the European Union without any great democratic input from national parliaments or the EU Parliament, in the context of often highly complex, confusing mixed public-private concerns—such as the European Police Agency, Europol, whose convoluted and untransparent organisational structure and projects are illustrated in Figure 5-2. These measures need to be underpinned with structures that protect the rule of law and make provision for accountability.

The creation of the state of emergency, encouraged by the growth of insecurity, calls for expulsion or containment of migrants and harsh treatment of an 'enemy within'. Habermas has provided a related explanation for a growth in insecurity, deriving from what he has described as the increasing colonisation by economic and bureaucratic 'systems' in modernity of 'lifeworlds' (meaning the shared values and understandings, developed through experience and contacts in groups such as families and communities). Lifeworlds relate to our values, identities and deeply held beliefs. Habermas has described the colonisation of lifeworlds by systems as a crisis, because the system media (money and power) have no legitimacy except that which the lifeworlds are able to provide. During modernity, lifeworlds responded to economic systemisation by establishing social welfare standards through the welfare state, thus furthering possibilities for community and strengthening of values; but lifeworlds have not been

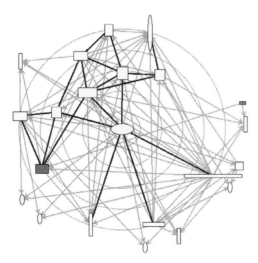

Figure 5-2: The governance of surveillance: an organisational chart of Europol, from Euro police blog post 'Europol: Operational Projects 2007', http://euro-police. noblogs.org/2009/01/europol-operational-projects-2007/ (accessed 4 January 2013)

so well adapted to globalisation.[86] There has been a confused mixture of reactions—on the one hand, a growth in religious fundamentalism and a desire for a return to the religious values of a pre-modern era and, on the other hand, increasing fragmentation and the development of postmodernism, with its retreat into subjectivity and partiality, in order to compete against the economic prerogatives of neoliberalism—with which, paradoxically, postmodernism shares a similar approach to globalisation:

> For different reasons, [postmodernism and neoliberalism] ultimately share the vision of the lifeworlds of individuals and small groups scattering, like distinct monads, across global, function-ally coordinated networks, rather than overlapping in the course of social integration in larger, multidimensional political entities.[87]

Conclusion

At this point, it is useful to recapitulate and consolidate the arguments proposed in this chapter as to why law currently plays its part in producing injustice. It is argued that the proliferation of legal pluralism and the consequent lack of clear lines of responsibility, accountability and authority, along with the increase in legal flexibility, a shift from government to governance, a move toward deregulation and contracting-out, and the dismantling of social welfare systems previously structured and supported by the state (often due to globalisation and market pressures, as with the austerity imposed by the Eurozone crisis) have transformed the nature of contemporary law, rendering it less susceptible to an account that characterises it in terms of clear structures, rules of recognition or Basic Norms. But along with this proliferation and fragmentation of legal forms have come increased insecurities and anxieties. At the same time, the focus of the state and that of international and transnational institutions on the provision of security has increased. This has led to an erosion of civil liberties and human rights, especially those of privacy and liberty of the person, and these encroachments may be attributable to a variety of sources, both public and private. So, in addition to a lack of accountability, the erosion of the rule of law due to pluralism and flexibility, and a weakening of social justice attributable to the ebbing away of the welfare state, there is also the

---

[86] It should be noted that Habermas, unlike many other contemporary theorists, does not believe that processes of fragmentation and colonisation of lifeworld are unstoppable but, on the contrary, argues that 'the project of Enlightenment' can be set back on its course by a normative framework and proceduralist paradigm for law. See J Habermas, 'Modernity: An Incomplete Project' in H Foster (ed), *The Anti-aesthetic* (Port Townsend, Bay Press, 1983) 3.

[87] J Habermas, *The Postnational Constellation* (Cambridge, Polity Press, 2000) 88.

debilitation of human rights caused by the greater emphasis on security, as well as the absence of the rule of law effected by situations such as those of the indefinite detention of prisoners in Guantanamo and Belmarsh.[88] All of these examples represent particular forms of injustice, and contemporary law has played its part in producing each of them. Law has shifted its shape and accommodated itself to perceived needs for greater flexibility, pluralism of authorities and sources, privatisation and contracting-out; a partial and unequal application of law to the benefit of elites (as in the application of global trade rules or the failure to prosecute those responsible for the financial crisis while vigorously enforcing laws against public protest); and pre-emptive and precautionary forms of 'justice' typical of the security state, namely the precaution of indefinite detention without trial or charge, and the introduction of new types of inchoate and incomplete offences, such as that of 'encouraging' terrorism.[89]

An interesting question is why people have been so willing to risk forfeiting their freedom. Why are they not more worried by these processes? Clearly there is a perceived need for security, but Michael Ignatieff has offered the explanation that strong measures actually appeal because people expect that as 'good citizens', they will not be affected.[90] They do not imagine for themselves the consequences as addressees of the law. In terms of a cost–benefit analysis, they accept higher potential restrictions on freedom if what they perceive to be the real scope of their freedom is stabilised.

This approach is both undesirable and unrealistic. First, most of the measures discussed above apply to *all* citizens. All communications data is retained, not just that of criminal suspects. We must all surrender biometric data to obtain passports or visas. We cannot predict what further use will be made of our data, nor to what destinations it will travel. These measures are subject to function creep and use of different purposes other than those originally foreseen for them. For example, European arrest warrants may be issued for offences that do not exist in a surrendering state, such as in the case of abortion, lustration and incitement to religious hatred,[91] where a surrendered individual is left unprotected by that country's domestic law.

---

[88] For a further discussion of such erosions of the rule of law, see below chs 7 and 8.

[89] S 1 of the UK Terrorism Act 2006 criminalises statements likely to be understood as encouraging terrorism. EU Framework Decision 2008/919/JHA specifically deals with the regulation and prohibition of incitement to terrorism. (EU Framework Decision of 28 November 2008 amending Framework Decision 2002/475/JHA on combating terrorism, (2008) OJ L 330).

[90] M Ignatieff, *The Lesser Evil: Political Ethics in an Age of Terror* (Princeton, Princeton University Press, 2004).

[91] Notably, abortion in Poland is prohibited as murder (and Poland issues about a third of all European arrest warrants received in the UK, for example). However, Belgium has now stated that abortion and euthanasia are not to be considered 'murder' for the purposes of the execution of the European arrest warrant: Art 5(4) Belgian Law implementing the European

Secondly, the approach highlighted by Ignatieff is undesirable because, as Günther has asserted,[92] the assumptions on which it rests annul the social contract. According to Immanuel Kant, the fundamental rule of the republican constitution is the impartial reciprocity of law-making, which guarantees the freedom and equality of all citizens. Freedom is identified as 'a warrant to obey no external laws except those to which I have been able to give my consent',[93] and equality as 'that relationship among citizens whereby no-one can put anyone else under a legal obligation without submitting simultaneously to a law which requires that he can be put under a similar obligation by another'.[94] This social contract does not work if I believe that the freedom-restricting law will not affect me (even if, as illustrated by, eg, EU data measures, they do in fact affect everyone).

Yet one need not be a Kantian to see the force of this argument.[95] For laws to be acceptable and function effectively, there must be reciprocity and participation of all in their making, engagement and dialogue of citizens, not mutual suspicion and lack of trust. Fuller, in his account of the rule of law,[96] stressed the reciprocity involved in good law-making, between citizen and law creator. Yet engagement and dialogue has not been greatly in evidence in the twenty-first-century security frenzy. Instead, it has built on a climate of insecurity and created untransparent laws that shore it up, threaten social cohesion and do not increase individual or collective security overall. In such a society, what happens to mutual trust and mutual recognition? Anyone is liable to become a potential suspect.

Beck has referred to an 'existential choice' between the regressive nationalism of surveillance states and the progressive multilateralism of cosmopolitan states. Rather than sacrificing rights, law, democracy and hospitality to the security of the Western citadel, Beck argues that the cosmopolitan state seeks security by means of human rights, international law, democracy and hospitality.[97] Beck's analysis is perhaps overly optimistic. Nevertheless,

---

Arrest Warrant—Loi du 19 December 2003. See *Moniteur Belge* (22 December 2003). Lustration (from Latin lustration—'purification by sacrifice') is used to denote 'purification' of state organisations from their 'sins' under the communist regime, and it is mainly used in the context of public life of post-communist Central and Eastern Europe. It is a policy barring officials and collaborators of a former regime from positions of public influence. Various states have adopted laws relating to lustration in Central and Eastern Europe, some of which were significantly stricter than others, and all of which were adopted in the early to mid-90s. See, eg, *Matyjek v Poland*, judgment of 24 April 2007.

[92] Günther (above n 85).
[93] I Kant, 'Perpetual Peace: A Philosophical Essay' in H Reiss (ed), *Kant: Political Writings* (Cambridge, Cambridge University Press, 1991).
[94] Ibid.
[95] Indeed, later chapters of this book explicitly reject Kant as the basis for a theory of justice.
[96] See Fuller (above n 32).
[97] U Beck, 'The Terrorist Threat: The World Risk Society Revisited' (2002) *Theory, Culture and Society* 43.

it reveals the great gulf between cosmopolitanism and the eclipse of the rule of law in the contemporary frenzy for surveillance, security and austerity.

At the very minimum, institutions of governance should be able to limit and constrain the potential for abuse of power. The situation is particularly critical on a global level, where very often even the minimal kinds of domestic constraints are absent. The new paradigm does not produce justice. Law after modernity produces its own particular types of injustice. What remedies may be proposed? A first step is surely the recognition that responsive, reflexive law, multifarious pluralism and transnationalism are not unalloyed goods. The next step is to examine the concept of justice in greater detail, seeking how it may be delivered, notwithstanding these challenges.

6

Law, Justice and Injustice

Figure 6-1: Angel Boligan, *Maze of Justice* (Cagle Cartoons, El Universal, Mexico City)

Justice is an emotive concept. Its meaning is far from clear, and yet everyone seems to agree that we should strive to eliminate injustice. As Amartya Sen has written:

> Parisians would not have stormed the Bastille, Gandhi would not have challenged the empire on which the sun used not to set, Martin Luther King would not

have fought white supremacy ... without their sense of manifest injustices that could be overcome.[1]

Most of us are not able to storm the Bastille, but we nonetheless may still experience a more generalised, undramatic desire for justice, for some more or less benign order of things to counteract the many injustices and wrongs on this planet. In an era when many people fear that the tragedy of the human condition is that we suffer and die in the midst of a meaningless world, justice holds out a promise of sense, of rendering in life. We also hope that somehow law can play its part in this—can help deliver on that promise and render more determinate some hidden, inchoate order.

Yet far from offering the promise of justice, law in the contemporary era can sometimes resemble the dystopian world of Franz Kafka's novel *The Trial*. In this famous work, Kafka's protagonist, Joseph K, is arrested and detained without ever being informed of the nature of the charges against him, nor of the evidence. It is a terrifying portrayal of a disjointed and nightmarish world in which power is abused, threatening regimes of detention and surveillance abound, and violence is institutionalised. There is no order, no justice, no sense to be made of Joseph K's predicament. Even officials appear not to comprehend the nature of their authority. Law is of labyrinthine complexity, an extremely bleak affair, riddled with surrealism, absurdity and madness, and justice unachievable. Yet this may in reality be the perception of law and justice for many people—that there is no clear rule of law, no rational legal system—and indeed, many critics saw *The Trial* as a commentary on Austrian law and procedure of Kafka's day.[2] Kafka's writings are also especially pertinent for legal theory, given that he was himself a lawyer writing about the law. Given the now regrettably familiar institution of 'indefinite detention', as it has been termed in Guantanamo Bay and in Belmarsh in the United Kingdom, it may be that a Kafkian account still has much to say of law in a world after modernity. It suggests a law that offers anxiety and despair rather than justice.

These next chapters consider the relationship of law to justice. This relationship is by no means straightforward. It is vexed but impossible to ignore. From earliest times, justice has been seen as a standard by which the law can be measured, or even as a quality inherent in law itself. Therefore it has proved as impossible for legal theory as for political theory to bypass the concept of justice. However, in the contemporary epoch, the question of justice has become ever more salient. Law is no longer solely a national product, underpinned by recognised

---

[1] A Sen, *The Idea of Justice* (London, Allen Lane, 2009) vii.

[2] T Zjolkowski, *The Mirror of Justice* (Princeton, Princeton University Press, 1997) 224.

institutional mechanisms for challenge and control, and the question of how law may deliver justice has become even more pressing although it is often strangely overlooked, overshadowed or displaced in the struggle to understand the ever more arcane forms that law is developing through the modalities of pluralism, flexibility and globalisation. In the context of the multiple legal pluralisms and overlapping hierarchies described in previous chapters, how may just outcomes be ensured if traditional mechanisms for control and accountability no longer apply? By what principles is law to be assessed, and those responsible for 'legal' measures to be held accountable? How to attribute motive or agency where injustice is fragmented, systemic and impersonal? Does the overwhelming complexity of the legal world diminish the prospects for justice? In these circumstances, justice becomes a crucial issue for legal theory. Yet it must first be asked: what is justice?

The Confusions of Justice

What is justice? Michael Sandel has answered this question in the following way:

> To ask whether a society is just is to ask how it distributes the things we prize—income and wealth, duties and rights, powers and opportunities, offices and honours. A just society distributes these goods in the right way; it gives each person his or her due. The hard questions begin when we ask what people are due, and why.[3]

Indeed. Interestingly, both Sandel and Sen use the same example to illustrate these 'hard questions'—who should take possession of a flute. Sen tells the story in this way: three children are quarrelling over who should have a flute. Anne claims she should have the flute because she can play it. Bob claims the flute because he is poor and has no toys of his own. Carla has spent many months making the flute and argues that it should be hers as the fruit of her labour. How do we decide between these claims?[4] This question proves very hard to answer.

Justice is part of our moral landscape.[5] According to Michael Walzer, nothing can be omitted, 'no feature of our common life can escape its

---

[3] M Sandel, *Justice: What's the Right Thing to Do?* (London, Allen Lane, 2009).

[4] Sen used this example in his book *The Idea of Justice*, published in the same year, 2009, as Sandel's *Justice*, although the example originates with Aristotle. Sen's answer, which this author shares, is that we may never reach a final ordering of plural values. Sandel has used the example in interviews he has given (eg, with *Prospect* magazine, January 2011), and he follows Aristotle in arguing that the person who can play the flute (ie, the person who possesses the relevant virtues to the greatest extent) should have the flute.

[5] W Sadurski, 'Social Justice and Legal Justice' (1984) 3 *Law and Philosophy* 329.

scrutiny.'[6] Yet Walzer's statement is over-inclusive, for there are good actions unrelated to justice, such as those of courage, truth and generosity; and there also exist morally unattractive ones, such as deceit, which may not always be unjust. Further, a person may be just and yet still be deficient in many other moral virtues. Indeed, justice was traditionally only one of the four cardinal virtues, the others being Prudence, Fortitude and Temperance (often joined by the three theological virtues of Faith, Hope and Charity)—but the notion of justice has survived into the twenty-first century more determinedly than the others.

And yet in the course of its survival into the era after modernity, the concept of justice has undergone some transformations and shifted its shape into something not always recognisable from its earlier manifestations. Its survival has involved some rather paradoxical transformations. For example, the remit of justice is now seen as encompassing the global arena,[7] and yet claims for justice may also demand more particularity, plurality, attention to individual circumstances, than the universalising imperatives of a 'modernist' narrative.[8] Justice has also been interpreted as requiring an awareness of dissymmetry rather than equivalence and equality,[9] and it may be required to take a 'reflexive'[10] rather than constant shape and to be able to work at multiple levels and across types of governance.

Yet there is no novelty in the suggestion that justice is susceptible to many interpretations. Notable accounts have suggested that it takes different forms according to context—Aristotle classified justice as having both a distributive and a corrective dimension;[11] other classifications divide it up as legal or social, substantive or procedural. Walzer has written of different 'spheres' of justice.[12] Demands for and understandings of justice are framed in many ways. Justice may appear subjective, relative and emotive. Indeed, the Scandinavian jurist Alf Ross proclaimed, 'Asking for justice is like banging on the table'; he saw it as no more rational than that. Ross

[6] M Walzer, *Spheres of Justice* (New York, Basic Books, 1983).

[7] See, eg, T Pogge (ed) *Global Justice* (Oxford, Blackwell, 2001); D Held, *Democracy and the Global Order: From the Modern State to Cosmopolitan Governance* (Stanford, Stanford University Press, 1996); and B Barry, *Theories of Justice* (London, Harvester Wheatsheaf, 1989). See also the further discussion of Pogge below.

[8] Eg, P Goodrich, 'Postmodern Justice' in A Sarat et al (eds), *Law and the Humanities* (Cambridge, Cambridge University Press, 2010); and C Douzinas and R Warrington, *Justice Miscarried: Ethics and Aesthetics in Law* (London, Harvester Wheatsheaf, 1994).

[9] Douzinas and Warrington (ibid).

[10] See, eg, N Fraser, *Scales of Justice: Reimagining Political Space in a Globalised World* (New York, Columbia University Press, 2008) 73.

[11] Aristotle, *Nichomachean Ethics*, Book V.

[12] Walzer (above n 6).

therefore dismissed the concept of justice as 'biological-emotional', believing the 'science' of law should abandon it.[13]

So justice is a contested subject, maybe even a utopian ideal. According to Jacques Derrida,[14] justice is unquantifiable; it is 'deconstruction' but—unlike law—is not deconstructible. This means that, for Derrida, justice is a complex of aporia—demanding immediate action yet infinite time, knowledge and wisdom in order to do 'justice'. Indeed, justice may operate as a surrogate for value in a modern 'valueless' world, holding out the promise or hope of what is right. Yet as Costas Douzinas has written, 'As origin or destiny, as nostalgia or prophesy, the presence of justice has been absent, edemic past or future arcadia always still to come. Absent meaningfulness, lacking values, the essence of modern myth.'[15] Gilles Deleuze and Félix Guattari, in their writings about Kafka, presented a similar interpretation. For them, justice represented the desire for what is lacking in our life, what we yearn for in an empty, valueless world: 'Justice is desire and not law.'[16] In this way, justice is rendered ephemeral, extremely subjective, a subject of our fantasies.

Those theorists who believe justice to be a constant, an ideal, unchanging in nature, regardless of the type of law to which it might be applied, face particular problems in the light of the analysis of law given in this book, as well as the challenges of postmodern jurisprudence and postmodern ethics. This is because for many theorists, justice, like law, is pluralist in nature, with no single, unifying concept. Contemporary theorists look to 'otherness' as the basis of a postmodern justice[17] and impose a mandate on law to recognise the 'demand of the suffering other' as 'the non-essential essence which the legal system needs in order to merit its necessary but currently absent claim to do justice'.[18] Such a demand requires us to recognise a plurality of different justices and mandates a new openness of scholarship to other disciplines, to pluralism, to difference.

Peter Goodrich has written:

[Derrida's] acknowledgement of the heteronomy of disciplines and knowledge fits well with the chaos of surfaces, of rhetorical fronts, of facades that Venturi and others had invoked in architecture and that Lyotard had already formulated neatly in stating that 'any attempt to state the law, for example, to place oneself in the

---

[13] A Ross, *On Law and Justice* (Berkeley, University of California Press, 1959) 274. This is an approach also taken by Hans Kelsen.

[14] J Derrida, 'Force of Law: The Mystical Foundation of Authority' in D Cornell et al (eds), *Deconstruction and the Possibility of Justice* (London, Routledge, 1992).

[15] C Douzinas, *Human Rights and Empire: The Political Philosophy of Cosmopolitanism* (London, Routledge Cavendish, 2007) 10 and 286.

[16] G Deleuze and F Guattari, *Kafka: Toward A Minor Literature*, D Polan (trans) (Minneapolis, University of Minnesota Press, 1986) 43.

[17] Douzinas and Warrington (above n 8) 17.

[18] Ibid, 19.

position of enunciator of the universal prescription is obviously infatuation itself and absolute injustice.' Derrida's warning is that to impose a universal principle of justice is to ensure injustice to some. Justice, and in this the postmodern accounts concur, is plurality.[19]

Postmodern accounts of justice, such as those of Derrida or Jean-François Lyotard, which relate it strictly to context, to different 'language games', seem to fit rather well with a multiplicity of laws. Yet such a conclusion is not necessarily a morally attractive one. A plurality of justices might not be only those of the suffering Other. If laws, such as those of the global *lex mercatoria*, may be privately created, then might this also be the case with justice? Should the concept of a private, tailor-made concept of justice be welcomed? Would this commit one to recognition of custom-made justice of large multinationals or private security firms in, for example, Iraq or Afghanistan? The issue of how to assess the justice of pluralistic law is an essential theme which will continue to be explored in the following chapters.

In this chapter, I foreground two issues that I believe are crucial to an understanding of justice and its connection to law in the era after modernity. First, I examine the nature of its relationship to law and the question of whether justice should be seen as an intrinsic and necessary part of the concept of law itself, as natural lawyers have tended to do over the ages, or as an external standard by which to assess law, a position with which positivists, legal realists and sceptics have felt more comfortable. I shall argue that there is scope for a particular *legal* understanding of justice, which will be elaborated in later chapters. Second, I consider the importance of understanding the relationship of law and justice on a global level. I conclude that a cosmopolitan approach, with a focus on human rights, including social rights, may at least provide a start to achieving justice internationally, although a more detailed discussion of human rights and cosmopolitanism is left for subsequent chapters. While a focus on justice in contexts beyond the state might seem to multiply an already well-populated field of candidate conceptions for justice, it is argued that if we are to take justice seriously, we cannot ignore its international dimensions, for it is in those contexts that some of today's most serious injustices occur. However, pervading the discussion in this chapter is also a reluctance to develop an idealist notion of justice. The conclusion will be rather that it is the fight against injustice that is crucial, and law can play its part in this endeavour.

---

[19] Goodrich (above n 8) 204, citing JF Lyotard and JL Thébaud, *Just Gaming* (Manchester, Manchester University Press, 1985) 99.

The Proximity of Justice to Law

Law and justice have a very close relationship, a special affinity. It is not by accident that judges take the title of 'justice', that government departments are named ministries of 'justice', that the frieze of the US Supreme Court contains the inscription 'Equal Justice under the Law'—regardless of whether any of these institutions or persons actually are just. People turn to law because they feel some sense of injustice, which they hope law will address. Law presents itself as a form of governance that is distinct from power and from personal rule, as an institution that can make legitimate demands on citizens, and it holds out the prospect of justice. As John Rawls most famously wrote, 'Justice is the first virtue of social institutions.'[20] This suggests the role of justice as an element in public life, unlike those now less popular virtues of Prudence or Fortitude or Temperance, which appear more private and individual in focus. Rawls' statement reminds us of the importance of justice to government and society, of its role in structuring institutions and as a yardstick of social co-operation (although this does not mean that justice should not also have other, less public locations, such as the family, the church or the workplace) and of its particularly close connection with law.

Leslie Green has described law as 'justice apt'.[21] Law may not be the only concept to be 'justice apt', but legal systems appear apt for appraisal as just or unjust in the way that other practices, such as rock-climbing, needlework or cookery are not.[22] Law may not always be just, but it is always possible and indeed often necessary to ask if it is actually just. Justice is seen as a peculiarly legal virtue. It plays its part in what Talcott Parsons referred to as 'the Hobbesian problem of order'—namely, that law is perceived as a preferable solution to organising society than private vengeance.[23] Justice also implies some sort of agency or human direction,[24] as something that may be organised, delivered or institutionalised. Injustice is not the same as misfortune, which is the result of nature or chance rather than human agency, nor is it to be equated with fate.

---

[20] J Rawls, *A Theory of Justice* (Cambridge, MA, Harvard University Press, 1971) 3.

[21] L Green, 'Positivism and the Inseparability of Law and Morals' (2008) 83 *New York University Law Review* 1035.

[22] I do not use Green's example of the composition of fugues here, as it is possible to argue that works of art such as great paintings or musical compositions have an ability to evoke our feeling for justice. Elaine Scarry, for example, in *On Beauty and Being Just* (Princeton, Princeton University Press, 2001) has argued that beauty, including the beauty to be found in great artistic achievements, continually renews our search for truth and presses us toward a greater concern for justice.

[23] Douzinas and Warrington (above n 8) 137.

[24] Unless one believes in the concept of 'divine' justice.

The Critique of Bureaucratised, Instrumental Justice

However, there is a need for caution, as the association of justice with law and public life has brought criticism. Certain types of jurisprudence characterise justice as a concept too often ensnared or implicated by Western male rationality, an emblem of the political arena and of work life, distant from the home, the family and an ethics of care.[25] Indeed, Aristotle wrote, 'When men have friends, they have no need of justice',[26] suggesting that justice has no place in the world of friendship or familial attachments. Even if the iconography of justice is very often feminine—whether of a blindfold female form or one armed with sword and scales—for most of history, women have been excluded from the legal profession and from the provision of justice.

The modern conception of bureaucratised, organised justice, which is closely linked to Max Weber's 'legal rationality', or the 'administration of justice', has been criticised for producing a 'social pathology', ie, a negative, institutional effect on individual lives.[27] Jürgen Habermas has interpreted this pathology as the colonisation of 'lifeworlds' by economic and bureaucratic systems throughout society.[28] Lifeworlds are those aspects of our lives that comprise family, friendship, religious association and so on. A primary example of this colonisation process is 'juridification', namely a hardening of relationships into legal categories. Justice, for Habermas, is embedded in a communicative process, which depends on a shared sense of what we believe to be right, stemming from our values, beliefs and practices. However, Habermas suggests that in the course of modernity, justice has become 'colonised' by abstract principles of formal law—principles that do not appear in our lifeworlds. In other words, 'modern' thought, including reasoning about justice, engages in an instrumental reasoning that is focused on means rather than ends, leading to the exploitation and colonisation of lifeworlds by instrumental values. In this way, justice has become instrumentalised, and in modernity, law and justice became de-coupled from a common sense (lifeworld) conception of what is believed to be just, fair and right. Justice has instead become juridification, and law as juridification has become a system that colonises the lifeworld.[29]

Earlier, pre-modern generations lacked the modern sense of justice as that of rational, bureaucratic decision-making and were more disposed

---

[25] See, eg, C Gilligan, *In a Different Voice* (Cambridge, MA, Harvard University Press, 1982).

[26] Aristotle, *Nichomachean Ethics*, Book VIIII 1:1155.

[27] Eg, A Honneth, *Leiden und Unbestimmtheit* (Stuttgart, Reclam, 2001).

[28] J Habermas, *Knowledge and Human Interests* (1968) (Cambridge, Polity Press, 1987); and J Habermas, *The Theory of Communicative Action: Reason and the Rationalization of Society*, vol 1, T McCarthy (trans) (Boston, Beacon Press, 1984).

[29] Habermas, *The Theory of Communicative Action* (ibid).

to conceive of justice in personal terms. As Douglas Hay has suggested, 'When authority is embodied in a direct personal relationship, men will often accept power, even enormously despotic power, when it comes from a "good king".'[30] This direct, personal sense of justice was lost in later modernity. However, much contemporary scholarship now rejects the association of justice with an official, formal rationality, stressing instead that justice is not and should not be restricted to the public sphere but can play a role in social spheres such as family and church, as well as courtrooms, Abu Ghraib and Guantánamo—in short 'wherever ... the plurality of subjects shows the unique and demanding face of the other'.[31] People are most likely to experience domination and injustice in the places where they spend their daily lives in the presence of more powerful others—families, schools, workplaces, shops, government departments and community organisations. A contemporary concept of justice should be capable of addressing these.

Some recent reconsidering of the concept of justice has fastened on the notion of 'restorative' justice, which is often discussed in tandem with the concepts of responsive and reflexive law, as a fitting complement to them. It is a process that aims to involve 'stakeholders' in injustice, gathering them together in 'conferences' collectively to resolve their grievances and deal with their implications for the future.[32] It is supposedly liberating and democratic, in that it aspires to put power in the hands of the people and aims to avoid potentially oppressive state structures such as prisons and courts by using more informal means of resolution.

Restorative justice has been employed in a wide range of matters, from criminal conduct to family welfare, disputes in school and the workplace, and increasingly in broader political conflicts, such as in the post-apartheid South African Truth and Reconciliation Commission and post-sectarian Northern Ireland. It has proved more popular in some jurisdictions than in others.[33] It is seen as attractive because it takes a deliberative form and draws some of its conceptual foundations from civic republicanism, in both its focus on deliberation and in promoting the perceived virtue of the active responsibility of wrongdoers. It also centres on empowerment and

---

[30] D Hay, 'Property, Authority and the Criminal law' in D Hay, P Linebaugh, JG Rule, FP Thompson and C Winslow (eds), *Albion's Fatal Tree: Crime and Society in Eighteenth-Century England* (New York, Pantheon Books, 1975) 39.

[31] Goodrich (above n 8) 205. This was also the case for Derrida, who believed that justice exceeds the bounds of law and the state to crucially involve our conduct with strangers. J Derrida, *On Cosmopolitanism and Forgiveness* (New York, Taylor and Francis, 2003).

[32] See, eg, J Braithwaite, *Restorative Justice and Responsive Regulation* (Oxford, Oxford University Press, 2002); and T Marshall, 'The Evolution of Restorative Justice in Britain' (1996) *European Journal of Criminal Policy and Research* 21.

[33] For example, New Zealand has a mandatory restorative justice programme in the case of juvenile crimes, whereas it is less likely to be available in the US, where it tends to operate at the margins of the criminal justice system.

non-domination—by giving people a forum in which to tell their stories and giving all stakeholders an opportunity to speak. Thus, responsibility is shifted from something imposed by the state to something that citizens autonomously take on themselves. Its focus is on justice in setting things right, justice in the healing process, rather than injustice in causing harm.

It is sometimes suggested that restorative justice involves an ethic of 'care' or a 'feminine' response compared to a 'justice' or masculine response, a distinction highlighted by Carol Gilligan in her book *In a Different Voice*, because it delivers a form of justice that is more personalised in nature and based on a concrete morality. Yet in some ways, it is more demanding as a concept of justice because it requires taking active responsibility. It is also suggested that it has more in common with premodern and indigenous justice practices rather than with the modern Western practice of justice.[34] In any case, it does seem to be a fragmented or hybrid justice form, with a mix of Western, bureaucratic justice and more informal methods—and it may therefore seem appropriate as a counterpart or partner to responsive and reflexive regulation.

Therefore, to summarise so far: the challenge is to avoid an overly bureaucratic, oppressive, instrumentalising conception of justice, while recognising that justice plays an especially important role in public life and within law in particular, necessitating some sort of general, perhaps even official, role for it, yet not ignoring all the other dimensions in which it also plays a part.

Intrinsic Connections: 'Legal' Justice?

One of the most salient questions of legal philosophy—or perhaps the most salient—focuses on the relationship between law and justice. Natural law is traditionally interpreted as making the claim that 'an unjust law is not law'. According to Cicero, 'Inherent in the very name of law is the sense and idea of choosing what is just and right',[35] suggesting justice as an intrinsic feature of law. The long pedigree of the natural law tradition holds that there exists a *necessary* connection between law and justice. Other accounts also see law and justice as necessarily linked: Aristotle isolated a specific

---

[34] J Consedine, *Restorative Justice: Healing the Effects of Crime* (Lyttelton, NZ, Ploughshare Publications, 1995).
[35] Cicero, *De Legibus I*, N Rudd and T Weidemann (eds) (Bristol, Bristol Classical Press, 1987).

concept of 'legal justice',[36] which is distinct from other aspects of justice, such as distributive and retributive justice.

Yet law and justice may be linked without the positing of an intrinsic connection. The concept of justice may be seen as external to law, as a measure by which law may be assessed as a standard, an ideal to which law should aspire. One may locate such a view in the Christian tradition, wherein justice is seen as realisable not within the City of Man but in the City of God.[37] Christianity proffers an eschatological perspective, with a promise of divine law, of justice in a world yet to come, in contrast to the inadequate, unjust existing one. Yet the distancing or 'diremption' of law from justice is by no means limited to a Christian, dualist perspective. It has been highlighted as a feature of the modern and postmodern eras by theorists who view justice as an ideal contrasted to the nihilism of law.[38]

Indeed, if law is simply associated and identified with the wielding of power, as asserted by, for example, Nietzscheans, Foucauldians and postmodern theorists, then injustice may in fact be seen as its inevitable consequence. Yet one need not be a postmodern pessimist to interpret justice as extrinsic to law. John Austin famously claimed that the existence of law was one thing, and its merit or demerit another—a succinct illustration of the legal positivist's insistence on the separation of law and morality.[39] Mainstream currents in late nineteenth- and early to mid-twentieth-century jurisprudence—legal positivism, formalism and legal realism—continued with this belief that neither morality nor justice could be a necessary part of law, thus leaving very little space for a legal concept of justice, other than in the most formal sense of treating like cases alike. Hans Kelsen even went so far as to reject the usefulness of justice as an external standard by which to appraise law (as he found justice to be too compromised by subjective standards).[40] One might, however, turn the legal positivists' argument on its head. It can be asserted that law is so powerful, with its abilities to coerce, punish, imprison, detain, confiscate and survey—it has such great reserves of force, and it claims the right to use this force—and so, therefore, it is crucial that law's actions should be guided by justice. Justice, seen in this way, is necessary to set a limit on law's power and to make it accountable.

---

[36] Aristotle, *Ethics*, JAK Thomson (trans) (London, Penguin, 1976) 198–200 [1137a32–1138a3].

[37] St Augustine, *The City of God* (London, Penguin classics, 2003).

[38] See, eg, Douzinas and Warrington (above n 8); and G Rose, *Mourning Becomes the Law* (Cambridge, Cambridge University Press, 1996).

[39] J Austin, *The Province of Jurisprudence Determined*, original edn 1832 (Cambridge, Cambridge University Press, 1995).

[40] H Kelsen, *The Pure Theory of Law*, M Knight (trans) (Clark, NJ, Law Book Exchange, 2005) 49 and 66–67.

Yet according to such positivist theories, how may law deliver justice? The problem of grounding law's authority and legitimacy has already been revealed in earlier chapters as a problem for positivism. If law's authority is perceived to lie neither with God nor with natural law, nor even with substantive customary standards limiting the discretion of judges, but rather with a formalism or rational legality, how may law claim authority or legitimacy or, *a fortiori*, deliver on its promise to do justice? The answer seems to be that law cannot do so in any clearly identifiable way. In the modern and postmodern eras, it has been suggested that we engage with the concept of democracy, of 'the sovereignty of the people', as the best candidate for the legitimacy and foundation of law, but relatively few theorists seek to make an explicit link between law's justice and democracy—although a notable theorist who has made this connection is Habermas.[41]

To raise the crucial connection between law and justice is also to allude to the ambiguity—is justice essential and intrinsic to law, or an external measure by which we assess law? Or perhaps it can be both, depending on how we understand justice? This vexed relationship between law and justice involves the issue of what Lon Fuller termed 'the law in quest of itself'.[42] Philip Selznick captured the complexity of the situation in this way:

> It is important to preserve the distinction between law as an operative system and justice as a moral ideal. But clear distinctions are compatible with—indeed they are important preconditions of—theories that trace connections and reveal dynamics. Law is not necessarily just, but it does promise justice. We must look to the theory of law and justice to understand why that promise exists and under what conditions it may be fulfilled or abridged.[43]

This, I believe, is the best way to conceptualise the relationship between law and justice, and one that I will work with in these chapters: *law is not necessarily just, but it does promise justice.*

There are many diverse and hidden dynamics in the rich relationship between law and justice. They do not give rise to one dominant conception of justice, nor one way in which the law can realise justice. However,

---

[41] And indeed such a link is particularly hard to make at a supra-national level, where there are few democratic institutions—a criticism that has been made of the EU on many occasions. But theorists who have made a link between transnational justice and democracy include: R Forst, 'Transnational Justice and Democracy', RECON Working Paper 2011/12, Oslo (2011); J Neyer, 'Justice, Not Democracy: Legitimacy in the EU' (2010) 48 *Journal of Common Market Studies* 903; P van Parijs, *Just Democracy: The Rawls–Machiavelli Programme* (Colchester, ECPR Press, 2011); and Sen, *The Idea of Justice* (above n 1).

[42] L Fuller, *The Law in Quest of Itself* (Boston, Beacon Press, 1999 reprint).

[43] P Selznick, *The Moral Commonwealth: Social Theory and the Promise of Community* (Berkeley, University of California Press, 1994) 443–44.

in subsequent chapters, I shall argue for a particular, legal, sense of justice—which I shall term 'critical legal justice', a more critical, nuanced application of the rule of law. Yet bearing in mind the ambiguity of the relationship of justice to law—extrinsic or intrinsic—I shall also argue that we look for justice beyond the law, partly in idealising the concept of human rights (and indeed the 'juridification' of human rights is not always satisfactory) and also by foregrounding our sharp awareness of *injustice*.

Can Justice Ever Be Transnational?

The second major issue I wish to foreground in this chapter is whether justice can operate beyond the confines of states or small communities. As Nancy Fraser has suggested, the metaphor of the 'scales of justice' evokes two images.[44] The first is the overly familiar image of the figure of impartial justice balancing conflicting claims. The second is that of the mapmaker whose scales are used to represent location, to plot spatial relationships.[45] Applied in this way to the concept of justice, this image raises the questions of where the boundaries of justice lie and on what scale should we be examining justice. In a post-Westphalian world, should we still look to state boundaries as delimiting the range of justice, or beyond, to a global dimension? Rather than balance, this metaphor evokes the activity of framing.

Rawls' theory of justice is perhaps the most prominent theory of justice in twentieth-century Western political philosophy. According to Rawls, one important principle of justice is that inequality will be permissible only if such unequal arrangements are for the benefit of the worst-off in society. This approach focuses on a distributive role for justice, the fact that we see justice as playing a crucial role in the distribution of societal 'goods'.[46] However, notably, the starkest inequalities today are illustrated by *global* comparisons. Previous chapters have illustrated the global nature of law—indeed, this book aims to highlight this increasing transnationalism and internationalism as a crucial element of law after modernity. Therefore, if law is becoming transnational, then surely the concept of justice should do so as well?

Clearly global *injustice* exists. For example, it is common knowledge that the richest one per cent of adults on the planet currently own about 40 per cent of global assets, and the richest 10 per cent of adults accounts for 85 per cent of the world's total wealth. In contrast, the bottom half of the world

---

[44] Fraser, *Scales of Justice* (above n 10).

[45] See also the discussion of this work on the 'mapping' and various scales of law, above ch 4.

[46] Although, as will be considered later, Rawls did not believe in the possibility of a 'global' distribution of resources.

adult population owns barely one per cent of global wealth.[47] More than 200 million people live in countries with an average life expectancy of less than 45 years. The average life expectancy at birth in 2008 was 49.2 years in the world's 48 poorest countries, compared to 78.8 for OECD nations.[48] According to UNICEF, 25,000 children die each day due to poverty. And they 'die quietly in some of the poorest villages on earth, far removed from the scrutiny and the conscience of the world. Being meek and weak in life makes these dying multitudes even more invisible in death.'[49] 1.4 million die each year from lack of access to safe drinking water and adequate sanitation.[50] And such life expectancy and inequality gaps are actually increasing. Figure 6-2, a map of child mortality, suggests how questions of justice may be 'reframed' to reveal their shocking proportions.

These statistics are sobering, evidence of such outrageous inequalities between rich and poor as to suggest not just misfortune of the worst-off but the *existence of injustice*. Such inequalities between the developed and developing world—more extreme even than the inequalities of Victorian England as presented by Charles Dickens—are of a magnitude not existing

Figure 6-2: The 'scale' of justice? A map of child mortality rates according to Worldmapper (http://www.worldmapper.org/), a website that re-sizes territories based on particular variables

[47] World Institute for Development Economics Research of the United Nations University (UNU-WIDER), 5 December 2006.
[48] WHO Commission on Social Determinants of Health, 'Closing the Gap in a Generation: Health Equity through Action on the Social Determinants of Health', Final Report (2008). See also T Honderich, *Violence for Equality: Inquiries in Political Philosophy* (London, Routledge, 1989).
[49] UNICEF, *The Progress of Nations 2000*, accessible at http://www.unicef.org/pon00/immu1.htm.
[50] United Nations Development Programme, *2007 Human Development Report* (HDR), 27 November 2007, 25.

within developed Western societies in recent times (although this is not to deny that inequality clearly exists within the developed world as well[51]). As Derrida has written,

> Never have violence, inequality, exclusion, famine, and thus economic oppression affected as many human beings in the history of the earth and humanity. Instead of singing the advent of the ideal of liberal democracy and of the capitalist market in the euphoria of the end of history ... let us never forget this macroscopic fact, made up of innumerable singular sites of suffering: no degree of progress allows one to ignore that never before, in absolute figures, have so many men, women and children been subjugated, starved or exterminated.[52]

A work that parallels Derrida's admonition in its bleakness is by the Danish sculptor Jens Galschiøt, entitled 'The Silent Death' (Figure 6-3). This work was one of many exhibited during the United Nations social summit in Copenhagen in 1995. 750 figures of children, made up of cloth and stuffed with gravel, were attached to benches, lampposts and buildings all over the city. The figures symbolised the 35,000 children who die every day on account of hunger and lack of medicine, primarily in the world's

Figure 6-3: Jens Galschiøt, *The Silent Death* (1995), courtesy of http://www.aidoh. dk (accessed 4 January 2013)

[51] See, eg, *Strategic Review of Health Inequalities in England Post-2010* (The Marmot Review), 11 February 2010.
[52] J Derrida, *Spectres of Marx* (London, Routledge, 1994) 85. See also A Sen, 'What Should Keep Us Awake at Night', address to the Indian Parliament (2008), abridged version published in (2009) 8 *Little Magazine*.

poorest countries. Additionally 13,000,000 certificates, one for each child that would die in 1995, were distributed.

These sober images—the map of child mortality and 'The Silent Death'—are displayed here to raise these issues of justice in their starkest and most shocking form—to confront us, as Galschiøt intended, with our own involvement in world poverty and injustice. It is not merely unfortunate or regrettable that such a small percentage of the world's population should enjoy so much of its wealth and the rest so little. Nor is it attributable only to an 'act of God', the product of unforeseeable and unavoidable natural acts. It is also unjust. There are issues of distribution, capability, responsibility and action here which can be translated into justice, although translating them into duties owed by specific states, persons or entities proves harder.[53]

Exploitative economic structures often underpin these sites of injustice. The poor, who make up these 'innumerable singular sites of suffering', are most of the time unable to challenge the forces responsible for their oppression—for within their own, often powerless or failing, states they are unlikely to find redress against oppressors or exploiters who occupy out-of-state, offshore areas of control, out of reach of justice. These oppressors include transnational enterprises, currency speculators, investors, more powerful states, national autocrats, as well as global 'governance' structures, all of which have participated in abusive practices but very often enjoy immunities from democratic control or accountability.[54] In such situations, globalisation wreaks injustice yet fails to provide corresponding justice mechanisms, and state institutions prove inadequate to the task. Global terror looms, almost as a symptom, if not an effect, of this state of affairs. A solution is needed on a different scale from that of the state but does not yet exist in any effective form. Fraser has referred to this as a problem of 'misframing', for she sees the question of the frame as itself a question of justice. Focused on 'the issues of who counts as a subject of justice, and what is the appropriate frame, the politics of framing comprises efforts to establish and consolidate, to contest and revise, the authoritative division of political space'.[55] The map of child mortality depicted by Figure 6-2 is a stark illustration of how these questions of justice may be 'reframed' to reveal their truly shocking dimensions—a different scale of justice.

Yet it is often suggested that it is problematic if not impossible to develop a global or transnational concept of justice. This raises two issues. First, is a global concept of justice impossible or incoherent?

---

[53] For such an attempt, see, eg, P Singer, *The Life You Can Save* (New York, Random House, 2010); and the work of Thomas Pogge, which is discussed below in the next section.

[54] These issues are also discussed in greater detail later in later chapters.

[55] Fraser (above n 10) 22.

And second, even if such a concept is feasible, is a global conception of justice in fact necessary to redress the global nature of injustice, or will localised or particular concepts of justice suffice? And further, what is the role of law in this, given the plurality of law and legislative systems at global level?

A Global Conception of Justice?

There are many theorists who believe that justice is only capable of having a local form or expression—that justice can function only within the nation state or smaller community, not across boundaries. Traditionally, during the Westphalian period, following Hobbesian theory, while states were perceived as arenas pacified by the civil social contract, the international sphere was regarded as still remaining a state of nature—although even within that framework, international law also operated to an extent.

Rawls, in his late career work *The Law of Peoples*,[56] denied the applicability in a global context of the twofold principles of justice that he articulated in his earlier *Theory of Justice* (namely, of equal access to basic liberties and, secondly, of the 'difference principle', which ensures that unequal social distributions are only permissible if they benefit the worst-off in society). Instead, he came to prefer something more like the principles of existing international law. Rawls believed his theory of justice to be inapplicable to the international arena, considering that, due to a lack of anything like an 'international society', justice could only be *interstatal* and not trans- or supra-national. He also confined justice between states to his first principle of justice, namely a matter of certain 'negative liberties', as opposed to any redistributional concept of justice, so limiting it to a right of states to self-determination that mirrors those rights of persons in his 'Original Position' to basic liberties.

So Rawls' theory, which, let us not forget, is the theory that many believe to be the greatest theory of justice of the twentieth century[57]—or indeed, of modern political philosophy—relies on traditional (or even outdated) international law principles and appears to lack the means of addressing the grossest injustices in the world today—namely, radical injustice at international level. Other philosophers such as Thomas Nagel have shared this

[56] J Rawls, *The Law of Peoples* (Cambridge, MA, Harvard University Press, 1999). See also Thomas Nagel, who also dismisses the idea of global justice on the basis that global government is not yet possible. T Nagel, 'The Problem of Global Justice' (2005) 33 *Philosophy and Public Affairs* 115.

[57] See Sen, who in *The Idea of Justice*, referred to reading the first drafts of Rawls' *Theory of Justice* as a young academic: 'Bliss was it that dawn to be alive.' Sen, *The Idea of Justice* (above n 1) 53. However, Sen is now more critical of Rawls' approach. See the discussion later in this chapter.

view, although Nagel's view derives from a somewhat different argument that justice depends on the coordinated conduct of large numbers of people that must be backed up by a centralised monopoly of force.[58] Even Sandel, who is perhaps the best-known contemporary theoretician of justice and is familiar from his engaging and accessible courses, televised debates and books on justice, seems reluctant to embrace a global concept of justice, focusing as he does on the production of justice as a creation of particular communities, working together to realise a communal concept of virtue, the 'common good', through a 'more robust public engagement with our moral disagreements'.[59] Such a shared sense of 'the common good' seems to require a community sufficiently closely bonded together to share a common teleological sense, rather than a desire to look beyond boundaries to more pluralistic reasoning about justice.

Theories such as those of Rawls and Nagel suggest that the lack of a shared identity or common demos with true cross-national bonds of solidarity and meaningful ties[60] raises real problems, particularly with regard to the level of mutual co-operation and engagement with others that seems necessary for social justice of a redistributive sort. There currently exists no deeply rooted supra-national community based on a substantive value consensus. Even the most developed supra-national community, the European Union, lacks a sense of mutual political belonging and solidarity, as the tortuous wranglings and failures to deal with the Eurozone crisis have demonstrated.[61]

However, a further concern is that a concept of global justice, even if it were possible, would conflict with other values, such as freedom or democratic self-government of peoples. Moreover, would a globalised conception of justice lead to a super-state, a world-governing Leviathan—an entity described by Kant as a 'soulless despotism' and a 'graveyard of freedom'?[62]

---

[58] See Nagel (above n 56), in which Nagel prefers to look to other standards such as 'minimal humanitarian morality'.

[59] Sandel (above n 3) 268.

[60] See, eg, R Bellamy, 'The Liberty of the Postmoderns? Market and Civic Freedom within the EU?' LSE Working Paper, 2009.

[61] On the lack of solidarity in the EU, particularly in the case of the Eurozone, see, for example, S Douglas-Scott, 'The Problem of Justice in the EU' in J Dickson and P Eleftheriadis (eds), *Philosophical Foundations of EU Law* (Oxford, Oxford University Press, 2012); and S Douglas-Scott, 'Rethinking Justice in the EU' in M Poiares Maduro and K Tuori (eds), *Rethinking EU Law* (Cambridge, Cambridge University Press, 2012). See also J Habermas, *The Divided West* (Cambridge, Polity Press, 2006), in which Habermas acknowledges the current lack of a shared demos within the EU, although he asserts the possibility of a future stronger EU identity grounded on a community of civic values rather than ethnic ties.

[62] I Kant, 'Perpetual Peace: A Philosophical Sketch' in HS Reiss (ed), *Kant: Political Writings* (Cambridge, Cambridge University Press, 1991) First Supplement.

Transnational Criminal Justice

So far, this discussion on the possibility of a global concept of justice has generally been concerned with distributive issues—of inequality of wealth and of poverty—which provide the focus for most contemporary theories of global justice. Accounts such as those of Rawls are distributive, yet justice in the global arena is not restricted to questions of distribution of wealth and social justice. Claims for redistribution have been supplemented by those for recognition—of identity, nationality, environmental rights and wrongs—which may also invoke a dimension of justice.

There are also, however, pressing issues of what Aristotle termed 'corrective' justice, which is concerned with restoring a balance that has been disturbed. Indeed, for most of its history, the philosophical literature has focused on corrective rather than distributive justice. Corrective justice is highly relevant in the field of criminal law.

Notably, crime has a decidedly global character in the twenty-first century. Since the end of the Second World War, 'crimes against humanity' have been perceived to be global in nature, and actions such as torture have now given rise to the universal jurisdiction of states to prosecute.[63] Furthermore, terrorists and organised crime gangs cross boundaries very easily (more easily than police forces), and this cross-boundary nature of crime, especially terrorism, makes cross-border solutions essential. Issues of transnational crime pose some of the most salient questions of justice today. In these circumstances, insistence on the nation state as the locus of criminal justice relies too heavily on other notions such as Weber's positivist concept of the state as having the monopoly of force. Twenty-first century international organisations such as the European Union are possessed of a wide range of institutions and bodies with powers that are not state-based. In the specific context of EU criminal law, some jurists point to a developing or even already existing 'harmonious convergence' in this area,[64] as evidenced by measures such as the EU-wide definition of terrorism.[65] Therefore, a shared conception of at least some aspects of criminal justice operates across state boundaries.

---

[63] See, for example, the UN Convention against Torture and Other Cruel, Inhuman or Degrading Treatment or Punishment (1984).

[64] M Delmas-Marty, one of the expert proponents of the *Corpus Juris* project (which aimed at unifying the rules of criminal law and procedure of the European Union Member States to combat fraud against EU financial interests), has asserted such a convergence, stating, 'It is beyond question that everywhere in Europe the criminal process has ceased to function within a closed circuit ... detaching itself from the artificial in order to approach the living, the machinery of criminal justice could move toward a greater functioning of the whole' and, at the same time, a 'lesser functioning of its constituent parts.' She terms this 'a new design of the legal landscape'. M Delmas-Marty, *Pour un droit commun* (Paris, Seuil, 1994).

[65] Council Framework Decision 2002/475/JHA of 13 June 2002 on combating terrorism.

Yet the difficulties of a transnational justice are just as salient in the criminal law field as in the search for a global distributive justice. Criminal justice is perceived as a matter that identifies the state. Criminal laws and procedures are cultural artefacts that reflect a wide, deep, embedded background, as much if not perhaps more than other types of laws, perhaps because they most directly involve the imposition of state force on individuals.[66] Jurists have been sceptical of the possibility of harmonising criminal law and justice provisions.[67] Pierre Legrand, for example, has taken a view directly opposed to 'harmonious convergence', perceiving a fundamental distinction between civil and common law systems.[68] He sees the two systems as having distinct *mentalités* which share no universal rationality or morality. At a functional level (that of rules), he allows that there may be similarities, but this is only the surface level of the legal system. We have to look beyond that to a regime's substructures, or its *epistèmes* (to use Foucaultian language). At this level, asserts Legrand, there is no clear evidence of convergence. This is because of different background theories or mindsets. In turn, different legal and political cultures give rise to different expressions of criminal justice, such as different provisions on jury trial, treatment of witnesses and rules of evidence. For example, the common law is inductive and empirical and resistant to axiomatisation. To attempt legal convergence results in what Gunther Teubner has called legal transplants as 'irritants'[69]—or an interference like that on the TV screen when

---

[66] It should be noted that although some convergence of accusatorial and inquisitorial systems took place as early as the eighteenth century, with continental systems responding to Enlightenment philosophy and the French Revolution, there has not been a great deal of convergence within, eg, the EU. There still exists mutual criticism—eg, of the common law's use of plea bargaining and the greater resources of its prosecutors—by continental systems, as well as criticisms of retention of the *Juge d'instruction* on the continent by Anglo-Saxons. The reconciling of different legal cultures, such as the combination of the accusatorial and inquisitorial, can be extremely problematic. For example, the London Charter was agreed after the Second World War to provide for the constitution and procedures of the Nuremberg trials. It specifically set up an international code of criminal procedure, which tried to bridge the gap between US/UK procedure and those of France and the Soviet Union. Aspects of the inquisitorial remained. But by today's standards the protections of the London Charter were minimal. There was no right to silence, nor the right to appeal, and contemporaries castigated the trials as unfair because of this uneasy compromise. More recently, the first defendant to appear before the ICTY challenged the limits on the defence's ability to cross-examine prosecution witnesses. There was a problem resulting from the struggle of the parties and judges to adapt a mix of doctrines to a hybrid situation.

[67] See, eg, P Legrand, 'The Impossibility of Legal Transplants' (1997) 4 *Maastricht Journal of European and Comparative Law*; G Teubner, 'Legal Irritants: Good Faith in British Law, or How Unifying Law Ends Up in New Differences' in F Snyder (ed), *The Europeanisation of Law: The Legal Effects of European Integration* (Oxford, Hart Publishing, 2000); and C Harlow, 'Voices of Difference in a Plural Community' in P Beaumont, C Lyons and N Walker (eds), *Convergence and Divergence in European Public Law* (Oxford, Hart Publishing, 2002).

[68] Legrand (ibid).

[69] Teubner (above n 67).

the picture is blocked. So the globalisation of criminal or corrective justice proves no easier to facilitate or theorise than does distributive justice.

Pluralism and Pessimism

A further point must also be borne in mind. Objections to the notion of global justice derive not only from those with statist or communitarian views. According to Fraser, justice is a complex concept, which must be contemplated in three, or even manifold dimensions.[70] On this account, a unitary global concept of justice, even if theoretically or practically possible, is inadequate—as a global concept denies to justice a multiplicity of perspectives, localities and frames.

A most anti-universalist, postmodern account such as Lyotard's asserts the pluralism of distinct and incompatible language games. Different concepts of justice are perceived as incommensurable, rather like a host of computer programmes that will not speak to each other. Lyotard's account rejects both the possibility and desirability of a global concept of justice. Fraser characterises this situation of incommensurability of different visions of justice as one of 'abnormal justice'—in which current theories of justice

Figure 6-4: Htein Lin, *Scale of Justice* (with the artist contemplating the scales of justice) (2010): a multiplicity of different claims? This work draws on the Myanmar artist's experience as a legal practitioner and also on the time he served as a political prisoner accused of planning opposition activities. Courtesy of Htein Lin

[70] See Nancy Fraser, who writes of a 'three dimensional theory of justice'. Fraser (above n 10) 16.

lack shared understandings and assumptions regarding the scope, agents, subjects and spaces of justice, and thus debates about justice have, as she puts it, a 'freewheeling character'.[71] Disputes over these very basic premises of justice are illustrated by, for example, the furore and misunderstanding over the Danish cartoons of the prophet Mohammed. Should this episode be interpreted as blindness to a clash of civilisations or as an exercise of liberal public reason? And yet the situation demands resolution.

One might ask, perhaps with a postmodern twist, how may we do justice to justice? Or as Goodrich has written, 'What then would it be for postmodern justice to be rendered, to be done?' Goodrich's own answer is sobering:

> The answer to that question, of course, is that there is no answer. Justice is an aporia, a suspension of judgement, the bold acknowledgement of an instance of uncertainty ... [P]ostmodern justice is an instance of law's entry into the multiplicity of language games, into the chaos of actually living institutions.[72]

Is this a conclusion that contemporary legal theory is bound to accept?

Such are the circumstances and quandaries of injustice in the era of law after modernity, which indeed may seem so perplexing as to require what the writer Joan Didion (in the course of a terrible year in which both her husband and daughter died) described as 'magical thinking'.[73] In other words, justice after modernity may require the irrational belief that one can bring about a circumstance or event by thinking about it or wishing for it—for how else are these problems to be resolved?

Transnational Justice

But perhaps necessity answers this question for us. Ultimately, global pressures, such as security and terrorist threats or the prospect of environmental disaster, not to mention the pressures imposed by the global financial markets, render solitary action by states acting singly futile—and productive of injustice. For example, issues of European integration, such as market integration and liberalisation at the expense of social justice, or a currency union without a fiscal union, will not be solved by states acting unilaterally. To continue the present pattern is to perpetuate a vicious cycle of

---

[71] Fraser (above n 10) 49. For accounts of 'abnormal' discourse, see, eg, JF Lyotard, *The Differend: Phrases in Dispute* (Minneapolis, University of Minnesota Press, 1988). See also Richard Rorty, who distinguishes 'normal' discourse as conducted 'within an agreed-open set of conventions about what counts as relevant contribution' and 'abnormal', which sets them aside or ignores them. R Rorty, *Philosophy and the Mirror of Nature* (Princeton, Princeton University Press, 1979) 320.
[72] Goodrich (above n 8) 208.
[73] J Didion, *The Year of Magical Thinking* (London, Fourth Estate, 2005).

insecurity and injustice. Greater regional integration and globalisation have given rise not only to a parallel growth in law beyond the state but also to particular injustices, which may be addressed only by the recognition that justice must be sought on a global level, as well as within states. If we are to remedy injustice, it is necessary to find legal solutions beyond the state.

And perhaps we should be aware of the irony of Pascal's comment, 'A funny justice that ends at a river. Truth this side of the Pyrenees. Error on that.'[74] The post-war growth of international law and human rights treaties, as well as the fast growing networks of global governance, serve to undermine state-bounded claims for the realm of justice. Pressing problems that cut across boundaries—such as environmental degradation and pollution, global poverty and terrorism—raise issues of justice that demand regional and global solutions. Indeed, many of the best-known accounts of justice have been avowedly cosmopolitan—eg, stoic cosmopolitanism, natural law or, indeed, even Kant's own account.[75]

These cosmopolitan sentiments have been reflected in the work of a growing number of theorists who disagree with Rawls' and Nagel's rejection of the possibility of a global theory of justice;[76] Unlike Rawls and Nagel, they do not see the lack of a global demos as a barrier. Habermas, for example, has advanced arguments for justice on a regional scale within the European Union (as well as on an international scale).[77] While Habermas has acknowledged that no overarching EU political identity currently exists, he asserts that civic solidarity across borders is possible if certain conditions are fulfilled. For Habermas, the key question is not whether an EU identity exists but whether processes of shared political opinion and will-formation can develop through public discourse, in the way that national identities were constructed in the nineteenth century, and so produce the type of popular support formerly attracted by the state.[78]

Thomas Pogge, World Poverty and Global Distributive Justice

Thomas Pogge is a theorist who has argued for a redistributive understanding of 'global justice' for some time. Notably, Pogge prefers the term 'global

---

[74] B Pascal, *Pensees*, AJ Krailsheimer (trans) (London, Penguin Books, 1966) 294.

[75] Kant (above n 62).

[76] For theories of justice applied to international level, see Pogge (ed), *Global Justice* (above n 7); Held, *Democracy and the Global Order* (above n 7); C Beitz, *Political Theory and International Relations* (Princeton, Princeton University Press, 1979) (looking to a Kantian justification of international justice principles); B Barry, *Theories of Justice* (London, Harvester Wheatsheaf, 1989); and M Nussbaum, 'Patriotism and Cosmopolitanism' in J Cohen (ed), *For Love of Country: Debating the Limits of Patriotism* (Boston, Beacon Press, 1996).

[77] Habermas, *The Divided West* (above n 61) 76.

[78] Ibid.

justice' to that of 'international justice', seeing the term 'international' as denoting an order of states as agents and redolent of a dualist world in which states were seen to possess both an internal sovereignty to manage their own affairs and an external sovereignty to manage their relations with other states. Pogge rejects this model of international relations because he sees it as overly reliant on the interests of governments, whom he does not believe to be the only morally relevant agents in international relations.

Pogge's argument focuses on the undeniable fact that around 2.5 billion humans live in conditions of severe poverty, deprived of basic necessities such as adequate food, safe drinking water, basic sanitation, adequate shelter, literacy and basic health care. One third of all human deaths on earth are from poverty-related causes, amounting to some 18 million annually, including over 10 million children under the age of five. Yet however immense a tragedy this may appear in human terms, the problem of world poverty is a relatively minor *economic* issue and should be resolvable. Pogge argues that an amount as small as that of one per cent of the national incomes of the developed world would be sufficient to end severe poverty worldwide and could be distributed, through the United Nations, to poor countries.[79]

Pogge's own theory is premised on the argument that the design of global and international institutions and the structures of world trade have had a central, causal impact on global poverty.[80] This is because of the nature of rules and practices developed by these international institutions. They operate rules that are shaped by the better-off and imposed on the worse-off in a manner which produces radical inequality and an uncompromising exclusion from natural resources. Further, Pogge believes this situation has emerged from and been caused by a shared and violent history which the developed and developing worlds have in common. So for example, World Trade Organization (WTO) rules have permitted wealthier countries to protect their manufacturers from the impact of cheap imports through the use of quota systems and tariffs. More affluent countries have also contributed to world poverty more indirectly by participating in the structuring of national institutions and policies of poorer countries, thus helping

---

[79] This approximates to an amount roughly equivalent to the direct cost to the taxpayer of bank bailouts during the financial crisis, which has been estimated as a little less than 1% GDP in the US and a little over 1% in the UK. Notably, this assessment in terms of direct costs of the bailout does not take into account the longer term costs of the financial crisis to society, such as those of unemployment and lost output. In 2010, Andrew Haldane, Executive Director for Financial Stability at the Bank of England, suggested that the financial crisis will in the end cost the world economy between US$60 trillion and US$200 trillion in lost GDP. For both of these figures, see A Haldane, 'The $100 Billion Question', available at http://www.bankofengland.co.uk/publications/Documents/speeches/2010/speech433.pdf.

[80] See, eg, T Pogge, *World Poverty and Human Rights*, 2nd edn (New Haven, Yale University Press, 2008).

to foster oppressive and corrupt governments. The cumulative effect of these practices is to impoverish those in poor countries and violate their human rights, and Pogge has argued that 'any institutional order is unjust if it foreseeably produces an avoidable massive human rights deficit.'[81] Yet most citizens in wealthier countries believe that there is nothing wrong in their behaviour.

The point of Pogge's argument is to illustrate the fact that the economic policies of wealthier countries, along with the practices of global economic institutions, have rendered these institutions, and the developed world, causally and morally responsible for the active impoverishment of the poor by economic means. In this way, Pogge can argue that wealthier countries have an actual enforceable *duty* to reduce poverty (to be fulfilled by means of an extra one per cent income tax in high-income countries).

Arguing in this way also enables Pogge to escape one of the more frequent charges made against global, or cosmopolitan,[82] theories of justice— namely that any supposed duty to take into account the interests of those outside of our own nations and communities and to ameliorate the poverty of those in the developing world must falter in the face of the obviously stronger claims of nation, community and family.[83] Pogge's response is that the stringency of most *negative* duties does not vary with compatriotism. I have no better reason not to murder a compatriot than I have not to murder a foreigner,[84] and the relevant negative duty in the case of world poverty is that of not imposing unjust societal institutions—and Pogge argues that this duty applies beyond states, to all human beings. In these circumstances, the radical inequality of world poverty manifests itself as an injustice that we have a duty to resolve.

Pogge's approach also avoids the difficulties of delineating the specific content of a positive duty to aid the poor by asserting the existence of a negative duty not to support unjust institutions. I believe that Pogge's work stands out from the myriad of theorising about justice beyond the state, in its ability to muster arguments that go beyond the idealism of much philosophical thought and instead specify in some detail the content of a global theory. As such, Pogge's work is amenable to the type of non-ideal theorising about justice I advocate later in this chapter.

---

[81] Ibid, 25.

[82] For more on cosmopolitanism and cosmopolitan theories, see below ch 10.

[83] Such arguments are made by, for example, Rawls in *The Law of Peoples* (above n 56), where he rules out the prospect of a global 'difference principle' of redistribution of wealth on this basis. David Miller also argues against this in, eg, D Miller, 'The Limits of Cosmopolitan Justice' in DR Mapel and T Nardin (eds), *International Society: Diverse Ethical Perspectives* (Princeton, Princeton University Press, 1998).

[84] See, eg, T Pogge, 'Cosmopolitanism: A Defence' (2002) 5 *Critical Review of International Social and Political Philosophy* 86–91.

Nevertheless, in a well-publicised article, Chandran Kukathas has made reference to the 'mirage of global justice',[85] arguing that the pursuit of global justice is not a worthy goal and that we should limit ourselves to more modest aims in establishing international institutions. Kukathas' main criticism is based on his argument that the pursuit of global justice requires a dangerous empowerment of elites, which would render supranational agencies formidably powerful. His conclusion is that the primary concern of all legal and political institutions should be not to secure justice but to limit power. He criticises theorists such as Pogge for arguing for a single standard of global justice, a standard that Kukathas believes to be unsustainable in the face of great diversity in ideas of social justice. Kukathas suggests that 'the outcome of their philosophical effort, is in effect, justification of rule by elites, guided by (and unchecked by anything other than) a commitment to justice.'[86] Yet Kukathas himself has offered no viable or feasible contribution to the problems of global poverty, other than expressing a hope for a growing moral convergence on these matters. Nor has he engaged with Pogge's specific argument that systematic institutional reform is needed because the present situation has been *caused* by the current institutional setup, thus giving rise to a specific, enforceable duty to redistribute wealth, given that present practices prevent any unilateral reform.

A focus on the actual, existing world rather than on an ideal state of affairs, such as Rawls' Original Position or postmodern utopian idealism, reminds us that injustice is the result of power allocations, imbalances and asymmetries; and such states of affairs are not natural or normal in the sense that it is a fact of nature that Switzerland is a mountainous country, and the Sahara is a desert. Pogge's approach is refreshingly realistic—grounded in the actual world, with its imbalances of power, and it builds a theory of global justice on that basis. It does not depend on some imagined Original Position that never existed. It stands firmly in the world as it actually is.

Contemporary writers such as Pogge and David Held are cosmopolitan in their wish to address justice at a global level, but both also stress the fundamental relationship of *power* to justice.[87] Held has argued that relations of power operate to produce major inequalities across the globe that are of such magnitude as to create significant violations of political liberty.[88] He has formulated a principle of 'nautonomy', namely the erosion of true autonomy and political participation by asymmetric inequalities of

[85] C Kukathas, 'The Mirage of Global Justice' (2006) 23 *Social Philosophy and Policy* 1–28.

[86] Ibid.

[87] Eg, Pogge, *World Poverty and Human Rights* (above n 80); and Held, *Democracy and the Global Order* (above n 7). See also IM Young, *Justice and the Politics of Difference* (Princeton, Princeton University Press, 1990).

[88] Held, *Democracy and the Global Order* (above n 7); and D Held, 'Sites of Power, Problems of Democracy' (1994) 19 *Alternatives* 221.

resources and income.[89] Framing questions of justice in this way reminds us that presently unjust situations derive from imbalances of power, from action already taken, and that rich countries, even if their citizens feel no solidarity with the global poor, cannot immunise themselves from consequences of their actions. Kant might have feared the concept of a world-governing Leviathan, but he famously wrote in *On Perpetual Peace* that 'a violation of rights in one part of the world is felt everywhere,'[90] a statement echoed by Martin Luther King, who wrote in 1963, in his *Letter from Birmingham City Jail*, 'Injustice anywhere is a threat to justice anywhere.'[91] Both statements reflect the interdependence of human life, and as Kant memorably stated, we are 'unavoidably side by side'.[92]

Justice after Modernity

The many conflicting and complex accounts of justice examined above are not unexpected. The fact of pluralism ensures that we live in a complex (legal) world, and justice presents itself as every bit as conflicting, multi-dimensional and paradoxical in nature as law. However, the discussion of justice so far does raise a quandary for legal theory. What direction should legal theory take if, on the one hand, it is wary of engaging in a certain type of reasoning about justice, reasoning that during modernity tended towards a universalistic and homogenising nature, but on the other hand, it wants to avoid the pessimistic, aporetic and ultimately perhaps disabling reasoning of a postmodern jurisprudence? How to avoid these undesirable conclusions? On the one hand, too uniform and constricting an account of justice; on the other, a recognition of a plurality of justices that seems almost unworkable in its fixity with the ideal and in its pessimism about the actual legal world. This is a challenge that I believe should be addressed, and the remainder of this book will attempt to do so.

Ideal and Non-ideal Theorising about Justice

In order to conclude this chapter's discussion of justice, it is necessary to consider a further distinction: that between ideal and non-ideal theorising about justice. This will require a different sort of engagement with Rawls' work—indeed, it might seem that in contemporary theorising about justice,

---

[89] Held, 'Sites of Power' (ibid) 197.
[90] Kant (above n 62) 108.
[91] ML King Jr, 'Letter from Birmingham Jail, April 16, 1963' in ML King, *Why We Can't Wait* (New York, Harper Collins, 1964) 79.
[92] Kant (above n 62) 114.

Rawls is liable to occupy the role that Derrida attributed to Karl Marx in the field of political economy—namely, that of 'fugitive spectre'.[93]

In *A Theory of Justice*, Rawls wrote:

> The intuitive idea is to split the theory of justice into two parts—the first, or ideal part, assumes a strict compliance and works out the principles that characterise a well ordered society ... and existing institutions can be judged in the light of this ideal conception.[94]

In contrast, 'non-ideal theory asks how this long-term goal might be achieved' and how to deal with cases of non-compliance.[95] Rawls described ideal theorising about justice as giving an account of 'a realistic utopia',[96] and it seems clear that in Rawls' work, it is ideal theory that was fundamental, with non-ideal theory taking second place and dependent on it. Indeed, Rawls wrote somewhat dismissively of non-ideal theory, 'I shall not attempt to give a systematic answer to these questions.'[97]

A distinction between ideal and non-ideal theorising by no means originates in the work of John Rawls, however. For example, in Plato's *Republic*, which is an extensive discussion of the nature of justice, the character Glaucon is critical of Socrates' idealist mode of theorising, arguing that Socrates relies on an unrealistic assumption that all will comply with such a conception of a just society; the question should instead be that of whether 'such an order of things is possible'.[98] This issue is resolved by Socrates in his prescription of a specific category of persons—'philosopher kings'—to be political guides and educators, an idealist solution to the problem of justice if ever there was one.

Sen's 'Idea of Justice' and Injustice

In recent years, there has been a shift toward non-ideal theorising about justice. The most notable exponent of this type of theorising is probably Nobel laureate Amartya Sen, who has been critical of accounts such as those of Rawls for being overly focused on an ideal, 'transcendental' theory of justice and, as a consequence, unable to offer practical guidance for remedying injustice in an increasingly borderless world. Sen has argued that 'A theory of justice that can serve as the basis of practical reason must include ways of judging how to reduce injustice and advance justice, rather than

---

[93] See Derrida, *Spectres of Marx* (above n 52).
[94] Rawls, *A Theory of Justice* (above n 20) 245–46.
[95] Rawls, *The Law of Peoples* (above n 56) 89.
[96] Ibid, 7
[97] Rawls, *A Theory of Justice* (above n 20) 216.
[98] Plato, *The Republic*, Books 5–6.

aiming only at the characterisation of perfectly just societies ...'[99] For Sen, Rawls' ideal theorising is exactly the wrong way to proceed, and those like Rawls who ask the question 'What is a just society?' are adopting what Sen calls a 'transcendental institutionalism'. Sen uses the term 'transcendental' because such theorising seeks to identify or construct an ideal of a perfectly just society, imagining another world abstracted from all recognisable identities, as is the case with Rawls' parties to the Original Position, behind a 'veil of ignorance'; Sen uses the term 'institutionalist' because such theorising seeks to identify what perfect institutional arrangements should be. Instead, Sen argues that we should seek a more practice-oriented approach to justice which engages in 'realisation focused comparisons'.

We have no reason to expect that a perfectly just society will be achievable in the near future or indeed ever. Given the inescapable diversity of human practices and capabilities, as well as the plurality and pluralism of values, there exists no common standard, no single unit of measurement for justice. Therefore, all that we can do is to make judgements of relative importance. What is needed is a theory of justice for an imperfect world, which will enable us to move from a situation of 'more unjust' to 'less unjust'. This is a comparative exercise, which cannot be assisted by transcendental theory. Instead, Sen's 'realisation focused comparison' emphasises a shared sense of *injustice* that enables people to agree that a given situation is unjust, even if they cannot agree on one single reason why they believe this is so.

Therefore, although Sen shares with theorists such as Kukathas the belief that the fact of diversity makes it difficult to advocate a single standard of social or distributive justice, in Sen's case this does not lead to the conclusion that the idea of global justice is a myth. Indeed, Sen believes that the most pressing instances of injustice occur at international level, that they need to be addressed and that it is just the very attachment to a demanding ideal of a perfect justice which *disables* us from finding the means to tackle global injustice. Ideal theories of justice require, at the very least, extremely sophisticated, developed institutions, such as those of the modern state, to implement them. Yet such an approach is disabling when it comes to the global arena, where organisational structures are weak and there is little prospect of sufficiently realised powerful institutions. As a result, theorists such as Rawls and Nagel deem global redistributive justice unlikely or impossible.

In contrast, Sen believes that we should focus on the plurality of reasons that may lead us to believe a situation to be unjust. For example, we may not agree on the reasons why the war in Iraq is unjust, but we may nonetheless agree that it is unjust. For Sen, a 'plurality of sustainable

---

[99] Sen, *The Idea of Justice* (above n 1) ix.

reasons' is a sufficient basis on which to act to decrease injustice.[100] Our starting point should be the reflection that our determination of what justice requires in a particular situation is initially motivated by feelings of injustice. Further reflection then requires us to look beyond a narrow, local conception of justice, to de-parochialise our thinking[101] (Sen has described this as a 'comparative broadening'[102]) and to acknowledge that there may exist more than just one unique reason for acting in a particular way. Sen draws on the work of theorists of the Scottish Enlightenment, particularly Adam Smith, who wrote, 'We are apt to feel too strongly whatever relates to ourselves ... The conversation of a friend brings us to a better, that of a stranger to a still better temper.'[103]

Yet is it any easier to identify and remedy injustice than it is to devise a theory of justice? Sen has illustrated his theory with examples of gross injustice that all might agree on, but is there any basis to believe that his theory is workable in the case of an injustice that is less flagrant than serious poverty, famine or even genocide? How are we to avoid injustice becoming an empty vessel that can be filled with any content depending on one's favourite theory of justice? The meaning of injustice is itself not always self-evident.

But perhaps this misses the point? The very aim of a non-ideal theorising such as Sen's is to avoid the tortuous search for a theory that may be operative in all situations, but rather to attain a workable response for an imperfect world. To achieve such a workable, pragmatic response requires us to establish and imbue in ourselves certain habits of mind and to be able to reason impartially and nonparochially. Notably, Sen's theory urges us to have trust in our capacity to identify injustice. We must therefore explore our sense of injustice, along with related feelings of moral outrage and indignation.[104] We identify injustice through our emotional responses— for example, we react with anger, horror or sympathy to a particular situation, and this provides a provisional judgement as to the occurrence of injustice.

However, this emotional reaction must, for Sen, be coupled with the exercise of reason. Although our emotions should not be ignored, it

---

[100] Ibid, 183.

[101] For example, Sen draws on classical Sanskrit thought to illustrate the relevance of traditions other than those of the dominant, contemporary Western discourse to theorise about justice. The distinction he draws is between two Sanskrit concepts, 'niti' and 'nyaya'. Whereas *niti* denotes organisational propriety and behavioural correctness, *nyaya* evokes a comprehensive conception of realised justice not linked to rules or institutions but, in Sen's words, to 'the world that actually emerges'. Sen, *The Idea of Justice* (above n 1) 20.

[102] Ibid, 170.

[103] A Smith, *The Theory of Moral Sentiments* (London, Clarendon Press, 1976) 125.

[104] See E Wolgast, *The Grammar of Justice* (Ithaca, Cornell University Press, 1987) for a similar focus on injustice and the role that our emotions play in its identification.

is necessary to deploy critical scrutiny to determine what lies beneath them.[105] Further, our decisions must be able to withstand public scrutiny, and so *public reason* is necessary to combat injustice.[106] Sen retains the Rawlsian notion of justice as fairness—namely, that the essential features of a just society are those features that will be seen to be fair by all reasonable people. Such a notion of justice as fairness requires impartiality and objectivity.

For Rawls, such impartiality was to be secured through the device of a hypothetical social contract, in the context of an Original Position operating under a veil of ignorance, whereby people have no information as to their own gender, wealth, race, parentage, etc. The purpose, for Rawls, of such a stipulated veil of ignorance is to eliminate personal bias from the choice of principles of justice and thus guarantee their fairness. However, while fairness might seem to demand impartiality, this need not lead to a singular, unique conception of a just society, for there exist diverse ways in which people may be impartial. Rawls' mode of impartiality rests on the contractual basis of his thought experiment, which assumes a clearly defined, closed, self-contained society. In such a group, the interests of non-contractors, namely those who do not belong to the focal group in the Original Position, such as future generations or foreigners, will have little weight. However, surely what is needed is to recognise a *plurality* of impartial perspectives, which do not rely on a particular *positional* objectivity or on 'closed' impartiality, in which one's moral evaluation of an act depends on the role that one plays.

Instead of an Original Position, Sen therefore prefers the approach to fairness adopted by Adam Smith, whose *Theory of Moral Sentiments* employed the notion of an 'impartial spectator'.[107] Smith's impartial spectator functions as a 'judge within', through which we may view our own actions from another perspective. For Smith, the impartial spectator was a creature produced by the moral power of the imagination, 'the man within the breast' who shapes the moral sensibility of an ethically sensitive person. It is not 'the eternal voice of conscience or of the deity; but in reality ... that of the world to which we belong.'[108] In Smith's own words:

> We conceive ourselves as acting in the presence of a person quite candid and equitable, of one who has no particular relation, either to ourselves, or to those

---

[105] Sen, *The Idea of Justice* (above n 1) 39.

[106] Ibid, 122.

[107] In making reference to Smith's *The Theory of Moral Sentiments*, Sen is part of a broader rehabilitation of Smith from the clutches of libertarian, free-market capitalism, which the more superficial but dominant reading of Smith's other major work, *The Wealth of Nations*, has given rise to.

[108] N Phillipson, *Adam Smith: An Enlightened Life* (London, Allen Lane, 2010) 157.

whose interests are affected by our conduct … who considers our conduct with the same indifference with which we regard that of other people.[109]

Smith also suggested that 'It is only by consulting this judge within us that we can make any proper comparisons between our own interests and those of other men.'[110] To follow this internal voice requires abstracting ourselves from the world in order to act morally. However, Smith's spectator does not just represent an ideal, for he requires one to look at issues 'with the eyes of other people' and from the viewpoint of 'real spectators'. Thus the plurality of impartial reasoning is ensured.

It is necessary, therefore, to diversify the sources of our theories and concepts in order to make the types of realisation-focused comparisons that Sen has urged. For Sen, justice is what emerges from public reason, although the thrust of his work is to avoid any final conclusions as to justice. Democracy therefore plays an important role in Sen's theorising, and it is through the exercise of global public reason rather than through ideal global institutions that he believes injustice may be identified and attacked.

Realist Thinking about Justice

Sen's focus on injustice as a starting point is indicative of a developing dissatisfaction with 'ideal' theory and a focus instead on achieving a notion of justice appropriate for guiding action in the world as it is. In adopting what the philosopher Raymond Geuss has criticised as an 'ethics first' approach, ideal theorising insists on, as Geuss has expressed it, 'the assumption of a separate discipline of Ethics that can be studied without locating it in the rest of life, and in relation to claims of history, sociology and ethics'.[111]

Kantian theory is often taken as the epitome of such ideal thought, with its claim that ethics can be constructed in a non-empirical manner, abstracted from human emotions, their particular history and geographical circumstances. 'Realist' philosophers such as Geuss, on the other hand, prefer to take as their starting point institutions as they actually are at any given time, as well as arguing that there is no one right or 'canonical' style of theorising about concepts such as justice or rights. Geuss has described his own mode of thinking as *orthogonal* to that of contemporary analytical political philosophy. Geuss also denies any clear distinction in his realist philosophy between the description of an institution and its evaluation, or

---

[109] A Smith, *The Theory of Moral Sentiments*, 3rd edn (London, T Cadell, 1777) 267.
[110] Ibid, 190.
[111] R Guess, *Philosophy and Real Politics* (Princeton, Princeton University Press, 2008) 7.

between fact and value, between 'is' and 'ought'—a way of proceeding to which this book is sympathetic and which has already been discussed and advocated in chapter two.

Such an approach has been shared by other philosophers such as Hannah Arendt and Bernard Williams, and both Williams and Geuss draw deeply on insights from Friedrich Nietzsche, in particular Nietzsche's critique of any attempt to ground morality as a source of value, whether in God, metaphysics or rationality. Nietzsche alerted philosophy to the gap between theorising and reality in moral practices, warning of the suspect character of 'official' accounts of morality.[112] Such an approach perceives idealist moralising to be a form of wishful thinking, viewing theories such as Rawls' as 'compensatory fantasy'.[113]

The British philosopher Bernard Williams, although working largely within the analytical philosophy tradition, was greatly influenced by Nietzsche. Williams believed that much of philosophy was a 'flight from reality'[114] which had 'simplified moral life' in ways he found egregious, 'failing to understand the heterogeneity of values, the tragic collisions between things we care for',[115] as well as the crucial roles that emotions play in our moral choices.

In a famous article entitled 'The Question of Machiavelli', Isaiah Berlin pondered 'the sheer number of interpretations of Machiavelli's political opinions', asking what it was that had proved so arresting to so many.[116] Berlin's own conclusion was that it was not only Machiavelli's realism 'or his advocacy of brutal or unscrupulous or ruthless politics that has so deeply upset so many later thinkers' but also the fact that Machiavelli's thesis contained the 'erschreckend' (terrifying) proposition: 'the belief that the correct, objectively valid solution to the question of how men should live can in principle be discovered is itself, in principle, not true'.[117] Berlin himself believed that moral values are plural, conflicting and often incommensurable, and concluded that it was this terrifying proposition, this 'awful truth' in Machiavelli's work, that has haunted the moral consciousness of men ever since:

Machiavelli's cardinal achievement is his uncovering of an insoluble dilemma, the planting of a permanent question mark in the path of posterity. It stems from his de facto recognition that ends equally ultimate, equally sacred, may contradict each other, that entire systems of value may come into collision without

---

[112] See, eg, Nietzsche, *On the Genealogy of Morals* (New York, Vintage, 1987 edition).

[113] R Guess, *Outside Ethics* (Princeton, Princeton University Press, 2005) 34.

[114] M Nussbaum, 'Bernard Williams: Tragedies, Hope, Justice' in D Calcutt (ed), *Reading Bernard Williams* (London, Routledge, 2008) 213.

[115] Ibid.

[116] I Berlin, 'The Question of Machiavelli' in R Adams (ed), *The Prince: A Revised Translation, Backgrounds, Interpretations, Marginalia* (New York, Norton, 1992) 206.

[117] Ibid, 225.

possibility of rational arbitration, and that not merely in exceptional circumstances, as a result of abnormality or accident or error—the clash of Antigone and Creon or in the story of Tristan—but (this was surely new) as part of the normal human situation.[118]

Williams also recognised the contingency of ethical belief and its relativity to particular forms of culture, stressing that our most valued ethical traditions are sustained only by contingent practices, social structures and traditions. The ideal presented by Kant—that human existence might be conceived as objectively just—and Aristotle's evocation of justice as 'a complete virtue'[119] are seen as beyond reach, and any notion of moral truth to be unrealisable. Instead, ethics is understood as a practical issue rather than a matter of idealist thinking, and to understand such issues, it is necessary to look more closely at our emotions and at the contribution they play to our moral life.

Injustice (Again)

The words of John Dewey are of relevance here:

> Men have constructed a strange dream world when they have supposed that without a fixed ideal of a remote good to inspire them, they have no inducement to get relief from present troubles ... [S]ufficient unto the day is the evil thereof. Sufficient it is to stimulate us to remedial action ... The physician is lost who would guide his activities by building up a picture of perfect health.[120]

Dewey's stimulation to the remedial action of 'the evil thereof' parallels Sen's call to remedy injustice, and both share a pragmatic approach.

A prioritising of injustice avoids an over-emphasis on ideals and takes account of the contextual inspiration for our sense of justice, the fact that we derive it from our experiences and responses to varieties of situations, and that we develop a sense of justice incrementally, through our feelings and the practices that surround it, from our earliest years. Our sense of justice is not gained rationally, through *a priori* reflection, but cumulatively, through experiences of its perceived opposite,[121] through the sensations of indignation or intolerability. These are the fundamental features of our moral lives. It is a sense of injury that comes first, which is then followed by a demand for justice, which explains the difficulty we experience in trying to explain in positive terms what justice is. Justice is secondary to injustice,

---

[118] Ibid.

[119] In the *Nichomachean Ethics*, Bk V, Aristotle described justice as a 'complete virtue', which encompasses all types of justice, as well as justice as a partial virtue, in the sense of distributive or corrective justice.

[120] J Dewey, *Human Nature and Conduct* (New York, Henry Holt, 1922) 282–83.

[121] See, eg, Wolgast (above n 104).

not an *a priori*, pre-existent value, enjoying its own Platonic existence in another world of ideal forms of moral concepts. Smith famously wrote:

> Mere justice is, upon most occasions, but a negative virtue, and only hinders us from hurting our neighbour. The man who barely abstains from violating either the person, or the estate, or the reputation of his neighbours, has surely very little positive merit. He fulfils, however, all the rules of what is peculiarly called justice, and does every thing which his equals can with propriety force him to do, or which they can punish him for not doing. We may often fulfil all the rules of justice by sitting still and doing nothing.[122]

Smith also insisted that resentment was 'the safeguard of justice and the security of innocence'.[123]

Judith Shklar has pointed out that we miss much if we focus only on justice, reducing injustice to the rejection and breakdown of justice, treating injustice as the anomaly. For Shklar, scepticism gives injustice its due, recognising that our judgements are often made in the dark, and that we should have doubts as to their validity.[124] This parallels Williams' view that we have no reason to believe that the world is fully intelligible to us, nor that it is receptive to our moral interests and purposes.[125] To believe otherwise is to engage in wishful thinking. Morality relies on sentiments, both positive and negative. Envy, jealousy, slight and perceived injury all play their part. Justice is a set of practices and procedures developed from our responses to injury and wrongdoing, a notion born of experience—of sympathy, compassion, pain, suffering and outrage.

A very famous pictorial image of injustice dating from the early 1300s exists in Giotto's *Injustitia*, part of his grisaille sequence of the Virtues and Vices for the Arena Chapel in Padua (Figure 6-5). This depicts Injustice in male form, fashioned as a tyrant who is armed with sword and an unpleasant forked spear, in contrast to the more usual female depiction of Justice and her usual sword and scales. The dress of Injustice resembles that of a judge, his expression is cold and cruel, his hands claw-like with long nails, a sinister fang-like tooth projecting up from his mouth. Below him are depicted scenes of robbery and violence, murder and rape. This figure sits within a broken, crenelated archway, which stands on a jagged ledge of rock—an unfriendly, destabilising landscape in which murder and mayhem hold sway, lacking any of the calm harmony and balance of more familiar images of justice. To contemporary eyes, Giotto's work might be interpreted as a medieval caricature, yet this image produces a forceful visceral reaction, provoking strong emotions of fear, horror and

---

[122] A Smith, *The Theory of Moral Sentiments*, DD Raphael and AL Macfie (eds) (Indianapolis, Liberty Fund, 1982) 82.

[123] Ibid, 79.

[124] J Shklar, 'Giving Injustice Its Due' (1989) 98 *Yale Law Journal* 1135.

[125] See, eg, B Williams, *Ethics and the Limits of Philosophy* (London, Fontana, 1985).

physical intimidation, reminding us of the immediacy of the emotional sources of morality—a psychological component too often ignored. We do not need to be expert in medieval iconography to understand the *Injustitia*. We *feel* its force.

Figure 6-5: Giotto, *Injustitia* (c 1306), Arena Chapel, Padua

Figure 6-6: Giotto, *Justitia* (c 1306), Arena Chapel, Padua

Contrast this image of *Injustitia*, then, with its counterpart, Giotto's representation of *Justitia* (Figure 6-6), the harmonious, orderly justice, which appears bland and insipid in comparison. Which is the more motivating? Which the more primordial?

Emotions and Justice

The argument then is that our sense of justice is secondary to and parasitic on our sense of injustice. Our sense of justice is derived from our sense of injustice, which in turn develops from a complex constellation of emotions, which provide a psychological basis from which moral theories may emerge.

Generally, however, philosophy has tended to prioritise rational thought over emotional response, although there have been notable exceptions to the philosophical subordination of emotions to reason—most particularly in the work of David Hume, Adam Smith, Charles Darwin and Friedrich Nietzsche. The Scottish philosophers of the Enlightenment, most particularly Hume and Smith, developed complex theories regarding the role that the emotions play in moral and social philosophy. They argued that the basis of morality lies in the emotions, not in reason. This emphasis on the role of sentiment in decision-making contrasts sharply with deontological theories such as Kant's, which have been founded on reason as a guide to human action. Hume, in *A Treatise of Human Nature*, however, argued that individuals morally evaluate the circumstances of others by imagining themselves in the observed situation. In this way, feelings of sympathy generate appropriate moral judgements.

It might be thought that to derive moral principles from human sentiment risks relativism—namely, the derivation of moral value from subjective emotional reactions to particular circumstances or events.[126] However, for Hume, this danger was avoided by his argument that *common* emotional reactions are experienced when human beings react to similar circumstances: 'the great resemblance among all human creatures' that 'must very much contribute to make us enter into the sentiments of others'.[127] For Hume, therefore, morality was founded on universal sentiments. To be sure, Hume distinguished two kinds of emotion—first, those self-interested emotions of the sort that Hobbes stressed in his theory of social contract as the origin of society, but also, on the other hand, those universal sentiments drawn from 'principles of humanity', which Hume believed formed the basis of moral judgements, thus refuting any claim that the emotions may only form the basis of negative, self-interested judgements, by stressing the role also played by sympathy and benevolence. However, it should be noted that in Hume's theory, reason also has its part to play, functioning as a calculator or instrument of analysis, aiding humans in understanding their emotions. Reason and emotion are therefore compounded and inseparable, working together in the formation of moral judgements, providing a motivation for moral action in a way that reason alone (in the cool and disengaged form it finds in rational philosophy) is unable to do.

---

[126] Hume himself, of course, famously criticised the practice of deriving value judgements from factual statements, in *A Treatise of Human Nature* (Book III, part I, section I) arguing that emotions, not reason, should be considered the proper basis of morals. For a strong expression of an emotivist view of ethics, see AJ Ayer, *Language, Truth and Logic* (London, Gollanz, 1936).

[127] D Hume, *A Treatise of Human Nature* (1739–40), LA Selby-Bigge (ed), revised by PH Nidditch, 2nd edn (Oxford, Clarendon Press, 1978) 318.

The work of Smith and the role that it plays in Sen's notion of justice have already been referenced. Smith, like Hume, believed that sensations of sympathy between humans and compassion for the misery of others are one of the most notable features of human existence. But along with Hume, he realised that not all of our emotional responses are an appropriate basis for the formation of moral judgements, and that there exists a need for judgements as to the propriety of our responses. It is Smith's 'impartial spectator' that enables the observation of emotional reactions from a more distant perspective and the capacity of emotions to render impartial judgements.

Therefore, these thinkers of the Scottish Enlightenment stressed the importance of emotion to our moral imagination; these emotions allow us to place ourselves in the circumstances of others and to feel sympathy and compassion. Furthermore, and crucially, recent work in neuroscience and psychology has strengthened the arguments of Smith and Hume, confirming that certain aspects of emotion and feeling are crucial for rationality.[128]

The key point here is that an account of justice that acknowledges both the role played by the emotions in identifying injustice and the contribution of our emotions to our reasoned ethical judgements not only more accurately represents the nature of our ethical thought but is better placed to motivate citizens. We place unrealistic demands on citizens if we start with justice as an ideal that is pre-existing, neutral and self-produced by a rational conception, such as in the work of Kant, who requires us to act 'not from inclination, but duty ... the necessity to act out of reverence for the law'.[129] Kant's standard is uninspiring for most people—it represents a distant icon, or even a delusion. It is injustice and its emotional sources that inspire most people. Philosophy and social psychology therefore are both crucial components of our moral reasoning.

Recognising this, however, requires not only a focus on positive emotions such as compassion and sympathy, but also a sense of envy, jealousy and revenge. Our sense of justice is inspired as much by thwarted expectations and frustrated desires, by visceral responses to injustice, as by sensations of sympathy with others. Altogether, seen in this way, justice is 'a way of

---

[128] For example, Jorge Moll et al have used neuroimaging techniques to identify the areas of the brain regions activated by basic and moral emotions; they have found that emotional experience is linked to moral appraisal. J Moll, R de Oliveira-Souza, et al, 'The Neural Correlates of Moral Sensitivity: A Functional Magnetic Resonance Imaging Investigation of Basic and Moral Emotions' (2002) 22 *Journal of Neuroscience* 2730–36. Antonio Damasio's study of the relationship between reason and emotion in patients with lesions of the ventro-medial prefrontal cortex of the brain has also demonstrated that emotion is central to reason. A Damasio, *Descartes' Error: Emotion, Reason, and the Human Brain* (New York, Putnam, 1994). More generally, see R Jeffery, 'Reason, Emotion, and the Problem of World Poverty: Moral Sentiment Theory and International Ethics' (2011) 3 *International Theory* 143–78.

[129] Kant (above n 62).

participating in the world, a composite set of feelings and affiliations, that link us ... with others.'[130] Justice is therefore 'a complex set of passions to be cultivated, not an abstract set of principles to be formulated, mastered and imposed on society,'[131] and its origins lie in the promptings of our most basic emotions.

An (Im)modest Response to the Confusion of Justice

Law cannot by itself establish justice. Yet it can place constraints on the exercise of power. Later chapters will examine how law does this—through the operation of a specifically *legal* justice, namely, the doctrine of the rule of law, as well as by enforcing certain human rights, and also through maintaining a larger accountability of power, whether it is exercised in the public or in the private domain.

My response to the confusion of justice is worked out within the ensuing chapters. It considers the issue of justice in various ways: justice as it operates within the law, through human rights, at global level, as well as from a perspective external to law. It is in some ways a modest response. It does not attempt to provide a complete theory of distributive justice or of social justice. Indeed, such an attempt may be ultimately futile. Rather, it concentrates, first, on what law can do. It seeks what is possible, the achievement of some sort of justice in the here and now—while acknowledging Derrida's point that justice can never fully be done, is always deferred in some way, is always still to come. But it refuses to accept this as a counsel of despair.

In another sense, the account provided in this book is not modest at all. It commits itself to an attempt for global justice and thus is cosmopolitan in outlook. In combination with this, it asserts the crucial importance of the rule of law both nationally and internationally, in conjunction with an accountability for the creation, promulgation and impact of all laws, public or private. Both cosmopolitanism and the rule of law are apt to be derided as too liberal, imperialistic even, the tools of an oppressive use of law by Western capitalistic culture. This approach seeks to reclaim them both from this derision and from the oppressive use to which they have sometimes been put, recognising that they do crucial work in a world in which power, in its many different forms, constantly seeks to usurp law.

Finally, I conclude this book with a meditation on injustice, as ever present and immediate, in a way in which the elusive concept of justice is not.

---

[130] R Solomon, *A Passion for Justice: Emotions and the Origins of the Social Contract* (Reading, MA, Addison-Wesley, 1990) 32.
[131] Ibid, 243.

There exists a deficit of injustice, which cannot be adequately redressed by any theory of justice. I consider how injustice motivates us and does its own work. It is crucial to act on feelings of injustice if we are not to sink into despair, depression or lethargy when faced with the complex, fragmentary pluralistic nature of law after modernity.

7

Legal Justice I: 'Maimed Justice' and the Rule of Law

The reflections of the last chapter revealed no single, overarching concept of justice and indeed suggested that such a thing is not possible. These pessimistic arguments might seem to amount to a counsel of despair. Is justice to be dismissed as a universalising myth, an impossible ideal or a partial tool of the powerful? Is there a way of escaping such pessimistic conclusions?

Chapter six also considered Amartya Sen's suggestion that perhaps we expect too much and set our goals for justice too high.[1] Justice need not be only about aspiring to achieve a perfectly just society, a transcendental ideal; it can also be a matter of actualities, of preventing manifest injustice in the world, of changes, large or small, to peoples' lives—whether it be the abolition of slavery or improvement of conditions in the workplace. In order to render this, it is not necessary to have a finely tuned, perfectly reasoned theory of justice. Furthermore, while law may not of itself embody a complete or perfect concept of justice, it is well placed to deter *injustice*. Therefore it is necessary to focus on how law may deter or prevent injustice, as well as on the ways in which *law itself* may be deterred from doing injustice.

In this chapter, I explore the concept of a *legal* justice, centred on the value of the rule of law. This notion of justice is best understood in negative terms, in line with the reflections of chapter six, in terms of its capacity to deter injustice. The rule of law plays a crucial role in restraining power. It is not a complete theory of justice in its own right. In this chapter, I engage with some general perceptions about the rule of law, as well as examining some catastrophic illustrations of its non-observance. In the next chapter, I take the discussion further, aiming to rebut some of the most pressing critiques of the rule of law, concluding with suggestions as to how the rule of law might be re-imagined or rehabilitated as critical legal justice for the twenty-first century.

---

[1] A Sen, *The Idea of Justice* (London, Allen Lane, 2009).

Maimed Justice

The Renaissance and early modern period produced a number of images of 'maimed justice'—of judges with their hands severed and corrupt judges suffering severe punishments. For example, the detail from the fresco illustrated in Figure 7-1 was painted in 1604 by the Vicenzan artist Cesare Giglio, for a room in the Town Hall of Geneva where the town councillors judged both civil and criminal cases.[2] The inspiration for the handless judges appears to be either Plutarch's *Moralia* or the writings of Diodorus of Sicily,[3] which describe how at Thebes, statues of judges were erected without hands to illustrate that justice was not to be influenced by gifts or diverted by friendship (as handless judges are unable to accept bribes). The councillors of Geneva, who commissioned the work, wished to convey the message that it is essential to the rule of law that justice should not be corrupted by bribes or influence, that power should not be abused or oppressive, and that justice should be unbiased.

Figure 7-1: Cesare Giglio, *Les juges aux mains coupées* (c 1604), Musee des Beaux Arts, Geneva

[2] Another reproduction of this work by Giglio can be found in DE Curtis and J Resnik, 'Images of Justice' (1987) 96 *Yale Law Journal* 1727, 1736. See also J Resnik and D Curtis, *Representing Justice: Invention, Controversy, and Rights in City-States and Democratic Courtrooms* (New Haven, Yale University Press, 2011).

[3] 'In Thebes,' Plutarch relates, 'there were set up statues of judges without hands, and the statue of the chief justice had its eyes closed, to indicate that justice is not influenced by gifts or by intercession.' Plutarch, *Moralia*, FC Babbit (trans) 355.A. Cf 'Diodorus of Sicily' in *Library of History*, 12 vols, CH Oldfather (trans) (Cambridge, MA, Harvard University Press, 1962) I.48.6. See C-N Robert, *La Justice dans ses Décors (XVe-XVIe siècles)* (Geneva, Librairie Droz, 2006) 93.

Today, we are familiar with less emotive images of justice—often in the form of a female figure with sword and scales astride such public buildings as the Old Bailey, or the image of 'blind' justice. In contrast, the maimed justice images now seem extreme and shocking. And yet, why should they? Does justice truly exist in a serene form in the world, as an achievable balancing of sword and scales? Or is justice not 'maimed' or corrupted too often? It may well be that the atavistic, 'maimed justice' images are closer to reality. I shall return to the notion of 'maimed' justice and injustice at the end of the book.

Both the images of 'blind' and of 'maimed' justice share an ambiguity—presenting justice as unbiased, incorruptible, closed to influence and power on the hand but, on the other, suggesting that human 'justice' is all too open to bias, bribes or cheating. It is for this very reason that the blindfold or the even more extreme measure of amputation have been imposed to prevent corruption—they reveal a lack of faith and absence of confidence in the virtue of justice. This impression of justice is relevant to the rule of law and its capacity to invoke our complex emotions about justice—our high hopes for it and yet also our perception that it is often damaged by all too human failings and abuse of power. This ambiguity also pervades my approach to justice, which recognises the necessity for constraints on power and abuse through legal means, thus realising a form of legal justice, but also acknowledges our strength of feeling over injustice as a powerful extra-legal intuition, which does its own work, inspiring us to fight corruption and iniquity.

A Common Conception of Justice? Justice and the Rule of Law

The Methodology of Impartiality

Because justice is such a contested concept, so difficult to agree upon, an approach that counsels proceduralism has been suggested, in the hope of achieving a fair assessment of competing claims that will satisfy everyone. A need for justice arises in conditions of conflict and strife,[4] when there is a myriad of competing and often incommensurable claims, predicated on different substantive notions of what is just, as discussed in the last chapter. In the absence of agreement or shared understanding as to the substance of justice, there is a turn to procedure. It is thought that justice may be assured by fair procedures, which in turn will ensure that outcomes are fair. Thus a limited, 'neutral' approach is counselled. In this way it is

---

[4] See, eg, S Hampshire, *Justice is Conflict* (London, Duckworth, 1999).

thought that outcomes can appear 'objective' and thereby counter the claim that to ask for justice is like 'banging on the table'.[5]

Perhaps the most famous twentieth-century account of justice, that of John Rawls, attempts to evade the contestability of justice by providing a theory of justice as fairness. This attempts to liberate justice from the biases of our personal circumstances, experiences and expectations. Rawls posited a 'veil of ignorance', a device employed in his 'Original Position', which is an attempt to put the 'Right' before any concept of the 'Good' so as to avoid any accusation of the partiality or bias derived from the subjective nature of values.[6] The veil of ignorance connotes a similar function as that of the blindfold of justice—not as extreme as 'maimed' justice but nonetheless a recognition of the abuses of bias and power.

If such an unbiased, objective account of justice were possible, then Rawls claimed it would acknowledge two principles: namely, first, equal access to civil liberties for all and, second, what he termed the 'difference principle', which requires that any societal inequalities should necessarily be for the benefit of all in society and most particularly of the least well off.[7] The problems of Rawls' particular device of neutrality (ie, the contractual 'Original Position' with its accompanying 'veil of ignorance') have already been discussed in the previous chapter—namely, the capacity of contractual devices to exclude those not in any original contract (such as foreigners or future generations) and its dependency on a 'positional' objectivity or 'closed' impartiality. For these reasons, Adam Smith's notion of an 'impartial spectator' has been proffered as preferable, since it does not require us to abstract ourselves from the actual world but instead recognises that there may be a plurality of impartial perspectives.

Rawls' theory, or at least the specific principles of justice that he derived from his methodological assumptions, have, however, been criticised from many perspectives, including both the left and right ends of the political spectrum. For egalitarians, Rawls privileged liberty over equality, placing the first principle of justice in lexical priority over the 'difference principle', and thus he deferred too much to liberal values. On the other hand, libertarians such as Robert Nozick have criticised him for failing to give sufficient protection to individual rights. Communitarians criticise Rawls for insufficient regard to virtue and the public good, in his placing the right over the good.

---

[5] A Ross, *On Law and Justice*, (London, Stevens and Sons, 1958) 274.

[6] The 'veil of ignorance' ensures that the group of people placed in the 'Original' (ie, pre-societal) position have no knowledge as to their personal circumstances in society—ie, whether they are rich or poor, healthy or ill, talented or stupid, young or old. J Rawls, *A Theory of Justice* (Cambridge, MA, Harvard University Press, 1971).

[7] Ibid.

Is it a criticism of proceduralism that supposedly neutral mechanisms such as Rawls' veil of ignorance may produce such contested outcomes? Or may one criticise some of the substantive outcomes of such deliberations while still adhering to a belief in the fairness of formal justice mechanisms and their ability to prevent injustice? It is not the purpose of this book to advocate Rawls' two substantive principles of justice, nor to debate their critique—an overabundance of works doing just that already exists. Yet there exists a strong intuition that power, position and status should not corrupt or 'maim' justice. Therefore it is suggested that despite the raging against it of certain postmodern critics, the *methodology* of impartiality (at least if envisioned as a notion more capable of pluralism than Rawls' social contract) may still have something to recommend it. In this way, we may achieve a theory of *legal* justice, which at the very least is designed to prevent law from increasing the injustice of the world.

The Rule of Law

The proceduralist approach has something in common with that favourite of liberal constitutionalism, the 'rule of law'—or at least with a certain conception of it. The rule of law is often seen as anathema to postmodern and critical theory because of its basis in the possibility of neutrality and of universal application—perceived as a justice of universal rules that can be sustained for all societies—and therefore is derided as an ideology, a 'totalising theory', of which we should be suspicious. These critiques will be considered in detail in the next chapter, but I believe they have been too fast to dismiss this classical part of liberal theory. For although the rule of law may not help us achieve perfectly just outcomes, nor deliver an impressive theory of ideal justice, it can help us to deter injustice.[8] It is not a complete theory of justice, nor does it claim to be so. Yet it does especially valuable work in preventing oppressive abuses of power, which cause injustice.

A first issue to be addressed, however, is a perceived connection between the rule of law and certain features that are often taken as characteristic of modern law. The rule of law might seem to be incompatible with the chaotic trajectories and complex forms of contemporary law, given its traditional association with stability, predictability, the model of rules and legal autonomy. If contemporary law appears to have moved away from autonomy, system and the model of rules, then how may it be constrained by

---

[8] Cf Sen, who has stated that his overall project is not to deliver a perfect theory of justice but 'to clarify how we can proceed to address questions of enhancing justice and removing injustice'. Sen (above n 1) ix.

structures that buck this trend, relying on supposedly 'rational', 'modern' notions of legal predictability and stability? Further, the rule of law also may appear at odds with the highly contested and political character of pluralism and post-national politics.[9] Yet contemporary advocates of the rule of law include many jurists who previously were antagonistic to it but now apparently support its values;[10] and it has always received support from others who might have been supposed to be critical of it.[11]

The key to this reconciling of rule of law with contestation and legal pluralism lies, I suggest, first and foremost in adhering strongly to the values that the rule of law protects—namely, in looking to its spirit rather than in an over-emphasis on the forms that it has taken in various contexts. However, I also hope to demonstrate that a belief in the rule of law does not commit one to a consequent belief in law as rules, nor in law as a strongly bounded, autonomous discipline. It does not commit one to the legal theory of legal positivism—nor to any other legal theory for that matter. Further, I will also argue that the rule of law does not violate substantive equality, nor is it blind to difference, because of its apparent focus on a philosophy of neutral, formal equality. To do all of this, however, it is necessary to reclaim the rule of law and to reimagine it as critical legal justice.

The Rule of Law as Legal Justice

The rule of law is what many theorists traditionally understand by the concept of 'legal justice'. It is therefore compatible with one of the aims of this book—to investigate and assess the possibility of justice *within* the law, to consider law's promise to do justice, rather than pursuing social and philosophical theories of justice more generally. For many, the rule of law plays a key role in the legitimacy of law—such legitimacy itself being somewhat of a holy grail, as previous chapters have explored. The rule of law has

---

[9] See, eg, N Krisch, *Beyond Constitutionalism* (Oxford, Oxford University Press, 2010) 69.

[10] For example, contrast A Hutchinson, 'The Rule of Law Revisited: Democracy and Courts' in D Dyzenhaus (ed), *Recrafting the Rule of Law* (Oxford, Hart Publishing, 1999) to his earlier work, which was critical of the rule of law, such as A Hutchinson and P Monahan (eds), *The Rule of Law: Ideal or Ideology* (Toronto, Carswell, 1987). Roberto Unger has also softened his attitude: compare his argument in 1976 that 'the very assumptions of the rule of law appear to be falsified by the reality of life in liberal society' (R Unger, *Law in Modern Society: Toward a Criticism of Social Theory* (New York, Free Press, 1976) 181) with this statement, 20 years later, in which he appeared to acknowledge that where the rule of law prevails, 'people enjoy security in a regime of rights.' R Unger, *What Should Legal Analysis Become?* (London, Verso, 1996) 64. See also R West, *Re-Imagining Justice: Progressive Interpretations of Formal Equality, Rights and the Rule of Law* (Aldershot, Ashgate, 2003).

[11] Eg, EP Thompson, who described the rule of law as 'an unqualified human good'. EP Thompson, *Whigs and Hunters* (London, Penguin Books, 1977) 266. See also F Neumann, *The Rule of Law: Political Theory and the Legal System in Modern Society* (Leamington Spa, Berg, 1986). Thompson's and Neumann's work are discussed below ch 8.

been described as a 'meta rule' about the importance and priority of legal rules.[12] It is a pervasive concept, as a recent commentary has stated:

> If celebratory rhetoric is to be believed, or money devoted to a cause regarded as a sign of its success, ours is the era of the rule of law. No one will be heard to denounce it, leaders of countries all round the world claim to have it, vast sums are spent to spread it.[13]

Yet what exactly is the relationship of the rule of law to law, and to justice? What do we understand by this vague and overused term, which, as much as justice, has so many conceptions, indeed almost a conceptual instability?

The rule of law has traditionally been seen to require state action to proceed by legal norms that are general in character, relatively clear, certain, public, prospective and stable, as well as recognising the equality of subjects before the law.[14] It stresses the fixed and stable enforcement of general principles—namely, legitimate expectations, formal rights of access to the courts, equality before the law. Its benefits can be stated simply. Observance of the rule of law enhances certainty, predictability and security, both among individuals and between citizens and government, as well as restricting governmental discretion. It restricts the abuse of power. Thus it has both private and public law functions—an attraction in the world of growing legal pluralism. Citizens are able to interact together, knowing in advance what rules will regulate conflicts, should there be any. Individuals also are able to know which actions are permitted and which prohibited.

These are perceived to be formal requirements of law rather than substantive content. Max Weber believed that what he termed 'formally rational' (ie, modern) law derives its legitimacy not from any substantive morality (a shared, common morality being hard to achieve in times of contested moral pluralism) but from formally rational propositions. Joseph Raz has even gone as far as to say that 'like a sharp knife, the rule of law is morally neutral.'[15] On this view, the rule of law does not have any moral value of itself. The rule of law, which presents itself as impartial, is appropriate in today's landscape of moral and legal pluralism. Adherence to the rule of law is perceived as necessary to ensure the legitimacy of law. Legitimacy thus overtakes morality as a significant benchmark of law.

---

[12] For further use of the idea of the rule of law as a 'meta rule', see G Palombella and N Walker, *Relocating the Rule of Law* (Oxford, Hart Publishing, 2009).

[13] M Krygier, 'Philip Selznick: Incipient Law, State Law and the Rule of Law' in J van Schooten and JM Verschuuren (eds), *The State Legislature and Non-State Law* (Cheltenham, Elgar, 2008).

[14] See J Raz, 'The Rule of Law and its Virtue' (1997) 93 *Law Quarterly Review* 195–202; and L Fuller, 'Positivism and Fidelity to Law: A Reply to Professor Hart' (1958) 71 *Harvard Law Review* 630. Both give similar but not identical accounts to this.

[15] Raz (ibid).

The attraction of the rule of law, however, is that it may also be explained in ways other than Weberian formal rationality. Indeed, the concept of legality goes back to classical times, to the Greeks. Yet one of the most familiar conceptions of the rule of law is that of the Victorian jurist Albert Venn Dicey. In his famous work *The Law of the Constitution*, Dicey identified the rule of law, along with parliamentary sovereignty, as one of the key characteristics of the Victorian constitution. Dicey divided the rule of law into three elements: the first was to exclude any government power in excess of the established law of the land; the second was the equal subjection of all to the ordinary law; and the third was that the law of the constitution was not to be derived from some body of fundamental law but to be articulated by judicial decisions in particular cases before the courts.[16]

Dicey's view is now perceived as somewhat anachronistic, especially for its refusal to countenance actual, specific governmental power as distinct in kind from that of the ordinary citizen (in any case, an inadequate description of government in Dicey's day). But what Dicey described as 'the predominance of the legal spirit'[17] does capture the constraints placed by law on the activity of government. Brian Simpson has attributed Dicey's singular treatment of the rule of law in part to the specific circumstances of his day, especially the legal cases and controversy surrounding the brutal suppression of insurrection in Jamaica by British colonial governor, Edward Eyre (and even earlier, to the Indian mutiny)—events that gave rise to the famous case *Phillips v Eyre*,[18] which Dicey discussed in *The Law of the Constitution*. Members of the British intelligentsia at the time, including John Stuart Mill, Charles Darwin and Thomas Huxley, wanted those of the Jamaican administration involved brought to trial for crimes against regular law,[19] and it was in this context that there arose a particular conception of government being bound by decisions of the ordinary courts.[20]

The concept of the rule of law also presents itself as a solution to the problem of human nature, as expressed by David Hume.[21] Both as individuals and as collectivities, humans act in a mixed variety of altruistic and selfish ways. Yet even if people act on good or altruistic motivations, they can never be sure what the consequences of actual behaviour will

---

[16] AV Dicey, *Introduction to the Study of the Law of the Constitution*, 8th edn (London, Macmillan, 1915).

[17] Ibid, 185.

[18] *Phillips v Eyre* (1870) LR 6 QB 1.

[19] See AWB Simpson, 'The Ideal of the Rule of Law' in AWB Simpson, *Leading Cases in the Common Law* (Oxford, Oxford University Press, 1995) 229.

[20] Although in the event, as Simpson has related it, Eyre escaped trial and was even awarded a pension by Disraeli.

[21] D Hume, *An Enquiry Concerning the Principles of Morals*, 3rd edn, LA Selby-Bigge and PH Nidditch (eds) (Oxford, Oxford University Press, 1975).

be. According to the Humean account of human nature, frequent and unpredictable errors of will, motive, judgement and reason will constantly combine to frustrate our aspirations for life as it ought to be. Furthermore, these individual failures are magnified to great and horrific complexity within larger groups. The rule of law addresses these problems by providing authoritative standards for all to observe in the pursuit of their own ends. These standards provide order, in that they establish legitimate expectations for such conduct. They also establish conventions for creating, interpreting and changing the rules. Thus, although it may be desirable that public virtue be the primary control on the government, as acknowledged by James Madison, 'experience has taught mankind the necessity of auxiliary precautions.'[22]

The allure of the rule of law can also be explained in psychoanalytic terms as enabling the overthrow of the powerful father figure (of power, brute force, wanton human desire), which is replaced with a totemic[23] rather than personal authority.[24]

So the function of the rule of law may be explained in a number of ways, satisfactory to a varied spectrum of theories. But all have in common the fact that the 'morally neutral' requirements of the rule of law are seen as helping to prevent arbitrary action by government, rendering those in power accountable. The rule of law aids government according to the law—the rule of laws, not the rule of men.[25] It ensures, in the words of Hans Kelsen,[26] that government, unlike King Midas, may not turn everything it touches to its preferred substance (in this case, law). Law must apply to the judiciary and to government itself.[27]

The rule of law is also often associated or even identified with the existence of the structural feature of the separation of powers of the state, which holds that those who formulate the laws should be distinct from those entrusted with their interpretation, application and enforcement. James Madison and Alexander Hamilton, writing in the eighteenth-century American context, stressed the theory of checks and balances (power must be placed against power, strength against strength) as a brake on power

---

[22] J Madison, 'The Federalist, No 51' in A Hamilton, J Madison and J Jay, *The Federalist* (1788), JE Cooke (ed) (Middletown, CT, Wesleyan University Press, 1961 edn).

[23] For further on this, see S Freud, *Totem and Taboo*, J Strachey (ed and trans) (London, Routledge and Kegan Paul, 1950).

[24] But the rule of law provides a rather less nebulous and fantasist object than Deleuze and Guattari's 'desire' or Lacan's *objet petit a*, which are discussed below chs 9 and 12.

[25] As also developed in the idea of the *Rechtsstaat*, for further on which, see N Barber, 'The Rechtsstaat and the Rule of Law' (2003) *University of Toronto Law Journal*.

[26] H Kelsen, *Pure Theory of Law*, M Knight (trans) (Berkeley, University of California Press, 1967) 161.

[27] This is what Mark Tushnet has referred to as a 'thin constitutionalism'. M Tushnet, *Taking The Constitution Away from the Courts* (Princeton, Princeton University Press, 2000).

and thus a way to ensure individual freedom.[28] Hannah Arendt, following Montesquieu,[29] believed that the legal limits characteristic of the rule of law could be best achieved by separating law-making into separate legislative and judicial functions. In contrast, in totalitarian systems, the three functions of law-making, executive and adjudication are often merged in one central system.

The rule of law is also sometimes linked with a commitment to some basic rights of the individual against the coercive power of the state and judicial review.[30] Indeed, in many recent debates over constitutionalism, there has been a tendency to define 'constitutionalism' as an approach based on the rule of law and judicial review, as opposed to an approach based on popular or parliamentary sovereignty.

Some conceptions of the rule of law build on these qualities to include further elements of substantive morality. For example, the International Commission of Jurists' New Delhi Declaration (1959) situated the rule of law at the centre of a social democratic political agenda.[31] 'Thick' theories of the rule of law tend to incorporate substantive notions of justice. They conceive the rule of law more broadly as a set of ideals, whether understood in terms of protection of substantive human rights, specific forms of organised government, or particular economic arrangements such as free market capitalism. Philip Selznick characterised these theories as 'more affirmative, more demanding, and in some ways a more risky point of view'.[32] These theories go beyond the abuse of power to include values that need affirmative protection by law. Examples of modern jurists who have advocated explicitly substantive rule of law theories include Ronald Dworkin, TRS Allan, Sir John Laws and John Finnis.[33] For Finnis, the rule of law, properly understood, comprises more than a *minima moralia*; indeed, as an element helping to ensure the goodness of law, it is part of

---

[28] A Hamilton, J Madison, J Jay and G Willis, *The Federalist Papers* (1788) (New York, Bantam Dell 2003).

[29] See, eg, H Arendt, *On Violence* (New York, Houghton Mifflin Harcourt, 1970).

[30] See, eg, T Bingham, *The Rule of Law* (London, Allen Lane, 2010). In Germany, for example, the concept of the *Rechtsstaat* is closely associated with judicial review for breach of basic rights. See, eg, L Pech, 'The Rule of Law as a Constitutional Principle of the European Union', Jean Monnet Working Papers No 04/09.

[31] International Commission of Jurists, *The Rule of Law in a Free Society: A Report of the International Congress of Jurists, New Delhi, January 1959* (Geneva, ICJ, 1959) 7–43; and International Commission of Jurists, 'The Rule of Law and Human Rights—Principles and Definitions' (1966).

[32] P Selznick, 'American Society and the Rule of Law' (2005–06) 33 *Syracuse Journal of International Law and Commerce* 29, 31.

[33] See, eg, R Dworkin, *Law's Empire* (Oxford, Hart Publishing, 1998); TRS Allan, *Constitutional Justice: A Liberal Theory of the Rule of Law* (Oxford, Oxford University Press, 2001); Sir J Laws, 'The Constitution: Morals and Rights' (1996) *Public Law* 622; and J Finnis, *Natural Law and Natural Rights* (Oxford, Clarendon Press, 1981).

a holistic theory of law's place in society. Judith Shklar[34] distinguished two models of the rule of law. One is that of imposing institutional restraints, following Montesquieu's doctrine of the separation of powers. The other model, that of the rule of law as 'the rule of reason', she derived from Aristotle and linked to modern-day theories such as those of Dworkin, with his initiatives of the 'super judge' Hercules and of sound moral reasoning.

These further aspirations for the rule of law highlight a range of benefits that extend beyond legality and the avoidance of arbitrariness to a more fulsome, rich notion of law. Yet the benefits of a 'thin' theory of the rule of law are often seen to lie in its very bareness, in its lack of prescription as to the substance of law. In its pared down form, the rule of law is of use to a very broad range of systems and societies. It makes no stipulation as to content and sets no necessary requirements as to democratic government. Raz perceives a fundamental problem with thick (or what Selznick has referred to as 'high-risk'[35]) theories:

> If the rule of law is the rule of the good law then to explain its nature is to propound a complete social philosophy. But if so the term lacks any useful function. We have no need to be converted to the rule of law just in order to discover that to believe in it is to believe that good should triumph.[36]

The rule of law as a means to justice also appears clearly capable of applying in conditions of legal pluralism and in the international arena. Transnational organisations such as the United Nations, the World Trade Organization and the European Union stress a commitment to the rule of law, although some of the self-professed commitment of international institutions is undoubtedly self-serving. For example, the rule of law is mentioned in the Preamble to the Universal Declaration on Human Rights (1948). It is entrenched in EU law (in Article 2 of the Treaty on European Union)[37] and is acknowledged by the European Court of Justice (ECJ) as a key principle of European constitutionalism in *Les Verts*, in which the ECJ referred to the EU treaties as a charter based on the rule of law.[38] The European Union is also more generally based on the notion of 'integration through law' and aspires to have its own form of the separation of powers, and checks and balances in the form of 'institutional balance',[39] even if, as I

---

[34] J Shklar, 'Political Theory and the Rule of Law' in A Hutchinson and P Monahan (eds), *The Rule of Law: Ideal or Ideology* (Toronto, Carswell, 1987) 1.

[35] Selznick (above n 32) 31.

[36] Raz (above n 14) 196.

[37] Although this may give rise to problems, as the rule of law is nowhere defined in the EU treaties, and different member states have different understandings of it, according to their diverse legal traditions (eg, *État de Droit* in France, *Rechtsstaat* in Germany and so on).

[38] Case 294/83 *Parti Ecologiste—'Les Verts' v European Parliament* [1986] ECR 1339.

[39] In Case 9/56 *Meroni & Co* [1958] ECR 133, the ECJ held that 'there can be seen in the balance of powers which is characteristic of the institutional structure of the Community a fundamental guarantee granted by the Treaty to the undertakings ... to which it applies.'

argue in the next chapter, the European Union has not in fact observed the rule of law as it should have done.[40] One may also consider the case law of the European Court of Human Rights, which has referred to the European Convention on Human Rights (ECHR) as 'a constitutional instrument of European public order'.[41] Conor Gearty, in a well-known article in 1993, referred to due process as a 'core unifying concept of the Convention and its case law'.[42] Notwithstanding Articles 8–11, which contain substantive rights to private and family life, freedom of religion, thought, expression and association, he suggested that the ECHR is principally a procedural charter, stressing the great use made of Articles 5, 6 and 7.[43] Gearty suggested a complex reading of due process, understood in three senses in an increasing level of generality: questions on fairness of trial, protection of minorities and fairness of the political process. He looked to the work of the American constitutional scholar Jon Ely[44] for elucidation of due process, which calls for fairer processes and a more participatory system.

Rule of Law: Thick or Thin? Or Neither?

Clearly, there exists more than one credible understanding of the rule of law. However, I also prefer to avoid an oppositional categorisation (frequently used in modernity) in terms of thick/thin, form/substance, strong/weak, hard/soft and so on, which has a tendency to oversimplify issues and set up apparently antithetical and even antagonistic categories that may wrongly suggest an irreconcilable or inimical relation which does not in fact exist. Nonetheless, there is merit in Raz's argument—the rule of law should be distinguishable from a complete legal philosophy.

Formal accounts do have a certain attraction in that they are more clearly capable of applying over a broader range of legal systems and different institutional settings. A substantive account such as Dworkin's, which centres around the judicial role, the possibility of coherence and integrity of legal systems, and the embrace of substantive legal/moral principles,

---

[40] For development of these arguments, see, eg, S Douglas-Scott, 'The Problem of Justice in the EU' in J Dickson and P Eleftheriadis (eds), *The Philosophical Foundations of EU Law* (Oxford, Oxford University Press, 2012).

[41] Case 15318/89 *Loizidou v Turkey* [1996] ECHR 70 (18 December 1996). The rule of law was first mentioned by the European Court of Human Rights in *Golder v UK* (1979) 1 EHRR 524, and the court has referred to it frequently ever since.

[42] C Gearty, 'The European Court of Human Rights and the Protection of Civil Liberties: An Overview' (1993) 52 *Cambridge Law Journal* 89–127.

[43] The great majority of cases are brought under these articles, which involve the right to liberty of the person (Art 5), the right to a fair trial (Art 6) and no punishment without law (Art 7).

[44] J Hart Ely, *Democracy and Distrust: A Theory of Judicial Review* (Cambridge, MA, Harvard University Press, 1980).

seems less than well adapted to the competing claims of pluralism and to demands of the regulatory state. Formal accounts that do not require such a principled coherence seem better suited to the contemporary legal space. However, rather than looking to the thinnest of theories, I argue that the rule of law incorporates human rights. Raz has argued:

> A non-democratic legal system, based on the denial of human rights, on extensive poverty, on racial segregation, sexual inequalities, and racial persecution may, in principle, conform to the requirements of the rule of law better than any of the legal systems of the more enlightened Western democracies ...[45]

However, human rights, as I argue below in chapter nine, have (rightly or wrongly) become so much part of our mindset, a first point for any vision of justice, that their recognition and enforcement is now seen as essential for the respect of human beings. Moreover, they have become juridified in a wealth of documents both national and international as essential standards that positive laws must observe. Even if there exists disagreement as to their exact nature and scope, there is broad agreement at a more general level and on the necessity of their legal enforcement, often—even usually—in the form of bills of rights, giving rise to judicial review. Human rights operate both as constraints on power and as preserving shields for individual autonomy and liberty—thus also fulfilling the essential functions of the rule of law. Therefore, I see them as necessary elements of the rule of law.[46] If forced to comply with categories, I would therefore describe the account of the rule of law advanced in this book as 'thin +'.

This brief discussion of the rule of law confirms that there exists no single model for the rule of law, no more than there is one for justice or democracy. Yet this should not mean that its value is lessened, nor that it may be dismissed as incoherent or essentially contested. Rather, it suggests that we should acknowledge that there exist different ways of furthering the values it serves. What are these values? Surely at the base of the rule of law lies the opposition to unrestrained, despotic power (and belief in the ability of law to control it), as well as a correlative emphasis on freedom and equality, which are enhanced by restraining power through law that is in sufficiently 'good shape'[47] to constrain and guide conduct.

In order to reclaim the rule of law, it is necessary to focus on these values rather than on specific, contingent, historical practices which have sometimes been used to further these values. Otherwise there is a danger of believing that contingent practices are in fact the essence of the rule of

---

[45] Raz (above n 14) 211.
[46] See Bingham (above n 30) for a similar view. For the view that German law strongly upholds this approach, see also Pech (above n 30), who urges EU law to do the same.
[47] J Waldron, 'Legal Pluralism and the Contrast between Hart's Jurisprudence and Fuller's' in P Cane (ed), *The Hart–Fuller Debate in the Twenty-First Century* (Oxford, Hart Publishing, 2010).

law—a fault that Dicey might be said to have committed by identifying the rule of law with its rather singular form under Victorian constitutional law. In this way, we may avoid the danger of 'goal displacement',[48] whereby practices introduced as a means to achieve the goals of the rule of law—for example, identifying it with a system of law as rules—become identified with the rule of law itself. So for example, 'principles of legality',[49] in their capacity to aid the calculability and transparency of the law and in turn enable people to plan their lives, may have served the aims of the rule of law at certain times, but they will not always be the best means to ensure the constraint of power.[50] An overemphasis on predictability, rule-bound behaviour and calculability may itself become oppressive. Furthermore, an overemphasis on one of the functions of the rule of law—its ability to guide conduct and protect personal autonomy—has resulted in a sometimes skewed understanding of the rule of law as a doctrine of libertarian philosophy and tool to protect private rights.[51] This has meant that the function of the rule of law as a constraint on power has sometimes been overlooked.

With its associations of order, regularity, proportionality and equality, there is something geometric or architectonic about the rule of law—a contrast with the 'chaos of surfaces' and 'rhetorical flows' of postmodernity. It therefore can seem to be the reverse of the chaotic trajectories and vortices of much contemporary law. The rule of law and contemporary governance (with its emphasis on flexible, responsive regulation) do not seem to be natural companions. The rule of law requires that standards, sometimes even described as 'rules', be applied to law. This may seem difficult in a legal world where 'the model of rules' is no longer clearly applicable. And yet the very fact of chaotic trajectories and perspectives might suggest a reason why this structural component is needed more than ever—as a bulwark against, a counterpoint to injustice, a means of containing the chaos of the legal universe. It does not require that actual, substantive laws form rule-like systems but rather that certain structural components be applied to shore up laws or even to eject them where necessary.

---

[48] M Krygier, 'False Dichotomies, Real Perplexities and the Rule of Law' in A Sajó (ed), *Human Rights with Modesty: The Problem of Universalism* (Leiden/Boston, Martinus Nijhoff, 2004) 251–77.

[49] Ie, requirements of lawmaking such as clarity, non-contradiction, absence of retroactivity and publicity.

[50] I discuss this further below ch 8.

[51] Such views are to be found in, eg, FA Hayek, *The Constitution of Liberty* (Chicago, University of Chicago Press, 1960); FA Hayek, 'Rules and Order' in FA Hayek, *Law, Legislation and Liberty: Volume I* (London, Routledge and Kegan Paul, 1973); and E-U Petersmann, 'How to Promote the International Rule of Law? Contributions by the World Trade Organization Appellate Review System' (1998) 1 *Journal of International Economic Law* 25 (as well as many other articles by Petersmann).

The Shameful Absence of the Rule of Law

Perhaps the strongest argument for observance of the values inherent in the rule of law is an awareness of what happens when it is not observed, when law seems to vanish, its constraints ignored by the state. As EP Thompson wrote, 'There is a very large difference, which twentieth-century experience ought to have made clear even to the most exalted thinker, between arbitrary extra-legal power and the rule of law.'[52]

Lon Fuller, Franz Neumann and Hannah Arendt all provide compelling accounts of the breakdown of law in totalitarian regimes of the twentieth century, of the ways in which failure to observe the safeguards of the rule of law resulted in an inability to create anything recognisable as 'law'.[53] Yet we do not have to look to the totalitarian twentieth century for examples of an absence of both justice and the rule of law. They are evident in the post-September 11, twenty-first century—notwithstanding that the United States issued a call for 'infinite justice' in its response to the 9/11 attacks.[54]

The attacks on the World Trade Center, the Pentagon and later in London and Madrid were clearly outrages, yet this does not justify the lacunae of justice created by the pugilistic responses by states. To start with, the US administration declared a 'war on terror', denoting terrorists as 'the enemy' rather than identifying them as criminal suspects, thereby removing them from the ambit of the criminal law. In Guantánamo, sited in Cuba and therefore nominally outside the jurisdiction of US courts, detainees were denied prisoner of war status and the protection of the Geneva Convention (1949). In this way, it was claimed that they might be detained indefinitely, as 'battlefield detainees' or 'unlawful combatants',[55] in the preferred language of the then US administration. Denied the protection of both the US Constitution or international law, these detainees were (in the extra-judicial words of Lord Steyn, at that time a judge of the

---

[52] EP Thompson, Postscript to 'The Rule of Law' in *Whigs and Hunters* (above n 11) 265.

[53] See, eg, Fuller (above n 14); Neumann, *The Rule of Law* (above n 11); F Neumann, *Behemoth: The Structure and Practice of National Socialism* (New York and Evanston, Harper Torchbooks, 1966); and H Arendt, *The Origins of Totalitarianism* (Cleveland, World Publishing Company, 1958).

[54] For further commentary on the term 'infinite justice', see A Roy, *The Algebra of Infinite Justice* (London, Flamingo, 2002).

[55] The US administration relied on the precedent in *Ex parte Quirin* 1942, Sct 317 US 1 31, in which the US Supreme Court described as an 'enemy combatant' anyone 'who without a uniform comes secretly through the lines for the purpose of waging war by destruction of life or property' and determined that such persons were not entitled to prisoner of war status and were to be 'regarded as offenders against the law of war subject to trial and punishment by military courts'. The US 2006 Military Commission defined an 'enemy illegal combatant' as 'anyone engaged in or supporting hostilities against the US', thereby suggesting that anyone opposing the government is at war with it.

UK House of Lords) in a legal 'black hole', 'a stain on American justice'.[56] They were classified as a unique class, denied rights as soldiers, as well as the protection of constitutional and criminal law. The US administration determined their classification—notably, mostly by the executive fiat of presidential orders.[57] Similarly, in the United Kingdom, foreign nationals were detained at Belmarsh, a high-security detention centre, in derogation from the protection of the ECHR, without limit and very often without access to lawyers of their choosing or to the courts.[58]

These detainees were therefore subject to a unique form of detention, not based on any proof of their alleged past wrongdoing but on assessments of their supposed dangerousness as 'enemy combatants' who might engage in terrorist acts if released. Their detention was justified as a *preventive* measure, because of the perceived *risk* of allowing them to remain free. Further, in the case of the United Kingdom, the government attempted to justify indefinite detention and derogation from normal human rights protections on the grounds that the United Kingdom was in a 'state of emergency'. Such a rationale allowed for potentially indefinite detention.[59] Regrettable parallels may be drawn with totalitarian regimes: Nazi Germany employed the concept of 'protective custody' (*Schützhaft*), which was broad enough in its scope to ensure that criminal suspects who were German nationals could be sent to concentration camps rather than to prison.[60]

In both the United States and the United Kingdom, detainees have obtained some limited access to judicial review, and some commentators believe that this has ameliorated the situation. The *Hamdi* and *Rasul* cases,[61] decided by the US Supreme Court, have been cited[62] as limiting the power of the executive, in that the applicants were at last able to rely

---

[56] See the comments of Lord Steyn in 'Guantánamo Bay: The Legal Black Hole' (2004) 53 *International and Comparative Law Quarterly* 1. For a discussion of 'black holes' more generally, see D Dyzenhaus, *The Construction of Law: Legality in a Time of Emergency* (Cambridge, Cambridge University Press, 2006).

[57] For example, by a presidential military order of 13 November 2001 (of hugely wide scope), US PMO, 'Detention, Treatment and Trial of Certain Non-citizens in the War against Terrorism', White House Press Release, 13 November 2001.

[58] Under Pt 4 of the Anti Terrorism, Crime and Security Act of 2001, which provided for the indefinite detention without trial of foreign nationals suspected of involvement in terrorism.

[59] They were, however, free to leave for their country of citizenship if they wished to do so. However, most chose not to do so, for fear of suffering ill treatment there. Nor could they be deported to those countries, as this would breach the ECHR Art 3 prohibition on torture and inhuman and degrading treatment, according to the ECtHRs in *Chahal v UK* (1996) 23 EHRR 413.

[60] For further on this, see Neumann, *Behemoth* (above n 53).

[61] *Rasul v Bush* 124 SCt 2686 (2004); and *Hamdi v Rumsfeld* 124 SCt 263 (2004). See also T Otty, 'Honour Bound to Defend Freedom? The Guantanamo Bay Litigation and the Fight for Fundamental Values in the War on Terror' (2008) *European Human Rights Law Review* 433.

[62] See, eg, Bingham (above n 30) ch 11.

on the writ of habeas corpus initially denied them, when a majority of the Supreme Court held they were within US 'territorial jurisdiction'. Justice John Paul Stevens, writing for the majority in *Rasul*, wrote, 'Executive imprisonment has been considered oppressive and lawless since King John at Runnymede ruled no free man should be imprisoned, disposed, outlawed or exiled save by the judgement of his peers or by the law of the land.'[63] In *A v Home Secretary (No 1)*[64] and subsequently *A v United Kingdom*,[65] first the House of Lords[66] and then the European Court of Human Rights found the UK government to be in breach of Article 5 of the ECHR (which outlines the right to liberty). The fact that under the UK detention regime only non-UK nationals were subjected to indefinite detention was found to be discriminatory by the courts, as well as disproportionate, and is a clear breach of the rule of law.[67] Also counter to the rule of law were the lack of protection from the US Constitution and from international law in the United States, and the application of a system of 'special immigration appeal tribunals' in the United Kingdom, whereby suspects were denied access to most of the information against them, as well as to lawyers of their choice.

However, it should be added that in neither of these sets of cases were the detainees freed by the Court decisions; nor was the Bush administration's activity deemed to be illegal. Notably, in *A v Home Secretary*, a majority of the House of Lords (by 8:1) was willing to accept the Government's argument that the United Kingdom was in 'a state of emergency threatening the life of the nation'. Nor did the Government's response to the Court's finding in *A* necessarily improve matters. The Government reacted to the House of Lords judgment by introducing 'control orders'[68]—in effect the imposition of curfews or house arrest. On later challenge in the House of Lords, the Court held that some but not all control orders deprived applicants of their liberty. These are disappointing results but do not indicate the irrelevance of the rule of law—rather, they indicate an inadequate application of it, with insufficient respect for human rights and too timorous employment by the courts.

---

[63] *Rasul v Bush* (above n 61).

[64] *A and Others v Secretary of State for the Home Department (No 1)* [2004] UKHL 56.

[65] *A v United Kingdom* (2009) 49 EHRR 29.

[66] As it then was, prior to its transformation into the UK Supreme Court in 2009.

[67] Adam Tomkins has suggested that this decision might indicate the beginnings of a 'judicial awakening' to the fact that the courts, even in cases of national security, had responded 'to ensure that the rule of law is respected'; although he also stated that this had been 'a long time coming'. A Tomkins, 'Readings of *A v Secretary of State for the Home Department*' (2005) *Public Law* 263.

[68] In 2011, the UK Coalition government replaced control orders with 'Terrorism Prevention and Investigation Measures' (TPIMs) in the Terrorism Prevention and Investigation Measures Act 2011, which still, however, retains many of the unsatisfactory elements of the old control order system.

Such conditions as those of the detainees in Guantánamo have been likened by the Italian philosopher Giorgio Agamben to that of the *homo sacer* or 'bare life' of the Roman Empire—namely, individuals who exist as exiles to the law, 'stripped of their political and biological lives'.[69] Agamben has used the expression 'biopolitics' to denote an exercise of power that captures and controls nature (and human nature) itself. Guantánamo has been described as 'a semiotic as well as a metaphysical construct ... The orange jump suits seem peculiar, the shackles, goggles, headphones, in which crouching detainees were initially kept in hot sun, more disturbing still.'[70] Such captivity is well captured by Goya's famous etching 'The Captivity is as Barbarous as the Crime' (Figure 7-2). It highlights the outrage of such detention, reminding us that such barbaric treatment by governments is nothing new but rather a further chapter in an on-going catalogue of injustice, abuse and ill-treatment by those in power. There is something almost pornographic about the images of detainees at Guantánamo (or Abu Ghraib)—an embarrassed, shameful excitement to them. Indeed, Ahdaf Soueif has located them within

Figure 7-2: Goya, 'The captivity is as barbarous as the crime', etching (original plate, 1810–14)

---

[69] G Agamben, *Homo Sacer: Sovereign Power and Bare Life* (Stanford, Stanford University Press, 1998). In fact, in ancient Rome, the term denoted a person who could be killed with impunity.
[70] I Ward, *Law, Text, Terror* (Cambridge, Cambridge University Press, 2009).

'the pornography of colonial occupation—a strategy of diminishing the conquered other'.[71]

Agamben has further identified Guantánamo as 'the space that is opened when the state of exception begins to become the rule'.[72] He continues, 'The detainees of Guantánamo ... are subject now only to raw power; they have no legal existence.'[73] Agamben has also likened these detainees to Jewish people who were stripped of their citizenship under the Nuremberg laws before they were placed in concentration camps. Indeed, their situation is redolent of Franz Kafka's *The Trial*, an observation that may be unoriginal but is nonetheless poignant. As a British detainee at Guantánamo, Moazzam Begg, has stated, 'I hadn't read Kafka, but I knew the expression Kafkaesque. It was happening to me.'[74]

There are many other instances of abandonment of the rule of law in the context of the 'war on terror'. For example, the practice of 'extraordinary rendition' whereby persons were detained—or abducted[75]—by US personnel abroad and then handed on to other states known to mistreat or torture prisoners. The US administration tried to present these actions as complying with the rule of law, but such attempts have been unconvincing.[76] One of the most extreme examples of unlawful conduct—more extreme even than leaving individuals in a legal black hole—concerns the use of torture. In 2006 the UN High Commission for Human Rights determined that the United States had committed acts which amounted to torture. This was denied by the US administration, which used the argument that ordinary definitions of torture could not be applied in these circumstances.[77]

---

[71] A Soueif, *Mezzaterra: Fragments from the Common Ground* (New York, Anchor Books, 2004).

[72] Agamben, *Homo Sacer* (above n 69) 168.

[73] Ibid. See also G Agamben, *State Of Exception* (Chicago, Chicago University Press, 2005). Perhaps unsurprisingly, Hardt and Negri agree: '[T]he state of exception has become permanent and general; the exception has become the rule, pervading both foreign relations and the homeland.' M Hardt and A Negri, *Multitude: War and Democracy in the Age of Empire* (London, Penguin, 2004) 7.

[74] M Begg, *Enemy Combatant* (London, Free Press, 2006).

[75] Practices of kidnapping a person abroad to bring them back to stand trial were found by the English courts to constitute a blatant and extremely serious failure to comply with the rule of law in *R v Horseferry Magistrates Court, ex p Bennett* (1994) 1 AC 42; and *R v Mullen* 2000 QB. Contrast *US v Alvarez-Machain* 504 US 655 (1992), in which the US Supreme Court found foreign kidnapping of a suspect no bar to trial in the United States.

[76] For equivocal views on the preservation of the rule of law, see, eg, R Wedgwood, 'The Fall of Saddam Hussein: Security Council Mandates and Pre-emptive Self-Defence' (2003) *American Journal of International Law* 577. For a thorough analysis of unlawful extraordinary rendition, see, eg, Council of Europe and European Parliament on Extraordinary Rendition: P6_TA (2006) 0316.

[77] An infamous 'torture memorandum' was written in April 2002 for the US Justice department by John Yoo and Jay Bybee at the request of then White House counsel Alberto Gonzales. The memorandum argued that as commander in chief, the President could order torture without fear of criminal liability. It also argued that in any case, the prohibition on torture did not include threats of death, as long as the threat of death was not imminent, nor

Indeed, articles started appearing with in the US press with titles such as 'Time to Think about Torture'[78]—notwithstanding the Eighth Amendment to the US Constitution, which prohibits 'cruel and unusual punishment', as well as the prohibitions on torture in Article 3 of the Geneva Convention and in Article 7 of the International Covenant on Civil and Political Rights (1966), to which the United States is a signatory. Nor were things a great deal better in the United Kingdom. Conor Gearty has set out a long list of UK laws in which human rights had been limited under anti-terror legislation, expressing the worry as to whether 'our civil liberties will still be here when we seek to pass them on to our children'.[79] The European Union has also been complicit in extraordinary rendition, EU states having permitted rendition operations to pass through their territories; and the EU has not made use of Article 7 of the Treaty on European Union (TEU), which permits enforcement actions (and suspension of EU membership) against those EU states that do not respect human rights.[80]

These examples demonstrate a shift in perception from 'normal' justice, in which basic safeguards of the rule of law apply (as imperfect as it might be), to instances of political or subjective or 'abnormal justice'—ie, established law does not play its part, and things are the worse for it. Guantánamo and Belmarsh reveal clear breaches of the rule of law and injustices on a primary and shameful level. Denying those incarcerated the protection of well-established national and international laws, access to lawyers of their choice or indeed to any lawyers in some cases, not to mention ill-treatment or even torture in confinement, are matters of shame and outrage. And importantly, these breaches of law appear glaring. When the US administration attempted to justify practices such as 'waterboarding' as not being torture, the duplicity and dishonesty in such conduct was recognised as blatant,[81] as was the fact that the law was not being followed.

Yet recourse to law has not always provided satisfactory remedies. The House of Lords, for example, agreed with the Government's assessment that the United Kingdom was in a state of emergency—indeed, in the United Kingdom and elsewhere, courts have too often been deferential to

---

prohibit the infliction of intense pain, as long as the pain did not rise to a severity associated with organ failure or death itself. See also P Sands, *Torture Team: Uncovering War Crimes in the Land of the Free* (London, Penguin, 2008); and M Danner, *Torture and Truth: America, Abu Ghraib and the War on Terror* (New York, New York Review Books, 2004).

[78] J Alter, 'Time to Think about Torture', *Newsweek* (5 November 2001).
[79] C Gearty, *Civil Liberties* (Oxford, Oxford University Press, 2007) 111–19.
[80] Art 7 (2) TEU states: 'The European Council ... may determine the existence of a serious and persistent breach by a Member State of the values referred to in Article 2, after inviting the Member State in question to submit its observations.'
[81] For further on this, see, eg, Sands (above n 77) 81–82 and 260.

the executive in cases of national security.[82] Lawsuits that reached the US Supreme Court did not result in the closure of Guantánamo. The House of Lords did not completely condemn control orders.[83] This suggests that judicial review will not always prove an adequate remedy when the rule of law has been abused.[84] This is highly regrettable. Sometimes, in the absence of overwhelming civil disobedience and with a weak legislature, the courts may be the only institutions sufficiently powerful to take on a strong executive. The overly deferential approach of the courts in the context of national security makes it easier for a government to ignore the rule of law. Again, this is not to castigate the rule of law as irrelevant but to regret that it has not been more vigorously enforced.

However, there is more than one way to assert and insist on the rule of law. Lawyers and courts, along with the public, have been willing to speak out against malpractice, ill-conduct and illegality.[85] There has also been widespread condemnation by the public and nongovernmental organisations (NGOs).[86] For example, the worldwide demonstrations in March 2003 against the war in Iraq, jointly commented on by Jürgen Habermas and Jacques Derrida,[87] indicated outrage at illegality, at the failure to

---

[82] For further examples, see, eg, the judgment of the majority in the UK case *Liversidge v Anderson* [1942] AC 206; and *Secretary of State for the Home Department v Rehman* [2001] UKHL 47 postscript of Lord Hoffmann, in which he stated that the 9/11 attacks underlined 'the need for the judicial arm of government to respect the decisions of ministers of the Crown'. Moreover, the attitudes of the UK courts and that of the ECtHRs towards governments' declarations of states of emergency have also been overly deferential. See, eg, the ECtHR case *Brannigan and McBride v United Kingdom* (1993) 17 EHRR 539. Such judgments tend to provide support for the statement of Brian Simpson that, in cases of national security, the courts wash their hands: AWB Simpson, *In the Highest Degree Odious: Wartime Detention without Trial* (Oxford, Oxford University Press, 1992).

[83] Eg, *Secretary of State for the Home Department v JJ* [2007] UKHL 45, in which, although the House of Lords held that an 18-hour curfew would be a deprivation of liberty, it appeared to suggest that a curfew for a shorter period of time, say 12 hours, would not be; nor did it condemn the general system of control orders.

[84] *R (Corner House Research and Others) v Director of the Serious Fraud Office* [2008] UKHL 60, in which the House of Lords upheld the decision of the UK Serious Fraud Office to discontinue the investigation of alleged corruption involving BAE System Plc over the Al Yamamah arms contract to Saudi Arabia, provides such a disappointing example.

[85] See, for example, Lord Steyn's extra-judicial writings on black holes; Sands (above n 77); G Pierce, *Dispatches from the Dark Side: On Torture and the Death of Justice* (London, Verso, 2010).

[86] For example, see the report of Amnesty International, 'Open Secret: Mounting Evidence of Europe's Complicity in Rendition and Secret Detention', available at http://www.amnesty .org.uk/uploads/documents/doc_21023.pdf (last accessed 29 November 2012).

[87] This took the form of an article entitled 'February 15th, or What Binds Europeans Together' (a reference to the day in 2003 when mass demonstrations against the Iraq War were held in many European cities) written by Jürgen Habermas and co-signed by Jacques Derrida, published in *Frankfurter Allgemeine Zeitung* on May 31, 2003, calling upon the nations of 'Kerneuropa' (what Donald Rumsfeld dismissively described as 'Old Europe'— France, Germany, Italy, Spain, Benelux and Portugal) to adopt a common foreign policy.

observe the rule of law and at injustice, which have all led to human suffering. We will return to this in the final chapter.

Such examples of disregard for the rule of law are of course not a novel feature of the post-9/11 world. It has been usual for governments to give themselves powers to deal with emergencies—usually wide executive powers, such as Presidential orders in the United States—ignoring or abolishing standard legal procedures and safeguards.[88] Sometimes positive law itself, however, provides for the exception, in advance of any perceived 'emergency'. This approach is today codified through the specific legal concept of derogation. Such treaty exceptions and constitutional provisions allowing for the limited suspension of law for limited periods of time have long been viewed as a compromise, given state sovereignty, which dictates the introduction of exceptional state measures during emergencies. Article 15 of the ECHR, which provides for derogation from certain articles in the Convention in 'time of war or other public emergency threatening the life of the nation', is one such example. It was also the subject of litigation in *A v Home Secretary*, discussed above.

The derogation model has been described as 'one of the greatest achievements of contemporary international law',[89] providing a compromise between state sovereignty, exigency and individual rights, although the term 'achievement' begs the question—what sort of gain has been made? In fact, the derogation mechanism is undesirable because it creates 'a space between fundamental rights and the rule of law'—amounting in effect to a 'double-layered constitutional system',[90] just at the time (ie, war, emergency) when human rights become most vulnerable to government interference. A further fear is that derogations become not mere spaces in between or additional, double layers but rather give rise to alternative 'legal' zones altogether. Times of exception threaten, as Mark Tushnet has suggested, a permanent condition of emergency in the light of the indeterminate, temporal threat of the 'war on terror', endangering the rule of law.[91] It is notable that the vast swathe of emergency legislation adopted in the United Kingdom to deal with the post-9/11 situation has not been repealed, thus threatening to become a permanent state of affairs. This recalls Arendt's analysis of Nazi and Stalinist law, which, she pointed out, involved the nominal continuation of many pre-totalitarian

---

[88] For an early statement of the executive prerogative, see J Locke, *Second Treatise of Government* (1690), P Laslett (ed) (Cambridge, Cambridge University Press, 1963) para 160.

[89] C Klein, 'Jaime Oraa, Human Rights in States of Emergency in International Law' (1993) 4 *European Journal of International Law* 134.

[90] T Hickman, 'Between Human Rights and the Rule of Law: Indefinite Detention and the Derogation Model of Constitutionalism' (2005) 68 *Modern Law Review* 655, 657.

[91] M Tushnet, 'Emergencies and the Idea of Constitutionalism' in M Tushnet (ed), *The Constitution in Wartime: Beyond Alarmism and Complacency* (Durham, NC, Duke University Press, 2005) 45.

measures, alongside the secret creation or retroactive adoption of 'shadow' laws and 'shadow ministries', which doubled for and covered the very same conduct.[92]

Even worse is the danger that exceptional measures become not merely spaces in between but actually occupy the whole 'legal' space, in fact abolishing law. Agamben, in his analysis of the state of exception, has emphasised it as existing *outside* the law rather than as a derogation for which specific provision is made by law. According to Agamben, the state of exception cannot be 'annexed' to the law but must be understood instead as law's 'other'; therefore 'the state of exception is not a state of law' but a 'space without law' and a 'zone of anomie'.[93]

In *The Origins of Totalitarianism*, Arendt also wrote about a parallel, extreme phenomenon, which results in violence.[94] She described regimes governed by the 'laws of terror' rather than the rule of law; those countries failed to have law in any recognisable sense but were furnished with terror instead, with its own relentless, ruthless 'laws'. Furthermore, Fuller, in the context of his famous debate with HLA Hart,[95] made a similar observation in opposing Hart's traditional positivist view that the Nazis had law but that it was bad law. For Fuller, Nazi Germany in fact failed to have any sort of law at all, because of its failure to comply with requirements of the 'inner morality of law', ultimately with the rule of law. In its absence, what the Nazi regime deemed to be 'law' lacked the presence, stability and salience of law. So what these writers have described is a situation in which law ceases to function: there is anomie, no law, and a former founding violence, or a law of terror, surfaces. These situations are extreme.

Carl Schmitt and the Suspension of the Law

In this context, reference to Carl Schmitt's work is instructive. Carl Schmitt directed most of his work against liberal theories of law and justice and indeed is often seen as presenting a very powerful critique of liberalism. We may view his critique as a strident, challenging critique of the rule of law (but of a very different complexion to the critiques that will be

---

[92] Arendt, *The Origins of Totalitarianism* (above n 53). See also Ernst Fraenkel, who theorised a concept of 'the dual state', which involved both a normative and a prerogative component. E Fraenkel, *The Dual State*, E Stills (trans) (Oxford, Oxford University Press, 1941). However, Franz Neumann, in *Behemoth* (above n 53), disagreed with Fraenkel, refusing to allow that the term 'law' could be given to any 'dual' or 'shadow' measures taken by the Nazis.

[93] Agamben, *State of Exception* (above n 73) 50–53.

[94] Arendt, *The Origins of Totalitarianism* (above n 53).

[95] Fuller (above n 14).

discussed in the next chapter). Schmitt formulated his theory under the conditions of the gravely unstable Weimar Germany and rise to power of the Nazi party, but what is extremely interesting is that very often a Schmittian analysis has been resurrected and applied (either consciously or unconsciously) in the context of the contemporary 'war on terror' and post-9/11 emergency measures.[96]

The 'state of emergency', or exception, a favoured subject for Schmitt,[97] involves the suspension of law and other constitutional guarantees, and the subjection of law to politics—a reversal of liberal law's order, in which rules are thought to govern, or at least structure, politics. The whole Nazi period in Germany might be described as one long state of exception. For Schmitt, exceptional times (those of crisis and war) 'are more interesting than the rule' because it is then that the sovereign must decide the exception, and law is determined.[98] For Schmitt, the liberal rule of law was simply unworkable in the unstable conditions of Weimar Germany and the emergencies facing the government. Schmitt, unlike Franz Neumann, with whom he debated, did not believe that the rule of law was salvageable. He argued that instead of government operating under general laws, what was essential was for a 'sovereign' to take control and to take decisions independently of any existing rules.[99] Thus Schmitt's legal philosophy is a 'decisionist' one, which supposedly enables political leaders more effectively to pursue the national interest.

It must be stressed that Schmitt's theory rests on a very singular, atavistic theory of politics—one that interprets (and gives no further meaning to) politics as a sphere of human activity rent by inexorable division between 'friend' and 'foe', a state of on-going violence and antagonism.[100] The 'foe' was never given any greater specification than this in Schmitt's work but is simply the Other, alien, an existential force not determined rationally. In such a situation, Schmitt believed political actions should be based on the active decisions of a strong leader and not on reason, discussion and justification, and he used the Weimar Republic as an illustration of what happens if strong sovereignty is missing. This decisionism leaves no room for what Schmitt perceived as 'naïve moralistic ideas like that of

---

[96] Ie, consciously by some academics who do not necessarily share Schmitt's view but find it salient in an analysis of the situation; less explicitly, in the case of, eg, the former Bush Administration and its categorisation of 'an axis of evil', a term used by former US President George W Bush in his State of the Union Address on 29 January 2002, and the phrase 'You're either with us or against us'—both of which are nonetheless indicative of a sharp Schmittian split along the lines of friend and foe.

[97] See, eg, C Schmitt, *Political Theology: Four Chapters on the Concept of Sovereignty*, G Schwab (trans) (Chicago, University of Chicago Press, 2005).

[98] Ibid, 15.

[99] Ibid.

[100] C Schmitt, *The Concept of the Political* (Chicago, University of Chicago Press, 1996).

the social contract or rule of law'.[101] So for Schmitt, political sovereignty was an act of decision-making about friend and foe, a situation of 'norm-less exception'.

Notably, Schmitt's theory rests on a particular notion of democracy quite distinct from any to be found in liberalism. For Schmitt, political strength depended on extensive homogeneity in society, which in turn relied on ethnic and/or national bonds and, for Schmitt, this was true democracy. Commitment to shared formal procedures of liberalism was rejected as inadequate by Schmitt because it does not produce the required degree of homogeneity.[102] Indeed, Schmitt's theory separates the rule of law from democracy, with which it is usually associated. This has all sorts of ramifications for multicultural and pluralist societies in which ethnic homogeneity is unlikely, and also for the possibility of commitment to and governance by transnational organisations such as the European Union. In contrast, contemporary theorists, such as Habermas, believe that in such pluralistic situations, attachments to shared values can achieve the degree of societal integration necessary. Such an example is furnished by the concept of 'constitutional patriotism' to a republican constitution, which Habermas has offered as the sole form of permissible national loyalty—in distinct contrast to what Habermas has specifically referred to as 'the *pre-political* crutches of nationality and community of fate',[103] thus illustrating a completely different concept of the political to that of Schmitt. Indeed, Schmitt's theory appears particularly unsuited to describe the current fragmented, pluralistic, legal landscape.

So it is the case that, in Schmitt's work, even normal law and rules ultimately depend on a sovereign, an entity only determined in exceptional times. Law is thus reasoned as subject to politics, which in the final instance is a matter of raw power. This analysis highlights violence and power as at the very heart of law, a point that is of course by no means limited to the work of Schmitt. Walter Benjamin's short 1921 essay 'Critique of Violence' strikingly claimed that there is something *rotten* in law—its original violence.[104] Benjamin argued that law and violence are inseparable, that all law is latent violence and that all violence is either law-making or law-preserving. Thus, for Benjamin, law amounted to a vicious circle of a violence, which determines what violence is justifiable—a mythical cycle

---

[101] W Scheuerman, *Between the Norm and the Exception: The Frankfurt School and the Rule of Law* (Cambridge, MA, Massachusetts Institute of Technology Press, 1997) 21.

[102] C Schmitt, *The Crisis of Parliamentary Democracy* (Cambridge, MA, Massachusetts Institute of Technology Press, 1988).

[103] J Habermas, 'Yet Again German Identity' in H James and M Stone (eds), *When the Wall Came Down* (New York, Routledge, 1992) 86, italics added. Habermas is discussed further below ch 10.

[104] W Benjamin, 'Critique of Violence' in P Dementz (ed), *Benjamin: Reflections, Essays, Aphorisms and Autobiographical Writings* (New York, Schocken, 1986) 286.

that Benjamin characterised as subject to endless repetition. Any nonviolent resolution of conflicts were seen by Benjamin as immaterial because they were dismissed as not 'legal'. Indeed, he argued that if they were to be legally codified, they too would become subject to force. For Benjamin, the only means of escape from this endless circle of violence would be either by way of a 'proletarian general strike' or by a 'pure' or 'divine violence'—a messianic force that would be law-destroying and might appear as a flash of revolutionary transcendence.[105]

Derrida, drawing on Benjamin,[106] asserted that all states emerge through violence—through revolutions, coups or civil wars—and therefore, there always exists this trace of violence and power behind even the apparently democratic state. Derrida's essay 'Force of Law' has already been mentioned in chapter two, where it was discussed in the context of justice. In that same piece, however, Derrida also stressed how the English term 'to enforce the law' reveals a decisive factor about law: it authorises the use of force. Robert Cover, in his famous essay 'Violence and the Word', has also defined law in terms of a mediated violence exclusively played out in 'the field of pain and death'; and he has identified an 'originary violence' in the founding of the United States at the time of the Revolutionary War.[107] Law, for Cover, presents itself as a paradox, as a promise of future justice that is, however, grounded in past and present violence. As Cover has written, 'Legal interpretive acts signal and occasion the imposition of violence upon others: a judge articulates her understanding of a text, and as a result, somebody loses his freedom, his property, his children, even his life.'[108]

Resisting Schmitt

It is one thing to identify and highlight the role played by violence and force in law. It is another to reduce law to violence or raw power. We may well ask why have there been so many references in the past 10 years to the work of the unattractive 'Crown Jurist of the Third Reich'.[109] The concept of a 'state of emergency' has resurfaced in the early twenty-first century (in a way unthinkable in the 1990s, when many Western politicians and intellectuals gave out the somewhat smug impression that 'the

---

[105] Ibid, 300.

[106] J Derrida, 'Force of Law: The Mystical Foundation of Authority' in D Cornell, M Rosenfeld and DG Carlson (eds), *Deconstruction and the Possibility of Justice* (New York, Routledge, 1992); and S Žižek, *Violence* (London, Profile Books, 2008).

[107] R Cover, 'Violence and the Word' (1986) 95 *Yale Law Journal* 1601.

[108] Ibid, 1601.

[109] A description of Schmitt usually attributed to the catholic, anti-communist, political theorist Waldemar Gurian, eg, W Gurian, 'Der N S Kronjurist Carl Schmitt als Mohr' (1936) 2 *Deutsche Briefe* 489–91.

end of history' or the age of Kant's 'Perpetual Peace' might have arrived), and Western states have taken unsavoury and often unlawful measures to deal with the 'war on terror'. The absence of the rule of law in locations such as Guantánamo is shameful, and therefore it is perhaps unsurprising that theorists invoke Schmitt. But need one revert to Schmitt's analysis and its contempt for the rule of law—even if it is tempered by Agamben or Derrida—to capture certain events of the early twenty-first century? And if Schmitt's analysis is indeed salient, what conclusions should be drawn? That the rule of law is a myth to be despised, because law is to be derived only from violence? Are we rendered powerless in a search for legal mechanisms of justice and accountability as a result, because we feel tempted by a certain forceful allure of these theorists' analyses, or is there some other route that may be taken, some exit route other than sovereign dictatorship or anomie? There is, of course, a sense in which Schmitt is useful as an exposé of the hypocrisy of the West in its claims to have acted in accordance with the rule of law. But Schmitt should not be relied upon as providing a complete and definitive analysis.

The turn to and great reliance on Schmitt's exceptionalist jurisprudence,[110] as well as the oppressive measures taken by governments, which give rise to the Schmittian analogies in the first place, do suggest an inability of jurisprudence to handle shocking events such as Guantánamo. They point to a certain impoverishment of juristic culture, an inability to defend or re-imagine the rule of law in these times. This is comparable to what Benjamin described as the 'tortured stupidity' of some of his leftist colleagues during the Weimar period, a 'negativistic quiet' and 'left-wing melancholy'.[111]

In chapter five it was suggested that the state's role is in danger of becoming diminished to that of 'security state' because, in the face of globalisation and private enterprise, it has become so powerless elsewhere. Therefore the state, or rather government, seeks to legitimise itself by declaring endless terrorist threats and states of emergency. But in so doing, the state actually increases insecurity and delegitimises itself, by its failure to observe longstanding liberties and procedures. Slavoj Žižek has accused the West of being complicit in the creation of the war on terror, providing the war on terror with a *raison d'être* and a convenient successor to the Cold War[112]—all of this productive of a discourse of fear in justification of the repressive measures.

---

[110] As well as that of other right-wing, or 'pragmatic', thinkers, such as Leo Strauss or Machiavelli.

[111] W Benjamin, *Selected Writings*, vol 2 (Cambridge, MA, Harvard University Press, 1999) 424.

[112] S Žižek, 'Are We in a War? Do We Have an Enemy?' (2002) *London Review of Books* 24.

In these circumstances, it becomes necessary to reaffirm a faith in law as offering at least the prospect of justice. For the danger of 'a depleted jurisprudential culture' is that it 'nurtures disillusion and indifference to those principles which define a liberal democratic society. The Fall of the Twin Towers was an appalling tragedy. But the fall of our belief in justice would be a far greater one.'[113] Undoubtedly, the weakness and fragility of our legal culture have been illustrated by the willingness with which governments have sacrificed justice and the rule of law as well as the ambiguous and doubtful responses of the courts and jurisprudence more generally. Yet this is not a time to abandon a hope for justice, nor to abandon law and jurisprudence. It is rather a time to make good on it, to cleave to hard-worked-for values of human rights, the rule of law and democracy. So Schmitt must be rejected as offering a jurisprudence of shame.

The preferable view, surely, is that counter-terrorism can and should be carried on under the rule of law, and 'abnormal justice' should be shunned. Law may not be completely autonomous, but this does not mean that it is only a matter of politics, brute force or decisionism. It is possible for laws to be created democratically and for structures, such as checks and balances and separation of powers, to be ensured, to protect against the abuse of power. Certainly, there have existed and do exist crises that are states of emergency, and such crises can never be completely prevented. However, when such exceptions exist, they create large gaps in law, or even an absence of law, rather than, as Schmitt would have it, an insight into law's very essence. Schmitt's account exaggerates the exception. Why should we think that the exception proves the rule?

Gearty has castigated the 'supercession of the criminal model based on justice and due process by a security model based on fear and suspicion'.[114] It is very important for 'exceptional' legislation to be promptly repealed and account rendered as an acknowledgement of law's capacity to assert itself over force. Therefore, prosecution for crimes (eg, of torture[115]) is essential. It is crucial that abuses such as those committed by the United States and the United Kingdom in the context of the war on terror should be accounted for. Such abuse breaks down the trust of citizens and alienates people from the legal system, leading to an absence of reciprocity between citizens and administration.[116]

---

[113] Ward (above n 70) 153.

[114] C Gearty, 'Human Rights in an Age of Counterterrorism', Oxford Amnesty lectures (2006).

[115] As well as prohibitions on the use of evidence obtained under torture—as alleged in *A v Secretary of State for the Home Department (No 2)* [2005] UKHL 71.

[116] Eric Holder, US Attorney General under the Obama Administration, stated (before he took office), 'Our government authorised the use of torture, approved of secret electronic surveillance against American citizens, secretly detained American citizens without due process of law, denied the writ of Habeas Corpus to hundreds of accused enemy combatants and

Yet how is such a reckoning to be provided? The argument has been made in the United States that, as the administration (or certain members of it at the very least) committed war crimes, it therefore should be prosecuted.[117] However, criminal prosecutions are unlikely, at least in the United States,[118] because of the retrospective immunity that was provided, for example, by the US Congress in the Military Commissions Act to officers involved in the interrogation of Al Quaeda suspects in the wake of September 11. Yet a lack of accountability, of reckoning, is unacceptable. In some countries such as Argentina, Chile and South Africa, truth and reconciliation commissions have been established as a way of approaching politically sensitive issues such as war crimes, while avoiding the political destabilisation that might be caused by direct prosecutions.[119] Such commissions, by permitting testimony to be taken in a public setting, allow for wide publicity about wrongdoing. But such commissions cannot themselves provide justice, if those implicated in the iniquity of previous regimes fail to acknowledge responsibility for past behaviour. There may still be a need for prosecutions. There should be acknowledgement of responsibility for crimes and high-level wrongdoing.

Furthermore, it becomes a necessity to look outside of law, to literature, to personal testaments of suffering and to art, in order to aid law's attempt to understand these situations. In this impoverished environment, as Ian Ward has suggested,[120] testamentary chronicles such as Clive Stafford Smith's account of being a lawyer at the Guantánamo military commissions and Moazzam Begg's account of his detention in Guantánamo, become essential supplements to our legal assessments of these situations.

Poetry conveys these experiences with immediacy. Stripped to 'bare humanity', some of the detainees at Guantánamo have turned to poetry[121] to express their pain, humiliation and denial of justice, and as a way of

---

authorised procedures that violated both international law and the US Constitution ... We owe the American people a reckoning.' Quoted in D Cole, 'What to Do about the Torturers?', *New York Review of Books* (15 January 2009). But it would seem that much of this reckoning has still to be provided.

[117] See M Ratner, *The Trial of Donald Rumsfeld: A Prosecution by Book'* (New York, New Press, 2008); and Sands (above n 77).

[118] Under international law, any country possesses universal jurisdiction to prosecute certain war crimes and crimes against humanity, regardless of where or by whom such crimes were committed. This was the basis of General Pinochet's arrest in London on a warrant from a Spanish magistrate. Crimes of universal jurisdiction under international law have been established by treaty, as well as by custom. Such treaties include, inter alia, the 1949 Geneva Conventions, the 1979 Hostage Taking Convention, the 1984 Torture Convention and the 1998 International Convention for the Suppression of Terrorist Bombings.

[119] Although in some countries such as Chile and Argentina, prosecutions occurred in spite of pardons also having been given.

[120] Ward (above n 70).

[121] Now published as M Falkoff (ed), *Poems for Guantanomo: The Detainees Speak* (Iowa City, University of Iowa Press, 2007).

salvaging some sanity and dignity. One such poem was famously written on a Styrofoam cup. For example, Siddiq Turkestani, who was held for four years at Guantánamo before his release in 2005, wrote hopefully, in 'Even in the Pain':

> Even if the pain of the wound increases,
> There must be a remedy to treat it.
> Even if the days in prison endure,
> There must be a day when we will get out.

Yet even this consolation of poetry was denied them by the American censors: most of this poetry was either confiscated or destroyed on the basis of raising an 'enhanced security risk'. Only those pieces written in English were likely to survive, supposedly because they could be security vetted, although even then —in a move calculated again to strip their creators of their humanity—they were liable to be castigated and destroyed as lacking artistic merit.[122]

Martha Nussbaum has argued that literature, by engaging our sympathy in lives very different from our own, thereby increases our imaginative capabilities, better equipping us to make the judgements that public life requires of us. Nussbaum does not suggest substituting empathetic imagining for a rule-bound moral reasoning; rather, she defends the literary imagination 'precisely because it seems … an essential ingredient of an ethical stance that asks us to concern ourselves with other people whose lives are distant from our own'.[123] It is thus, as already argued in chapter six, essential to draw on our emotions—a view defended as essential to ethical reasoning by Smith in *The Theory of Moral Sentiments*.[124] Nussbaum has also drawn on Smith's model of the 'judicious spectator', who she suggests 'will give no group or individual special indulgence or favor on account of their relationship to her' but, on the other hand, whose 'neutrality does not require a lofty distance from the social realities of the case' and who is enjoined 'to examine those realities searchingly, with imaginative and emotional responses'.[125]

Simone Weil argued that it is 'the human voice' that we need to hear, not the 'shrill nagging' of legal arguments, claims and counterclaims.[126] These 'supplementary texts'—personal testaments, plays and poetry—do what law itself cannot always do: they provide us with accounts of suffering, the experiences of both terrorist and victim, of grief and rage, and give

---

[122] See ibid.

[123] M Nussbaum, *Poetic Justice: The Literary Imagination and Public Life* (Boston, Beacon Press, 1997) xvi.

[124] A Smith, *The Theory of Moral Sentiments* (London, Clarendon Press, 1976) 125.

[125] M Nussbaum, 'Poets as Judges: Judicial Rhetoric and the Literary Imagination' (1995) 62(4) *University of Chicago Law Review* 1477, 1482.

[126] S Weil, 'Human Personality' in S Miles (ed), *Simone Weil: An Anthology* (New York, Grove Press, 1986) 51.

us a much richer account of injustice. Indeed, they may do 'justice' and function as a 'counterterrorism strategy' that contrasts with the shameful response of governments, antiterrorist legislation and detention camps. In this way, Ward has suggested, we can address 'a second black hole'—that of voice.[127] By supplementing law with texts of suffering, by approaching these texts as a judicious spectator while also remaining aware of people's emotional responses, law may be rendered fair and may achieve its promise of justice. In this way, we may reclaim the rule of law.

Finally, it is important to recognise the way in which, in engaging in the conduct described in this section, governments not only subvert the rule of law but actually wage war upon it. Kant and Hegel both elaborated a theory in which the sanction restores the law, and in this sense the sanction is actually due to *law itself*, as well as to the victim. Punishment has as its first function to mend a public disorder. The extreme disregard for the rule of law in the context of the war on terror and the consequences that arise from it present a very strong case for the continued importance of the rule of law today. Without the rule of law, we risk giving free reign to all the coercive power that governments can summon, surely turning Leviathan into Frankenstein's monster.[128]

Figure 7-3: John Heartfield, 'Der Henker und die Gerechtigkeit' (1933) © The Heartfield Community of Heirs/VG Bild-Kunst, Bonn; and DACS, London 2012: maimed justice for our times?

---

[127] Ward (above n 70).
[128] N MacCormick, 'The Ethics of Legalism' (1989) 2 *Ratio Juris* 184, 188.

8

Legal Justice II: Reclaiming the Rule of Law from its 'Dark Side'—Critical Legal Justice

I have argued that regardless of the complexities and quagmires of justice, it is possible to identify a particular type of justice that is integral to law. Moreover, it is vital in an era of ever-increasing pluralism, complexity and globalisation that this legal justice be maintained if law is to deliver on its claim to do justice. Observing the rule of law is a means of delivering legal justice. This is not a complete theory of justice, as it leaves room for extra-legal types of justice; nor does legal justice always ensure that justice is done. Indeed, in a sense, it is not a theory of justice at all but should perhaps more properly be understood in terms of the arguments in chapter six, in negative terms,[1] as a means of deterring injustice—ensuring that law does not of itself contribute to the already manifold injustices in the word. It therefore provides an example of non-ideal thinking about justice, as it works to combat the harm that law can actually do. Without the fulfilment of legal justice, law is liable to become fiat, dictat, discretion, whim, coercion and abuse.

The rule of law is at the core of legal justice, and yet the rule of law is clearly not without its detractors. Earlier in his career, Allan Hutchinson attacked it in the following way:

> The rule of law is a sham; the esoteric and convoluted nature of legal discourse is an accommodating screen to obscure its indeterminacy and the inescapable element of judicial choice ... [L]egal discourse is only a stylised element of political discourse.[2]

Hutchinson's onslaught is fairly typical of postmodern critiques of law, which interpret law as a function of power and politics, warning us not to

---

[1] Indeed, Joseph Raz has described the rule of law as a 'negative virtue'. J Raz, 'The Rule of Law and its Virtue' (1977) 93 *Law Quarterly Review* 195.

[2] A Hutchinson, *Dwelling on the Threshold* (Toronto, Carswell, 1988) 40.

be beguiled by the apparently 'neutral' objective nature of the formal rule of law. Jurists have tended to take polarised views of the nature of the rule of law, viewing it either as ideal or as ideology, good or bad. As Judith Shklar has suggested, the rule of law has tended to be seen as 'a football in a game between friends and enemies of free market liberalism'.[3] Yet these oppositions present a false dichotomy.[4] It is not necessary to choose between only these stark formulations of the rule of law.

The crucial question is surely rather this one: is it possible to affirm the rule of law without remaining committed to a traditional account of rules and rule following?[5] In other words, is it possible to embrace the rule of law as a means to justice without either, on the one hand, turning to legal positivism or formalism based on a model of rules or, on the other, denigrating the rule of law in a postmodern critique of law as based on ideology or power? May the rule of law and the functions that it serves be reclaimed for law after modernity?

In order to determine whether this is possible, it will be necessary to examine a variety of different critiques of the rule of law, to determine their strength. Carl Schmitt's critique from the right of the spectrum has already been considered in the previous chapter and found wanting. In this chapter, I shall consider the following. First, what I shall call the 'impoverishment critique', which is that the rule of law as a theory of justice is too thin to be of any salience, and that it depends upon the adoption of a positivist or formalist theory of law not unlike those rejected in the first part of this book. If this critique were successful, it would be fatal to my advocacy of the rule of law, given the earlier claims of this book. Second, I examine attacks on the rule of law as a manifestation of perceived unattractive aspects of liberalism in one way or another—what Brian Tamanaha has referred to as 'the dark side' of the rule of law.[6] Such arguments tend to regard law pessimistically as the instrument of the powerful. These include attacks from postmodern legal theory, feminist jurisprudence and critical race theory, as well as the Marxist critique, shading into modern attacks on the 'Washington consensus' which see capitalism as 'global plunder'.

These critiques present a powerful challenge to the view I wish to present, namely that we must strive to protect and enforce the rule of law as a means to justice in an era of increasing complexity, globalisation and

---

[3] J Shklar, 'Political Theory and the Rule of Law' in A Hutchinson and P Monahan (eds), *The Rule of Law: Ideal or Ideology* (Toronto, Carswell, 1987) 16.

[4] See M Krygier, 'False Dichotomies, True Perplexities and the Rule of Law' in A Sajó (ed), *Human Rights with Modesty: The Problem of Universalism* (Leiden, Martinus Nijhof, 2004) 251.

[5] A question asked by Margaret Radin. See M Radin, 'Reconsidering the Rule of Law' (1989) 69 *Boston University Law Review* 781.

[6] B Tamanaha, 'The Dark Side of the Relationship between the Rule of Law and Liberalism' (2008) 3 *New York University Journal of Law and Liberty* 516.

privatisation of law. I hope to demonstrate how, in spite of these powerful challenges to its efficacy and value, the rule of law remains a valid and necessary means to justice and accountability of the myriad forms of law that now exist.

The Critiques

The Impoverishment Critique

This critique is aimed at 'thin' theories and sees the rule of law as being too closely linked to legal formalism and legal positivism and therefore subject to their defects. Formalism presents law as purified, closed and formal, and has already been encountered in this book. Formalism's aim is to depersonalise power and circumscribe discretion, and it is part of a wider attempt, like the closely related approach of legalism, to isolate law from politics and ethics, as an autonomous discipline. The critique derides formal justice and formal, or thin, versions of the rule of law as 'morally impoverished', 'the shabby remnant of the sum total of virtues that was once called justice' where now 'only a *minima moralia* remains'.[7] Agnes Heller finds this legal justice to be 'a cold virtue, sometimes even a cruel one', and indeed, the traditional image of justice, with the scales balancing behaviour and sword threatening punishment, can seem chilling as well as austere—and even more so the images of 'maimed' justice.[8] This chilling nature (which perhaps carries a whiff of brimstone) is also captured by Grant Gilmore, who wrote: 'In Hell, there will be nothing but law, and due process will be meticulously observed.'[9] A formal justice that, for example, executes only all left-handed people, whether rich or poor, would indeed be seen as cold and cruel.

HLA Hart wrote about the 'peculiarly intimate connection between law and justice',[10] highlighting the law's special and explicit concern for treating like cases alike, in a universal, rule-like manner. But Hart also stressed that this sense was only a partial account of justice and that it needed to be supplemented by a substantive account of justice—ie, what in fact constitutes a 'like' case, the implication being that formal justice is, of itself, inadequate, or at least incomplete. Hart's approach, along with the hypothetical execution of all left-handed people, seems therefore to confirm the view that formal justice is 'impoverished', or at least incomplete.

[7] A Heller, *Beyond Justice* (New York, Blackwell, 1987).
[8] See above ch 7.
[9] G Gilmore, *The Ages of American Law* (New Haven, Yale University Press, 1977) 111.
[10] HLA Hart, *The Concept of Law*, 2nd edn (Oxford, Clarendon Press, 1994) 157.

Joseph Raz has stressed the capacity of the rule of law to function like a sharp knife—ie, amorally.[11] It is also frequently pointed out, by positivists as well as by postmodern theory, that adherence to the (thin) rule of law may be compatible with great wrongdoing: 'Racial, religious and all manner of discrimination are not only compatible with but often instituted by general rules.'[12] This is in line with Raz's belief that law is not of itself morally valuable and that its distinguishing feature lies in its claim to offer authoritative reasons for action. The rule of law serves this purpose because in order for law to be able to claim authority in this way, it must be capable of guiding behaviour, which conformity with rule of law principles of legality enables it to be.

Yet Lon Fuller stressed the link of the rule of law with freedom, describing his eight canons or principles of legality as 'the inner morality of law'[13]. He argued for the intimate association of these canons with a moral view of the relation between citizen and state, and with their ability to support normative grounds for believing that citizens have a moral obligation to obey the law. He believed that they indicated and mandated an element of reciprocity between government and citizen, established by the observation of certain types of rules. Although in the context of the Hart–Fuller debate, Hart famously suggested that Fuller's 'internal morality of law' consists of no more than principles of efficiency, which could be 'compatible with very great iniquity',[14] Fuller vehemently denied Hart's critique. Fuller believed that compliance with the principles of legality increased the capacity of law to become *good* law, and that it was actually hard, if not impossible, for a regime bent on immoral or unsavoury ends to achieve them through the rule of law.[15] He gave Nazi Germany as an example, which, he felt, far from using formally viable laws to achieve substantively immoral ends, had actually failed to produce 'law' at all,[16] due to its near complete lack of consistency, publicity, clarity and coherence.

The experience of actions taken in the course of the 'war on terror' (discussed in the previous chapter) also suggests that the rule of law, along with human rights, is likely to be lost in a search for 'expedient' measures. John Finnis has made a similar point. Against the standard complaint that tyranny is logically possible under the rule of law, Finnis has pointed out

[11] In his later work, Raz has suggested that the rule of law has moral value in certain democracies on account of its contribution to democratic governance. See, eg, J Raz, 'The Politics of the Rule of Law' in J Raz, *Ethics in the Public Domain* (Oxford, Oxford University Press, 1994).

[12] J Raz, *The Authority of Law* (Oxford, Oxford University Press, 1983) 216.

[13] L Fuller, 'Positivism and Fidelity to Law: A Reply to Professor Hart' (1958) 71 *Harvard Law Review* 630.

[14] See Hart (above n 10) 207.

[15] Fuller, 'Positivism and Fidelity to Law' (above n 13).

[16] An opinion that was shared by Franz Neumann in F Neumann, *Behemoth: The Structure and Practice of National Socialism* (New York and Evanston, Harper Torchbooks, 1966).

that it is most unlikely, for the practical reason that a 'tyranny devoted to pernicious ends has no self-sufficient reason to submit itself to the discipline of the rule of law'.[17] It is true that the rule of law does not guarantee the values that justify it, and tactically motivated tyrants might attempt to use the form without permitting the substance to prevail. But in such a case, adherence to the rule of law 'systematically restricts the government's freedom of manoeuvre'.[18]

Fuller also stressed the capacity of the rule of law to treat people with respect as equals, writing, 'To judge an individual's actions by unpublished or retrospective laws ... is to convey to him your indifference as to his powers of self-determination.'[19] He also described the predictability and certainty that he denoted as characteristic of the rule of law as necessary to 'secure to the subjects of authority the dignity of self-direction and freedom from certain forms of manipulation.'[20] As Finnis, drawing on Fuller's work, has reminded us, 'Individuals can only be selves—ie, have the "dignity" of being "responsible agents"—if they are not made to live their lives for the convenience of others but are allowed and assisted to create a subsisting identity across a "lifetime".'[21] Philip Selznick, writing in *The Moral Commonwealth*, suggested that the guarantee of the formal justice of the rule of law is in some sort of way a vehicle or conduit for more substantive justice, in that it nurtures a greater commitment to respect for persons, self-restraint in the use of power.[22] In other words, law contains the germ of substantive justice in its concern for formal justice; consistency and the treatment of like cases alike are not just empty, barren propositions but necessary components in the quest for substantive justice.

These responses to the impoverishment critique are persuasive indications that thin versions of the rule of law are not productive of only an impoverished, diminished justice. It suggests that even if we do not embrace a 'thick' notion[23] of the rule of law, the values that the rule of law serves are nonetheless variegated or levelled—on the one hand, a 'cynical' aspect requiring the simple function of constraining power and its abuse; on the other, a more aspirational one of enabling individuals to plan their lives productively and securely in the context of a transparent, reciprocal administration of law.

---

[17] J Finnis, *Natural Law and Natural Rights* (Oxford, Clarendon Press, 1980) 273.
[18] Ibid, 274.
[19] L Fuller, *The Morality of Law* (New Haven, Yale University Press, 1964) 162.
[20] Ibid.
[21] Finnis (above n 17) 272.
[22] P Selznick, *The Moral Commonwealth: Social Theory and the Promise of Community* (Berkeley, University of California Press, 1992).
[23] And of course it is also worth remembering that many of those who assert the value of the rule of law adhere to a 'thick' concept of it (eg, Ronald Dworkin and John Finnis), in which case the 'impoverishment' critique will have very little purchase.

The Rule of Law Does Not Commit One to the Model of Rules

Many advocates of the rule of law have insisted that it should be a 'law of rules'[24] and see it as necessarily connected to the positivist theory of law. Raz has written, 'It is on the whole wise legal policy to use rules as much as possible for regulating legal behaviour because they are more certain than principles and lend themselves more easily to uniform and predictable application.'[25] Yet even positivists recognise that law is arguable in character and cannot always provide optimal security or predictability.[26] One need not be a believer in formal, mechanical rule-bound law to support the value of the rule of law.

The view that I am proposing holds that rules do exist but not necessarily in such a way as to automatically mandate outcomes in a coherent, fully determined way without further interpretation. The vast legal machinery of contemporary states and the technical nature of law-making render precisely drafted laws unfeasible. Not all of law is composed of rules, and policy, principles and vaguer standards also play their part in legal reasoning. Law is not completely autonomous in the sense that rules apply independently of the interpretation that judges give them. Yet neither is legal reasoning only an exercise of unconstrained judicial power. As Hutchinson has written, we are not faced with a 'stark choice between a foundationalist account of law and adjudiciation with coherent, determinate answers, or capitulation to faithless world in which arbitrary power and ideologies run amok.'[27] So rules do not always rule, but there are still some constraints. Nor does this account lead one to believe in some sort of Dworkinian judicial discretion constrained by the requirements of integrity, to render law coherent and principled, if not a seamless web. In the actual legal world, judges do not embody Dworkin's ideal judge, Hercules, and the constraints that operate on judges are less exalted but still present. Hutchinson's belief in the 'good faith' efforts of most judicial reasoning better captures the messy terrain of judging. Rules, principles, standards and so on all operate within particular contexts and historical circumstances, adding greater variety, flexibility and further dimensions, as well as less stability and certainty to legal reasoning and the rule of law. These further dimensions of context, history and place reduce the autonomy of legal reasoning.

[24] Eg, A Scalia, 'The Rule of Law as a Law of Rules' (1989) 56 *University of Chicago Law Review* 1175; and T Campbell, *The Legal Theory of Ethical Positivism* (Aldershot, Dartmouth, 1996).

[25] J Raz, 'Legal Principles and the Limits of Law' (1972) 81 *Yale Law Journal* 823, 841.

[26] See, eg, N MacCormick, 'Rhetoric and the Rule of Law' in D Dyzenhaus (ed), *Recrafting the Rule of Law* (Oxford, Hart Publishing, 1999).

[27] A Hutchinson, 'The Rule of Law Revisited: Democracy and Courts' in Dyzenhaus (ed) (ibid), which is more recent than Hutchinson's earlier critique of the rule of law.

So it should not be thought that observance of the rule of law requires subjection to legal formalism, nor to the tenets of legal positivism, whether legal positivism is seen as entailing the delineation of law from morality or as being based on a model of law as rules. As Shklar suggested in her book, *Legalism*, it is one thing to favour a *Rechtsstaat*, but it is quite another to separate law and morals.[28] It is quite possible for both positivists and anti-positivists to endorse the rule of law, as evidenced by the fact that both Raz and Fuller (as well as a host of others, including EP Thompson and Franz Neumann) have done so. Modern welfare states demonstrate that liberalism and capitalism can indeed be organised in ways that provide for social welfare without danger of governmental tyranny and excessive discretion, notwithstanding the warnings of AV Dicey and Friedrich von Hayek. Indeed, on the contrary, the rule of law may function so as to nurture and construct the public sphere rather than frustrate it, protecting against brutal conduct, often within the private sphere.[29] Many redistributive rules (eg, property tax, capital gains tax) aspire to provide social justice but can be formulated as general rules applicable to all, consistently with the rule of law. Acknowledging and supporting such measures is one way in which the rule of law can be reclaimed from legal formalism.

The Critique of the Rule of Law as Liberal Law

A further series of critiques attack the rule of law not so much for an impoverished formalism and legalism but rather for its association with the broader doctrine of liberalism and associated notions. In particular, these critiques assault the rule of law for its connection with the perceived 'totalising' and universalising doctrine of liberalism and its lack of attention to the Other. In this context, these jurisprudential approaches have some sort of affinity, and they also share features of the 'impoverishment critique' above.

Postmodern and 'Outsider' Critique

One may express the postmodern jurisprudence critique in the following way. It rejects the ideal of impartiality (which it sees as intrinsic to the rule of law) and proceeds from the observation that the account of legality

---

[28] J Shklar, *Legalism: Law and Ideology* (Cambridge, MA, Harvard University Press, 1964).

[29] For an account that stresses this aspect of the rule of law, see B Kriegel, *The State and the Rule of Law* (Princeton, Princeton University Press, 1995). Kriegel, a French theorist and former associate of Foucault, reclaims the rule of law for the left, arguing against anti-statism, through a re-reading of early modern writers, including, inter alia, Hobbes and Bodin.

found in the rule of law consists of 'a demand for equality in the abstract and for repetition. Concrete individuals are turned into legal subjects and changeable characteristics are subsumed under ... types and roles ... [which] negate the singularity of the other.'[30] This approach shares with Marxist and neo-Marxist critiques the claim that the rule of law fails to consider the inescapable difference of humanity, the constant otherness of existence—a difference requiring the immediate action yet infinite time, knowledge and wisdom stipulated by Jacques Derrida in 'The Force of Law' as necessary to doing justice.[31]

Feminist jurisprudence highlights the perceived character of the rule of law as counter to women's material and existential circumstances of connectedness and intimacy—a viewpoint that has led to a commitment to anti-legalism and to an 'ethic of care'.[32] According to these views, the impartiality required by the rule of law and formal theories of justice is unattainable and undesirable. This critique claims further consequences: 'Within the law we are fated to be "unfaithful" to otherness ... If classification in and of itself is thought to be violence against singularity, then law inevitably perpetuates that violence.'[33] So it is alleged that the desire for neutrality and impartiality results in violence against the Other for not recognising the Other's singularity, its specific characteristics—a force and violence of law at the very centre of a concept of justice.

But this critique rests on mistaken assumptions about the rule of law and a naiveté about the kinds of social relations that might be possible in its absence. This critique also assumes too much. First, surely the rule of law does recognise otherness and singularity because the requirements that it sets—that law be predictable, open, impartial, etc—are set as requirements for the very reason that they help to ensure that each individual's very different qualities, hopes and ambitions are respected, that each is treated as an individual, able to pursue his or her different agenda within the structures set by law. Mary Wollstonecraft's *A Vindication of the Rights of Women* very forcefully makes the point that the rights of women must be protected just as much as the rights of man[34]—ie, justice must have a universal reach, precisely in order to recognise and give the Other its due. All too often categorisation of difference and otherness has been used to defeat

[30] C Douzinas and R Warrington, *Justice Miscarried: Ethics and Aesthetics in Law* (Brighton, Harvester Wheatsheaf, 1995) 230.

[31] J Derrida, 'Force of Law: The Mystical Foundation of Authority' in D Cornell, M Rosenfeld and DG Carlson (eds), *Deconstruction and the Possibility of Justice* (London, Routledge, 1992).

[32] Eg, the work of Carol Gilligan. C Gilligan, *In a Different Voice* (Cambridge, MA, Harvard University Press, 1982).

[33] D Cornell, 'Post-Structuralism, the Ethical Relation and the Law' (1987–88) 9 *Cardozo Law Review* 1587, 1591.

[34] M Wollstonecraft, *A Vindication of the Rights of Men and a Vindication of the Rights of Woman* (Cambridge, Cambridge University Press 1995).

claims for recognition of identity, as in the US Supreme Court decision in *Plessy v Ferguson* in 1896,[35] in which the Court held that the federal Constitution's Fourteenth Amendment requirement of equal protection under the law could be construed as 'separate but equal'—'separate' treatment being different from and, in reality, not equal at all. The judgment thus justified racial segregation for a further 60 years, until the Court's subsequent decision in *Brown v Board of Education*.[36] Indeed, the undeniable disadvantage that has been suffered by women and by members of cultural minorities in modern society should be seen not as a failure of the rule of law itself but rather as a failure of society to respect and realise the values of the rule of law.

On the contrary, the alternatives proposed to the rule of law—such as a politics of recognition or an ethic of care—might actually function to the detriment of disadvantaged groups. They seem to be advocated on the basis of some sort of face-to-face relationship, or at least a direct, caring community, which is somehow perceived as possible in the absence of the more formal requirements of equality imposed by the rule of law. Yet such arrangements may work to further disadvantage those already treated unequally. These critiques fail to capture the sense in which law operates in the public sphere—a sphere not overly characterised by care and consideration and recognition of the Other, regardless of how desirable such an ethic of consideration for strangers might appear to be. As Patricia Williams has written, those who are discriminated against and disadvantaged seek not intimacy but the status of 'bargainers of separate worth, distinct power, sufficient rights'.[37]

Robin West has found 'an ethical imperative' in 'the demand of legal justice', arguing:

> Surely, the greatest injustice ... is the wrongheaded insistence that some human beings are to be used by, rather than be an equal part of, our community. Because they are not part of our community of equals, they can be treated differently in spite of apparent similarities ... The rule of law, and the mandate of legal justice it implies, might be best understood today as a bulwark—institutional, to be sure, but also deeply ingrained in our nature—against our human tendency to self-servingly do otherwise.[38]

---

[35] *Plessy v Ferguson* 163 US 537 (1896).

[36] *Brown v Board of Education of Topeka, Kansas* 347 US 483 (1954).

[37] P Williams, *The Alchemy of Race and Rights* (Cambridge, MA, Harvard University Press, 1991).

[38] R West, 'Is the Rule of Law Cosmopolitan?' (2000) 19 *Quinnipiac Law Review* 259. West is another theorist who has moderated a formerly aggressive critique of the rule of law. In 1993, West wrote that modern jurisprudence was masculine in large part because of its commitment to the rule of law, a concept that she found counter to women's 'material and existential circumstance of connection and intimacy'. R West, 'Jurisprudence and Gender' in P Smith (ed), *Feminist Jurisprudence* (Oxford, Oxford University Press, 1993) 520.

Nor does the rule of law *prevent* a more substantive justice, on account of embedded circumstances, from application. It sets a necessary minimum. Different regimes may then go further, by redistributing wealth through tax or promoting disadvantaged groups through positive action. Nothing about the rule of law dictates only the applicability of formal theories of justice; nor does it deny the possibility of redistributive justice.

The Critique of Indeterminacy

However, this critique of the rule of law as liberal law also takes a further direction that is distinct from but often muddled with the first. This further critique, shared by some postmodern theorists and critical legal studies (CLS) and neo-Marxist scholars alike, as well as some public law scholars, focuses once again on the indeterminacy of law. In other words, this further critique is strongly antagonistic to the 'model of rules' critique already dismissed in the last section. Yet rather than criticising the model of rules as impoverished, it dismisses it as impossible and unrealisable. From this perspective, the certainty and determinacy of a formal concept of justice and the rule of law are simply unattainable. All law is seen as matter of interpretation, with an endlessly arguable quality, illustrated by the existence of a large area of judicial discretion. This further critique interprets as highly exaggerated the capacity of the rule of law to achieve legal certainty—and asserts that law is merely what the judge says it is. West has cited as an example of this sort of critique the action of Professor Frank Michelman of Yale University, who refused to sign a 'letter of protest' from 700 law professors to the *New York Times* in 2001, which was directed against the US Supreme Court decision in the case of *Bush v Gore*.[39] The decision was widely interpreted as illegitimate judicial law-making, in breach of the judicial duty of fidelity to law. West has interpreted Michelman's refusal as, at least in part, prompted by his acceptance of the power of the sceptical CLS critique, which in seeing all judicial interpretation as an exercise of power, leaves no function for rule of law values that might have been offended by the *Bush v Gore* decision.[40] According to the indeterminacy critique,

> There just isn't some mosaic or tapestry or seamless web of prior material-statutes, codes, decisions, constitutions, texts, primary documents, and all the inferences one can possibly draw from all of that—from which it follows that

[39] *Bush v Gore* 531 US 98 (2000). In *Bush v Gore,* the US Supreme Court ruled that the system devised by the Florida Supreme Court to recount the votes cast in the state during the 2000 US presidential election violated the equal protection clause of the 14th Amendment to the federal Constitution. The Court stopped the recount process, allowing George W Bush to become President of the United States.

[40] See R West, *Re-Imagining Justice: Progressive Interpretations of Formal Equality, Rights and the Rule of Law* (Aldershot, Ashgate, 2003).

Bush v Gore was wrong ... Whatever disgust or anger or betrayal we feel is political, pure and simple, not legal. There is no determinate legal ground to stand on, if one wishes to cloak that disgust in the rule of law, once one grasps the inescapable meaning of even moderate versions of the indeterminacy thesis. If we're angry, we're angry as politically involved citizens, not as professional upholders of the rule of law.[41]

However, the indeterminacy thesis is overstated. We are neither bound by strongly determinate rules; nor, on the other hand, is it completely unrealistic to believe in the possibility of fair and regular administration of laws in the conditions of post-industrial global capitalism. The argument of this book has been that law is not the autonomous concept that some modern theorists have asserted it to be. Therefore the law will always be indeterminate to a certain extent. Yet this does not mean that indeterminacy can never be contained and managed, at least to some extent, by legal norms which possess the general attributes of clarity, generality, publicity and so on. There surely exists a certain element of creativity in interpretation, and opportunities for activist or politically motivated judges to manipulate texts according to their will, especially with (all too often) poorly drafted legal provisions. But there also exist concern for clarity in drafting and initiatives to aid it, as well as outrage at apparently 'political' decisions such as *Bush v Gore* (and its UK counterparts, such as *Bromley v GLC*,[42] in which the House of Lords appeared to give a very partial, 'political' interpretation of the law regarding the ability of the Greater London Council, then authority for London, to reduce fares on the London underground). The more recent UK *Cornerhouse*[43] decision may also be criticised on these grounds. In this case, the House of Lords ruled that the Director of the UK Serious Fraud Office (SFO) had acted legally in terminating the SFO's investigation into alleged corruption by British Aerospace (BAE) Systems in its dealings in Saudi Arabia. The SFO decision followed lobbying by BAE and threats from Saudi officials to cut off intelligence links with the United Kingdom if the investigation proceeded. This was widely criticised as a judgement in which supposed political and national security considerations triumphed over the rule of law. Such reactions reveal, at the very least, an expectation that interpretation not be calculated on political grounds. Moreover, the strength of these reactions suggests that we do not see these 'political' decisions as the norm; we do believe certain institutional constraints and structures apply to legal decision-making.

---

[41] As expressed but not personally held by R West, 'Reconstructing the Rule of Law' (2001–02) 90 *Georgetown Law Journal* 215, 216.

[42] *Bromley London Borough Council v Greater London Council* [1983] AC 768.

[43] *R (Corner House Research and Others) v Director of the Serious Fraud Office* [2008] UKHL 60.

Marxist/Neo-Marxist, Other 'Equality' Critiques and the 'Affinity' of the Rule of Law with Capitalism

This section examines a cluster of critiques that attack the rule of law from the left, principally for its perceived ability to cause or further inequality—to frustrate social purposes on account of its 'neutral' principles.

The rule of law undoubtedly has a powerful legitimating function. As such, it may be manipulated by cynical governments who play lip service to its tenets while in fact flouting them. Such cynicism, as has been noted, 'tarnishes' the rule of law and debases its value. There is what Tamanaha has described as 'a dark side to the rule of law'.[44] It is also undeniable that the rule of law has a connection with a certain type of liberalism, which serves as basis for some criticism of it. A trajectory may be mapped out from John Locke through Karl Marx and Max Weber to Friedrich von Hayek, and the thrust of these arguments posits an 'elective affinity' between the rule of law and capitalism.[45] And capitalism of course has its dark side, too. This connection of the rule of law to capitalism is acknowledged both by liberals and by their opponents. In the case of English law, this link can be dated back to the seventeenth century and the connection drawn between law, government and property. The rule of law has played a historical role in protecting private property and freedom of contract,[46] especially when it was used to support a concept of fundamental rights conceived in terms of a right to accumulate private wealth. As has been strongly expressed:

> The Glorious Revolution of 1688 established the freedom not of men, but of men of property. Its apologist, John Locke, distorted the oldest arguments of natural law to justify the liberty of wealth from all political and moral controls ... "Government" declared John Locke, "has no other end but the preservation of property ..." Again and again the voices of money and power declared the sacredness of property in terms hitherto reserved for human life. Banks were credited with souls, and the circulation of gold likened to that of blood.[47]

Unfortunately, such a view of banking continued into the twenty-first century.

---

[44] Tamanaha (above n 6).

[45] See, eg, W Scheuerman, *Frankfurt School Perspectives on Globalization, Democracy, and the Law* (New York, Routledge, 2008); and W Scheuerman, 'Economic Globalization and the Rule of Law' (1999) 6 *Constellations*.

[46] For further on this, see, eg, N Ferguson, 'The Rule of Law and its Enemies', BBC Reith Lectures (2012).

[47] D Hay, 'Property, Authority and the Criminal Law' in D Hay et al (eds), *Albion's Fatal Tree* (New York, Pantheon Books, 1975) 18, citing J Locke, *Second Treatise of Civil Government* (1690) (Oxford, Basil Blackwell, 1982) s 85.

Both liberal and critical accounts highlight certain features as indicative of this connection between capitalism and the rule of law. For example, it might seem that capitalism and economic development require certainty, predictability and security in order to flourish. By securing these measures, it is possible to ensure the stability of contract law and predict the costs and benefits of particular transactions. The origins of the European Union can be explained in this way. Ordo-liberals justified the creation and existence of the European Union by its capacity to support free market rights, guaranteeing private property and exchange of goods, based around the economic nexus, or even 'constitution', of the Treaty of Rome.[48] The rule of law offers protective functions for business, sheltering trade against political arbitrariness and expropriation of property rights,[49] and it has sometimes served as an ideal partner for market capitalism. Thus capitalism is able to focus on commerce rather than on shielding its existing efforts from capricious conduct.

Allegory of the Freedom of Trade, painted by the seventeenth-century Netherlands artist Gerard de Lairesse, captures these links very appositely. De Lairesse's painting, illustrated in Figure 8-1, is interesting because the figure of trade it depicts employs much of the iconography of justice. The female figure, representing trade, sits on high, in much the glorious way in which justice is usually portrayed, in one hand a merchant's hat balanced on a stick in sceptre like fashion, in the other a baton held up like a torch of freedom. Winged cherubs rush to place a naval crown on the figure (symbolising the freedom of the seas, very important to Dutch trade at the time).

Interestingly, this painting was once displayed in a wealthy Dutch burgomaster's house but is now located in the Peace Palace in The Hague, the sometime site of the Treaty of Westphalia painting that was discussed in chapter one, thus identifying international trade not only with justice but now also with peace. Indeed, security is another theme in the other two

---

[48] See, eg, H-P Ipsen, 'Europaische Verfassung—Nationale Verfassung' (1987) *Europarecht* 195.

[49] However, this does not necessarily give rise to an excessively formalistic or codified law. The English common law courts have had a long tradition of protecting property. Brian Tamanaha has cited Jacob Viner regarding Coke in *Dr Bonham's Case*: 'It was in this period [the late sixteenth and early seventeenth century] that Sir Edward Coke appealed to the common law as a traditional barrier to the interference by government with the economic and other "freedoms" of the individual.' J Viner, 'The Intellectual History of Laissez Faire' (1959) *Journal of Law and Economics* 45, 55. Tamanaha (above n 6) considers this to be evidence of the stand of the common law courts against the King in order to protect freedom of enterprise. The willingness of the common law courts to protect freedom of enterprise and the development of the rule of law in this way may also go some way toward explaining Weber's 'England problem'—namely, the question of how the stability and clarity in law necessary for the progress of capitalism could be provided by the uncodified common law system.

Figure 8-1: Gerard de Lairesse, *Allegory of the Freedom of Trade* (1672), ceiling painting, Peace Palace, The Hague

panels of the ceiling of which this work forms a part.[50] So capitalism, the freedom of trade, is portrayed as an allegory of the just society, bringing with it security and peace. The capacity of trade to function as an allegory of freedom continues to this day. For example, the twin towers of the World Trade Center, which were destroyed on 11 September, were sited next to 'Liberty Plaza', and it seems that the building designed to replace the twin towers in New York may be named 'Freedom Tower'.

In addition to these calculable and protective functions of the rule of law, the dimensions of time and space are also relevant. Capitalism has preferred law to be stable over time in order to aid planning and coordinated action.[51] To appreciate this need, William Scheuerman has asked us to

> ... imagine a merchant trading in the backwoods of North America in the late eighteenth century, whose business relied on long and risky voyages from a port city on the coast ... to the frontier ... It would make economic sense to seek tax laws unlikely to change during the course of his travels, a stable system of contracts, and many other predicable legal norms and practices ... In short, familiar

---

[50] Lairesse named the triptych *Allegory on Concord, Freedom and Security*. The triptych has been known for some time as 'The Triumph of Peace', although it is actually an allegory of the city of Amsterdam as a protector of freedom. Further information is available at http://www.triomfdervrede.nl/ (accessed 6 December 2012).

[51] RH Fallon, 'The Rule of Law as a Concept in Constitutional Discourse' (1997) 97(1) *Columbia Law Review* 1, 38.

features of the rule of law would serve as a powerful tool for counteracting uncertainties generated by the distance and duration of economic exchange …[52]

In this way, the rule of law functioned as an attempt to render time and space manageable. Scheuerman in fact has likened these developments in law to the development of maps and clocks, referring to 'ever more precise, systematic models of time and space measurement':

> Just as modern clock and mapmakers carved time and space into homogeneous units possessing an ever more precise and systematic character, so too did modern legal reformers imagine a complementary legal universe consisting of rationally ordered, uniform abstract concepts and norms, as well as formalistic modes of decision-making ideally no less predictable than the operations of a modern clock or reliable than a good map … [L]ike rational maps and clocks, the modern rule of law implicitly rested on the aspiration to render both time and space rationally manageable. One crucial way in which it achieved this task was by reducing economic uncertainty based on the distance and duration of commercial exchange.[53]

One point, however, to highlight at this stage, is that these conditions—stability, certainty, predictability—which were favourable to eighteenth-century capitalism do not necessarily apply in the twenty-first century, in an era where, on the contrary, multinational enterprises (MNEs) and commerce prefer flexible, responsive solutions—a state of affairs, already discussed in earlier chapters, that suggests that the close link between a certain notion of the rule of law and capitalism may be dissolving. This is a significant point and will be developed further later in this chapter.

For the present, I want to focus on the ways in which the perceived link with capitalism has been seen to tarnish the rule of law. Marx himself laid out no express theory as to the nature of justice, although to be sure, he strongly believed that freedom and justice could not be fully realised within capitalism. He believed that ideally, 'equal rights' presupposed a domination-free, democratic community. However, he asserted that under capitalism, the legal form of individual rights had taken a proprietary and antagonistic form which permitted individuals to pursue selfish interests without any regard for humanity.[54] Marx therefore concluded that legal rights radically isolate persons from each other and, because of their formal nature, also permit vast inequalities of power and wealth. Formal equality

---

[52] WE Scheuerman, *Liberal Democracy and the Social Acceleration of time* (Baltimore, Johns Hopkins University Press, 2004) 156.

[53] W Scheuerman, 'Globalisation and the Fate of Law' in Dyzenhaus (ed) (above n 26) 252. See also EP Thompson, 'Time, Work-Discipline and Industrial Capitalism' (1967) 38 *Past and Present* 56–97; and J Urry, 'The Sociology of Time and Space' in B Turner (ed), *The Blackwell Companion to Social Theory* (Oxford, Blackwell, 1996) 369–95.

[54] See K Marx, 'On the Jewish Question' in J Waldron (ed), *Nonsense upon Stilts: Bentham, Burke and Marx on the Rights of Man* (London, Methuen, 1987).

before the law can be compatible with a great deal of social and material inequality.

Later critical theorists (eg, those of the Frankfurt School) and radical theorists of the 1960s and 1970s also derided the rule of law, believing it incapable of delivering on its promises, creating instead a 'false consciousness'. Moreover, it has been suggested that 'The principle aim of Marxist jurisprudence is to criticise the central piece of liberal political philosophy, the ideal called the rule of law.'[55] Therefore, in focusing on its close ties with capitalism, Marxist and critical theory have insisted that this supposed universal, formal, neutral rule of law is in fact a concept inseparable from a particular kind of social and political order—indeed, one that has considerable consequences for society. The rule of law is understood as not ethically neutral but facilitative of a particular way of life, namely capitalism. Later critiques share with Marx the assertion that treating as formally equal entities of vastly different power undermines the rule of law itself. Thus it is possible for corporations to exploit their great financial resources to vigorously protect certain rights, such as property or business confidentiality in antitrust cases, to the detriment of 'just' outcomes. Contrast, for example, the difference within the English common law between the use of economic tort law to outlaw trade union activity[56] on the one hand and, on the other, its failure to develop competition law to deal with cartels and the restrictive practices of dominant commercial concerns. Commerce is given a free rein, while trade union activity is curbed. This critique also employs the concept of hegemony to argue that in these circumstances, power is achieved by a combination of force and the actual consent of those oppressed.[57]

The Rule of Law, Justice and Democracy

At this stage, I want to include a critique that is closely related to those that deride the rule of law as unable to deliver true equality. This related critique focuses on a supposed inability of the rule of law to deliver social justice, based on its perceived conflict with democracy. Although the rule of law has functioned and often thrived in democracies, it is sometimes suggested that there is a conflict between the rule of law and the will of the people as expressed in legislation. Dicey viewed the rule of law as a

---

[55] H Collins, *Marxism and Law* (Oxford, Oxford University Press, 1982) 1.

[56] See, eg, *Taff Vale Railway Co v Amalgamated Society of Railway Servants* [1901] UKHL 1, in which the House of Lords held that unions can be liable for loss of profits to employers that was caused by taking strike action. This decision caused outrage and was reversed by the Trade Disputes Act 1906.

[57] For further on the concept of hegemony, see A Gramsci, *Prison Notebooks* (New York, Columbia University Press, 2007).

companion principle to UK parliamentary sovereignty, but there does exist a tension between these principles, and it has even been suggested that this tension is capable of generating a 'constitutional crisis'.[58] This tension arises from the fact that the rule of law operates to check legislation by way of procedural standards (and by human rights in its 'thicker' versions), and so judges should have the power to scrutinise and even invalidate legislation, as well as administrative acts. Indeed, in *Dr Bonham's Case* (which admittedly predated Britain's parliamentary democracy),[59] Chief Justice Sir Edward Coke claimed that a statute contrary to common right and reason would be declared void by the courts, and although no recorded case exists in which the UK judiciary have actually invalidated legislation, recent case law suggests that the English judiciary may be ready to give especially careful scrutiny to legislation that it sees as a threat to the rule of law.[60]

In other jurisdictions, the threat is actualised by the existence of constitutionally authorised, supposedly 'counter-majoritarian' judicial review, for example as it exists in the United States, where the Supreme Court has the power to strike down both federal and state legislation that conflicts with the federal Constitution. This gives the judiciary the ability to thwart policies adopted by a democratically elected legislature—especially pernicious when democracy is viewed as the means by which a community is able to escape from a neoliberal, capitalist conception of the individual as rights-bearing property holder, as Marx's 'isolated monad', in favour of a more altruistic welfare community. It is undeniable that judges have sometimes used a particular conception of the rule of law to thwart more democratic, empowering ideals. In the early twentieth century, for example, the US Supreme Court in deciding the case of *Lochner*,[61] struck down a law limiting the amount of hours which employees could be required to work, on the ground that this law infringed the liberty of autonomous, contractual bargaining rights. Such decisions lend weight to the criticism that the rule of law can defeat democratic purposes. Numerous other examples abound of judges interpreting rights in oppressive and anti-democratic ways.[62] Voices from the right, such as Hayek, have also noted this tension between the rule of law and democracy, in this case perceiving the legislation of the

---

[58] See, for example, V Bogdanor, 'The Sovereignty of Parliament and the Rule of Law', *Magna Carta Lecture* (June 2006).

[59] *Dr Bonham's Case* (1610) 8 Co Rep 107a, 114a CP.

[60] See, eg, Lady Hale in *Jackson*: 'The courts will treat with particular suspicion (and might even reject) any attempt to subvert the rule of law by removing governmental action affecting the rights of the individual from judicial scrutiny.' *Jackson v Attorney General* [2005] UKHL 56.

[61] *Lochner v New York*, 198 US 45 (1905).

[62] A parallel may be drawn with the English case of *Roberts v Hopwood* [1925] AC, in which the House of Lords struck down a minimum wage policy. Many further examples are given in K Ewing and C Gearty, *Freedom under Thatcher: Civil Liberties in Modern Britain* (Oxford, Oxford University Press, 1990).

welfare or social state as a threat to the rule of law, because of its perceived over-emphasis on discretionary powers.[63]

However, both types of critique, from right and left, rely on too crude a concept of the rule of law, derived from an ideology of libertarianism which over-emphasises the capacity of the rule of law to protect personal autonomy and over-simplifies democracy as majority governance. A law may be unjust if it is created in a way that is undemocratic. But justice and democracy are, of course, not identical. A democratic decision that denies fundamental rights to a minority, if taken on a crudely 'democratic' majoritarian basis, may itself be unjust. In fact, judicial review may contribute to democratic governance by providing access to justice for those who have been deprived of their rights, as well as by preventing government from abusing its power. Judges may have used the notion of the rule of law to defend an ideologically based interventionist approach counter to democratic ideals, but this does not mean that the rule of law may not also be used to further democratic, emancipatory ends—as it has sometimes been employed in invalidating oppressive, rights-restricting legislation adopted by states in the name of fighting the 'war on terror'.[64] Nor does it mean that legislation adopted in furtherance of the welfare state will automatically be found to be in conflict of rule of law principles, notwithstanding ideological tirades such as that of Lord Hewart's *The New Despotism*,[65] written in England in the 1920s against the growing administrative social state.

International Injustice

Even if the rule of law does not threaten democracy, this group of critiques poses a strong challenge to its application in the contemporary international situation. The Marxist critique finds close allies among those who interpret global injustice as a product of the manipulation of law through liberal concepts applied globally through the capitalist 'Washington consensus'.[66] The last half-century has witnessed the spread of neoliberal reforms across the world, in what has been described as an 'economic constitutionalism'.[67]

---

[63] Indeed, the setup of the UK welfare state was supported by a system of administrative law and tribunals—often bypassing the formal court system.

[64] Eg, the case of *A v Home Secretary* (discussed in the previous chapter).

[65] In this work, Lord Hewart, the Lord Chief Justice of England, compared the growth of administrative practices in the UK to the despotism of the Stuart kings, writing 'The strategy is different, but the goal is the same. It is to subordinate Parliament, to evade the courts and to render the will or caprice of the executive unfettered and supreme.' Lord Hewart of Bury, *The New Despotism* (London, Ernest Benn, 1929) 17.

[66] The 'Washington Consensus' was an economic plan proposed by the World Bank and the International Monetary Fund in 1990, supposedly as a template for economic reform in Latin America and elsewhere. For a general account, see D Harvey, *A Brief History of Neoliberalism* (Oxford, Oxford University Press, 2005).

[67] For further on 'economic constitutionalism', see below ch 11.

Loans to developing countries from the International Monetary Fund (IMF) and World Bank have been conditional on those countries undertaking reforms linked to so-called 'good governance', such as reducing market and trade barriers, privatisation, the protection of property and enforcement of contracts, as well ensuring the free flow of capital. These 'reforms' supposedly reproduce the economic and legal conditions of the developed world, yet this has not been the result. As has been pithily remarked, 'You buy habeas corpus and end up with Habitat Corporation.'[68]

Figure 8-2 presents the work of the Danish sculptor Jens Galschiøt. The piece is entitled *Survival of the Fattest*,[69] and it was displayed in Copenhagen Harbour in December 2009 at the time of the G15 climate change summit, along with several other large cast iron sculptures by Galschiøt.

Survival of the Fattest depicts a grossly obese European *Justitia*, actually bearing the scales of justice in her right hand, being carried on the shoulders of a starving African man. Galschiøt has said that the sculpture represents the 'self-righteousness of the rich world', which sits on the backs of the poor while pretending to do justice. *Survival of the Fattest* was deliberately placed next to Edvard Eriksen's famous bronze statue *The Little Mermaid*, in a bid to

Figure 8-2: Jens Galschiøt, *Survival of the Fattest* (2002), as exhibited in Copenhagen Harbour at the Copenhagen Climate Summit in 2009, courtesy of http://www. aidoh.dk (accessed 4 January 2013): an allegory of free trade for our times?

[68] K Nicolaidis, 'Can a Post-colonial Power Export the Rule of Law? Element of a General Framework' in G Palombella and N Walker (eds), *Relocating the Rule of Law* (Oxford, Hart Publishing, 2008) 143.

[69] To be accurate, 'Survival of the Fattest' was jointly created by Galschiøt and fellow artist Lars Calmar in 1992.

ensure international attention. In doing this, Galschiøt juxtaposed the famous mythical subject of Hans Christian Andersen's fairy tale next to the shocking but undeniable realism of his work, as if perhaps to suggest that the goals of the wealthy nations at the climate change conference might be little more than fairy tales. It is a striking work, beautiful in its way, but borne out of a compulsion to change things, to shock people into doing justice. The chimneys at the other side of the harbour, billowing out smoke, also add to the irony, conveying an image of a duplicitous West, profiting off the backs of the poor and polluting the environment, all the while appearing to work hard to prevent global warming. This work provides a poignant contrast to the earlier allegory of trade by de Lairesse (see above Figure 8-1).

Chapter six described some of the graphic injustices of poverty, and law has been portrayed as complicit in the developing nature of this world poverty. Indeed, law's perceived role in international injustice is a theme running through these chapters. Wade Mansell, Belinda Meteyard and Alan Thomson, in their critical and highly stimulating introduction to law, for example, highlight four legal concepts, stipulated as intrinsically connected with the rule of law, which they see as 'enabling the West to maintain a façade of rectitude while taking Third World wealth'.[70] They identify these four concepts as property, contract, debt and legal personality. They relate a sorry story of how wealth has been transferred from poor to rich, and exploited peoples have actually paid for their own oppression, which has been secured by means of reckless financial investments by Wall Street financiers and the complicity of international institutions such as the IMF and World Bank.

By this account, contract law secures legal complicity in global inequality, making Third World debt possible because of capitalism's insistence and focus on a perceived formal equality which has ignored the true relative bargaining power of parties. This produces a situation that Laura Nader and Ugo Mattei have described as 'global plunder'[71]—namely, what they characterise as 'imperial' uses of the rule of law in the context of a less than ideal practice of distributive justice. Nader and Mattei liken the rule of law to the oppressive practices of the Crusades, the slave trade, the occupation of 'terra nulla' in the United States, as well as the exploitative activities of the East India Company, which made a fortune for its shareholders. They also point out that the rule of law was ironically one of the justifications for the recent war in Iraq, which was widely perceived to be illegal. They also cite as another example of 'plunder' the actions of Paul Bremer, the US administrator and head of the Coalition Provisional Authority in Iraq charged with overseeing Iraq's reconstruction. Bremer was criticised for

---

[70] W Mansell, B Meteyard and A Thomson, *A Critical Introduction to Law* (London, Routledge Cavendish, 2004). See also U Nader and L Mattei, *Plunder: When the Rule of Law is Illegal* (Oxford, Wiley-Blackwell, 2008).

[71] Nader and Mattei (ibid).

allowing 100 per cent foreign ownership of Iraqi business and granting foreign contractors immunity from Iraqi laws—practices actually illegal under the international Hague regulations of 1907, which stipulate that a defeated society may not be transformed into the victors' own likeness.[72]

Indeed, Mattei and Nader see this imperialist 'plunder' as the rule rather than the exception. While the Enron scandal and indefinite detention at Guantánamo are usually perceived as exceptional scandals in a society governed by the rule of law, in their view this is not so. The reality, as they see it, is of corporate capitalist exploitation, which results in a world in which workers are victimised, innocents killed and people starve and die young. Therefore, for Nader and Mattei, the dominant, positive image of the rule of law is false and does not capture its darker side. They see this false representation of the rule of law as issuing from the mistaken idea, or rather ideology, that good law is autonomous and separate from society and its institutions non-political and non-distributive rather than proactive.

There has also been a general critique and targeting[73] of international institutions such as the IMF and World Bank as complicit in this plunder. These institutions of the 'Washington Consensus' are undeniably undemocratic. Based in Washington, DC, neither the World Bank nor the IMF operate on the basis of one vote for each of their members; the US has a dominant role, and larger vote share, in both and is able to veto measures. However, the World Trade Organization WTO presents itself as embodying the rule of law in world trade. After squabbling and disagreements in the WTO ministerial conference in Seattle in 1999, the then Secretary General of the WTO, Mike Moore, concluded his speech in the following way:

> ... [P]eople do want global rules. If the WTO did not exist, people would be crying out for a forum in which governments negotiated rules, ratified by national parliaments, that promote free trade and provide a transparent and predictable framework for business ... That is what the WTO is. We do not lay down the law. We uphold the rule of law. The alternative is the law of the jungle, where might makes right and the little guy doesn't get a look in.[74]

Yet in contrast, the UN High Commissioner for Human Rights has suggested that WTO rules are based on grossly unfair assumptions and reflect an agenda that serves only to promote dominant corporatist interests: 'For certain sectors of humanity, particularly the developing countries in the South, the WTO is a veritable nightmare.'[75]

---

[72] Ibid, 115.

[73] Nader and Mattei have described the IMF and World Bank as the 'vulgate' of financial institutions. Nader and Mattei (above n 70) 35.

[74] M Moore, 'The Backlash against Globalisation', speech (Ottawa, 26 October 2000).

[75] UN Economic and Social Council Commission Human Rights, 'Preliminary Report: The Realisation of Economic, Social and Cultural Rights: Globalisation Admits Impact on the Full Enjoyment of Human Rights' UN DocE/CN.4/Sub.2/2000.

The IMF attaches austerity programmes to its rescue of countries, insisting that they reduce spending on welfare and wages, liberalise trade practices and privatise—in effect focus on deregulation and openness to Western investment. These practices have been much criticised, for example, by Joseph Stiglitz, a former chief economist with the World Bank.[76] In this way, there has been a shift from loans designed to support economic projects and infrastructure, to those designed to support institutional reform in a way attractive to Western capitalist investors. Additionally, prices have been fixed in commodity markets through speculation rather than by primary producers controlling prices. A further notable feature of 'good governance' initiatives of development aid is the strikingly anti-democratic way in which the programmes are implemented. These programmes usually impose harsh social and economic conditions as the price of development, which are naturally unpopular with local electorates and so likely to be imposed autocratically by those countries' leaders,[77] rather than with the populations' consent. Significantly, although the rule of law is heralded as important, and the World Bank trumpets its 'rule of law' index,[78] the most influential sources for assessing a country's 'rule of law score' are usually commercially based, such as those of the US Heritage Foundation.[79] All of these factors put together involve a particular notion of rule of law with an extremely heavy focus on property law rights.

We might add to this critique the apparent skewed protection of financial interests in the context of the recent financial crisis. There has been a notable lack of prosecutions, notwithstanding such egregious examples of apparently unlawful conduct as securities fraud, accounting fraud, money laundering and the manipulation of interest rates. In contrast, the law has been vigorously enforced against those protesting against the excesses of capitalism, such as the various Occupy movements. For example, a recent report found not only robust law enforcement against the 'Occupy Wall Street' movement but also numerous human rights violations, including baseless arrests, dispersal of peaceful assemblies and unjustified closures of public spaces.[80] This asymmetry suggests a privileging of powerful corporate interests, leaving some actors above the law.

---

[76] J Stiglitz, *Globalisation and its Discontents* (New York, Norton, 2002).

[77] For further on this, see Mansell, Meteyard and Thomson (above n 70) ch 9.

[78] See M Thomas, 'What Do the Worldwide Governance Indicators Measure?', *European Journal of Development Research* (16 July 2009).

[79] Ibid.

[80] Global Justice Clinic (NYU School of Law) and the Walter Leitner International Human Rights Clinic at the Leitner Center for International Law and Justice (Fordham Law School), 'Suppressing Protest: Human Rights Violations in the US Response to Occupy Wall Street', Protest and Assembly Rights Project (2012).

Against the Critiques

There is much to be said for this critique, which highlights the deficiencies of a rule-of-law version of justice that, by applying the same rule to different and unequal people, or by applying and enforcing the law in discriminatory ways, produces inequality and ensures that the ideology of the market governs. It illustrates a massive gap between the promise of justice held out by the rule of law and the practices of capitalism and abusive states. The alternative for most such critics is to turn to an account that focuses on substantive social justice, to be brought about by political means instead.

The Abuse of the Rule of Law

However, there are two ways in which all of these supposed 'anti-liberal' critiques fail to give credit to the rule of law as a means for assessing legitimacy and justice. The first is that they fail to account sufficiently for the fact that many of the situations they describe are ones in which the rule of law and its principles have been *abused* and usurped (especially in the context of 'global plunder') and its features and components distorted, or substantive features imported which do not necessarily belong to it (such as overemphasis on property rights). These abuses might be characterised as what Habermas has called 'distorted communication'. They also employ instrumental reason—the use of the 'language' of human rights and the rule of law with the ulterior aim of market colonisation, rather than human rights and justice as ends in themselves.[81]

Few of the situations discussed by 'anti-liberal' critiques are actually ones in which morally obnoxious, substantive laws have been enforced and imposed in ways compliant with the rule of law (ie, clearly, unambiguously and transparently). For example, Mansell et al critique the shift in contractual arrangements for money lending to developing countries since the end of the Second World War because it has involved a move from formerly clear terms and conditions and fixed-term interest rates to a situation where it is now much easier for one (more powerful) party to unilaterally alter a contract, especially interest rates. This shift has aided the transfer of wealth from rich to poor, and in this way, it has become possible for scarce resources to be taken from those in abject poverty to enrich those who already enjoy massive material wealth. Such a shift with such consequences is clearly shameful but hardly the result of transparent, unambiguous rule of law conditions. Rather, it is the result of their

---

[81] J Habermas, *The Divided West* (Cambridge, Polity Press, 2006) 16.

opposite. Is contract law to blame for this, as the critique of liberalism suggests? In this context, the relevant 'contracts' may simply be managerial orders written up in 'legalese' but lacking the party autonomy (at least on the employee's side) and formal attributes of contract law. This is a point acknowledged by PS Atiyah, who has written that the decline of classical liberal contract law in the twentieth century was partly caused by the rise of global corporate power.[82] The move from clear contractual terms to those favouring the dominant party is not an example of the rule of law in action but rather one of the thwarting of its principles. The remedy for this type of abuse or bad faith is surely not to dispense with some sort of rule of law altogether but to ensure that it is not corrupted. Likewise, the paucity of prosecutions of bankers while public protest laws are rigorously or even erroneously enforced is an illustration not of the rule of law but of its opposite—a partial application of law in favour of one sector of society.

Another example of failure to observe the rule of law is offered by the recent measures taken to deal with the Eurozone crisis. The European Union is a market par excellence, having created an economic constitution,[83] and an example of integration through law as much as political agreement. But it has not always observed the rule of law. Since the onset of the crisis, EU states and institutions have limped from summit to summit, instigating a seemingly incessant series of measures in an ad hoc and reactive way. New measures on economic governance have been adopted and austerity measures institutionalised through mandatory limits on public spending and adjustment of labour market policies in favour of more flexibility and lower wages. What is particularly notable, however, is that many of these measures seem to bring the European Union into conflict with human rights, with its own treaties and proclaimed values. For example, the Lisbon Treaty sets the objective of 'a highly competitive social market economy'.[84] It would be hard to argue that Eurozone reforms that require states to monitor labour law and lower wages to ensure competitiveness are compatible with a social market economy. Likewise, the stipulation that 'sustainability of pensions, health care and social benefits' should be the primary means of ensuring 'sound public finances' seems to fly in the face of the provisions of Article 9 of the Treaty on the Functioning of the European Union (TFEU), which states:

> In defining and implementing its policies and activities, the Union shall take
> into account ... the promotion of a high level of employment, the guarantee of

---

[82] PS Atiyah, The *Rise and Fall of Freedom of Contract* (Oxford, Clarendon Press, 1985) 571.

[83] On this, see, eg, M Poiares Maduro, *We the Court: The European Court of Justice and the European Economic Constitution* (Oxford, Hart Publishing, 1998).

[84] Art 3(3) Treaty on European Union (TEU).

adequate social protection, the fight against social exclusion, and a high level of education, training and protection of human health.

Nor do measures that impose unilateral cuts on wages, pensions and public spending and restrict collective bargaining enhance the objective of social justice set out in Article 3 of the Treaty on European Union (TEU). Furthermore, the conditionality clauses in the bailout agreements, which impose restrictions on the availability of collective bargaining, show little concern for the special status of the social partners recognised by Article 152 of the TFEU[85] and may infringe the right to collective bargaining and freedom of association laid out in the EU Charter of Fundamental Rights. The rule of law and proceduralism in the European Union have been attacked as insisting on 'integration through law'. Such 'integration through law' has been evident in some of the case law of the Court of Justice, in the pressing of free movement principles which ignore policy and social market interests. Yet the *lack* of the rule of law has been glaring and damaging in areas of EU affairs—in this instance, in the imposition of conditions on Member States that do not accord with the European Union's own treaty provisions.

Flexible, Complex Regulation Threatens Equality

The second way in which 'anti-liberal' critiques fail to give credit to the rule of law is by failing to take into account a change in legal and business practices. This change involves an increasing preference for flexible regulation rather than predictability and stability.[86] Many of the practices so castigated rely not on formal rule of law but on anti-formalist practices designed with very specific interests of business in mind, indeed on highly complex financial trading rules akin to gambling. Here, a short reflection and diversion into the work of Neumann is instructive and valuable.

---

[85] Art 152 TFEU states: 'The Union recognises and promotes the role of the social partners at its level, taking into account the diversity of national systems. It shall facilitate dialogue between the social partners, respecting their autonomy.' Further, all 27 EU member States have ratified International Labour Organization (ILO) Convention No 154 on the promotion of collective bargaining and ILO Convention No 87 on freedom of association. Greek Trade Unions complained to the ILO regarding the imposition of bailout conditions, in particular restrictions on collective bargaining. In this context, the CEACR (2011) Report of the Committee of Experts on the Application of Conventions and Recommendations) of the ILO held that 'restrictions on collective bargaining should only be imposed as exceptional measures and only to the extent necessary, without exceeding a reasonable period' (p 83).

[86] See above chs 3 and 5.

Neumann, an anti-Nazi legal theorist working in Weimar Germany,[87] might not appear to be the most obvious ally of the rule of law against the Marxist critique of global capitalism (especially as he himself was a member of the Frankfurt critical theory school), but in fact, in his work he sought to rehabilitate the rule of law and ascribe an ethical function to it. Neumann had his legal training within a Weberian-Marxist intellectual framework, which minimises law's normative and democratic qualities, but Neumann's own life circumstances also influenced his work. He had participated in the workers' uprisings in Germany in 1918–19 and practised labour law as well as working as a legal adviser for the SPD, the Social Democratic Party.[88] He also participated in a famous 'dialogue', or rather debate, with Carl Schmitt.[89] In his writings on Weimar Germany, Neumann crucially noted growing anti-formalist trends in business law, which appeared to reduce capitalism's traditional reliance on stable, predictable laws, its traditional 'elective affinity' with formal law. Large monopolistic enterprises were able to manipulate law creation and application and by their economic power produce measures that suited their needs rather than general laws applicable to all.

Neumann acknowledged, along with many others, that in Weimar Germany there existed a crisis of the rule of law, but unlike many of his contemporaries, he thought that the solution to this crisis could be found in the rule of law itself, which he believed had unfulfilled potential to support democracy. Neumann asserted that the answer to the crisis was not to undermine the rule of law but to transform society in a democratic and anti-capitalist direction.[90] For him, the troublesome, undemocratic aspect of the rule of law lay in the way it had been manipulated by capitalism. Indeed, in his 1944 work, *Behemoth*,[91] Neumann traced Nazi Germany's subsequent annihilation of rational, formal law to earlier capitalist abuses denying equal application of the rule of law. To counter this, there could be departure from the formal rule of law to redistribute private property—a shifting of the understanding of the rule of law from one dominated by

---

[87] The post-WWI Weimar Constitution had attempted to reconcile economic liberties and social rights. Indeed, it was unique at the time for doing this.

[88] Ie, *Sozialdemokratische Partei Deutschlands*, the German Social Democratic party.

[89] For further on, this see W Scheuerman, *Between the Norm and the Exception: The Frankfurt School and the Rule of Law* (Cambridge, MA, Massachusetts Institute of Technology Press, 1994).

[90] F Neumann, 'The Change in the Function of law in Modern Society' in W Scheuerman (ed), *The Rule of Law Under Siege: Selected Essays of Franz L Neumann and Otto Kirchheimer* (Berkeley, University of California Press, 1996); and F Neumann, 'The Social Significance of the Basic Laws in the Weimar Constitution' in O Kirchheimer and F Neumann, *Social Democracy and the Rule of Law*, K Tribe (ed) (London, Allen & Unwin, 1987). See also R Cotterrell, 'The Rule of Law in Transition: Revisiting Franz Neumann's Sociology of Legality' (1996) *Social and Legal Studies* 456.

[91] Neumann, *Behemoth* (above n 16).

economic liberalism to one rooted in social democratic formulations. He believed social and political relations of equality could actually enhance the rule of law. If property were to be more equally divided, there would be less danger of social crises and panics, and of crime committed against property, and all the unpredictability that follow from these. Further, he considered that access to justice and to good lawyers could and should be more fairly distributed, in keeping with general principles of equality, which would apply (in Lockean terminology) to 'the favourite at court', as much as to 'the countryman at plough'.[92]

Neumann asserted that ambiguous laws presented a danger to democracy, because they could be used to advance the needs of social elites. (In this, his thinking was very much in line with traditional liberal theorists such as Locke and Jeremy Bentham.) Therefore, for Neumann it was essential to preserve formal law as an element of the liberal democratic heritage, even in a post-capitalist legal order. In this way, Neumann's approach provides a more optimistic prognosis for rescuing, reinventing and rendering more robust the rule of law—in contrast to the pessimism of other members of the Frankfurt School, such as Theodor Adorno and Max Horkheimer, or Herbert Marcuse.[93]

Likewise, contemporary law today possesses similar anti-formal trends— often flexible and discretionary, with vague clauses and general principles. It illustrates growing ad hoc, discretionary trends rather than traditional virtues associated with the rule of law. Neumann's analysis, however, illustrates how a dissatisfaction with law's links with capitalism, as well as concern over legal indeterminacy, need not lead to rejection of the rule of law, deconstruction nor the trashing of law. It also reminds us that an urge to de-formalise law and to scorn the rule of law, such as that embodied by the Marxist critique and CLS, is not the only route towards social transformation.

The Need for the Rule of Law

It is undeniable that law can be used both to mask power and to legitimate it, and it often does so most effectively when using respected tools and beliefs. Global poverty has been exacerbated by manipulation through law. The *notion* of a neutral, autonomous apolitical rule of law has helped propagate injustice—indeed, even some situations that we perceive to be very grave injustices. These critiques help to unmask and deconstruct the

---

[92] Locke (above n 47) ch 11.
[93] See, eg, M Horkheimer and T Adorno, *Dialectic of Englightenment: Philosophical Fragments (1947)*, GS Noerr (ed), E Jephcott (trans) (Stanford, Stanford University Press, 2002); and H Marcuse, *One-Dimensional Man* (Boston, Beacon, 1964).

hidden politics of a dominant conception of justice. Yet is the rule of law totally discredited? Or to rephrase the question: Can the rule of law be salvaged and given a radical reinterpretation while resisting the siren song of legal liberalism?[94] I believe that it can.

One may concede that the rule of law has too often been manipulated in such a way as to frustrate more inclusive participation and progressive policies—but does this fact rule out the possibility of it being used as part of a more emancipatory programme? This question is often obscured by a dogmatic, polarised jurisprudence which asserts either that the rule of law produces neutral, objective rules or that it is subject to the politically inde-terminate results of power relations. In other words, there is a stark choice between rigid stability or chaos. As Hutchinson has suggested in his later work, which is more friendly to the rule of law, 'a more nuanced, less crass appreciation of the rule of law ... is needed.'[95] Similarly, West has writ-ten, 'We need a progressive jurisprudence—a jurisprudence that embraces rather than resists, and then re-interprets, our liberal commitment to the rule of law.'[96] What is needed is the realisation that the rule of law must be created and fought for. It does not exist by itself as a manifes-tation of some sort of Platonic form but is the product of struggle and action.

While respect for the rule of law is of course not a guarantee of the good society, it is hard to have the good society without it. It is able to constrain both private and public coercion—both the Hobbesian state of nature and the Leviathan that Hobbes introduced as the solution to the state of nature. In its positing of principles of certainty, generality, equality, as well as pro-spective, knowable and stable law and structural features such as a separa-tion of powers and possibly natural justice, it embodies the belief that law is something other than raw power or assertion of will. The rule of law has met challenges to it in previous centuries, such as during the reign of the Stuart kings in the seventeenth century, as well as the growth of formal-ism in the nineteenth century and formalism's decline in the twentieth and twenty-first centuries. So it is surely capable of weathering the challenges of a post-Enlightenment world.

I have tried to explain why certain critiques such as the CLS and Marxist ones are misguided, to the extent that they posit the rule of law as a *cause*, responsible for societal wrongs rather than as a tool that has been abused and manipulated by the powerful, and why, on the contrary, adherence to the rule of law is important as a weapon against injustice, as well as embodying legal justice. Law is not completely autonomous, but

---

[94] Hutchinson, 'The Rule of Law Revisited' (above n 27).
[95] Ibid.
[96] West, *Re-imagining Justice* (above n 40) 9.

neither is it only a function of power relations or fatally indeterminate. It can still be valuable.

Reclaiming the Rule of Law?

The rule of law can be reclaimed both from its overly formalist image, which is embedded in classic liberalism, and from the castigations of its critics. In this context, it is useful to remember EP Thompson's defence of the rule of law. Thompson famously described the rule of law as an 'unqualified human good',[97] rejecting the orthodox Marxist position that it creates a false consciousness which separates law from politics, enabling the powerful to manipulate its forms to their own advantage. Thompson accepted that the rule of law was ideology. But he understood it as an ideology that operated to require ruling classes to acknowledge constraints on how they governed. Thompson also rejected the nihilism of the Marxist critique, expressing his opinion thus: 'Law surely *is* an instrument of class power, but that is not all it is.'[98] Such an approach, however, took its toll on Thompson—he was ostracised by many of his colleagues on the left.[99]

Thompson has been criticised for taking a confused approach to law. Robert Fine has found his approach to be contradictory, and he alleges that Thompson appeared to interpret law as both idealist and materialist, producing both freedom and domination, commitment and alienation.[100] In other words, Thompson both idealised the rule of law and championed anti-nomianism.Thompson himself admitted that his position was 'a precarious ledge'.[101] However, Thompson embraced this contrariness as a unity of opposites,[102] explaining it in this way:

> We reach, then, not a simple conclusion (law = class power) but a complex and contradictory one. On the one hand, it is true that law did mediate existent class relations to the advantage of the rulers ... [O]n the other hand, the law mediated these class relations through legal forms, which imposed again and again, inhibitions on the actions of the rulers ... The rhetoric and rules of a society are a great deal more than sham. In the same moment they may modify, in profound ways, the behaviour of the powerful, and mystify the powerless. They may disguise the

---

[97] EP Thompson, *Whigs and Hunters* (London, Penguin Books, 1977) 266.

[98] Ibid.

[99] Thompson had already left the communist party and become a socialist humanist.

[100] R Fine, 'The Rule of Law and Muggletonian Marxism: The Perplexities of Edward Thompson' (1994) 21 *Journal of Law and Society* 193.

[101] Thompson, *Whigs and Hunters* (above n 97) 264.

[102] Indeed, Fine prefaced his article 'The Rule of Law and Muggletonian Marxism' (ibid) with the following quote by Thompson on William Blake: 'Against the "single vision" of mechanical materialism, Blake sought, and succeeded, to think coexistent "contrary states" and to marry heaven and hell.' See EP Thompson, *The Poverty of Theory and Other Essays* (London, Merlin Press, 1978) 305.

true realities of power, but at the same time, they may curb that power and check its intrusions. And it is from within that very rhetoric that a radical critique of the society is developed: the reformers of the 1790s appeared first of all clothed in the rhetoric of Locke and Blackstone.[103]

Thompson's main point still stands, full of importance. As Thompson wrote:

If the law is evidently partial and unjust, then it will mask nothing, legitimise nothing, contribute nothing to any class's hegemony. The essential precondition for the effectiveness of law, in its function as ideology, is that it shall display an independence from gross manipulation and shall seem to be just. It cannot seem to be so without upholding its own logic and criteria of equity; indeed, on occasion, by actually *being* just ... Even rulers need to legitimate their power.[104]

Therefore, for Thompson, the law is not *merely* ideology nor *only* the tool of the ruling classes.

Thompson then continued with his now famous claim that 'the rule of law itself, the imposing of effective inhibitions upon power and the defence of the citizen from power's all-intrusive claims, seems to me to be an unqualified human good ... a cultural achievement of universal significance', adding that to deny this good 'in this dangerous century when the resources and pretensions of power continue to enlarge, [is] a desperate error of intellectual abstraction ... a self-fulfilling error ... which encourages us to disarm ourselves before power.'[105]

In fact, writing in the 1970s and early 1980s, Thompson perceived the main threat to the rule of law to come from the state, from modern governments, which he believed had lopped off the branches of 'the tree of liberty' and were 'the main muggers of the Constitution'.[106] He suggested that 'even the most exalted thinker' should be able to note the difference between a state based on the rule of law and one based on arbitrary authority. This is surely relevant in the context of the current 'war on terror' and the threat it poses to our civil liberties—arguments already explored in the last chapter. It has been traditional for both left and right to attack state power for abuse and despotism, linking state sovereignty with absolutism and perceiving it as the most major threat to the rule of law. Yet Thompson's defence of the rule of law also works if private or global forces pose the threat. Thompson believed that law could and should function as a form of mediation, to impose 'effective inhibitions on power'.

Thompson also wrote as an historian, and his writing reminds us that the rule of law is a child of history, moulded in the seventeenth-century

---

[103] Thompson, *Whigs and Hunters* (above n 97) 264–65.
[104] Ibid, 253.
[105] Ibid, 266.
[106] EP Thompson, 'Introduction' to I Blunt et al, *Review of Security and the State: Collected edition of State Research bulletins (1978)* (London, Julian Friedmann Books, 1978) i.

English civil war, by struggles of those such as John Hampden, as well as a timeless ideal of law as equity. He reminds us of the importance of the common law in eighteenth-century England as an 'alternative notation of law' to codified systems such as Roman jurisprudence, because it was more 'flexible and unprincipled ... more available as a medium through which social conflict could find expression', noting its export to the United States, India and certain African countries. He therefore found it 'important to re-examine the pretensions of the imperial donor'.[107] Thompson wrote about the rule of law in the context of the English eighteenth-century 'Black Acts', which imposed disproportionate, severe punishments for poaching, as an example of bad law. As Douglas Hay has written, in the eighteenth century, 'in place of police ... propertied Englishmen had a fat and swelling sheaf of laws which threatened thieves with death'.[108] Thompson saw these severe laws as the result of the fact that law had been captured by certain interests, and classes had 'grabbed hold of the law, throttled it', noting that 'the Hanoverian Whigs of the 1720s and 30s were a hard lot of men. And they remind us that stability, no less than revolution, may have its own kind of terror.'[109] Thompson even noted that it might be wise to end his work there, with that comment, but nevertheless continued to write:

> I sit here in my study, at the age of fifty, the desk and the floor piled high with five years of notes, xeroxes, rejected drafts, the clock once again moving into the small hours, and see myself, in a lucid instant, as an anachronism. Why have I spent these years trying to find out what could, in its essential structures, have been known without any investigation at all?[110]

Yet Thompson's many late nights were not in vain. For, Thompson concluded, *his research did matter* because the law can be used to restrain the powerful, to check abuse. 'It is only when we follow through the intricacies of the [law's] operation that we can show what it was worth, how it was bent.'[111] He added that we might feel contempt for those such as the eighteenth-century English prime minister Sir Robert Walpole, or for those judges who had manipulated the law, 'but we feel contempt not because we are contemptuous of the notion of just and equitable law but because the notion has been betrayed by its professors'.[112] Thompson stressed:

> I do not lay any claim as to the abstract extra-historical impartiality of these rules ... I am not starry-eyed about this ... [I insist] only on the obvious point, which

---

[107] Thompson, *Whigs and Hunters* (above n 97) 267.
[108] Hay (above n 47) 18.
[109] Thompson, *Whigs and Hunters* (above n 97) 258.
[110] Ibid, 260.
[111] Ibid, 268.
[112] Ibid.

some Marxist historians have overlooked, that there is a difference between power and the rule of law.[113]

To be sure, Thompson does provide us with a somewhat contradictory account of law, one which acknowledges both law's ability to function as ideology, to aid those in power and, at the same time, its ability to do the reverse—to constrain the powerful. Fine is in a sense right in his criticism. But this is only because law *itself* is complex and contradictory—an example of the 'both/and', incapable of being captured by modern, straightjacket theories of law. The subtlety and sensitivity of Thompson's approach lies in his recognition of this fact.

Hay, a legal historian, expressed in *Albion's Fatal Tree* observations that are similar to Thompson's, based on Hay's own historical study of justice in eighteenth-century England. Hay described how after the constitutional struggles in the seventeenth century had helped to establish the rule of law, 'justice' became an 'evocative' word in the eighteenth century, in spite of draconian punishments (usually the death penalty) for minor breaches of the criminal law. Law, though it served the interests of the propertied classes, was indeed something other than the creature of the ruling classes, and 'equality before the law' meant that no one, including the aristocracy, was exempt from its extreme penalties. Hay cited Lord Mansfield's finding against the executive use of general warrants in *Entick v Carrington* as evidence for this, as well as the colourful fact that in 1760, Lord Ferrars, who killed his steward, was hanged in his silver brocade wedding suit but 'dissected like a common criminal'. Moreover, 'later in the century this event was often recalled as irrefutable proof of the justice of English society.'[114] Thus, the public could accept that law stood by formal procedures, which provided, at least in enough cases, evidence of its equal application and justice (even if a sometimes rough sort) for all.

Indeed, the notion of the justice of English law, 'of wicked Lord Ferrars, of juries, habeas corpus',[115] became leading themes in anti-Jacobin popular literature, a powerful weapon in the French revolution, as evidenced by James Gillray's satirical print (Figure 8-3), which illustrates the French 'tree of liberty' in contrast to English justice. Such expressions are an ideological weapon to be sure, and most beloved of conservatives. However, for this weapon to have functioned effectively, it had to be rooted in fact, in efficacy—in the circumstances that Hay and Thompson described.

---

[113] Ibid, 266.
[114] Hay (above n 47) 34.
[115] Ibid.

The Tree of LIBERTY...with, the Devil tempting John Bull.

Figure 8-3: James Gillray, 'The Tree of Liberty with the Devil Tempting John Bull' (1798), US Library of Congress, Prints and Photographs Division

Gillray captured the rooted and organic nature of English justice, picturing the devil springing from behind the French tree of liberty, his serpentine form coiling round the trunk of the tree. The Rights of Man grow from one of the French tree's branches, but they grow from a trunk formed of 'Opposition' with its roots in 'Envy', 'Ambition' and 'Disappointment'. The Devil fails to tempt John Bull with the rotten, forbidden fruit of this tree of liberty, for John Bull has already filled his pockets with fruit from the tree of English justice, which, in contrast to the French tree of liberty, bears wholesome fruit. This is not to suggest the bloated slovenly John Bull of Gillray's print as a model for the application of the rule of law, let alone justice, but rather to illustrate the somewhat paradoxical nature of the rule of law, which was noted by Thompson. By forcing all—rich and poor—to observe it, by actually having to do what it claims to do, the rule of law may bear a 'wholesome fruit' for law and justice.

The Rule of Law Transfigured: Critical Legal Justice

The rule of law need not be reduced to conservative, neoliberal understandings. It may be reclaimed. I have preferred to recast it as critical legal justice in order to adopt the methods and tenets of a critical tradition going back to Kant and to capture insights of legal realism and the critical legal studies movement, as well as to be alert to the snares of an uncritical approach to the rule of law. Furthermore, recasting the rule of law as critical legal justice acknowledges it as a form of *justice*. What is crucial, as Martin Krygier has highlighted,[116] is to recognise and identify the rule of law in terms of the values that inspire and underpin it—its ability to impose effective inhibitions on power, to prevent abuse and oppression but also to enable law to do some more ambitious works as a field of human aspiration, as a realm of value. In other words, it is crucial to identify the rule of law by the good that it does, rather than by the contingent forms that it has taken at different times. Otherwise, there is a danger that it will simply be identified with those contingent forms—with legality and formalism, with capitalism or with Dicey's vision of the Victorian constitution. Therefore it is vital that it is seen in terms of its ends and values; otherwise, there is a real prospect of 'goal displacement'—of institutions and practices once used as a means of achieving certain goals becoming reified as the only way of achieving those ends. In this way, goals become identified with the means of achieving them; the goals, values and the 'lifeworld' of the rule of law become instrumentalised.

The rule of law serves the apparently straightforward function of restraining the abuse of power. Yet it is itself not always straightforward. Earlier chapters of this book have considered and warned of the danger of having to choose between exclusive and binary alternatives—the 'either/or', the false dichotomy. Krygier has described the rule of law as a 'layered phenomenon', insisting that we keep separate its point from the forms it should take—avoiding 'a melodramatic once and for all choice'.[117] The rule of law has its contradictions, its opposites, its 'both/ands'. Its nature may shift, using different means to fulfil its values in different contexts. The rule of law may be seen as providing accommodation between some sort of *yin* and *yang*, or between an idealist, aspirational Apollonian rule-like order for law and a Dionysian undisciplined fury of politics,[118] between formalism and chaos, the contradictory and contrarian impulses noted by Thompson, an almost Hegelian dialectic, in the interplay of law and power, as evidenced by, eg, the seventeeth-century battles between the monarchy and Lord Chief Justice Coke over the royal prerogative, or in the law suits in the United Kingdom and the United States over indefinite detention in the war on terror.

Ruti Teitel has also suggested that there exists 'a tension between the rule of law as backward looking and forward looking, as settled versus

---

[116] Krygier (above n 4) 251–77.
[117] Ibid, 251.
[118] West, *Re-imagining Justice* (above n 40) 5.

dynamic'.[119] The rule of law also *restrains*—ie, inhibits power as well as *enables*—by making a space for a realm of aspiration through law. As Selznick recognised, it is a blend of scepticism and confidence. And it will fulfil these functions in different ways in different times. It has been argued that the rule of law is best seen as contingent on historical circumstances. In this way it can protect the various forms of pluralism. As already stressed, it is a minimum. It is necessary—there can be no fair and just system without it, yet it will not always be sufficient to ensure such a system.

This may sound vague. There is no detailed blueprint for institutional design, no formula for its realisation. Yet there are some requirements that need to be complied with, although this may be done in different ways over different times. They relate to the key values that the rule of law serves. It must be possible to constrain power. Law must be administered and implemented in ways that are not arbitrary. Law must also be sufficiently intelligible and public so that people may be able to comply with it and use it to guide and plan their lives. Finally, it is very important to acknowledge that for it to exist, it is necessary that people *believe* in and be committed to the rule of law. Trust and belief in law must be nurtured and earned, which is not very likely if only elites have access to law creation and enforcement. The rule of law also thrives on the reciprocity that Fuller wrote about. Evidence suggests that compliance with, for example, tax laws will be greatly increased if people believe they are being treated with respect and procedural fairness by revenue authorities, in addition to believing that tax laws are substantively, distributively fair.[120] Similarly, the dissymmetry between the lack of prosecutions of those responsible for the financial crisis and fraudulent financial management on the one hand and the vigorous prosecution and criminalisation of those protesting in various 'Occupy' movements, on the other hand, creates a dissonance, a lack of reciprocity, in which law is perceived as exploitation, and confidence and faith in law is eroded.

The European Union as a Microcosm for Critical Legal Justice

The European Union may be examined as one final case study here. Indeed, the contemporary European Union is perhaps particularly apposite for such a purpose, as it exhibits many of the key traits of law after modernity that are discussed in this book—pluralism, transnationalism and loss of sovereignty, adoption of new types of law and concepts (eg, directives, direct effect) and flexibility and governance by experts; and it therefore poses

---

[119] R Teitel, 'Transitional Rule of Law' in AM Krygier, A Czarnota and W Sadurski (eds), *The Rule of Law after Communism* (Aldershot, Ashgate, 2003).

[120] J Braithwaite, *Restorative Justice and Responsive Regulation* (Oxford, Oxford University Press, 2001).

salient problems for the possibility of transnational justice. A further threat to the rule of law is raised by the European Union and its Member States' response to the crisis of its currency, which as already suggested, has been characterised by a continuous flurry of untransparent and undemocratic measures, distancing economic governance from the control of elected governments and national parliaments, in an extremely complex and confusing melée of arrangements of EU law and international agreements between states. Indeed, the contemporary European Union provides a particularly apposite candidate for the application of critical legal justice, as I have argued elsewhere.[121]

The European Union presents extraordinary obstacles to the accomplishment of a transnational theory of justice. At present,[122] its problems seem almost insurmountable, as the European Union itself is facing the prospect of either disintegration[123] or the imposition of a fiscal union which its citizens would not wish for it. Neither of these prospects seems palatable. The byzantine complexity of EU operations renders injustice and lack of accountability all the more likely, and also renders justice all the more difficult to achieve. A monist, universalising type of justice risks deadening the vibrancy of the Union's many legal cultures, of failing to do justice in many singular instant cases. An alternative embrace of plural justices risks the creation of a neo-medieval world of private, self-serving justices or of failing to meet some very real needs for an overarching transnational justice.

The way forward, I suggest, both for the European Union and more generally, lies in just this very reimagining of the rule of law in a critical, dynamic way—in rejecting pessimism yet also realising and acknowledging that flexible, reflexive legal pluralism brings its own problems that may find their solutions only through the reimagining and reworking of some rather old ideas of classical legal thought into the theory of critical legal justice. Many of the most glaring injustices within the European Union, for example, derive from: its failure to observe some basic fundamental requirements and procedures (eg, lack of access to justice in certain areas, such as EU measures on criminal law[124] or the inflexible, individual standing requirements for judicial review under the pre-Lisbon Article 230

---

[121] S Douglas-Scott, 'The Problem of Justice in the EU' in J Dickson and P Eleftheriadis (eds), *Philosophical Foundations of EU Law* (Oxford, Oxford University Press, 2012); and S Douglas-Scott, 'Rethinking Justice for the EU' in MP Maduro and K Tuori (eds), *Rethinking EU Law* (Cambridge, Cambridge University Press, 2013).

[122] Ie, the early second decade of the twenty-first century.

[123] See comments in J Fischer, 'Europe and the "New German question"', (6 April 2011).

[124] At least prior to the amendments of the 2009 Lisbon Treaty. Before the implementation of the Lisbon Treaty, it was extremely difficult for individual applicants to bring direct challenges in the EU courts to EU criminal law measures, and also difficult in any other type of measure.

EC); overuse of broad, vague principles and standards, which engender unpredictability; and less than transparent law-making that is slanted towards executive law-making (eg, a large amount of delegated law-making by the (unelected) European Commission, along with excessive use of confusing comitology procedures[125]). Economic and monetary union (EMU) is a prime example of this sort of lack of transparency. As one author has recently commented:

> The EU's economic governance rules fail the test of transparency, because of their near-total complexity and unreadability, scattered across a dozen primary, secondary and soft-law sources, with more to come. This might be justifiable if the subject-matter of these rules were a technical issue like chemicals regulation, but it is hardly acceptable that the basic rules on the EU's coordination and control of fundamental national economic decisions are essentially unintelligible.[126]

Part of the problem has been too great a reliance on 'output' legitimacy—ie, on efficient and effective results, irrespective of the means used to achieve them. Remedying many of these situations requires no overarching substantive theory of justice for the European Union but rather recourse to a more formal, legal justice through the means of observance of the rule of law.[127] If more attention were paid to the rule of law at all stages of the EU law-making process, then it would be possible to prevent some conflicts and particular clashes of pluralism occurring. For example, the introduction of the European Arrest Warrant (EAW) provoked an extraordinary amount of litigation (both in national courts and in the European Court of Justice (ECJ)) with regard to human rights and the failure to respect national identities by eradicating long-held constitutional prohibitions against extradition of a state's own citizens. The EAW legislative measure was crafted in great haste as an EU response to the attacks of September 11, with democratic institutions, such as national parliaments, poorly informed, often being sent out-of-date information, and they were therefore unable properly to set democratic controls on its content.[128] If the EAW had been debated and adopted in a context of more carefully thought through processes, then the scope for later human rights challenges to it, as well as clashes of a pluralist nature, would have been lessened, along with the opportunities for national

---

[125] 'Comitology' is a process whereby a large number of committees with a membership appointed by EU member states are used to manage or scrutinise many types of legislation in the EU. This process has been criticised on a number of occasions for its undemocratic nature, and scandalously, it has proved difficult to ascertain the exact number of committees operating in this way.

[126] S Peers, 'Analysis: Draft Agreement on Reinforced Economic Union (REU Treaty)', *Statewatch* (21 December 2011).

[127] See, eg, S Douglas-Scott, 'The Rule of Law in the European Union: Putting the Security into the "Area of Freedom, Security and Justice"' (2004) 29 *European Law Review* 219.

[128] For further on this, see ibid, 116.

supreme courts to pronounce on the status of EU law in apparently defiant ways, evoking the perils of radical pluralism. In this way, attention to critical legal justice could work to strengthen the rule of law in the face of pluralism, rather than allowing the development of a situation in which a destructive pluralism appears inevitable. Likewise, the EU's response to the Eurozone crisis stores up future problems, due to its lack of observance of the rule of law.

There is a need for thoughtful law-making which is capable of producing virtuous rather than the present vicious circles, in which globalisation, or greater EU integration, leads to injustice.

Conclusion

If people neither expect nor insist on the rule of law when officials move to compromise its application, it becomes too readily corrupted and replaced by rule of power. Scepticism wreaks its own damage. Aleksandr Solzhenitsyn pointed to the absence of such a tradition of law as the basic explanation for the failure of the Russian people to resist the Bolshevik takeover, which was carried out through nocturnal arrests and ad hoc political trials and executions.[129] This is why it is important that breaches of the rule of law committed by those in government (eg, at Guantánamo) be accounted for, so that a firm and progressive tradition of and belief in the rule of law be maintained. The rule of law, understood as critical legal justice, must be fought for and is the product of continuous struggle.

It has been argued that although the rule of law may not help us achieve perfectly just outcomes nor deliver an impressive theory of ideal justice, it can help to deter injustice. It is not a complete vision of justice and may operate in tandem with the enforcement of human rights and a quest for social justice. In proposing the theory of critical legal justice, I have attempted to escape from the binary either/or and from the thick/thin categorisations that beset both the rule of law and, indeed, modern conceptions of law more generally. Such juxtapositions and oppositions fail to capture the complexities of contemporary law. The key to this recasting of the rule of law as critical legal justice and to reconciling of the rule of law with complex or even chaotic legal pluralism lies in adhering strongly to the *values* that the rule of law protects—namely, in looking to its spirit rather than in over-focusing on the forms that it has taken in various contexts.

---

[129] A Solzhenitsyn, *The Gulag Archipelago*, vol 3, H Willetts (trans) (New York, Harper and Row, 1978).

I have also argued that it is necessary to rescue, reinvent and render more robust the rule of law, following in the footsteps of theorists such as Neumann and Selznick. My argument is that the rule of law, understood and recast as critical legal justice, can bring about some sort of justice in the here and now, while recognising Derrida's point that justice can never fully be done, is always deferred in some way, is always still to come. Critical legal justice concentrates on what law *can* do and *should* do. It seeks what is possible. Moreover, it ultimately commits itself to an attempt for global justice and thus is cosmopolitan in outlook. It asserts the crucial importance of the rule of law both nationally and internationally, in conjunction with an accountability for the creation, promulgation and impact of all laws, public or private. It takes seriously the contemporary dilemma posed by complex pluralism, in terms of its under-provision of accountability and justice, a problem that seems to have been under-researched in legal theory.

As a form of *legal* justice, critical legal justice provides a distinctly legal solution to the problems of pluralism. The rule of law (and sometimes even human rights law) is apt to be derided as too liberal, imperialistic even—the tool of an oppressive use of law by Western capitalistic culture. This approach seeks to reclaim the rule of law from this derision, and in doing so, it recasts the rule of law in the particular form of critical legal justice—as a concept of justice rather than an anodyne, formal concept.

I end this chapter with a literary analogy. A model for critical legal justice might be that of Dr Rieux in Albert Camus' *La Peste*, who in the face of the terrible adversity of plague, quietly and determinedly gets on with his work as a doctor. This should also be the message—not to be detracted by the emotional and intellectual fireworks of writers such as Schmitt, nor by the nihilism and reductionisms of those who cast all law as only an exercise of power. The sniping against the rule of law by postmodern and latter-day Marxist critics is reminiscent of the image used by Zygmunt Bauman of the snake destroying its own tail.[130] In this way, critique can destroy the very foundations necessary for justice to thrive. Better to keep on, struggle on, using the rule of law to fight injustice, because without it, law is deficient, 'maimed' even.

---

[130] Z Bauman, *Postmodern Ethics* (Oxford, Blackwell 1993).

9

The Enigma of Human Rights

For many people, the search for a moral element in law begins inevitably with a turn to human rights. It has become commonplace to describe human rights as a 'secular religion' for our times[1] or, according to Boaventura de Sousa Santos, as a 'political esperanto'—a creed that has displaced other once favoured concepts such as distributive justice or equality.[2] Whatever their theoretical or ideological persuasions, theorists agree on the apparent present ubiquity of human rights. Generally, human rights are seen as praiseworthy: it is hard to deride the 'idea' of human rights (as opposed to less than optimal interpretations or applications of them). Indeed, one might even think that human rights have overtaken or at least colonised the concept of justice, given their centrality to the Western moral landscape. The idea of human rights seems exciting and inspiring, in comparison to the more sober notion of the rule of law, even if it is imagined as critical legal justice.

However, this smug introduction aside, there are some very real problems. Politically, human rights may be at the fore, a marching banner of any politician, cause or global movement that wishes to claim a moral high ground, but conceptually, there exists a great deal of scepticism as to what human rights actually are—a scepticism that is partly the product of so many (different and competing) causes and movements claiming them for themselves. There is a feeling that human rights represent a displacement or 'transference', that they are actually a metaphor for many other things—for legitimacy, protest or, as in the case of EU law, sovereignty (ie, the ability of a state to determine what are perceived as foundational moral matters for itself, rather than cede those to a transnational authority).[3] Conor Gearty has used the metaphor of human rights as a 'mask'—for

---

[1] E Wiesel, 'A Tribute to Human Rights' in Y Danieli, E Stamatopoulou and C Dias (eds), *The Universal Declaration of Human Rights: Fifty Years and Beyond* (Amityville, NY, Baywood, 1999).

[2] B de Sousa Santos, *Toward a New Common Sense: Law, Science and Politics in the Paradigmatic Transition* (London, Butterworths, 1995) 348.

[3] Witness the current vogue for and volume of literature about human rights in the EU—most of which has little to do with substantive contents of rights or outcomes of their application but rather more to do with highly complex discussions of jurisdiction, competence and struggle over the terrain of human rights (as discussed above ch 4).

truth, legality or security—to capture the way in which they are used as ciphers for other things.[4] Can they be truly valuable, then, as weapons against injustice?

So contemporary scholarship tends to problematise human rights. Gearty, in his Hamlyn lectures entitled '*Can Human Rights Survive?*' has analysed them in terms of three crises: authority, legalism and national security. Marie Benedicte Dembour has asked the very question 'Who Believes in Human Rights?' as the title of her book,[5] and Costas Douzinas tellingly entitles his book (not, in fact, a work of a totally sceptical nature) *The End of Human Rights*. Therefore, we find ambivalence and doubt in the human rights scholarship. As Andrew Williams has noted, the characterisation of human rights as 'esperanto' by de Sousa Santos implies a certain sense of frustration. However attractive the notion of a universal language of human rights may be, 'its acceptance or even relevance in the world is open to doubt. The likening of human rights to Esperanto suggests something "'quaint", perhaps whimsical, a potentially dispiriting association suggesting a lack of "connection" with people's daily experiences'.[6] Indeed, the majority of scholarship identifies considerable conceptual problems for human rights—what Gearty terms the crisis of their authority.[7]

Given that human rights now occupies such a wide ethical field and such a prominent position in our moral consciousness, it is vital to be able to justify this prominence and pre-eminence, in order for human rights to, as Gearty has put it, 'work its magic'. This use of the word 'magic' is revealing—for the embrace of human rights takes us beyond rational attachment to the attribution of an almost supernatural force, identified in terms of religion, but also to a more esoteric magic or 'alchemy'.[8] It is very important to understand this facet of human rights—our belief, even in secular societies, of its ability to work magic, an almost irrational belief in its power. Indeed, the enduring nature of human rights is inexplicable if we ignore this dimension. I will return to this feature later in the chapter.

However, there is another aspect to human rights discussion and scholarship that lies a world away from alchemy. Human rights also invoke what Upendra Baxi has termed a 'weariness' and 'wariness'[9]—a feeling

---

[4] C Gearty, *Can Human Rights Survive?* (Cambridge, Cambridge University Press, 2006).

[5] M-B Dembour, *Who Believes in Human Rights? Reflections on the European Convention* (Cambridge, Cambridge University Press, 2006).

[6] A Williams, 'Human Rights and Law: Between Sufferance and Insufferability' (2007) *Law Quarterly Review* 132.

[7] Gearty, *Can Human Rights Survive?* (above n 4).

[8] Eg, P Williams, *The Alchemy of Race and Rights* (Harvard, MA, Harvard University Press, 1991); A Sachs, *The Strange Alchemy of Life and Law* (Oxford, Oxford University Press, 2010), which is a work by a South African constitutional court judge discussing human rights cases.

[9] U Baxi, 'Voices of Suffering and the Future of Human Rights' (1998) *Transnational Law and Contemporary Problems* 125.

that they are overused, worn out, unfit for purpose or even an obstacle to justice rather than a means of providing it. A consideration of human rights involves an awareness of their almost Janus-faced characteristics—of the weary and the jaded, as well as the magical.

In the remainder of this chapter I will proceed by means of three analyses. First, I shall consider some conceptual problems that beset human rights, for if human rights truly lack clear conceptual foundations, they may not be best placed to resolve those issues of chaos and disorder within law identified in this book. However, I am aware that a search for strong conceptual foundations and justifications perhaps merely reveals a residual preference for unity and certainty—which is perhaps impossible to achieve in any case. It might be that the very malleability of human rights is what makes them appropriate for use in the complexities of contemporary law.

My second analysis, following in the footsteps of Gearty and many others, examines the role of human rights in law. Law tends to the conservative rather than the radical and is not remarkable as a progressive force in society. Much scholarship of a critical nature focuses on perceived dangers of legalising human rights, of thus petrifying them, removing their emancipatory potential. These critiques warn of the corruption of human rights by law, that if the moral imperatives of human rights are contorted and made misshapen, then human rights become not a means of ensuring law's justice but the reverse. Karl Marx provides one of the earliest and most notable examples of this type of critique of formal and legal rights,[10] and his critique still has resonance today. So this is a danger to be aware of. Yet this book is written from the perspective of *law* after modernity, and the present aim is to locate an ethical dimension for law. The fear of possibly stultifying consequences of juridification cannot (at least at this stage) deter this investigation, although it may ultimately lead to negative conclusions.

The third and final investigation in this chapter concerns the possibility of human rights as a normative resolution to dilemmas of complexity and pluralism in the contemporary legal space. It assumes human rights as a concept and as existing in positive law, but works with the concerns and worries identified in investigations one and two. So to summarise: overall, my enquiry takes shape in a pattern of concentric circles, set out in Figure 9-1 below, and seeks to ascertain if the disadvantages and ambiguities identified in human rights may be turned to strengths—whether they may in the end be capable of performing some sort of magic, a transformation of law into justice.

---

[10] K Marx, 'On the Jewish Question' in J Waldron (ed), *Nonsense upon Stilts: Bentham, Burke and Marx on the Rights of Man* (London, Methuen, 1987).

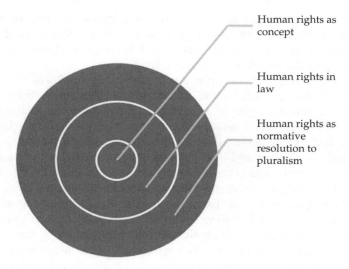

Human rights as concept

Human rights in law

Human rights as normative resolution to pluralism

Figure 9-1: Concentric analysis of human rights

A Conceptual Lack of Clarity

The conceptual lack of clarity with regard to human rights has long been a preoccupation for many, going at least as far back as Jeremy Bentham's condemnation of the 'pestiferous and pestilential' French Declaration of the Rights of Man and the Citizen (1789) as 'nonsense on stilts'.[11] The philosopher Raymond Geuss has similarly taken Robert Nozick to task for assuming too much and explaining too little, in a work that rests on a particular theory of rights. In the much quoted first sentence of his book *Anarchy, State and Utopia,* Nozick wrote, 'Individuals have rights, and there are things no person or group may do to them (without violating their rights).'[12] Geuss has pithily complained:

> [Nozick] then allows that bald statement to lie flapping and gasping for breath like a large, moribund fish on the deck of a trawler, with no further analysis or discussion, and proceeds to draw consequences from it ... The existence of rights that (all) individuals 'have' is, he seems to think, to be taken for granted, and requires no further argumentative support.[13]

---

[11] J Bentham, *Anarchical Fallacies* (Edinburgh, William Tait, 1843).
[12] R Nozick, *Anarchy, State and Utopia* (New York, Basic Books, 1974) ix.
[13] R Geuss, *Philosophy and Real Politics* (Princeton, Princeton University Press, 2008) 64.

Are human rights conceptually incoherent? It is common to start accounts of human rights with statements such as 'human rights are what you have by virtue of being human', and such a statement has a satisfying simplicity to it. Yet one is immediately minded of Carl Schmitt's famous comment 'Whoever invokes humanity wishes to cheat.'[14] The invocation of human nature (along with God or other supposed universal justifications for human rights) simply raises too many questions. What is so special about human nature that it gives rise to rights, when it seems that venality is as much a common feature of humankind as dignity?

To derive rights from human nature also too easily enables the exclusion of those interests not counted as 'human', as, for example, in the past—women, certain ethnic or religious groups and so on. It also raises the question of why human nature should only have been perceived as sufficiently important to give rise to rights as late as the eighteenth century, becoming a base for the declarations of rights in America and France. Prior to this period, rights were conceptualised as particularistic in nature, for example, as the rights of Englishmen, if they were classified as rights at all. Oppressed Europeans in the Middle Ages, for example, would have been far more likely to look to an avenging angel or patron saint for relief. So to locate human rights in humanity creates as many problems as it solves.

Since a fundamental aim of human rights is to guide and constrain the actions of society, one approach is to offer human rights as those rights that can be delivered by the one correct or best moral theory. But naturally, all are not agreed as to which is the best moral theory, let alone whether substantive moral theory should be the starting point. Lack of clarity about human rights not only relates to a scepticism as to their viable existence but also follows from the huge range of different substantive moral theories from which they are drawn. There are many accounts of the conceptual nature of human rights. Contrast the following: 'If human rights are the rights one has simply because one is a human being, as they usually are thought to be, then they are held "universally" by all human beings.'[15] 'Human rights do not belong to humans and do not follow the dictates of humanity; they construct humans.'[16] Or how about: 'The idea of human rights is ineliminably religious, and any notion of the dignity of the human person is at risk if its religious origins are denied.'[17] Or yet again: 'I take it

---

[14] C Schmitt, *The Concept of the Political* (1932), G Schwab (trans) (Chicago, University of Chicago Press, 1996). In fact Schmitt was modifying an earlier quotation from Proudhon.

[15] J Donnelly, *Universal Human Rights in Theory and Practice*, 2nd edn (Ithaca, Cornell University Press, 2003) 1.

[16] C Douzinas, *The End of Human Rights: Critical Thought at the Turn of the Century* (Oxford, Hart Publishing, 2000).

[17] M Perry, *The Idea of Human Rights* (New York, Oxford University Press, 1998).

as axiomatic that the historic mission of "contemporary" human rights is to give voice to human suffering, to make it visible, and to ameliorate it.'[18]

A multitude of further descriptions could be given, variously different in nature, and taken together, they quash any hope that there is any common conceptual core or even an identifiable 'family resemblance'[19] in the notion. Wesley Hohfeld identified in 1913 the different conceptual uses of rights within the law in an attempt for clarity in the way we use them.[20] Yet accounts of human rights are not only varied in nature but even competitive—human rights are variously perceived as universal or differentiated, pertaining to human nature or socially constructed, a product of discourse or an objectifiably identifiable moral concept. They cannot be all of these things. Nor does it help to identify human rights as attributes of overriding importance, for this does not tell us which attributes should be considered of overriding importance.

In the face of this, one solution is to agree on the practical uses for human rights but to avoid or bypass any attempt to pinpoint an agreed definition. Jacques Maritain, for example, in his 1954 'The Rights of Man', described how 'proponents of violently opposed ideologies' would announce at UNESCO meetings, 'We agree on these rights providing we are not asked why.'[21] Likewise, Michael Ignatieff has written, 'People may not agree why we have rights, but they can agree that they need them.'[22]

However attractive this view might appear as a pragmatic compromise, it is troubling, for the existence and identifications of human rights are bound up with the very justifications we use for them. For example, a Nozickian who believes that rights always operate as side constraints in the context of a night watchman state is unlikely to recognise a right to holidays with pay, to be paid out of general taxation, as a human right. Aiming for adherence to a pragmatic consensus also brings dangers—namely, that a focus on consensus slips into a dangerous utilitarian inclination toward dispensing with rights when it appears in the public interest to do so—as Ignatieff himself seems to have conceded. In *The Lesser Evil: Ethics in an Age of Terror*, Ignatieff suggested that it may sometimes be necessary to suspend certain rights in times of emergency in order to secure national security, a

---

[18] U Baxi, *The Future of Human Rights*, 2nd edn (Oxford, Oxford University Press, 2006) 6.

[19] After the Wittgensteinian term. Marie-Benedicte Dembour has investigated the possibility of a family resemblance as a conceptual tool for the understanding of human rights but finds it unworkable in this context. See Dembour (above n 5).

[20] See, eg, W Hohfeld, 'Some Fundamental Legal Conceptions as Applied in Judicial Reasoning' (1913) 23 *Yale Law Journal* 16.

[21] J Maritain, 'The Rights of Man' in J Maritain, *Man and the State* (Washington, DC, Catholic University of America Press, 1998).

[22] M Ignatieff, *The Lesser Evil: Political Ethics in an Age of Terror* (Princeton, Princeton University Press, 2004).

concession that underlines his statement elsewhere in the book that 'The fundamental moral commitment entailed by rights is not to respect, and certainly not to worship. It is to deliberation.'[23]

Where to go in this quagmire of conceptual uncertainty? Does a rejection of a universal foundation for human rights commit one to a morass of relativism or particularism, in which rights can appear to mean whatever we want for whomever we want? A binary classification is often adopted to distinguish between 'foundational' and 'anti-foundational' approaches. However, while it may be helpful to classify theories to the extent that it helps us to map out history and scholarship of human rights in a systematic way, this sort of binary thinking (eg, universal/particular, foundational/anti-foundational) is best avoided if one aims to move beyond the stalemate and perplexity that has dogged rights. In the next sections, I examine some different theories of human rights, not with the aim of a comprehensive overview of this literature but rather with an eye to some of the underlying concerns that may have prompted these theories and accounts in the first place. This will then enable me to take a somewhat different perspective on the conceptual confusions of human rights.

Foundations

Liberal Rights

It is a conventional approach to start with 'liberal' theories. I follow the convention not because these necessarily appear to be examples of the best and foremost theorising about rights but because they are bound up historically with the origins of the notion of human rights, although they continue to be presented in recognisable form today.

Liberal thought often grounds human rights in the premise of some sort of social contract—a crucial concept of modernity that also does important work to explain the creation of law's authority. This (hypothetical) contract, allegedly formed by individuals with government, was deemed necessary in order to protect the rights to liberty and property which supposedly exist in a state of nature but cannot be effectively maintained in such a state. The notion of such a social contract influenced the framers of the US Constitution, and versions of social contract theory are to be found in the work of Thomas Hobbes, John Locke and Jean-Jacques Rousseau, as well as, more latterly, John Rawls. Social contract theory implicitly or explicitly posits free and equal individual beings who can rationally bargain in order to ensure the benefits of government. But the notion of a social contract,

---

[23] Ibid.

even if thought of as heuristic in form, is tendentious. People have never been free and equal in that way, and in, for example, the forming of the contract that is the US federal Constitution, many parties were quite definitely excluded from this process—notably women, slaves and native Americans. And this invocation of a bargaining-type process, with each out to maximise his or her essential self-interest, brings to mind Max Weber's characterisation of law as a community of strangers.[24] Or in the more extreme expression of Hobbes, 'Every man enemy to every man.'[25]

The social contract was deemed necessary to protect natural rights. A fundamental premise for liberal rights lies in autonomy, evident in the form given to the rights these theories tend to prefer—privacy, free expression, liberty, property—all vital to us if we are to be autonomous beings. Rights are considered to be those things you have by virtue of being autonomous, according to one particular analysis (given, for example, by HLA Hart[26]) of the concept of a right. If you do not have the will or sufficient autonomy to bargain away, or waive, the right, then you cannot possess it in the first place. This of course can be problematic for those beings who, for whatever reason, have been singled out as not conforming to the autonomy model in the first place—for example, at various times, children, mental incompetents and even women.

For others, this liberal tradition is clearly linked to the best way of theorising about rights. For example, James Griffin, author of a recently acclaimed work, *On Human Rights*, has found 'the best substantive account'

> ... to be in the spirit of this tradition and to take the following form: Human rights can then be seen as protections of our human standing ... or personhood ... To be an agent, in the fullest sense of which we are capable, one must (first) choose one's own path through life—that I not be dominated or controlled by someone or something else (call it 'autonomy'). And (second) one's choice must be real; one must have at least a certain minimum education and information. And having chosen, one must then be able to act; that is, one must have at least the minimum protection of resources as capabilities that it takes (call all of this 'minimum protection'). And ... (third) others must also not forcibly stop one from what one sees as a worthwhile life (call this 'liberty').[27]

This is Griffin's 'central intuitive idea',[28] and I have quoted it at length as a paradigm example of a well-regarded, contemporary human rights theory in the liberal tradition (although it should be mentioned that Griffin's account is notable and quite rare in its aspiration to provide a *substantive*

---

[24] See A Kronman, *Max Weber* (Stanford, Stanford University Press, 1983) 110.
[25] T Hobbes, *Leviathan* (1651), CB MacPherson (ed) (London, Penguin Classics 1968) ch 13.
[26] HLA Hart, 'Are There any Natural Rights?' (1955) 64 *Philosophical Review* 175–91.
[27] J Griffin, *On Human Rights* (Oxford, Oxford University Press, 2008) 33.
[28] Ibid.

account of human rights, namely one that claims to identify those rights we actually have). Griffin's account is centred on the notion of *agency* rather than happiness, flourishing, needs or suffering, seeking to provide clear foundations for human rights, and it has at its roots the philosophies of John Locke and Immanuel Kant. Griffin sees it as his work to complete the 'Enlightenment project' by providing this notion of human rights with greater determinacy than it possessed during the Enlightenment.[29]

Griffin's resulting candidates for human rights are largely civil and political, and his focus is on protecting individual autonomy from state action. But his focus on human agency as the foundation nails human rights to a monistic,[30] partial grounding for them—unattractive to those who look to human rights not for an expression of an historically grounded Western value of autonomy but for a more immediate relief from human suffering, a protection of those very people who are not autonomous. For too many, the liberal notion of human rights is grounded in a bourgeois, 'possessive individualism'[31] that corrupts the very moral purposes which human rights are meant to serve. Such an account enables the use of rights for selfish, consumer-led claims, bolstering images of the active, atomistic, autonomous rights bearer who is willing to assert a right against the community. This was Marx's message in his essay 'On the Jewish Question', in which he criticised human rights:

> None of the so-called rights of man, therefore, go beyond egoistic man, beyond man as a member of civil society—that is, an individual withdrawn into himself, into the confines of his private interests and private caprice, and separated from the community.[32]

Ronald Dworkin's account of 'rights as trumps' proceeds from a similar commitment to liberal philosophy but takes a rather different form.[33] Dworkin's theory also requires that government not interfere with individual choices and be neutral as to what constitutes the good life, in order to protect the equal concern and respect for every individual which he believes to be at the foundation of liberalism. However, his reasoning has taken a particular form in order to avoid what he identifies as an especial

---

[29] This he holds in common with Jürgen Habermas, who sees modernity as an 'unfinished project'. See, eg, J Habermas, 'Modernity: An Unfinished Project' in M Passerin d'Entreves and S Benhabib (eds), *Habermas and the Unfinished Project of Modernity* (Cambridge, Polity Press, 1996).

[30] See, however, the work of John Tasioulas for a sympathetic critique of Griffin from a more pluralistic perspective, eg, J Tasioulas, 'Human Rights, Universality and the Values of Personhood: Retracing Griffin's Steps' (2002) 10 *European Journal of Philosophy* 79–100.

[31] See, eg, CB Macpherson, *The Political Theory of Possessive Individualism: Hobbes to Locke* (Oxford, Clarendon Press, 1962).

[32] Marx (above n 10).

[33] R Dworkin, 'Rights as Trumps' in J Waldron (ed), *Theories of Rights* (Oxford, Oxford University Press, 1984) 153–67.

pitfall of utilitarian reasoning—namely, a flaw of representative democracy that, in the calculation of the aggregated general welfare, what Dworkin terms 'external' preferences will be allowed into the calculus. These are preferences that relate not to my own particular interest but those that concern my preferences for what others are able to do, which, according to Dworkin, involve a 'double counting' that destroys the very basis of utilitarianism, namely that everyone is to count for one, and no one is to count for more than one.[34] Therefore, for Dworkin, it is necessary to have a scheme of civil rights to protect against this double counting and to ensure that, in the general distribution of goods and opportunities, no one suffer a disadvantage because of what others think of them. To do this it is necessary to give protection to those areas of conflict most at threat from external preferences, and this protection will take the form of rights that function as trump cards. This will be a variable list of rights, as the external preferences of the majority will vary over time. However, it is to be noted that these rights as trumps will function as paramount against the general good, and government will be unable to deny them, even if it would be in the collective good to do so. In those cases, the balancing exercises and weighing of interests that have become familiar features of rights litigation will not be applicable, and the now ubiquitous proportionality doctrine will not be available for use.

This approach might seem salutary in an environment where the state has too often attempted to dilute rights in the name of a claimed public good of security, justifying indefinite detention or a reinterpretation of torture on this basis. A right not to be tortured seems to be an obvious candidate for rights as trumps if ever there were one. However, external preferences, if they function at all,[35] are just as likely to be exercised against instances of pornography that portray women in humiliating and subversive roles, or against hate speech, which advocates the rights of neo-Nazis to march with swastikas. If rights as trumps are to function to outlaw communal attempts to prohibit such behaviour, they result in a very strong protection of free speech such as that found under the US First Amendment.[36] Indeed, Dworkin's theory will produce a limited, but to many disagreeable, list of rights recognising the interests of those who wish to be free to pursue their own conception of the good, however flawed that might appear to others, on the strength of protecting autonomous choices from the tyranny

---

[34] See R Dworkin, 'Do We Have a Right to Pornography?' (1981) *Oxford Journal of Legal Studies* 177–212.

[35] Some would doubt this basis of Dworkin's argument, eg, HLA Hart, 'Between Utility and Rights' (1980) 79(5) *Columbia Law Review*.

[36] Eg, *Collin v Smith*, 578 F.2d 1197 (1978). See also C Mackinnon, *Only Words* (Cambridge, MA, Harvard University Press, 1993) for a critique to this approach to freedom of speech.

of majority preferences. A good example of this is provided by *Snyder v Phelps*,[37] a case in which the US Supreme Court held that a military funeral protest by Fred Phelps' Westboro Baptist Church was protected by the First Amendment and did not give rise to civil liability under the state law torts of intentional infliction of emotional distress or invasion of privacy. The facts of the case were particularly arresting: the self-styled religious group from the Westboro Baptist Church in Kansas had chosen to picket US military funerals, claiming that the deaths of US soldiers in Iraq and Afghanistan were God's punishment for America's acceptance of homosexuality. They carried banners reading, for example, 'Thank God for dead soldiers'.

Rights as trumps will also rule out protection of any competing interests of those injured by that exercise of autonomy—namely those who are insulted, diminished or silenced by exercises of, eg, hate speech or pornography. In this instance, the right is justified as existing precisely because it is the right to act in what others perceive as a disagreeable way, indeed a right to do wrong.[38] Slavoj Žižek has conveyed this critique of Dworkin's rights thesis in his condemnation of rights as rights to break the Ten Commandments: 'What is the right to privacy but the right to commit adultery? The right to religion but the right to worship false Gods?'[39]

Not every liberal theorist attempts a justification and articulation which leads to the necessity of overriding the common good in such a categorical way as Dworkin, but accounts such of those of Griffin and Dworkin, with their focus on agency and autonomous choice, may lead to a culture in which 'self-respect and dignity depend on being in a position to make strident querulous, adversarial claims'—what Waldron has termed the 'muscular and self-asserted individualism of rights'.[40]

Indeed, it is undeniable that a result of a wider, cultural stress on autonomy has been that courts have on occasion treated the choice of the parties as beyond challenge, regardless of the fairness of exchange or the existence of hard and unconscionable bargains. Courts became unwilling to question, for example, the adequacy of consideration in contract law. Extreme examples of the fulfilment of the parties' will can be seen in the widely cited American employment contract cases *Lochner v New York* and *Coppage v Kansas*, decided by the US Supreme Court in the early

---

[37] *Snyder v Phelps*, 562 US, 131 S Ct 1207 (2011). Contrast *CPS v Mohammad Razaul Haque and Emdadur Choudhury* (2011), in which the defendants were found guilty of public order offences for burning poppies and chanting 'British soldiers burn in hell' on Remembrance Day.

[38] As in Dworkin's theory of rights. See also J Waldron, 'A Right to Do Wrong' (1981) 92 *Ethics* 21; and J Raz, 'The Nature of Rights' (1984) 93 *Mind* 194–214.

[39] S Žižek, 'Against Human Rights' (2005) *New Left Review*.

[40] J Waldron, 'Nonsense upon Stilts? A Reply' in Waldron (ed), *Nonsense upon Stilts* (above n 10) 196 (emphasis in original).

part of the twentieth century.[41] In *Lochner*, the Supreme Court found unconstitutional a state law designed to protect employees of a bakery from excessively long working hours, and in *Coppage* it found a state law that outlawed 'yellow dog' contracts (ie, those banning workers from joining trade unions) to be invalid. In both cases, the basis of the Court's reasoning was that such state legislation invaded the private contractual right which was to be found 'included in the right of personal liberty and the right of private property and partaking of the nature of each'. The fact that labourers might not be in a sufficiently autonomous bargaining position to be able freely to bargain themselves into an excessively long working day was not considered by the Supreme Court.

The European Court of Justice (ECJ) has been also criticised for developing a rights jurisprudence that overly focuses on bourgeois market rights.[42] A formative influence on the EU Single Market was an ordo-liberal economic theory of the market in which market freedoms are seen as intrinsic to the notion of human dignity, as well as upholding a theory of contract and private property rights. Thus, rather than uplifting economic rights to the same status as a right to human dignity, it might be said that under this vision, human dignity is achieved by the functioning of a free and equal market society. This brings a danger of what Terry Eagleton has termed 'commercial humanism', by which the citizen is defined not by political virtue but by rights to and in things.[43] This in turn raises the prospect of a commodification of rights whereby rights become tools for corporations to further profit and prosperity, legitimising accumulation of wealth through the veneer of human rights. Competition becomes a virtue rather than merely a business practice.[44]

But to leave the matter here is to oversimplify. Human rights—even those rights that appear very closely linked to autonomy and individualism, such as the right to privacy—and their justifications are too complex and prone to differing interpretations for overly general conclusions. Privacy provides an illustrative example. *Legally*, it is a modern concept and is still not expressly recognised in US constitutional law—although it has been upheld in some famous case law.[45] Nonetheless, it is, perhaps perversely, in the US constitutional context that privacy, in its immanent yet non-explicit form, has been subject to most criticism.

---

[41] *Lochner v New York*, 198 US 45 (1905); and *Coppage v Kansas*, 236 US 1 (1915).

[42] Eg, Case C-438/05 *Viking Line* [2007] ECR I-10779; and Case C-341/05 *Laval* [2007] ECR-I 11767.

[43] T Eagleton, 'Freedom and Interpretation' in S Shute and S Hurley (eds), *Oxford Amnesty Lectures: On Human Rights* (New York, Basic Books, 1993).

[44] See, eg, N Ferguson, *Civilization: The West and the Rest* (London, Allen Lane, 2011) in which a whole chapter is devoted to free competition, claiming a crucial role for it in the West's long dominance.

[45] Eg, *Griswold v Connecticut*, 381 US 479 (1965).

Mary-Anne Glendon sees the right to privacy as at the heart of the atomistic lone rights bearer of US law, responsible for a lack of community, responsibility and fellow-feeling.[46] Because the courts have been too willing to recognise 'zones of privacy', she has argued, we have created a society in which rights are viewed as isolated monads, possessions of the individual, to be enforced as good things for ourselves, apart from society. Yet Glendon has suggested that this approach is not endemic. In Europe, she asserts, they do things differently. In particular, she cites the right to abortion, which is so often derived from a woman's right to privacy in both jurisdictions yet is usually coupled with other features in European jurisdictions, such as actions, responsibilities or even further rights, which can take us out of isolation and link us with our community—eg, funding for abortion, counselling and so on. Perhaps Glendon exaggerates the contrast. What is interesting is that the situation is not clear-cut but rather shot through with ambivalences. If privacy lies at the heart of the concept of the autonomous rights bearer, why then is it still expressly not protected under US constitutional law? This ambivalence about privacy seems to express late-modern ambiguities about the individual and about rights. Just how much of it do we want in any case? When does it become privation? When does it conflict with freedom of expression? We are simply not sure how much autonomy, privacy or individualism we have or want. And it seems that law nicely reflects these ambiguities.

A parallel can be drawn to feminist critiques of the Cartesian *cogito*,[47] which perceive it as a male, self-identical subject that excludes women as supposedly passive, non-rational beings. Yet as Renate Salecl has reminded us, these feminist challenges lose some of their force when we recall that in the seventeenth century, some women embraced the *cogito* as a liberating idea,[48] regarding it as a way to overcome patriarchal domination by confirming that 'mind has no sex'.[49]

Human Rights and Suffering

A very different approach to human rights, proceeding partly in reaction to those accounts that stress agency and autonomy, is one which concentrates on the link between human suffering and the need for human rights, and aims to take this link between human rights and suffering seriously.[50] The focus is on that part of human rights which Gearty characterises as 'all bad news'[51]—the part that seeks to protect humans from the violence

---

[46] MA Glendon, *Rights Talk* (New York, Free Press, 1991).
[47] See E Harth, *Cartesian Women* (Ithaca, Cornell University Press, 1992).
[48] R Salecl, *The Spoils of Freedom* (London, Routledge, 1994) 115.
[49] Harth (above n 47) 73.
[50] Uprenda Baxi, Andrew Williams and Klaus Günther are notable exponents of this view.
[51] Gearty, *Can Human Rights Survive?* (above n 4).

and suffering of torture, inhuman treatment, death and displacement, rather than enabling the already articulate to become more so. It sees human rights as a process by which pain and suffering are overcome.[52] It requires us to be sensitive to those who suffer pain, humiliation and fear, and enables those experiences to be articulated as injustice rather than misfortune, fate or the victim's own fault.

Different theorists express their reasoning differently, but in each case there is an initial empathy, an awareness of the existence of a suffering 'Other' and a context or history of exclusion of that Other's voice by selective discrimination or dehumanising of them. This approach acknowledges the emotion underlying human rights, rather than grounding them in reason or autonomy. It locates human rights in our 'visceral register',[53] acknowledging biological sources—compassion, sympathy and emotion. The rights bearer takes on a very different character—no longer robust and assertive

Figure 9-2: 'This is just a duplicate', Amnesty International exhibit at the Mannheim Art Gallery

Figure 9-3: Inscription on the exhibit at the Mannheim Art Gallery, depicted above in Figure 9-2

---

[52] K Günther, 'The Legacies of Injustice and Fear' in P Alston and J Weiler (eds), *The European Union and Human Rights* (Oxford, Oxford University Press, 1997) 117.
[53] Donnelly (above n 15).

but suffering and weak, an image drawn from memories of massacre and genocide, the face of an Amnesty campaign. (See Figures 9-2 and 9-3.)

These images provide a counterpoint to the smug, self-congratulatory talk that can pervade human rights organisations, where human rights appear to be in the hands of an international elite that presents them as a matter of good news. In contrast is the stark fact that over 90 per cent of applications to the European Court of Human Rights (ECtHR) are rejected as 'inadmissible' and are therefore overlooked.

In Klaus Günther's account, a human right becomes the conceptual framework for a rejection of a concrete historical experience of injustice and fear; it becomes the means of articulating suffering, a way for victims to regain voice and control.[54] In this way, human rights have a performative aspect, a capacity to transform the experience of a victim into a viable claim.[55]

Other interpretations that found human rights on suffering owe much to the philosophy of Emmanuel Levinas, for whom the attempt to articulate an obligation toward the Other provides the only possible basis for ethical action.[56] For Levinas, who turns much of Western philosophy on its head, ethics precedes both autonomy and ontology, placing hugely demanding obligations on us. In Levinas' philosophy, ethics has at its root 'face-to-face encounters', or intersubjective relations, which are asymmetrical and emphasise the Other. The most basic and crucial aspect of experience is therefore not that of individuals with natural rights but the immediacy of intersubjectivity. And rather than reason providing the foundations for ethics, it is ethics that provides the basis for reason. Human rights then take on a very different form and, rather than being manifestations of individual entitlements, become an acknowledgement of an absolute and inexhaustible obligation to each and every other human being—grounded in sensibility rather than in reason.

Levinas has emphasised that human rights are, originally and absolutely, 'the rights of the other',[57] which always have priority over my own needs and interests, and that they are not grounded in goodwill, mutuality or reciprocity on my part, but rather in 'Justice as the Other's due, as an absolute and inescapable command'.[58] The suffering of the Other is translated not as misfortune but as *injustice*. So this is an ethical call of complete altruism, requiring an ethical life of 'asymmetry', in which 'the ego is the only

---

[54] Günther (above n 52).

[55] For a philosophical view of relevance, see M Fricker, *Epistemic Injustice: Power and the Ethics of Knowing* (Oxford, Oxford University Press, 2007).

[56] See, eg, E Levinas, *Alterity and Transcendence* (New York, Columbia University Press, 1999).

[57] Ibid, 129.

[58] E Levinas, *Entre Nous: On Thinking-of-the-Other* (New York, Columbia University Press, 1998) 103.

one who has no rights'.[59] Levinas has suggested that this constitutes an 'original' right that is prior to law and politics; and all human rights flow from here.[60]

Theories such as those of Levinas seem to place impossible, 'infinitely demanding'[61] obligations on us, stretching beyond the state and its emotional and affective ties, almost unintelligible outside of a comprehensive religious framework. Why would we accept the demand of the Other, outside of a faith that transcends our everyday lives? Surely, outside of religion, such a faith is impossible to manufacture and certainly not derivable from reason. But perhaps that is the point.

Discourse Theories

Intersubjectivity is not the focus of only Levinasian ethics. Many contemporary theories of ethics also look to process or to 'discourse' as a basis for ethical concepts, including human rights. Rather than perceiving human rights as inherent in human nature or emanating from some prior moral theory, this approach sees human rights as both the framework for and the product of informed, open, public discussion, which is able to produce a consensus. Such an approach seems preferable in an environment where there is far less confidence in the notion of 'universal' or self-evident rights than in the eighteenth century. Instead, rights can be seen as results of public deliberation, exchange and argument, through which meanings and outcomes are negotiated and argued for. Or they can be seen as the product of what Rawls termed an 'overlapping consensus'[62]—achieved by deliberation of those with different world views and no shared comprehensive overview. This approach enables us to acknowledge human rights as enmeshed in a political process. It acknowledges the important place that talk about rights occupies in our world, that it is a language universally recognised and used, even if it is used in different ways for different purposes.

In some cases, discourse theories come close to embracing rights only as a political strategy, or rights as rhetorical tools and effective ways to mobilise argument—an approach that comes close to a Rortyan scepticism

---

[59] 'To approach the Other is to put into question my freedom, my spontaneity as a living being, my control over things, this freedom of a "moving force," this impetuosity of the current to which everything is permitted, even murder.' E Levinas, *Totality and Infinity* (Pittsburgh, Duquesne University Press, 1969) 303.

[60] See Levinas' brief essay 'On the Rights of Man and the Rights of Others' in E Levinas, *Outside the Subject*, MB Smith (trans) (Stanford, Stanford University Press, 1994).

[61] S Critchley, *Infinitely Demanding* (New York, Verso, 2007).

[62] J Rawls, 'The Idea of an Overlapping Consensus' (1987) 7 *Oxford Journal of Legal Studies* 1–25.

or irony,[63] which sees the value of rights only in their ability to move and mobilise support, to tell sentimental and moving stories. Viewed this way, however engaged they may be in a struggle to secure progressive aims or to mitigate suffering, human rights are conceived in nominalist terms only, a product solely of (perceived) contingent discussion and debate. Other discourse approaches seek a more grounded basis—one that aims to provide a more satisfactory justification for human rights and to avoid the pitfalls of relativism, without being implicated in a dubious moral realism of natural rights or overblown claims of universality.

The work of Jürgen Habermas is a notable example of this latter approach. He has presented an idealised, or counterfactual, conception of practical discourse in the 'discourse principle', reliant on an ideal speech situation, which provides, 'Just those actions and norms are valid to which all possibly affected persons could agree as participants in rational discourses.'[64] It will be noted that Habermas' discourse ethics relies on some very strong assumptions about the capacity of persons for moral dialogue. It rests on idealisations, impossible in the existing world—for the ideal speech situation is to be a dialogue that is completely free and un-coerced, in which no force prevails but that of the better argument. Indeed, it might even be said to function as a hypothetical thought experiment, analogous to Rawls' 'Original Position'.

Habermas has incorporated and institutionalised in his discourse ethics both democratic theory and a system of rights and law-making. He argues that we should understand human rights as 'the rights citizens must accord one another if they want to legitimately regulate their living together by means of positive law'.[65] According to Habermas, rights are neither pre-existing entitlements that individuals possess prior to any political discourse or engagement, nor created by or dependent on the results of such discourse. Rather, rights are what enable public deliberation within democratic fora, in which all persons can regard themselves as both authors and subjects of the law. In Habermas' terms, human rights and popular sovereignty—or alternately put, private autonomy and public autonomy— are 'co-original' and mutually support each other.[66] In this way, Habermas avoids the critique of a liberal conception of rights, which, in basing rights on rational autonomy, is derided as conceptualising rights as pre-political and conceived not only without regard to public good but in opposition to society, as rights against the state, debilitating the public realm.

---

[63] Eg, R Rorty, *Contingency, Irony, Solidarity* (Cambridge, Cambridge University Press, 1989).
[64] J Habermas, *Between Facts and Norms* (Cambridge, MA, Massachusetts Institute of Technology Press, 1998) 107.
[65] Ibid, 82.
[66] Ibid.

Habermas has also argued that human rights have a dual nature. They are not merely moral rights but are 'Janus-faced'—on the one hand relating to law and on the other to morality. He has written that the concept of human rights 'does not have its origins in morality, but rather bears the imprint of the modern concept of individual liberties, hence of a specifically juridical concept'.[67] However, for Habermas, human rights are not merely positively enacted legal rights, for, like moral norms, they claim universal validity, and their justification can be exclusively moral.

This is unsatisfactory. While attractive in its optimism (and in its motivation to avoid deriving rights from some metaphysical concept of private autonomy), there is a certain emptiness at the core of such an approach. What is the content of these rights? Unlike substantive liberal theorists such as Griffin, Habermas does not give us a means of identifying which rights are human rights, leaving so much up to the end-product of discussion. Habermas has acknowledged that 'this paradigm of law, unlike the liberal and social welfare models, no longer favours a particular ideal of society, a particular vision of the good life, or even a particular political option'.[68] This offers no real motivation for political engagement. As Habermas himself has acknowledged, in contemporary Western democracies, the conditions of this ideal speech situation, of unconstrained communication, are rarely satisfied, and it is more likely that bargaining 'may rely on power and mutual threats'; and 'social power relations cannot be neutralised in the way rational discourse supposes.'[69] How may the overwhelming power of the market and the media, as well as of political propaganda and advertising, be countered to provide the conditions for undistorted communication? The absence of almost any regulation of political campaign financing and advertising in the United States[70] provides a glaring example of just how distorted communication that is supposedly democratic can be, and it renders Habermas' theory naively idealistic. Indeed, it has been dismissed by one writer as 'a neo-Kantian transcendental deduction of conditions of necessity of the contemporary German constitutional state.'[71]

Seyla Benhabib's discursive approach is somewhat different from that of Habermas. Benhabib shares with Habermas the conviction that universal human rights and popular sovereignty, or the norms of private and public autonomy, constitute two necessary foundations for democratic states. However, while her account of human rights is grounded in discourse, she provides a particular elaboration of the products of this discourse, which

---

[67] Ibid.
[68] Ibid, 445.
[69] Ibid, 186.
[70] Following the US Supreme Court decision in *Buckley v Valeo*, 424 US 1 (1976).
[71] B Bowring, *The Degradation of the International Legal Order* (Oxford, Routledge Cavendish, 2008) 105.

she terms 'democratic iterations'.[72] The concept of 'iterations' is borrowed from Jacques Derrida[73] and involves a process of 'linguistic, legal, cultural and political "repetitions-in-transformation" which not only change established understandings but also transform what passes as the valid'.[74] In this way, citizens are not passively co-opted into uncritical adoptions of the law. Instead, Benhabib has argued that it is possible to understand the people as author and interpreter of their laws, even if, in circumstances of globalisation and post-national law-making, the laws stem from distant international agreements negotiated by treaties. It is still possible, she asserts, for progressive normative and legal change to take place—through the repeated engagement with and redefining of certain norms, new morals, customs and social practices are created. Benhabib has characterised this as a 'jurisgenerative' politics, namely one which 'includes the augmentation of the meaning of rights claims and the growth of the political authorship by ordinary individuals'.[75] She believes that this ultimately leads to a more inclusionary politics. The process requires both 'outsiders' and 'insiders' to engage with and dispute rights and their meanings; it requires constant negotiation and redefinition in order to achieve new laws that assure a more inclusionary political milieu.

As an illustration of this process, Benhabib has cited *L' Affaire du Foulard* in France, which commenced in 1989 when three girls were suspended from a state school for wearing the Moslem headscarf, an affair that has become even more controversial since the legislation banning the burka in all public places came into force in France in 2011. This situation presents a clash between (modern) French traditions of secularity and the right of freedom of religion and the adoption of a particular cultural norm. Such clashes of rights and values present one of the main contemporary challenges to rights theory. Benhabib has characterised the girls' actions in contesting the French ban as 'no less than a process of democratic iteration and cultural resignification',[76] transforming them into agents in their own right. She has asserted that democratic iteration establishes a dialectic between rights and identities in democracies in which differences can be negotiated and contradictions between universal rights mediated. In this way, different national conceptions of justice, or different interpretations of rights, are not made impossible or disallowed. Therefore, for Benhabib, resistance, agency and dialogue drive the process of negotiating between democratic rights and national identities.

---

[72] See S Benhabib, *Another Cosmopolitanism: Hospitality, Sovereignty and Democratic Iterations* (Oxford, Oxford University Press, 2006).
[73] See J Derrida, *Of Hospitality* (Stanford, Stanford University Press, 2000).
[74] Benhabib (above n 72) 48.
[75] Ibid, 49.
[76] Ibid, 63.

Discourse theories take account of some important features of human rights—the fact that there is little agreement as to the foundations of rights, that different people seem to have different understandings of what rights are and also that discussion, negotiation and redefinition appear to be part of their very being. It also conveys the ways in which the broad, vague abstract propositions of charters are converted into specific contexts, thus enabling a reconciliation of the universal and the particular, an acknowledgement that rights are an on-going conversation. Discourse theories also represent a step away from a search for secure ontological foundation for rights towards a recognition of the role that language and discourse play in constructing our identities—a role emphasised by postmodern and post-structural writers such as Michel Foucault and Jacques Derrida. Yet there are, of course, disadvantages to conceiving rights in this way. Discourse theories are liable to render human rights only as valuable as a particular discourse allows them to be, and discourse can operate for the harmful as well as for the good; it is capable of being hijacked by the powerful in society, creating an environment far removed from any ideal speech situation of un-coerced consensus. It also seems to omit the categorical force that seems so important for rights: if rights are liable to constant renegotiation, is there anything that may not be bargained for and bargained away? The recent highly publicised attempted redefinitions of torture provide just one example.[77] Benhabib's *Affaire du Foulard*, which is on-going in several European countries, is far from taking the shape of an obviously empowering democratic iteration, as successive legal challenges have highlighted an indeterminacy and lack of articulation of rights in this context.[78]

Scepticism

I would categorise rights scepticism as just as much a part of human rights discussion and theorising, rather than cast it in opposition to it. Scepticism toward human rights has been in existence for as long as human rights have been considered important—as soon as the eighteenth-century declarations of rights came into being, critics such as Bentham and Burke were voicing their opposition to them. Latter-day critiques of rights such as critical legal studies (CLS) and postmodern approaches merely continue the debate in our times. Scepticism and critique is a conversation that human rights has with itself, constantly interrogating its own suppositions and scope. Apart from those rare beings whose belief in human rights takes the

---

[77] See, eg, B Schlink, 'The Problem with Torture Lite' (2007) 29 *Cardozo Law Review* 86.
[78] See *R (Begum) v Governors of Denbigh High School* [2006] UKHL 15, the culmination of one particular lawsuit in the UK.

form of a certain moral realism, all other accounts work within some sort of sceptical framework. For example, those who believe human rights to be a product of socially and politically constructed discourse are sceptical of alleged pre-political foundations; those who relate human rights directly to human suffering refuse to countenance an account of human rights that appears to enhance the abilities of already enabled autonomous beings. Sceptical accounts of human rights are both valuable and destructive—Bentham's critique of nonsense on stilts highlights the wobbly conceptual foundations of rights, still shaky 200 years later;[79] Marx's critique points out the way in which rights are misused, appropriated and tools of ideology, a possession of the dominant class, of the capitalist bourgeoisie of his day—and of today.[80]

It is almost impossible to abjure any touch of scepticism. Marie Benedicte Dembour captures this issue nicely with the very title of her book *Who Believes in Human Rights?*[81] She has acknowledged that the book grew out of both an attraction to and a discomfort with human rights, and she has admitted an uncertainty as to which should take precedence. Her book is a carefully considered attempt to work out this ambivalence.

There is indeed a dilemma. Human rights bring with them so much promise and ambition—of a self-evidence, universality, inalienability, not to mention their very existence. They are presented as 'values for a godless age',[82] and as such, who would not to embrace them? Even if on closer inspection, these promises seem incapable of being fulfilled—no adequate foundation can be found for them, and they are just as often used cynically as earnestly—they are still available as a rhetorical resource, more powerful perhaps than any other moral resource for law today. Even those most sceptical of what law has become see human rights as a means of returning ethics to law, acknowledging their utopian, emancipatory possibilities.[83]

Yet the ambivalence will not go away. Each of the three accounts of human rights examined earlier is unsatisfactory. Insofar as they resolve one issue (eg, the need for a secure foundation), they result in another problem (namely, the undesirable or unsatisfactory nature of that foundation). One can understand and sympathise with many of the arguments marshalled by each of these accounts, such that elements of each appear persuasive. We can acknowledge that rights are not part of the moral fabric of the universe, but we still see it as desirable that we can point to some sort of durable foundation that would explain the categorical force we wish them

---

[79] J Bentham, 'Nonsense on Stilts' in J Waldron (ed), *Nonsense upon Stilts* (above n 10).
[80] Marx (above n 10).
[81] Dembour (above n 5).
[82] F Klug, *Values for a Godless Age: The Story of the United Kingdom's New Bill of Rights* (Harmondsworth, Penguin, 2000).
[83] Eg, Douzinas (above n 16).

to possess. We recognise the part they play in expressing and acting on our feelings of empathy and compassion for others, a drive that may be hardwired into our biology[84] but also seems to have been foregrounded over the last 200 years, located in a particular historical and cultural context. We recognise the way in which human rights are created and fought for by discussion, and yet we still see them as something more—possessing that little element of magic that moves them beyond mere social construct. It seems that all of this is going on at once. Endless debates and dialogues take place over the nature, content and manipulation of human rights, rather in the way that, for example, arcane Christian religious doctrine was debated in the past—Reformation/counter-Reformation, orthodoxy/heterodoxy, Rome/Byzantium, often conflicting and contradictory, and yet people continued to believe in a Christian God. And crucially perhaps, while all of this is going on, we neglect to look at outcomes. To what extent do human rights actually improve people' lives? To what extent do they lend an ethical dimension to law? In the midst of all this discussion, these questions are too often forgotten.

Having expressed these ambivalent and ambiguous thoughts of my own, I will conclude this section with two observations, which I believe shed light on the conflicting nature of human rights today. First, why did human rights come to prominence at the time they did? Those who deny a universal status to human rights are quick to point out that it is hard to claim universality and self-evidence for them when they were only recognised as such from the eighteenth century on. This is an important insight, because the foregrounding, or perhaps invention of, human rights in the eighteenth century has shaped their very being, leaving us with a very strong, particular notion of them. And second, why then are we still so preoccupied with human rights 250 years on?

Why *Then*: An Historical Investigation

How can human rights be recognised as universal in nature if they did not exist as a recognisable concept before the eighteenth century? Although Roman law contained the concept of *ius*, and the doctrine of 'natural' rights can be traced to the medieval period and beyond, there is no direct line or relationship between these concepts and the modern concept of

---

[84] On the connections between Darwinian theory and human rights, see C Gearty, 'The Holism of Human Rights: Linking Religion, Ethics and Public Life' (2004) 6 *European Human Rights Law Review* 605–9, 608. See also D Krebs, 'The Evolution of a Sense of Justice' in J Duntley and T Shackleford (eds), *Evolutionary Forensic Psychology: Darwinian Foundations of Crime and Law* (Oxford, Oxford University Press, 2008) 230–46; and S Baron-Cohen, *The Science of Evil: On Empathy and the Origins of Human Cruelty* (New York, Basic Books, 2011).

human rights, or even to the modern concept of natural rights. The English Bill of Rights (1689) refers to 'ancient rights and liberties' established by English law and history, not to self-evident and universal rights; and until well into the first half of the eighteenth century, most English writing continued to look to the historically based rights of the freeborn Englishman and not the universal rights of man. Yet as Lynne Hunt has pointed out, somewhere between 1689 and 1776 (the date of the American Declaration of Independence and of George Mason's Virginia Bill of Rights) a shift took place, and rights that had previously been viewed as pertaining only to particular persons, under particular traditions, became transformed into human rights, which all could lay claim to.[85] Why did this happen?

Hunt locates the origins of the term 'rights of man' in the 1760s, in Rousseau's *Social Contract*, although Rousseau himself gave no definition of the term there.[86] But shortly thereafter, definitions were given: Condorcet defined the rights of man to include security of the person and of property, impartial and fair justice, and the right to contribute to the formulation of the laws.[87] Blackstone defined them in his commentaries as 'the natural liberty of mankind ... the absolute rights of man, considered as a free agent'.[88]

Hunt's explanation for the appearance of and focus on human rights in the late eighteenth century is based on a changing notion of the self in that period. Liberal theories tend to identify human rights with autonomy, as already mentioned. Rights are linked to a recognition of persons as separate individuals who are capable of moral judgement. This emphasis was partly a product of seventeenth-century revolutions of political thought, ranging across the Levellers, Lockean philosophy and Grotius' juristic work. However, Hunt has highlighted this definition of self in terms of not only autonomy but also a growing empathy—suggesting that it became possible to think in terms of rights when there was a strengthened awareness that others were like oneself. So the birth of human rights was rooted as much in emotion as on reason.

Human rights are most clearly at issue when we are conscious of their violation. They emerge from sentiment and what Diderot termed an 'interior feeling'.[89] Equal possession of universal rights would be meaningless and empty if equality were not internalised by means of a sympathetic reaching out to others and awareness of their likeness to ourselves. So for Hunt,

---

[85] L Hunt, *Inventing Human Rights* (New York, Norton, 2007).

[86] J-J Rousseau, *The Social Contract and Other Later Political Writings*, V Gourevitch (ed) (Cambridge, Cambridge University Press, 1997).

[87] N de Condorcet, 'On the Influence of the American Revolution in Europe' in *Condorcet: Selected Writings*, KM Baker (trans and ed) (Indianapolis, Bobbs-Merrill Company, 1976).

[88] Sir William Blackstone, *Commentaries on the Laws of England*, vol 1 (Oxford, Clarendon, 1765) 121.

[89] D Diderot and J le Rond d'Alembert, *Encyclopedie*, vol 5 (1755) 115–16.

autonomy and empathy were the co-original roots at the origins of human rights. Their evolution can be traced over a period of time in which individuals became viewed as increasingly independent, and this, asserts Hunt, was quite literally embodied in physical processes, as well as a mental awareness—in an increasing sense of the need for privacy, as well as a growing sense of the need for separation, and a shame of bodily functions.

It is often stated that privacy is a creature of the modern age—that the rise of industrial society, ubiquitous technology and modern overcrowded society have created a desire for escape, for a space, a 'zone of privacy', whether from a too-powerful government or just one's neighbours. This view is perhaps somewhat tendentious. After all, like individualism, privacy has a number of senses, many of which would have been familiar to classical and medieval society. In pre-modern times, there was a sense in which privacy connoted 'privation' or deprivation,[90] an absence of something valuable (ie, society?). But there was also a value in solitude, in self-examination, as exemplified by the Christian mystics, such as St Augustine. Yet Hunt is right to highlight the evidence and import of greater respect for bodily integrity and clearer lines of demarcation between individual bodies produced by an increase of shame as to bodily functions and an emphasis on bodily decorum—an evolution of notions of interiority and depth of psyche. It might seem unrealistic to trace a growing empathy in a century when penal practices such as the Bloody Code in England flourished, when capital punishment could be imposed for the most minor of offences and torture could still be carried out. Yet torture had already become a focus of criticism with Montesquieu's *The Spirit of the Laws* in 1748, which was followed by Beccaria's rejection of the death penalty in his 1764 Treatise.[91] There had grown a new awareness that torture could brutalise both its victim and its spectators. Hunt has linked the growth of sympathy for others to a culture of reading epistolary novels in the eighteenth century, such as Samuel Richardson's *Pamela* and Rousseau's *Julie*. These enabled readers to identify and empathise with other, ordinary characters, enabling a realisation that others could think, feel and experience things like oneself.

To be sure, empathy did not spring out of nowhere in the eighteenth century: it is a capacity of biological origin, rooted in our brains. Altruism and empathy are as much dispositions and part of the human condition as egoism and venality.[92] The importance of emotions in the formation of our

---

[90] See, eg, H Arendt, *The Human Condition*, 2nd edn (Chicago, University of Chicago Press, 1998) Part II.

[91] C Beccaria, *On Crimes and Punishments, and Other Writings (1764)*, R Bellamy, R Davies and V Cox (eds) (Cambridge, Cambridge University Press, 1995).

[92] Gearty, *Can Human Rights Survive?* (above n 4); and J Decety and PL Jackson, 'The Functional Architecture of Human Empathy' (2004) *Behavioral and Cognitive Neuroscience Review* 71.

sense of justice has already been emphasised in chapter six, and works such as those of David Hume and Adam Smith, who built their philosophical theories from an awareness of human nature and the emotions, are highly relevant. Notably, Smith, best known for *The Wealth of Nations*, was also the author of the earlier *Theory of Moral Sentiments*, a work of a quite different nature. In this work he explained, by use of the example of torture, how we identify and sympathise with another even if others are strangers to us: 'We enter as it were into his body and becoming some measure him.'[93] 'Sympathy' is just that fellow-feeling induced by trying to put oneself in another's place and imagining how you would feel. Smith located conscience in the sympathetic feelings of spectators. As spectators of the actions of others, we imagine how we would feel in their situation. If we might share their motives, we approve of their action. If not, we disapprove. That knowledge forms conscience, an imagined 'impartial spectator' who informs us whether an action is right or wrong.

This openness to sympathy and the ability to imagine oneself in another's place in turn opens the door to the possibility of a wider ranging corpus of rights, extending beyond one's own countrymen and class, and even if neither the American nor the French eighteenth-century declarations went so far as to open up rights to women or, in the case of the United States, slaves, many groups who had previously been denied rights (eg, Jews and Protestants in France) began to be conceived as rights holders.

Hunt's historical investigation into the origins of human rights in the eighteenth century seems to me persuasive. Although it is impossible to do justice to the depth and richness of her analysis in this short discussion here, there is much to be said for an account that looks to changing meanings of the self over time and the importance of the way in which individual minds understand social and cultural contexts, as well as the salient features of those cultures themselves. The eighteenth-century mind-set is an important backdrop to the growth and dissemination of human rights and underlines their singular historical and Western origins. Feelings of empathy of course are possible in any time and culture, and neuroscience[94] tells us that they may be part of our biology, but their particular alliance with a certain bourgeois liberal philosophy explains how these features of selfhood morphed into human rights in the eighteenth century. It highlights an important dimension of human rights—they concern our subjectivity, not only our social context. They, of necessity, concern how we think, act and believe, and put into focus our actions and beliefs as ethical subjects, and also subjects as of the law. However much a postmodern philosophy

---

[93] A Smith, *The Theory of Moral Sentiments* (London, A Millar in the Strand, 1759).
[94] See references above, especially Baron-Cohen (above n 84).

may feel it necessary to efface the subject,[95] human rights bring back this focus on our personhood—on our existence as ethical beings, not as the social constructs of language.

Why Are We Still so Preoccupied with Human Rights?

We are of course no longer living in the eighteenth century. Whatever changes and events may help and explain the origins of human rights, we are a long way from an empathy provoked by reading the novels of Richardson, and too many of us no longer believe in Kantian autonomy or the categorical imperative. Subsequent developments and a growth of nationalism in the nineteenth century, with a focus on ethnic ties rather than a universally shared humanity, explain why human rights as a doctrine was somewhat eclipsed in the nineteenth century. Although the horrors of twentieth-century totalitarianism and genocide may explain the impetus to draft universal charters and declarations of rights in the post-war period, such horrors might just as easily have convinced us that 'inalienable' and 'universal' rights are incapable of mitigating human cruelty and serve no purpose. Why then does our preoccupation with rights continue? Why do they continue to bewitch us?

If a combination of rational philosophy and a turn to empathy helps explain the (rather particular, historical) origins of human rights, then I believe a very different philosophical and factual turn helps to explain our continued obsession with them. That framework is one of nihilism and disappointment. In this context—namely, one in which social and religious motivations are absent for many people—human rights are the closest we have to moral motivation, exerting a powerful symbolic supplement relating to endless proliferating desires which will never leave us, a hoped-for substitute for our feelings of meaninglessness and lack. Because they relate to and respond to these primeval desires and urges, human rights are almost impossible to fulfil, so will always leave us unsatisfied, seeking more, pushing new claims.

Simon Critchley has suggested that modern philosophy arises not out of wonder but out of disappointment and lack of fulfilment, a fear of our limitations, despite the many Promethean myths of overcoming the

---

[95] In his earlier work, for example, Michel Foucault wrote of man being effaced like writing in the sand: 'As the archaeology of our thought easily shows, man is an invention of recent date. And one perhaps nearing its end. If those arrangements were to disappear as they appeared ... then one can certainly wager that Man would be erased like a face drawn in sand at the edge of the sea.' These are the closing lines of M Foucault, *The Order of Things: An Archaeology of the Human Sciences* (London, Routledge, 2002).

human condition.[96] We sense these limits but have great difficulty in accepting them and living with them. This disappointment, if we locate it philosophically, starts with Friedrich Nietzsche,[97] or perhaps even earlier. Nietzsche denied not only an ordering of the world by moral principles but teleology as well: there is no external cause, no final principles. We sense a breakdown of order, an absence of transcendence or any other basis for objective value. All seems meaningless. Religion has, for many, become something known only by its absence in secular society, even if much of the world is in fact moving either into a 'post-secular age'[98] or into fundamentalism of an almost biblical nature, often in reaction to the apparent absence of value in Western life. There is something lacking, and it is a lack we are uncomfortable with, as many have found little to replace it with.

Likewise, there exists a deficit in the political realm. We inhabit a violently unjust world in which there is a corrosion of political structures, as well as a public apathy in exercising once hard fought for rights to vote. Secular liberal democracy exerts no real motivating force. In a culture in which governance is experienced as 'banal' positivism,[99] devoid of any ethically compelling nature, law is too often felt only as externally binding by coercion and not internally binding or compelling. In Hartian terms, few citizens experience an 'internal point of view'.[100] In these circumstances, governments seize the chance to exert some sort of control by exercising a politics of fear and security, promoted by announcements of states of emergency and declarations of war on terror.

In the face of these two crises of religion and politics, Critchley has noted that one response is nihilism, which takes a variety of forms. One can conclude that everything is meaningless in a world devoid of value and so seek to destroy this world. The perception that active destruction is necessary to transform a will to nothingness into some sort of affirmation usually means an embrace of militant means, whether through Maoism or Al Qaeda. Passive nihilists, on the other hand, also take the view that the world is meaningless, find liberal humanism pointless, and any suggestion of progress illusionary; but they retreat into themselves and their own projects—what Nietzsche described as 'European

---

[96] Critchley (above n 61).

[97] See, eg, F Nietzsche, *On the Genealogy of Morals*, D Smith (trans) (Oxford, Oxford World's Classics, 1996).

[98] See, eg, J Habermas, 'Religion in the Public Sphere' (2006) 14 *European Journal of Philosophy* 1–25.

[99] For an exploration of the concept of 'banal' positivism, see above ch 2.

[100] For further on the 'internal point of view', see HLA Hart, *The Concept of Law* (Oxford, Clarendon Press, 1961); and the discussion above ch 2.

Buddhism' or a 'dampening of the feeling of life, mechanical activity, modest pleasures'.[101]

I would add to the religious and political crises discussed by Critchley another crucial element, closely related to nihilism. This is a crisis of the self. For many recent philosophers and social theorists, such as Foucault, our belief in our individuality or our autonomy is a myth, born from our having been 'normalised' by modern life—we are not individuals but 'subjects'. Likewise, Louis Althusser and other late Marxists have suggested that we have only an 'imaginary' centre of our lived life, which provokes us into experiencing ourselves as autonomous individuals.[102] Hidden to us are the structures and conditions that produced us. One such structure is the law, which concretises and constructs a figure of a free and responsible agent as a measure against which the state can be judged. However, according to this account, the sovereign will of the individual is not prior to the law but instead generated by the law's functioning. These theories suggest that nobody is free of this misconception—even modern legal scholars may have been acculturated to believe that they are relatively autonomous selves, but they are trapped like mice in a maze.[103] This is a depressing picture, making us wonder just where we could turn for change. How can we free ourselves if we have been so thoroughly taken over by the normalising activities and discourses of modern life? They seem to leave absolutely no room for selfhood. In this way, even aspects of the law that we might think of as liberating turn out to be no such thing, as they simply reinforce a dominant ideology—although we are too stamped and marked by this ideology to be aware of our incarceration.

A dystopian impression of selfhood is also produced by writers who rely on psychoanalytic tools to argue that the self is not a unity at all but rather a fragmented being, lacking any harmony in itself. Instead of the autonomous self, Sigmund Freud presented us with the repressed self, caught up in its submerged desires and impulses, divided or fragmented into the rational and the irrational subconscious. Our identity, our sense of self, is nothing but a contingent formation that depends on the crucial, idiosyncratic contingencies of our past. There is no autonomy, no Kantian free will. I cannot be in control of myself, because my actions can be caused by desires over which I am not necessarily in control, by the *id*, the subconscious. This makes a nonsense of the picture of individuality presented earlier, of autonomous rights bearers, of free will, and also of disciplines such as law and economics—for how can we be rational self-maximisers

---

[101] Nietzsche (above n 97) 114.

[102] L Althusser, *Lenin and Philosophy and Other Essays* (London, Monthly Review Press, 1971).

[103] P Gabel and D Kennedy, *Roll over Beethoven* (1984) 36 *Stanford Law Review* 1, 3. See also P Schlag, 'The Problem of the Subject' (1991) 69 *Texas Law Review* 1627.

if deeper forces propel us against our interests, or if we sense alienation regarding our own activities?

Freud offered psychoanalysis as a tool for self-mastery, acknowledging that the ego may try to replace blind, instinctual actions by rational and coherent plans. No such help, however, seems to lie at hand from post-modern psychoanalytic influences, which interpret the self as irredeemably fragmented. Constantly seeking a unity in which we found ourselves submerged in infancy and have ever since been trying to retrieve, we are beguiled by our own image into thinking ourselves whole, trying to retrieve that unity for the rest of our lives, beguiled by the 'symbolic' order of language,[104] which we use as a means to try to fulfil our personhood, to grasp ownership of ourselves. But this is never possible. Something always remains that cannot be symbolised, cannot be expressed—something that Jacques Lacan called the *Real*, which leads us through an endless quest, a succession of searches, journeys, misappropriations of *objets petit a*[105] in our struggle for fulfilment—to no avail. The Real always resists this symbolism, and we are left with constant desire, lack even, a struggle to come to terms with what cannot be expressed.[106]

The arcane psychoanalytic language of Lacan seems a long way from the formalism, the control, the order of much modern jurisprudence. At one and the same time, we use legal precedents, cite *A v B*, suggest that we are responsible for our actions and so must be punished for them, but also observe the theories of Freud and Lacan. We suffer postmodern anxiety and notice that in this culture of late capitalism, there are as many depressed persons on medication as there are 'possessive individuals'. Perhaps the one cannot exist without the other. Have we become schizophrenic in our conception of personhood? And how should law respond to this, if so? Does it continue to portray individuality as unified? Or perhaps, if we are to go along with Foucault or CLS, how are we to know, 'normalised' as we are? How can the law respond to any such fragmentation and conquest of the self?

The problematic nature of contemporary personhood is evoked by an image from the artist Cindy Sherman (Figure 9-4). It is one of a series of self-portraits that imitates the style of old still photographs which were used to advertise movies. At the same time, however, the photo subverts the genre, because it is not based on any real film. The portrait is unsettling, the expression on Sherman's face hard to read but troubled and ambiguous, provoking a reading of solitude and anxiety but also subtle conflict

---

[104] J Lacan, *Écrits: The First Complete Edition in English*, B Fink (trans) (New York, WW Norton, 2006).

[105] In the context of Lacanian psychoanalysis, the 'objet petit a' signifies an unattainable object of desire. See ibid.

[106] Ibid.

Figure 9-4: Cindy Sherman, *Untitled Film Still 21* (1978) Courtesy of the artist and Metro Pictures

or even threat—of the powerlessness of the lone female in the megalithic metropolis of the modern city. Overall, the mood is uncertain, evoking a lack of confidence, a troubled self-awareness.

The film critic Arthur Danto has suggested that Sherman's film still series might be read as metaphors for the meaning of existence in the troubled, contemporary age:

> I can think of no oeuvre which addresses us in our common humanity and at the same time induces the most advanced speculations on Post-Modernity, no images which say something profound about the feminine condition and yet touch us at a level beyond sexual difference. They are wry, arch, clever works, smart, sharp and cool. But they are among the rare works of recent decades that rise to the demand on great art, that it embody the transformative metaphors for the meaning of human reality.[107]

For Critchley, the task of philosophy is how to respond to this motivational and moral deficit in order to resist nihilism, and he sees philosophical activism as a militant response to nihilism. He believes a motivating, empowering concept of ethics to be necessary, one capable of facing down

---

[107] A Danto, 'Photography and Performance: Cindy Sherman's Stills' in *Sherman: Untitled Film Stills* (London, Jonathan Cape, 1990) 14.

the drift of the present. He looks to a counter-position of an alternative approach, an ethics that is based on the Other's demand, one side, radical, and unfulfillable—indeed, one that has much in common with the Levinasian view examined earlier.[108]

However, I believe that this is exactly how human rights come into the picture and play a role. Not that they necessarily can do so satisfactorily. That lack of satisfaction in fact helps us to explain its continuing perplexities. Faced with the despair and prospect of nihilism, with feelings of lack of control over even our own identity, we search for something to give meaning to our lives. The law of legal positivism, stripped of any necessary identification with morality, is not an admirable candidate for this. Yet we keep searching, and human rights play the role of Lacan's *petit objet a*, hopeless objects of our desire.[109] Just as Western society engages in a rampant consumerism in a search for a hopeless meaning, which can never satiate our desire, so we look to human rights, which are the nearest thing we have to religion or magic, for attainment of our fantasy. There is always an excess of demand over need. Rights legalise our desire and give public recognition to the subject's wishes.[110] As objects of our fantasy, their content remains to be filled by ourselves. And this explains why their content is so different and impossible to achieve, why we cannot agree on a definition. Human rights symbolise our very lack, but they also signify it and prevent it from being fulfilled.

A psychoanalytic reading of human rights helps us to understand the very conflicting and ambivalent role they play in our legal thought. Although so many of us may feel sceptical (whether of a liberal, radical or postmodern perspective), we find it very hard if not impossible to let them go. They are the objects of our fantasies, a phantasmal supplement which is the best hope we have for an ethical dimension in law, however unsatisfactory their practice may be. And this is why we continue believing in human rights, even when faced with impossibly conflicting and competing accounts, and often so little practical good by way of outcomes. They are all we have left by way of magic or religion, or supplement for it, and we cannot give them up. The ultimate in disillusion would be to succumb to a human rights nihilism, whereby we face up to human rights as in themselves not only lacking in any foundations but also devalued and devoid of any morality, and acknowledge that they are indeed devoid of meaning, or rather empty shells, ciphers for whatever content, often that of a dominating powerful ideology. Most of us are unwilling to confront our nihilism on this scale, to face up to it, so we turn instead to the demanding (but perhaps hopeless) prospect of an ethical engagement with human rights. It is the best that we

---

[108] Critchley (above n 61).

[109] For an expression of these views, see Douzinas (above n 16); and R Salecl, 'Rights in Feminist and Psychoanalytic Perspective' (1995) *Cardozo Law Review* 1121.

[110] Salecl (ibid).

are left with, and rather like believing in fairies, if we try to hard enough, we may just be able to prove they exist.

Juridification of Human Rights

These, then, are the dilemmas and ambiguities of human rights. We cannot do without them, but they always fail to satisfy us. Their transposition into law only further complicates things. There are of course those such as Bentham for whom the concept of a right makes sense only within a legal setting—without this, for Bentham, it is a meaningless 'anarchical fallacy'.[111] For others, the reverse is the case. Converting human rights into law involves what Gearty has described as a 'Faustian bargain'.[112] Law is not notable for its radical, progressive nature, and the translation of rights into law risks jettisoning any emancipatory force rights may have, even setting them in opposition to politics, as something pre-political (derived in good liberal tradition from our status as autonomous beings in the state of nature, prior to the social contract), capable of overriding political agreements on the common good. Douzinas has claimed that we have now come to a point in time when we have lost human rights, due to their conversion from a language of rebellion and emancipation to 'a criterion of state legitimacy and a new type of positive law'.[113] Hence the title of his book, *The End of Human Rights*. Therefore, law is seen as damaging rights, a view clearly expressed in collections of sceptical essays on rights, one of which has a section specifically entitled 'Failures of Juridification'.[114]

The more straightforward ways in which law is perceived as harmful to rights relate to law's procedures: the way in which claiming rights in law is perceived as inherently antagonistic, encouraging litigation, constructed around a paradigm in which there are only two parties, diminishing any role for a residual public interest. It has also been described as converting the relationship between the citizen and the state into one of quasi-contract, whereby a Bill of Rights becomes a list of clauses in a contract of good government.[115] Once human rights are situated in this way, so the argument goes, they lose their transformative effect and become stagnant, overriding political culture. The legalisation of human rights is thus antithetical to a promotion of human rights that, as discussed in the last section, sees its mission as the relief of suffering.

---

[111] Bentham, *Anarchical Fallacies* (above n 11).

[112] Gearty, *Can Human Rights Survive?* (above n 4).

[113] Douzinas (above n 16) 380.

[114] T Campbell and A Tomkins (eds), *Sceptical Essays on Human Rights* (Oxford, Oxford University Press, 2003).

[115] A Tomkins, 'Introduction' in Campbell and Tomkins (eds) (ibid).

Andrew Williams has made the point directly. For him, the law itself is formed on sufferance rather than insufferability.[116] By this, he means a toleration of suffering, a failure to act, and a denial of human rights. This tolerance is illustrated by the following examples: the relativisation of torture and debates as to whether certain activities qualify as torture in human rights covenants; or the constant applications of jurisdiction and legal boundaries in order to remove human rights violations from any possible remedy. Although there exists a limited principle of universal jurisdiction for the most serious crimes such as torture,[117] national legal sovereignty is still usually the norm, territorialising disputes or partitioning them according to various jurisdictional limits—depending on the nature of the action or personal involvement.

EU law provides another excellent example here. The scope of EU law has become the main determining factor as to whether any human rights violation may be pleaded, but this jurisdictional limit is complex in the extreme,[118] transforming legal argument and the legal literature into a debate about the arcane limits of the European Union's competences rather than focusing on human rights. In one case, a claimant was able to successfully plead the application of Article 8 ECHR on the right to family life, through a (really rather tenuous) connection to EU law;[119] but in other cases, the ECJ has been unwilling to extend the scope of EU law. Thus a claimant was not able to rely on freedom of expression to contest the banning of a five-pointed star in Hungary as a former totalitarian symbol, because the ECJ held there to be insufficient links with EU law.[120]

Another contemporary legal debate as to jurisdiction concerns the liability for human rights violations committed outside of national territory but within the control of the alleged perpetrator, an issue with which both national and international courts have been engaged. Most notably, the ECtHR found liability for death and injury caused by the actions of British soldiers in Iraq.[121] A further 'boundary' dispute concerns the standing of claimants. The ECJ is notorious for interpreting the EU treaty standing provisions for individuals in direct actions for judicial review so strictly that the more people who claim that their rights have been violated, the harder it is to satisfy the test—which appears illogical to say the least.[122] All of these legal requirements serve to bracket or demote the main subject of

---

[116] A Williams, 'Between Sufferance and Insufferability' (above n 6).

[117] The United Nations Convention against Torture (1984) requires signatory states to adopt national laws that are based on the concept of universal jurisdiction.

[118] Examples may be found in, eg, Case 5/88 *Wachauf* [1989] ECR 2609; and, more recently, Case C-34/09 *Ruiz Zambrano* [2011] ECR I-0000.

[119] Case C-60/00 *Carpenter* [2002] ECR I-6279.

[120] Case C-328/04 *Attila Vajnai* [2005] ECR I-8577.

[121] *Al-Skeini and Others v the United Kingdom* (No 55721/07), judgment of 7 July 2011.

[122] Case 25/62 *Plaumann v Commission* [1963] ECR 95.

the litigation, the claim that rights have been violated. Instead, such legal requirements prompt endless litigation over preliminary, collateral, procedural matters which very often dispose of the cases.

Indeed, we could go even further and maintain that human rights have been effaced or elided out of law, even when they are given prominent place in legal documents of rights, which put rights claims at centre stage and do not require preliminary questions of jurisdiction or scope. We may grant that the range of interests that have been asserted in and accepted by courts, whether national or international, in contemporary human rights litigation is wide-ranging. For example, the right to keep a dog, 'property' in the form of milk quotas, and a right to feed pigeons in public squares have all been accepted as interests protected by legally binding fundamental rights.[123] This wide ranging nature of rights has been especially evident in the ECJ, which, until the declaration of the EU Charter of Fundamental Rights in 2000 lacked a binding charter but was nevertheless ecumenical in its approach, willing to assert as rights a great variety of interests and rights that were protected in EU national constitutions or in the ECHR.

However, this expansive embrace of a wide variety of interests should not be interpreted as necessarily improving the protection of human rights. Very few rights are drafted as absolutes. One example of a right drafted in absolute terms, without limitations or exceptions, is the prohibition on torture and inhuman and degrading treatment in Article 3 ECHR and other international human rights instruments. But there are very few such other rights drafted in this way. For a great many rights, it is usual to include in the rights document a limitation provision, either in a second paragraph following the declaration of the right itself, setting out specific limits to that right (as in Articles 8–11 ECHR) or a more general limitations provision, such as in the Canadian Charter or in the EU Charter of Fundamental Rights, which is drafted in the following manner:

Article 52

Scope and Interpretation of Rights and Principles

1. Any limitation on the exercise of the rights and freedoms recognised by this Charter must be provided for by law and respect the essence of those rights and freedoms. Subject to the principle of proportionality, limitations may be made only if they are necessary and genuinely meet objectives of general interest recognised by the Union or the need to protect the rights and freedoms of others.

In this way, the key issue in rights litigation shifts away from interpretation of the right itself to a focus on whether the state interference with that

---

[123] See Case No 6825/74 *X v Iceland* 5 DR 86 (18 May 1976) (right to keep a dog); Case 5/88 *Wachauf v Federal Republic of Germany* [1989] ECR 2609 (milk quotas); and BVerfGE 54, 143 (right to feed pigeons in public squares).

right has been in pursuance of a legitimate interest and, if so, whether that interference was proportionate. Indeed, the key issue becomes that of proportionality. This translates into a balancing exercise, an investigation of countervailing concerns.

Mattias Kumm has suggested that we could classify this justification exercise as an exercise of public reason (a welcome one, in his view).[124] This elision of rights might be comforting to those who fear that the public good is very often omitted in rights litigation, with a too prominent focus on the interest of the selfish rights bearer. However, this assessment of the proportionality of state action is only as good as the reasoning and motives of those engaging in it, and in human rights litigation this will be either senior national judiciary or those of international courts such as the ECJ or ECtHR. Are they better placed than public policymakers to decide what are almost always controversial decisions concerning questions of social policy, allocation of resources or issues of public morality? Judges do not, unlike Plato's fictional guardians, have any especial knowledge of justice, and *pace* Dworkin's ideal judge Hercules, they are not philosopher kings. For some such as Kumm, they exercise a type of public reason that should be seen as a crucial aspect of liberal public democracy. Indeed, he believes the role of judges in these cases to be every bit as vital to democracy as the decisions of elected politicians—it being the especial wisdom of judges to know which questions to ask and how to test the coherence of government views and force public authorities to defend themselves. This, Kumm believes, promotes a practice of the critical, reasoned, exercise of public claims relating to justice. But here is a (forcefully put) alternative view by James Allan:

> The Human Rights Act, no less than the US Bill of Rights or the Canadian Charter of Rights, has created a situation in which the judges' view of what the rights respecting outcome is magically transmogrifies into the correct view. What *they say* our rights are, in effect, gets equated to what our rights actually are, as though these are not highly contentious issues over which committees of ex-lawyers have no pipeline to God, no special expertise, and no obvious grounds for being deferred to.[125]

Both views, namely those of academics such as Kumm, who have a faith in the ability of rights-based review to turn into Socratic contestation, and those of sceptics such as Allan, are too extreme, too overblown. South African constitutional court judge Albie Sachs, in a chapter of his book *The Strange Alchemy of Life and Law* that specifically focuses on proportionality,

---

[124] M Kumm, 'The Idea of Socratic Contestation and the Right to Justification: The Point of Rights-Based Proportionality Review' (2010) *Law & Ethics of Human Rights* 1.

[125] J Allan, 'Bills of Rights: Doin' the Sankey Hanky Panky' in T Campbell, KD Ewing and A Tomkins (eds), *The Legal Protection of Human Rights: Sceptical Essays* (Oxford, Oxford University Press, 2011). By 'ex lawyers' he means judges (108).

illustrates and conveys the sincerity of a judge grappling with crucial, value-laden questions under the rubric of proportionality.[126] He outlines why he believes that sometimes it is an advantage for judges, who are not directly accountable to the electorate, to take decisions without being subject to the undue populist pressures that politicians might face. Yet counter-examples of regrettable, poorly reasoned judicial decisions can also be found.[127] Human rights are subject to both legal and political manipulation, and it seems futile to highlight the one without recognising the other. What is important overall are *outcomes*—whether the use of human rights actually improves people's lives. And here, what does indeed seem to be the case is that the heavy, cumbersome operation of the law too often obscures and overwhelms the urgency and immediacy of rights claims, shifting time, effort and (above all) money onto contingent, technical issues, giving support to Williams' claim that law too often suffers and tolerates the intolerable, leaving one ambivalent as to the desirability of a juridification of human rights.

The discussion above illustrates how rights claims can be exhausted by the weighty, technical, often casuistic operation of the law. However, a further challenge to the juridification of rights suggests a more sinister operation of the law—that rights are prone to a particular ideological manipulation by the powerful to transform them into the very reverse of the emancipatory message they supposedly proclaim, a means whereby they are mutated from the radical into the reactionary. This critique is similar to the critique of the rule of law considered in earlier chapters and merits further consideration.

The very transformation of the radical into the reactionary may ironically be made possible because of the false promise of rights; their very success as ideology lies in the fact that we may be blinded by their light, by their claim to be liberating and emancipatory, so we miss their cynical manipulation. This is something we should beware of. It is all too easy to become entranced by the beguiling language of rights into believing that more legalisation of rights must be progressive. But experience does not necessarily bear this out.

The protection of the rights of egoistic man enabled the judiciary to debilitate progressive legislation, in cases such as *Lochner*, in which the right to liberty might have been eloquently proclaimed by the Supreme Court but not to the advantage of those manual workers whom the New

---

[126] A Sachs, 'Human Dignity and Proportionality' in Sachs, *The Strange Alchemy of Life and Law* (above n 8).

[127] My personal choices might be: from the UK House of Lords, *Bromley London Borough Council v Greater London Council* HL [1983] 1 AC 768; from the US Supreme Court, *Bowers v Hardwick*, 478 US 186 (1986); and from the ECtHR, *Otto Preminger-Institut v Austria* (13470/87) [1994] ECHR 26.

York legislation had tried to shield from working over-long hours. Instead, in this case, freedom of contract operated to reinforce the positions of those who were already socially privileged. The creation and insertion of an unwritten Bill of Rights by the ECJ into an organisation originally created as a free market (namely the European Union), by its very nature celebrating capital, at first appears commendable, as do the efforts of those such as Ernst-Ulrich Petersmann, who aims to inscribe a rights jurisprudence into WTO law. The European Union now possesses a binding, written, wide-ranging Charter of Fundamental Rights, which is far broader in ambit than the ECHR and refreshing in its efforts to maintain the indivisibility of civil and political rights on the one hand and socioeconomic rights on the other. However, what has been notable to date has been the willingness of the ECJ to select as rights issues those that are capable of aiding capital and business in its drive for a freer market. The right to the confidentiality of business information has been just as energetically furthered by the ECJ as have rights to asylum or immigration. Furthermore, in cases such as *Viking* and *Laval*, the ECJ has placed a right to free movement (of business rights) above any collective rights of bargaining or industrial action.[128] Gearty has also discussed how Bills of Rights were inserted into post-war German and Italian constitutions with the specific aim of maintaining a capitalist status quo, thus pre-empting any more radical socialist legislation.[129]

Sometimes law has been blatant, excluding individuals from 'personhood' and from the possession of rights, as it did with women and people of colour in much of the nineteenth and twentieth centuries, lumping them together with imbeciles, infants and those lacking capacity. Yet because law presents itself as neutral, this bad faith is not always apparent. In this way, law can operate as ideology, creating a false consciousness and lack of awareness of our true situation. For CLS adherents, and in the words of populist language, we are already 'pods', and the body snatchers have taken over.[130] This sort of critique is well known to feminism and critical race theory and has been adopted by writers of a postmodern orientation, including Foucault, who described us as the victims of the ideology of a disciplinary society, beings constructed by modernity.[131] We may think, according to the Enlightenment project, that we are free, but this is not the case, as we are 'disciplined' into certain forms of life by the forces of power operating upon us.

There is something in the 'bad faith' argument. Certain groups have been treated appallingly by the law, denied the status of personhood and human rights. Cases like *Lochner* now even seem to have a dishonest air

---

[128] *Viking Line* (above n 42); and *Laval* (above n 42).
[129] Gearty, *Can Human Rights Survive?* (above n 4) ch 1.
[130] P Gabel and D Kennedy, *Roll over Beethoven* (1984) 36 *Stanford Law Review* 1, 3.
[131] M Foucault, *History of Sexuality*, vols I–III (New York, Pantheon, 1978).

about them—a covering up of what's really going on. But, aside from nineteenth-century formalism, with its excesses of abstract individualism, it is not clear that the conspiracy theory really works. Law is not completely imbued with the ideology of a self-serving elite. For all that arguments have been made against law as an instrument of oppression, it is still possible to find examples in which the law has also operated in an imaginative and impassioned way, and so it is too simplistic to claim that law, even, or especially, at its most supposedly liberating in the guise of human rights, is an exercise of bad faith. Applications and interpretations of human rights are too varied for simplification.

Although a liberal or perhaps neoliberal conception of human rights, derived from the roots of human rights in personal autonomy, has been used to propel rights jurisprudence in a certain direction, there are countervailing tendencies. For example, the jurisprudence of freedom of expression takes many, often competing forms. On the one hand, in the American constitutional law context at least, the First Amendment sometimes seems to have an almost absolute force. Cross-burning and flag-burning have in the past been interpreted by the US Supreme Court as acts of individual expression meriting the protection of the First Amendment, even when offence, outrage and upset are created as a result.[132] The community interests (think of neo-Nazis marching through Skokie, a predominately Jewish suburb of Chicago, whose residents were not able to prevent this rally because of the First Amendment[133]) are given less consideration, and particular types of harm, such as intimidation by racist and hate speech, go unrecognised, without remedy. The US case law on campaign financing appears, through the rather thinly disguised veil of the First Amendment, to serve only to prop up the abilities of wealthy corporations to manipulate politics. On the other hand, in the form in which we find it in the ECHR[134] and in the constitutional law of most European states, free expression, while highly valued, must sometimes give way to societal interests. A neo-Nazi may not always get up in a rally and vent his opinion that 'Hitler was right'; and remembrance ceremonies may not always be disrupted in the name of free speech.[135]

---

[132] Eg, *RAV v City of St Paul*, 505 US 377 (1992); and *Texas v Johnson*, 491 US 397 (1989).

[133] *Collin v Smith*, 578F.2d1197 (1978); and *Snyder v Phelps*, 562 US 131 S Ct 1207 (2011).

[134] Art 10 ECHR provides the right to freedom of expression, subject to certain restrictions that are 'in accordance with law' and 'necessary in a democratic society'.

[135] In 1994, the German Constitutional Court upheld a ban on Holocaust denial, preventing a meeting in Munich, where 'revisionist historian' David Irving was to question the Holocaust. BVerfGE 90, 241 (1994). For further on this, see S Douglas-Scott, 'The Hatefulness of Protected Speech: A Comparison of the American and European Approaches' (1999) 7 *William and Mary Bill of Rights Journal* 305.

The juridification of rights is not so much an exercise in bad faith (although it has sometimes been this) as one of complexity, sometimes confusion, and greatly varied interpretation. There are many ambiguities here, paralleling EP Thompson's defence of the rule of law. Manipulation certainly exists, but in many different directions. If judges are of a neo-liberal bent, then rights, too, may well take that turn. Rights are not the neutral, pre-political tools that a certain liberal theory presents them as. But nor are they ideology. They are capable of deterring injustice. They are more like empty vessels, prone to be filled with all sorts of content and, most likely of all, clogged up in the vast, arcane machinery of the law.

Pluralism, Complexity and Human Rights

There has been a body of scholarship that suggests human rights could provide some sort of solution both to the messiness of law's complexity and to the apparently irresolvable problems of pluralism discussed in previous chapters. If so, then human rights might indeed be a holy grail. As long as all law respects human rights, then there will be this in common—a means to ascertain some sort of golden thread in the complexity and chaos. It is an attractive prospect. Yet the discussion so far suggests that human rights bring a complexity, disorder and incoherence of their own—indeed a pluralism of their own, and a legal pluralism as well, insofar as human rights have legal force. In this case, seeking resolution through human rights would just add to the complexity.

There is no doubt that every legal player would wish to claim an adherence to human rights—as discussed, human rights present the closet we possess to a common religion. As Andrew Williams has suggested:

> The power of the *language* and *practice* of human rights rests in their exceptional ability to draw people together in a community, to channel social aspirations, to provide a means of expressing arguments for social change, to guide and frame those in authority in their policy and decision-making, to impose significant control on the exercise of power, and to provide respect for one's identity as an individual human being *and* as a member of different and interlocking communities.[136]

This comprehensive account of human rights explains their attraction to so many different constituencies and their ubiquity. It suggests that here we have a something capable of instilling a sense of commonality to guide institutional behaviour.

---

[136] A Williams, 'Promoting Justice after Lisbon' (2010) *Oxford Journal of Legal Studies* 682.

Yash Ghai has highlighted the way in which human rights can appeal to a great variety of cultures and legal systems (despite their apparent origins in eighteenth-century Europe) and the ways in which rights can be used with success in mediating complex ethnic and cultural claims.[137] Where culture itself presents a lack of homogeneity, rights can be ahead of that culture and provide a stronger material basis for agreement. Ghai believes that a regime of rights, because of its inherent diversity, proves an attractive foundation for intercultural dialogues and the promotion of a consensus. He also believes that rights need no longer be seen as inextricably belonging to the dominant tradition based on individual autonomy but can, for, example provide for groups to be the subject of rights, allowing for the recognition of claims not based on individual autonomy or identity:

> For multicultural states, human rights as a negotiated understanding of the acceptable framework for coexistence and the respect for each culture are more important than for mono-cultural or mono-ethnic societies, where other forms of solidarity or identity can be invoked or minimized to cope with conflicts. In other words, it is precisely where the concepts and conceptions of rights are most difficult that they are most needed. The task is difficult, but possible, even if it may not always be completely successful. And most states are today multicultural, whether as a result of immigration or because their people are finding new identities.[138]

In a wide-ranging, empirical survey of a number of countries and rights regimes, Ghai concludes that rights are used not merely as protections against the state but also as instruments for the distribution of resources and as a basis of both identity and a social vision of society. For Ghai, they are not necessarily deeply held values but a mode of discourse for advancing and justifying claims. We might also cite the judicial vogue for conversations in terms of rights (eg, citations of rights of other jurisdictions in the US case of *Lawrence v Texas*, which extended a right of privacy to homosexual couples).[139]

However, the discussion earlier in this chapter suggests that rights are every bit as conflicting and incoherent as the disputes they are supposed to resolve. A legal space such as that in Europe illustrates the complexity and multiplicity of human rights. In Europe, they operate at national, EU,

---

[137] Eg, Y Ghai, 'Universalism and Relativism: Human Rights as a Framework for Negotiating Interethnic Claims' (1999) 21 *Cardozo Law Review* 1095–140. See also W Twining (ed), *Human Rights, Southern Voices: Francis Deng, Abdullahi An-Na'im, Yash Ghai and Upendra Baxi* (Cambridge, Cambridge University Press, 2009).

[138] Ghai (ibid) 1102.

[139] *Lawrence v Texas*, 123 S Ct 2472 (2003). In this case, the Court relied in part on foreign sources of authority, directly citing the European Court of Human Rights and the UK Wolfenden Report to the British Parliament. The Court's citation was highly criticised in Justice Scalia's dissent, which suggested that the 'Court's discussion of ... foreign views [was] meaningless dicta'.

ECHR and international level, often productive of the very complexity and pluralism that they are supposed to resolve. What is the relation between these different regimes of rights? How are they supposed to interact? Are the rights at these different levels in any way interchangeable or equivalent? There exists much debate and discussion today about the desirability of domesticating or maintaining an autonomy of different regimes of human rights. A great deal of scholarship and judicial writing is focused on just this question. For example, English judges have suggested a lack of comprehension on the part of Strasbourg judges of the common law system and a need for the English judiciary to develop a jurisprudence of rights suitable for the specific system of the common law.[140] There is also a great deal of scholarship on the need for the European Union to develop its own autonomous human rights jurisprudence, and to date, the ECJ seems to have developed rights in such a way as to emphasise or promote economic and commercial rights. Members of the US Supreme Court judiciary have denied the relevance of overseas rights jurisprudence to US law.[141] This suggests a lack of compatibility or interchangeability of rights at different legal levels.

Furthermore, as the earlier part of this chapter has sought to illustrate, human rights possess many attempted justifications and conceptual clarifications. Hohfeld identified four different concepts of rights, some allied to a particular correlative duty in the form of a claim right, whereas others presenting themselves as immunities or liberties are possessed on the basis that others have no duties or powers regarding the rights holder.[142] The different theoretical justifications of rights examined earlier in this chapter lead to very different ideas as to who possesses rights and the types of rights that they possess. Furthermore, one of the most crucial questions today concerns conflicts of rights—how are we to determine the solution to a conflict between freedom of expression and the right to privacy, for example?[143] There is no clear answer to any one of these questions, suggesting a very significant moral indeterminacy at play here.

And yet perhaps human rights are the best we can do? Whatever the source of conflict, there is still the essence of a common language here,

---

[140] See Lord Hoffmann, 'The Universality of Human Rights', Judicial Studies Board Annual Lecture (19 March 2009), available at http://www.judiciary.gov.uk/media/speeches/2009/speech-lord-hoffman-19032009 (accessed 10 December 2012).

[141] Eg, Scalia's dissent in *Lawrence v Texas* (above n 139). But contrast the view of Justice Breyer. See further N Dorsen (ed), 'The Relevance of Foreign Legal Materials in US Constitutional Cases: A Conversation between Justice Antonin Scalia and Justice Stephen Breyer' (2005) 3 *International Journal of Constitutional Law* 519–41.

[142] W Hohfeld, 'Fundamental Legal Conceptions as Applied in Judicial Reasoning' (1917) 26 *Yale Law Journal* 710.

[143] This conflict is exemplified by the *von Hannover* case in the ECtHR: *von Hannover v Germany* [2004] Application No 59320/00.

a currency that all can understand, even if it is interpreted differently, a means of importing morality and ethics into law, the basis for substantive justice, a reminder that we should not tolerate the intolerable, suffer the insufferable. As Douzinas has written, 'Human rights are the necessary and impossible claim of law to justice.'[144] Chapter four highlighted the problems of finding a 'meta-principle' or fragile balance for pluralism. Chapter five considered the many injustices of law after modernity, and chapter six suggested that there exists no overarching theory of justice capable of helping us to remedy these injustices. If the rule of law, reimagined as critical legal justice, is a vital tool for deterring injustice, then human rights, however unsatisfactory they may appear, are also essential moral ingredients for law after modernity, both operating within the law, as ingredients of critical legal justice, and functioning outside of it, as elusive ideals or aspirations. Human rights seem to be our best chance, accompanied by an almost desperate faith in their ability to fill the void. Although Gearty has reminded us that 'there is no certainty of a happy ending',[145] he also stated at the very end of his lectures, 'The human rights language ... is the best way we have of securing a hearing without killing to do so.'[146] Both statements are applicable and germane to the enigma of human rights.

---

[144] Douzinas (above n 16) 380.
[145] Gearty, *Can Human Rights Survive?* (above n 4) 1.
[146] Ibid, 157.

10

Critical Legal Justice and Beyond: Cosmopolitanism

In chapters seven and eight it was argued that the rule of law should be extended and enhanced as critical legal justice, and some illustrations were offered of how this might be possible. This chapter looks more closely at the global arena and at the claim that cosmopolitanism operates as an application of the rule of law internationally.

Cosmopolitanism

Cosmopolitanism is frequently presented as a compelling approach to justice at the global level and as a means of addressing some of the quandaries of justice beyond the state. Typical accounts of cosmopolitanism stress that cosmopolitanism is founded on universalism, in that it claims to respect all forms of difference among human beings. It would also point out that cosmopolitanism presents an openness to other peoples, cultures and experiences, urging mutual recognition and respect of others as equals in the context of multiple differences. Cosmopolitanism evinces concern for others without demanding that they become like us, and it has particular regard to human rights. However, introduced in this way, cosmopolitanism connotes a utopian ideal and needs greater explication to demonstrate its relevance and workability as a form of the rule of law transferred to global level. Regrettably, however, cosmopolitanism has suffered from a lack of definition.

Cosmopolitanism is in fact an ancient idea. People have always travelled across the globe for all sorts of reasons, including commerce, conquest and discovery. Cosmopolitanism has its roots in the stoic philosophies of the ancient Greeks and later in the mix and melée of the vast Roman empire and the notion of the *civus romanus* (which was notably, however, not a status open to all). But most of the resonances of cosmopolitanism are far more modern. Immanuel Kant is often credited as responsible for reviving it in the eighteenth century, as he recognised the interconnectedness of humankind and used practical reason to argue for the rational necessity of cosmopolitanism in his short work *Perpetual Peace*.[1] Indeed, cosmopolitanism itself has sometimes been interpreted as a creature of late and post-modernity. For example, the Portuguese author Fernando Pessoa perceived it as an emerging global, common, hybrid self-consciousness of formerly subjugated peoples,[2] and cosmopolitanism is argued to have increased relevance in the globalisation of the late twentieth and early twenty-first centuries.[3]

In the twenty-first century, cosmopolitanism urges a focus on human rights, on world citizenship rather than on nationality; and cosmopolitan norms are now derived from the notion of individuals as moral and legal persons. Notably, these cosmopolitan norms (provided by, eg, international human rights treaties) directly endow individuals rather than states, the traditional subjects of international law. Thus cosmopolitanism involves a departure from nationalism and realism in international relations, a rejection of the Westphalian idea of state sovereignty, by recognising that human rights set limits on what states may do to their subjects, that state limits may sometimes be crossed in the name of humanitarian intervention, and that individuals may be prosecuted for crimes against humanity in states other than those of their nationality or other than where those crimes took place.

Cosmopolitanism is not the only possible attempt for international justice beyond the sovereign state. Philosophical theories of justice beyond the state were already considered in chapter six of this volume, including those such as Thomas Pogge's, which argue for a global redistributive justice. In the next chapter, I shall look closely at ways in which justice and accountability may be secured for informal and more reflexive types of law. Cosmopolitanism does not go so far as to recommend a world government or legislature, so it does not really take the form of an attempted global constitutionalism, and indeed, Kant stigmatised the idea of a world government as a soulless despotism.[4] Such a government exists now no more than it did in Kant's day. However, current problems of account-

---

[1] But see the earlier example of Montesquieu's *Persian Letters* (1721).

[2] This was written in the context of Pessoa setting out the manifesto for the journal *Orpheu* in 1915, quoted in R Jara, 'A Design for Modernity in the Margins' in AL Geist and JB Monleón (eds), *Modernism and Its Margins: Reinscribing Cultural Modernity from Spain and Latin America* (New York, Garland Publishing, 1999) 282–83.

[3] See, eg, D Archibugi, *Cosmopolitics* (London, Verso, 2004); U Beck, *Cosmopolitan Vision* (Cambridge, Polity, 2006); S Benhabib, *The Rights of Others: Aliens, Residents and Citizens* (Cambridge, Cambridge University Press, 2004); R Fine, *Cosmopolitanism* (London, Routledge, 2007); D Held, *Democracy and the Global Order* (Stanford, Stanford University Press, 1995); D Held, *Cosmopolitanism: Ideals and Realities* (Cambridge, Polity, 2010); D Harvey, *Cosmopolitanism and the Geographies of Freedom* (New York, Columbia University Press, 2009); and J Habermas, *The Divided West* (Cambridge, Polity, 2006).

[4] See I Kant, 'Perpetual Peace' in H Reiss (ed), *Kant: Political Writings* (Cambridge, Cambridge University Press, 1991).

ability and democracy at that global level, and the lack of a global public space, render such an institution desirable for some, if hard to achieve. On the other hand, what currently do exist are various international institutions, many of which are concerned with the mechanisms of global capitalism, including the World Trade Organization (WTO), the World Bank and the International Monetary Fund (IMF). A few other international institutions have broader competences, most notably the United Nations. Furthermore, there are also various other international movements that have been founded almost as an antithesis to world government, based and justified around resistance to global capitalism, generally lacking unifying principles, and aligned around some sort of principles of resistance to power. One such is the World Social Forum, formed in deliberate opposition to the World Economic Forum at Davos, and modelled on anarchist principles.[5] Theories such as Jean-François Lyotard's, which urges recognition of a global plurality of justices,[6] are also conceived in direct opposition to any cosmopolitan universalism, instead arguing for a radical pluralism (given what Lyotard perceived to be a world of unbridgeable gaps).

Global resistance movements have definite value, but cosmopolitanism might appear to have greater strength, given that it claims to muster norms of international law in its name. Yet rather like the rule of law, to which it is closely related, cosmopolitanism occupies an ambiguous place in theory today. It is derided by some as idealistic and utopian, but interpreted by others as a cloak for twenty-first-century imperialism, a latter day reinvention of oppressive Western 'universalism'. Yet it also has a wide variety of adherents among both liberal and postmodern theorists.[7] Cosmopolitanism is sometimes a pragmatic approach, which may also, almost paradoxically, seem unrealistic in the face of the violence, suffering and disillusion of the modern and postmodern worlds. It may also appear too liberal, too rooted in a discredited universalism for the chaotic, unsystematic legal spaces described in previous chapters. However, I believe this is not the case. It is in fact a way of achieving the 'both/and' described in chapter foura way of linking the universal and the particular, a synthesis of modern humanism and postmodern identity politics.[8] It acknowledges that reality is complex. Cosmopolitanism may itself be characterised both as an *outlook*a way of envisioning the world, a form of consciousness, an 'internal point of view' for law as well as an actual *state of affairs*, describing existing social

---

[5] Another example is provided by the various 'Occupy' movements of 2011 and 2012.

[6] Eg, J-F Lyotard and J-F Thébaud, *Just Gaming*, W Godzich (trans) (Minneapolis, University of Minnesota Press, 1985).

[7] For example, Robert Fine, Jürgen Habermas, David Held, Paul Gilroy and Kwame Anthony Appiah.

[8] See, eg, Fine (above n 3); and Beck (above n 3).

phenomena in the world, so it may also be examined from an 'external point of view'.

Perpetual Peace

Kant is of fundamental importance in understanding cosmopolitanism. He was the first modern philosopher to acknowledge that issues of international relations could not be ignored, and he reasoned on them in *Perpetual Peace: A Philosophical Sketch*, first published in 1795.[9] In this, as in several others of his works written around this time, Kant was influenced by the events of the French Revolution, and his political theory reveals a focus on human freedom, as well as connections to Kant's view on Enlightenment, which he saw as a dynamic process leading to self-emancipation.[10] The cosmopolitanism Kant argued for in *Perpetual Peace* is linked to his analysis of and arguments for republicanism in his other works,[11] and it is aimed at providing a coherent and consistent account of the moral, social, political and international spheres as a whole. Kant's arguments are based on practical reason and are sometimes known as the 'democratic peace' theory, implying an intrinsic connection between democracy, law and international peace. Also, notably, law plays a crucial role in these works, specifically in establishing principles of right, of just actions. Taken in all, Kant's work was influential in shaping the doctrine of the *Rechtstaat*, the just state grounded in reason, which sustains peace.

In the international arena, as in other areas, Kant argued that ethical action ought to be based on maxims capable of being formalised as universal laws. Kant's most important arguments are found in the second part of *Perpetual Peace*, in which he sets out three definitive articles. The first article requires the civil constitution of any state to be republican. This he thought necessary because despotism deprives the individual of freedom as co-legislator and creator of the law that binds him. Yet Kant went beyond this to insist that the rule of law be extended to relations between states. The second definitive article therefore concerns the relations of states to each other *ius gentium*, or international law and requires that the international order be based on a federation of free states that would abolish war among themselves. Kant argued that war results from the lack of the rule of law internationally, undermining properly constituted political order by causing human misery and leading to despotic rule. His third article extends beyond relationships between states to concern the relationship of states and individuals to each other, which Kant took to follow from common

---

[9] Found in Reiss (ed) (above n 4).

[10] I Kant, 'What is Enlightenment?' in Reiss (ed) (above n 4).

[11] See, eg, I Kant, 'The Metaphysics of Morals' in Reiss (ed) (above n 4).

membership of the universal state of mankind (*'ius cosmopoliticum'*, or cosmopolitan right)and it is here that we find his theory of cosmopolitanism. It holds that cosmopolitan obligations should be limited to 'universal hospitality', the right of a stranger not to be treated with hostility.

Kant's cosmopolitan right is limited in scope. Although it is a right of hospitality and not mere philanthropy, it is much more restricted than what already exists in today's European Union, for example. The right to hospitality involves no right of asylum, nor any right of permanent residence. Indeed, hospitality is a concept amenable to deconstruction, as Jacques Derrida showed.[12] For Derrida, 'hospitality' belonged to two radically distinct orders. The first, 'unconditional' hospitality, connotes a giving without limit, but the latter, 'conditional' hospitality, is finite in nature—necessarily so, because otherwise the host would be dispossessed of all of his or her possessions. Kant's hospitality is clearly conditional and limited to visiting another place. Perhaps it is limited because Kant insisted that the parties to these definitive articles be republics, which he believed would not persecute their citizens, and so further rights of asylum would not be necessary. This is overly optimistic, however, as history has shown us. Derrida's deconstruction also highlights the ambiguity of the (surprisingly related) terms 'host' and 'hostility', which share the same etymological root, generating a problematic overlap of meaning.[13] Hosts may be hostile. These ambiguities are evident in Europe today, where third-country nationals have very reduced rights in comparison with EU citizens, and even some EU citizens are treated as second class—a situation that Etienne Balibar has referred to as 'apartheid in Europe'.[14] Thus, hospitality harbours more than the trace of its hostility.

Kant provided a limited account of international justice. Although it sets out a desirable minimum, sadly not even yet reached by large areas of the world, in its limitation of cosmopolitan rights to that of hospitality, it is very cautious. Jürgen Habermas, for example, has been critical of its minimal nature.[15] Additionally, aside from the limited scope of hospitality, there is the question of how it is to be enforced. Kant's cosmopolitan principles

---

[12] J Derrida, *On Cosmopolitanism and Forgiveness*, M Dooley and M Hughes (trans) (London, Routledge, 2001). See also B Honig, 'Another Cosmopolitanism? Law and Politics in the New Europe: A Response to Seyla Benhabib' in S Benhabib (ed), *Another Cosmopolitanism*, Berkeley Tanner Lectures Series (Oxford, Oxford University Press, 2008).

[13] The two words share the same Latin root. See J Derrida, *Of Hospitality*, R Bowlby (trans) (Stanford, Stanford University Press, 2000) 77. Derrida emphasises their connectedness by merging them and inventing the word *'hostipitality'*, which simultaneously connotes acceptance and rejection.

[14] E Balibar, *We the People of Europe? Reflections of Transnational Citizenship* (Princeton, Princeton University Press, 2004).

[15] J Habermas, 'Kant's Idea of Perpetual Peace with the Benefit of 200 Years' Hindsight' in J Bohman and M Lutz-Bachmann (eds), *Perpetual Peace: Essays on Kant's Cosmopolitan Ideal* (Cambridge, Massachusetts Institute of Technology Press, 1997).

were apparently legal rather than moral rights,[16] and he envisaged the rule of law as a political project, not one of technical expertise,[17] with the emphasis on citizens as the authors of their own laws. Yet Kant stipulated no mechanism for their enforcement and specifically denied the possibility or desirability of a world state. Further, Kant's cosmopolitanism seems to run in tandem with and perhaps to depend on a rather discredited modern belief in the amelioration and linear progress of the human condition. Kant believed that he could discern a historical process toward the achievement of cosmopolitan ideals, arguing that humanity was moving toward the formation of a 'cosmopolitan system of general political security' through the means of impersonal forces of commerce and interaction of peoples in a shared globe.[18] In the twenty-first century, we are far less certain of the progress of humankind, and today's globalisation has not been orderly but contradictory and fragmentary.

Taking Cosmopolitanism into the Twenty-First Century: Habermas and International Justice

Cosmopolitanism in the twenty-first century does not maintain all of the features and arguments of Kant's *Perpetual Peace*. Although many states still occupy a strong position in the world, continuing the Westphalian order of Kant's day, there undoubtedly now exists a multi-layered global order—what has been described as 'a different architectonic',[19] which lends itself to a different type of cosmopolitanism. Many contemporary social and political theorists recommend a generally cosmopolitan approach (for example, David Held, Daniele Archibugi, Ulrich Beck, Robert Fine and Seyla Benhabib), often with a nod in acknowledgement of a postmodern ordering, as in the case of Beck, who has written of a 'post-universal' cosmopolitanism.[20]

However, this discussion will focus mainly on Habermas' cosmopolitanism, largely because Habermas has placed a greater focus on law than many of these other theorists, indeed adopting a fully worked out theory

---

[16] The German word *Recht* may refer both to 'law' and to 'right' (ie, just principles), but Kant in Perpetual Peace specifically refers to a '*ius cosmopoliticum*'. Nevertheless, Habermas has argued that Kant could not have had a legal obligation in mind, since 'his federation of nations was not organised around organs . . . that could acquire coercive authority'. Habermas, 'Kant's Idea of Perpetual Peace' (ibid) 117.

[17] Contrast the EU, which is often derided as an arena of 'technocrats' or 'eurocrats'.

[18] I Kant, 'Idea for a Universal History with a Cosmopolitan Purpose' in Reiss (ed) (above n 4).

[19] Fine (above n 3) 40.

[20] See Held, *Cosmopolitanism: Ideals and Realities* (above n 3); Archibugi (above n 3); Beck (above n 3); Fine (above n 3); and Benhabib, *The Rights of Others* (above n 3).

of law that acts as a basis for his cosmopolitanism. Habermas has provided conceptual arguments for a rule of law regime whereby laws are legitimated if they can be justified as self-imposed by those subject to them, and as satisfying universal norms such as those in universal human rights.[21] Habermas' critique of Kant's cosmopolitanism as too limited has already mentioned. Indeed, Habermas sometimes applies what Karl-Otto Apel has described as the technique of 'thinking with Kant against Kant'.[22] Habermas' cosmopolitan theory is based on 'mutual respect' rather than hospitality. But like Kant, Habermas derives his cosmopolitanism from his more general theory. There is much of value in Habermas' account of law, explaining the ambition of law to deliver justice, so my discussion on cosmopolitanism will dwell on it for some time because of the useful insights into the nature of law and justice which it delivers, although I shall argue that Habermas' form of cosmopolitanism is ultimately unrealisable.

In *Between Facts and Norms*, Habermas considered the question of how valid law is possible. Habermas argued that democracy is the only possible grounding for law's legitimacy in late modernity.[23] Law is legitimised by embodying the concurring and united will of free and equal citizens who are the authors of the law to which they are subject. Habermas' principle of universalisability holds that 'just those norms are valid to which all possibly affected persons could agree as participants in rational discourse',[24] and it is clearly related to Kant's categorical imperative.[25] However, unlike Kant's categorical imperative, Habermas' theory is dialogical and discursive in nature, taking all relevant interests into account, and it avoids some of the more troubling, metaphysical aspects of Kant's theorising about justice, which have been touched on in chapter six. Habermas' theory emphasises procedure over substance and is closely linked to his belief in communicative rationality.[26]

How does Habermas' more general theory give rise to cosmopolitanism? Already, on a very basic exposition of Habermas' theory, one can see that many of the non-state, private or global norms discussed in previous chapters are unlikely to satisfy the principle of universalizability. In no way

---

[21] J Habermas, *Between Facts and Norms* (Cambridge, Massachusetts Institute of Technology Press, 1996).

[22] K Apel, 'Kant's Perpetual Peace as Historical Prognosis from the Point of View of Moral Duty' in Bohman and Lutz-Bachmann (eds) (above n 15).

[23] See also the discussion of Habermas' account of law, above ch 2.

[24] Habermas, *Between Facts and Norms* (above n 21) 132.

[25] Kant asserted that the fundamental principle of morality is a *categorical imperative*. One formulation of it requires us to 'act only in accordance with that maxim through which you can at the same time will that it become a universal law'. I Kant, *Groundwork of the Metaphysics of Morals*, M Gregor and J Timmermann (eds) (Cambridge, Cambridge University Press, 2012) 4:421.

[26] J Habermas, *Theory of Communicative Action* (Boston, Beacon Press, 1985). Discussed above ch 2.

would all possibly affected persons have agreed to many of these measures. Yet Habermas has insisted that his theory is workable in a pluralist society in which there are competing conceptions of the good and no substantive consensus on values; this is due to the existence of 'a consensus on the procedures for the legitimate enactment of laws and the legitimate exercise of power'.[27]

To understand the nature of Habermas' theory, it is necessary first to understand his reasoning in the context of the state. The starting point for Habermas' cosmopolitanism is his suggestion that the concept of the nation state is regressive—a response to problems caused by modernity, such as the demise of religious tradition, the lack of a homogeneous set of values, and the growth of urbanisation.[28] Faced with these problems, nationhood presented itself as a new, rooted and workable basis of societal and communal relations (although, in fact, the idea of the nation was mostly contrived out of invented traditions and fictional histories).[29] Notwithstanding this concoction, the nation and its engendering of national consciousness proved to be very effective at creating bonds of solidarity between unrelated citizens with no family ties. However, while the nation state has proved efficacious in these ways and has had its social achievements, it has also proved dangerous as an idea and ideology, by distinguishing those who belong from those who do not, by its suppression of minorities and by its dependency on affective or emotional relations, which Habermas terms pre-discursive, not the product of reason, and readily manoeuvred by elites. Nationalism arises all too easily when nations are already under threat. This continues to be the case in the twenty-first century, when states are under threat from a globalisation that creates pressing problems of economic migration, poverty, environmental catastrophe and multinational exploitation.

In the face of all of this, Habermas has asserted that in the contemporary era, it is only within the context of a *Rechtsgemeinschaft* that national traditions, practices and affiliations may be affirmed and espoused. A *Rechtsgemeinschaft* may be defined as a lawful community of free and equal citizens, in contrast to a *Volksgemeinschaft*, which unites around ethnic identity. Affiliation to the *Rechtsgemeinschaft* takes the form of 'constitutional patriotism'. This has been promoted by Habermas as a bridge between the particular and the universal by offering the possibility

---

[27] J Habermas, *The Inclusion of the Other* (Cambridge, Massachusetts Institute of Technology Press, 2000) 225.

[28] For these and further arguments made by Habermas, which are explored immediately below, see J Habermas, 'The European Nation State, Its Achievements and Its Limitations: On the Past and Future of Sovereignty and Citizenship' (1996) 9(2) *Ratio Juris* 135.

[29] See B Anderson, *Imagined Communities: Reflections on the Origin and Spread of Nationalism*, 2nd edn (London, Verso, 2006); and E Hobsbawm (ed), *The Invention of Tradition* (Cambridge, Cambridge University Press, 1992).

of identification with one's nation and a self-consciousness of citizenship, but one anchored in the universal principles of the constitutional state. In a *Rechtsgemeinschaft*, positive law must be evaluated according to universal concepts of the constitution. So in Habermasian theory, the constitution would seem to take the place of a moral filter such as that of natural law, and it may help to surmount the loss of meaning in our lives that was alluded to by Max Weber,[30] and the concomitant crisis of kinship and the yearning for a shared and meaningful identity. For Habermas, the constitution is the form of law that 'a community of free and equal citizens gives itself'. Habermas understands the constitution as distinct from the state and as the ultimate source of the transformation of state power by law, because it reverses the capacity of law to serve as an instrument of power. Further, as an example of the rule of law, the constitution may contribute to a sense of attachment and commitment to a polity and hence may help overcome disenchantment.[31]

Habermas' approach might, however, seem to over idealise the constitution, rather in the way that the ideal speech situation carries a lot of weight in his general theory.[32] Clearly not all constitutions would be able to bear this weight. Constitutional patriotism also has very strong roots in the postwar German situation, in which strong and painful memories of earlier twentieth-century nationalistic excesses under the Nazi regime rendered it necessary to rebuild national identity. And indeed, the term 'constitutional patriotism' originates in Germany.[33]

The European Union as a Cosmopolitan Project?

The link to cosmopolitanism more specifically comes about in this way. Notwithstanding the close connection of 'constitutional patriotism' with recent German history, Habermas has applied the concept to both European and international integration. In the context of Europe, he has applied reasoning analogous to the German example—the 'learning from

[30] Eg, M Weber, *The Protestant Ethic and the Spirit of Capitalism* (London, George Allen & Unwin, 1948) 183.

[31] Habermas, *The Divided West* (above n 3) 131.

[32] For further on the ideal speech situation, see above ch 2.

[33] It would appear that the term '*Verfassungspatriotismus*' was first used by the political scientist Dolf Sternberger in the German national newspaper *Frankfurter Allgemeine Zeitung* on 23 May 1979 to mark the thirtieth anniversary of the German Constitution. Habermas first used the term in the context of the bitter '*historiker Streit*' in Germany in the 1980s, in which there was a reassessment by some German historians of Germany's past, along with an urging by some historians of the cessation of German reparations to Israel, and a more dominant German role in the world to reflect Germany's reborn economic power. For Habermas, this revisionism was pointless and atavistic, and he argued strongly that the only appropriate patriotism would be grounded in universal principles of the constitutional state.

catastrophe' of twentieth-century history—to highlight and warn against the risks of a Europe of nation states in economic and political competition rather than in co-operation with each other. Habermas has also taken account of Theodor Adorno's categorical imperative (which imposes a duty to ensure that 'Auschwitz would not repeat itself, that nothing similar would happen again'[34]), arguing that advocating the political union of Europe could be seen as a way to advance this aim.

Habermas further developed these thoughts in *Does Europe need a Constitution?* which was written in 2001, around the time of the debates about the now defunct European Constitution. Habermas considered how, in the twenty-first century, one of the aims of the original European Economic Community (EEC)—keeping the peace—might seem to have lost its immediate post-war resonance (although the relevance of keeping the peace survives, as the challenges of what was formerly Yugoslavia showed us in the 1990s). However, as a common project, Europe has always had further rationales other than that of peace—(namely, economic prosperity and the benefits of the Common Market), and yet in order to gain legitimation, Europe needs shared values beyond those instrumentalised in pursuance of economic gain, which lack an affective dimension and do not really bind people together.[35] Habermas suggested that Europe could take its part in countering the worrying social consequences of globalisation that national governments are unable to counter by acting alone.[36] This has some normative appeal for those who take a critical view of the impact of globalisation, and it could function to place constraints on some legal developments criticised earlier in this book. Habermas therefore called for a 'catalytic constitution'[37] for Europe to take this process further.

Indeed, in the early 2000s, the European Union made distinct attempts to embed the rule of law more deeply by drafting a 'Constitution' that was supposed to engage and motivate its citizens, inspire solidarity and provide further legitimation for the Union. However, this project of a written Constitution ultimately failed,[38] as it did not engage the European public

---

[34] T Adorno, *Negative Dialectics*, EB Ashton (trans) (New York, Seabury Press, 1966) 365.

[35] See also A Williams, *The Ethos of Europe: Values, Law and Justice in the European Union* (Cambridge, Cambridge University Press, 2010).

[36] Such consequences include the constraints placed by deregulating markets, such as to lower taxes and wages, which generates increasing inequalities.

[37] J Habermas, 'Why Europe Needs a Constitution?' (2001) 11 *New Left Review* 5–26.

[38] Many would assert that the EU already has, and for many years has had, a constitution, in the same way in which the UK has a Constitution, albeit not a codified one but one based on existing treaties and foundational documents. See, eg, J-C Piris, 'Does the European Union have a Constitution? Does It Need One?' (1999) 24 *European Law Review* 557; F Mancini, 'The Making of a Constitution for Europe' (1990) 100 *Yale Law Journal* 2403; and more generally, S Douglas-Scott, *Constitutional Law of the European Union* (London, Longman,

and was deemed unworkable after 'no' votes in the constitutional treaty referenda in France and the Netherlands. Indeed, the European public and the EU Member States seem reluctant even to accept some basic tenets of the Union's more longstanding constitution (ie, with a small 'c') for example, by rejecting the longstanding doctrine of the primacy of EU law in some cases.[39] Some countries, especially in central and eastern Europe, have feared a loss of their newly gained sovereignty at the hands of the European Union[40] and have thus been unwilling to cede primacy in case of conflicts to EU law. This reflects a reluctance to engage and commit fully to the EU project, to see it as a source of the sort of shared values within the *Rechtsgemeinschaft* that Habermas urges. The European public does not feel a 'constitutional patriotism' toward the European Union, and it has not, in Hartian terms, adopted an 'internal point of view' toward EU law.

For laws to be acceptable and to function effectively, there must be reciprocity and participation of all in their making, engagement and dialogue of citizens, not mutual suspicion and lack of trust. As already noted, Lon Fuller, in his account of the rule of law, stressed the reciprocity involved in good law-making, between citizen and law-creator.[41] Yet engagement and dialogue has not been greatly evident in the twenty-first-century European Union. On the contrary, for example, reciprocity and mutual recognition have been lacking in the context of EU criminal law, as evidenced by reactions to the European Arrest Warrant and a reluctance to trust other Member States' criminal laws and to treat them as equivalent to domestic ones.[42] The mutual respect that would seem to be a hallmark requirement of cosmopolitanism is lacking.

2002). Notably, the existing EU 'constitution' was driven in particular by the European Court of Justice rather than by acts of collective self-determination by any European 'demos'.

[39] The doctrine of supremacy of EEC law was originally established in Case 6/64 *Flaminio Costa v ENEL* [1964] ECR 585.

[40] On this, see, eg, W Sadurski, "'Solange, Chapter 3'": Constitutional Courts in Central Europe' (2008) 14 *European Law Journal*.

[41] For this, see L Fuller, *The Morality of Law* (New Haven, Yale University Press, 1964); and further above ch 8, esp the section on 'The Impoverishment Critique'.

[42] The European Arrest Warrant (EAW) (Framework Decision 2002/584/JHA 1 (EU) on the European arrest warrant and the surrender procedures between Member States OJ [2002] L 190/1) was seen as ignoring traditional safeguards on extradition such as requirement of dual criminality or protection of citizens. It thus provoked both a flurry of litigation, much of it in national courts, and a series of judicial reflections on the vexed relationship between EU and national law. Indeed, it resulted in what might be termed anarchy, given the non-application of the EAW (and release of terrorist suspects) in countries such as Germany, which found its implementation unlawful. See, eg, the Polish Constitutional Court, *Re Enforcement of a European Arrest Warrant* [2006] 1 CMLR 36; and Judgment of the German Constitutional Court of 18 July 2005, 2 BvR 2236/04.

Likewise, the Eurozone has seen a lack of solidarity between Member States.[43] Who benefits from the 'solidarity' measures of the bailouts, which have been undertaken with reluctance and only under conditions of extreme austerity? It would seem to be indebted banks and creditors in other EU Member States and elsewhere, rather than the citizens of the states in difficulty, who must face years of shrinking wages, unemployment and shrivelling public services and welfare. The handling of the Eurozone crisis also reveals a very serious deficit of democracy in the European Union, which must surely be of particular concern to a theorist such as Habermas, who stresses democracy as a crucial underpinning to law's legitimacy. Elected politicians (prime ministers, in the case of Greece and Italy) have been forced out of office, to be replaced by unelected bureaucrats or 'economic experts' with no electoral mandate. National budgets will become as much the property of EU institutions as of national governments and parliaments.[44] This is hugely troubling. All of these measures were adopted with little debate and a minimum of public awareness. Indeed, most Europeans have little idea that these changes, involving such inroads into their governments' economic sovereignty, have taken place. The EU and Member States response to the crisis of its currency has been characterised by a continuous flurry of untransparent and undemocratic measures, distancing economic governance from the control of elected governments and national parliaments, in an extremely complex and confusing mêlée of arrangements of EU law and international agreements between the states. The contemporary European Union thus does not provide an encouraging example of a *Rechtsgemeinschaft*.

The Lack of an Adequate Public Sphere

Habermas has expressed the opinion that the Enlightenment project can be put back on track by a commitment to a normatively grounded procedural

---

[43] In the context of the EU and the Euro, notably Art 125(1) TFEU, which could be seen as a 'no solidarity clause', provides:

> The Union shall not be liable for or assume the commitments of central governments, regional, local or other public authorities, other bodies governed by public law, or public undertakings of any Member State, without prejudice to mutual financial guarantees for the joint execution of a specific project. A Member State shall not be liable for or assume the commitments of central governments, regional, local or other public authorities, other bodies governed by public law, or public undertakings of another Member State, without prejudice to mutual financial guarantees for the joint execution of a specific project.

It was necessary to introduce new measures, notably the ESM, in order to make provision for future loans to troubled Member States, as well as to engage the IMF in the bailouts.

[44] For details, see Council briefing of 8 November 2011, accessible at http://www.consilium.europa.eu/uedocs/cms_data/docs/pressdata/en/ecofin/125952.pdf (accessed 12 December 2012).

paradigm of law, as he conceived it in *Between Facts and Norms*. Yet it is undoubtedly challenging to work with a Habermasian paradigm in an international setting. One problem of applying Habermasian theory to the European Union or indeed, beyond that, to the international arena, lies in the absence of a *demos* and of a public sphere. How may a Habermasian, normatively grounded, discursive procedural paradigm function in an organisation such as the European Union, in which so many decisions are taken by unelected bureaucrats or by executives (ie, Member State governments) whose decisions are not adequately scrutinised by parliaments?[45] Can a Habermasian principle of universalisability truly apply in this context?

The public sphere and communicative rationality have always played very important roles in Habermas' work, and he focused on them as early as 1962, in *The Structural Transformation of the Public Sphere*,[46] which treats accounts of dialogue in coffeehouses in eighteenth-century England as an excellent example of fora in which people come together voluntarily and participate as equals in public debate and discussion. However, Habermas acknowledged that, since the eighteenth century, the public sphere has declined and been manipulated by the mass media, interest groups and elites, leading to the etiolation and deterioration of democratic politics and instead a focus on instrumental reason and a crisis of legitimacy. 'System'—namely those self-regulating systems of economy, bureaucracy and administration, governed by powerful (often financial) elites—have come to dominate 'lifeworlds' that traditionally provided the basis for a shared identity and 'a social integration based on mutual understanding, intersubjective shared norms and collective values'.[47] In the context of globalisation, market relations have undermined social welfare policy and social justice. As Fritz Scharpf has expressed it in the specific context of the European Union:

European integration has created a constitutional asymmetry between policies promoting market efficiencies and policies promoting social protection and equality. National welfare states are legally and economically constrained by European rules of economic integration, liberalisation, and competition law, whereas efforts to adopt European social policies are politically impeded by the diversity of national welfare states, differing not only in levels of economic development and hence in their ability to pay for social transfers and services but, even more significantly, in their normative aspirations and institutional structures.[48]

---

[45] As in the case, for example, of EU 'comitology' (ie, the bureaucratic committees that dispense much of the EU's business) procedures.

[46] J Habermas, *The Structural Transformation of the Public Sphere* (Cambridge, MA, Massachusetts Institute of Technology Press, 1991 edn).

[47] J Habermas, *The Postnational Constellation: Political Essays* (Cambridge, Polity, 2001) 82.

[48] F Scharpf, 'The European Social Model: Coping with the Challenges of Diversity', MPIfG Working Paper 02/8. See also John Gray, who has denigrated the 'late twentieth-century, free-market experiment attempt to legitimate . . . severe limits on the scope and content of

Formerly robust social welfare systems are under threat in an austerity-based ideology driven by markets, and fragmentation, postmodernism and pluralism, as alternatives, have proved to be no match for the heavy demands of neoliberal orthodoxy.

However, unlike other Frankfurt school members such as Adorno and Max Horkheimer, who were deeply pessimistic over the decline of the public sphere and the conquest and invasion of lifeworlds by instrumental reason, Habermas has remained optimistic, focusing on the need for improved institutional design. He has carried over this optimism to the European context, believing in the possible formation of a civic and voluntaristic rather than ethnic identity in Europe, one that is capable of fostering an abstract solidarity between strangers going beyond national boundaries. Moreover, this voluntaristic identity would not be dominated by the market, as in the contemporary European Union. Yet given the democratic shortcomings, lack of a public sphere or notion of collective identity and self-determination, and over-dominance of market rationality in the European Union, it is hard to see how such optimism may be sustained. Habermas' theory may be prescriptively attractive, but in the absence of improved institutional design of the type he aspires to, it does not amount to an accurate description of the contemporary European Union.[49]

Indeed, to seek to apply cosmopolitanism as a theory to the European Union would appear to misunderstand the nature of either cosmopolitanism or the European Union (or both). Constitutional patriotism and shared values (derived by discursive means, based on universal principles and also capable of fostering solidarity) may be desirable, but they do not currently exist, and prospects for their achievement do not seem very high. Further, the contemporary European Union is not based solely on the sorts of universal norms that underpin cosmopolitanism. A desire for peace and non-discrimination might appear universal, but the EU Single Market is a particularistic and ideological concept. Moreover, the European Union is a bounded community. It excludes non-EU citizens from the enjoyment of most of its rights (as reflected in its critical designation as 'fortress Europe'). Why should the advanced nature of EU integration be interpreted as representing a contemporary cosmopolitan form? It represents a greater fusion of standards and norms than traditional cosmopolitanism, lacks the democratic, discursive elements that a Habermasian cosmopolitanism would seem to require, and not all EU norms are universalisable in the sense that the Habermasian principle of universalisability requires.

democratic control over economic life'. J Gray, *False Dawn: The Delusions of Global Capitalism* (London, Granta Books, 2002) 9.

[49] For Habermas' more recent reflections on the EU, see J Habermas, *Europe: The Faltering Project* (Cambridge, Polity, 2009); and J Habermas, *Zur Verfassung Europas: Ein Essay* (Frankfurt, Suhrkamp, 2011).

International law poses even greater challenges to a theorist such as Habermas, who places so much importance on democracy and on a vibrant public sphere. Yet it might be argued that the lack of democracy at international level is more manageable than the democratic deficit of the European Union, given that international law, unlike the European Union, is at present so limited in its scope and focus. International laws, due to their restricted purview, do not intrude on lifeworlds to the extent that more wide-reaching EU laws do. Nonetheless, international law is testing for democracy—treaties are usually the prerogative of the Executive,[50] bypassing legislatures. Furthermore, international organisations such as the WTO are not very democratic.[51]

Notwithstanding its challenges, Habermas also looks to the construction of the rule of law in the international arena, to a constitutionalisation of international law, based on principles of equal sovereignty, human rights and the priority of international law over state law.[52] The constitutionalisation of international law might be interpreted as a response to Carl Schmitt, an attempt to overcome the excesses and abuses of a national sovereignty based on 'friend and foe', but can international law carry this weight? International law is not armed with effective means of enforceability. For example, the International Court of Justice (ICJ) has not been willing to empower itself with a strong power of judicial review in the same way that the US Supreme Court did in *Marbury v Madison*, or that the European Court of Justice (ECJ) did in *Van Gend en Loos*.[53] In any case, as discussed, in the far more developed arena of EU law, the concept of constitutionalisation has been bitterly attacked on various grounds—some not necessarily regressive and nationalistic but rather based on the European Union's unbalanced emphasis on deep market integration and the continuously expansive membership of states, without equivalent social integration or democratic underpinnings.

---

[50] The Ponsonby Rules in the UK traditionally operated as a constitutional convention requiring the laying of the instruments of international treaties before the UK Parliament for at least 21 days before the ratification of treaties by the executive, but it did not give Parliament any control over executive action. Part 2 of the UK Constitutional Reform and Governance Act 2010 on the ratification of treaties now puts Parliamentary scrutiny of treaties on a statutory footing, although it does little to change the Ponsonby Rules.

[51] It is notable that neither the World Bank nor the IMF, which are based in Washington DC, operates on the basis of one vote for each of their members. The US has a dominant role and a larger vote share in both organisations and is able to veto measures.

[52] J Habermas, 'Does the Constitution of International Law Still Have a Chance?' in Habermas, *The Divided West* (above n 3). See also G Borradori (ed), *Philosophy in a Time of Terror: Dialogues with Jurgen Habermas and Jacques Derrida* (Chicago, Chicago University Press, 2004) 31.

[53] *Marbury v Madi*son 1 Cranch (5 US) 137 (1803); and Case 26/62 *Van Gend en Loos* [1963] ECR 1. On this, see D Halberstam, 'Constitutionalism and Pluralism in *Marbury* and *Van Gend*' in MP Maduro and L Azoulai (eds), *The Past and the Future of EU Law: Revisiting the Classics on the Fiftieth Anniversary of the Rome Treaty* (Oxford, Hart Publishing, 2008).

Yet 'constitutionalisation' has many senses,[54] and in the context of international law it may take the thinnest of forms, which may be little more than a recognition, ordering and priority of certain humanitarian and human rights norms. It has been suggested that 'constitutionalisation' need not involve an act of will by the people, nor a specific subject, unlike constitutionalism, which is perceived to require some sort of act of self-determination. Beyond this spare form, a postnational constitutionalism might not seem to be viable. Transnational identities, if they may be said to exist at all, are very thin in nature and unlikely to replace state or ethnic-based identities for the foreseeable future. There is at present no global sentiment of constitutional patriotism. Habermas seems to have acknowledged this and has suggested in later work that the constitutionalisation of international law need not take a comprehensive form but rather a power-limiting form at global level, thus building on the values of the rule of law.

Habermas envisions postnational constitutionalism as supplementing rather than replacing national patriotism. Rather than any form of world government, what Habermas seems to have in mind is some sort of inter-locking system of institutions and jurisdictions, with federal-like features that could permit and promote the integration of various types and layers of identity. But it is important that such a constitutionalism should not enable the exploitative structures mentioned in chapters six and eight to flourish,[55] nor allow powerful economic interests to limit the power of the state and its ability to regulate in critical areas. A global concept of constitutionalism should not overly focus on the right to trade, certainly not at the expense of other types of social integration. Given the lack of any viable public sphere or workable concept of democracy at global level, the limited ambitions for global constitutionalism seem apposite, as Habermas has recognised in his more recent work, urging a power-limiting rather than comprehensive constitutionalism in the international arena. This corresponds more clearly to the motivations of critical legal justice.

Other theories have also attempted to work out an application of cosmopolitanism at international level. For example, Benhabib has urged

---

[54] For different uses of the terms 'constitutionalism' and 'constitutionalisation', see M Loughlin and P Dobner (eds), *The Twilight of Constitutionalism?* (Oxford, Oxford University Press, 2009); and J Klabbers, A Peters and G Ulfstein, *The Constitutionalisation of International Law* (Oxford, Oxford University Press, 2009).

[55] Nonetheless, this approach has been criticised by some theorists as possibly legitimating what should be critiqued and providing affirmation for deficient structures. See, eg, N Krisch, *Beyond Constitutionalism: The Pluralist Structure of Postnational Law* (Oxford, Oxford University Press, 2010) 57. See also discussions of 'constitutionalism lite' in, eg, J Klabbers, 'Constitutionalism Lite' (2004) 1 *International Organizations Law Review* 31; and C Harlow, 'Global Administrative Law: The Quest for Principles and Values' (2006) 17 *European Journal of International Law* 187.

a 'republican federalism',[56] a constitutionalising structure of a set of inter-locking institutions, each with responsibility and accountability to each other. In this way, she believes that new modalities for the exercise of federalism may be created. However, Benhabib has complemented this by stressing the importance of what she calls 'democratic iterations',[57] a concept originating in Derrida's deconstruction theory, in which every iteration of a term asserts but also changes the understanding of a word, adapting its meaning, making it one's own and marking it as a creation of all and everyone. She has termed this process a 'jurisgenerative politics'.[58] A cosmopolitan, democratic iteration involves border-crossing and inter-locking—a creative and transformative approach to the meaning of rights and other concepts, whose meaning can be transformed by iterations in conversations and arguments across borders.

As an illustration of the transformative power of democratic iterations, she has pointed to the headscarf debate in France,[59] where three young Moslem women took on the received view of the French state as essentially secular, contesting it with different interpretations of freedom of expression and religion. In this way, Benhabib has asserted, the will of democratic majorities can be reconciled through public argument and deliberation in acts of democratic iterations. Yet once again this depends on the possibility of a robust public sphere in which to express and assert these iterations. Furthermore, while the concept of democratic iterations might be a useful conceptual tool for a more inclusive, demotic reworking of certain terms whose interpretations have been too long dominated by elites, the connec-tion between and the achievement of cosmopolitan ethical norms is by no means clear. All sorts of movements might utilise democratic iterations (for example, the Tea Party movement in the United States), but this does not mean that the products of their debates and deliberations will be cosmopol-itan in nature. In the context of the headscarf affair, for example, different jurisdictions have taken different approaches, with France and the United Kingdom taking very diverse approaches. Moreover, when the European Court of Human Rights determined the *Leyla Sahin* case,[60] which origi-nated in Turkey, it was willing to leave a large margin of appreciation to Turkey, finding no breach of the freedom of religion under the European Convention on Human Rights (ECHR), allowing Turkey to adopt a secu-lar approach and to ban the wearing of the headscarf in state universities.

---

[56] S Benhabib, 'Twilight of Sovereignty or the Emergence of Cosmopolitan Norms? Rethinking Citizenship in Volatile Times' in H Gautney, O Dahbour, A Dawson and N Smith (eds), *Democracy, States, and the Struggle for Global Justice* (London, Routledge, 2009).

[57] See, eg, S Benhabib, 'Democratic Iterations: The Local, the National and the Global' in Benhabib (ed), *Another Cosmopolitanism* (above n 12).

[58] Benhabib, 'Democratic Iterations' (ibid).

[59] '*L'affaire du foulard*' discussed in Benhabib, 'Democratic Iterations' (above n 57).

[60] *Leyla Sahin v Turkey* App No 44774/98 [2007] 44 EHRR 5 (Grand Chamber).

This suggests that democratic iterations do not always make their mark on national laws and approaches, and Benhabib's cosmopolitanism may be no more effectual than that of Habermas.

The Critique of Cosmopolitanism

Writers such as Habermas seek to extend and enhance more traditional concepts of cosmopolitanism. I have argued that there are problems with this extension, requiring as it does the means for a democratic involvement and/or discursive application in law-making that is hard to apply in the transnational arena. Yet there is a critique to be made even of more limited ambitions of cosmopolitanism.

For example, cosmopolitanism aligns itself with a universal concern for 'humanity'—but what is meant by this concept? Can it bear the conceptual weight cosmopolitans attach to it? Can the notion of humanity actually encourage solidarity? Will it encourage us to empathise and think of others as 'us', to have 'we feelings'? 'Humanity' appears less emotive and stirring than the more ideologically suspect concept of nationality. The anthropologist Claude Lévi-Strauss pointed out that a universal concern with humanity, with human beings as equals, is a reflection of the modern age. Past eras were more concerned with status,[61] whether someone was citizen or slave, noble or peasant. However, since the second World War, 'humanity' has come to the fore as a postholder for concern to prevent the reoccurrence of unimaginable conduct and the greatest atrocities, as in the introduction of the concept of 'crimes against humanity', which signifies criminal conduct of the greatest evil. Yet what is this 'humanity' in the context of these crimes of international law? In whose names are these prosecutions brought? Does it denote humanity at large, or the international community, or even groups of powerful states? Pessoa reflects the ambivalence of such a cosmopolitanism in the following piece of writing:

> They spoke to me of people, and of humanity.
> But I've never seen people, or humanity.
> I've seen various people, astonishingly dissimilar,
> Each separated from the next by unpeopled space.[62]

This captures the sense in which at the centre of cosmopolitanism sits something of a vacuum, attributable to the ambiguous nature of humanity.

Another common criticism of cosmopolitanism attacks its alleged universalism. Universalism presents itself as an attractive openness to other ways and practices. However, Derrida, for example, highlighted the 'alienness'

---

[61] See, eg, above ch 2.

[62] F Pessoa, *The Collected Poems of Alberto Caeiro* (Exeter, Shearsman Books, 2007).

of a universalism that seeks to subsume the new or the foreign within categories whose fundamental characteristics remain unchanged by any encounter with newcomers. Some critiques go further, alleging that universalism not only maintains its own unchanging characteristics but is actually hostile to otherness. For example, Balibar has criticised the existence of an 'apartheid' in Europe, in which, using Derridean terminology, the 'hosts' are 'hostile', and foreign immigrants are perceived as second-class citizens, as 'metics'[63] or even as the 'internal enemy'.[64] The charge is that the Kantian categorical imperative, the Rawlsian 'veil of ignorance' and even Habermas' discursive perspective function inadequately in an environment where individuals and communities wish to maintain their particular allegiances and identities, declining any 'comprehensive' outlook.[65] Religious fundamentalism, for example, looks not to any universal reason but instead regards the tenets of its particular religion as absolute. Richard Rorty,[66] in a general attack on the Enlightenment as 'the wrong project', argued for a sceptical anti-universalism—a belief in and admission of the historical contingency of our own beliefs, motivated partly by the conviction that socalled universalism and humanism have in the past proved to be far from universal and humanist. Postmodern writers such as Lyotard have called for an end to grand metanarratives such as that of universalism, demanding an anti-realism in metaphysics, along with scepticism in epistemology.

The critique of cosmopolitan universalism therefore derides it as hypocritical, seeing beneath its alleged universal concern for humanity either cultural assumptions that remain intact or even a desire for global domination. In brief, the allegation is that cosmopolitanism is a mask for Western values. This criticism is not limited to postmodern and communitarian authors. Schmitt referred to a concern for humanity as the hypocrisy of the great powers, declaring that 'he who invokes humanity wants to cheat' and deriding the Nuremberg trials (in which Schmitt himself was indicted) as 'victor's justice'.[67] Universalism has been castigated as an exercise in self-deception,[68] which, if it leads to military action in the name

---

[63] '*Metic*' was the ancient Greek term for resident alien.

[64] Balibar (above n 14).

[65] See, eg, J Tully, *Strange Multiplicity: Constitutionalism in an Age of Diversity (The Seeley Lectures)* (Cambridge, Cambridge University Press, 1995) chs 2 and 3; and C Taylor, 'The Politics of Recognition' in A Gutmann (ed), *Multiculturalism: Examining the Politics of Recognition* (Princeton, Princeton University Press, 1994) 36.

[66] See, eg, R Rorty, 'Justice as Larger Loyalty' in P Cheah and B Robbins (eds), *Cosmopolitics: Thinking and Feeling beyond the Nation* (Minneapolis, University of Minnesota Press, 1998).

[67] C Schmitt, *The Concept of the Political*, G Schwab (trans) (Chicago, University of Chicago Press, 1996) 54.

[68] See, for example, T Brennan, 'Cosmopolitanism and Internationalism' in D Archibugi (ed), *Debating Cosmopolitics* (London, Verso, 2003); and P Gowan, 'The New Liberal Cosmopolitanism' in D Archibugi (ed), *Debating Cosmopolitics* (London, Verso, 2003).

of humanity, becomes what Paul Gilroy has described as an 'armoured cosmopolitanism'.[69] Jacques Rancière has provided one of the most extreme critiques of cosmopolitan rights on a global scale, asserting that they ultimately amount only to a right of invasion, which denies the essence of human rights.[70] Although human rights have been described as 'values for a godless age',[71] their tendency to become a universal moral language that subsumes other moral discourses has already been noted. [72]

Cosmopolitan humanism and universalism have been presented as something new and improved in the twenty-first century. It is supposedly different, honest and unlike the universalism of previous imperialist generations, such as Victorian colonisers and empire-builders. And yet Gilroy has reminded us that such claims to benevolence are nothing new: nineteenth-century imperialists also relied on 'benign humanitarianism' in their empire-building, justifying the scramble for Africa, for example, in the name of peace, as exemplified by Joseph Chamberlain's 'messianic civilisationism'.[73] The problem is that a universal scale has in fact often been used as a device to measure the 'civilised' or 'desirable' characteristics of other peoples, and thus it has facilitated differential or abusive treatment of migrants in the twenty-first century as much as the colonial ill-treatment of 'backward' societies in the nineteenth century.[74]

There are responses to these claims. One counter is that there was clearly less of universalism and the rule of law in Victorian imperialism than at first glance. Just as contemporary global institutions such as the IMF and World Bank may not provide shining examples of equal treatment and the rule of law, so the nineteenth-century colonial practices of the East India company or of occupying states, which applied different rules for indigenous populations than for the colonial governors, also failed to observe the rule of law and its requirement of equal treatment. They did not provide genuine examples of universalism or cosmopolitanism but instead illustrated a pernicious partiality. Hannah Arendt's response to the critique of

---

[69] P Gilroy, *After Empire: Melancholia or Convivial Culture* (London, Routledge, 2004).

[70] J Rancière, 'Who is the Subject of the Rights of Man?' (2004) *South Atlantic Quarterly* 297–310.

[71] F Klug, *Values for a Godless Age: the History of the Human Rights Act and its Political and Legal Consequences* (London, Penguin, 2000).

[72] See, eg, W Twining (ed), *Human Rights, Southern Voices* (Cambridge, Cambridge University Press, 2009); and U Baxi, *Human Rights in a Posthuman World* (New Delhi, Oxford University Press, 2007). See also above ch 9.

[73] Gilroy (above n 69). Chamberlain declared in 1893, 'It is our duty to take our share in the work of civilization in Africa.' Quoted in N Palmer and H Perkins, *International Relations* (Boston, Houghton Mifflin, 1969) 186. However, Andrew Roberts has argued, 'Chamberlain's messianic belief in colonies and imperial expansion . . . resulted in the Boer War, the British Empire's Vietnam.' A Roberts, 'Salisbury: The Empire Builder Who Never Was' (1999) 49 *History Today*.

[74] D Manderson, 'Not Yet: Aboriginal People and the Deferral of the Rule of Law' (2008) 29/30 *ARENA*.

universalism was to stress that the only universalism possible in the modern age is one of rights—of 'the right to have rights'.[75] This response denies the premise of the rights critique (a premise that seeks to undermine the very concept and practice of human rights) and provides another reason for cosmopolitan law to focus on human rights.

Furthermore, contemporary cosmopolitans argue that they do not vaunt grand, homogenising metanarratives of universalism but instead seek a reconciliation of the universal and the plural incompatible with homogenising claims, labelling such efforts as 'post-universalism'.[76] A prominent defender of this type of cosmopolitanism is Anthony Appiah.[77] In Appiah's opinion, cosmopolitanism actively resists the forms of 'universalising' humanism, such as those of the Victorian missionaries who attempted to impose their purportedly superior ways. Appiah's approach is to urge us not to interpret cosmopolitanism as a belief in objective human nature with guaranteed foundations, because it is almost impossible to agree with others on such a level of principle. In Appiah's view, agreement on such a fundamental level is not in fact necessary, as we can already identify so many more points of agreement on a local and contingent level. He sees cosmopolitan agreement as taking place on a contingent, particular level rather than that of universals.

Other theorists have also proposed techniques to avoid the dangers of an imperialist cosmopolitanism. For example, Iris Marion Young interpreted the ideal city life as a 'being together' of strangers who seek no overarching group identity, community or loyalty yet remain open to an 'unassimilated otherness'.[78] In this way, different groups would never be completely outside of nor estranged from each other. Gilroy has noted the value of estrangement from the cultural habits one is born into, suggesting that we must learn to procure a systematic disloyalty to our civilisation if we are to understand it, to interact equitably with others.[79] He has proposed a new 'geopiety', prompted by the vision of the first photos of Earth from space, an image of the globe not as limitless but as small and fragile, requiring a common consideration of imperilled existence, a 'planetarity' rather than globalisation.[80]

---

[75] H Arendt, *The Origins of Totalitarianism* (Boston, Houghton Mifflin Harcourt, 1973).

[76] See, eg, Beck (above n 3); and P Berman, 'Conflict of Laws, Globalization, and Cosmopolitan Pluralism' (2005) 51 *Wayne Law Review* 1105, 1113, who sees cosmopolitanism as 'a middle ground between universalism on the one hand and strict territoriality on the other . . . and that it seeks to understand multiple affiliations'.

[77] A Appiah, 'Citizens of the World' in MJ Gibney (ed), *Globalising Rights: Oxford Amnesty Lectures 1999* (Oxford, Oxford University Press, 2003).

[78] IM Young, 'The Ideal of Community and the Politics of Difference' in L Nicholson (ed), *Feminism/Postmodernism* (London, Routledge, 1989) 317.

[79] Gilroy (above n 69).

[80] Ibid.

Figure 10-1: Earth rising, as seen from the moon—an inspiration for 'planetarity'?

Cosmopolitan 'Law'?

Yet one of the strongest critiques of cosmopolitanism (and perhaps the most salient, for the purposes of this book) questions the very possibility of a *cosmopolitan law*. For many theorists who appear to be avowedly cosmopolitan, such as Kant and Habermas, law plays an important role. Yet what exactly is cosmopolitan law? Which legal, moral and political principles inform it? Is cosmopolitan law limited to measures that are humanitarian in nature, with the individual at their centre (such as international human rights or principles regulating crimes against humanity and humanitarian intervention), or should it also include the vast growth in measures regulating international business and trade, which are considered to be of a great importance in international communication (to the benefit of global capitalism)? Kant interpreted cosmopolitan law as expressing the equal moral worth of persons in the 'universal community',[81] yet he limited its scope to the right of universal hospitality. The attempts of latter-day cosmopolitans such as Habermas to extend cosmopolitanism to the transnational sphere would result in a considerable extension of the concept of cosmopolitan 'law', well beyond that envisioned by Kant.

The basis of cosmopolitan law and legal theory would seem to be the notion that law ought to be underpinned and constrained by principles of universal worth, respect and justice. But this is a very abstract statement,

[81] See Reiss (ed) (above n 4) 108.

normative in nature. It does not amount to a set of positive laws. It prompts two further questions. First, does cosmopolitan law already exist as an array of positive laws embodying these principles of universal human worth and justice? Second, does cosmopolitanism rather operate as a critical theory, functioning as a standard of review for existing laws? It is certainly the case that much writing about cosmopolitanism is normative in form, prescribing a desirable state of affairs rather than describing an existing state of affairs. But if this is its totality, then we cannot really say that cosmopolitan law exists as such. (There is also the third possibility: that cosmopolitanism functions *both* as a set of existing laws and as a standard of appraisal for positive law—thus expressing the 'both/and' motif familiar throughout this book. I will return to this.)

So the nature of the question amounts to this: can we say that the vague, normative principles of cosmopolitanism (which are necessarily vague because the concepts from which they derive—ie, 'humanity', 'universal respect'—are likewise extremely broad and abstract) also give rise to legal provisions? If so, what is the basis for them? What are their formal sources? What duties and rights do they create? Which institutions are necessary to enforce them?

Let us start with some basics—sources. As Pavlos Eleftheriadis has argued, cosmopolitan law seems to lack a strict theory of sources.[82] Lacking a singular, bounded, state community, it cannot rely on traditional theories which evoke bounded theories for the origins of law, such as contractarian theories; nor can cosmopolitanism point to unified, hierarchical sources of law in the way that twentieth-century theories of legal positivism did (however successful or unsuccessful such attempts at grounding state law have actually been in practice). Some candidates for cosmopolitan 'law' (namely, those that take the form of, eg, international human rights treaties) might seem to be grounded in the usual sources of international law (ie, the agreement of sovereign states), but not all examples of what we might wish to call positive cosmopolitan law take this form.

If the traditional sources of law do not apply, then what might be the basis for cosmopolitan law? One might be tempted to fall back on a tradition natural law argument for its existence. The emperor Marcus Aurelius referred to 'the natural law of fellowship'.[83] Natural law might provide a viable basis for a law of 'common humanity'. John Rawls also described what he perceived to be a 'fundamental natural duty of justice' requiring us to 'support and comply with just institutions'.[84] But notably, as the main basis for his theory of justice, Rawls used the social contract device of the

---

[82] P Eleftheriadis, 'Cosmopolitan Law' (2003) 9(2) *European Law Journal* 241.
[83] Marcus Aurelius, *Meditations* (London, Penguin Classics, 2006 edition) Bk III.
[84] J Rawls, *Theory of Justice* (Cambridge, MA, Belknap Press of Harvard University Press, 1971) 115.

Original Position rather than natural duties, resulting in a theory of justice applying for the most part only within states.

Eleftheriadis, who has provided one of the most thorough theories of cosmopolitan law, grounds it in a 'substantive code of political morality' operating internationally,[85] which he takes to be the result of near-universal agreement in principle, in the vast majority of states, over a set of basic principles of good government. These principles of political morality, he has suggested, are based not necessarily on formal sources of law but on the persuasive force of fundamental common principles of political justice. They are not metaphysical in nature, as natural law is, but rather the result of a political consensus, and they therefore avoid some of the traditional criticisms of natural law—notably, that it is an inappropriate theory for a post-metaphysical age. Many of these principles of political morality also take concrete legal form as treaties or other forms of international law—for example, international human rights treaties and humanitarian law, or conventions stipulating universal jurisdiction for the prosecution of certain crimes, such as torture, piracy, hijacking or genocide.[86]

The assertion of a universal jurisdiction reflects certain universal commitments towards all persons, wherever situated, and also the view that no atrocious crime should go unpunished. It also seeks to guarantee that there exist no morally arbitrary judgements among persons, at least as far as these extreme crimes are concerned. The creation of the International Criminal Court is evidence of a cosmopolitan law providing a residual forum for prosecution, ensuring that for certain crimes, prosecution should always be a possibility.[87] Courts have also shown an awareness of and a critical attitude toward the existence of 'legal black holes', whereby individuals have been unable to bring claims to protect their human rights. For example, the US Supreme Court rejected the argument of the US government that the Geneva Conventions on the humanitarian treatment of prisoners and victims of war did not apply to what they chose to term 'enemy combatants' captured in Afghanistan.[88] The UK House of Lords acknowledged the existence of universal norms of *jus cogens*, including torture in the *Pinochet* case.[89]

---

[85] Eleftheriadis (above n 82) 251.

[86] Universal jurisdiction is a principle of public international law in which states can claim criminal jurisdiction over persons whose alleged crimes were committed outside the prosecuting state's jurisdiction, regardless of nationality, country of residence or any other relation with the prosecuting state. Crimes of universal jurisdiction under international law have been established by treaty, as well as by custom. Such treaties include, inter alia, the Geneva Conventions (1949), the Hostage Taking Convention (1979), the Torture Convention (1984) and the International Convention for the Suppression of Terrorist Bombings (1998).

[87] With the few exceptions of those states that have not signed up to the ICC, including, notably, the US.

[88] *US v Hamdan* 126 SCt.

[89] *R v Bow Street Magistrates, ex p Pinochet Ugarte (No 3)* [1999] 2 All ER 97.

These laws together form a corpus of positive, cosmopolitan law, crystallising around a concern for equal respect for human beings, derived not from contractarian nor from legalistic, rationalistic accounts of law but from a consensus of opinion in their desirability and worth. They differ from traditional international law in exemplifying a derogation from the state sovereignty doctrine, as they place distinct limits on what states may do to citizens and enable individuals to bring claims, regardless of traditional rules of jurisdiction. So to this extent, cosmopolitan law may be said to exist in a positive form. Figure 10-2, a photograph of portions of the former Berlin Wall placed in front of the European Court of Human Rights, poignantly illustrates this dimension of cosmopolitan law. For the Court not only applies a form of cosmopolitan law (namely, international human rights law) but also has had to determine the human rights implications of the shooting of those who sought to escape over the Berlin Wall from former East Germany.[90]

However, does cosmopolitan 'law' extend beyond these humanitarian, human rights norms and crimes of universal jurisdiction? Clearly, some theorists believe that it does. Habermas' arguments have already been discussed. Eleftheriadis, for his part, has classified the European Union

Figure 10-2: A piece of the Berlin Wall in front of the European Court of Human Rights, Strasbourg: cosmopolitan law breaking boundaries?

[90] App Nos 34044/96, 35532/97 and 44801/98 *Streletz, Kefler, Krenz v BRD*, ECtHR (22 March 2001).

as 'a cosmopolitan legal order', as 'an example of the new category of cosmopolitan law: the four freedoms,[91] the principle of non-discrimination and proportionality'.[92] Yet as I have already argued, the features of the European Union (for example, its Single Market, its energetic competition policy) go beyond the enforcement of laws based on universal human respect to encompass more specific, partial forms of law. *A fortiori*, this applies to those types of measures being enacted in the austerity drive underpinning the EU response to the euro crisis.

To be sure, EU or international business regulations clearly play an important part in the creation of a law beyond the state. Kant most certainly stressed the importance of trade to the growth of cosmopolitanism,[93] and free trade has undoubtedly been of huge importance to the EU project.[94] Jeremy Waldron, in the context of a dialogue with Benhabib over cosmopolitanism, suggested that cosmopolitanism occurs in more 'mundane' encounters than she had allowed for, through the frequent interactions of commerce, which 'coalesce into informal norms, which reflect relations between people in non-state created ways'.[95] Waldron argued that these interactions are truly democratic, because they are generated through ordinary life in which there exist 'no problematic or invidious exclusions'.[96] Yet once again, we should be very cautious here. The global economic and business communities may perhaps be 'cosmopolitan' in nature, to the extent that they build relations between different parts of the world[97] and play their part in creating a certain worldly cosmopolitanism (populated by international executives, bankers and lawyers, who read the *Financial Times, Economist* and *Wall Street Journal,* and stock up thousands of air miles); but they do not really seem to be based on any great desire to promote mutual respect and equality between anybody other than the already rather uniform economic and business communities. The concern for humanity is limited. In Habermasian terms, they are liable to represent strategic action and distorted communication—for example, when the language of universal human rights is used only to open markets or protect property rights; when the free movement of

---

[91] The four 'fundamental freedoms' of EU law are the free movement of goods, services, persons and capital.

[92] Eleftheriadis (above n 82) 259.

[93] See, eg, Kant, 'Perpetual Peace' (above n 4); and Kant, 'Idea for a Universal History' (above n 18).

[94] See, eg, Eleftheriadis (above n 82). In the context of the WTO, see also E-U Petersmann, 'Human Rights, International Economic Law and "Constitutional Justice"' (2008) *European Journal of International Law* 769.

[95] J Waldron, 'Cosmopolitanism Norms' in Benhabib (ed) (above n 12) 84–95.

[96] Ibid, 97.

[97] See, eg, E-U Petersmann, 'European and International Constitutional Law: Time for Promoting Cosmopolitan Democracy in the WTO' in G de Burca and J Scott (eds), *The European Union and the World Trade Organization* (Oxford, Hart Publishing, 2001).

goods or capital is classified as a fundamental right;[98] or when economic globalisation is seen as the only path to well-being, its products not as manufactured goods but as desirable lifestyle choices.

These types of transnational laws and measures will be considered in the next chapter. However, it is suggested that in this context, cosmopolitanism operates better as a *critique* or standard of review of laws such as those of the European Union or WTO, rather than as an *embodiment* of those laws. David Held, for example, has suggested that there is a need for a bridge between human rights law and international economic law—between a formal commitment to impartial treatment for all and a geopolitics all too often driven by special interests—if what he terms 'nautonomy' (namely, 'the assymetrical production and distribution of life-chances which limits and erodes the possibilities of political participation'[99]) is not to prevail. A flavour of the irony of this commercial sort of 'cosmopolitanism' is caught by Figure 10-3, an image of a Starbucks cup bearing one in a series of 'inspirational quotes'. In this case, the words are from the curator of a leading 'conference' of thinkers favouring global over national citizenship, which might perhaps place Kant's 'world citizen' in the minds of many consuming their daily shot of caffeine (produced, however, by a global corporation and costing more than the daily wages of many workers around the world).

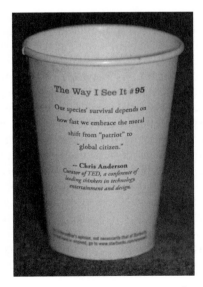

Figure 10-3: A cosmopolitan cup courtesy of Starbucks?

[98] This has long been a criticism of the case law of the European Court of Justice on fundamental rights. For a seminal critique, see J Coppel and A O'Neill, 'The European Court of Justice: Taking Rights Seriously?' (1992) 29 *Common Market Law Review* 669.

[99] Held, *Democracy and the Global Order* (above n 3) 210.

Conclusion

Cosmopolitanism may be criticised both for being too idealistic, bland and ineffectual and for being frequently unenforceable in practice, thus failing to take us beyond Kant's (legally unenforceable) right to hospitality. This would be unfair. There have been achievements: the wide ambit of the post-war international human rights movement, the prosecution of war crimes and crimes against humanity, the fact that some former and present leaders are afraid to travel abroad for fear of recriminations due to past conduct, after the precedent set by the *Pinochet* case. Cosmopolitanism puts both individual rights and individual responsibility at the centre of international law and seeks to construct a sense of universal responsibility, distinct from the power of mightier states to intervene and act as 'global police'. To be sure, cosmopolitanism may be usurped by power, but as Fine has pointed out, criticism can fall short of what it seeks to criticise.[100] One may concede that the meaning of cosmopolitanism has sometimes been hijacked. However, as with the rule of law, the fact that the coinage of cosmopolitanism is sometimes debased should not diminish its value. Cosmopolitanism is a constructive attempt to render justice globally, even if it has not always succeeded, and power, self-interest and contingency, have too often played their part in world history.[101] To be sure, intervention in other jurisdictions may be an exercise of twenty-first-century imperialism. But on other occasions, resistance to intervention (eg, in the event of genocide) in the name of anti-imperialism may simply serve to glorify and legitimate violence. Cosmopolitanism recognises this.

For the present, cosmopolitanism's main concern is with relations and appreciation of interconnectedness between people. Its impact on justice and law is as yet rather limited—at least to human rights and other very fundamental norms. Although it evinces a concern for human suffering, it does not intrude very deeply into the field of social justice, certainly not to the extent of establishing clear obligations, although Pogge's argument for a global, redistributive justice, discussed in chapter six, presents an extremely strong case, carefully crafted in terms of negative duties.

Fine's suggestion is that we should think in terms of 'a cosmopolitan research agenda' rather than in terms of a fixed state to be achieved.[102] Cosmopolitanism presents both a challenge to modern ways of thinking (particularly the tendency to identify some socially situated, contingent particularism with the interests of humanity as a whole) and also a challenge to the postmodernist identification of universalism with the

---

[100] Fine (above n 3).
[101] Ibid, ch 1.
[102] Ibid, Conclusion.

suppression of difference and the exclusion of the Other. Cosmopolitanism is therefore complex in nature, apposite to a complex age. Fine has interpreted it as 'cathedral-like' in structure, rather than taking the classic form of an ancient Greek temple. This is because it is hybrid, fluid, reflecting both social systems in constant flux and metamorphic tensions; it recognises the complexity of human aspirations, which should not and cannot be circumscribed by national fantasies and primordial communities.[103] Yet perhaps no single architectural style adequately captures the notion of cosmopolitanism. I would suggest that it has greater affinity with a complete city—in its span, fluidity, motion and mixture of ideas and views.

I have taken some time to consider what cosmopolitanism, and in particular, cosmopolitan law, amounts to. Earlier in this book, I identified a transnational element, a crossing of boundaries, as a key element of law after modernity. Cosmopolitan law exemplifies this. However, I have also been critical of the capacity of contemporary law to provoke injustice and have suggested a need for mechanisms to ameliorate this. For many theorists, cosmopolitanism denotes an ethical outlook, a normative approach of a universal nature. But cosmopolitan law is more than mere outlook and takes the form of enforceable laws. But they are limited in nature—mainly to human rights—and as such, also subject to the critique and ambiguities of human rights detailed in chapter nine. Furthermore, the accounts and theories of cosmopolitan law by authors such as Habermas and Eleftheriadis seem overly ambitious. Cosmopolitan law does not take us much beyond international human rights law, with humanitarian law and universal jurisdiction (aspects of an international rule of law) appended. As a *moral* theory, cosmopolitanism has greater ambitions, but they have not yet been realised in law, and for reasons given earlier in the chapter, I believe them to be unrealistic, too often based on the type of ideal thinking criticised in chapter six, if not ultimately unrealisable. These more ambitious elements of cosmopolitan theory may function as an ethical critique of existing laws but do not constitute a form of *legal* justice. Their ability to deter injustice is limited.

---

[103] See, eg, J Waldron, 'Minority Cultures and the Cosmopolitan Alternative' in W Kymlicka (ed), *The Rights of Minority Cultures* (Oxford, Oxford University Press, 1995).

11

Beyond Cosmopolitanism: The Murky World of Governance and Global 'Justice'

The subject of cosmopolitanism has become complicated by the tendency of some authors to expand it beyond its natural and coherent sense to include within its ambit international business regulation, economic constitutionalism and strategies of good governance—and to capitalise on cosmopolitanism's normative core by claiming these forms of regulation as a type of 'global justice'. This chapter argues that this conjunction is wrong and confused in at least two ways. First, these interactions, practices and measures are not forms of cosmopolitanism. Second, they are not examples of global justice or a global rule of law.

In this chapter, I pay particular attention to situations in which 'formal' law may be thin on the ground. This is especially visible in the growth of informal, flexible, private or non-state 'governance' organisations and networks, which undermine accountability and the possibility of justice. Much writing about 'global justice' is of a very vague nature, mixing together different concepts such as 'global constitutionalism', 'economic constitutionalism', 'global pluralism', governance and so on, often aiming to bring them all under the umbrella of some sort of nebulous cosmopolitanism. In this chapter, I seek to unravel this confusion in order to determine which, if any, of these notions are actually effective as forms of justice, or at least constraints on injustice. The conclusion is that most operate as forms of global 'regulation' rather than justice and are themselves in need of checks and constraints.

Much contemporary law concerns a subject matter rather different from that which lies at the basis of the human-centred focus of cosmopolitanism (discussed in the last chapter). Rather than human rights, contemporary law tends to concern a different form of regulation—trade in goods, supply of utilities, standards for financial or other professional services. To be sure, where this regulation has an international dimension to it, then it has its own sort of 'cosmopolitanism' and international connectedness. Jeremy Waldron's critique of theorists such as Seyla Benhabib for having insufficient regard to 'the dense thicket of rules that sustain our life together ...

because we don't like commerce' has already been cited in the last chapter, and Waldron's suggestion is that cosmopolitanism should focus as much on 'quotidian norms' as for example on 'l'affaire du foulard'.[1]

Kant was interested in trade and its possibilities, as well as its wrongs, but as we have already seen, his vision of the rule of law was based on the right of peoples to give themselves a civil constitution, not only on technical expertise and commercial transactions. As I have already argued, it is hard to conceive of the vast body of international trade, finance and business regulation as cosmopolitan in nature, although it may be that cosmopolitan norms may function as a *critique* of them in some cases.[2] Too much of contemporary corporate, commercial or financial law is rather nebulous and shadowy in nature, indicative of a regard for powerful private interests rather than the 'living democracy' that Waldron suggests, and reflective not of a universal regard for humanity and respect for others but of economic transactions generating all sorts of externalities, over which those affected have very little power. The remainder of this chapter considers how, or indeed if, the values of cosmopolitanism and critical legal justice might be satisfied in the field of global commercial interactions and in the more amorphous, opaque regions of law and governance.

It has already been argued in this book that existing arrangements of governance and 'reflexive' regulation have a structural impact that may wreak injustice. In the transformation from a command-and-control archetype to the contemporary regulatory state, the nature of law-making, or regulation more generally, has become dispersed and fragmentary. One of the most pressing questions of legal theory has been how law's coercion may be justified,[3] and yet when power and coercion switch from the public to the non-state sphere, there is insufficient investigation into the constraints that operate on this swiftly growing force. The power of coercion is so formidable that it must be located within a framework of a maximum of checks and balances. At the very minimum, critical legal justice requires that institutions of governance should be able to limit and constrain the potential for abuse of power. What principles and/or standards should be applied? Public law has over some time developed a set of principles to constrain the exercise of power—such as duties to act fairly, to hear both sides, to give reasons, to act proportionately—as well as imposed structural principles such as the rule of law, democracy

---

[1] J Waldron, 'Cosmopolitan Norms' in S Benhabib (ed), *Another Cosmopolitanism*, Berkeley Tanner Lectures Series (Oxford, Oxford University Press, 2008) 84–95.

[2] Contra the views of Waldron and Ernst-Ulrich Petersmann. See, eg, E-U Petersmann, 'European and International Constitutional Law: Time for Promoting Cosmopolitan Democracy in the WTO' in G de Burca and J Scott (eds), *The European Union and the World Trade Organization* (Oxford, Hart Publishing, 2001).

[3] See, eg, R Dworkin, *Law's Empire* (Cambridge, MA, Harvard University Press, 1986).

and separation of powers, and substantive principles of human rights. However, many, if not most, of these principles have little purchase in the private law domain. Yet powerful private interests, such as corporations or trade unions, often wield considerable power—indeed, sometimes in excess of that of states. Their actions should be subject to standards capable of controlling the abuse of power,[4] but most of the time they are not, unless the institution concerned may be characterised as some sort of 'public body' or as exercising some sort of 'public function'.[5] The controls of public law are usually still seen as somehow inapplicable to control private power. Instead, a much lighter touch of regulation is applied, and different standards operate to constrain actions of private parties, such as unconscionability, good faith or the 'neighbour principle', when contract, property rights or negligent action are at issue. This is partly because private law has been perceived as focused on different concerns, and the autonomy of private individuals taken to require protection from state interference. Such an approach derives from a more general liberal desire to leave space for individuals to pursue their own conception of the good, free from government interference. The capacity to choose is prioritised over the constraint of power. This includes freedom to conclude contracts, buy property, move capital, conduct a business, trade, etc. In contrast, the state is seen as wielding vast amounts of potentially invasive power and thus needing the constraints of public law principles. Yet the rule of law is also based on the value of individual autonomy, and critical legal justice requires not only the predictability and stability necessary for individual choice but also the constraint of power. Law's virtue is not only that of ordered liberty and consistency.

The situation is particularly critical on a global level, where even the minimal kinds of domestic constraints are usually absent. Decisions taken at international level are distant from the usual accountability mechanisms of representative democracy. There exists no world government or global demos in whose name governance takes place. Although much norm creation has shifted to a global level, prospects for democratic governance beyond the nation state are uncertain. Moreover, in spite of talk of 'economic constitutionalism',[6] there is no effective world constitutional system

---

[4] See, eg, Sir John Laws, 'Public Law and Employment Law: Abuse of Power' (1997) *Public Law* 466; and D Oliver, *Common Values and the Public–Private Divide* (Cambridge, Cambridge University Press, 1999).

[5] These are the tests under UK public law. See, eg, *YL v Birmingham City Council* [2007] UKHL 27, in the context of when a duty to observe human rights applies.

[6] Eg, E-U Petersmann, *Constitutional Functions and Constitutional Problems of International Economic Law* (Fribourg, University of Fribourg Press, 1991); and DZ Cass, 'The "Constitutionalization" of International Trade Law: Judicial Norm-Generation as the Engine of Constitutional Development in International Trade' (2001) 12 *European Journal of International Law* 39.

that constrains power in an institutionalised way, through mechanisms such as checks and balances. Nor does there appear to be a great desire for an international power-constraining constitution of the Habermasian sort. This has unfortunate consequences. There exists a high degree of fragmentation of international institutions—with different institutions serving different purposes, without any overarching authority. The weakness and fragmentation of global governance and lack of effective regulation, along with an exclusionary mode of operation (ie, one in which those who manage and oversee institutional operations are not usually the same as those who bear the consequences of those same institutional actions[7]) have allowed the growth of risk and, ultimately, have led to crisis—for example, in the financial and environmental fields.[8]

In these circumstances, some authors have hailed the growth of a 'global administrative law' and urge (or even argue for the current existence of) a set of principles that could ameliorate this situation by imposing controls on global regulation and helping to address the fragmented nature of governance at global level.[9] Such principles are largely procedural in nature, and like the already established principles in national systems of administrative law, they are largely derived from the rule of law to ensure that a system of checks and balances on decision-taking is applied, in order to control power. The emergence of such global principles has been viewed as a common trend in global governance, with the attraction that principles are more flexible than cumbersome procedures of international treaties—making them particularly desirable as a form of constraint on decentred areas of governance. However, there exists a lack of agreement as to the identity of global administrative principles and, indeed, on whether they exist at all. A list of *desiderata* might include: fairness, rationality, accountability, legality, impartiality, access to grievance procedures and openness. However, not all of these principles are observed equally in all jurisdictions, and it is doubtful if there could be said to be a consensus for their application on a global scale. What exists at present is evidence for only a very limited application of some principles in the context of some international administrative law proceedings.[10]

---

[7] See section 'Accountability' below.

[8] D Held, *Cosmopolitanism: Ideals and Realities* (Cambridge, Polity Press, 2010) ch 6.

[9] On the growth of a global administrative law, see generally B Kingsbury, RB Stewart, N Krisch, 'The Emergence of Global Administrative Law' (2005) 68 *Law and Contemporary Problems* 15; and (more critically) C Harlow, 'Global Administrative Law: The Quest for Principles and Values' (2006) 17 *European Journal of International Law* 187.

[10] Eg, for emergence of a duty to give reasons. See WTO Appellate Body, United States— *Import Prohibition of Certain Shrimp and Shrimp Products*, WT/DS58/AB/R Doc No 98-3899 (12 October 1998).

However, one of the attractions of such a common set of principles is that it could be applied across a wide range of entities and governance structures. According to one set of scholars:

> Global administrative bodies include formal intergovernmental regulatory bodies, informal intergovernmental regulatory networks and coordination arrangements, national regulatory bodies operating with reference to an international intergovernmental regime, hybrid public-private regulatory bodies, and some private regulatory bodies exercising transnational governance functions of particular public significance.[11]

As the authors acknowledged, defining global administrative bodies in this way would require 'that much of global governance can be understood and analysed as administrative action',[12] including, as subjects of global administration, individuals, corporations, nongovernment organisations (NGOs) and other collectivities, as well as states. At present, the application of a set of global administrative principles has the status of a normative project rather than reflecting the existence of a state of affairs. Moreover, there are different normative arguments for application of administrative principles: internal administrative accountability, protection of private rights or the rights of states, and promotion of democracy.[13] While there exists scope for an application of global principles on all of these levels, the argument of this book is that it is particularly important that such principles reflect critical legal justice rather than the private rights application of rule of law preferred by neoliberalism and more prevalent among international institutions to date, which has given corporate concerns a dominance in dispute settlement and has led to an emphasis on economic rights and the interests of companies over human rights. With regard to the third candidate for a normative underpinning of global principles (ie, implementing democracy), as has already been argued, scope for democracy at international level is extremely limited, and suggestions such as those of Anne-Marie Slaughter[14] (or Waldron) as to the democracy of international networks or commercial interactions risk privileging the transactions of elites. These principles remain *desiderata*, evidence perhaps of a growing trend, but nothing more concrete as yet.

Reflexive Justice?

In the absence of an existent set of global administrative principles, we must look elsewhere for avenues for critical legal justice. In parallel with

---

[11] Kingsbury, Stewart and Krisch (above n 9) 17.
[12] Ibid, 17.
[13] Ibid, 43.
[14] AM Slaughter, *A New World Order* (Princeton, Princeton University Press, 2004).

Gunther Teubner's notion of 'reflexive law', it has been suggested that what is needed is a 'reflexive' notion of justice,[15] which would be able to work at multiple levels and across types of governance. In this complex situation, talk tends to be of 'good governance strategies',[16] and efficiency and effectiveness are valued over the rule of law, public law values or international democracy. Such good governance strategies have as their aim an increase in both organisational effectiveness and legitimacy. Appropriately for a pluralism of laws, there are many different such strategies, which may be applied simultaneously by any organisation. A move away from public law values to governance strategies tends to reflect a view that the rule of law is inappropriate for contemporary regulation,[17] that it is too associated with the law of rules and with precise and determinate provisions to be appropriate for reflexive governance. The value placed on rendering regulation calculable in advance, by means of use of generally applicable rules and principles, has been seen as incompatible with flexible, informal, facilitative governance. Rather, the drift has been toward a non-hierarchical approach that assists parties in self-regulation or in finding suitable regulatory solutions. In such situations, law does not seem to be in charge, and there is less scope for critical legal justice. Indeed, reflexive justice has a tendency to be as problematic as reflexive law. The critical question is whether such 'good governance' strategies are capable of checking injustice. Generally, they are not. This deserves a closer look.

For example, one strategy is related to Max Weber's focus on the benefits of expert bureaucratic governance. In this way, legitimacy is gained by the efficient and 'optimific' results of supposedly neutral, expert policymaking. Such an approach has been recommended and in fact operates to a certain extent within the European Union.[18] What Fritz Scharpf has characterised as 'output legitimacy'—the problem-solving quality of laws and rules[19]—means that a political system and specific policies may be legitimated by their success. In contrast, 'input legitimacy' refers to a particular quality of a decision-making process leading to laws and rules, and the view that those who are forced to comply with the rules ought to have an input in the rule-making processes. 'Output legitimacy' is lighter in

---

[15] See, eg, N Fraser, *Scales of Justice* (New York, Columbia University Press, 2009) 73.

[16] The IMF, World Bank and OECD stress good governance. See, eg, the good governance factsheet on the IMF website at http://www.imf.org/external/np/exr/facts/gov.htm (accessed 14 December 2012). See also European Commission White Paper on European Governance (WPEG), COM(2001) 428 final [2001] OJ C287/1, which highlights five 'good governance' principles: openness, participation, accountability, effectiveness and coherence.

[17] For further on this, see L McDonald, 'The Rule of Law and the New Regulatory State' (2004) 33 *Common Law World Review* 197, who repudiates this view.

[18] See, eg, A Moravcsik, 'Reassessing Legitimacy in the European Union' (2002) 40 *Journal of Common Market Studies* 603.

[19] F Scharpf, *Regieren in Europa* (Frankfurt, Campus Verlag, 1999); and F Scharpf, *Governing in Europe: Effective and Democratic?* (Oxford, Oxford University Press, 1999).

touch and operates as a governance strategy, unlike input legitimacy, which is more closely related to some sort of democratic engagement.

There is also a theory of good governance that rests on clarity and transparency of measures, features of which are closely related to the values of the rule of law. For example, the World Bank, along with most other international organisations, now provides annual reports and other documents containing detailed information about its work and projects on its website. Other mechanisms such as 'corporate social responsibility' are also currently in vogue.

Accountability

Perhaps the most often used term (to the point of tiresomeness) in the good governance scholarship is the concept of accountability. Accountability is a fairly recent concept,[20] a creature of the past couple of decades, with, as its name suggests, its origins in the worlds of audit and accountancy. Yet it has come to be seen as a panacea in the contemporary world of governance, especially useful and applicable in situations where democratic governance may not be possible. Deirdre Curtin has written:

> Accountability is one of those golden concepts that are relatively uncontested in the sense that everyone intuitively agrees that public institutions or authorities should render account publicly for the use of their mandates and the manner in which public money is spent.[21]

For this reason, I spend time discussing this concept from the distant (to legal theory) world of bookkeeping and inventory because of its apparent usefulness, even as a tool for legal theory and a means to justice.

Accountability may be able to step in and, to some extent, fulfil the contemporary role of democracy in rendering law legitimate. Indeed, it has been suggested that accountability, with its associations with the world of New Public Management,[22] its companiability with market economies and categorisation of the citizen as consumer (along with the 'three Es' of economy, efficacy and effectiveness) may be about to join the classical

---

[20] Although accountability (if not by that name) has always been of importance in the field of administrative law, requiring that officials and institutions be accountable to those affected by their decisions.

[21] D Curtin, *Executive Power of the European Union* (Oxford, Oxford University Press, 2009) 246.

[22] The doctrines of NPM involve 'a focus on management, performance appraisal and efficiency; the use of agencies which deal with each other on a user-pay basis; the use of quasi-markets and contracting out to foster competition; cost-cutting; and a style of management which emphasizes, among other things, output targets, limited term contracts, monetary incentives and freedom to manage.' UK Parliament, HL Select Committee Report on the Public Service (1997–98) HL 55.

constitutional trilogy of sovereignty, rule of law and separation of powers.[23] However, its usefulness may be diminished because of its capacity to mean different things to different people. Jerry Mashaw has described it as 'protean'—'a placeholder for multiple contemporary anxieties'.[24]

What do we understand by accountability? Would it be a worthy place-holder in constitutional and legal theory? Even more importantly, could it be a means of achieving justice in the complex legal world of today? What is meant by saying that regulation is unaccountable? Ruth Grant and Robert Keohane have defined it in this way:

> Accountability, as we use the term, implies that some actors have the right to hold other actors to a set of standards, to judge whether they have fulfilled their responsibilities in the light of these standards, and to impose sanctions if they determine that these responsibilities have not been met.[25]

One of the most significant aspects of accountability is that, unlike some features of the rule of law[26] or checks and balances, accountability mechanisms always operate *after the fact*, exposing the actions of power to view, judging and sanctioning them. Accountability is useful because it can aid in identifying particular responsibilities of identifiable individuals. It is an important check on the exercise of power—decision-makers are less likely to abuse their discretion if they know that at some stage they will have to explain and justify their decisions. It can also operate in the absence of pubic law and can apply to non-state actors.

Note that accountability has a relationship with legitimacy—adequate accountability mechanisms may help render regulation legitimate—but the nature of this relationship is not automatically clear. It will depend on the standards by which those in power are held accountable and may also depend on whether accountability is seen either in terms of a relationship between a deliberate transfer or delegation in power by one organisation or principal to another (which will usually be more managerial in nature and focus on *internal* accountability structures[27]) or in terms of a relationship between the actions of those in power and those who are affected by power or suffer its consequences—which is more likely to be seen in terms of mechanisms of accountability *external* to an organisation or structure. These mechanisms may not always be very satisfactory. For example,

---

[23] See C Harlow, *Accountability in the European Union* (Oxford, Oxford University Press, 2002) 7.

[24] JL Mashaw, 'Accountability and Institutional Design: Some Thoughts on the Grammar of Governance' in M Dowdle (ed), *Public Accountability: Designs, Dilemmas and Experiences* (Cambridge, Cambridge University Press, 2006) 115.

[25] RW Grant and RO Keohane, 'Accountability and Abuses of Power in World Politics' (2005) 99(1) *American Political Science Review* 29.

[26] Unless the process of judicial review is considered a feature of the rule of law, as it is in some 'thick' theories, as discussed above chs 7 and 8.

[27] As argued in Grant and Keohane (above n 25).

in the context of the Eurozone crisis, accountability for managing state budgets within the levels set by the relevant Eurozone laws and the EU Stability Pact now appear to lie with the unelected EU Commission (which may bring enforcement proceedings against Member States) or with EU bureaucrats,[28] rather than with national parliaments or national electorates. This will not be satisfactory to citizens who will feel little link between the act of electing a government responsible for public spending and subsequent ways of holding that government to account.[29] Also, over the past decades, there has been a shift from systems of political accountability, such as the concept of 'responsibility' (which was the term traditionally used, for example, in British constitutional law, to describe the relationship between ministers of the Crown and Parliament) to other types of accountability, due to the fact that power has shifted from the public to the private sphere or to independent agencies; and so accountability has become distanced from political, democratic channels.[30]

Notably, what many governance mechanisms appear to have in common is a problem with *external* accountability. While many multinational enterprises (MNEs) have complex internal accountability systems of their management and board of directors to shareholders,[31] there may exist no external accountability to many of the people on whom their actions have effect. Accountability has too often been of an *exclusionary* sort in which there exists an acute problem of responsibility in relation to the costs and

---

[28] From 2012, under the 'Six Pack' of legislation adopted late in 2011, the European Parliament and Commission will have the power to scrutinise national budgets before even national parliaments have the chance to do so. If Member States fail to reduce their debts or refuse budgetary suggestions from Brussels, they can be subject to enforcement measures, which can lead to fines of up to .05% of GDP. A very notable feature of the EU/ECB/IMF 'bailouts' to Greece has been the conditions imposed, according to which the Greek economy is subject to supervision by unelected economists from outside of Greece. For details on the 'Six Pack' of legislation, see Council briefing of 8 November 2011, accessible at http://www.consilium.europa.eu/uedocs/cms_data/docs/pressdata/en/ecofin/125952.pdf (accessed 14 December 2012).

[29] In the *Euro Rescue Package*, Bundesverfassungsgericht [BVerfG] 7 Sept 2011, 2 BVR 987/10, the German Constitutional Court considered analogous arguments concerning the right to vote and the principle of democracy in Germany in the context of Euro bailout rescue packages. The complainants had argued that the bailout was a breach of the right to democratic representation (Arts 20 and 28 of the German Constitution) by restricting Parliament's control over its own budget, and also a breach of the voting right (Art 38 of the Constitution) because it could lead to a transfer of rights, authorities and tasks to the EU as a supranational organisation. However, the Court held that the German government was permitted to agree multimillion euro bailouts for Greece, Portugal and Ireland, provided that the German Parliament retained responsibility for public spending.

[30] On this, see, eg, A Tomkins, 'Political Accountability in the United Kingdom' in L Verhey, H Broeksteeg and I Van den Driessche (eds), *Political Accountability in Europe: Which Way Forward?* (Groningen, Europa Law Publishing, 2008) 243.

[31] Although internal accountability to shareholders is usually limited to the narrow confines of profit-making.

externalities of crises.[32] As David Held has suggested, the distribution of costs and risks has not been commensurate with the arrangements of their governance.[33] A regressive approach has been taken to decision-making. There exists not only a capacity problem in which international institutions are not fit for the manifold tasks of managing global risks, but also a *responsibility* problem, with an asymmetry between institutional action and its effects, due to the prevalent exclusionary model with little external accountability. Moreover, the impacts and externalities on these excluded parties are undoubtedly great. The results of the global financial crisis—such as deteriorating terms of trade and reduced availability of credit—cause slow rates of growth not just in those Western countries whose banks were at the centre of the crisis but also in Third World countries—with devastating effects, greater poverty, starvation and more deaths, especially among children and infants.

Criticism has already been made of organisations such as the World Trade Organization (WTO) and International Monetary Fund (IMF) in earlier chapters for their capacity to cause injustice, but it should be noted that even when the suggestion is made (as, for example, by Ernst Ulrich Petersmann[34]) that the WTO has a 'rights-based constitution'—which suggests a normative basis for international economic organisations—in fact, such proposals still emphasise economic rights, market freedoms and property rights. In other words, they give individuals such as investors, traders and corporations rights they can enforce directly rather than enforceable rights for those suffering from abusive trading practices. Once again, this is an exclusionary model and is a very limited form of accountability.

A further, related problem is that international law has failed to articulate human rights *obligations* for corporations,[35] yet again excluding the possibility of external accountability for human rights violating actions; and attempts to subject corporations to, for example, the jurisdiction of the International Criminal Court have failed. Once again, external accountability is lacking.

---

[32] For example, membership of the IMF is very broad, but its voting procedures are weighted, with the US carrying disproportionate weight. Private interests have been shown to influence the IMF through lobbying US Congress. The Basel Committee on Banking Supervision, which regulates banking standards, exerts a highly exclusionary membership, with no formal representation of developing countries.

[33] Held (above n 8) ch 6.

[34] Eg, E-U Petersmann, 'The WTO Constitution and Human Rights' (2000) 3(1) *Journal of International Economic Law* 19.

[35] Contrast the position under the UK Human Rights Act, whereby private bodies may be liable for breaches of human rights if they qualify as 'functional' public authorities—in itself a vexed concept. For further on this, see, eg, M Freedland, 'Law, Public Services and Citizenship: New Domains, New Regimes?' in M Freedland and S Sciarra (eds), *Public Services and Citizenship in European Law* (Oxford, Oxford University Press, 1998); and L Turano, 'Charitable Trusts and the Public Service: The Public Accountability of Private Care Providers' (2007) 18 *Kings Law Journal.*

This is an area that cosmopolitanism and human rights clearly has not succeeded in penetrating. In contrast, Nancy Fraser has proposed what she terms the 'all affected principle', which would mean that 'all those affected by a given social structure or institution have moral standing as subjects of justice'.[36] Although this principle might be an attractive candidate for a post-Westphalian framework for justice, it would not amount to *legal* redress.

In sum, the problem is that many more people are influenced by actions of non-state (as well as state) bodies than can influence them internally through internal lines of accountability. Further, while it may be the case that some transformative movements are creating new fora—transnational public spaces in which issues of injustice can be raised, such as the World Social Forum[37]—generally there is a distinct lack of institutions in which such issues can be aired, and even where they do exist, as in the case of the World Social Forum, matters are *aired* rather than redress provided. Such fora also suffer from what, in the context of international institutions, has been termed the 'joint decision trap'[38]—namely, the greater the amount of participants, the harder it is to reach decisions.

The nebulous, poorly defined and inarticulate nature of many law-creating mechanisms poses a significant challenge to accountability. How to identify those who should be accountable when it is not clear who exactly has taken the action in the first place? Colin Scott has written of 'extended account-ability structures' and models of 'interdependency'—examples of multi-polar accountability, originating in regulatory theory, in which actors have to account to different bodies for different activities. Scott cites the British Treasury as an example of such a structure.[39] This approach allows for accountability to be dispersed and spread around systems. However, such interdependency may not provide sufficient checks. For example, account-ability mechanisms were investigated in the context of the debacle over the resignation over the whole of the European Commission in 1996 due to instances of fraud and mismanagement. The Committee of Independent Experts, which was specifically tasked with investigating how this had come about, stated, 'It is difficult to find anyone who has even the slightest sense

---

[36] Fraser (above n 15) 25, a test which she later changed to 'all subjected' at 66.

[37] According to its own publicity, 'The World Social Forum is an open meeting place where social movements, networks, NGOs and other civil society organizations opposed to neo-liberalism and a world dominated by capital or by any form of imperialism come together to pursue their thinking, to debate ideas democratically, for formulate proposals, share their experiences freely and network for effective action.' See http://fsm2011.org/en/wsf-2011 (accessed 14 December 2012).

[38] F Scharpf, 'The Joint-Decision Trap: Lessons from German Federalism and European Integration' (1988) 66(2) *Public Administration* 239–78.

[39] See C Scott, 'Accountability in the Regulatory State' (2000) 27 *Journal of Law and Society* 35.

of responsibility.'[40] The Committee rejected an interdependency model of accountability as inadequate, preferring instead a model based more clearly on traditional government structures. The inference is that interdependency models may make it too easy to shift responsibility.

Such flexible monitoring involves adopting overlapping roles, which are shifting and blurred, and such non-hierarchical forms may appear incoherent.[41] Indeed, Scott has mused, 'If there are only non-hierarchical relations ... then perhaps there is no regulation at all in a narrow sense.'[42] Such flexibility undermines confidence in the ability of regulation to handle social problems. As Susan Strange has written, 'In a world of multiple, diffused authority, each of us shares Pinocchio's problems: our individual consciences are our only guide.'[43]

Some types of accountability favoured as modern governance strategies involve few or no external constraints and are simply too nebulous or weak to be effective. For example, the strategy of 'exit' can in theory operate as a form of accountability.[44] Corporations may think carefully about the impact of their actions on their market share, because consumers are liable to switch brands for a variety of reasons, including their dislike of abusive corporate behaviour. Yet consumers are not the only, nor even the most sizeable, body to be affected by a company's behaviour. Employees of

[40] See Harlow, *Accountability in the European Union* (above n 23) 184.

[41] See for example, the work of Janine Wedel, who has considered the example of 'flex groups'. The terms 'flex group' and 'flex players' have been used to describe informal units in which flexible players gain influence by promoting each other for influential positions and by co-ordinating their efforts to achieve mutually beneficial goals. Wedel gives as an example of 'flex groups' the US 'neo-cons'. For example, Richard Perle was not a full member of the Bush administration but instead chaired the Defense Policy Board, which was a Pentagon advisory board with a mixed private–public character, apparently allowing for more flexibility of action. The ambiguity of such structures actually enhances influence, and flex groups create 'not quite state not quite private organisations', duplicating divisions and bodies of government to bypass and override otherwise relevant entities and processes. Their private agendas conflict with the public interest, but crucially, they are not subject to the same accountability and ethics requirements as government employees. J Wedel, 'Blurring the State–Private Divide: Flex Organizations and the Decline of Accountability' in M Spoor (ed), *Globalisation, Poverty and Conflict: A Critical 'Development' Reader* (Dordrecht, Kluwer Academic Publishers, 2004) 217.

[42] C Scott, 'Analyzing Regulatory Space: Fragmented Resources and Institutional Design' (2001) *Public Law* 329, 352.

[43] S Strange, *The Retreat of the State: The Diffusion of Power in the World Economy* (Cambridge, Cambridge University Press, 1996) 199.

[44] The term 'exit' is taken from Albert O Hirschman's seminal work *Exit, Voice and Loyalty: Responses to Decline in Firms, Organizations, and States* (Cambridge, MA, Harvard University Press, 1970), which distinguishes between different ways of reacting to deterioration in corporations and, more generally, to dissatisfaction with organisations. 'Exit' involves the member leaving the organisation or the customer switching to a competing product, and 'voice' involves members or customers agitating and exerting influence for change from within. 'Loyalty' functions to retard 'exit' and permits 'voice' to play its proper role.

companies, those in its immediate environment, may be far distant from the ultimate consumers of the product.

In the wake of the urge to private parties to 'responsibilise', another type of governance strategy considered important in the corporate context is that of 'corporate social responsibility'. Transnational campaigns against child labour in sweatshops owned by Nike or against activities of oil companies such as Shell (for example, Greenpeace's 'Brent Spar' campaign[45]) have set the agenda for the emergence of a new transnational norm governing corporate behaviour. The doctrine of corporate social responsibility exhorts large corporate enterprises to integrate ethics and international human rights, as well as environmental norms, into business practices. This supposedly increases the external accountability of firms.

Admittedly, a number of global governance arrangements have arisen to improve corporate social responsibility, such as the Dow Jones Sustainability Index and the UN Global Compact, which consists of companies voluntarily agreeing to comply with international human rights or environmental norms. However, the effectiveness of corporate social responsibility is questionable. It has largely taken the form of soft law—of voluntary codes and standards—and therefore does not qualify as a form of critical *legal* justice. And the fact that corporations are generally not bound by human rights law (although they may often profit from it as supposed 'victims' of violations) remains. A further problem is that MNEs have shaped corporate social responsibility in their own image, to fit their own concerns, including it for example in MBA courses, so it has tended to display an instrumental rationalism. The act of shaping a type of responsibility tailored to the needs of particular companies does not comply with the rule of law canon which operates generally.

So in general, accountability mechanisms do not function as effectively as might be desirable. In spite of the fact that, as Onora O'Neill has written, in recent times, a search for greater accountability 'has penetrated all our lives, like great draughts of Heineken's, reaching parts that supposedly less developed forms of accountability did not reach',[46] accountability remains underdeveloped, and its existing mechanisms, such as they operate in the private sphere, are barely adequate for the work that has to be done. Private law accountability—obtainable through litigation—is only

---

[45] Brent Spar was a 14,500 tonne oil platform operated by Shell UK in the North Sea. When it was considered to be of no further value, Shell decided, with the support of the UK Government, to dump the entire facility in the Atlantic Ocean. Greenpeace took action against Shell as part of its long-running campaign against ocean dumping. As a result of Greenpeace's sustained campaign, Shell eventually reversed its decision and agreed to dismantle and recycle the platform on land. See, eg, L Bennie, 'Brent Spar, Atlantic Oil and Greenpeace' (1998) 51(3) *Parliamentary Affairs* 397.

[46] O O'Neill, 'Called to Account: A Question of Trust' in O O'Neill, *A Question of Trust: The BBC Reith Lectures 2002* (Cambridge, Cambridge University Press, 2002) 45.

affordable for a tiny, wealthy number and may, in any case, be inadequate to deal with grosser abuses of power, which are immune from principles that operate in the public sphere. Market accountability has only a small effect—in any case, switching consumer choices makes very little difference where injustices hurt those other than the consumer. Part of the problem is that accountability in world politics is inextricably constrained by power relationships—a feature recognised by the function of the rule of law in its role of constraining power. *Power* is necessary to hold others accountable. The poor and disempowered, especially in the small developing countries of the global south, lack the capacity systematically to hold powerful actors accountable. It should also be emphasised that, in any case, domestic accountability will often be insufficient to make up the shortfall, as even democratic states will tend to act in biased ways toward noncitizens.[47]

Also, accountability tends to be haphazard. It will often be the case that the issues which come to the attention of the public are not even the most important abuses of power. It is also problematic that with the increase in knowledge-based policymaking, many participants in governance have expert knowledge, and this poses serious challenges of accountability, for who has enough counter-expertise to control the experts?

For some, the answer is not 'more accountability' but more intelligently designed accountability systems: 'The point is not to design a comprehensive, ideal accountability system but rather to figure out how to limit abuses of power in a world with a wide variety of power wielders and without a centralised government.'[48] I agree with this sentiment, but finding effective ways to limit such abuses remains highly problematic. Furthermore, as the discussion above illustrates, *law* can also sometimes play a very limited role.

Restorative and Responsive Justice

One final strategy to remedy injustice will be considered—the contemporary movement to understand justice as 'restorative' or 'responsive'. This strategy is worthy of specific reflection on account of its nomenclature, which denotes it specifically as a type of 'justice', as well as on account of its close relations to responsive and reflexive law. Restorative justice and its connections with responsive and reflexive law has already been mentioned in chapter six.[49] There is clearly also a connection between

---

[47] This is given as one of the rationales for the existence of the EU by Miguel Poiares Maduro. See MP Maduro, 'Europe and the Constitution: What if This Is as Good as it Gets?' in JHH Weiler and M Wind (eds), *European Constitutionalism Beyond the State* (Cambridge, Cambridge University Press, 2003).

[48] Grant and Keohane (above n 25) 41.

[49] Above ch 6, 'The Critique of Bureaucratised, Instrumental Justice'.

restorative justice and accountability. Restorative justice is concerned with responsibility, and accountability is concerned with giving a public account of that for which one is responsible. Restorative justice advocates argue that horizontal, deliberative accountability to others within a restorative justice circle may be more effective than hierarchical accountability in the criminal justice system. For example, the police may be more likely to account for use of excessive force during arrest to a mother who pleads directly that her son has been unfairly treated, than in a court case where the mother may have no role at all unless she is called as a witness. Restorative justice is also perceived to satisfy a need for face-to-face, emotional communication, which can be more productive in creating commitment to follow through.

Restorative justice has been argued as a civic republican strategy to widen the circles of deliberative accountability.[50] Yet there is also a need for restorative justice to be *exercised* accountably and for external accountability to be possible, such as recourse to the courts, through a residual right to appeal. Perhaps just because restorative justice proponents are willing to present it as 'a natural authentic type of justice',[51] there has been a tendency for it to eschew formal methods of accountability, preferring instead more informal, unofficial methods, such as a deliberative accountability conducted directly by participants themselves. However, there are dangers posed by informal justice—not least oppression by the dominant and strong. Important safeguards achieved through law should not be omitted. For example, human rights of both victims and offenders must be respected, and punishments must not take excessive, degrading and humiliating forms. If such safeguards are not observed, then restorative justice can degrade into cruel and oppressive informal justice—into vigilante movements or the forms of *charivari* (namely, popular, demotic justice, often accompanied by rough music) that once took place in Europe.[52] It has been suggested that 'democracy is enriched when the justice of the people and the justice of the law each become more vulnerable to the other'.[53] Yet it is important that more informal restorative justice practices be integrated into external accountability processes and the rule of law.

---

[50] See, eg, J Braithwaite, 'Accountability and Responsibility through Restorative Justice' in M Dowdle (ed), *Rethinking Public Accountability* (Cambridge, Cambridge University Press, 2006).

[51] D Roche, 'Gluttons for Restorative Justice' (2003) 32(4) *Economy and Society*.

[52] This type of justice took the form of traditional customs and rituals in which some form of embarrassing punishment was imposed on those who offended the community, accompanied by noise and ridicule. See, eg, EP Thompson, '"Rough Music": Le Charivari Anglais' (1972) 27 *Annales: Economics, Societies, Civilizations* 286.

[53] J Braithwaite and C Parker, 'Restorative Justice is Republican Justice' in L Walgrave and G Bazemore (eds), *Restoring Juvenile Justice* (New York, Criminal Justice Press, 1999).

For the time being, restorative justice plays a relatively small role[54] in most jurisdictions.[55] Indeed, it is usually applied only in the cases of offenders who have already admitted guilt, dealing with punishment rather than the fact-finding stage. It is also much more likely to be used in the case of small-scale rather than serious crime (with the exception of truth and reconciliation commissions).

Perhaps the closest connection with 'reflexive' law is to be found in notions such as Braithwaite's proposal of a 'responsive' justice as a meta-regulatory project,[56] to provide responsive and restorative justice for the whole body of law. His aspiration is that the justice of the people 'bubble up' into the justice of the law through direct emotional engagement of stakeholders in the particularities of justice. Braithwaite's inspiration lies in the works of James Madison and Tom Paine, and the hope is for 'empowered civic virtue, with power checking power, not only in government, but in society as a whole'.[57] In this way, it is hoped it will give rise to a sort of republic federalism, in which state regulators check and monitor business custom and law, and both in their turn be checked by vigilant NGOs and social movements.

For theorists such as Braithwaite, 'responsive' justice is founded on the premise that the healing of injustice is more likely when undominated deliberation is possible among stakeholders regarding injustice and the remedies for it. In this context, Christine Parker, for example, has suggested as a responsive, regulatory idea a requirement that organisations (regardless of whether public or private) above a certain size produce an access to justice plan, concerning all injustices which their activities might provoke, such as to consumers if a business, or to prisoners if incarceration, and that very large organisations should be required to report annually and publicly on the internet on their performance under the plan.[58] Under Parker's plan they would have to demonstrate to independent auditors that they had improved access to justice over the last reporting period. Parker's suggestion is based on the reduction of injustice through *prevention* rather than its redress through dispute resolution—and it highlights the fact that dispute prevention is cheaper than litigation. At present industries dominate the courtrooms. Nevertheless, to free up courts from corporate disputes and give voice to the less powerful through restorative justice appears somewhat aspirational or utopian, and also depends on building up social

---

[54] Braithwaite, 'Accountability and Responsibility through Restorative Justice' (above n 50).

[55] D Roche, *Accountability in Restorative Justice* (Oxford, Clarendon Press, 2003) 3.

[56] J Braithwaite, *Restorative Justice and Responsive Regulation* (New York, Oxford University Press, 2002); and Braithwaite and Parker (above n 53). See also C Parker, C Scott, N Lacey and J Braithwaite (eds), *Regulating Law* (Oxford, Oxford University Press, 2004).

[57] Braithwaite, *Restorative Justice and Responsive Regulation* (ibid).

[58] C Parker, *The Open Corporation* (Melbourne, Cambridge University Press, 2002).

movements that are crucial to transforming law. Braithwaite himself fears that before this can happen, there will need to be a yet greater crisis in confidence and further crises of injustice. So this does not seem to be the strongest of strategies for reducing injustice at present.

Reinforcing Critical Legal Justice

The discussion of the last sections indicates that a search for a more reflex-ive justice, complementary to governance strategies, has not been very satisfactory. Can these relatively new principles and 'governance strategies' aid and supplement older control mechanisms such as the rule of law, separation of powers and judicial review? The hope is that these new strat-egies and mechanisms will provide checks and balances for each other, just as federalism and the separation of powers have traditionally been a major check on central state power. Notably, many of these strategies—such as corporate social responsibility and responsive justice—are not legal as such, and take us beyond critical legal justice. In many cases, their ability to deter injustice is very limited. It is questionable whether the public interest can be adequately ensured by these new forms, and the fear is that these new mechanisms may also be colonised by particular interests. Whatever the mode of governance, there is still a need for bureaucratic and regulatory discretion to be subject to clear, predictable and operative constraints, such as those applied by the rule of law.

Arguments that dismiss the rule of law as irrelevant miss the very important point that there exists a need for the constraints, checks and balances, discipline and supervision which the rule of law can provide. Further, the rule of law may be applied as critical legal justice in the con-temporary context without reverting to an overly formalistic or fetishistic focus on rules and without the neo-liberal preoccupation with individual autonomy and private rights, as argued in the last chapters. Most impor-tantly, critical legal justice should ensure that regulation be answerable to clear, predictable, legally enforceable controls that operate on constraints on power. Critical legal justice primarily operates the rule of law through the lens of preventing capricious, arbitrary and unaccountable regulation and decision-making, in both the private and public sectors in contrast to the role of the rule of law understood as protecting individual autonomy and private rights through predictable rules.[59]

Philip Selznick, although he promulgated a complex theory of the rule of law, defined it simply as 'the progressive reduction of arbitrariness in

---

[59] For a similar argument, see McDonald (above n 17) 219.

law and its administration',[60] associating arbitrariness with such features as capriciousness, wilfulness and absence of reasoned justification. Selznick's work is particularly relevant because of his attention to inchoate and incipient law, not just law in fact and textbooks. Selznick believed that the concepts of public law and of due process, as a common law of governance, should be applied, 'whereby the rule of law may be extended to areas hitherto controlled only by concepts of private law ... wherever the social function of governing is performed, wherever some men rule and others are ruled'.[61] He also argued that these standards were necessary to rebalance social asymmetries created by property, contract and corporate law, which he saw as being overly individual-centred, domination-centred and ignoring important power relations. Indeed, he believed these public law standards should lie at the heart of the law of governance. Such standards might not guarantee social justice but do help render those in power accountable. Selznick also argued that 'the exercise of power must be justified. From this it is but a step to the view that reasons must be given to defend official acts. Reasons invite evaluation and evaluation requires development of public standards.'[62] Overall, he believed that the current heterarchical, flexible character of regulation, networks and governance 'create[s] a demand for restraint and accountability, for countervailing institutions, for a conception of the organization that yields a theory of authority ... a quest for the corporate conscience'.[63] 'What is at stake is the capacity of organisations to do justice.'[64]

We may also return to Lon Fuller, who in his later work described law as 'an extension of the universal human tendency to improve conditions by stabilizing interactional expectancies'.[65] Yet it is just this very stabilisation of interactional tendencies that has been lost in the drive toward ever more flexible regulation. Contemporary good governance measures and 'light-touch' accountability show little chance of redressing this drift, of reducing the capacity of institutions to do injustice. And of course it is crucial to remember that whatever is to be done should be measured not only by standards of effectiveness, efficiency and legitimacy but also by the criteria of justice and equality.

Constraints need to be placed on power, whatever form it takes; accountability of democratically elected bodies needs to be exercised over the spending of public money; and values of fairness and accountability

---

[60] P Selznick, 'Sociology and Natural Law' (1961) 6 *Natural Law Forum* 84.

[61] P Selznick, *Law, Society, and Industrial Justice* (New York, Russell Sage Foundation, 1969) 259.

[62] Ibid, 30.

[63] Ibid, 67.

[64] Ibid, 72.

[65] LL Fuller, 'Human Interaction and the Law' in K Winston (ed), *The Principles of Social Order* (Durham, NC, Duke University Press, 1981) 219–20.

need to be observed, whatever the source of regulation—public or private. Yet in an era of flexibility and self-regulation, there has been a diminution in formal legal structures. How may administrations or power bases be constrained in the absence of formal constraints? One is reminded of Zygmunt Bauman's characterisation of postmodernity as a desert—of life without the paved paths and clearly signposted roads that give a clear sense of safety and direction to our movements, and where footprints and distinguishing marks are erased by the lightest of winds.[66] In this sense, the contemporary legal world is desert-like.

Anarchic Resistance to Injustice

A final reflection takes us beyond the boundaries of law. As Simon Critchley has noted, there exists a large gulf between a sharp awareness of injustice and a perception that liberal democracy is not in good shape.[67] He has argued that what is needed is a motivating, empowering concept of ethics, one capable of facing down the drift of the present. A positivist conception of law, stripped of any necessary identification with morality, is not an admirable candidate for this. The 'brave new world' of legal pluralism presents yet further challenges—of a lack of accountability and possible chaos and confusion, of the 'desert' of contemporary law. The lack of such a motivation may prompt despair and nihilism, as was discussed above in chapter nine in the context of human rights.

An alternative to such nihilism has been offered by radical or even utopian strategies to obtain justice. Critchley's candidate for a motivating, empowering concept of ethics is based on his own conception of ethical subjectivity as riven by an infinite demand, although moderated by a self-mocking humour. What he has proposed as an alternative to nihilism (or liberal capitalism) is an ethics based on the experience of the Other (derived, inter alia, from the work of Emmanuel Levinas). He has argued that, as human beings, we are faced with an infinite, ethical demand from the Other, a demand that we have no way of satisfying. This is a primordial debt to the Other that takes the form of an obsessive and insatiable responsibility—a responsibility that Levinas himself described as 'anarchic'.[68] Critchley has proposed humour as a means of sublimating the problem, in psychoanalytic mode, a comic acknowledgement of the

---

[66] Z Bauman, *Legislators and Interpreters: On Modernity, Postmodernity and Intellectuals* (Ithaca, Cornell University Press, 1987).

[67] S Critchley, *Infinitely Demanding* (London, Verso, 2007) ch 1.

[68] E Levinas, *Otherwise than Being or Beyond Essence* (Pittsburgh, Duquesne University Press, 1998) 100–1.

inadequacy of the subject, which transforms feelings of self-violence into a chastened self-understanding.

This is no mere work of ethical subjectivity or human psychology, however, for Critchley argues that this anarchic Levinasian ethical demand, which disrupts the autonomy of the subject, provides both a model and a motivation for the anarchic disruption of the state. This provides a 'meta-political moment' that justifies anarchism as an ethical practice, leading to a politics of resistance.[69] Therefore, Critchley has advocated a politics that is resolutely anti-statist, a politics that seeks not to take control of state power but rather to create 'interstitial' distance within the state.[70] It is a politics of resistance to the state, one that constantly confronts the state with impossible demands and denounces the limitations of state mechanisms. Critchley denounces a state of affairs in which capitalism continuously perpetuates itself and ingests and transforms all opposing ideologies, arguing that therefore a new motivating politics must be distanced from the state, taking the form of anti-war movements, ecological organisations, protest against racist or sexist abuses, and other forms of local self-organisation. Critchley has described these movements as possessing a 'carnivalesque humour deployed as a political strategy', one that 'combines street-theatre, festival, performance art and what might be described as forms of non-violent warfare' in a 'new language of civil disobedience'.[71]

Critchley's anarchic politics of resistance is one of a number of strategies of progressive politics. For example, Boaventura de Sousa Santos has described and praised a 'counter-hegemonic' globalisation—a new model of social regulation based on voluntary participation of stakeholders—and has praised the World Social Forum as 'the first critical utopia of the twenty-first century'.[72] The World Social Forum, which was conceived as 'an open space' in contradistinction to the World Economic Forum in Davos, has already been discussed in this chapter. It takes a distinctive, non-hierarchical form, with a horizontal organisation structure, is not divided according to political parties and is also non-deliberative, modelled on anarchistic spaces and formed with the aim of articulating social and political objectives, as well as protest and resistance.[73]

---

[69] Critchley (above n 67).

[70] Ibid, 11.

[71] Ibid, 123.

[72] B de Sousa Santos, 'The World Social Forum and the Global Left' (2008) *Politics & Society* 15.

[73] However, it has been accused of producing its own lack of transparency and tyranny of structurelessness, an unregulated space that can produce inequalities. For a discussion of the World Social Forum, see H Gautney, 'Is Another State Possible?' in H Gautney, O Dahbour,

There also exist new forms of deliberation across cultural, linguistic and national boundaries, such as those that occur online, using innovative forms of software and social networks. These stimulate new forms of communication and social empathy, along with a commitment to justice and a fight against oppression, extending beyond empathy to actions in support of others.[74] The Internet comprises many types of 'iterations', democratic or not, which are broadcast and accessed but also recast, distorted and given alternative or opposite meanings, which are accessible to vast audiences. The power of such fora was illustrated by the counter-governmental protests in the Arab Spring and by the Chinese government's attempts to control Google China.

In a work of great scope that sometimes appears to be situated more in the realm of fiction or fantasy than in political theory, Michael Hardt and Antonio Negri posited a spontaneous revolt of a self-constituting 'multitude'—ie, the scattered, wretched and disaffected of the earth, existing as a collective subject. Hardt and Negri have also rejected a strategy of organised politics, looking rather to a diffuse but extensive popular desire for liberty, emanating from the 'multitude'.[75] As in their discussion of 'empire', there is more than a hint of the messianic in their vision—suggesting the possibility of destabilisation by even apparently insignificant, marginal events. They have noted that the most visible and significant contemporary rebellions have been those such as Tiananmen and Zapatista, which were local, in contrast to the global WTO protests in Seattle and Genoa. Critchley has also highlighted the indigenous nature of much contemporary political resistance.

Critchley's theory is particularly interesting because it is one of the most philosophically carefully worked through attempts to theorise a progressive politics, and Critchley himself has also had some personal involvement with the recent Occupy movements. While I do not agree with all aspects of Critchley's argument, I find it compelling in its diagnosis of the contemporary disappointment of the times and stimulating in its search for an alternative ethics of motivation—hence my discussion of his work in more than one chapter of this book. However, in particular, I find Critchley's Levinasian brand of 'infinitely demanding' ethics too impossible, in its demands on the subject, to serve as a motivation for political action. Further work is surely necessary to explain the relationship between his particular brand of ethics, based on the private individual's relationship to and relentless responsibility for the Other, and the

A Dawson and N Smith (eds), *Democracy and the State in the Struggle for Global Justice* (New York, Routledge, 2009).

[74] CC Gould, 'Envisioning Transnational Democracy: Cross-border Communities and Regional Human Rights Frameworks' in Gautney et al (eds) (ibid).

[75] M Hardt and A Negri, *Multitude* (London, Penguin, 2005).

Figure 11-1: A 'carnivalesque' notion of justice? Photograph by Carsten Koall of a statue of Justice in Roemer Square (Frankfurt, Germany), masked during a 'Blockupy' anti-capitalism protest on 17 May 2012, courtesy of Getty Images

formation of more cohesive political movements. While appreciating the role that satirical and parodical protest may play in promoting alterative visions, it is doubtful whether such 'carnivalesque' movements will be sufficient to transform the present political landscape, without underpinnings of stronger legal tools. For an illustration of a 'carnivalesque' approach to protest, see Figure 11-1.

However, theories such as Critchley's are undoubtedly valuable as an inspiration toward revitalising progressive politics, 'especially so in the present ideological atmosphere of disillusionment'.[76] Richard Falk has argued:

> This rich tradition reminds us strongly of the relevance of anti-state traditions of reflection and political engagement, as well as the indispensable role of cooperation, nonviolence, community, small-scale social organisation and local solutions for human material needs if the aspiration for a just and sustainable society is ever to be rescued from its utopian greenhouse.[77]

However, Falk has also noted that the risk of all such approaches is that the only change possible is of a very minor and local variety.

---

[76] R Falk, 'Anarchism without "Anarchism": Searching for Progressive Politics in the Early Twenty-First Century' (2010) 40 *Millennium: Journal of International Studies* 1.
[77] Ibid, 5.

By using the term 'anarchic', Critchley not only places himself in the context of a long philosophical and political tradition but also raises the question of the relationship of an anarchist theory such as his to law. Such a theory clearly attacks laws, which it takes to be unjust—but does it also require a rejection of law altogether? If so, such a theory would be beyond the ambit of the project of this book, which though at times highly critical of the law, does not reject it totally as a concept or practice and, in particular, seeks a critical *legal* justice. While I share a willingness to critique those particular juridical practices in which a minority have managed to monopolise power for exploitative ends, I do not argue for the total expulsion of law from society. In chapter two, I argued for a complex and nuanced understanding of the role of law in society, but I did not deny law's role in conflict resolution, nor the capacity of coercion and sanctions to maintain order—a baseline 'banal' positivism assumes at least this much. In particular, law can serve a critical function, not only in maintaining order but also in controlling power, particularly the powerful private interests discussed earlier in this chapter. An anarchistic account risks annihilating this important legal weapon against injustice and oppression. Indeed, law may sometimes be the only factor sufficiently powerful to take on these concerns.

While there may be scope for articulating an account of law that could facilitate rather than repress a social or subjective operation of anarchy such as Critchley's (ie, an anarchy that would not seek the undoing of law and would not be a resolute resistance to law), such an articulation is beyond the scope of this book. So while political resistance (however diffuse) insofar as it takes the form of an attack on unjust law with an impulse to its abolition or reform, may be embraced, the total rejection of law may not. It risks making the contemporary landscape even more desert-like.

12

Conclusion: Law and Justice after Modernity

Diagnosis and Critique

At a most general level, the argument of the book is that both law and the ways in which we understand law have changed, and a former legal paradigm has been supplanted. This transformation has taken place over time, in the course of a passage from the modern to a postmodern era (although opinions differ as how to date these periods of time). During the period of modernity, law was identified or understood in terms of certain attributes, such as a belief in or stipulation of its autonomy, an association or identification of law with 'state' law and an inclination to systematise laws into ordered legal 'systems'—although modern law is probably best understood in terms of 'family resemblances', as not every law or example of legal theorising possessed every one of these attributes. In the contemporary era, it has become much harder to identify law with these characteristics. Law has become more diffuse and plural in character and its connection with the state undermined.

I have also argued that law must be understood in its cultural context, in the sense that law is both a cultural object, and that we improve law if we interpret and assess it in a cultural light. I have suggested that the relationship between law and culture is a complex one, of 'co-implication', not simplistically causal but rather one that illuminates and enriches our understanding of law. An interdisciplinary approach, looking to law's undeniable relationship with a broader culture, is also a way of resisting both a reductionist approach to law (namely one that adopts an economic, instrumentalist logic), which has tended to dominate Western law for the past 300 years, and also the acontextual and unhistorical view of law as doctrinal science.

I have examined more closely the claims that have been made for law as an autonomous discipline. This has required a broad-ranging enquiry into legal theory, interrogating the nature of law. Claims for legal autonomy are characteristic of a certain 'modern' type of legal thought, such as the positivism of Hans Kelsen, which seeks to portray law as a 'pure' discipline that must be understood as distinct and free-standing, independent of politics, culture and history. The original motivation for attributing autonomy to law served a clarificatory purpose, supporting the claim that if law were independent of religion or morality, it could serve a mediating role of independent authority. However, the claims for autonomy are unsustainable. Law's techniques of practical reason and its methods of interpretation are not categorically different from non-legal applications. It is impossible to find a singular, distinguishing feature of law to separate it from non-law. Problems of closure are even more pressing at the level of law's ultimate foundations, which are inevitably non-legal. Law cannot be self-grounded but rests on something else—that something else being drawn from a large range of possibilities. Ultimately, the source identified as law's foundation tends to be the expression of a particular point of view or of a particular period of time. For example, the 'sovereign' was designated at a time when parliamentary sovereignty tended to be absolute.

I have also argued in this book that law is an 'open' concept, not to be understood as homogeneous, insular and closed but instead as encompassing very plural entities and diverse opportunities; moreover, the designation 'law' is often a product of those who have an investment in identifying law in a certain way. Nonetheless, such a wide account may seem to efface and collapse law out of independent existence—the very fear of those modern theorists who insisted on legal autonomy in the first place. Therefore, even those who insist on a contextual understanding of law also concede that it may be necessary provisionally to identify some sort of 'organising concept' of law. I have suggested that, in this context, a 'banal' positivism may be employed, allowing for law's distinctness in a weak way, in terms of a claim to authority (a claim which may not, however, always be justified) and in terms of a function of co-ordination that, although it may take the form of human flourishing for some, for others amounts to an amoral capacity for organisation. However, law may also seek to distinguish itself by its 'aptness for justice'.[1] Law may not always be just, but it is always possible and indeed often necessary to ask if it is actually just. Therefore, law—even understood within the very general organisational concept of 'banal' positivism—may claim distinctiveness, by virtue of its role in addressing conflict in society and its 'aptness' for justice; and though this distinctiveness may fail to render law unique or completely autonomous from other elements in society, it helps to explain law's claim to do so.

However, I have also argued that in order to gain greater insight into the nature of law, it is necessary to study law from many different perspectives,

---

[1] L Green, 'Positivism and the Inseparability of Law and Morals' (2008) 83 *New York University Law Review* 1035.

including but not limited to those of legal participants, such as lawyers and judges. It is necessary to take account of law's history, as well as its origins in society, and in different types of society, which will produce different types of law and different concepts of law. I have adopted what Brian Simpson described as an 'anti-grand theory' theory of legal scholarship.

I have then noted the impulse for an organisational clarity, a search for unity in law and a rendering of law as systematic; this tendency for cohesion is apparent in much modern theorising about law. This approach fails to acknowledge the multidimensionality, complexity and lack of unity of laws. In the present age, major landmarks of modern law seem to have lost their prominence in a way that produces many crossings and fluidities of law. State sovereignty has become weaker in a post-Westphalian age, and government and governance no longer necessarily follow the structures of state sovereignty. Rather, law is made up of cross-references, strange loops and alternative hierarchies. Modern law's schematisations may be interpreted as in themselves 'symbolic forms' that are mental constructions and categorisations of space, no longer workable in present times. There are few orderly perspectives to be found in the contemporary legal world. Theories and conceptualisations of law must therefore now adapt.

In the face of this more nebulous, indeterminate prospect, how to conceptualise law? I have argued that legal pluralism (namely, a state of affairs for any social field in which behaviour pursuant to more than one legal order occurs) should now be seen as the most convincing and workable theory of law. Legal pluralism is not, however, itself uncomplicated. Many pluralists also include the further and distinct claim that not all law-like phenomena have their source in institutionalised law. Legal pluralism is also usually taken to imply more than just a plurality of laws; it can include situations in which two or more legal systems coexist in the same societal field, sometimes in a contradictory way, in which each may have equally plausible claims to authority. In this way, pluralism introduces incommensurability as a feature of legal life to be reckoned with, and rather than a centralised unity of the legal field, legal relationships are seen to be characterised by the heterarchical interactions of different levels and sources of law. Notably, one crucial strand in contemporary pluralism is situated at transnational or global level, where a rich and often competing proliferation of rules and norms are to be found. A common response to pluralism, whether at national, regional or international level, is to seek to structure and stabilise the proliferating institutions and rationalities by way of meta-principles or by some sort of 'order of orders'.[2]

---

[2] N Walker, 'Beyond Boundary Disputes and Basic Grids: Mapping the Global Disorder of Normative Orders' (2008) 6 *International Journal of Constitutional Law* 373.

Unlike some contemporary theorists, I do not believe that pluralism, plurality, interlegality and the like are necessarily normatively superior (as opposed to more descriptively accurate) to those monist or dualist accounts that cleave to notions of a more unified legal space. On the contrary, it is important to be aware that legal pluralism brings with it increased risks of a lack of accountability, of self-regulating institutions and of localised laws being captured by special interests.

Yet legal pluralism has not paid a great deal of attention to such questions. The social fact of multiple legal orders says nothing as to their moral worthiness or capacity for justice. By its very definition, pluralism acknowledges the possibility of contradictory laws, of different legal orders imposing competing demands on citizens—a legal space that is not, as Jeremy Waldron has put it, 'in good shape'.[3] This conclusion opens up a dilemma for those of us who see pluralism as empirically plausible but seek some sort of justice or morality within law itself. This is because it works against pluralism as a normative theory or as an 'ethical positioning', in the sense that pluralism appears to run the risk of opening up too many opportunities for abuse of power and law, of undermining the rule of law, of glorying in the beauty and wonder of a *Carina Nebula*, without sufficiently acknowledging its black holes.

The first four chapters of the book presented law as a complex, pluralist phenomenon not readily capable of systematisation, in contrast to an earlier paradigm of a more formal, autonomous, systematic law. In the next sections of the book, however, my argument departed from many postmodern and pluralist accounts of law, which have embraced pluralism as normatively attractive and as a viable ethical positioning. I raised the question of whether this is actually a transformation that should be welcomed.

In particular, many situations exist in which there is either a weak or, indeed, no functioning rule of law. This is visible in the growth of informal, flexible, private or non-state 'governance' organisations and networks. This undermines accountability and the possibility of justice. Justice is further compromised in the global arena, where there exists either little or no trace at all of formerly familiar mechanisms of state accountability. Too little attention has been paid to this. Therefore, I have argued that complexity, fragmentation, pluralism of laws and globalisation can perpetuate injustice. Additionally, what is also particularly dismaying about these 'little or no rule of law' situations is that they are in part implicated by a politics of fear and security, which gives rise to a growing spiral of further injustices and destruction of human rights.

---

[3] J Waldron, 'Legal Pluralism and the Contrast between Hart's Jurisprudence and Fuller's' in P Cane (ed), *The Hart–Fuller Debate in the Twenty-First Century* (Oxford, Hart Publishing, 2010).

I have argued that justice becomes a key issue for law in the era of legal pluralism. Rather than, or at least in addition to, questions of ordering or interpreting pluralism, we should ask how justice is achievable, given this complexity.

***

So ends the diagnostic and critical part of the argument. One might leave it there. As Brecht wrote, 'Nothing but *ad hominem* abuse; that's better than nothing.' ('*Nichts als Beschimpfungen, das ist mehr als nichts.*'[4]) By one argument, the diagnosis of injustice speaks for itself. This is the case with much critical theory, which is solely negative in nature, whether diagnostic or deconstructive. Yet law stands in a particular position vis-à-vis justice. Law is not merely a theoretical pursuit, an academic discipline. Law is also practical in nature: lawyers, judges and others daily face the necessity of actually doing justice in their application and enforcement of the law. There would be a certain inadequacy to a project such as this one, which investigates law after modernity, if it failed to attend to law's task of doing justice.

Justice

Identifying a positive, constructive element for law after modernity proves harder than diagnosis and critique, and there are no ready answers. Justice is multifarious in nature, perceived as both a 'complete' virtue and as singular and particular in nature, taking on a variety of forms, dependent on context—substantive, formal, redistributive, corrective, social, legal and so on. All of these forms may be plural in dimension, varying according to context (local, national or global), making us aware of the 'scale' of justice and requiring a cartography of justice itself. Justice appears as a mystery or labyrinth, and the search for justice as a Herculean endeavour. In the face of this, I have argued that two specific points are of relevance to law after modernity.

First, I have argued that justice has a specific *legal* sense—that law has a specific relationship with or 'aptness' for justice. It may not be just, but it holds out a promise of justice. We should attend to this. Second, and beyond this legal sense (which in itself is not uncomplicated), lies the vastness of justice in all of its dimensions, which is still perplexing. Here, I

---

[4] B Brecht, *Schriften sur Politik und Gesellschaft, 1919–56* (Frankfurt, Suhrkampf, 1974) 311.

have argued that we should seek to avoid 'ideal' theorising about justice. There exists a tendency in much political philosophy to posit transcendental, speculative systems of justice, such as those of Immanuel Kant or John Rawls. There is a vast array of these theories—an often tempting array—from which we might pick and choose according to preference. However, their idealism renders them ultimately unrealisable, even if Rawls made reference to a 'realistic utopia'.[5] In spite of all of this theorising, we continue to live in a violently unjust world.

Along with being unworkable, these theories lack another quality. In their conception as the products of reason, they lack the necessary elements for motivation. I have argued that our sense of justice is derived from our sense of injustice, which in turn develops from a complex constellation of emotions, which provide a psychological basis from which moral theories may emerge. Reason and emotion are therefore compounded and inseparable, and work together in the formation of moral judgements, providing a motivation for moral action in a way that reason alone (in the cool and disengaged form it finds in rational philosophy) is unable to do. The key point here is that an account of justice that acknowledges the role played by the emotions in identifying injustice and the contribution of our emotions to our reasoned ethical judgements not only more accurately represents the nature of our ethical thought but is better placed to *motivate* citizens. The argument, then, is that our sense of justice is secondary to and parasitic on our sense of injustice. We place unrealistic demands on citizens if we start with justice as an ideal that is pre-existing, neutral and self-produced by a rational conception. I have adopted Amartya Sen's argument that it is not necessary that we have a fully worked-out, fine-tuned theory of justice in order to remedy injustice.[6] A situation may be perceived as unjust for a variety of reasons, and they come together to provoke us to act.

In the remainder of the book, I have built on these arguments. I have recast the rule of law as critical legal justice, understood in what I call a 'thin+' sense (ie, incorporating legally enforceable human rights). In other words, critical legal justice is a form of 'legal justice' that can enforce law's promise to do justice. It 'fleshes out' law's aptness for justice. However, I do not argue for critical legal justice and human rights as examples of a transcendental, idealist theory—a temptation to which human rights are particularly prone. Both the rule of law and human rights may be argued for on the basis of a myriad of definitions—for example, in the case of human rights, on the basis of liberal theory, Levinasian theory based on the demand of the other, and discourse theory—but no single theory can provide an entirely satisfactory grounding for their apparent

---

[5] J Rawls, *The Law of Peoples* (Cambridge, MA, Harvard University Press, 1999) 7.
[6] A Sen, *The Idea of Justice* (London, Allen Lane, 2009).

desirability. I have argued that we should avoid any temptations to assert their transcendental foundations and instead accept their existence, to use a prosaic term, as elements in the legal toolbox. Critical legal justice and human rights provide a background theory of justice (itself the product of a practical consensus around a variety of different accounts) within which law can operate. Understood in a non-perfectionist, non-ideal sense, they offer an operational theory of justice, a meaningful mechanism by which legal institutions may avoid causing injustice—and thereby contribute to a better world. There exists a sufficient consensus for us to embrace their use.

I have also argued that we must be aware of the historical context within which the rule of law and human rights operate. Neither the rule of law nor human rights are timeless concepts; they are rather the developments of particular periods in history. They are also, most especially in the case of human rights, the reflection of a particular psychological desire for the ineffable, or unnameable, which we convert into justice—a desire that can never properly be fulfilled and is particularly strongly felt in a post-metaphysical, post-traditional and (for many, but by no means all) post-religious age. We must bear this in mind and acknowledge that the rule of law and human rights will always be problematic and will always achieve less than our great expectations of them.

However, with regard to law's more practical duties, the rule of law and human rights function as important weapons against injustice, going some way to fulfilling law's identification as a concept and practice that is 'justice apt'. The rule of law—in its elements of public, prospective law, rights to equality of treatment, an independent judiciary, a fair assessment of evidence, and rights of appeal—is affirmative of many crucial elements of justice within law, an illustration of how law may demonstrate an aptness for justice and aspire to make good on its proclaimed ideals. Human rights, in spite of their apparent indeterminacy, can be meaningful and achieve change when they function within legal structures, even if their 'juridifica-tion' is liable to deaden some of their initial emancipatory promise. The application of critical legal justice involves, at its best, a remorseless and pervasive holding to account and attention to the detail of law-making and transparency. This is not to argue that the rule of law exhausts justice but rather that it is an essential element of it.

I have also argued for cosmopolitanism as an extension of the rule of law and human rights at the global level. However, a close examination reveals that the legal form of cosmopolitanism is very limited at present, and many legal elements described as examples of 'cosmopolitanism' or 'global jus-tice' in fact have very little, or even nothing, to do with either.

Therefore the diagnosis or critique of law after modernity need not extend to the dismissal of these apparent inventions of legal modernity (ie, the rule of law and human rights), provided that we approach them with care. They are not so devalued that we would be better off without them. In this way, I reject the arguments of those postmodern writers who argue that the rule of law or human rights are part of the corrupted body of modern law and may only function abusively. For example, I reject the argument that the rule of law operates only as a tool of capitalism and of global plunder. On the contrary, provided that we use them with care (ie, do not cleave to an understanding of the rule of law in which the free market, property rights and negative liberty dominate), they are valuable weapons against injustice.

Resistance and Demanding Justice

Despite my rejection of pessimistic or nihilistic views of law's role, I nonetheless return to an ideal of justice outside of the law. The rule of law, however recast, will never overcome the feeling of lack we experience at injustice, the desire for something more. It is unlikely that any banners will be unfurled, any revolutions started, in the name of critical legal justice.

Figure 12-1: A common image of justice

DER HENKER UND DIE GERECHTIGKEIT

Göring im Reichstagsbrand-Prozeß. Für mich ist das Recht etwas Blutvolles

Figure 12-2: John Heartfield, *The Executioner and Justice* (1933) with the caption 'For me, Justice is something bloody'© Heartfield Community of Heirs/VG Bild-Kunst, Bonn; and DACS, London 2012

I conclude with some visual images to help make this point. The usual image of justice (see Figure 12-1), with the scales displayed above, is often found on the roofs or in the vicinity of law courts, and it is readily associated with the rule of law. However, this image is bland and less emotive or captivating than the two further images of justice in Figures 12-2 and 12-3, which represent 'maimed' justice or injustice.

We have already encountered the image in Figure 12-2 at the end of chapter seven, as an example of the 'maimed justice' prevalent in times of war or of other abrogations of the rule of law. This image was created by John Heartfield (born Helmut Herzfeld), a German artist and member of the Dada group, whose work was banned by the Nazis and who fled Germany before the Second World War. This image, entitled 'The Executioner and Justice', shows the mutilated and shattered figure of Justice, who, in place of the usual blindfold, has a bandaged head to illustrate Goering's words from the Reichstag fire trial, which are captioned underneath: 'For me, Justice is something bloody' (or maybe 'lively', the German is ambiguous). This is a portrayal of a justice that has been abused and defiled. Heartfield used his work as a political medium, aiming to undermine Nazi propaganda through the use of satiric artistic representation and by appropriating and reusing images to artistic effect—rendering tangible their ideological content. Works such as these were often on the cover of the German *Workers' Illustrated Newspaper,* which sold very well at newsstands in Weimar Germany and contributed to the incendiary atmosphere of the times as a means of popular agitation against injustice.

Let us also return once more to Jens Galschiøt's 'Survival of the Fattest' (Figure 12-3), first visited in chapter eight. This time, however, I have chosen another image of the same work. In this illustration, we see the work close up, away from its location in Copenhagen Harbour during the climate change summit. Indeed, the work has been displayed in many locations.

At the centre is the same obese European 'Justitia', her eyes closed rather than blindfolded, to illustrate a justice that is degenerating into a refusal to observe or notice obvious injustice, holding up the diminutive scales as a symbol of justice. Behind her, however, are an oversized set of scales, eight metres high. On one side of these scales hangs a dead cow, suspended by its legs, and on the other a number of emaciated Third World people, outweighed by the ponderous, corpulent, dead cow. Galschiøt's point here is, as he has expressed it:

> The grotesque fact that each cow in the EU receives a subvention of 800 US dollars to block the poor countries from selling their products on the European market... In the rich part of the world our main scourge is obesity due to over-consumption while people in the Third World are dying of hunger. The misery

Figure 12-3: Jens Galschiøt, *Survival of the Fattest* (centre), displayed along with Galschiøt's works *Mad Cow Disease and Hunger March* at the WTO summit in Hong Kong (2005), courtesy of http://www.aidoh.dk (accessed 4 January 2013)

is creating floods of immigrants. In a desperate attempt to entrench ourselves and preserve our privileges we resort to measures so harsh that we betray our ideals of humanism and democracy.[7]

This sculpture confronts our notions of justice head on and reveals their hypocrisy.

The point I wish to make is this. As I have already argued, it is extremely difficult to agree upon a theory of justice in the abstract. This contrasts with the readiness with which we experience *injustice*, the immediacy of emotion that injustice provokes. The world that we inhabit is violently unjust. Costas Douzinas and Adam Gearey have referred to the 'great paradox', in which

> We are surrounded by injustice, but we do not know where justice lies ... We know injustice when we come across it ... but when we discuss qualities of justice both certainty and emotion recede ... Justice and its opposite are not symmetrical.[8]

As they also note, justice is far more likely to move people in its breach than as an academic exercise or 'piece of rhetoric that fails to convince or enthuse'.[9] Justice is therefore something of a philosophical failure. It is *injustice* that motivates and propels action. Hence, Figures 12-2 and 12-3 seem far more compelling than Figure 12-1. These striking images bring home the point with great immediacy.

However, several things follow from the observation that we have a keenly felt sense of injustice that may be distinguished from attempts to formulate coherent theories of justice. First, it may provoke pessimism or even despair or nihilism—a propulsion that has already been noted in this book. There exists a large gulf between a keen awareness of injustice and a perception that liberal democracy is not in good shape, and that there is little that can be done to improve it. Institutions of the Establishment are permeated with scandal, whether it be politicians fiddling with expenses, bankers gambling away millions and still claiming huge bonuses, the press engaged in illegal phone hacking with the complicity of the police, or EU states lurching from summit to summit in their efforts to solve the Eurozone crisis.

Politics fails to motivate, and philosophical attempts to reach a coherent theory of justice are unlikely to reassure a sceptical public. There exists both a moral and a motivational deficit.[10] In these circumstances, law

---

[7] 'Dead Cow and Starving Africans in Danish Capital', available at http://www.aidoh.dk/new-struct/and-Projects/Happenings/Global-Week-of-Action/GB-Copenhagen.htm (accessed 13 December 2012).

[8] C Douzinas and A Geary, *Critical Jurisprudence: The Political Philosophy of Justice* (Oxford, Hart Publishing, 2005) 28.

[9] Ibid, 109.

[10] S Critchley, *Infinitely Demanding* (London, Verso, 2007) ch 1.

is experienced as coercive or regulatory but not as internally binding. A respect for law, or political institutions, is not part of the mind-set, nor part of the disposition of our subjectivity.[11] In these circumstances, some populations identify themselves and seek coherence by turning inward toward some atavistic, racist, xenophobic self-identifications—a move sadly on the increase and encouraged by certain elements of the media. Others turn inward in a different way, to a sort of passive nihilism, what Nietzsche described as a 'European Buddhism', away from political or active life, to a focus on the self and individualist concerns.

Simon Critchley's point, discussed in chapters nine and eleven of this book, is that what is needed is a motivating, empowering concept of ethics, one capable of facing down the drift of the present. A positivist conception of law, stripped of any necessary identification with morality, is not an admirable candidate for this. The 'brave new world' of legal pluralism presents yet further challenges—of a lack of accountability and possible chaos and confusion. Critchley's own argument, as discussed in chapter eleven, is based on his conception of ethical subjectivity as riven by an infinite demand, although moderated by a self-mocking humour. This, Critchley has argued, provides a parallel motivation for the anarchic disruption of the state. While I have some sympathy with Critchley's advocacy of a 'politics of resistance' in the face of apparently intractable injustice, whether of the state or of private enterprise, ultimately I find his Levinasian brand of 'infinitely demanding' ethics too impossibly demanding and exacting to motivate people to action, and his 'carnivalesque' humour resistance strategy inadequate as a form of resistance to power.

Instead, in the absence of any motivating concept of politics or ideal of justice, for many, human rights have taken on this role (and for many, they have become the nearest thing to religion or magic in a secular age). This partly explains the current vogue for human rights and its ability to overshadow and render almost old fashioned other moral or political discourse. However, as I argue in chapter nine, human rights can never fulfil this role satisfactorily, and that lack of satisfaction helps to explain its continuing perplexities. Faced with the despair and prospect of nihilism, feelings of lack of control, even despair of our own identity, we search for something to give meaning to our lives. Human rights play the role of Jacques Lacan's *petit objet a*, hopeless objects of our desire.[12] Just as Western society engages in a rampant consumerism in a search for a hopeless meaning, which can never satiate our desire, so we look to human rights, which are the nearest thing we have to religion or magic, for attainment of our fantasy. There is

---

[11] Ibid.
[12] Cf C Douzinas, *The End of Human Rights: Critical Thought at the Turn of the Century* (Oxford, Hart Publishing, 2000); and R Salecl, 'Rights in Feminist and Psychoanalytic Perspective' (1995) *Cardozo Law Review* 1121.

always an excess of demand over need. Human rights symbolise our very lack but also signify it and prevent it from being fulfilled.

The ultimate in disillusion would be to succumb to a human rights nihilism, whereby we face up to human rights not just as lacking in foundations but as in themselves devalued and devoid of any morality, and acknowledge that they are empty shells, ciphers for whatever content (often that of a dominating powerful ideology). Most of us are unwilling to confront our nihilism on this scale, to face up to it, so we turn instead to the demanding (but perhaps hopeless) prospect of an ethical engagement with human rights.

Where does this leave justice? If we move beyond human rights to a more general notion of justice, then perhaps we should acknowledge that in the twenty-first century, justice is somewhat of a philosophical failure. Yet it is still a powerful intuition, and injustice provokes strong emotion. Although I argue that transcendental theories of justice, for all their aspirations to a 'realistic utopia', fail to motivate, this does not mean that we can have no aspirations for justice. The imagination has an important role to play, and works of art can inspire and engage us. This is why artists such as Galschiøt use their art to fight injustice in the world, to provoke strong emotion. Galschiøt encourages viewers to use their own imagination to work with his art, as part of a fight against injustice, writing, 'In my work with sculptures and happenings, I try to ask why and how our ethical and moral self-understanding is connected to global and local reality. I leave it to the spectators to work out the answers for themselves.'[13] Works of art, by engaging our sympathy in lives very different from our own, force us to confront these ideas through forceful images, thereby countering Max Weber's dismal characterisation of our times—'rationalisation and intellectualisation and, above all ... the disenchantment of the world'.[14] Art thereby increases our imaginative capabilities, better equipping us to make the judgements that public life requires of us, forcing us through imaginative reception to change our attitudes in radical ways.

Perhaps justice is best envisaged as a discourse of absence, something that does not belong to the order of being, is always desired, to come, unachieved. There is an excess of demand over need. As an object of our fantasies, the content of justice is always subjective and indeterminate. We are left with a sense of *injustice* as a motivator, a call to resistance, instilling us with a sense of responsibility to some sort of action—in Sen's words, 'a matter of actualities, of preventing manifest injustice in the world, of changes, large or small, to people's lives—the abolition of slavery, improvement of conditions in the workplace—realisation of an improvement in

---

[13] 'Jens Galschiøt: Portrait of a Sculptor', available at http://www.aidoh.dk/new-struct/About-Jens-Galschiot/CV.pdf (accessed 13 December 2012).
[14] M Weber, 'Science as a Vocation' in H Gerth and CW Mills (eds), *From Max Weber: Essays in Sociology* (New York, Oxford University Press, 1991) 155.

the lives of actual peoples.'[15] This, I think, should be the response to the injustice of law after modernity—one of resistance and action, of scepticism, scrutiny and critique. We should look closely at each legal measure adopted and resist greater infringements of our liberty in the name of security. We should demand transparency and resist measures that violate human rights. We should also work on our imagination and aspire to something better—rather than agonising over a finely tuned theory of justice.

> 'I promised to show you a map of the world you say but this is a mural
> then yes let it be these are small distinctions
> where do we see it from is the question'

> Adrienne Rich, 'An Atlas of the Difficult World'
> A Rich, *An Atlas of the Difficult World* (WW Norton and Co, 1991).

---

[15] Sen (above n 6) ch 1.

Index

Index

Index

networks, 148–9, 155
Neumann, Franz, 229, 238, 253, 271–3,
    284
New Guinea, 109
New Public Management, 365
New Zealand, 183n33
Nietzsche, Friedrich, 143, 185, 207, 211,
    313–14
nihilism, 53, 101, 143, 275, 312, 313,
    316–17, 377, 393, 394–5
Nike, 371
Nonet, Philippe, 62, 84, 135, 148–9
Northern Ireland, 85, 183
Nozick, Robert, 218, 290
Nuremberg trials, 347
Nussbaum, Martha, 244

Occupy movement, 162, 268, 281, 380
'officious bystander,' 6
Old Bailey, 217
O'Neill, Onora, 371
Open Method of Coordination (OMC),
    62, 125
ordo-liberalism, 259, 298
organised crime, 193
Orwell, George, 159, 160
output legitimacy, 283, 364–5

Paine, Tom, 374
Pandectists, 73, 80
Panofsky, Erwin, 96–8, 99
Panopticon, 160, 161
Paracelsus, 140
Parker, Christine, 374
parliamentary sovereignty, 49, 222, 224,
    263, 384
Parsons, Talcott, 71, 181
Pascal, Blaise, 47, 49, 197
Pashukanis, Evgeny, 54
Peers, S, 283
Perry, M, 291
perspective, 94–100
Pessoa, Fernando, 330, 346
Petersmann, Ernst-Ulrich, 323, 368
philosopher kings, 202, 321
Picasso, Pablo, 99–100
Plato, 5, 25, 202, 209, 274, 321
pluralism see legal pluralism
Plutarch, 216
poetry, 26, 243–4
Pogge, Thomas, 153, 197–200, 330, 356
Polanyi, Karl, 12
Polybius, 155
positivism:
    20th century, 20
    autonomy of law, 29–30
    banal positivism, 65–8, 114–16, 313,
        381, 384

common law and, 71–3
divided sovereignty and, 76–7
evaluation of legal theory and, 50
hard positivism, 37–8
justice and law, 66–7, 185–6
law and morality, 41, 42–3
legal pluralism and, 107, 377, 394
living law and, 92
meanings, 19
mechanical jurisprudence, 80
nihilism and, 317
rule of law and, 220, 249–53
Pospisil, Leopold, 109
Postema, Gerald, 36–7
Poster, Mark, 160
postmodernism:
    concepts, 14–18
    crisis of values, 27
    literature, 101–4
poverty: world poverty, 187–91, 197–201
principles of law, 83, 121–3, 128
Prirogine, Ilya, 139
privacy:
    business information, 323
    rise of right to, 310
    United States, 298–9, 326
privatisation:
    dispute resolution, 157–8
    governance, 161–5
    security, 161, 180
professional bodies, 91
property rights, 118, 258, 259, 298,
    354–5
    see also capitalism
proportionality principle, 91, 126, 128, 228,
    320–2, 354
prudence, 178, 181
psychoanalysis, 223, 314, 315, 317,
    377–8
Pynchon, Thomas, 81, 101–2, 103, 121,
    136–7

quantum mechanics, 94

Rancière, Jacques, 348
Rawls, John:
    geometric ideal, 74
    justice
        critique, 218–19
        fairness, 218
        fundamental duty, 351–2
        global justice, 191, 192, 197,
            199n83, 203
        ideal and non-ideal theory, 201–2, 203
        neutrality, 218
        priority, 24, 181
        redistributive role, 187, 193, 199n83
        speculative system, 388